Frank Clifford is a writer, lecturer and Astro-Palmistry consultant. He began teaching himself astrology and palmistry at the age of 16 and wrote his first astrology book seven years later. Around this time he founded a publishing company and edited/published seven books during 1999-2000, including the landmark *Astrology in the Year Zero* and two pop guides to the astrology of love and sex. Frank's biographical data compendium is included in the world's best-selling astrology software *Solar Fire*. His first full-length book on hand analysis, *Palmistry 4 Today*, was acclaimed and has been translated into Spanish, Dutch and Italian.

In the last twelve months Frank has been interviewed on *LBC*, *BBC London Live* and regional BBC stations, as well as profiled in *The Guardian*, *Good Health* and numerous regional newspapers. Frank has also appeared on TV discussing palmistry and astrology and taking part in phone-ins. He writes the monthly horoscope column for the family magazine *Candis* and has written and recorded astrology columns and phonelines for *Marie Claire*. He teaches for The London School of Astrology and has devised a palmistry course, which is being used by the British Astrological and Psychic Society. Frank is a regular at corporate events reading palms and birth charts.

Frank can be contacted at info@flareuk.com or c/o Flare Publications, P.O.Box 10126, London NW3 7WD.

By the same author:

Palmistry 4 Today (June 2002, published by Rider)
Venus: Your Key to Love (November 2000)
Mars: Your Burning Desires (November 2000)
The Essentials of Hand Analysis (February 1999)
British Entertainers: the Astrological Profiles (2nd ed., Sep 1997)
British Entertainers: the Astrological Profiles (1st ed., May 1997)
The Clifford Data Compendium (Solar Fire program, May 1997, revised 2000)

Forthcoming titles:

Hand-Reading (to be published by Pyramid, 2004)
Birth Charts: Horoscopes of the Famous (2004)

Published by Frank Clifford and Flare Publications:

Astrology in the Year Zero by Garry Phillipson (November 2000)
The Draconic Chart by Rev. Pamela Crane (January 2000)
The Sun Sign Reader by Joan Revill (January 2000)
Shorthand of the Soul by David Hayward (October 1999)

All book titles are available via Amazon.com, Amazon.co.uk and Flareuk.com

British Entertainers
the astrological profiles

Frank C. Clifford

Flare Astro-Profiles Series
www.flareuk.com

First edition published in May 1997 by Flare Publications.
Second edition published in September 1997 by Flare Publications.
Third edition, fully revised and updated – published in June 2003 by Flare Publications.

A catalogue record for the book is available from the British Library.

ISBN 1-903353-01-7

Astrological charts generated using Io Edition.

Cover design: Daniel St. John Smith
Illustrations: Judith Wardle

Printed by MPG Books, Victoria Square, Bodmin, Cornwall PL31 1EB
01208 73266, www.mpgltd.co.uk

The author welcomes further contributions or corrections to this book.
To contact him please enclose an SAE and write c/o Flare Publications, P.O. Box 10126, London NW3 7WD, England, UK. Email: info@flareuk.com

www.flareuk.com

The author would like to thank the following collectors – their efforts are in this book:

Joan Abel, T.J. Andrews, Julie Argyle, Ananda Bagley, Zerda Barlow, Jane Bennett, Nick Dagan Best, Arthur Blackwell, Laura Boomer, Grazia Bordoni, Nandon Bosma, Arthyr Chadbourne, Karen Christino, Linda Clark, Betty Collins, Chryss Craswell, Boris Cristoff, Nalini Kanta Das, Frederick Davies, Sally Davis, Patrick Deimar, Martine Delamere, Lorri dePasqua, Ruth Dewey, David Dozier, Margaret Dunford, Roger Elliot, Ruth Elliot, John Etherington, Nancy Ewart, Lorraine Exley, Cyril Fagan, Kim Farnell, David Fisher, Adam Fronteras, Caroline Gerard, Richard Geyman, Tashi Grady, Fiona Graham, B. Granite, Russell Grant, John E. Greig, Lesley Griffiths, Judy Hall, Jenni Harte, Dana Haynes, David Hayward, Garry Heaton, Gillian Helfgott, Dana Holliday, Prue Hollingshead, Blanca Holmes, Maggie Hyde, Eve Jackson, Jayj Jacobs, Kathleen Johnson, Mark Johnson, Stephanie Johnson, Tony Joseph, Carol Kanada, Brian Kelly, Debbi Kempton-Smith, Babs Kirby, Sally Kirkman, Ralph Kraum, Misty Kuceris, Magpie Latham, Bettina Lee, Mary Lee Lewis, Phillip Lindsay, Jo Logan, Gary Lorig, D. Martini, Tony Matthews, Valerie Matthews, Frances McEvoy, Mary McFadden, Craig McIntosh, John McKay-Clements, Liz Medler, Neal Meredith, Suzanne Michaud, John Naylor, Paul Newman, Ruth Nobel, Barbara Norris, Ruth Hale Oliver, Marjorie Orr, Lynne Palmer, Marc Penfield, Bob Prince, Reina James Reinstein, Joan Revill, Ian Richards, Amy Rodden, Lois Rodden, Paul Rosner, Helene Schnitzer, Sy Scholfield, Victoria Shaw, Bill Sheeran, Rosemary Shields, Dori Sipper, Christeen Skinner, Neil Spencer, Zane Stein, Edwin C. Steinbrecher, Pauline Stone, Barry Street, Jane Struthers, Janey Stubbs, Dennis Sutton, Hans-Hinrich Taeger, Jon Taylor, Penny Thornton, Pete Watson, Peter West, Richard West, Thelma & Tom Wilson, Scott Withers, Paul Wright, Greg Young.
Apologies to anyone I have missed out!

Dedicated to my Dad, Frank Clifford,
who died while I was writing this book

And to Lois Rodden for her inspiration and guidance

To Roberto, Mum, Helen, Filly and Sue, who have given me their love and support

A special thank you to astrologers
Caroline Gerard, Sy Scholfield, David Fisher, Grazia Bordoni and Darby Costello

Many thanks to Daniel St.John Smith and Judith Wardle for the cover and artwork

Below are the glyphs featured in the Essentials section,
and most can be found on the birth charts presented in the book:

♈	aries	☉	the sun	AS	ascendant
♉	taurus	☽	the moon	MC	midheaven
♊	gemini	☿	mercury	☌	conjunction
♋	cancer	♀	venus	☍	opposition
♌	leo	♂	mars	△	trine
♍	virgo	♃	jupiter	▱	square
♎	libra	♄	saturn	⌲	semi-sextile
♏	scorpio	♅	uranus	⚹	sextile
♐	sagittarius	♆	neptune	⚻	quincunx
♑	capricorn	♇	pluto	∠	semi-square
♒	aquarius	⚷	chiron	⚼	sesquisquare
♓	pisces	☊☋	north/south node	℞	retrograde

Data and Abbreviations

The data for each astro-profile are presented as follows: Date, time (in 24 hour clock), time zone, place, co-ordinates (exact for Scottish locations). Source. Rodden Rating (see below for details).

New data information or profiles (20% added since the first edition) are indicated by the symbol ✪

Data that are unverified or have conflicting information are indicated by the symbol 💣

> Please note that these unverified data are presented to aid further investigation and are not intended to be used for research studies. As data are the foundations of astrological study, it is important to use only accurate, sourced data. Please always use the original source (e.g. Gerard q. birth certificate) rather than simply a reference (e.g. From the book British Entertainers). Be wary, too, of 6am quotes!

All data in this volume have been classified using the simple Rodden Rating system:

> AA – Data from birth certificate (BC), hospital or governmental birth records, family bibles, baby books, family written records. Included here are websites, books and articles that quote an official document. N.B. In England birth times are found on the BCs of twins only. 'AA' data are the best evidence of accurate information.

> A – Data from the individual, family member, intimate friend or associate. Included here are newspaper birth announcements and where times are given within a 'window of time' of thirty minutes, e.g. "Between 15.45 and 16.00."

> B – Data from biographies, autobiographies and official websites where no other source is given.

> C – Caution, data not verified. No source, a vague or untrustworthy source, rectified/speculative data, "personal" ambiguous sources, unnamed biographies that cannot be checked and approximate birth times outside half an hour ("early morning", "between 2 and 4 am").

> DD – Dirty Data. Two or more unsubstantiated quotes of time or date, indicating that at least one (possibly all) has been rectified without designation. Any unverified data that are contradicted by another unverified source.

GMT/GDT/GWT/MET: Greenwich Mean/Daylight (Summer)/War/Euro Time (18/2/68 to 31/10/71)
DGDT: Double Greenwich Daylight Time (active for periods during WWII)
RR: Rodden Rating, the system of classifying data according to accuracy (see above)
TR: Transits, the movements of the planets (see page 11)
FCC: The author, Frank C. Clifford
Gerard: Researcher/Astrologer Caroline Gerard, Edinburgh, Scotland
BC: Birth Certificate
EQHS: The Equal House System (see page 11)

Foreword

by Lois M. Rodden

The most valuable books in our library are our reference books. Among them, data collections stand out as the basic tool in our study of astrology. Without them our study is entirely theoretical. Moreover, when we look at the charts of family and friends, we need examples of Mars in the 1st house or Jupiter conjunct the MC to see how this has worked out in the lives of other people. As devoted as we are in our study of astrology, without horoscopes to examine, we cannot see how the planets work in real lives.

Through the early 20th century much of the data available was speculative or rectified. Fortunately, pioneers in the field of data collecting began showing us data that have come from birth records, from biographies and from interviews, data that can be validated. Frank Clifford is one of those pioneers who is dedicated to finding the real data, not just hearsay. In his *British Entertainers* he has investigated resources of fellow data-collectors, biographies and interviews and has personally sleuthed backstage, through websites and in correspondence to reach public figures.

In 1996 Frank travelled to California to visit me and talk with other California astrologers, a tight-knit community of data collectors who are delighted to share a new 'find' – an item of virgin data that has just turned up. Frank was getting data from hard-to-get places with his perseverance (and more than a little charm). He soon proved to be one of our best collectors, not only for the data that he contributes to the community but for his dedication to fastidious accuracy and reporting.

In *British Entertainers* Frank presents some 800 data with a biography and a noted data source. Almost half of the data are presented in chart form as well. He uses the Rodden Rating of AA-A-B-C-DD in order that one may immediately trust the integrity of the publication. Unfortunately there are still astrology books in print that present data that are unreliable, and with *British Entertainers* it is reassuring to know that the data can be trusted.

I'll join Dana Holliday and Edwin Steinbrecher in thanking Frank Clifford for *British Entertainers*, an admirable addition to every astrologer's research library.

Lois M. Rodden
AstroDatabank
www.astrodatabank.com

New Features

There are a number of new features and changes to this third edition, which is twice as large (140,000 words) as its predecessor. Firstly the format is A to Z rather than by category. There are over 800 profiles with full data and source, plus one hundred untimed or non-British data, and charts for a handful of quintessential British TV shows. Many profiles have extended biographies and the book contains thousands of dated events. (Where exact event dates are in dispute I have used estimates such as "mid-February" and "end of the month".)

Symbols ✪●✸

Data are sometimes updated, verified or contradicted. For those who have bought previous editions, I have introduced two symbols that will help to identify the profiles that present:
– New entries or updated information (since the first edition) ✪
– Unverified data sources ●✸

Chart Wheels – Two House Systems in One!

There are over 350 chart wheels, all calculated using the Placidus house system. You'll notice an extra wheel around each chart – this is for those who prefer to look at charts using Equal house (EQHS). *For EQHS users although this grid is not numbered it shouldn't take long before you feel comfortable counting from the Ascendant (or Descendant) to obtain a planet's Equal house position.* For example, in the chart presented, Sun and Mercury fall in the 1st Placidean house but using the simple grid you can see that they fall within the 2nd Equal house grid (second grid anti-clockwise from the Ascendant). In this horoscope most planets move house: Pluto moves from the Placidean 7th to EQHS 8th, Uranus from the 3rd to the 5th etc. (Some points, like Mars and the Node in this chart, will require rechecking

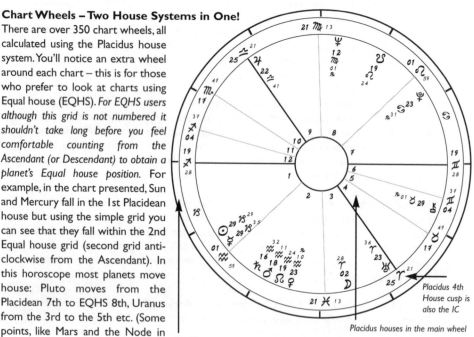

Placidus 4th House cusp is also the IC

Placidus houses in the main wheel

First Equal house grid (beginning from the Ascendant) – not numbered

the Ascendant degree.) For EQHS users the numbered houses next to the inner wheel will soon appear irrelevant but the main (bold) angle axes (Asc-Dsc and MC-IC) will stand out clearly. My chart comments about houses in this book refer to EQHS because, after ten years of comparing house systems, this method of division stands up as the clearest in describing the mundane areas of life.

On occasion, when there are conflicting data, two chart wheels have been printed for the reader's discernment.

Speaking Your Chart

Q Astrology comes alive when we read quotes from and about people. This new section presents almost two hundred quotes, which required wading through many of the 5000 clippings and books I have! They offer insights into the personalities and horoscopes of the entertainers.

Australian Data Section

From page 306 there are 30 timed data of Australian entertainers who are well-known in the UK.

Essentials *One*

the motivations of each sign (particularly for Ascendant and Moon placements) and essence of each house

Aries ♈
assertive • pioneering
energetic • competitive
impulsive • independent
me-first • pugnacious
intolerant

Taurus ♉
practical • dependable
sensual • artistic
steadfast • conservative
possessive • materialistic
stubborn

Gemini ♊
articulate • versatile
sociable • quick-witted
clever • adaptable
restless • changeable
fickle

Cancer ♋
tenacious • nurturing
sensitive • intuitive
patriotic • sympathetic
manipulative • self-pitying
moody

Leo ♌
creative • unique
supportive • dramatic
magnanimous • proud
autocratic • boastful
pretentious

Virgo ♍
efficient • discriminating
industrious • methodical
seeking perfection
exacting • critical
pedantic • petty

Libra ♎
diplomatic • persuasive
peace-loving • refined
cooperative • charming
insincere • superficial
indecisive

Scorpio ♏
powerful • insightful
passionate • enigmatic
determined • intense
secretive • jealous
compulsive

Sagittarius ♐
spiritual • optimistic
lucky • adventurous
broadminded • athletic
exaggerative • blunt
self-indulgent

Capricorn ♑
hardworking • serious
responsible • committed
scrupulous • traditional
controlling • inhibited
social-climbing

Aquarius ♒
humanitarian • idealistic
independent • inventive
progressive • rebellious
strong-minded
impersonal • intolerant

Pisces ♓
imaginative • romantic
devoted • compassionate
intuitive • artistic
lazy • fatalistic
selfish

1st House
public face we most naturally slip into • appearance

2nd House
possessions • money • resources • physical body • earning potential

3rd House
communication • bonding with a live audience • radio • voice and delivery

4th House
home • family • property

5th House
audience • following • love affairs • attitude to performing • stage fright

6th House
health • work routine • habits • service • conveyor belt of production

7th House
partnerships • fan base

8th House
investments • lawsuits

9th House
media • talk shows • education • travel

10th House
career avenues • life path • our view of the 'big outside world'

11th House
advisors • friends • contacts • social issues • a focused, politicised audience

12th House
'down time' • behind-the-scenes work • rehearsals • alter-ego/protective mask

Ascendant
personal worldview • behaviour on stage • general personality

Descendant
others' reactions • what we project, provoke and attract

MC
reputation • vocation • parental inheritance • aspirations

IC
personal and psychological motivations • roots

Essentials *Two*

the essence of each planet and its relationship to entertainment – these are expanded upon in the profiles

The Sun – *ego, identity, life force, potential*
   The archetype an actor seeks to play on film and stage (because of a desire to personify the Sun's role and message).

The Moon – *instinct, emotion, basic needs, longings, mother, emotional memory*
   Rapport with an audience; instant feedback; relaying everyday life situations, habits and routines; consumer shows and current affairs; intuitive sense of musical trends; expressive, imaginative, sentimental and lyrical ways of communicating; popularity that waxes and wanes.

Mercury – *intellectual interests, expressiveness, reasoning, persuasion, communication, exchange*
   Word play and association; verbal dexterity; quick one-liners; improvisation; stand-up; catchphrases; memory for scripts and facts, figures and data.

Venus – *relating, luxury, art, romance*
   Charming and easy-going lightweights; fighting to be taken seriously; known for romantic escapades; pleasant rapport with an audience where feedback is essential; manufactured pop star puppet.

Mars – *energy, initiative, aggression, will, individuality*
   Endurance and fighting spirit; surviving and staying 'on top'; resilience after countless rejections; stage/screen impact and 'presence'; biting wit with a definite target; exposing injustice and fighting for the underdog; comedy as a soap-box; hard and fast physical, sexual and 'rude' humour.

Jupiter – *expansion, quests, morality, indulgence*
   Superstitions; opportunities and lucky breaks; fighting to maintain a benevolent reputation; larger-than-life characters; playing god; philanthropy; exhibitionism; 'blue' and lavatorial humour; literal, physical and verbal slip-ups; idealism 'tripped up' by life; exaggeration; pranks; finding humour in mishaps; publicity and hype; publicity seekers; TV gloss; the diva; excessive lifestyles; gospel music.

Saturn – *parental authority, restrictions, the law of cause and effect, life lessons*
   The comedy straightman; being typecast; catchphrases; backbone to withstand long hours, little pay, no thanks and rejection; discipline to practice for years; opera; a long apprenticeship; becoming an established 'name' later in life; emerging from humble beginnings; country music; laconic, ironic, hard-done by humour; cursed with bad luck and accustomed to being able to predict it – 'knowing my luck'; 'why me?' situations; darker humour from a dissatisfaction with life and 'the system'.

Uranus – *sudden change, collective ideals, innovation, the extraordinary*
   Overnight success (and back to obscurity again!); sudden changes/reversals in career path; success from new fads (disco, rave) or one-offs; censorship; daring to voice others' true opinions; provocative; anarchic; innovative; the tearing down of established comic rules; smashing convention; jazz music.

Neptune – *escapism, belief, illusion, lack of direction*
   Charisma; longevity; stage presence; trends and glamour for which the masses yearn; mania; descension into drugs/drink and delusion; ability to be many diverse characters; chameleon-like; legends whose reputations live on after their untimely death from excess or self-destructive habits.

Pluto – *obsessions, secrets, group dynamic, political undercurrents, regeneration, inevitability*
   Controlling force behind the scenes; cult followings and shows; obsessive fans; the major sign of generational influence and power; career resurrection; black humour; satire; comedy with political or social undertones; use of language as a weapon; communicating taboos; shaping public opinion.

Chiron – *sacrifice, defiance, wound*
   The area of our life where we must learn more about our worth and, if necessary, accept that sacrifices must be made; what we're prepared to risk and fight for but inevitably what we may need to sacrifice or change in a fundamental way.

Planetary Strength

I have often noted when a planet is strong – i.e. when the planet dominates the life and character. From my research this occurs when a planet is conjunct the Sun or Moon or has just passed one of the four chart angles (particularly the Asc and MC) – *found above the angles in the Placidus 12th, 9th, 6th and 3rd* (the Gauquelins found this in their research of character traits and planetary symbolism).

House Systems may continue to provoke much debate, but I switched to Equal house (EQHS) ten years ago and find it superior for a clarity of understanding and interpretation in the mundane areas of life. The MC/IC axis is still a major point of reference, but it adds another dynamic to the chart. (It was reassuring to discover that major researcher/collector Lois Rodden settled on EQHS too!)

Retrograde planets, according to Rodden, take on an interior but dramatic impact in our development before reaching maturity and being influential in our adulthood, eg. Saturn retrograde points to early restrictions, duty or responsibilities, but an ability to tackle these later in a larger arena. With four or more retrograde planets we have intense early experiences followed by a pause until we are ready to develop. Then we have a 'second chance' in our lives with a more solid foundation (noticeable in many entertainers' charts who 'comeback'). **Stationary** planets (not shown on the charts in this book) make a potent mark on our lives, personally and professionally.

Planets – Signs – Houses – Rulerships – Aspects – Configurations – Orbs

Planets are *dynamic energies*, **signs** are the particular *qualities and characteristics these energies work through*, and the **house** a planet is placed in is the *area of life* where the themes of the planet are most vivid. **Rulers** of each house (e.g. the Sun rules the house cusp that Leo's found on) *colour the meaning of the house and its affairs*. **Aspects** are the angular relationships between two points and *link the energies and drives represented by the planets*. Neutral and hard aspects (conjunction, square, opposition, quincunx, sesquisquare) are character-making, productive aspects, inclined towards activity. Soft aspects (trine, sextile) are associated with in-born talents or opportunities that need effort to manifest productively. We are motivated to act out our hard aspects (particularly squares and oppositions, but not always to our benefit) but can waste the soft, less-challenging ones. A conjunction (0°) with a personal planet or point indicates traits prominent in our innate character. With an opposition (180°) we must integrate the planetary energies to achieve their potential, or our lives swing from one stance to the other. We face these polarities head-on through one-to-one relationships. A trine (120°) points to talents and lucky breaks – being in the right place at the right time. A sextile (60°) is a gift or opportunity often passed up and regretted. A square (90°) represents challenges and obstacles we are compelled to face and overcome in order to achieve success and express our will. A quincunx (150°, aka inconjunct) suggests a crisis that will have been in the background for some time and must now be resolved immediately. The sesquisquare (135°, aka sesquiquadrate) is a disruption which can lead us down new, unexpected and original paths. Aspect **configurations** mentioned in the text are: the Grand Trine (a dose of talent in need of tough aspects to produce something more than inertia!); the Grand Cross (a major challenge with the potential for greatness if the issues presented by the aspects are successfully channelled); and the T-Square (which is half a Grand Cross, and points to an area of productivity and tension). An **orb** is *the deviation of an exact aspect between two points in a horoscope*. I believe it is wise to be generous with orbs in the birth chart, although major chart themes will show up in many ways regardless of adding an extra two degrees or so!

Transits

In the profiles only **transits** (TR) have been noted (where appropriate). These planetary movements (particularly over the Sun, Moon, Ascendant, Descendant, MC and IC) reflect our personal timing, our periods of growth and development, and signal change from our existing life pattern. Transits of the outer planets often signal new phases in our life (the inner planets are daily and mood-related periods). **Jupiter transits** can bring success, opportunity, publicity, travel, bursts of fame and fortune if we have prepared and worked hard – otherwise they can be shallow 'feel-good' times or even major let-downs. **Saturn transits** highlight areas in our life that need attention and bring us rewards only if we have followed the path of personal growth. **Uranus transits** disrupt our lives, can turn situations around from fame to obscurity and back again. They are the easiest to time; they tend to be spot on to the degree. **Neptune transits**, on the other hand, will leave us feeling bewildered before and after exactitude. We can perform our most creative work when Neptune passes over a potent point in our horoscope, but more often than not, it is a period of disillusionment – things were not quite what they appeared to be and secure, emotional crutches are dissolving. **Pluto transits** bring hidden truths to the surface are are non-negotiable. We may need lose what we think we value in order to be reborn – old patterns must be destroyed to move on.

AC/DC

Formed in 1973 in Australia, AC/DC have enjoyed 30 years of cult following – due as much to their stage gimmicks and theatrics as to their music (note both Young brothers have Jupiter prominent). Malcolm and brother Angus Young played their first gig with the band in Sydney on 31 December 1973. Soon after the first single was produced in July 1974, the lineup changed to include the band's ex-chauffeur Bon Scott (apparently rejected from the Australian Army for being "socially maladjusted"). The first album, *High Voltage*, was released in February 1975, before they relocated to London the following January and established a fanbase. On 20 February 1980 (following TR Neptune on his MC,

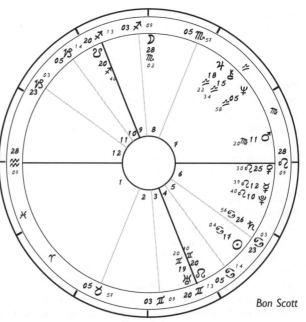

Bon Scott

and an Eclipse on his Ascendant just four days earlier) Scott choked on his own vomit after a whisky binge. After Scott's death, Brian Johnson (b. 5 October 1947, Newcastle, England) was appointed lead singer, and his first album with the group, *Back in Black*, topped the UK chart. They went on to become one of the world's top stadium acts. From the late 1980s sporadic tours and album releases followed, including the October 1990 smash release, *The Razor's Edge*.

Bon Scott

b. 9 July 1946, 23.20 GDT, Maternity Hospital, Forfar, Scotland, 56N39, 02W53.
Gerard q. BC (Ronald Belford Scott). RR: AA.

Angus Young

b. 31 March 1955, 20.10 GMT, Skerryvore Road, Glasgow, Scotland, 55N52, 04W10.
Gerard q. BC (Angus McKinnon Young). RR: AA.

Malcolm Young

b. 6 January 1953, 14.05 GMT, Bernard Street, Glasgow, Scotland, 55N51, 04W12.
Gerard q. BC. RR: AA.

Adamski

✪ b. 4 December 1967, 21.40 GMT, London, England, 51N30, 0W10.
Laura Boomer q. him (Adam Tinley). RR: A.

A former acid-house keyboard player on instrumental dance tracks, Adamski hit #1 in the UK with the record *Killer* in May 1990. Electronics whiz Tinley, under the name of Stupid Babies, had hit the Indie Top Five with the *The Babysitters* at age eleven. In 1998 he resurfaced with a new recording.

Dawn Addams

◐ b. 21 September 1930, 08.00 GDT, Felixstowe, England, 51N58, 01E20.
Church of Light q. Theodoseus in Predictions. RR: C.

Actress who made her West End debut in *Charley's Aunt* on 22 December 1949. Addams arrived in Hollywood in 1950 and made a string of moderate films, with the exception of Chaplin's *A King in New York* (1957), the commercial pinnacle of her career. Better known for her love affairs, Addams also married twice. The first was to Prince Vittorio Massimo in 1954 and the couple had a son Prince Stefano on 10 January 1955. The couple separated in 1958 and divorced in 1971 (the year TR Pluto crossed her Sun-Mercury). A seven-year custody battled ensued, which was eventually won by the father. Addams retired after her second marriage in 1974. D. 7 May 1985, London, cancer.

Pete Agnew – see Nazareth

Brian Aherne

> b. 2 May 1902, 10.40 GMT, King's Norton, England, 52N24, 01W56.
> From his autobiography, A Proper Job (1969), p. 3, which states his father was informed at 11 am, so presumably a short while beforehand. RR: B.

With an Aries MC and Mars elevated, prodigious Aherne was a child actor from 3. On 26 December 1913 he made his West End debut in *Where the Rainbow Ends*. Later he was popular in silent films before moving to Broadway in 1931 (during TR Uranus to MC) for *The Barretts of Wimpole Street* (which opened on 9 February 1931). Two years later he went to Hollywood and starred with Cary Grant (qv) in *Sylvia Scarlett* (which premiered on 9 January 1936). Aherne garnered an Oscar nomination for *Juarez* in 1939. The latter film was released in April 1939 (as TR Saturn passed Aherne's MC). Known to be aloof, Aherne was married (from 20 August 1939 to early June 1944) to actress Joan Fontaine*. His second marriage was from 27 January 1946 to his death on 10 February 1986.

John Alderton – see Pauline Collins

Sophie Aldred

✪ b. 20 August 1962, 06.00 GDT, Greenwich, London, England, 51N29, 0W00.
> Misty Kuceris q. her personally (exact place in London from various websites). RR: A.

Aldred served as assistant Ace to Sylvester McCoy (qv) in the long-running TV show *Doctor Who* from 1987-8. Rebellious from the age of 16, Aldred fought her biggest battle with anorexia for five years from age 17, before a kidney infection highlighted her plight (Uranus, usually prominent in the charts of anorexics, conjuncts the Sun and Ascendant). She is known to be impressionable, optimistic and extroverted (an elevated Moon in Aries and MC ruler Venus in Libra). In September 1996 she co-hosted the paranormal series *It's A Mystery*. Aldred married on 12 July 1997 and the couple had a son, born 10 February 2000.

Jean Alexander

> b. 11 October 1926, 03.00 GMT, Liverpool, England, 53N25, 02W55.
> FCC q. her. (N.B. Some sources incorrectly state 24 February 1926; her autobiography gives 1926 and refers to her birthday being late in the year, after summer.) RR: A.

At four years of age, Jean Alexander almost died from pneumonia. Her first job – which she grudgingly worked at for five years – was as a librarian (no doubt helped by having a studious Virgo Ascendant!). Then she joined the Adelphi Guild Theatre in Macclesfield and toured with its players. Alexander worked in repertory for the next 11 years with a quiet determination (there's little fanfare with a Virgo/Libra combination). Her first stage appearance was in Somerset Maugham's *Sheppy*, a part she was asked to audition for in late July 1949 (as TR Saturn ventured towards the Ascendant). She also starred – on 27 April 1959 – in *A View from the Bridge*. She was asked to join the cast of *Coronation Street* in February 1964

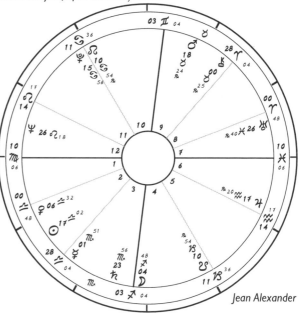

Jean Alexander

---

* Joan Fontaine b. 22 October 1917, 06.00 JST (-9), Tokyo, Japan, 35N42, 139E46. Church of Light q. Fontaine's mother to Gilbert Ibarra, "dawn." RR: A.

(with TR Uranus on Ascendant), and first appeared on the show on 10 June 1964. She brought comedy and pathos with Virgoan detail to the role of busybody Hilda Ogden and it established her as one of the nation's best loved actresses. On 23 May 1985 she won the Royal Television Award for Best Performance of 1984-5. During Summer 1987 she decided to leave the series and her last appearance was on Christmas Day of that year. Although her career has slowed down considerably since she left, Jean Alexander has appeared in TV's *Boon*, the film *Scandal*, and the comedy series *Last of the Summer Wine*. From 20 September 1996 she was appearing in adverts for repeat showings of *Coronation Street*, with a reputed £50,000 fee for the 40-second commercial. In April 2003 she was seen in the TV series *Heartbeat*. Alexander has never married and admits to being a virgin and, with the Moon and Saturn flanking the IC, is known to be intensely private.

John Alford
✪ b. 30 October 1971, 07.55 MET, Glasgow, Scotland, 55N51, 04W14.
   Gerard q. BC (John James Walter Shannon). RR: AA.
Brooding pinup singer and actor who starred in *Grange Hill* and *London's Burning*. An undercover drugs bust in August 1997 (TR Uranus square Sun) led to his arrest. He was found guilty and sentenced to seven months imprisonment in late May 1999. After serving his sentence he lost an appeal in September 2000 to clear his name.

Marc Almond
✪ b. 9 July 1957, 05.00 GDT, Southport, England, 53N39, 03W01.
   Garry Heaton q. his letter (year confirmed by FCC at Registry). (N.B. In his autobiography *Tainted Life* (Sidgwick & Jackson, 1999), Almond states he is a Cancerian with a Leo Ascendant. The book contains no further reference to a birth time.) RR: A.

Flamboyant and theatrical singer (with a Uranus, Venus and Mars conjunction in Leo) Almond founded the influential electronica outfit Soft Cell with David Ball (b. 3 May 1959, Blackpool, England), and together they played their first gig in December 1979 (a few months after the Lunar Eclipse on Almond's MC). Their first single release, *Tainted Love*, topped the British charts in September 1981 and went on to be the year's biggest seller (eventually notching up sales of 1.1 million units). After a few follow-up hits the duo split and Almond embarked upon a solo career while battling addiction to ecstasy, cocaine and the sleeping pill Halcion (spending half a million pounds on his habit). Although he has been unable to match the success of Soft Cell. Almond did score two notable hits in April 1985 (*I Feel Love* with Bronski Beat) and January 1989 (the melodramatic #1 *Something's Gotten Hold of My Heart* with Gene Pitney). He remains an interesting and eloquent interviewee and

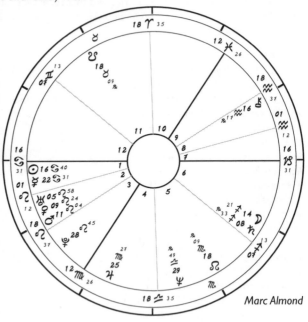
Marc Almond

wrote a popular autobiography. In September 2002 he released a Soft Cell comeback album, *Cruelty Without Beauty*.

Q "My father was a violent alcoholic and the mood swings and beatings were terrible. I think marriage was forced on him when my mother got pregnant with me. So I was a symbol of everything that he thought had ruined his life."
Were you bullied at school? "I was an effeminate asthmatic stammerer, so what do you think? That's why so many damaged people end up in the entertainment industry – they're running away from the playground taunts, getting their worth reaffirmed by their fans and number one singles." (Marc Almond, *You*, 10/10/99)
"I always loved the spotlight. I didn't feel the outsider. People gave me their love... I enjoy building up and knocking down. I enjoy risks and – this must be a flaw in my personality – if I have a good love affair and roses are growing round the door, I have to cut the heads off the roses." (Marc Almond, *Q*, August 1992)

John Altman
b. 2 March 1952, 03.15 GMT, Reading, England, 51N28, 0W59.
FCC q. him. RR: A.

With a Neptunian overtone and Moon in Taurus, a career in music had always appealed to Altman, but in 1975 he chose acting instead. During his salad days, major transits from Neptune (on Ascendant), Saturn and Pluto (on MC) in late 1982 coincided with a personal nadir – he was unemployed, had a hernia and had come out of a destructive relationship. From the start of BBC's *EastEnders* in February 1985, he portrayed Nick Cotton, widely considered the nastiest character on TV. Known, however, as one of the nicest men in show business, Altman has since appeared sporadically in the show, turning up to torment his long-suffering mum, played by June Brown (qv). His sinister "Hello, Ma" was even a catchphrase in gay discos as a pickup line! Altman has taken advantage of his TV character by playing pantomime villains, perfecting his theatrical King Rat act (perhaps the birth time is a few minutes later, giving Altman a Scorpio MC). Before his TV success he made appearances in *An American Werewolf in London*, *Quadrophenia* and *Return of the Jedi*, and in 1984 he filmed *Higher Mortals* and *To Die For*, a comedy about AIDS. Altman met his future wife, actress Brigitte, in early 1985. In August 1989 his daughter Rosanna was snatched at Waterloo Station. Fortunately, she was quickly rescued, unharmed.

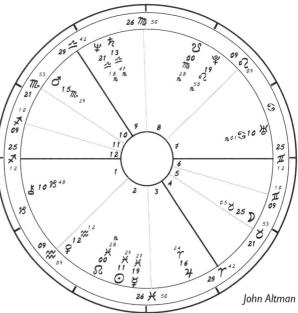

John Altman

Ian Anderson
b. 10 August 1947, 07.30 GDT, Maternity Hospital, Dunfermline, Scotland, 56N04, 03W28.
FCC q. BC (Ian Scott Anderson). RR: AA.

Rock singer, songwriter and flautist who formed the blues group Blades in 1963, which developed into the John Evan Band, the John Evan Smash, and finally Jethro Tull. The band's final incarnation was fixed during a pivotal meeting in December 1967 (with TR Jupiter on his Ascendant and TR Neptune on IC). With a heavyweight stellium in Leo, Anderson soon assumed full control of the band's material. Gaining national attention from August 1968 (TR Neptune over his IC again), the band proceeded to win a strong following in the US from October 1971 (TR Saturn at EQHS 10th). Consecutive chart-topping concept albums followed and their popularity peaked with the worldwide broadcast to a 400 million audience of a Madison Square Garden concert on 9 October 1978. Anderson is recognised as an extroverted and distinctive stage performer (best demonstrated astrologically by Mars-Uranus in the 10th). With Pluto involved in a heavy Leo stellium square abundant Jupiter, Anderson's professional highs were matched by personal lows in the 70s, including the death of band-

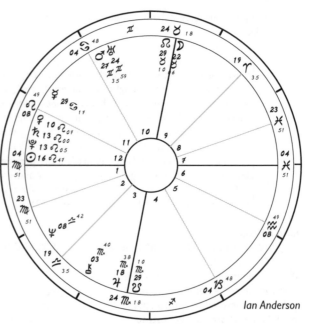

Ian Anderson

member John Glascock (on 17 November 1979, TR Uranus opposite Moon). Nevertheless Anderson reemerged with a solo album in November 1983. A year's sabbatical in 1985 was taken to recover from recurring throat problems. (Chart factors indicating prominence appear to be the MC ruler Venus conjunct Saturn, Pluto and Sun in Leo, an aggressively defiant Mars-Uranus in the 10th, and a long, albeit fluctuating, popularity with Moon on the MC opposite Jupiter. An interesting feature, too, is the unaspected Mercury, suggesting his impact as a songwriter.) After 35 years, Anderson, also a successful entrepreneur, is the only remaining original member of Jethro Tull. Recent album releases include *Divinities* (September 1998) and *The Secret Language of Birds* (March 2000). Anderson married on 7 February 1970, and also won notice for his parallel career as a Laird-like fish farmer.

Jean Anderson

b. 12 December 1907, 13.00 GMT, Eastbourne, England, 50N46, 0E17.
FCC q. her for the date, year and place. Time is speculative. RR: C.
Much-loved veteran of stage, screen and television, Anderson is best known as the tough meddling matriarch in BBC's drama series *The Brothers* (March 1972 to December 1976), which commanded eleven million viewers each week. She waved goodbye to her elegant persona in October 1982 when she joined the cast of *Tenko* for two years as gutsy POW Joss Holbrook. Originally Anderson was a violinist and had also played tennis at junior Wimbledon before studying at RADA with a view to teaching. She ran the Players' Theatre in London during the Second World War and made her film debut in *The Mark of Cain* (1947). Anderson cites *A Town Like Alice* (1956), *The Kidnappers* (1953) and *Lucky Jim* (1957) as her favourite film roles. She made her belated Broadway debut in 1987. She was married from August 1934 until early 1949.

Tom Anderson

b. 29 August 1910, 23.00 GMT, Moorfield, Eshaness, Northmavine, Shetland, 60N00, 01W35.
Gerard q. BC (Thomas James Anderson). RR: AA.
Renowned fiddler and composer of more than 500 tunes, mostly of the Shetland fiddling style (note the lyrical Moon is closely conjunct the Ascendant). Anderson donated his collection to Stirling University in 1980, where he taught Summer School for some years. He was awarded an MBE in 1977. D. 1991.

Eamonn Andrews

b. 19 December 1922, 08.00 GMT, Dublin, Ireland, 53N20, 06W15.

From him to the Astrological Association some years ago. RR: A.

Popular compere best known for fronting the celebrity surprise show *This Is Your Life*, which ran from July 1955 to 1964 and 1969-87. A boxer in his youth (a former All-Ireland Amateur Junior Middleweight Champion), in 1939 Andrews moved into Radio Eireann, eventually working as a sports commentator for BBC radio from 1950 (a regular every Saturday for twelve years). Although often embarrassed, awkward and self-effacing on air (Moon in Capricorn, Saturn on MC), nevertheless he made a successful transition to television in July 1951 with the hugely popular *What's My Line?* (see Lady Isobel Barnett, qv), which made him a household name. His *Eamonn Andrews Show*, the Britain's first chat

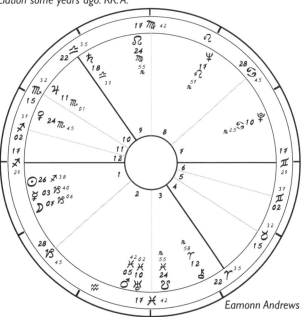

Eamonn Andrews

show, debuted on 1 October 1964 at 23.05. It was poorly received, with Andrews often appearing ill at ease, but the show limped on until 1969. The devoutly religious Andrews (the Jupiter and Saturn overtones) was voted Top Television Personality of the Year four times (Mercury-Moon opposite Pluto attests to his popularity and prominence). D. 5 November 1987, London, heart disease.

Julie Andrews

b. 1 October 1935, 06.00 GDT, Walton-on-Thames, England, 51N24, 0W25.

From Julie Andrews by J. Cottrell (Mayflower, 1969), p. 14, "approximately 6:00 am." RR: B.

Talented leading lady of stage and film. Andrews was a child musical prodigy with a four-octave range who toured in vaudeville and became a sensation at age 12 (as TR Uranus crossed her MC). Her parents had divorced when she was four, and she had been left in a typical Libran predicament of attempting to please both sides. Her mother was a no-nonsense lady who kept young Julie's feet on the ground. With Virgo Rising and Venus prominent, Andrews's mastery of the good-natured, erudite, prim and proper governess in both *Mary Poppins* (August 1964, plus an Academy Award) and *The Sound of Music* (March 1965) made her an international star and the world's top box office attraction for two years (Ascendant/MC ruler Mercury squares Pluto). The former coincided with TR Neptune over her Moon, suggesting the enduring worldwide popularity and devotion that the film evoked. Andrews's wholesome image is perhaps a product of a Virgo Ascendant, Sun in Libra and its ruler, Venus, in Virgo – she is often described as optimistic, earnest, driven and 'in control'. Before her success on film, she was praised for major roles on stage. *The Boy Friend* from 30 September 1954 was her first outing to Broadway, and on 15 March 1956 she began three and a half years of performing eight songs a night as Eliza Doolittle in *My Fair Lady* (her last performance was on 8 August 1959). She teamed up with comedienne Carol Burnett at Carnegie Hall in 1962 and won an Emmy. Andrews married in May 1959, divorcing nine years later on the grounds of cruelty (when TR Uranus moved over the Ascendant) but the couple remained friends. She married again in November 1969 and the following year, she had her first major film disappointment with *Darling Lili* (as TR Pluto crossed her Ascendant). A sugary weekly TV series from September 1972 to April 1973 failed, reflecting the new wave turning away from all-round entertainers of Andrews's stature. Her on-screen persona has hindered offers of more diverse roles. Her film triumph in *Victor, Victoria* (March

1982) marked one move against typecasting (Virgo prominent can exude an androgynous image). A second, the film *10*, was well received in October 1978 (as TR Saturn was near to crossing her Ascendant). Her stage revival of *Victor, Victoria* (722 performances, from November 1995 to 8 June 1997) betrayed the range and quality of voice she once had, although critics welcomed her return to Broadway after 33 years. She left the show suffering from a bacterial infection on her vocal chords and a throat operation later that year was said to have ruined her voice. When in May 1999 she was (wrongly) alleged to have been treated at a clinic for dependency on painkillers, amid rumours of marital separation – she took the

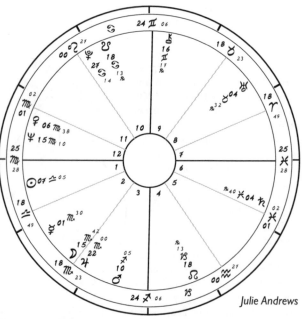

Julie Andrews

tabloids to court (she had been at the clinic to discuss bereavement and the loss of her voice). In June 2002 she volunteered to undergo a risky operation to restore her voice. In late 2001 she starred in the Disney film The Princess Diaries and in October 2002 she was named the 59th Greatest Briton of all time. Andrews portrayed Gertrude Lawrence (qv) in the flop film *Star!* and Maria Von Trapp* in *The Sound of Music*. A look at her synastry with the latter reveals that Andrews's Sun conjuncts Von Trapp's Moon in Libra, while Pluto conjuncts Von Trapp's MC (both helped Andrews to introduce von Trapp's dramatic, adventurous life to a worldwide audience in a wholesome way). *Mary Poppins* was written by Pamela Travers**. Again the synastry is fascinating: JA's MC conjunct PT's Neptune; JA's Neptune on PT's Moon; JA's Venus conjunct PT's Mercury; JA's Mercury on PT's Jupiter.

> "Julie Andrews is a person where extremes meet, both wilful and strong but peculiarly brittle, vulnerable... She's all modesty, self-deprecation. She'd never be boastful enough to think she was just amazingly talented... She has a hopefulness that age just never knocked out of her... I imagine it's excruciating for her to show pain, because she'd see it as weakness. You suddenly realise why she's so adept at sorting out everyone else's problems. Because, of course, we all teach what we need to learn. She so readily jumps into the role of a mythical, capable creature. Inside there's turmoil. That's what's so attractive about her." (Chrissy Iley, *The Sunday Times Magazine*, c.2000)
>
> Q "Discipline is the foundation which leaves me free to fly. If I've got discipline I can take chances. You could call it tradition. You could call it good manners. You could call it knowing how to work hard, but I call it discipline. If you have that, you can really take off, because you've always got that shelf to fall back on." (Julie Andrews, *The Sunday Times Magazine*, c.2000)
>
> "Subtle male and female shadings of personality aside, the world has been trying to figure out the hidden dimensions of this actress for some time now, and Julie's own attempts at showing us her inner self have been mighty inconclusive. For years she's tried to shed layers of her prim screen persona, only to reveal more flawless Limoges beneath." (Timothy White, *The Entertainers*, Billboard Books, 1998)

* Maria Von Trapp b. 25 January 1905, 23.50 MET, on a train en route to Tirol, Austria, 47N48, 13E02. From her autobiography, Maria, My Own Story, p. 12. RR: B.
** Pamela Travers b. 9 August 1899, 12.00 AEST (-10), Maryborough, Australia, 37S03, 143E45. Frances McEvoy q. her. RR: A.

Jack Anthony

b. 4 September 1900, 11.45 GMT, Glasgow, Scotland, 55N52, 04W15.

Gerard q. BC (John Herbertson). RR: AA.

Professional comedian (from 1926), best known for his regular pantomime work (with his catchphrase "Nae better at a'!") at the Pavilion Theatre, Glasgow, from 1931 to his retirement, when he settled down as a hotel owner in Dunbar. Anthony died from a stroke, 28 February 1962, 19.15 GMT, Dunbar (Gerard q. Death Certificate).

George Arliss

◖ *b. 10 April 1868, 00.30 GMT, London, England, 51N30, 0W10.*

From Church of Light, no source (Sabian Symbols #44 gives 00.06 LMT; also 1869 given). RR: DD.

A highly-respected actor of stage and screen, Arliss made his stage debut at 18 in September 1886. In 1902 an American stage tour brought him both film and theatre offers in the USA, where he remained for 20 years specialising in villainous roles. He won the Academy Award for *Disraeli* (released 2 October 1929) on 5 November 1930. Arliss married on 16 September 1899. D. 5 February 1946.

Jane Asher

b. 5 April 1946, 22.00 GMT, London, England, 51N30, 0W10.

FCC q. her. RR: A.

Actress, businesswoman, cook and writer, often perceived as prim and "giving off a general image of ladylike perfection" (MC in Virgo). Asher made her first professional acting appearance at 5 in the film *Mandy*, and won acclaim in *The Greengage Summer* (1961). In 1976 she joined the National Theatre. She lived with cartoonist Gerald Scarfe for ten years before they secretly married in 1983, and she is a successful mother of three. Asher has gained fame for a variety of reasons: as Paul McCartney's (qv) 'posh dollybird' and muse for four years from the age of 17 until 20 July 1968 (she has remained silently dignified about the relationship); for acting roles in *Alfie* (1966) and *Brideshead Revisited* (1981); as a cosy cake-baker with a string of

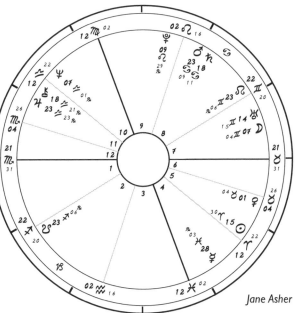

Jane Asher

cookery books; and most recently, as a novelist (*The Longing*, published October 1996). Although Asher's Sun is in the dramatic 5th house, her retrograde planets (including Mercury, ruling the MC) demonstrate that her true vocation came through her later efforts as a writer and cook (Venus in Taurus). She makes the occasional acting appearance, and a while back starred in the television drama *Closing Numbers* as a woman coming to terms with her bisexual husband's infidelity; with this project Asher added to her impressive range. In January 2003 she joined the cast of the revamped soap *Crossroads* as the power-crazy hotel boss (releasing her Aries-Scorpio inner bitch!).

Peter Asher – see Gordon Waller

Michael Aspel

> b. 12 January 1933, 04.00 GMT, Battersea, London, England, 51N28, 0W10.
> FCC q. him. RR: A.

Television's Mr Smoothie, known for his relaxed and charming manner in such programmes as *Ask Aspel* (1970-4, 1976-81), *Give Us a Clue* (1979-83), *Aspel and Company* (1984-93), *Strange... But True?* and, from 2000, *Antiques Roadshow*. In October 1988 he replaced Eamonn Andrews (qv) on *This Is Your Life* (Aspel quit in early June 2003). Aspel began his career as an actor with BBC radio (1954-7) then moved into TV announcing (1957-60) and news reading (1960-8). He was also a presenter of *Crackerjack* (1968-70, 1972-4). Aspel's horoscope carries the major significators for TV presenting to a wide audience: authoritative Jupiter prominent for self-promotion (on MC with Mars), Pluto aspecting Moon, Mercury or Sun (Pluto

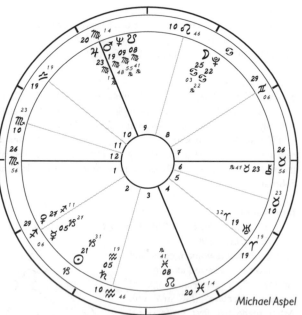

Michael Aspel

conjuncts Moon and opposes Sun). Interestingly, Aspel has only one planet in an Air sign in his horoscope – suggesting the desire to communicate is demonstrated more vividly from the above significators. In addition there are strong EQHS connections in the chart between the 3rd (talk shows and presenting), 5th (audience) and 9th (TV/Media) with his EQHS 10th and MC (Aspel has 5th rulers Jupiter (on MC) and Neptune in 10th, his 3rd ruler is placed in 3rd, and 9th ruler Moon conjuncts Pluto). Aspel has survived turbulent times in his private life. In 1971, and again in June 1988, he suffered heavy financial losses from investments. In January 1989 he flew to Australia to comfort his dying son (who had been diagnosed with cancer in November 1986). He separated from his third wife Lizzie Power (best known for her on-going performance in *EastEnders*) in May 1995.

Margot Asquith

> b. 2 February 1864, 03.30 GMT, The Glen, Traquair, Scotland, 55N36, 03W03.
> Gerard q. BC (Alice Emma Margaret Tennant). RR: AA.

With a Libra MC and the Moon and Jupiter Rising, Margot Asquith was an extravagant, sparkling society hostess (from 1881) who married Herbert Asquith (Liberal P.M. from 12 April 1908 to 7 December 1916) and after his resignation wrote a set of indiscreet autobiographies (Jupiter conjunct her Sagittarian Ascendant). Asquith was sharp and uncompromising (Moon in Scorpio, Sun in Aquarius square Pluto), and her influential friends included Gladstone and Virginia Woolf. D. 28 July 1945.

AVERAGE WHITE BAND

This soul-influenced band formed in 1971, with a first gig in July 1972 and a debut album in 1973. With natal Uranus on the MC, McIntosh's sudden death from a heroin overdose on 23 September 1974 acted as a catalyst in the band's fortunes (Gorrie, whose own life was saved by Cher, had TR Uranus square Sun, and TR Mars-Pluto on Neptune, ruler of hard drugs). McIntosh was replaced by Steve Ferrone (b. 25 April 1950, Brighton, England) and the band soon began to achieve commercial success and critical acclaim with the album *AWB*, hitting the top of the US charts in February 1975. By 1980 a failed album had signalled the demise of the group but Gorrie (who went on to release a solo album in 1985), Ball and McIntyre reformed in August 1989, performing at small venues in the UK and USA. In 1997 they toured again to promote *Soul Tattoo*. Hamish Stuart was born 8 October 1949 in Glasgow.

Roger Ball
    b. 4 June 1944, 16.25 DGDT, Broughty Ferry, Scotland, 56N28, 02W52.
    Gerard q. BC (Roger Alister Ball). RR: AA.
Malcolm 'Molly' Duncan
    b. 24 August 1945, 01.40 GDT, Montrose, Scotland, 56N42, 02W28.
    Gerard q. BC (Malcolm Stuart Duncan). RR: AA.
Alan Gorrie
    b. 19 July 1946, 09.00 GDT, Perth, Scotland, 56N23, 03W27.
    Gerard q. BC (Alan Edward William Gorrie). RR: AA.
Robbie McIntosh
    b. 2 May 1950, 16.30 GDT, Maryfield Hospital, Dundee, Scotland, 56N28, 02W58.
    Gerard q. BC (Robert Rattray Stewart McIntosh). RR: AA.
Owen 'Onnie' McIntyre
    b. 25 September 1945, 12.30 GDT, Lennox Castle, Scotland, 55N59, 04W14.
    Gerard q. BC (Owen McIntyre). RR: AA.

Mick Avory – see The Kinks
Alan Ayckbourn – see Belinda Giblin, Australian Data

Pam Ayres
    b. 14 March 1947, 21.00 GMT, Stanford in the Vale, Cotswolds, England, 51N38, 01W32.
    David Fisher q. a letter from Ayres's secretary, which quotes a telephone conversation with Ayres. RR: A.

Gifted raconteur and poet, popular since her discovery – in 1975 at age 28 – on *Opportunity Knocks*. A loner at school, Ayres soon discovered the power her comedic talents had over her classmates. Prior to her 'overnight fame' she had worked tirelessly to break onto the national stage (retrograde Saturn is on the MC, suggesting the long struggle and the typecasting that followed). She even published and distributed her own pamphlet of verse, which sold 7,000 copies. She made her radio debut in Autumn 1974, when TR Uranus hit the Ascendant). Following her contest win, Ayres left her day job in an office on 13 February 1976 to concentrate on her writing. She admits that she spent the next 20 years adjusting and learning how to do the job (Mercury in Pisces quincunx Pluto on the MC). Ayres married her manager Dudley Russell in July 1982 (TR Pluto on Ascendant) and gave birth to their first son that December. Her husband helped her out of a legal problem with her previous agent, who had tricked her into signing over copyright of her work some years before. In early 1994 she was back for a six-month sell-out tour entitled *The Works*. With three 5th House planets, she has a devoted following who appreciate her trademark doggerel verse, yokel accent, and reassuring everyday colloquial anthems.

Pam Ayres

Mel B – see Spice Girls
Tom Bailey – see Alannah Currie

Isobel Baillie

> b. 9 March 1895, 03.15 GMT, Wilton, Roxburghshire, Scotland, 55N25, 02W48.
> Gerard q. BC (Isabella Baillie). RR: AA.

Hailed as one of the great oratorio singers of the century (a strong Saturn on the MC), Dame Isobel Baillie made her debut in 1921 and achieved universal praise for her opening season in London two years later. She gave over one thousand performances of Handel's *Messiah*. D. 24 September 1983.

Aly Bain

> b. 15 May 1946, 01.45 GDT, Lerwick, Scotland, 60N09, 01W09.
> Gerard q. BC (Alistair Bain). RR: AA.

Acclaimed and influential fiddler (with Pluto square both Moon and Mercury) who studied under Tom Anderson (qv). Professional from 1968, Bain joined up with singer-guitarist Mike Whellans for tours and recordings, culminating in a sold-out Carnegie Hall concert in 1989 as a member of the quartet Boys of the Lough. An eponymous solo album had been released in 1984, featuring Shetland fiddle tunes and tunes from other countries. Later Bain merged classical and folk styles on his album *Follow the Moonstone*. He was awarded an MBE in 1994 and in 1999 was given a doctorate from the Royal Scottish Academy of Music and Drama. In November 2001 he released a Celtic-Nordic album project, *Fully Rigged*.

Ian Bairnson

> b. 3 August 1953, 03.30 GDT, Maternity Hospital, Lerwick, Scotland, 60N09, 01W09.
> Gerard q. BC (Ian John MacGregor Bairnson). RR: AA.

Guitarist, bassist, percussionist, singer and songwriter who has leant his talents to a variety of acts, including Alan Parsons. He joined Pilot in 1974 and the band reached the top of the British charts in February 1975 (when TR Jupiter had passed over his MC). The band soon dissolved and Bairnson played on Kate Bush's first album.

Cheryl Baker

✪ b. 8 March 1954, 13.00 GMT, Bethnal Green, London, England, 51N32, 0W03.
> From her to an astrologer on BBC1's The Eleventh Hour (November 1996). RR: A.

Baker (born Rita Crudgington) was a member of the pop group Bucks Fizz, formed to represent the UK in the Eurovision Song Contest on 4 April 1981. Their song, *Making Your Mind Up*, won and became the first of three chart-toppers for the band (Baker had scored a hit in May 1978 with a previous contest entry). With Cancer on the Ascendant Baker, ambitious and tenacious, was the 'mumsy' girl member of the group (Jay Aston had the sexy image and posed semi-nude). At 23.00 on 11 December 1984 the group sustained serious injuries in a road accident in Newcastle (for Cheryl, TR Uranus was conjunct Mars, and TR Neptune squared MC). Minor hits and a change in line-up followed their recovery, but the

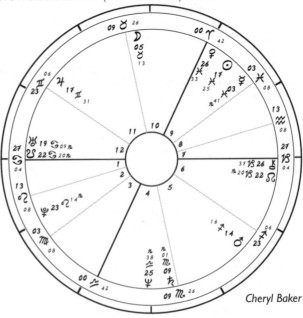

Cheryl Baker

original band dissolved in 1989. With youthful Venus on the MC and five retrograde planets, Baker moved into a second career presenting children's TV and accepting promotional work with her twin girls (born by Caesarean just after midnight on 20 June 1994 in North London after a third stab at IVF treatment). She attributes her career success not to a remarkable talent but rather to the luck of being in the right place at the right time.

Tom Baker

☄ b. 20 January 1934, 05.50 GMT, Liverpool, England, 53N25, 02W55.
David Fisher q. a letter from Jean Diamond, Baker's agent for 05.40. Misty Kuceris (Mercury Hour, January 1991) q. him for 06.10; and a letter from him in October 1984 states "I believe it was 5.20 or 6.20." Times of birth range from 05.20 to 06.20. Mid-time arbitrary. RR: C.

Actor best known for being the fourth (and most popular) eccentric *Doctor Who*, appearing regularly from the twelfth season in December 1974 to March 81 (he was working on a building site at the time he was cast). He has also appeared in *Medics* and as the sexually awakened priest in *The Life and Loves of a She Devil*. For years he hosted a children's factual show, *The Book Tower*, and in 1999 wrote a children's book, *The Boy Who Kicked Pigs*. Baker grew up in poverty and ran away from home at 15 and entered a monastery for six years. After marriage in 1960, he admits to having tried to kill his mother-in-law. A nervous breakdown followed the collapse of this marriage in 1965, before he was rescued by minor stage roles and work as a labourer. Baker married again in 1980 and for a third time in 1987.

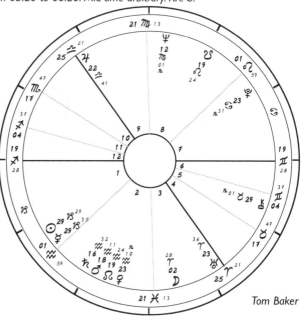

Tom Baker

Q "He is a huge presence of naughtiness, a sort of biblical Noah, with a warm booming voice... the archetypal overgrown schoolboy." (Joanna Pitman, *Metro*, 30/10/99)
"When you're brought up as I was, with no self-regard; when you are brought up to feel the awful guilt of being worthless... it means that you're actually capable of accepting terrible things and believing that that's what you deserve... so I carried on because somewhere in my madness and confusion and idiocy, I felt that it was part of this martyrdom that I'd always wanted, that I was worthless." (Tom Baker, *Metro*, 30/10/99)

Joan Bakewell

✪ b. 16 April 1933, 22.30 GDT, Stockport, England, 53N25, 02W10.
FCC q. a reliable private source, who obtained the data from Bakewell. RR: A.

Intelligent and articulate presenter of BBC's *Heart of the Matter*, on which various issues are explored and debated. She won the Richard Dimbleby Award in 1994 for journalism. A recent biography on Harold Pinter* detailed a long affair between the playwright and Bakewell. Often referred to by her sobriquet as the Thinking Man's Crumpet, she is infamous for having changed her Northern accent overnight whilst at Cambridge. Bakewell has also appeared in *Late Night Line Up* and *Reports Action*. In October 2000 she spoke of her relationship with her mother (Moon in Capricorn opposite Pluto and square Uranus-Venus-Sun) and the damage to it caused by the beating she received for stealing:

---

* Harold Pinter b. 10 October 1930, 14.00 GMT, London, England, 51N30, 0W10. Joan Revill q. him. RR: A.

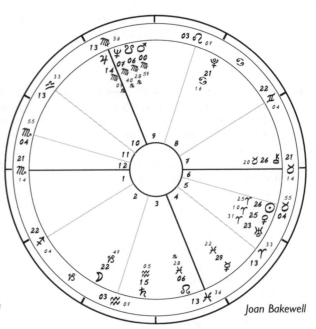

Joan Bakewell

"I was one of the results of my mother's efforts... I was required to have perfect manners, good school reports... and to maintain a reputation for moral behaviour that brought credit on the family... [After the beating] I grew adept at concealing these petty errors while my mother, suspicious but without proof, couldn't break my resolve... That early tension survived. And with it went the knowledge that she would, if she could, impose her own will on mine." (J. Bakewell, *Mail on Sunday*, 29/10/2000)

David Ball – see Marc Almond
Roger Ball – see Average White Band
Tony Banks – see Genesis

Ian Bannen

b. 29 June 1928, 05.00 GDT, Maternity Hospital, Airdrie, Scotland, 55N52, 04W00.
Gerard q. BC (Ian Edmund Bannen). RR: AA.

A stage actor from Summer 1947 (*Armlet of Jade*), Bannen appeared on TV from March 1955 and graduated to supporting and lead film roles. He appeared in *The Flight of the Phoenix* (1965), for which he won an Oscar nomination. Other notable work includes *Jesus of Nazareth* (TV, 1977) and the film *Hope and Glory* (1987), but Bannen turned down the lucrative lead role in *Hawaii Five-O*. On leaving school he had joined the army and even considered becoming a monk. Bannen had a long battle with drink (Moon square Neptune) until hepatitis forced him to give it up. D. 3 November 1999, car crash.

Bill Barclay

✪ *b. 22 February 1943, 21.15 GDT, South Lorne Place, Leith, Scotland, 55N58, 03W10.*
Gerard q. BC (William Pryde Barclay). RR: AA.

Comedy singer, actor and radio host who supported Elton John (qv) and Rod Stewart (qv) in the 70s.

Ronnie Barker

✪ *b. 25 September 1929, 14.00 GDT, Bedford, England, 52N08, 0W29.*
Pete Watson q. Barker's letter. RR: A.

Barker was one of the most famous comedy faces on British TV, thanks to leading roles in *Open All Hours* (20 February 1976 to 6 December 1985, when TR Uranus conjunct his Ascendant), *Porridge* (5 September 1974 to 25 March 1977, when TR Neptune conjunct his Ascendant) and his comedy partnership with Ronnie Corbett (qv). In fact Barker has always worked best alongside a comedy actor of equal calibre (the Libra MC). With Corbett in *The Two Ronnies* (1971-87) they regularly topped the TV ratings. Barker's chart has a number of powerful success indicators: Moon-Jupiter on the Descendant is trine Mars-Mercury on the MC, as well as being opposite Saturn on the Ascendant. These features point to his comedic talent and temperament: the larger-than-life characters (Moon-Jupiter), the saucy humour (Mars-MC), and dead-pan delivery in *Porridge* (Saturn-Ascendant – the character Norman Stanley Fletcher was 'born' on 2 February 1932). Although an angular Saturn is synonymous with being typecast, Barker's chart clearly has too many features (including MC ruler Venus conjunct Neptune) for him to be anything but versatile. Barker, who worked on his characters by developing the make-up and clothes rather than the personality, even lampooned eccentric astronomer Patrick Moore* (the synastry is marvellous: Barker's Jupiter on Moore's Ascendant for his hilarious send-up, Barker's Sun conjunct Moore's Moon, and Barker's MC on Moore's rigid Saturn, plus Ascendants opposite one another). Retiring in 1988 to run an antiques business, he emerged for a small role in a drama about Churchill.

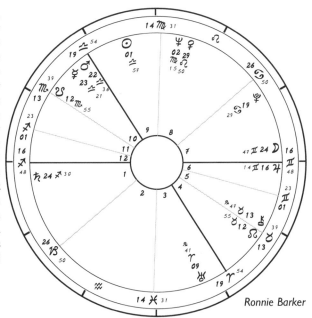

Ronnie Barker

Gary Barlow – see Take That

Jimmy Barnes

✪ b. 28 April 1956, 16.30 GDT, Maternity Hospital, Glasgow, Scotland, 55N51, 04W14.
Gerard q. BC (James Dixon Swan). RR: AA.

Singer who formed the hard rock band Cold Chisel in Australia in 1977 before going solo in 1984.

Isobel Barnett

b. 30 June 1918, 21.15 GDT, Holburn, Aberdeen, Scotland, 57N09, 02W07.
Gerard q. BC (Isobel Morag Marshall). RR: AA.

Elegant TV personality who won the attention of millions as a panelist on the quiz show *What's My Line?* (from July 1953). Married to Sir Geoffrey Barnett, a Mayor of Leicester, she had given up practising medicine to rear their son (MC ruler Mars opposite Moon-Chiron suggests the sacrifice). Extremely image-conscious with an air of superiority, she basked in publicity and the superficiality of her status (Sagittarian Ascendant, Jupiter on Descendant). When the 7th House is strongly tenanted, others' opinions matter most. As her popularity faded, she began shoplifting in 1978. Apprehended for her attention-seeking, she was prosecuted on 17 October 1980 and committed suicide two days later (TR Jupiter on EQHS 10th, TR Saturn on Mars).

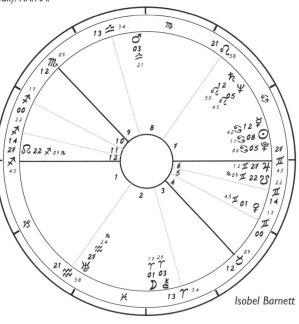

Isobel Barnett

* Patrick Moore b. 4 March 1923, 10.00 GMT, Pinner, England, 51N36, 0W23. From his book *Can you Speak Venusian?* RR: B.

Wendy Barrie

b. 18 April 1912, 15.15 GMT, London, England, 51N30, 0W10.
Ralph Kraum (in Astro-Science, Fall 1942) q. her. RR: A.

Barrie began her stage career in 1930 and the following year moved into films. A contract brought her to Hollywood for a couple of dozen films (from 1936) before her relationship with a mobster made her an unsafe bet for film roles (note 7th House ruler Neptune squares MC ruler Mercury – the association tarnished her reputation). With Jupiter in the EQHS 3rd on the IC, Barrie began one of TV's earliest talk shows (in 1949). D. 2 February 1978, Englewood, New Jersey.

John Barrowman

b. 11 March 1967, 17.25 GMT, Robroyston Hospital, Glasgow, Scotland, 55N54, 04W11.
Gerard q. BC (John Scot Barrowman). RR: AA.

Intense, versatile and a natural on stage, John Barrowman spread his talents in the direction of the West End theatre and regular children's television, before tackling TV in the US by appearing in night-time soaps. By 1998 Barrowman had tasted success in every medium in which he had worked (note the healthy dose of talent and luck from his grand trine of Neptune-Jupiter-Sun/Moon/Saturn). After arriving in England in 1989, audiences watched the part Scottish, part American-accented entertainer present Saturday morning television for children. During this time he was also appearing in some six West End musicals (*Anything Goes, Miss Saigon, Matador, The Phantom of the Opera, Rope, Hair*). A year after starring

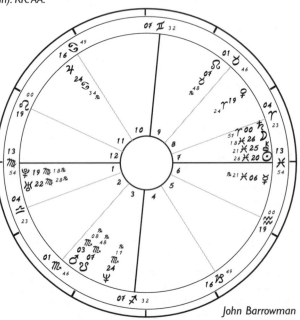

John Barrowman

alongside Betty Buckley in the London production of *Sunset Boulevard*, he was approached to star in the US drama *Central Park West*, which began in September 1995, and later appeared in *Titans*. (Back in 1984, to further his professional ambitions, Barrowman had become a naturalised American.) Prominence is shown vividly in his horoscope with Pluto and Uranus Rising opposite his Sun-Moon in Pisces, although relationship dramas may equally dominate his life. Mercury retrograde in Pisces (ruling the MC) and five more retrograde planets suggest his restlessness will result in him moving on and finding a new direction.

Michael Barrymore

b. 4 May 1952, 08.00 GDT, Bermondsey, London, England, 51N30, 0W05.
Old Moore's Almanac 1995 q. his agency (verified by FCC). (N.B. His Ascendant may be Gemini, which was rising from approximately 06.15 to 07.59.) RR: A.

Rake-thin, hyperactive TV presenter and manic quiz-master (MC ruler Uranus in 1st House), Barrymore (born Michael Parker) was the highest-paid man in British show business before a series of bizarre and tragic events turned the public against him. With a Moon in Virgo making three trines and two sextiles, he was loved for his game show *Strike it Lucky* (later *Strike it Rich*) broadcast from 1986, and for poking fun (sometimes cruelly) at members of the public in a number of other shows, but often not knowing where to draw the line of good taste or respect. Nevertheless his talent lay in audience participation and this was ground-breaking. His father, a violent and chronic drinker, walked out on Michael and his mother when Michael was 11 (natal Pluto on the IC). He joined a rock and roll band before becoming a Butlin's Redcoat. From a January 1973 audition to perform as a stand-up comedian, what followed were a number of lean years trying to establish himself. Barrymore appeared on *New Faces* in 1975 and met his future wife. He married on 10 June 1976 (the year he was declared bankrupt) and his fiercely protective wife/manager Cheryl steered his career, providing his Virgoan Moon with the personal order and stability it craved. He was booked on TV's *London Night Out* in 1982 which led to Thames TV commissioning six half-hour shows for him. A Royal Variety Performance in 1983 led to a Saturday night slot with *Strike it Lucky*, which garnered 14 million viewers at its peak. Soon Barrymore was a household name. When his beloved father-in-law died on 3 November 1990, Barrymore

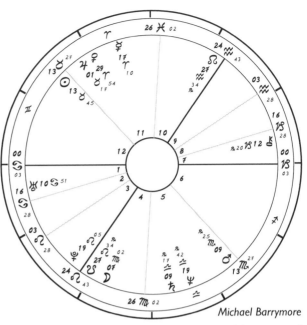

Michael Barrymore

was devastated and suffered a nervous breakdown. His marriage began to crumble and he continued his hard-drinking lifestyle until Spring 1993, when he sought professional help in a rehab clinic (as TR Saturn and Pluto aspected the MC). After wrestling with his sexuality for many years, he revealed his homosexuality during a live programme on London's Spectrum Radio (23 August 1995, at around 02.00), and in Summer 1995, reports of his on-again, off-again marriage kept the tabloids busy (elevated Mercury opposite Neptune). The couple split for good in October 1997 (their divorce was granted on 23 December) and Barrymore married his male partner in Hawaii in 1999, with talk of adopting children, but they too split in March 2001. By this time Barrymore's drinking had been seriously affecting him professionally and personally – he was fast becoming a loose cannon. He checked into rehab in May 1996, at a time when his show, *My Kind of People*, was axed. His mother, with whom he was estranged for eight years, died on 22 September 2001. His vulnerability endeared him to his public (he won an unprecedented number of TV awards and signed a £2.5 million contract with ITV) until an event that occurred during the early hours of 31 March 2001 (as TR Uranus conjunct Barrymore's MC). A man, Stuart Lubbock, was found unconscious in Barrymore's swimming pool, having suffered a "serious sexual trauma" (he was pronounced dead in hospital at 08.32). A Total Eclipse on 21 June 2001 (conjunct Barrymore's Ascendant, with TR Uranus retracking over the MC) followed his arrest for drug offences on 6 June (later bailed without charge). Barrymore fled the country to seek therapy (as TR Jupiter crossed his Ascendant) and his career was left in tatters. On 13 September 2002 an open verdict was given at the young man's inquest. Barrymore's former wife and manager, Cheryl, published an explosive biography in October 2002 about their life together. (According to the book, *Catch a Falling Star*, Robson, p. 10, she was born on 22 March 1950 in the East End Maternity Hospital, London.) Cheryl was born with Venus opposite Pluto, both square Moon in Taurus, and Sun in Aries opposite Mars in Libra. She wrote of her turbulent life with her ex-husband, recounting stories of his alleged violence towards her. Barrymore, who was sacked in September 2002, was playing to small audiences in New Zealand in April 2003 in an attempt to rebuild his career. Barrymore is known to be fragile, hypersensitive and self-critical (Mercury opposite Neptune, Moon in Virgo) with a deep-seated melancholy. His recent behaviour has had him labelled self-destructive and reckless.

> Q "He could take the once-sterile TV formats and make them compulsively watchable by the sheer force of his personality... It was the note of excitement, even danger, he brought to his work... Barrymore seemed to walk an even higher, more delicate tightrope than his peers." (David Thomas, *Daily Mail*, 5/6/01)

Mike Barson

b. 21 April 1958, 07.30 GDT, Millerfield Place, Edinburgh, Scotland, 55N57, 03W11.
Gerard q. BC (Michael Barson). RR: AA.

Founding member and keyboard-player of ska-influenced group Madness, which achieved 14 UK Top Ten hits between 1980 and 1983. Having helped form the bluebeat-based band Invaders in 1976, Barson played his first gig with them on 30 June 1977. Renamed Madness in January 1979, the group released a first single that September. In December 1983, after their most commercially successful year in the USA, Barson announced his intention to leave and settle in Holland with his wife, a move that sounded the death knell for the group (Barson's TR Uranus conjunct Descendant, TR Pluto opposite Sun). The group announced its own split on 1 September 1986. In June 1992 they reformed to perform two concerts in Finsbury Park, London. Madstock, as it became known, continued for a further four summers.

Martin Bashir

✪   b. 19 January 1963, 12.30 GMT, London, 51N30, 0W10.
From him to FCC via a private source. RR: A.

A TV interviewer, Bashir was famously an accessory in Princess Diana's revenge interview on *Panorama* in November 1995. (Diana's Jupiter — indiscreet and publicity-hungry — conjuncts his MC and confessional Saturn is on his Sun; his Mars conjoins her explosive Uranus triggering her T-Square). With that interview (prepared and filmed in secret), he made his reputation (TR Uranus, his MC ruler, conjunct Sun), and later interviewed notorious nanny Louise Woodward. Bashir made the headlines in early February 2003 when his interview with Michael Jackson (filmed over eight months) was shown. Bashir was heavily criticised for his approach, and Jackson aired his own footage of the filming a week later.

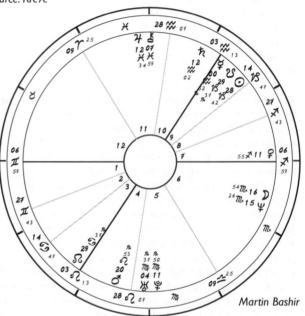

Martin Bashir

Shirley Bassey

☾   b. 8 January 1937, 09.00 GMT, Tiger Bay, Cardiff, Wales, 51N29, 03W13.
David Fisher q. Roger Elliot, original source not known. RR: C.

Celebrated singer and camp diva (Jupiter prominently placed in a Gauquelin zone) with a panache for attacking songs with the sheer power and range of her voice ('Bassey the Belter' — Pluto opposing Mercury, possibly on the Ascendant). Sales of her singles and albums in the UK place her above all other British female vocalists, and Bassey has scored two chart-toppers (February 1959 and September 1961, when TR Jupiter crossed the 09.00 MC and Ascendant respectively). Discovered in 1955, and a star from Christmas 1955 (TR Saturn on Moon and later MC), she had her first hit in 1957, and by the early 60s was headlining in New York (1961) and Las Vegas (Americans called her the "Musical High Priestess of Soul and Sex"). Top entertainment awards in 1976 and 1977 attested to her longevity and popularity, and her three Bond film tunes contributed to her ranking as one of the Top 100 most famous people of the twentieth century. She moved to Switzerland in 1969 and announced her semi-retirement in 1981, before embarking on numerous comebacks in the 80s (the possible Moon-MC suggests popularity that waxes and wanes — phases in and out of the spotlight).

She had once loved Peter Finch (qv) and was distraught at his death on 14 January 1977. She is a private person living a public life and refuses to discuss in detail the deaths of those closest to her, including the tragedy that befell her daughter, found in a river on 7 September 1985 (the death was thought to have been suicide). Bassey continues to delight audiences and, in 1996, her show-stopping performances brought her back into the limelight, as did a guest appearance on a pop hit in 1997, *History Repeating*. Since the early 90s she has lived in Monte Carlo. On 10 April 2003 she was awarded France's Legion d'Honneur, and there was talk of marriage.

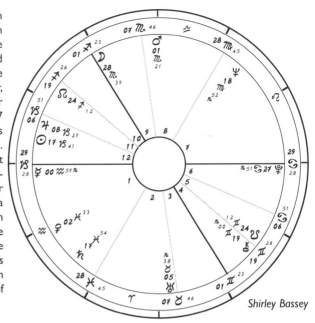

Shirley Bassey

Q "She still performs with the same air of wounded optimism, as if she really believes in the power of spangled dresses, feline movements of the head, and loud, forcefully pronounced words... She projects a blindness to pain, a need to keep smiling through." (William Leith, *Night & Day*, 16/6/96)

Stanley Baxter

b. 24 May 1926, 02.15 GDT, Glasgow, Scotland, 55N52, 04W17.
Gerard q. BC (Stanley Livingston Baxter). RR: AA.

Versatile comic actor and impressionist (Sun in Gemini square MC ruler Jupiter on the Ascendant) known for his nervous disposition, and for his masterful use of the split-screen technique on his television shows. A perfectionist, Baxter's professional debut was at the Edinburgh Festival production in 1948. Pantomime (the strong Jupiter) from 1949 brought much stage work until his breakthrough with two popular television series, *Stanley Baxter On...* in 1960 (when TR Uranus moved over his Descendant), and later *The Stanley Baxter Show* (1967-1971). His career was resurrected for Channel 4 in 1995. On 13 December 1997 Baxter won a Lifetime Achievement Award at the British Comedy Awards (TR Jupiter on Ascendant).

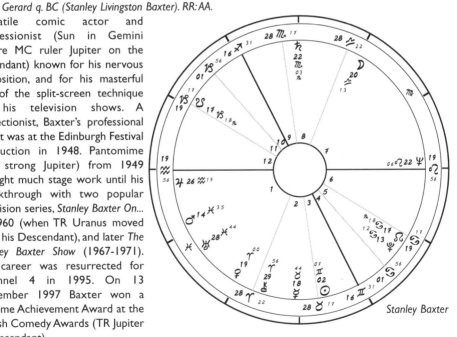

Stanley Baxter

BAY CITY ROLLERS

A 70s tennybop sensation, the Longmuir brothers and their band won their first big break in 1971 and scored their first chart hit that October. Wood and McKeown joined them in January 1973. Between October 1971 and October 1976 the tartan-clad band achieved ten consecutive Top Ten hits and won millions of teenage fans. The peak of their success occurred during 1975 with back-to-back #1 hits in Britain, and in February 1976 they earned a place at the top of the US chart. During the 70s they sold 70 million records. Alan Longmuir retired from the band in April 1976 (replaced by Ian Mitchell, who was later replaced by Pat McGlynn in late 1977) and aimed to win back a personal life. What followed was one personal disaster after another for the remaining members: suicide attempts, a conviction of gross indecency against teenage boys (the band's manager, in May 1982), and McKeown, the colourful front man, being charged with reckless driving after hitting and killing a 75-year-old widow. In addition the band realised in 1985 that they were owed millions of pounds in royalties. Alan Longmuir, a plumber by trade, was bitter and angry at the money owed to him and went on to suffer from depression (Uranus and Sagittarius are usually highlighted in the charts of those with on-going depression, and Longmuir has Sun-Uranus opposite a Moon-Jupiter conjunction in Sagittarius). Drink problems (Neptune squares Mercury-Venus) and a marriage break-up followed

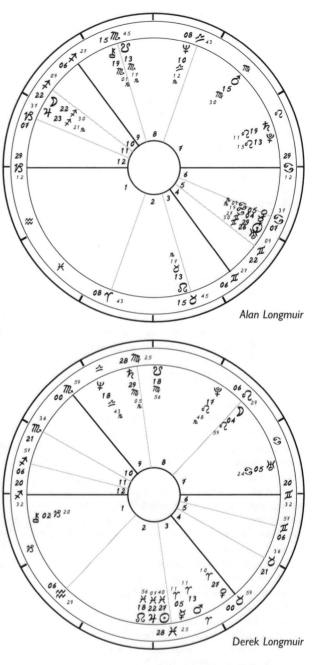

Alan Longmuir

Derek Longmuir

in 1990. On 1 February 1997 (TR Neptune towards his Ascendant), two years after recovering from a heart attack, Alan suffered a stroke (from a blood clot on his brain). Since then the band have reunited and, with the exception of Derek Longmuir, toured in Japan and America. Derek Longmuir became a registered nurse in Edinburgh in 1995 and (following TR Neptune opposite his Moon) appeared in court on 3 March 2000 admitting possession of photos of child pornography. At the time of the raid he was said to be living with a 15 year-old boy he had met in Portugal.

Alan Longmuir

> b. 20 June 1948, 23.35 GDT, Simpson Memorial Maternity Pavilion, Edinburgh, Scotland, 55N57, 03W12.
>
> Gerard q. BC. RR: AA.

Derek Longmuir

> b. 19 March 1951, 02.25 GMT, Western General Hospital, Edinburgh, Scotland, 55N57, 03W13.
>
> Gerard q. BC. RR: AA.

Pat McGlynn

> b. 31 March 1958, 17.25 GMT, The Jewel, Edinburgh, Scotland, 55N56, 03W07.
>
> Gerard q. BC (Patrick James McGlynn). RR: AA.

Leslie McKeown

> b. 12 November 1955, 10.10 GMT, Simpson Memorial Maternity Pavilion, Edinburgh, Scotland, 55N57, 03W12.
>
> Gerard q. BC (Leslie Richard McKeown). RR: AA.

Stuart Wood

> b. 25 February 1957, 17.05 GMT, Simpson Memorial Maternity Pavilion, Edinburgh, Scotland, 55N57, 03W12.
>
> Gerard q. BC. RR: AA.

Other members without full data: Eric Faulkner (b. 21 October 1955, Edinburgh) and Ian Mitchell (b. 22 August 1958).

Ian Bayne – see Runrig

Stephanie Beacham

(Confidential data)

Independent actress with a strong Gemini overtone in her chart (plus Moon and Venus strongly placed). Beacham has often been cast in glamorous and predatory parts, making a career out of the posh, sexy bitch (*Dynasty* co-creator Richard Pollack said that she can say "hello" on the telephone and sound bitchy!). Beacham is best known for her continuing role in *The Colbys* and later *Dynasty* (acting like a evil pantomime queen and being paid $20,000 a week to do so!). Beacham became famous in lead roles in the British TV series *Connie* (the part was written as a heavily disguised tribute to Margaret Thatcher!) and *Tenko* (from late October 1981). She was born with no hearing in her right ear and reduced hearing in her left. Passionate about ballet as a teenager, she was rejected by the Royal Ballet School. At 23 she stripped for *Playboy* and promptly lost her cosmetics advertising job. Beacham was discovered in 1971 and cast in Michael Winner's 1972 film *The Nightcomers* with Marlon Brando. Ironically the legend goes that later she was blacklisted in Hollywood for not posing nude to promote the film. She gave up work in 1974 when she married, but the marriage dissolved in the mid-80s. After 'chasing the dollar' and moving to Los Angeles in May 1985 to take the role in *The Colbys*, she returned to England in 1996 to nurse both parents (her mother died in 1998 and her father died in May 1999). Beacham joined the cast of *Bad Girls* in May 2003.

THE BEATLES

•1957, July 6 – Lennon, a member of The Quarry Men Skiffle Group, meets McCartney after a gig.

•1957, Oct 18 – McCartney makes his debut with Lennon's band.

•1958, July 15 – Lennon's mother dies in a road accident.

•1958, Aug – Harrison joins the band, and they record a demo.

•1960, Jan – Stuart Sutcliffe (qv) joins on bass.

•1960, Oct 15 – Starr first plays with the newly-named Beatles.

•1961, Nov 9 – Brian Epstein (qv) meets the band for the first time (he signs them two months later, and to a five-year contract in October 1962).

•1962, May 9 – They sign a contract with EMI.

•1962, Aug 14 – Starr replaces Pete Best (b. 24 November 1941, Madras, India), who was fired.

•1962, Aug 23 – Lennon marries Cynthia Powell (she sues him for divorce in August 1968, finalised on 8 November).

•1963 – Domination of the international music scene begins.

•1963, May – The first of eleven consecutive #1 British releases.

•1963, Sep – *She Loves You* tops the charts, and soon becomes the biggest selling UK single until McCartney's *Mull of Kintyre*.

•1964, Feb 7 – They arrive at JFK Airport, Queen, NY at 13.35; and perform on the *Ed Sullivan Show* two days later.

•1966, Jan 21 – Harrison marries Patti Boyd in Epsom.

•1966, Mar 4 – Lennon is quoted as saying the Beatles are bigger than Jesus.

•1968, Feb 16 & 18 – The band travels to India for two months of transcendental meditation study.

•1968, Jul 1 – Lennon publicly declares his love for Yoko Ono (they had met on 9 November 1966).

•1968, Nov 29 – Lennon is fined for possession of cannabis (after a police raid on 18 October).

•1969, Mar 12 – McCartney marries Linda Eastman.

•1969, Mar 20 – Lennon marries Yoko Ono; they begin their 'Bed-In' the following day in Amsterdam.

•1970, Feb 29 – Lennon's US visa runs out, beginning a three-year fight to stay in America.

•1970, Apr 9 – McCartney quits the group. He files suit on 31 December 1970 to dissolve the enterprise (agreed in court on 12 March 1971).

•1971, Jan – Harrison's hit *My Sweet Lord* tops the UK chart.

•1971, Oct – Lennon's album *Imagine* hits US and UK #1.

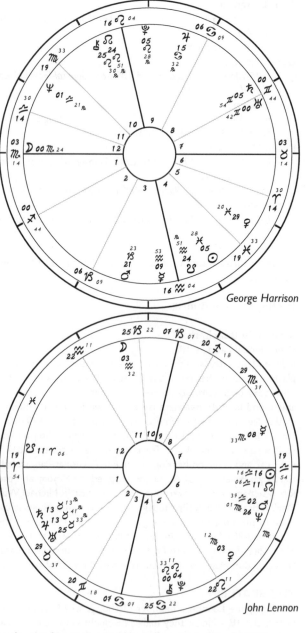

George Harrison

John Lennon

•1972, Feb 9 – McCartney appears live for the first time with Wings (formed in August 1971).

•1975, July 17 – Starr is divorced.

•1975, Oct 9 – Lennon's son Sean is born, and Lennon retires for five years.

•1976, Jan 19 – The band are offered $30 million to reform.

•1976, Aug 31 – Harrison is found guilty of plagiarism.

•1976, Sep 7 – McCartney acquires the publishing rights to Buddy Holly's songs.

•1977, June 9 – Harrison's marriage is officially dissolved (he remarries on 2 September 1978).

•1977, Dec 3 – McCartney's song *Mull of Kintyre* hits UK #1, eventually selling two million copies.

•1979, Apr – Starr undergoes a life-saving intestinal operation.

•1979, Nov 28 – Starr's home in Los Angeles is destroyed by fire.

- 1980, Jan 16 – McCartney is jailed in Japan for drug possession.
- 1980, Dec 8 – Lennon is gunned down at 22.50 EST in New York. He dies at 23.30.
- 1981, Feb – Lennon has his third consecutive posthumous UK chart-topper.
- 1981, Apr 27 – Starr marries Barbara Bach.
- 1982, Apr – McCartney's duet with Stevie Wonder tops the UK charts.
- 1983, Dec – McCartney's duet with Michael Jackson hits US #1.
- 1985, Aug – Michael Jackson buys the entire Lennon-McCartney music catalogue.
- 1988, Jan – Harrison tops the US chart with *Got My Mind Set On You*.
- 1995, Nov – McCartney begins a performing arts school in Liverpool inspired by the film *Fame* (it opens in January 1996).
- 1995, Dec – The recording *Free As A Bird* and the album *Anthology Volume 1* top the charts.
- 1996, Sep – Linda McCartney continues to battle breast cancer after an operation in December 1995.
- 1998, Apr 17 – Linda dies.
- 1999, Dec 30 – Harrison is stabbed in his home by an intruder at 03.30 GMT.
- 2001, Nov 29 – George Harrison dies at 13.30 PST, Los Angeles.

Extra event dates from astrologer-writer Nick Dagan Best (stellardweller@hotmail.com), quoting *The Complete Beatles Chronicle* by Mark Lewisohn (Harmony, 1992).

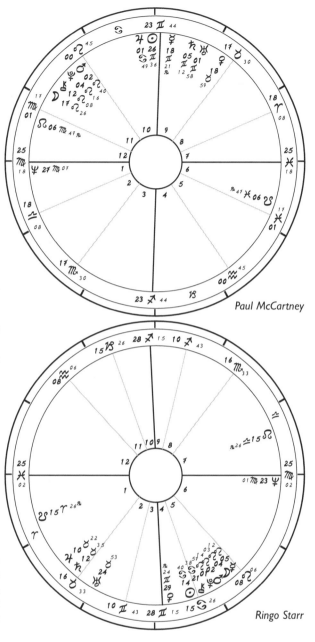

Paul McCartney

Ringo Starr

One would expect the group's members to have repetitive themes of success in their charts. Here are the most outstanding outer planetary and angular contacts:
- Harrison – Pluto on MC opposite Mercury, both square Moon on Ascendant. Sun, ruler of MC, square Saturn-Uranus. Jupiter and Moon in Gauquelin Plus Zones.
- Lennon – Pluto opposite Moon in 10th, both square Mercury in 7th.
- McCartney – Jupiter-Sun-Mercury on MC (in a Gauquelin Plus Zone). MC ruler Mercury on MC.
- Starr – Pluto conjunct Moon and Mercury.

McCartney's Jupiter influence (rather than Pluto prominent) attests to different personal motivations and character. The Neptune placement suggests his longevity and nostalgic songs.

George Harrison

○ *b. 25 February 1943, 00.10 GDT, Liverpool, England, 53N25, 02W55.*

● *Jayj Jacobs q. a 2002 radio show, Beatle Brunch, in which Harrison's sister was interviewed, "She said she was confused by her brother's statements concerning the change in his birth date and time because she had a birth record in hand – in her mother's handwriting – saying he was born at 12:10 am on the 25th. She also said that her mother was awake and aware of the birth." (N.B. In an interview with Billboard magazine, 5 December 1992 Harrison states, "I only recently learned after all these years that the calendar date and time of my own birth have always been off by one calendar day and about half an hour on the clock." The time given out was 23.42. Tashi Grady q. him personally and states, "rectified by him and his astrologer to 11.52.19 pm," giving 0 Scorpio Rising.) RR: AA?*

John Lennon

b. 9 October 1940, 18.30 GDT, Liverpool, England, 53N25, 02W55.

From Pauline Stone, who obtained the data from an aunt present at Lennon's birth. RR: A.

Paul McCartney

b. 18 June 1942, 14.00 DGDT, Liverpool, England, 53N25, 02W55.

Tom Hopke (Nalini Kanta Das) q. Linda McCartney. RR: A.

Ringo Starr

○ *b. 7 July 1940, 00.05 GDT, Liverpool, England, 53N25, 02W55.*

Lynne Palmer q. him (same in the biography The Beatles by H. Davies, "just after midnight"). RR: A.

Other Data:

Julian Lennon

b. 8 April 1963, 07.45 GDT, Liverpool, England, 53N25, 02W55.

David Fisher q. a letter from Christina Rose, May 1985 (Cynthia Lennon gives the same birth time in the book, A Twist of Lennon). RR: A.

Son of John Lennon (qv) and Yoko Ono (qv, The Beatles). He began his own singing career (braving inevitable comparisons to his father) with a debut album in 1984.

Sean Taro Lennon

b. 9 October 1975, 02.00 EDT, Manhattan, New York, USA, 40N46, 73W59.

BC in hand from Lois M. Rodden. RR: AA.

Son of John Lennon (qv) and Yoko Ono (qv). He made his singing debut at age 9 on his mother's album.

Linda McCartney

○ *b. 24 September 1941. 10.00 EDT, New York, NY, USA, 40N43, 74W00.*

Nalini Kanta Das q. her. RR: A.

Wife of Paul McCartney. Their first daughter Mary was born on 29 August 1969 at 01.30 in London (from The Beatles Encyclopedia by Bill Harry, Virgin, 2000).

Yoko Ono

b. 18 February 1933, 20.30 JST (-9), Tokyo, Japan, 35N42, 139E46.

Roger Elliot q. her. RR: A.

A bohemian performer and avant-garde artist, Ono is still held responsible for breaking-up the band (note Descendant ruler Mars is conjunct Neptune, and Neptune is opposed by Mercury in 'patsy' Pisces – the opposition aspect relates to partnerships). The couple married days after a Jupiter-Uranus conjunction and Ono was widowed when the Jupiter-Saturn conjunction of December 1980 crossed her Ascendant (TR Uranus was also on solar arc Ascendant).

Mark David Chapman

b. 10 May 1955, 19.30 CST, Fort Worth, Texas, 32N44, 97W19.

D. Martinie q. a private source, validated. RR: A.

Sociopath and murderer. Obsessed with Salinger's classic *The Catcher in the Rye*, Chapman fatally shot John Lennon (qv) in front of his wife Yoko Ono (qv) outside Lennon's Manhattan apartment, The Dakota. The connections between killer and idol are vivid: Chapman's Moon conjuncts Lennon's MC, Chapman's Venus is on Lennon's Ascendant, and Chapman's Descendant is conjunct Lennon's Uranus. Chapman was given life-imprisonment on 24 August 1981, and has since become somewhat of a media celebrity in America. Chapman had married a Japanese travel agent in 1979, and had ended the marriage weeks before the murder.

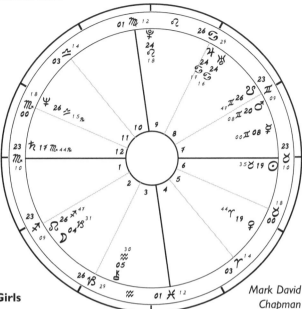

Mark David Chapman

Victoria Beckham – see Spice Girls

BEE GEES

•1958 – The Gibb family, including the child performers Barry, Robin and Maurice, emigrate to Australia. Two years later, the brothers make their TV debut in Australia.

•1963, Jan – The toothsome Gibb brothers (eccentric highly-strung Robin, stable Maurice, and perfectionist Barry) sign a recording contract and are named the Bee Gees.

•1965, Sep – Bee Gees begin a run of hit records in Australia, becoming known for their three-part harmonies led by Robin's falsetto.

•1967, Feb – Bee Gees sign a five-year management contract with Robert Stigwood (qv). They begin to have international hits, and in October 1967, a US #1.

•1968, Sep – Barry Gibb announces his intention to split from the band. But Robin is the one to leave (in March 1969) and have several solo successes.

•1969, Feb 18 – Maurice Gibb marries Lulu (qv).

•1971, Aug – Having reunited in early 1971, they have another US #1 but interest in the band soon wanes, and Maurice is drinking heavily. (From 1971 to 1974 they are in a musical dead zone until they relocate to the USA.)

•1975, Aug – *Jive Talkin'* hits US #1.

•1975, Oct 17 – Maurice remarries.

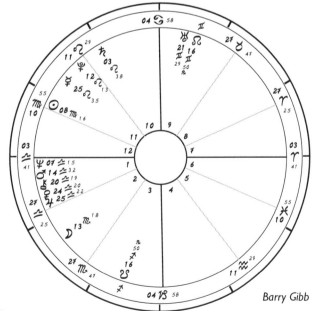

Barry Gibb

* Robert Stigwood b. 16 April 1934, 03.10 SAST (-9.5 = - 9hrs 30 mins), Adelaide, Australia, 34S55, 138E35. *From Signs of the Stars by Frederick Davies. No source. RR: C.*

•1977, Dec – *How Deep Is Your Love* is the first of six consecutive US #1s (to June 1979).

•1978 – Bee Gees top the charts with the album *Saturday Night Fever*, which eventually sells 30 million copies. The soundtrack marks the peak of the disco movement and the brothers are immortalised by their trademark hairy-chests, white suits and ball-breaking falsetto. On 18 March the top 4 songs on the US chart are all written by the brothers.

•1980, Oct 2 – Bee Gees sue Stigwood for $200 million.

•1981, Jan – Barry Gibb's duet with Streisand hits #3 on the US charts. Later the group write *Heartbreaker* for Dionne Warwick, *Islands in the Stream*, the double-million seller for Kenny Rogers and Dolly Parton, and *Chain Reaction* for Diana Ross.

• 1985, Jul 1 – Robin (who first married in December 1968) marries his girlfriend of five years; they continue to have an open, bisexual relationship.

•1987, Oct – They hit #1 in the UK with *You Win Again*.

•1991, Oct – Maurice Gibb seeks help for his drug problem after threatening his family with a gun.

•1997, Feb – Bee Gees are awarded a Brit Award for their contribution to British music.

•2002, Jan – Bee Gees are awarded the CBE.

•2003, Jan 12 – Maurice Gibb dies at 00:45 in Miami after an intestinal blockage and heart attack (on 8 January). His brothers announce their intention to investigate the hospital in Miami, as well as the end of the Bee Gees.

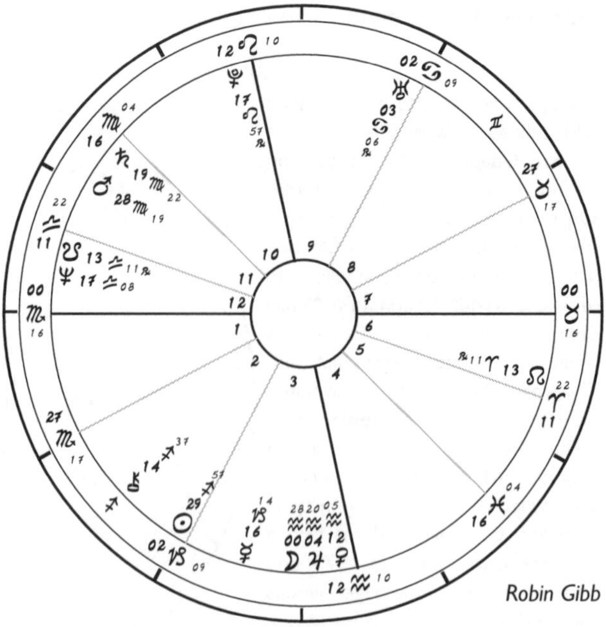

Robin Gibb

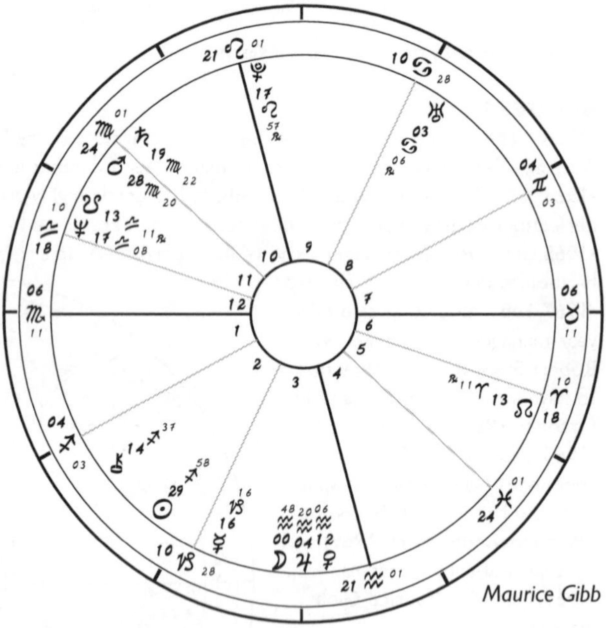

Maurice Gibb

Barry Gibb
   b. 1 September 1946, 09.00 GDT, Douglas, Isle of Man, 54N09, 04W28.
   Tashi Grady q. Gibb's mother for Birth Record. RR: AA.

Robin Gibb
   b. 22 December 1949, 03.15 GMT, Douglas, Isle of Man, 54N09, 04W28.
   BC in hand from Edwin C. Steinbrecher (Robin Hugh Gibb). RR: AA.

Maurice Gibb
   b. 22 December 1949, 03.50 GMT, Douglas, Isle of Man, 54N09, 04W28.
   BC in hand from Edwin C. Steinbrecher (Maurice Ernest Gibb). RR: AA.

Other data:

Ashley Robert Gibb
> b. 8 September 1977, 10.05 EDT (+4), Miami, Florida, USA, 26N46, 80W12.
> Tashi Grady q. Ashley's parents for BC. RR: AA.

Second son of Linda and Barry Gibb.

Barbara Gibb
> b. 17 November 1920, 23.58 GMT, Manchester, England, 53N30, 02W15.
> Tashi Grady q. her. RR: A.

Mother of Barry, Maurice, Robin and Andy Gibb.

Berry Gibb
> b. 29 September 1964, 22.30 AEST (-10), Sydney, Australia, 33S52, 151E13.
> Tashi Grady q. Berry's mother for Birth Record. RR: AA.

Sister of Barry, Maurice, Robin and Andy Gibb. Singer and actress.

Linda Gibb
> b. 11 May 1950, 18.35 GDT, Edinburgh, Scotland, 55N57, 03W13.
> Tashi Grady q. Linda Gibb for BC. RR: AA.

Wife of Barry Gibb.

Michael Gibb
> b. 1 December 1984, 05.30 EDT, Miami, Florida, 26N46, 80W12.
> Tashi Grady q. Michael's parents for BC. (N.B. This corrects an error in Lois Rodden's data book
> AstroData IV.) RR: AA.

Fourth son of Linda and Barry Gibb.

Stephen Gibb
> b. 1 December 1973, 23.56 GMT, London, England, 51N30, 0W10.
> Tashi Grady q. Stephen's parents for Birth Record. RR: AA.

First son of Linda and Barry Gibb.

Travis Gibb
> b. 10 January 1981, 05.55 EST (+5), Miami, Florida, 26N46, 80W12.
> Tashi Grady q. Travis's parents for BC. RR: AA.

Third son of Linda and Barry Gibb.

Maggie Bell
> b. 12 January 1945, 00.45 GDT, Great Western Road, Glasgow, Scotland, 55N53, 04W19.
> Gerard q. BC (Margaret Bell). RR: AA.

Foxy-voiced Bell made her recording debut in 1966 with Bobby Kerr under the name Frankie and Johnny. She became a popular live performer (Neptune Rising) with soul-based group Stone the Crows from 1970, having partnered guitarist Leslie Harvey (qv) from 1967. She was touted as Scotland's answer to Janis Joplin, and her press release at the time insisted that she would loosen her vocal chords by gargling with gravel! She won several top vocalist awards before tragedy struck on 3 May 1972 (Lunar Eclipse on her Pluto): Harvey died after being electrocuted onstage in Swansea. Several solo albums (including *Queen of the Night*, 1974) and a UK Top 40 single in April-May 1978 failed to reignite this much under-rated singer's career. Bell performed the stunning rock track for the popular television series, *Taggart*, starring Mark McManus (qv). After a 1989 album release, *Crimes of the Heart*, she retired from the music business.

Lynda Bellingham

b. 31 May 1948, 15.00 EDT (+4), Montreal, Canada, 45N31, 73W34.

FCC q. her, from her parents. RR: A.

Actress who gained a sexy image on TV but is fondly remembered for playing home-centred mother roles (Venus on MC in Cancer). She appeared in *General Hospital* (September 1972 until March 1975, when TR Pluto crossed her Ascendant), *Angels, Z Cars, Doctor Who, All Creatures Great and Small* (January 1988 to 1990), the comedy *Second Thoughts* (November 1988 to July 1992) and its spin-off *Faith in the Future*. She is widely known as the mother in the Oxo TV adverts, a role she won in September 1983. In late December 1999 the Press revealed that her private life was far from her perfect TV image (Neptune squares Venus-MC). As TR Pluto opposed her Sun, a court heard her testify that she was a battered wife, a victim of physical

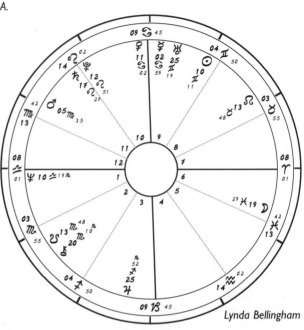

Lynda Bellingham

abuse throughout her 15-year marriage. Her ex-husband admitted to stalking her between September 1997 (after their split) and July 1999, and was placed under a seven-year restraining order. Her dramatic personal life took another twist in March 2002 (TR Saturn on Sun) when, after a lengthy hate campaign, a mentally-ill former tenant tried to firebomb her home. Bellingham was unhurt. The trial reached court in February 2003 and the culprit was ordered to remain indefinitely at a mental home.

David Benson

b. 11 January 1962, 09.05 GMT, Oxford, 51N46, 01W15.

FCC q. him, from BC (a twin). RR: AA.

A canny actor and impersonator (MC ruler Jupiter Rising) with five 12th House planets (aiding his ability to become someone else on stage). Benson conceived the outstanding one-man show *Think No Evil of Us... My Life with Kenneth Williams* in October 1994, and took it to the Edinburgh Festival on 12 August 1996 for a three-week run. In January 1997 he began a national tour to rave reviews, receiving praise from those who had known Williams (qv) personally. The show revealed the man beneath the much-loved incarnations whilst cleverly unravelling Benson's own childhood memories. His connection to Williams dates back to 10 December 1975, when the *Carry On* star read out the then-13-

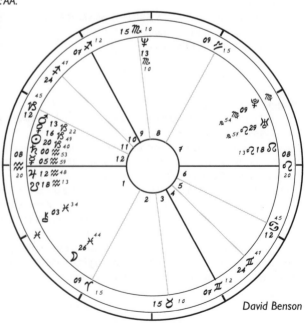

David Benson

year-old Benson's competition-winning story *The Rag and Bone Man* on *Jackanory* at 4 pm. In January 1998 he played Noel Coward (qv) in his first TV role, *Goodnight Sweetheart* (TR Pluto on MC and TR Uranus on Ascendant). The synastry between Benson and his subjects is remarkable. With Williams: Benson's Ascendant conjuncts KW's Venus, they have opposing Ascendant signs, Jupiters conjunct, his Pluto opposes KW's Mercury, his Moon conjuncts KW's Uranus, his Mars opposes KW's Pluto, his Mercury on KW's Descendant. Benson's connections with Coward are interesting, too: Coward's Mercury-Uranus flanks Benson's MC, both Venus placements are exactly conjunct, and Coward's IC conjuncts Benson's Saturn. After a tour about the death of Princess Diana, Benson toured with *Being Frank*, a tribute to Frankie Howerd (qv). Although there is some direct synastry (Benson's Sun conjuncts FH's Saturn, and Moon on FH's Chiron) Benson's chart suggests that he will be best remembered for his Williams work, which he brought back to the London stage in April 2003.

Michael Bentine – see The Goons
Pete Best – see The Beatles

Sean Biggerstaff
✪ b. 15 March 1983, 21.35 GMT, South General Hospital, Glasgow, Scotland, 55N53, 04W19.
Gerard q. BC. RR: AA.
Young actor who appeared as Gryffindor captain Oliver Wood in the *Harry Potter* films (from 2001).

Christopher Biggins
💣 b. 16 December 1948, 00.00 GMT, Oldham, England, 53N33, 02W07.
FCC q. his letter. (N.B. The letter was unclear whether the birth time was midnight beginning or ending 16th December.) RR: C.

Flamboyant professional celebrity and jovial, larger-than-life actor-presenter with a cult following who has, in recent years, taken to appearing in self-parodying roles (*Absolutely Fabulous*). As well as children's programmes and a season with Cilla Black (qv) on TV's *Surprise, Surprise* (1984-5), Biggins has been impressive in dramatic roles, such as those in *Poldark* (October 1975 to December 1977) and *I, Claudius* (September to December 1976). He was featured in *The Rocky Horror Picture Show* with Tim Curry (qv) and the much-loved comedies *Porridge* (September 1974 to March 1977) and *Rentaghost*. Biggins had an ordeal in October 1994 when he was falsely accused of shoplifting.

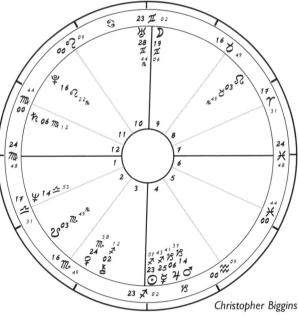
Christopher Biggins

The publicity capped a difficult twelve months during which he had been convicted of drink-driving the previous November. Biggins is a seasoned pantomime dame and regular party-goer. As a child Biggins had ambitions to become a vicar.

Jackie Bird
b. 31 July 1962, 00.25 GDT, Maternity Hospital, Bellshill, Scotland, 55N50, 04W01.
Gerard q. BC (Jacqueline MacPherson). RR: AA.
Respected newsreader on Scottish television with a competitive and cynical edge (Saturn prominent). She was sent to perform at nightclubs from the age of 11 (Saturn retrograde has to grow up quickly), before proof-reading on *Jackie* magazine and inventing its horoscope columns. Later a

journalist with tabloids, she moved into television presenting and reporting, before returning to Glasgow to read the news for BBC Scotland (Bird's EQHS chart has key indicators of professional respect and journalistic opportunities – 10th House ruler Jupiter in 10th trines co-ruler Neptune in 6th, while she has a strong 3rd House and Gemini Rising).

Jane Birkin

● b. 14 December 1946, 11.00 GMT, London, England, 51N30, 0W10.
  Grazia Bordoni q. Amica magazine, original source not known. RR: C.

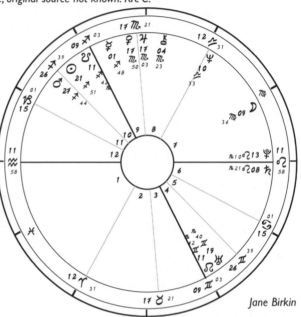

Jane Birkin

Former sex kitten and wild child who has gone on to be revered as an actress and recording artist in France. A renowned sexual exhibitionist who epitomised Swinging London (Venus-Jupiter in Scorpio and Sun-Mars in Sagittarius opposite Uranus), Birkin simulated sex on a pop record and film with her Svengali-husband Serge Gainsbourg*. Their sensual hit, *Je T'Aime... Moi Non Plus*, was banned in Britain but nevertheless shot to #1 in the charts in October 1969. Birkin starred in *Evil Under the Sun* (1982) and is the mother of actress Charlotte Gainsbourg (qv). She went into a deep depression after Serge's death on 2 March 1991, followed days later by her father's. Both events heralded the end of her second marriage. (The deaths were preceded by a Lunar Eclipse, which fell on her Saturn and possibly her Descendant.) In May 2003 she embarked upon a tour of Gainsbourg's songs.

Cilla Black

○ b. 27 May 1943, 08.00 DGDT, Liverpool, England, 53N25, 02W55.
● *David Fisher q. Martine Delamere who obtained the data from Black's agent. (N.B. Black has said on TV that she doesn't know her exact time of birth.) RR: C.*

Brassy girl-next-door vocalist-turned-TV presenter. With tremendous self-belief Priscilla Mary White transformed herself from typist and part-time hairdresser to become Britain's most successful girl singer during the 60s. Renamed Cilla Black, she made her debut at Liverpool's Cavern Club on 25 January 1963 and signed a recording contract in July, having been championed by John Lennon (qv). She had eleven Top Ten hits from 1964 to 1971 (two #1s, late February and May 1964, as TR Saturn crossed her 08.00 MC). Black married Bobby Willis in 1969 and let him manage and steer her career as deal-maker and business advisor (Mars in Pisces opposite Neptune). Her singing success continued until work dried up in the early 70s, so she effectively retired to bring up her family (the possible Cancer Ascendant). When Black returned to the spotlight ten years later (after a sparky chat show appearance around her 40th birthday renewed interest in her) she began two hugely popular TV series: *Surprise Surprise*, from 1984 (with Christopher Biggins, qv) and *Blind Date* from 1985. With alarming regularity she leant her foghorn voice to the former show and her vocal performances each week – after she had instigated a tear-jerking family reunion for a member of her audience – remain memorable for a number of reasons. Both ventures were tackled with a thorough professionalism and Black has always managed to present a 'real', comfortable persona on television, even if the Press continue to promote her champagne lifestyle (Venus-Jupiter). Intensely private, Black suffered a

---

* Serge Gainsbourg b. 2 April 1928, 04.45 GMT, Paris, France, 48N52, 02E20. Gauquelin q. BC. RR: AA.

personal loss when her mother died in early October 1996. In July 1999 her husband-manager was diagnosed with inoperable liver and lung cancer. He died on 23 October 1999, leaving Cilla grief-stricken. In love with the limelight and driven to remain at the top of her profession, she continued to work, took steps to reinvent her image and in late 2001 there was talk of her relaunching her singing career. In May 2002 there was much speculation about her being replaced on *Blind Date* because of falling ratings. The show was revamped but Black announced on live TV on 4 January 2003 that she was quitting at the end of the current (19th) series in March. In 2003 new music, a TV documentary and autobiography, *What's it all About?*, were in the offing.

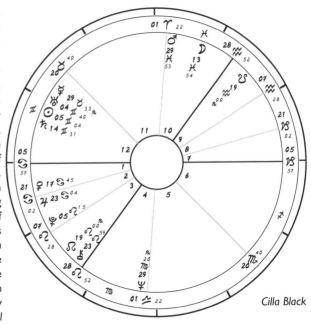

Cilla Black

> Q
> "Our Cilla is an experienced innocent, a professional unsophisticate and her personal life is beyond reproach... One of her other self-images, which she's worked well to perfect, is self-deprecation." (Hunter Davies, *Daily Mail*, 8/5/95)
> "Her all-embracing personality undermines her self-confessed obsession with stardom and how she has survived almost 40 years of varying fashions and trends in show business." (David Wigg, *Daily Mail Weekend*, 7/12/02)

Isobel Black

b. 27 December 1943, 12.30 GDT, Edinburgh, Scotland, 55N57, 03W12.
Gerard q. BC (Isobel Primrose Black). RR: AA.

Actress with numerous TV credits, including the long-running drama, *The Troubleshooters*, in which her role ran from 1967-1972. She is married with three daughters.

Tony Blackburn

b. 29 January 1943, 02.00 GDT, Guildford, Surrey, England, 51N14, 0W35.
From his autobiography, *The Living Legend* (place and year confirmed by FCC at Registry). RR: B.

Long-time radio disc jockey known for his outspokenness, joviality and his corny jokes, Blackburn had immediate success when he began on Radio One at 07.00 GDT on 30 September 1967 in London (the Moon in the radio station's birth chart is conjunct Blackburn's MC). He had begun in pirate radio for Radio Caroline South in 1964 after being a compere, singer and guitarist in a ten-piece band at 16. At Caroline he pioneered the personalised name jingle, but Blackburn was hungry for wider success and joined Radio One. His breakfast show launched him as a national phenomenon, and with nearly 20 million listeners he was considered the most important man in British broadcasting. Blackburn promoted himself in every medium and the public related to him as the boy next door (Moon-Ascendant) who lived the glamorous life (Leo MC). He was demoted in 1973 to an afternoon show but remained a loose canon, expressing his forthright views on family morality. In September 1979 he lost his daily show, then moved into children's radio before quitting Radio One in 1984. A stint with Radio London followed until he was sacked in April 1988 (he left on 25 April). Blackburn trebled his salary with a move to Capital Radio in 1988, launching Capital Gold. With his Moon and Jupiter falling in significant areas of the chart (and Moon square Pluto), he hit a popular chord with listeners for years, although some see him as an amiable buffoon desperate to hold on to his fame. A loner since childhood, Blackburn is known to be ambitious and obsessed with his work, but was inconsolable after his wife of four years left him in October 1976 (TR Uranus on Ascendant and approaching a square to his Sun). Blackburn became addicted to tranquillisers and Valium for 5 years, sharing his depression with his listeners. (Note Sun opposite Pluto T-square Moon in Scorpio.) Finally in March 1978 radio bosses took him off the air for a two-week break. In June 1992 he married for the second time (TR Saturn conjunct IC) and became a father at age 54. His media profile was raised in late August 2002 (as TR

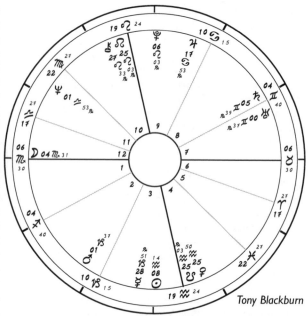

Tony Blackburn

Jupiter crossed his EQHS 10th) when he joined fellow celebrities in the Australian outback for the TV game show *I'm a Celebrity – Get Me Out of Here!*, and emerged the winner on 8 September 2002 (with TR Neptune conjunct MC ruler Sun and TR Uranus conjunct Venus, there was talk of new shows and even a Christmas single to add to his 18 previous releases and two albums).

Honor Blackman

b. 22 August 1925, 06.00 GDT, Plaistow, London, England, 51N32, 0E03.

FCC q. her for data except year (confirmed at Registry). RR: A.

Blackman was the first of Steed's leading ladies in *The Avengers*, signing to the television series in June 1962 (TR Uranus conjunct Ascendant and Sun). Her first episode was transmitted on 22 December 1962. She hung up her kinky boots, quitting the series in September 1963, and went to Hollywood to star as Pussy Galore alongside Sean Connery (qv) in *Goldfinger* (released in Britain in September 1964). Such glamorous parts, though, hindered her ambitions to play the classic roles. With Mars conjunct Sun on the Ascendant in Leo, imperious Blackman 'inherited' her determination from her influential but undemonstrative father (who died in 1971), although Honor admitted she was emotionally estranged from him (Leo Sun conjunct Neptune). Always a tough battler, Blackman used her physical attributes to great advantage in *The Avengers*, a show that required strength and endurance. Blackman has spoken candidly of her nervous breakdown at 29 – following the collapse of her

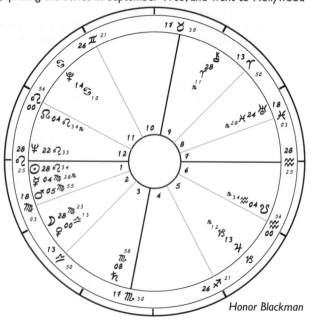

Honor Blackman

eight-year marriage, she spent three weeks at a mental hospital (Moon, ruler of EQHS 12th, opposes Uranus, ruler of 7th), and later healed with four years of psychoanalysis. She made a successful TV comeback with the top-rated *The Upper Hand* (airing from May 1990). In January 1997 she published a book on keeping youthful.

Q "People tell me [I'm strong], but I don't think I am at all. I see myself as being so weak, I have to put on a pretend strong front... [My father] brought me up to suppress all my emotions. Perhaps that's why I became an actress." (Honor Blackman, *Daily Mail*, 31/1/2000)

Norman Blake – see Teenage Fanclub

Brian Blessed

b. 9 October 1936, 04.00 GMT, Mexborough, England, 53N30, 01W17.
FCC q. him (Blessed's autobiography The Dynamite Kid (Bloomsbury) tells of his mother seeing him for the first time at 05.00). RR: A.

Blessed suffered a nervous breakdown in his teens after a critical write-up of his first starring stage role (the experience 'toughened up' the fragile Moon square Uranus, and Neptune Rising in his chart). He made his name in *Z-Cars*, went on to perform with the RSC, and later starred in the acclaimed BBC production *I, Claudius* (September to December 1976). Blessed also made regular appearances in the first series of *Blackadder* (June to July 1983). With Mars and Jupiter in prominent positions, his is a rugged and titanic presence, courageous and unafraid to be vulnerable. Adept in a number of sports Blessed has taken to regularly assaulting Mount Everest (April 1990 and October 1993 saw the first two attempts to reach the summit) and there was talk of aiming to be the oldest man to reach the summit in a climb scheduled for March 2003. He signed up to play Hamlet's father in Kenneth Branagh's (qv) film of the play (released February 1997). Married twice, his first marriage lasted from 1958 to January 1975.

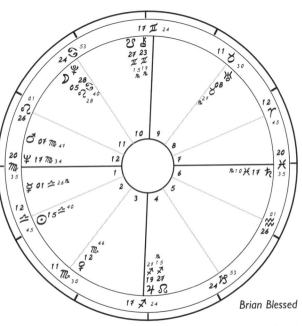

Brian Blessed

Q "Everything I know about life I've learnt from women, they're my heroes; 99% of men bore the arse off me. I've always been physically very strong... which means men behave competitively towards me... When I was at school I was fascinated by nature. I knew the names of every butterfly and newt, but I was told to stop dreaming, which is an appalling thing to say to a child. So I retreated into my head... With [my daughter] I was always interested in what this young, pure brain had to say. What she had to teach me. I found that intriguing and I tried to bring her magic all the time. Fairy stories, beauty, flowers, animals – magic! We'd invent stories. I couldn't care less about teaching her the bloody alphabet... It is so important to be vulnerable... We must never, ever, lose the child in us. That is the gateway to so much progress." (Brian Blessed, *The Sunday Times Magazine*, c.1999)

Q "He has an ability to really lift people. It's his way of displaying his love and affection, his team spirit... When he's working he is 100% full on, providing the energy that everyone else feeds off. But afterwards, no one can find him because he's disappeared... He has a huge need to retreat, to be on his own, to be still and quiet... Underneath the jolly exterior there's a lot of insecurity. He is vulnerable... Dad has big passions and big depressions. His Everest obsession was very difficult to deal with... I think it was the ultimate physical challenge, a spiritual and physical quest, his holy grail. He used to say that a real adventure must involve danger... He still has an amazing temper. Ignorance in general and cruelty to animals make him absolutely livid... He doesn't care about money. He probably has quite bad financial skills; most of his money is spent on his climbing obsession." (Blessed's daughter Rosalind, *The Sunday Times Magazine*, c.1999)

Morris Blythman

b. 25 September 1919, 00.15 GDT, Inverkeithing, Scotland, 56N02, 03W24.
Gerard q. BC (Robert Morris Blythman). RR: AA.

Poet and influential songwriter in the 50s Glasgow folk revival, known for acidic and biting political pieces deriving from a combination of Marxist ideology and Scottish Nationalism (Pluto squares Mercury, Sun and Moon, which are placed in the EQHS 3rd). He also wrote under the pseudonym of Thurso Berwick.

Dirk Bogarde

b. 28 March 1921, 08.30 GMT, Twickenham, England, 51N27, 0W20.
From his autobiography, A Postillion Struck By Lightning (Chatto & Windus, 1977). RR: B.

The son of the Art Editor of *The Times*, Derek Niven Van den Bogaerde had an idyllic childhood in the company of his nanny, but in 1934 was sent away to Scotland when his brother was born. He made his first appearance on stage in December 1939 before he served in the army from May 1941. He reappeared on stage in February 1947 and his performance in *Power Without Glory* landed him a movie contract. *Doctor in the House* (1954), the first in a series of successful 'Doctor' comedies, brought national stardom for Bogarde and by the late 50s, he was a top box office draw, 'the idol of the Odeons' and Britain's top sex symbol. Success in America eluded him until *Victim* was released there in February

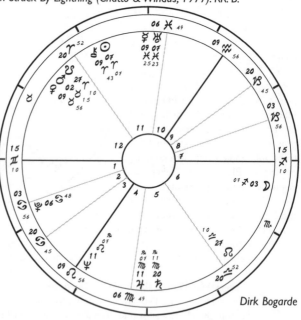

Dirk Bogarde

1962 (before TR Saturn hit the MC), and he often maintained that his Rank film contract prevented him from achieving the worldwide success he felt he deserved. *Victim* shattered his clean-cut image and Bogarde soon excelled in a variety of dangerous roles. Bogarde was a gifted painter and born writer, establishing a reputation with a series of lucid best-selling autobiographies published from 1977 (Mercury in Pisces conjunct MC ruler Uranus, both square Moon). The media made much of his life-long obsession to conceal his homosexuality. Personally private, discreet and mysterious (which others thought of as aloof, controlled and arrogant – Aquarius MC), in his seven volumes of autobiography Bogarde never once acknowledges his 50-year relationship with actor Tony Forwood, who died in May 1988 (TR Pluto opposite Venus). Two years earlier he had burned most of his private papers and scrapbooks. After suffering two strokes in 1996, Bogarde died on 8 May 1999 from a heart attack. Co-star Charlotte Rampling (qv) said he possessed an eternally young spirit (the Aries-Gemini-Sagittarius combination, with Ascendant ruler Mercury in Pisces).

Q
"[His acting makes] it possible for the spectator to actually feel that they are inside his thoughts and know what he's thinking. It's about silence and it's about allowing the camera to invade you. It's a magnetic quality. You are compelled to look... He was one of the great raconteurs with his wit and with his sarcasm... his bitchiness, tenderness and impossible moods." (Charlotte Rampling, *Radio Times*, 15/12/01)

"He was capable of huge gentleness, but he was also waspish, humiliating, intolerant." (Nicholas Shakespeare, *Radio Times*, 15/12/01)

"Highly professional – with a hint of menace." (His nurse, Sheila Maclean)

"He was a very discerning sort of man. He could see into you. He knew what made you tick... He had rather quick judgments about people, and [was] very intuitive and insightful." (James Fox, as quoted in TV's *Legends*)

Marc Bolan

b. 30 September 1947, 12.30 GDT, Hackney, London, England, 51N33, 0W03.
Adam Fronteras q. Bolan on Wax Records Company literature, information from his parents (same data in the biography Marc Bolan). RR: A.

A former model and skiffle group founder (in Summer 1957), Mark Feld signed a record deal in August 1965 and as a homage to his idol Bob Dylan reinvented himself as Marc Bo(b Dy)lan. Original, charismatic and bohemian, he was an underground hero (Jupiter in Scorpio conjunct Sagittarius Rising), a glamorous, androgynous figure (Neptune conjunct Sun, opposite Moon), once famously telling an interviewer that he lived "in a twilight world of drugs, booze and kinky sex." After a number of solo recordings he formed T. Rex in late 1967, and the band were soon at the forefront of the new glam rock movement. In July 1971 they scored their biggest hit with the single *Get It On* and in March 1972 they were filmed during two sold-

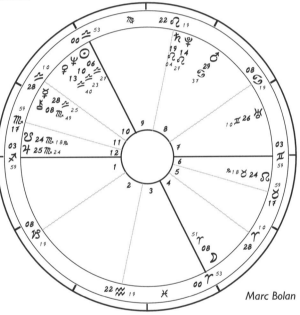

Marc Bolan

out Wembley Arena concerts. Bolan left his wife in June 1973 and began an affair with singer Gloria Jones; their son, Rolan Seymour Feld, was born on 26 September 1975. As the hits dried up in 1976 and the savage reviews began, he turned to comfort eating. His Saturn Return in Summer 1977 saw him revitalised, healthier and feeling as though he'd been 'born again'. Tragedy struck at 05.00 on 16 September 1977, in London, when Bolan was killed in a car accident, keeping the Neptunian image frozen in time and guaranteeing musical immortality (TR Pluto conjunct MC ruler Venus). Previously unreleased material and many reissues proved popular for over a decade after his death. In mid-September 2001 his son appeared on stage with his father's first band, John's Children, and continued to search for the millions of pounds owed from his father's royalties.

Q
"One of the most charismatic performers in British pop. His self-confidence and ambition led T-Rex to define the glam-rock era... Marc liked to be in control and had a self-belief that bordered on the messianic." (Lisa Sewards, *Daily Mail Weekend*, 1/3/03)

Derek Bond

b. 26 January 1920, 17.30 GMT, Glasgow, Scotland, 55N52, 04W17.

Gerard q. BC (Derek William Douglas Bond). RR: AA.

Leading actor of stage from 1937 and British films from 1946. During the war he served with the British Grenadier Guards and was awarded the Military Cross. Actors with solid reputations and an 'appropriate' temperament invariably have a prominent Jupiter, as discovered by the Gauquelins (Bond has Jupiter Rising in Leo in 12th). From 1984 to 1986 he was president of British Actors Equity (Jupiter conjunct Leo Ascendant).

Samantha Bond

❂ *b. 27 November 1961, 09.00 GMT, London, England, 51N30, 0W10.*

FCC has Bond's letter in hand (from a trusted colleague), which quotes her mother's memory. Year and place confirmed at Registry. RR: A.

A member of the Royal Shakespeare Company, Bond has toured extensively on the UK and US stage, but is most famous for playing Miss Moneypenny in the James Bond films (the first was in *GoldenEye*, released November 1995, as TR Jupiter crossed the Ascendant). She has also appeared on TV many times, often in murder mysteries and thrillers.

Bono

b. 10 May 1960, 02.00 GDT, Dublin, Ireland, 53N20, 06W15.

Edwin Steinbrecher q. a mutual friend, from him, "two on the dot." RR: A.

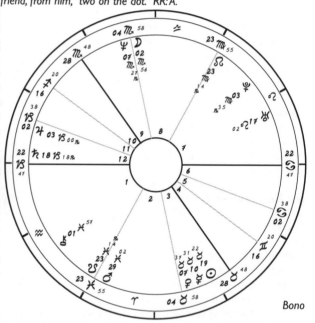

Bono

Distinctive vocalist Bono (Paul David Hewson) formed the band Feedback in 1976 before changing its name to U2 the following year. In November 1977 the band came together and Bono began dating his future wife. After winning a talent contest in March 1978, U2 were signed up and began winning a strong following, gaining major chart success in Ireland by early 1980 (TR Pluto conjunct EQHS 10th). Their major UK and US breakthrough occurred after extensive tours in 1981 (again, TR Pluto conjunct 10th, TR Jupiter conjunct EQHS 10th, TR Uranus on MC) and with the help of college radio in the US. During 1983-4 they became the most popular band in the UK, with chart-topping discs and awards. By early 1985 they were headlining in America and named the Band of the 80s by *Rolling Stone* magazine (TR Saturn on MC). The band were an even greater commercial success after the release of *The Joshua Tree* (1987). After 100 million albums and 14 Grammys, U2 were recently voted the Best Band in the World, and Bono topped Q magazine's list of the 50 Most Powerful People in Music because of his political influence (Scorpio MC). Bono shares the charismatic rock star conjunction of Moon-Neptune in Scorpio with Michael Hutchence (qv, Australian Data) but is steadied by the 'normal bloke' aspect of Saturn Rising in Capricorn. He has been married for over 20 years and has remained free of scandal, although he has at times battled booze. Bono has been able to utilise that Moon-Neptune in Scorpio by turning crusader for a number of humanitarian causes (issues with Scorpionic themes of crisis, tragedy and life-death issues – for those who have suffered because of politics and war). In May 2003 a non-musical 'talking tour' was planned for the US, highlighting the need for African aid.

Q "He appears to be a rock cliche, just enough for everyone to identify with him. And then, once you're hooked, you realise that he encompasses the most bizarre set of contradictions. He can write songs about Martin Luther King, have high ideals and talk about his love of John Hume, yet insists that "In myself, I'm capable of aggression of a really brutal kind"... His Christianity has always been a weird and yet necessary ingredient of those perfect rock songs... The death of Bono's mother when he was 14 was a defining moment... It pushed him in two directions at once, towards the emotional exorcism offered by punk rock and the meditative space to be found in Christianity." (Chrissy Iley, *Evening Standard*, 17/8/01)

Roy Boulting – see Hayley Mills

David Bowie

✪ *b. 8 January 1947, 09.00 GMT, Brixton, London, England, 51N28, 0W06.*
From the biography Alias David Bowie by Peter & Leni Gillman (Hodder & Stoughton, 1986), p. 41 (same time in Backstage Passes by his wife Angela Bowie and Patrick Carr). (N.B. Bowie gave Gary Lorig a time of 09.30 (Asc: 15 Aquarius). There is another time of "just before midnight" in the biography David Bowie (1975) by David Douglas, p. 3, with a Libra Ascendant but no source, and is likely to be literary license.) RR: B.

An enigmatic, mercurial singer-songwriter-actor whose work is considered by many to represent the zenith of rock. Bowie, heavily influenced as a child by Little Richard, released his first single, *Liza Jane*, in June 1964 with the band King Bees. A debut solo single was released in April 1966. In June 1969 he signed a recording contract and met his future wife Angela Barnett (they married on 20 March 1970 and were divorced in February 1980). The following year saw personal changes in his life, including his father's death and his brother being committed to a mental institution. Bowie's first album success occurred in June 1972 (when TR Neptune conjunct his MC) with his stage alter-ego Ziggy Stardust (a character he

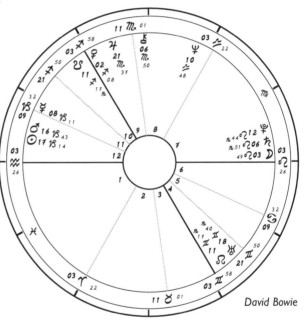

David Bowie

portrayed until Summer 1973, when he announced his 'retirement' on 3 July). Bowie's theatrical presence proved equally as charismatic when he took to the Broadway stage in *The Elephant Man* from September 1980 to 3 January 1981 (he had opened in Denver on 19 July 1980). Later that year with group Queen, he topped the UK charts with *Under Pressure*. Back on 27 April 1976 when Bowie's Nazi memorabilia were confiscated, he made the infamous remark that Britain would benefit from a fascist leader – adding that it was a post he would like to fill some day. Bowie's continuing artistic evolution and chameleon-like persona can be described by the prominent Neptune (square to Mercury, Mars and Sun), whilst his generational influence can be seen by the angular Moon-Saturn-Pluto conjunction. He scored a commercial triumph in 1983 with the album *Let's Dance* (with TR Uranus hovering near his MC). In early 1997 he celebrated a highly-publicised 50th birthday alcohol-free and with an album of jungle music. In October 2002 he was named the 29th Greatest Briton of all time, the same month he released his 26th album, *Heathen*. Bowie has his own art and music websites and has been married to model Iman since 6 June 1992. In February 2003 *The Mail on Sunday's Rich Report* estimated his fortune at £100 million.

Boy George

○ *b. 14 June 1961, 02.30 GDT, Bexley, Kent, England, 51N26, 0E10.*

● *From him to Laura Boomer, checking with his mother a couple of times to clear-up confusion surrounding various conflicting birth times (including 00.45 – Pisces Rising). (N.B. Another birth time of 02.50 was sent to Garry Heaton scribbled on a postcard from George's office in 1997 (perhaps the 5 and 3 were unclear or the chart had been rectified?). Previously Russell Grant had quoted George's mother for 00:45.) RR: A?*

By 30, singer-songwriter Boy George – witty and articulate, with an infectious love of campy melodrama – had lived a remarkable life of glamorous highs and drug-ridden lows (note the dominant opposition of Venus-Neptune). Influenced by David Bowie (qv, note the synastry), Boy George was the first 80s genderbender and the decade's ultimate pop icon. After being expelled from school on 29 September 1976 and spending a few years as a minor fashion icon in London, he made his stage debut with Bow Wow Wow in late February 1981. His individual sense of style and outlandish clothes became an armour for him. George presented a fearless front and often fought people who ridiculed or upset him (this defensive trait has

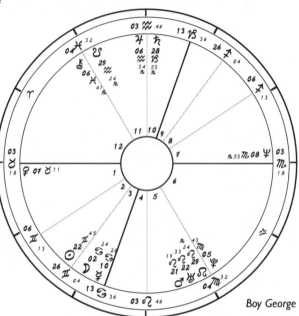

Boy George

also seen him appear in court for assault in recent times). Overnight he became a source of fascination in Britain after his new band Culture Club had a chart-topper in October 1982 with *Do You Really Want to Hurt Me* (six and a half million copies sold worldwide). He was soon the most famous pop face on the planet (note the marketable Venus-Neptune opposition on the Ascendant/Descendant axis, suggesting a visual image that crossed all boundaries, fascinated the public, had them speculating his gender and created a worldwide media sensation). Yet rather than developing a threatening sexual persona, he became an asexual mumsy doll-like creation loved by girls and grannies (note the Taurus and Cancer influence!). He famously said (in early October 1983) that he'd prefer a cup of tea to sex. By September 1983 he was enjoying success from the single *Karma Chameleon* (UK sales of 1.4 million) and an album that would eventually sell 16 million copies. At the time of his chart success he was also involved in a love-hate relationship with band drummer Jon Moss (born 11 September 1957). George's drug habit was out of control by late 1985 and the Press made much of his shenanigans with singer Marilyn. A media frenzy and foxhunt accompanied his fall from grace during June-July 1986, as George struggled to overcome his heroin addiction (with TR Pluto on Descendant he was crucified by the Press). He was fined for heroin possession on 30 July 1986 and his houseguest died in his home five days later. In February 1987 he confirmed the group's split, cleaned up his act and had a first solo #1 in March. He has, over time, adopted numerous religions and faiths (Neptune on the Descendant). He wrote a witty, compulsive autobiography in 1995, with revealing insights into his intense partnerships and roller-coaster life. In 1997 he was unsuccessfully sued for libel over recollections in the book (he won the case on 29 April). A Culture Club reunion tour took place in Summer 1998 (with a hit that October) and George has established himself as a top DJ – a diva of the decks. He developed a musical, *Taboo*, in April 2001, which chronicled life in the New Romantic period and in 2002 (as TR Saturn crossed his Sun) he played the role of performance artiste Leigh Bowery in the show (the show headed for Broadway in April 2003). In October 2002 he was named the 46th Greatest Briton of all time. (*Take it Like a Man* by Boy George with Spencer Bright, Sidgwick & Jackson, 1995.)

"If I'm in a mood... it tends to permeate everything around me." (Boy George, as quoted in BBC's *Gimme a Freak*, 2002)

"I wanted people to like me so badly that I ended up being too nice... There was a part of me that really wanted to be 'lock up your sons' and the reality was that I wasn't really like that.. I could never really build my career on this mystery... my whole thing was about being accessible, that's why it worked." (Boy George, as quoted in BBC's *Omnibus: Boy Next Door?*)

Q

"The ultimate rebel ends up dead. All the best people in pop, the legends, are dead. Some people say I've sold out but I haven't, I've cashed in." (Boy George, *The Face*, c.1986)

Billy Boyd
✪ b. 28 August 1968, 10.10 MET, Maternity Hospital, Glasgow, Scotland, 55N51, 04W14.
   Gerard q. BC (Wiliam Boyd). RR: AA.
Singer and actor who played Peregrin 'Pippin' Took in the *Lord of the Rings* films (from 2001). Boyd attended the Royal Scottish Academy of Music and Drama. In 2002 he topped a poll of the 100 Most Eligible Men in Scotland.

Billy Bragg
✪ b. 20 December 1957, 04.00 GMT, Barking, London, England, 51N33, 0E06.
   Neil Spencer q. him. RR: A.

A sincere songwriter with a strong political sensibility, Steven William Bragg (nicknamed "The Bard of Barking") is a committed left-wing political performer and leading figure of protest pop (note Pluto-MC and the Sagittarius-Scorpio influence). His first release was with the punk/R&B band Riff Raff in May 1978 (TR Saturn near MC, TR Uranus near Ascendant). When the band split, Bragg joined the army in 1981 but bought himself out of the military after only 90 days. In 1982 he began a maverick tour of the UK in a bus and train, playing small venues and working men's clubs, ready at a moment's notice to fill in as support for almost any act. He was fast developing a reputation as an original singer-songwriter of note, with lyrics full of passion,

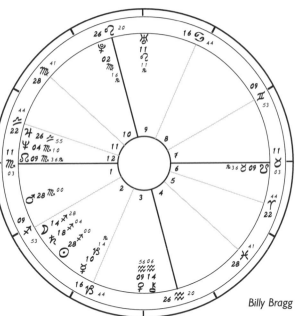

Billy Bragg

anger and wit. In July 1983 (TR Neptune conjunct Sun) a two-track mini-album *Life's a Riot With Spy Vs. Spy* was released and Bragg made his radio debut on John Peel's (qv) Radio One show. Bragg insisted the album be sold at a below-average selling price and it eventually sold 150,000 copies. Commercial success followed in the next few years and Bragg leant his name to a number of political causes, including the Miners' Strike. On 21 November 1985 Red Wedge was launched and Bragg toured with a number of prominent musicians and singers in 1986 to raise left-wing awareness around the country. On 2 November 1986 he was arrested outside the airbase in Norfolk during an anti-nuclear demonstration. Kirsty MacColl recorded his song, *A New England*, which hit the Top Ten in February 1985. On 21 May 1988 he hit #1 with *She's Leaving Home* as one side of a double A-side benefit record. In September 1991 his most commercial album, *Don't Try This At Home*, was released. In 1999 he was a regular presenter on BBC Radio 2 and a new album *England, Half-English*, followed in 2002.

Melvyn Bragg

b. 6 October 1939, 00.10 GDT, Carlisle, England, 54N54, 02W55.
David Fisher q. his letter, "approximately 12.10 am." RR: A.

Editor and presenter of *The South Bank Show*, once a prestigious arts programme and winner of 87 major awards, which first aired in January 1978 and continues to the present day. Bragg joined the BBC as a radio producer in 1961 and began writing for the *New Statesman*. After stints as a TV producer-writer on *Monitor* and presenter of *Second House* in 1973, Bragg became the Head of Arts for London Weekend Television in 1982. His sixteenth novel *Credo* was a religious tale set in the seventeenth century. Bragg has also written *Rich*, the biography of Richard Burton (qv) and his sex scenes in *A Time to Dance* caused a furore when the novel was filmed for television. Bragg was married for ten years before his wife committed suicide in 1971, and he was also

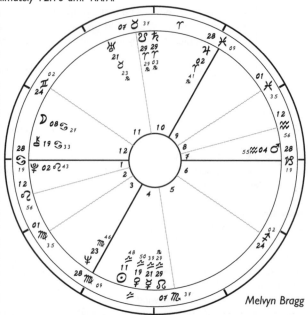

Melvyn Bragg

deeply affected by the death of his father in 1994. He has spoken of his bouts of severe depression. Bragg remarried in 1973. The presence of Jupiter on the MC and Moon also in a Gauquelin Plus Zone are strong indicators of Bragg's interest in literature, theatre and cinema, as well his professional standing, success and authority. His horoscope suggests the temperament for a career in politics.

Kenneth Branagh

b. 10 December 1960, 16.50 GMT, Belfast, Northern Ireland, 54N25, 05W55.
From his autobiography, Beginning (Chatto & Windus, 1989), p. 11, "In the late afternoon... it was about ten minutes to five... just in time for the football results." RR: B.

A youthful and pioneering actor-director, Branagh moved to London in 1971 and won his first break in late January 1982 when he was invited to join the RSC. At the same time he was awarded a role in *Another Country*. Whilst at the RSC he developed a reputation for brilliance and the sort of temperament that usually accompanies prodigious talent (Jupiter is angular and his MC ruler Uranus falls on the IC). Tired of the RSC's relative conservatism, Branagh (with the MC in Aquarius) formed his own Renaissance Theatre Company and eventually directed and starred in the film version of *Henry V* in late 1989 (as TR Uranus crossed his Descendant

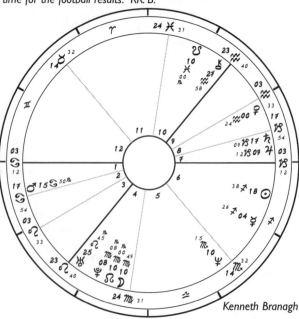

Kenneth Branagh

and just prior to his Saturn Return). Critics were soon comparing his talent to that of Laurence Olivier (qv). The films *Dead Again* (1991) and *Much Ado About Nothing* (1993) demonstrated his talent for intensity and creative flair on screen, although he has also encountered a few commercial and critical failures in the early 90s (*Frankenstein* and *Peter's Friends*). His *Hamlet* was released in February 1997. There are clear astrological signs of Branagh's success in the performing arts. The most vivid is the Moon-Pluto conjunction square Mercury. He married Emma Thompson (b. 15 April 1959, London) in August 1989 (TR Jupiter over Ascendant) but they separated in 1996. Although Emma's Moon is in touchy, sensitive Cancer (Branagh's Ascendant sign), her Mars is conjunct his Ascendant suggesting a dynamic, creative professional atmosphere which can result in a combative, stubborn home environment. To their credit, neither has spoken at length in public of their personal split. With early success Branagh was depicted by the media as a brash egomaniac, but is someone who does not take himself too seriously.

Gyles Brandreth

b. 8 March 1948, 20.00 MET (-1), British Forces Hospital, Wuppertal, Germany, 51N16, 07E11.
Caroline Gerard q. his letter, 27/6/1996. RR: A.

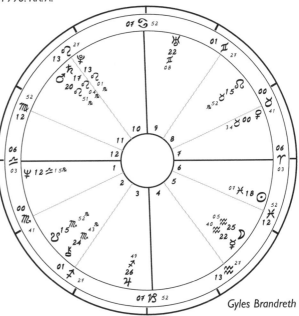

Gyles Brandreth

Versatile TV presenter, writer and businessman, who for so long led a double-life as flamboyant court-jester and serious intellectual (picture a combination of Noddy and Einstein). As TR Uranus crossed his Ascendant he was discovered by a TV producer in September 1969, and Brandreth, Students' Union president at Oxford, featured on *A Child of the Sixties* (December 1969). He proved an instant success as a competent interviewer (the 3rd, 5th and 9th are strongly connected – the rulers are in these houses and in aspect to one another). A Solar Eclipse fell opposite his Sun around the former date. At the time he expressed an interest in a political career. Before making his move, Brandreth (with Libra Rising and MC in Cancer) became a pleasant, popular celebrity on TV, where he could make good use of his intelligence on shows such as *Countdown*, and also of the fancy, sometimes bizarre, sweaters sent in by viewers when he greeted the nation each morning on *TV-am*. With Moon-Mercury conjunct in inventive Aquarius in the creative 5th House, Brandreth's company has produced over one hundred games and books, from a biography of John Gielgud to Knock Knock jokes. Brandreth also holds world records for the longest screen kiss and the longest after-dinner speech (twelve-and-a-half hours). He was elected a Conservative Member of Parliament in May 1992 (weeks before a Solar Eclipse occurred on his MC), before losing his seat in May 1997 (weeks after the Solar Eclipse conjunct his Sun). In April 1999 Brandreth, who never made much of an impact politically, broke the code by publishing his Parliamentary diaries, which chronicled his five years in the Commons. In August 2002 (TR Saturn opposite Jupiter) he appeared in *Zipp!* at the Edinburgh Fringe Festival. The show, a homage to 100 musicals in 90 minutes, moved to the West End in late January 2003 and officially opened on 4 February.

Richard Branson

b. 18 July 1950, 07.00 GDT, Blackheath, England, 51N28, 0E01.

FCC q. Branson's mother, via his secretary (N.B. L & L for Blackheath). RR: A.

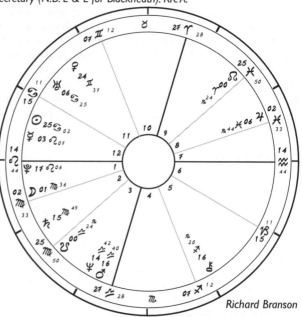

Richard Branson

Branson, with tremendous instinct and self-belief, began his career hustling for advertising in a telephone box for his *Student* magazine (first published on 26 January 1968). By 20 he had a thriving business and 40 employees. His first unexpected success came when he signed Mike Oldfield (b. 15 May 1953, Reading) to his Virgin label in November 1971 (TR Uranus conjunct MC ruler Mars), and had a media phenomenon on his hands when Virgin released the Sex Pistols' album in October 1977 (TR Pluto conjunct MC ruler Mars). Branson forced his way into the music business with a hands-on approach, originally offering up to 60% off any album on any label. His company Virgin became synonymous with value for money, informality and an emphasis on service (Virgo Moon). Jupiter (ruler of the 5th and 8th) is the handle of the chart in the 7th trine Uranus (7th House ruler) in the 11th – suggesting opportunities for taking advantage of fortunate contacts, investing and building upon creative ventures, as well as a reputation for philanthropy. By 32 Branson's empire consisted of 50 companies with a turnover of £50 million. His companies promote a wide range of products from software, music and video to property and travel (the importance of his brand name, focus on customer service and personal agenda is best shown by Pluto Rising and Moon in Virgo). Raised by an adventurous and competitive mother (MC in Aries, Moon opposite Jupiter), Branson was taught to be self-reliant and enterprising. One character-building event occurred when she dropped him off in a field in Devon and asked him to find his way home. He was four years old. Branson emulated her achievements with his own record-breaking daredevil antics in later years, and his need to challenge the media establishment demonstrate his pioneering Aries MC (the MC also accounts for his image as a schoolboy adventurer). With many polarities in his nature, he has been a maverick in the music industry yet so often represents the establishment; ostensibly an exhibitionist and publicity-seeker (adopting the showmanship and bravado of his Leo Ascendant), he is shy and awkward one-to-one (Sun in Cancer square MC). To many, the private man remains an enigma. He is known to have little interest in music (signing people for personal reasons), and he does not appear to have a passionate opinion about anything. Some critics see his domination in various markets as hiding a personal agenda (certainly a Virgo Moon has a mission to systematically 'clean up' the world and tidy it into manageable and governable pieces). Branson has commented that he would like to see the brand name Virgin everywhere – a Virgin world of cola, megastores, cinemas, radio, music and TV. Although his businesses have suffered in recent years, in February 2003 *The Mail on Sunday's Rich Report* estimated his fortune at £1.2 billion. He has married twice (22 July 1972, separated Summer 1974, and from December 1989). (*Richard Branson – The Inside Story* by Mick Brown, Headline, 1994.)

> Q "I'm always looking at details and striving to get them right. [Money] enables you to indulge in fantastic challenges, fantastic ways of testing yourself to the limits... At times when I could live happily ever after, I will throw my life, my family and my business partners into turmoil by getting into another survival battle." (Richard Branson, as quoted in *Reflections on Success* by Martyn Lewis, Lennard, 1997)

Ewen Bremner

✪ b. 11 December 1970, 19.34 MET, Elsie Inglis Maternity Hospital, Edinburgh, Scotland, 55N57, 03W10. Gerard q. BC. RR: AA.

Actor who is best remembered for his roles in *Trainspotting* (February 1996) and *The Acid House* (1998). His Venus is conjunct writer Irvine Welsh's (qv) MC, and Jupiter on Welsh's Moon.

Rory Bremner

b. 6 April 1961, 21.05 GDT, Edinburgh, Scotland, 55N57, 03W12.
Gerard q. BC (Roderick Keith Ogilvy Bremner). RR: AA.

Acclaimed comedian and impersonator. Bremner won his first break in August 1981 at the Edinburgh Festival in *The Importance of Being Varnished*, but continued other jobs the following year, including teaching English in Paris. Before hitting the comedy circuit in Britain (he was discovered by Terry Wogan and asked to appear on the very first *Wogan* show), he worked in a supermarket and impersonated Prince Charles on French and German radio. In the 80s he put his personal life on hold and concentrated fully on establishing his reputation. He even hit the pop charts with a spoof cricket-based pastiche in July 1985. At the end of the 80s he developed an eating disorder and went through a period of depression and

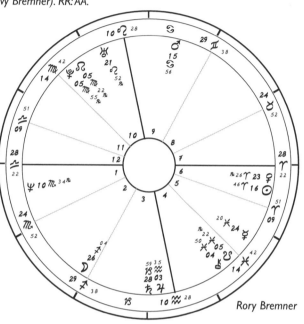

Rory Bremner

low self-esteem. His marriage in January 1987 lasted seven years (a more tranquil Bremner would remarry on 11 September 1999). With the Venus and Mars emphasis (both strongly positioned plus the Sun in Aries and Libra Rising), Bremner is able to present his sharp brand of comedy to an enthusiastic audience, although he has never taken the anarchic, alternative comedy route of his contemporaries (Uranus is in a Grand Trine with no hard aspects – his comedy has been described as "politically toothless"). After Princess Diana's infamous *Panorama* interview, Bremner dedicated a series of hilarious and unforgettable sketches to the approval-seeking Queen of Hearts (Bremner's Venus is conjunct Diana's IC). Bremner's work as Tony Blair is memorable (again Bremner's Venus is conjunct Blair's Mercury, and his Sun is conjunct Blair's Venus). The Venusian synastry points to highly popular and accessible, but unthreatening, portrayals. Bremner has Moon in Sagittarius trine 10th House Uranus grand trine (Ascendant ruler) Venus in 6th for wit, inventiveness and popularity.

> Q
>
> "It is impossible not to think of all [his] mimicry as being a side-stepping defence mechanism. He is very amusing, provocative company, but I imagine rather wilful... This emotional evasiveness is, possibly, why his past relationships (until his second marriage) seem to have been such a disaster area... He is, basically, a walking set of contradictions." (Lucy Cavendish, *Evening Standard*, 23/9/02)
>
> "I'm pretty schizophrenic. For years, in my twenties, it was all work, work, work and everything suffered. My health went, my relationships were strained. I think my mind went. Even then I started looking for balance, but I couldn't find anything... I've always been torn between two conflicting things: appearing on television as compared to performing live; living in the countryside or in London; seeking other people's approval and then being bullish when they voice an opinion. It's endless." (Rory Bremner, *Evening Standard*, 23/9/02)

Richard Briers

   b. 14 January 1934, 00.30 GMT, Merton, England, 51N25, 0W12.

   FCC q. him, from his parents. RR: A.

Leading British actor whose first professional role was in *Hamlet* at RADA in 1955 (when TR Uranus crossed his MC). Briers was class clown until he fell in love with Shakespeare at age 12. After a number of TV and theatre comedy roles as the silly ass or jovial fool (Jupiter Rising), Briers had the skill, temperament and luck to hit the big time with *The Good Life* (from April 1975 – as TR Saturn headed towards the EQHS 10th and over the MC – until it ended in June 1978). He followed it with *Ever Decreasing Circles* (29 January 1984, TR Jupiter conjunct Moon, to December 1989). In the latter, Briers played the irritatingly exacting husband to perfection (a market cornered by Capricorn, particularly when in the Virgo

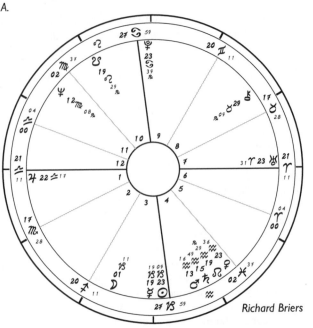

Richard Briers

decan of the sign! Briers has the Moon, Sun and Mercury positioned in Capricorn). Personally he is known for his driving energy and huge temper (marks of a cardinal Grand Cross and a Mars-Saturn conjunction). Briers suffered from extreme stage fright for some years (EQHS 3rd and 5th House rulers are opposing each other on the Ascendant-Descendant axis, and part of his Grand Cross life challenge). In January 1990 he returned to his Shakespearean roots by taking on the role of *King Lear* for a world tour with Kenneth Branagh's (qv) Renaissance Company. Branagh helped Briers expand his range and gain further stage credibility (Branagh's Saturn conjuncts Briers's Mercury, and his MC conjuncts Briers's Venus – perhaps Briers was a comedy favourite of Branagh's). Briers was on the New Year's Honours list of 1989 in line for an OBE. Recently he starred in the TV series *Monarch of the Glen*.

> Q "My father's life did me a big favour because he made me cautious. I've never lived beyond my means and don't spend a lot because I may not earn again, or get ill." (Richard Briers, *Radio Times*, c.1991)

Geoff Britton

   b. 1 August 1943, 15.30 DGDT, Lewisham, London, England, 51N27, 0W01.

   From him to Magpie Latham, "about 3.30 pm." RR: A.

Hugely experienced drummer with bands Gun, East of Eden, Wild Angels Wings, Rough Diamond, Raphael Ravenscroft, Key, and Manfred Mann's Earthband (with an album in March 1979).

Tim Brooke-Taylor

   b. 17 July 1940, 11.00 GDT, Buxton, England, 53N15, 01W55.

   Data from Suzanne Michaud, original source not known. RR: C.

Actor, comedian and writer who began his entertainment career in the Cambridge Footlights revues (1962-3) after a year-long stint teaching and travelling. The second revue transferred to the West End for five months. He then invested nine months with ATV on production until July 1964 before embarking on a revue revival in New York, which led to other work in the States. In May 1965 Brooke-Taylor returned to England and later appeared in *On the Braden Beat*, before starring in and writing two series of *At Last the 1948 Show* with members of Monty Python (qv). Since then he has taken part in theatre farce, children's television, quiz shows and the hugely popular and ridiculous series *The Goodies* (November 1970 to February 1982), as the patriotic coward and upper-class twit. He also starred in *Me and My Girl* (August 1984 to November 1988). Brooke-Taylor joined the cast of the revamped soap *Crossroads* in Spring 2003 (TR Saturn conjunct MC) but was killed off after a week. He married in 1968.

Elkie Brooks

b. 25 February 1945, 20.00 GDT, Salford, Lancashire, England, 53N28, 02W18.
Julie Argyle q. Brooks personally. RR: A.

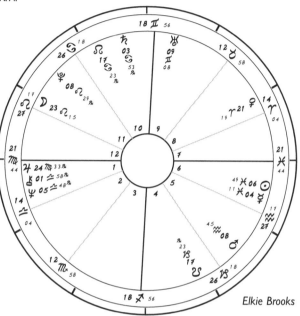

Elkie Brooks

After stints with various bands from the early 60s (as "Manchester's answer to Brenda Lee"), Brooks (Elaine Bookbinder) embarked on a solo career in 1974. But it took until 1977 (at age 32) before she became famous for her expressive approach to dramatic love songs and ballads. Brooks's hits include two Top Ten hits in 1977, a hit album in November 1981, and a further chart smash in January 1987, *No More the Fool*. Six years later she embarked upon a 49-date UK tour. On 8 March 2003 she began appearing on the reality TV show *Reborn in the USA*, performing with other 70s and 80s stars across America each week before UK viewers voted which star they'd like to send home. Brooks, the eldest in the group and popular with audiences, was voted off in week four on 29 March.

BROS

•1987, Apr – Bros sign a recording deal. The Goss twins, whose father had left when they were five years old, had met Logan in 1980 and asked him to join their band. Matt was the songwriter and front man of the group, despite having been introverted for a long time after his parents split.
•1988, Feb – First hit of a banner year. Enormous hype and instant teen fandom follow (TR Uranus hits both Luke's and Matt's MC during the year, and in March, TR Jupiter conjuncts Logan's MC ruler Sun).
•1988, June – First chart-topper.
•1989, Jan – Logan, the least popular/hyped member, leaves the group, later suing the Goss twins.

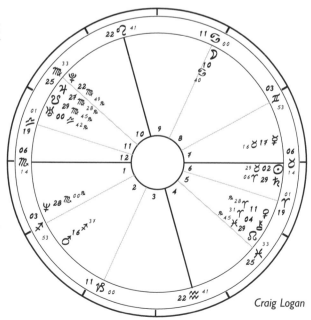

Craig Logan

- 1990 – A drunk driver kills the Goss' step-sister (their mother had remarried in July 1976).
- 1991, Oct – After 14 millions albums and 11 hit singles, the group have their last chart hit in the UK. They are later burdened with financial worries from their excessive lifestyles (both Jupiters are angular) and management difficulties in the 80s. Matt Goss moves to Los Angeles and secures a solo record deal. Luke Goss finds himself broke and unemployed.
- 1995, Aug – Matt Goss releases a comeback album *The Key*.
- 1995, Sep – Logan becomes the international marketing manager at EMI Records.
- 1996, Mar – Luke Goss moves into stage acting.
- 1997, Apr 27 – Luke Goss begins appearing in the musical *What a Feeling* with Sonia (qv).
- 2001, Feb – It is announced that Luke Goss will appear alongside Wesley Snipes in the $60 million action sequel *Blade 2*.

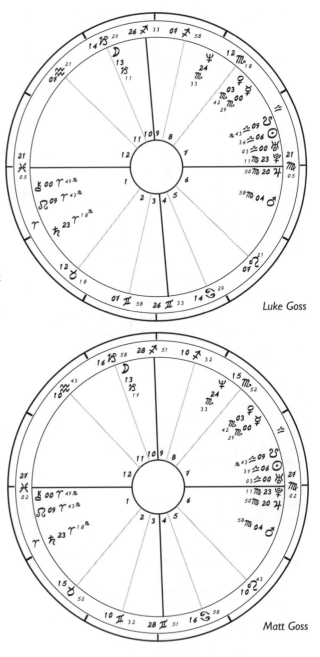

Luke Goss

Matt Goss

Luke Goss
b. 29 September 1968, 18.11 MET, Lewisham, London, England, 51N27, 0W01. BC in hand (a twin, Luke Damon Goss). RR: AA.

Matt Goss
b. 29 September 1968, 18.21 MET, Lewisham, London, England, 51N27, 0W01. BC in hand (a twin, Matthew Weston Goss). RR: AA.

Craig Logan
b. 22 April 1969, 20.50 MET, Maternity Hospital, Kirkcaldy, Scotland, 56N07, 03W09. Gerard q. BC (Craig William Logan). RR: AA.

Janet Brown

b. 14 December 1923, 07.45 GMT, Rutherglen, Scotland, 55N50, 04W12.
Gerard q. BC. RR: AA.

Comedienne and impressionist (Jupiter Rising in Sagittarius, Sun in Sagittarius) who won a strong following for her astute impersonation of Margaret Thatcher during the 80s. Brown made her first stage and radio appearances at age 13. Subsequent stage performances in London (1945) and radio shows led to her own series on Radio Scotland in 1949 and a film debut in *Mr Gillie* (1950). She starred with husband Peter Butterworth (of *Carry On* fame) in the 1954 sitcom *Friends and Neighbours*. Other comedy series began in January 1963 (*The TV Lark*, radio) and August 1974 (*Mr Digby, Darling*, TV) before her career revival as Thatcher. Brown's Venus and MC fall across Thatcher's all-important cardinal T-Square, and her new career was sparked off when Thatcher became PM (TR Saturn near EQHS 10th, TR Pluto over MC). Venus is important in their synastry because Brown's impersonation, unlike Steve Nallon's (qv) or Angela Thorne's (qv), was gentle, gracious, and admired by the lady herself. In September 1996 she opened in a national tour of Charles Dickens's *Hard Times*. In 2000 Brown appeared in the short-lived sitcom *Rhona* starring Rhona Cameron (qv).

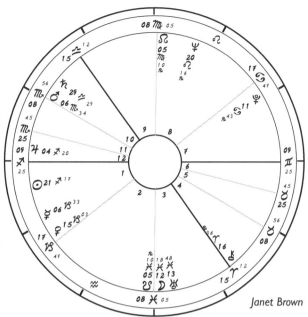

Janet Brown

June Brown

(Confidential Data)

Original actress, known (and typecast) for her portrayals of neurotics, Brown became a national TV icon as Dot Cotton (in *EastEnders*, from its start in February 1985). Viewers loved ignorant, religious, chain-smoking Dot, who was a victim of her own hot flushes and nasty treatment from vile son Nick (John Altman, qv) and layabout husband Charlie. With her chart ruler on the MC, Brown won fame during her second Saturn Return. She left *EastEnders* in June 1993 (her final appearance aired in late August that year) and the show soon lost its humour and character. She was, however, persuaded to return in April 1997. Brown is strongly interested in palmistry and astrology. With her tough T-Square she learned from an early age to cope with death: she lost her brother, sister, uncle, grandparents, mother and father when young. Later, tragedy struck when her husband of seven years committed suicide – Brown was then 30. This extraordinary talent met her second husband a year later and gave birth to six children in seven years.

Melanie Brown – see Spice Girls

Ronnie Browne

b. 20 August 1937, 00.45 GDT, central Edinburgh, Scotland, 55N57, 03W12.
Gerard q. BC (Ronald Grant). RR: AA.

Musician, singer and portrait-painter. Ronnie Browne co-founded the Corries Folk Trio in 1961 whilst studying at the Edinburgh College of Art. In 1966 he put his teaching career on hold to tour with the group. Corries became one of Scotland's most popular folk acts with best-selling albums, national television shows and concerts, before one member's untimely death on 12 August 1990 (Solar Eclipse on Browne's Pluto in 1st). Browne went solo.

Ian Bruce

✪ b. 21 June 1956, 00.02 GDT, Maternity Hospital, Glasgow, Scotland, 55N51, 04W14.
Gerard q. BC (Ian Morris Bruce). RR: AA.

Folk singer who released his first album with brother Fraser in May 1981 before going solo in 1988.

Jack Bruce

b. 14 May 1943, 02.10 DGDT, Bishopbriggs, Glasgow, Scotland, 55N55, 04W14.
Gerard q. BC (John Simon Asher Bruce). RR: AA.

Legendary rock bassist known for his free-spirited approach to music and his improvisational skill (Mercury conjunct Uranus in 5th in Gemini). Bruce joined the R&B circuit when he moved to London at 19, first with Alexis Korner and later with the Graham Bond Organisation. He formed Cream with Ginger Baker and Eric Clapton (qv) in July 1966 and the band soon gained a strong international following (as TR Neptune crossed Bruce's MC). They sold 35 million albums but in July 1968 Cream announced they would split in November 1968. They reconciled briefly for a concert in January 1993. His solo career continued in the 90s with over a dozen albums to his credit, including *A Question of Time* (1990). During the late 90s he toured with Ringo Starr's (qv) All Star Band along with Peter Frampton (qv) and others, and in 2001 he released *Shadows in the Air*.

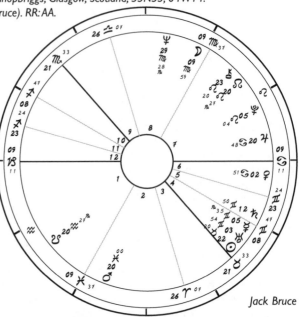

Jack Bruce

Ken Bruce

✪ b. 2 February 1951, 04.30 GMT, Glasgow, Scotland, 55N53, 04W15.
Marjorie Orr q. him. RR: A.

British disc jockey.

Tom Buchan

b. 19 June 1931, 11.10 GDT, Broomhill, Glasgow, Scotland, 55N53, 04W20.
Gerard q. BC (Thomas Buchanan Buchan). RR: AA.

A poet and prolific playwright ahead of his time (a strong Gemini-Virgo chart fuels the desire to communicate), Buchan was a literary giant who was never given the respect he deserved from Scotland's literary community nor the credit for creating a particular theatre style (his MC has only two major aspects, and the Moon, Saturn and Jupiter are not in the Gauquelin areas of recognition in the chart). In 1968 Buchan was appointed senior lecturer in English and Drama at Clydebank Technical College, and in 1973 he began as editor of the magazine *Scottish International*. He began Billy Connolly's (qv) career with the 1972 comedy *The Great Northern Welly Boot Show* (Buchan's Pluto is conjunct Connolly's MC suggesting this starmaking influence).

Isobel Buchanan

b. 15 March 1954, 03.35 GMT, Robroyston Hospital, Glasgow, Scotland, 55N54, 04W11.
Gerard q. BC (Isobel Wilson Buchanan). RR: AA.

Soprano (Ascendant ruler Saturn on the MC square Moon) with the Australian Opera (1975-8) who first trained at the Royal Scottish Academy of Music and Drama. Buchanan became a sensation in the late 70s in Europe and America. She married actor Jonathan Hyde in 1980.

Jack Buchanan

✪   *b. 2 April 1890, 01.40 GMT, Helensburgh, Scotland, 56N00, 04W44.*
     Gerard q. BC (Walter John Buchanan). RR: AA.

Buchanan made his music hall debut in 1911, but was booed off the stage. The management quickly brought down the curtain and hit him on the head. The audience's jeers turned to sympathetic laughter and thereafter the management paid him to do the routine twice nightly! In 1915 he began in the play *Tonight's the Night*, which brought him stardom. Buchanan then made a move into films, very often as a suave dancer in top hat and tails. D. 20 October 1957.

Charlie Burchill – see Simple Minds

Eric Burdon

     b. 11 May 1941, 00.00 Midnight (10th/11th) DGDT, Newcastle-upon-Tyne, England, 54N59, 01W35.
     From him to Jenni Harte. RR: A.

Singer and songwriter, originally lead vocalist with The Animals, and heralded as one of the finest white Blues singers of his era. The Animals were signed in January 1964 and hit #1 in Britain in July (TR Jupiter conjunct Sun, TR Pluto conjunct EQHS 10th) and the USA that September (TR Uranus conjunct EQHS 10th). During September 1966 the band, amid increasing musical differences and allegations of drug use, agreed to split (TR Neptune opposite Sun), but Burdon remained to form Eric Burdon & the Animals. Their song *The House of the Rising Sun* secured musical immortality for the band. In January 1970 Burdon joined the black jazz and rock band Nite Shift after he failed to win acting roles in Hollywood. A new band, as Eric

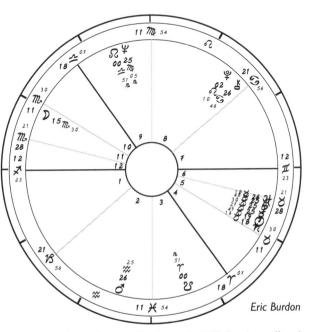

Eric Burdon

Burdon and War, released the US hit *Spill the Wine* later that year. During early 1971 Burdon suffered burnout and War, continuing to tour without him, became a leading 70s funk band. At the time of Hendrix's death on 18 September 1970, Burdon gained publicity after claiming to have a suicide note in his possession. In October 1972 and August 1973 Burdon's hits with the Animals were reissued and charted (TR Uranus on MC). He reemerged on the scene in March 1977 with a new album (Jupiter Return). Burdon has a spectacular stellium in his chart highlighting his bursts of fame, brilliant performances and health/addiction problems. In 1986 he released an autobiography, *I Used to be an Animal But I'm Alright Now*, and a solo album of the same name in 1988. He continued to tour in the 90s and reformed the New Animals in 1999.

John Burgess

     b. 11 March 1934, 10.40 GMT, Aberdeen, Scotland, 57N09, 02W07.
     Gerard q. BC (John Davie Burgess). RR: AA.

Childhood bagpipe lessons brought prodigy Burgess numerous accolades in junior and professional competitions, and later the title "The King of the Highland Pipers" (Burgess has MC ruler Saturn conjunct the MC for professional respect, and Moon opposite Pluto for distinction – part of a Grand Cross). His albums in the 70s were popular and Burgess was awarded the MBE in 1989.

Richard Burton

🜨 *b. 10 November 1925, 14.30 GMT, Pontrhydyfen, Wales, 52N17, 03W51.*
Frances McEvoy q. him to his friend Alfred Baruth for "midafternoon just before his siblings came home from school." Speculative time. RR: C.

The son of a coal miner, Burton made his stage debut on 22 November 1943 before embarking upon a three-year stint with the RAF (1944-7). After a film debut in 1948 he quickly established a reputation as an actor with a commanding presence and a fine speaking voice. It was during the long filming of *Cleopatra* (shooting began in September 1960 – TR Jupiter on MC; the film premiered in June 1963) with future wife Elizabeth Taylor (qv), that Burton became a worldwide celebrity. Their first scenes together were in January 1962 (TR Pluto conjunct Moon). Their tempestuous on-again off-again romance assured good copy for newspapers across the world for years, as did his infamous rages and on-going battle with

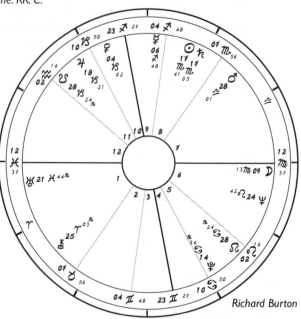

Richard Burton

alcohol (the Sun-Neptune square and possible Pisces Ascendant). His 1964 *Hamlet* was the theatrical event of the decade. He married on 5 February 1949, and later married Taylor twice (15 March 1964 to 26 June 1974, and 10 October 1975 to 30 July 1976). D. 5 August 1984, brain haemorrhage.

Max Bygraves

b. 16 October 1922, 05.30 GMT, Rotherhithe, London, England, 51N30, 0W02.
FCC q. him. (N.B. His autobiography I Wanna Tell You a Story (W.H. Allen, 1976), p. 13, relates how his father returned after losing a boxing match in the afternoon to his new-born son "born a few hours earlier.") RR: A.

Perennial singalong entertainer, family entertainer and comedian, much loved by the nostalgic (Cancer MC's ruler Moon is conjunct Neptune for longevity, nostalgia and popular song mixed with gentle patter). Walter William Bygraves became a professional comedian and singer after the Second World War, and in May 1946 began his first tour (after TR Saturn had crossed the MC). A son was born on 14 July 1946, two days before Bygraves got his big break opening at Sheffield's Moss Empire Theatre. Bygraves, often-impersonated for his catchphrases (Saturn-Ascendant), which included "I wanna tell you a story", was a

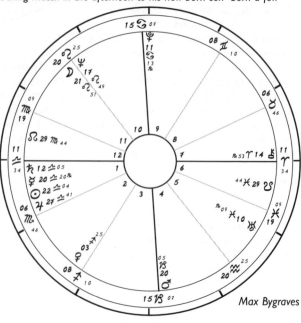

Max Bygraves

regular contributor to Royal Variety Performances, and was bumbling host of the quiz show Family Fortunes for a while. In 1996 he celebrated 50 years in show business. In May 1999 Bygraves was diagnosed with a rare ear infection that threatened to end his long career. In September 2002, however, he was promoting his work and a new book.

> Q | "I'm better than the rest. No entertainer in Britain has my pedigree and I'm clean. No one has ever heard a four-letter word from me on stage." (Max Bygraves, *Daily Mail*, c.1996)

David Byrne

b. 14 May 1952, 14.00 GDT, Overton Maternity Hospital, Alexandria, Dunbartonshire, Scotland, 56N00, 04W35.

Gerard q. BC. RR: AA.

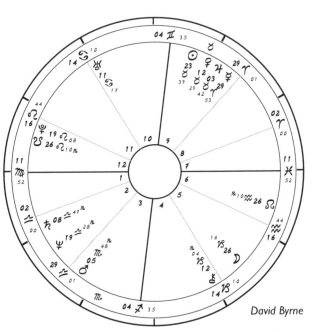

David Byrne

Educated in the USA, Byrne established a group in September 1974 with two fellow design students and named it Talking Heads in May 1975. A first gig was staged a month later and the trio signed a recording contract in November 1976. The initial fruit of their labours charted in the US in Spring 1978 and the band quickly developed a new-wave rock following on both sides of the Atlantic. Talking Heads began charting in Britain in 1981, at the time of major commercial developments in the group. Byrne, quirky and innovative (with Ascendant/MC ruler Mercury conjunct a prominent Jupiter), is known for experimenting with images on the band's videos. His film, *True Stories*, premiered in July 1986. With Talking Heads popularising crossover African and Latin American rhythms, Byrne began his global music label Luaka Bop in the late 80s, with a mission to bring world music into the mainstream. Talking Heads made their last live appearance on 18 July 1989.

> Q | "In performance, and as the 'compere' in his film *True Stories*, David Byrne comes across as the epitome of Wasp uptightness, nervy and ill at ease. Perhaps that's why his obsession, in Talking Heads and as a solo artist, has been with shedding the white man's burden of self-consciousness... But Byrne is very far from the repressed, twitchy egghead. Rather, he's laid-back, genial and humorous in a low-key sort of way." (Simon Reynolds, *The Observer*, 23/6/91)

John Byrne

b. 6 January 1940, 08.10 GMT, Barshaw Hospital, Paisley, Scotland, 55N51, 04W23.

Gerard q. BC. RR: AA.

Dramatist and stage designer best known for his work on the television series *Tutti Frutti* (March 1987) with Robbie Coltrane (qv), and *Your Cheatin' Heart*. Byrne's first play, entitled *Writer's Cramp*, was produced at the Edinburgh Festival Fringe in August 1977.

Mel C – see Spice Girls

Marti Caine

b. 26 January 1945, 15.15 GDT, Sheffield, England, 53N23, 01W30.

David Fisher q. her letter. RR: A.

Energetic and gutsy, Caine won *New Faces* in 1974 (during the year TR Jupiter crossed her MC and TR Saturn passed over her Ascendant) and its Gala Final in 1975. With a Sun-Pluto opposition and Saturn retrograde on her Ascendant, Caine had a life of hardship, with any rewards being a result of her own fighting spirit and hard work. Her father died when she was seven (TR Uranus on Ascendant) and she was sent to a children's home at eleven. Later at 12, her grandfather abused her. A beauty contest winner at 14, she spent the next couple of years modelling (as TR Pluto crossed the IC). She fell pregnant at 16 and married a womaniser (they separated in May 1978). Her mother died when she was 22. Out of financial necessity

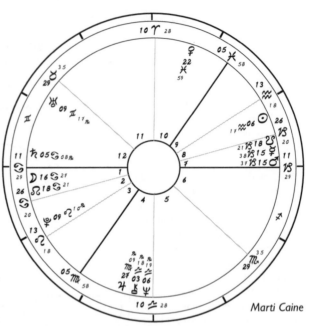

Marti Caine

and with two children to raise, Caine embarked on the club rounds as a singer with a zaniness and repartee that won her quite a following. She was a fanatically tidy housewife by day and played the working men's clubs by night for 15 years before securing a regular TV spot. From 1986 she presented *New Faces* with a maternal approach to contestants who were in the same position she had once been herself. As she was preparing for Christmas pantomime in 1988 (Lunar Eclipse on MC), Caine revealed she was living with an incurable lymphatic cancer (in September 1988 doctors had given her 18 months to live). She had a bone marrow transplant in 1993. Caine was preparing for her annual pantomime season in 1995 when she became seriously ill again and lost her battle. Her autobiography is entitled *A Coward's Chronicle*. D. 4 November 1995.

Q

"[My mother] drank to forget the pain and then it was too late, she was hooked on booze... [Being molested by my grandfather] damaged me and gave me a streak of recklessness. He was responsible for so many of my rash actions, getting pregnant at 16 for instance... My real name is Lynne Stringer and Lynne is different to Marti Caine. Marti is arrogant and pushy, the one that gets me into trouble. She's the one that opens her mouth and says the wrong thing. I'm aware when she takes over. It's conscious schizophrenia because the face alters and the chin comes forwards. Marti Caine is infinitely more aggressive than I am and she's saved my bacon a lot of times." (Marti Caine, *Daily Mail*, 19/8/95)

"My confidence is totally on the surface. I sometimes feel the softness I inherited from my mother and I have to hide it deliberately because I don't want to be crushed. You can bleed for people and my mother did. She took on the worries of the world... I'm always grateful for my tough childhood... So many people in show business come from a deprived background you've got to laugh or you'd go mad. Adversity breeds either comedy or bitterness." (Marti Caine, *Daily Mail*, 6/11/95)

Michael Caine

b. 14 March 1933, 10.03 GMT, Rotherhithe, London, England, 51N30, 0W02.

From his autobiography, What's It All About (Arrow, 1993), p. 5, "I was born in the Charity wing of St Olave's Hospital, Rotherhithe on Tuesday, 14 March 1933 at a few minutes after ten o'clock in the morning." RR: B.

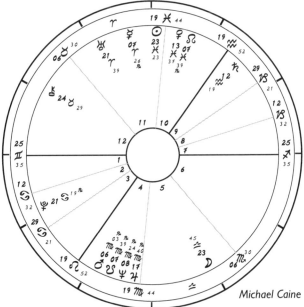

Michael Caine

A highly popular actor and personality from the early 60s and now influential amongst the Hollywood elite (a Saturn type rebels but often later 'becomes' the establishment). A violent and aggressive youth, Caine later channelled his energies and immense ambition into acting, although he was to endure a long apprenticeship (the prominent Saturn). Originally a filing clerk and messenger boy with a film company from August 1950, he won his first minor break in 1952 but gave up acting when he married two years later. The union was dissolved in 1956 and his father died early that year, with Caine narrowly escaping a nervous breakdown. The film *Zulu* proved to be the turning point in early 1963 (during his Saturn Return) and his reputation grew steadily. But it was as the womanising *Alfie* the following year that Caine achieved stardom and broke the mould as a genuine working class successful actor who didn't have film star looks (Saturn-MC in Aquarius). He was then typecast (Saturn-MC) as the tough rogue and laconic anti-hero. His success in America began with his role as Harry Palmer in *The Ipcress File* (August 1965, TR Jupiter on Ascendant), and *Alfie* was released there twelve months later. Since then he has made film appearances in *Dressed to Kill* (July 1980), *Educating Rita* (1983), and *Hannah and Her Sisters* (February 1986, Oscar, Best Supporting Actor). Caine has shown versatility (Gemini Ascendant) in over 70 films, although he is a victim of media intellectual snobbery and is criticised for often playing the same character type (Saturn prominent is an impressionist's dream target, too, although *not a lot of people know that*). His acting career was revived with *The Cider House Rules* (for which he won his second Oscar to add to two Baftas and three Golden Globes) and *The Quiet American* (premiered in the UK on 29 November 2002, as TR Saturn moved towards his Ascendant). Caine has always had an ambiguous relationship with Britain and used his Bafta Fellowship speech in April 2000 (TR Uranus on MC) to confess that he always felt an outsider in his own country and profession (Aquarius MC). This 'chip' on his shoulder has led some to believe he is obsessed with the British class system (Saturn on the MC in Aquarius) but he is more driven by a need for respect. He was knighted on 16 November 2000. Caine has been married since 8 January 1973. Caine's mother died on 12 December 1989 and a tabloid revealed (on 12 May 1991, TR Pluto square MC) that she had taken a secret to her grave: that Michael had a half-brother in a mental hospital.

> Q "I never had a natural respect for anybody. Even when I was young, no matter how old you were or how grand you were, you had to earn it." (Michael Caine, *Vanity Fair*, 12/92)
> "He is a natural pedagogue who likes to acquire information himself and then pass it on, regardless of whether anyone is interested... In my opinion, what he hates is not the [British class] system per se, but the fact that he was born into the wrong part of it... The chip on his shoulder is not really about class at all, but about attention, being listened to and taken seriously... You discover that he doesn't suffer fools gladly, that he doesn't trust anyone readily, that he is very serious about money, that he is a puritan." (Lynn Barber, *Vanity Fair*, 12/92)

Christine Cairns

> *b. 11 February 1959, 22.20 GMT, Saltcoats, Ayrshire, Scotland, 55N38, 04W47.*
> *Gerard q. BC (Christina Wilson Cairns). RR: AA.*

Mezzo-soprano (with MC ruler Moon angular and square Saturn). Cairns's singing career took off in 1985 with a worldwide tour with André Previn and the Los Angeles Philharmonic.

John Cale

✪ *b. 9 March 1942, 08.10 GWT, Garnant, West Glamorgan, Wales, 52N00 04W00 (L&L is approximate).*
> *John McKay-Clements q. a letter from Cale. RR: A.*

A child piano prodigy, Cale was awarded with his first BBC radio broadcast at the age of five. Cale is best known for his contribution to the band Velvet Underground. He is also a composer (highly respected for his work on soundtracks), record producer, and a recent album *Songs for Drella* with Lou Reed told of their experiences with Andy Warhol.

Simon Callow

> *b. 15 June 1949, 07.00 GDT, London, England, 51N30, 0W10.*
> *FCC q. him ("Caesarean birth, therefore precise to the minute"). RR: A.*

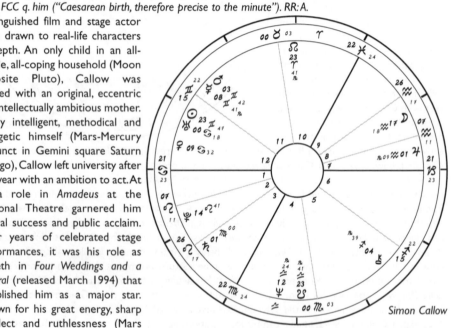

Simon Callow

Distinguished film and stage actor often drawn to real-life characters of depth. An only child in an all-female, all-coping household (Moon opposite Pluto), Callow was blessed with an original, eccentric and intellectually ambitious mother. Highly intelligent, methodical and energetic himself (Mars-Mercury conjunct in Gemini square Saturn in Virgo), Callow left university after one year with an ambition to act. At 30 a role in *Amadeus* at the National Theatre garnered him critical success and public acclaim. After years of celebrated stage performances, it was his role as Gareth in *Four Weddings and a Funeral* (released March 1994) that established him as a major star. Known for his great energy, sharp intellect and ruthlessness (Mars conjunct Mercury in Gemini, Moon-Pluto), Callow was also one of the first actors to publicly announce his homosexuality. Callow wrote of his intense, sensual friendship with theatrical agent Peggy Ramsay in *Love is Where it Falls*. He has also penned highly-detailed biographies on Orson Welles* and Charles Laughton**. The synastry between Callow and Welles is fascinating: Moons conjunct, Callow's MC conjunct Welles's Jupiter, Callow's Sun conjunct Welles's Ascendant. Callow's Venus conjuncts Charles Laughton's Sun, and his Sun opposes Laughton's Neptune, and Mars opposes Uranus.

> Q "I hated every moment of being a child. I saw no advantage in it at all. I hated the vulnerability, the dependency and the fact that one wasn't taken seriously enough... I was very small and fat, so I developed a sharp tongue to deal with other children. Also I was an exhibitionist – I wanted laughter and admiration." (Simon Callow, *You*, 19/5/02)

---

* Orson Welles b. 6 May 1915, 07.00 CST (+6), Kenosha, Wisconsin, USA, 42N35, 87W49. Note from Birth Registry in hand from Steinbrecher. RR: AA.

** Charles Laughton b. 1 July 1899, Scarborough, England.

Doreen Cameron
> b. 17 August 1949, 14.55 GDT, Glasgow, Scotland, 55N53, 04W19.
> Gerard q. BC. RR: AA.

Stage and television actress who has worked to promote working-class and anti-capitalist theatre. Cameron lived in the Middle East for four years teaching Drama and English. Stage performances include *Educating Rita*, though she is best known for her continuing role on the television soap *Take the High Road* (1990-4).

Rhona Cameron
✪ b. 27 September 1965, 16.20 GDT, Dundee, Scotland, 56N28, 02W59.
> From BC. RR: AA.

Stand-up comedian. Cameron won Channel 4's So You Think You're Funny Award in 1992 and three years later toured Britain with *The Jack Dee Show*. A regular at the Edinburgh Fringe Festival, she also co-hosted four series of *Gaytime TV* on BBC2. While filming the latter show she won a bronze medal for swimming at the 1998 Gay Games. In July 2000 own TV sitcom, *Rhona*, aired but the series, which was Britain's first lesbian sitcom, suffered from bad reviews and low viewing figures. In 2002 she appeared on the West End stage with *The Vagina Monologues* and made an impact on the summer TV hit *I'm a Celebrity – Get Me Out of Here!*, in which the woman with Mars conjunct MC in Scorpio (and

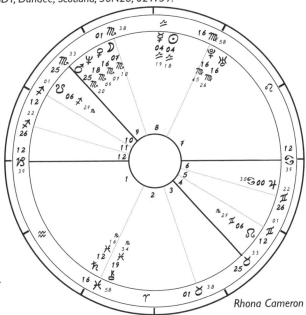

Rhona Cameron

three other planets in Scorpio) managed to provoke, antagonise and argue with the entire cast of minor celebrity contestants (TR Uranus was square MC-Mars).

Ian Campbell
✪ b. 10 June 1933, 05.45 GDT, Aberdeen, Scotland, 57N09, 02W08.
> Gerard q. BC. RR: AA.

Left-wing folk singer who released his first album in 1962. His sons Ali and Robin formed UB40.

Peter Capaldi
✪ b. 14 April 1958, 20.30 GMT, Balornock, Glasgow, Scotland, 55N53, 04W14.
> Gerard q. BC (Peter Dougan Capaldi). RR: AA.

Seasoned actor known nationally for his role in *Crow Road* (1997) and for his Oscar-winning short film *Franz Kafka's It's a Wonderful Life*. He played George Harrison (qv) in *John and Yoko: A Love Story* (1985).

Captain Sensible
> b. 24 April 1954, 05.00 GDT, Balham, London, England, 51N27, 0W08.
> Marjorie Orr q. him. RR: A.

Originally the bass guitarist of the punk band the Damned (and still a punk at heart), Ray Burns developed alter-ego Captain Sensible and hit the top of the charts in the UK during July 1982 with *Happy Talk* (which made chart history with the biggest jump to the pole position – 33 to 1). The last ten years of his recording life have brought a number of difficulties, yet Burns continues to make music and in 1996 reformed the Damned.

Elizabeth Carling

✪ b. 20 October 1967, 14.30 GDT, Middlesborough, England, 54N35, 01W14.
FCC q. BC in hand (a twin). RR: AA.

Actress best known for her role in the comedy *Goodnight Sweetheart*, which aired for four years. Liz Carling's first love is singing and in mid-1999 she released a spin-off album from the series on which she sang a number of 40s standards. In her teenage years Carling joined a short-lived pop group called Replay and played the club circuit. At 18 she joined the National Youth Theatre and was soon starring in pantomimes and musicals. Later she landed a role in the series *Boon* with Michael Elphick (qv) and *Barbara* with Gwen Taylor. Carling was romantically involved with actor Neil Morrissey (b. 4 July 1962, Stafford, England. From him to FCC.) for seven years until 1998, when their breakup made tabloid headlines (Descendant ruler Moon opposite Neptune-MC).

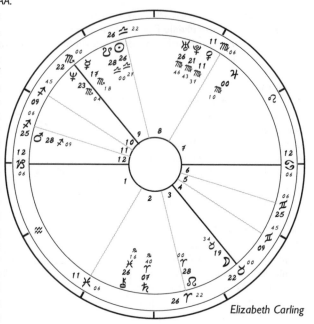

Elizabeth Carling

Robert Carlyle

✪ b. 14 April 1961, 05.15 GDT, Glasgow, Scotland, 55N52, 04W16.
Gerard q. BC. RR: AA.

Anarchic and versatile actor who terrified cinemagoers and made the big time in the surprise hit film of 1996, *Trainspotting* (released February that year). He became a major box office star in the film *The Full Monty*, the second most successful British film of all time. He won a Bafta for his role as the single dad struggling for respect. Since then he has given a number of impressive performances in a remarkable range of roles, including *Angela's Ashes* (released January 2000), and is known to push himself to extraordinary lengths in search of details that will make a performance more believable. Carlyle has a talent of immersing himself into roles, 'becoming' the characters he portrays (Pisces Rising), and is best remembered for playing a number of dysfunctional

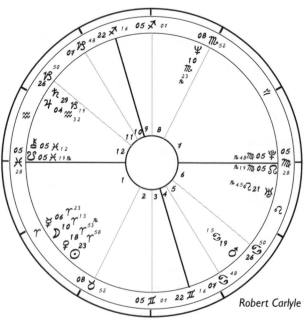

Robert Carlyle

or psychotic men on film (no doubt tapping into his dominant Pluto, which is conjunct the Descendant). Carlyle was raised by his dad when his mother left at age four – he admits that from then on it was him and his dad against the world. He considered acting only shortly after his 21st birthday and secured a place at the Royal Scottish Academy of Music and Drama in Autumn 1982. Carlyle has gone on to become one of the UK's most bankable actors ("It's hard to be that stressed when you are earning £40,000 a week," he has said, with Sun-Venus in 2nd trine Uranus in 6th, Grand Trine MC). Carlyle married on 29 December 1997 and attempts to live an uncomplicated, quiet life two miles from where he was born.

> Q "Robert himself is not much given to introspection. But he acknowledges that he finds it easier to identify with losers than winners. "I have always been interested in people who are marginalised in some way, people slightly outside society." Although Carlyle is an intensely private man, there is a warmth and a sensitivity behind the dour demeanour." (Lester Middlehurst, *Daily Mail*, 11/1/2000)

Ian Carr

b. 21 April 1933, 20.00 GDT, Charwood Maternity Home, Dumfries, Scotland, 55N04, 03W36.
Gerard q. BC (Ian Henry Randell Carr). RR: AA.

Carr's career as a teacher, writer and broadcaster, as well as an important jazz musician and composer, spans 30 years (Jazz, a Uranian music form, is shown by his Uranus-Venus-Sun conjunction, with Venus ruling the Ascendant and Sun ruling the MC). From 1960-2 he played with the EmCee Five and later recorded five albums as co-leader of the Rendell-Carr quintet (1963 to July 1969). September 1969 saw the launch of the influential Nucleus, pioneering jazz-rock fusion. His books include *Miles Davis* (1982), *Keith Jarrett: The Man and His Music* (1991) and *Jazz: The Rough Guide* (1995). In 1982 he became an associate professor with the Guildhall School of Music and was awarded the Calabria Award for outstanding contribution in the field of jazz.

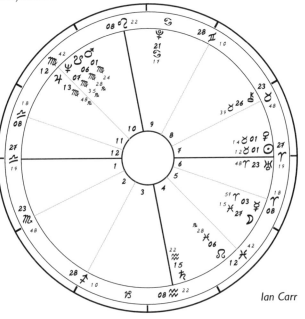

Ian Carr

Walter Carr

b. 1 April 1925, 06.30 GMT, Larkhall, Scotland, 55N44, 03W58.
Gerard q. BC (Robert Carr). RR: AA.

Actor and comic chiefly known for roles in comedy and as a pantomime dame. From musical revue at age 7, he became a singer, dancer and comedian in 1940 (in May and June that year both TR Jupiter and TR Saturn crossed his Ascendant). Variety concerts with Gracie Fields (qv) led to Carr joining the company at the Royal Lyceum Theatre in Edinburgh. (Pantomime appears to be a Jupiter-influenced pursuit, and Carr has Jupiter on his MC.)

Madeleine Carroll

● b. 26 February 1906, 15.00 GMT, West Bromwich, England, 52N31, 01W56.
  Church of Light q. Tucker, "data from her in 1935." Tucker had an article in Dell in which he stated
  00.40, but the chart was calculated for 12.40. RR: DD.

Carroll was briefly employed as a French teacher before making her stage debut in 1927, and later her film career involved a number of diverse roles. Her cool beauty attracted Alfred Hitchcock (qv) and he cast her in The Thirty Nine Steps (1935) and Secret Agent (1936). Her popularity resulted in an invitation to join Twentieth Century Fox in 1936, the first English rose to succeed there, and she made The Prisoner of Zenda in 1937. Carroll was involved in war relief from 1942 (awarded the Legion d'Honneur), but her patriotism led to the decline and, by 1949, the end of her career. She married and divorced four times (25 August 1931 to 12 December 1939, 14 February 1942 to 8 May 1946, 13 July 1946 to 1949, and 1 September 1950 to 22 January 1965). Carroll became a recluse in 1983 following the death of her daughter. D. 2 October 1987, Marbella, gall bladder cancer.

CARRY ON FILMS

Lavatorial humour, saucy seaside postcard innuendo and unrequited lust were all part of the formula in the Carry On films, each of which was made on a shoe-string budget in a breathless six-week schedule. The films are still popular in the form of TV reruns and compilation clips in spite, or perhaps because, of the current wave of political correctness in comedy. Peter Rogers and Gerald Thomas (b. 10 December 1920, Hull) produced 31 films with a semi-regular team, of which some played exaggerated versions of themselves. (The Carry On Companion by Robert Ross, Batsford, 1996.) Carry On performers featured in this book are: Roy Castle, Julian Clary, Bernard Cribbins, Barry Cryer, Fenella Fielding, Sid James, Maureen Lipman, Bob Monkhouse, Joan Sims, Kenneth Williams and Barbara Windsor.

Frank Carson

  b. 6 November 1926, 09.45 GMT, Belfast, Ireland, 54N35, 05W55.
  Marjorie Orr q. him. RR: A.

Uninhibited wise-cracking comedian whose repertoire includes blue humour (Jupiter squares four planets) and a fondness for ending a joke with a laugh because, "It's the way I tell 'em." (Astrologically, catchphrases are Mercurial in nature, and research reveals Saturn and Sagittarius are often prominent — Carson has Mercury Rising in Sagittarius, and Saturn conjunct Ascendant.) Discovered on Opportunity Knocks, Carson was later featured in The Comedians (1971-3), a TV showcase for top comics performing before a live audience. Carson is a devout Catholic, does extensive charity fundraising and was, for a time, Mayor of Balbriggan, Ireland.

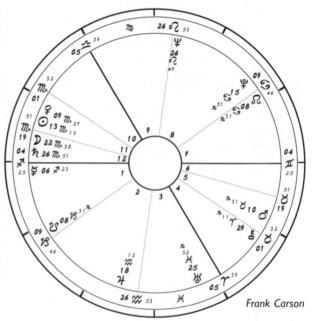

Frank Carson

Michael Cashman

b. 17 December 1950, 06.15 GMT, London, England, 51N30, 0W10.

FCC q. him, from his parents. RR: A.

A former child actor from age 12 (he appeared in *Oliver!*), Cashman was a successful actor and singer before moving into politics. In *EastEnders* Cashman played the first multi-dimensional gay character on a soap, and did so with sensitivity from August 1986 (TR Saturn on Ascendant) until the character left in February 1989. Although he will forever be associated with the role (Saturn on the MC), Cashman (a double Sagittarian) has become a spokesman for gay rights, and was one of the founding members and directors of the charity Stonewall in 1988, dedicated to eroding prejudice and ignorance (Sagittarius aims to break down barriers). He was elected as a Labour Party Member of the European Parliament for the West Midlands

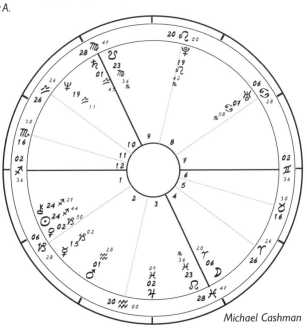

Michael Cashman

at the elections on 10 June 1999. Cashman has spoken of his abuse by a paedophile at age 9 as well as being raped at 18. Cashman has lived with his partner since January 1984.

Roy Castle

b. 31 August 1932, 18.00 GDT, Huddersfield, England, 53N39, 01W47.

Marjorie Orr q. him. RR: A.

Companionable and uncomplicated personality best known for the long-running series *Record Breakers* (from 1972, with Norris McWhirter, qv). Castle turned professional in 1953 and a Royal Variety Performance later made him a star. He was a singer, dancer, instrumentalist and actor (film credits including *Carry On Up the Khyber*). Audiences admired his sense of fun, his dedication (he set and broke his own world records during the *Record Breakers* series), and later his dignity and courage in the face of adversity during his fight against lung cancer (often surprising others with his black humour). The first symptoms of the disease were evident on 19 January 1992 (TR Neptune conjunct Ascendant and opposite Mars). Castle was diagnosed on 17 March (TR Uranus conjunct Ascendant

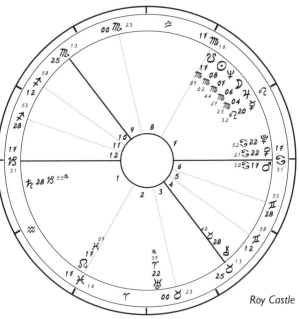

Roy Castle

and opposite Mars, TR Jupiter conjunct Sun and Neptune in EQHS 8th), and was given the all-clear in June. With Saturn backbone and Mars fighting spirit, Castle campaigned vigorously against smoking. He believed he had developed cancer via passive smoking during years of playing the trumpet in smoky clubs. The disease returned in November 1993 (TR Pluto on MC) and developed rapidly in May 1994. During that summer he participated in a Tour of Hope to raise £12 million for a new cancer centre. He was married for 31 years and had four children. Back in 1974, his wife had suffered a severe depression and Castle spent the next several years drinking heavily. The difficulties he later encountered as well as his great achievements in a number of areas are shown vividly in his remarkable chart: stellium in Virgo in sesquisquare Uranus; MC ruler Pluto conjunct EQHS 10th ruler Venus in 7th, square Uranus, T-square Saturn; Capricorn Rising and Saturn in 1st; Mars on Descendant. Castle's parents were opposites: his stage struck mother was fiercely ambitious, humourless and overprotective of Roy, while his father was easy-going and kind. D. 2 September 1994 (TR Saturn opposite Sun, TR Uranus opposite Venus, TR Pluto on MC). (*Now and Then: An Autobiography*, Robson Books, 1994.)

Q "Roy was very gentle. He loved people, he never trod on anybody. He hated anybody being done down but he didn't have very high self-esteem at all. He always had to have it bolstered, he was easily brought down." (His widow, Fiona Castle, *Daily Mail*, 22/10/94)

Jacqueline Chadwick – see Jacqueline Pirie

Judith Chalmers
* b. 10 October 1935, 10.10 GMT, Manchester, England, 53N30, 02W15.
 From BBC North's LifeLines, 17 March 1982. Original source not known. RR: C.
Perennially tanned television presenter of *Wish You Were Here?* since its conception in 1973. Chalmers was a child actor from 13, working on BBC Radio's *Children's Hour*. With poise she hosted *Miss World* and many royal film premieres for a number of years. During the late 50s she was a regional TV announcer and from 1970 presented *Women's Hour* for four years. She has confessed to being unable to manage her finances. Chalmers was awarded a CBE in June 1994.

Charles Chaplin
 b. 16 April 1889, 20.00 GMT, Walworth, London, England, 51N29, 0W05.
 From Chaplin's autobiography, *My Autobiography* (Penguin, 1966), p. 13. RR: B.
An actor, mimic, comedian, composer and pioneer and, in the tradition of a strong Scorpionic chart, both a much-acclaimed and much-maligned genius. Chaplin first performed at 4 (in January 1894), rescuing his mother when her voice cracked on stage. The family were sent to the workhouse on 30 May 1896. Chaplin signed with a theatrical agent in February 1908 (TR Jupiter conjunct EQHS 10th) and toured America in 1910 for two years. He began work on his first film, *Making a Living*, on 16 January 1914. But his comic talent was first appreciated fully upon the release of *The Tramp* in April 1915, and his humour is best characterised by the strongly aspected Moon Rising in political Scorpio (it opposes Mars for physical humour, and squares Saturn for pathos). The Aries influence (and Uranus opposite Mercury) added a need for perfection and anarchy, while elevated Saturn added a methodical, solitary nature. His life and work have been covered by hundreds of thorough biographies, but the key events in his life (as is so often the case when Scorpio is on the Ascendant) and changes in reputation are vividly reflected in transits over the angles of his chart:
    First Saturn conjunct MC – he signed a million-dollar contract and formed United Artists (January to April 1919); Second Saturn-MC – his reputation was damaged by a smear campaign regarding his political stance (April to July 1947); First Saturn conjunct Ascendant – poverty-stricken with a sick mother; Second Saturn-Ascendant – physical exhaustion and the release of *The Gold Rush* (August 1925, also TR Neptune to MC); Third Saturn-Ascendant – allegations against him of Communist sympathies; Pluto conjunct MC – branded a Communist, Chaplin had his films banned and he was denied a visa back into the USA (September to October 1952). (N.B. Jupiter transits invariably heralded difficult times, lawsuits and major losses.)

Chaplin refused to conform (Sun in Aries, Mercury opposite Uranus) and in forging his own path, achieved a level of distinction unparalleled in his day (Jupiter sesquisquares MC). With an elevated Saturn, political and moral slurs and an insatiable appetite for young women (Moon opposed by a Venus-Mars conjunction in the 7th) did much to overshadow his achievements, but his early film performances demonstrate one of the finest of all craftsmen at work. Chaplin first married on 23 October 1918 until 13 November 1920, remarried in November 1924 (which lasted until 10 January 1927, with a divorce on 25 August 1928), took Paulette Goddard down the aisle in June 1936 (until they divorced on 4 June 1942), and

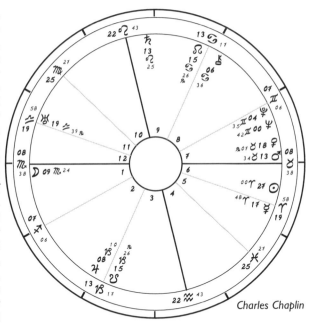

Charles Chaplin

married Oona O'Neill on 16 June 1943. In December 1944 he was in court fighting a paternity suit, but was acquitted in mid-April after a retrial (TR Pluto conjunct EQHS 10th). Chaplin's portrayal by Robert Downey Jr* in the eponymous 1992 film was, according to Chaplin's daughter Geraldine (qv), as though her father's spirit had inhabited Downey during filming. Both have the signs Aries and Taurus strong in their charts. Downey's Ascendant conjuncts Chaplin's Saturn, Downey's Sun-Mercury conjuncts Chaplin's Mercury within four degrees, Downey's Moon conjuncts Chaplin's Venus. Chaplin completed his last film on 11 May 1966. He was awarded a star on the Hollywood Walk of Fame on 10 April 1972, six days before he received an honorary Oscar. He died on Christmas Day 1977, but on 1 March 1978 his body was stolen from its grave (and found 16 days later). O'Neill died on 27 September 1991 (TR Pluto opposite Venus in 7th).

Geraldine Chaplin

b. 31 July 1944, 23.14 PWT (+7), Santa Monica, California, USA, 34N01, 118W29.
BC in hand from Thelma & Tom Wilson, via Lois Rodden (Geraldine Leigh Chaplin). RR: AA.

Chaplin, the eldest daughter of Charles Chaplin (qv), began her professional career as a dancer with the Royal Ballet in England. She was featured in *Doctor Zhivago* (released 22 December 1965) and since then has had roles in many internationally successful films.

Michael Chaplin

b. 6 March 1946, 22.25 PST (+8), Santa Monica, California, USA, 34N01, 118W29.
BC in hand from Thelma & Tom Wilson, via Lois Rodden (Michael John Chaplin). RR: AA.

Actor, screenwriter and producer son of Charles Chaplin (qv).

Sydney Chaplin

b. 30 March 1926, 08.50 PST (+8), Beverly Hills, California, USA, 34N04, 118W24.
BC in hand from Thelma & Tom Wilson, via Lois Rodden (Sidney Earl Chaplin). (N.B. Different spelling of first name on BC.) RR: AA.

Son of Charles Chaplin (qv). At nine months old his parents instigated a bitter divorce case, ending in a million-dollar settlement in favour of his mother in August 1927. Chaplin made his film debut in his father's film *Limelight* (1952), but his career shone more brightly on the Broadway stage, where he was, in part, able to escape his father's huge shadow (Jupiter conjunct MC).

---

* Robert Downey Jr b. 4 April 1965, 13.10 EST (+5), New York, USA, 40N43, 74W00. From him. RR: A.

Graham Chapman – see Monty Python

Ian Charleson
> b. 11 August 1949, 08.20 GDT, Eastern General Hospital, Edinburgh, Scotland, 55N58, 03W09.
> Gerard q. BC (John Charleson). RR: AA.

Considered to be one of the leading actors of his generation, Ian Charleson had a distinguished career. He appeared as Hamlet with the Cambridge Theatre Company before taking up with the RSC. One memorable film was *Chariots of Fire* (US premiere, September 1981, Lunar Eclipse conjunct Jupiter), directed by David Puttnam (qv) and co-starring Nigel Havers (qv). Before his death he had given a memorable performance in *Hamlet* for the National Theatre. D. 6 January 1990, scepticaemia (AIDS-related, TR Neptune opposite 8th ruler Mars).

Keith Chegwin
> b. 17 January 1957, 13.35 GMT, Walton, England, 53N28, 03W00.
> FCC q. BC (a twin). RR: AA.

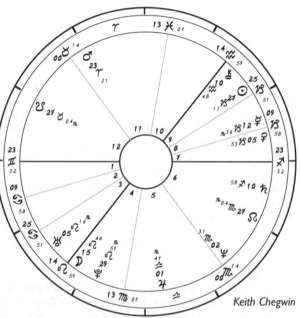

Keith Chegwin

Youthful TV personality who became famous as the out-and-about presenter in *Multi-Coloured Swap Shop*, broadcast from 7 October 1976 (TR Pluto square Mercury, and Sun ruler Saturn conjunct Moon) to 1982 and later, as the host of *Cheggers Plays Pop*. In his autobiography he wrote at length of his battle with alcohol. He admitted his addiction on live TV on 5 November 1992. Chegwin had originally checked into a clinic on 1 November 1991 (TR Pluto square MC) for five weeks. Seven months after he quit drinking, he began an acrimonious divorce to end his 11-year marriage. He had a second chance at TV success when TR Saturn moved across the MC, and on 12 April 1993 a sober Chegwin appeared on the vulgar TV magazine show *The Word*. This revived his career and soon afterwards he was asked to join *The Big Breakfast* show on 16 August 1993 (and proved a surprisingly popular choice after years of being viewed as unfashionable and irritating). Chegwin shocked viewers when he appeared nude in the one-off game show *Naked Jungle* (6 June 2000, TR Pluto conjunct MC ruler Saturn), Channel 5's attempt to rake in viewers. The show became notorious, as did Chegwin for his small part in it. After an acrimonious divorce from his TV co-presenter, he married again in 2000. (*Shaken But Not Stirred* by Keith Chegwin, Coronet, 1994.)

George Chisholm
> b. 29 March 1915, 07.05 GMT, Glasgow, Scotland, 55N51, 04W12.
> Gerard q. BC. RR: AA.

One of the few jazz greats to emerge from Britain. Arriving in London in 1936, Chisholm, inspired by Jack Teagarden, joined dance bands before moving on to the contemporary jazz scene (Moon in Virgo, EQHS 10th ruler Uranus elevated). He worked with diverse talents such as Fats Waller and Benny Carter. In 1952 he joined the BBC Show Band. Many TV appearances in the late 50s and early 60s (including *The Goon Show*) brought his technique as a jazz soloist, eccentric dress sense and irreverent humour to a large audience (Ascendant ruler in Aquarius in EQHS 10th, Uranus square Ascendant). He continued to perform after heart surgery (1982) until 1995, two years before his death.

Melanie Chisholm – see Spice Girls

Julie Christie

✪   b. 14 or 15 April 1940, Chubwa, Assam (near Dibrugarh 27N29, 94E54), India.

☞   Marc Penfield's rectification gave 14 April 1941, 10.00 LMT, Shillong, India, 25N34 91E53. FCC q. her for "no idea of the time of birth." Julia and Derek Parker give 23.30 IST, no source. 1940 and Chukua also given. Sy Scholfield reports that the Times (18 April 1940, p. 1) lists her birth as 15 April 1940 in Chubwa, Assam: CHRISTIE. – On April 15, 1940, at Chubwa, Assam, to Rosemary (nee Ramsden), wife of Frank Sr. J. Christie – a daughter (Julie). Scholfield suggests the date could be a misprint. RR: DD.

Private and beguiling stage/film actress, who made her acting debut in 1957 on stage. Christie was in films from 1962, had a lead role in *Billy Liar* (1963) and became a quintessential symbol of the 60s. The 1965 film *Darling* made her an international star – Oscar and New York Film Critics awards followed. Other films include *Dr Zhivago* (released December 1965), *The Go-Between* (1971) and *Don't Look Now* (1973). She was Kenneth Branagh's (qv) choice for Gertrude in his film *Hamlet* (released February 1997). Reclusive and bewildered by the public's fascination with her, she has since spent many years dedicating her time to ecological awareness and human and animal rights awareness.

Madeleine Christie

✪   b. 18 January 1904, 03.55 GMT, Corstorphine, Edinburgh, Scotland, 55N56, 03W17.
    Gerard q. BC (Madeleine Elsie Jane Christie). RR: AA.

Durable actress of film, stage and television. Having trained as an actress and singer, Christie enjoyed an international career spanning six decades. She made radio appearances in *Mrs Dale's Diary* and had a TV role in *Dr Finlay's Casebook*. She was widowed in 1950. D. 2 February 1996.

Charlotte Church

✪   b. 21 February 1986, 22.28 GMT, Cardiff, Wales, 51N29, 03W13.
    Bill Sheeran q. Sunday Times (26/11/2000), which serialised her autobiography Voice of an Angel.
    Pamela Crane q. the book for 22.30. RR: B.

Discovered in July 1997 at age eleven, soprano Charlotte Church has gone on to become the world's biggest selling classical artist of recent times. After auditioning for the Sony record chairman in February 1998 and signing an album deal with Sony that Summer, her first two albums, *Voice of an Angel* and *Charlotte Church*, sold in excess of five million copies in the UK and USA (note her Moon in Leo, on the MC square Pluto, is the chart handle). In November 2000 the lawsuit of her former manager (who had discovered her but was sacked in January 2000) reached the High Court in London (TR Neptune conjunct IC and TR Pluto conjunct Mars in 2nd and square Venus). He was suing for a cut of her £15 million fortune. Thoroughly professional and appearing well-adjusted, Charlotte is now managed by her "fiery and emotional" mother. Leo MC and Sun-Jupiter, however, suggests a prima donna in the making. Tabloids had a field day when, in October 2002, she was thought to be going 'off the rails' when caught visiting her DJ boyfriend, defying her mother and… smoking a cigarette!

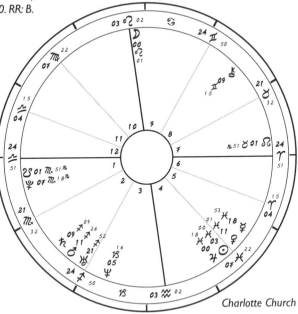

Charlotte Church

Diane Cilento – see Sean Connery

Eric Clapton

b. 30 March 1945, 20.45 GDT, Ripley, England, 51N18, 0W29.
Arthur Blackwell q. R. F. Nobel, who was told by Clapton that his grandmother believed the birth to have taken place between 20.30 and 21.00. Many years later, however, Janey Stubbs q. him for 05.30 (24 Aquarius Rising). Both charts are presented for the reader's discernment. RR: DD.

The world's premier rock guitarist. From October 1963 Clapton was a member of The Yardbirds, who signed a music deal in February 1964. Replaced by Jeff Beck on 27 March 1965, he joined the Bluesbreakers until July 1966, when he formed Cream. A series of health worries have led to periods of obscurity: by April 1971 he had become a recluse due to his drug habit (TR Uranus opposite Sun) and he underwent treatment in November 1973 (TR Uranus on Libra Ascendant). In April 1981 he was hospitalised for bleeding ulcers (TR Pluto on Libra Ascendant). His status as a true superstar-survivor was sealed when he performed an *Unplugged* session in January 1992. Clapton married on 27 March 1979. His son Conor* fell to his death shortly after 11.00 on 20 March 1991 (a Lunar Eclipse in January 1991 was conjunct his father's Pluto). Clapton won multiple Grammys for his musical tribute to his son, *Tears in Heaven* (from the album *Crossroads*). Clapton's childhood and faith in people was marred by the discovery at age nine that his parents were, in fact, his grandparents and the woman whom he thought was his sister, but whom he barely knew, was his mother ("I became frightened of being lied to and of broken promises"). He admits to being an "egomaniac with an inferiority complex" and describes himself as compulsive (his evening chart has the Moon in Scorpio square Pluto) but has steered clear of drink and drugs since 1987. In February 2003 *The Mail on Sunday's Rich Report* estimated his fortune at £115 million.

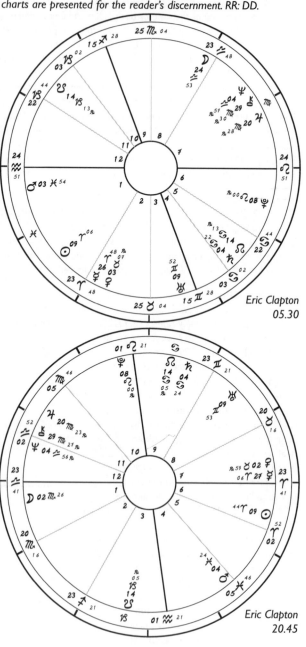

Eric Clapton
05.30

Eric Clapton
20.45

---

* Conor Clapton b. 21 August 1986, 06.20 GDT, London, England, 51N30, 0W10. Grazia Bordoni q. the TV news. RR: A.

"I'm a very habitual person, and I like nothing more in my life than to have a kind of routine... My dedication to my music has driven everyone away... An isolated, cold, rather intimidating, generally selfish person to be around. That's what my occupation has done to me." (Eric Clapton, Q, 01/90)

Graeme Clark – see Wet Wet Wet

Michael Clark
✪ b. 29 May 1962, 21.00 GDT, Aberdeen, Scotland, 57N09, 02W08.
Gerard q. BC. RR: AA.

Clark is a dancer and choreographer who began attending dancing lessons at age 4. At 13 he was given a place at the Royal Ballet School in London, moved on to Ballet Rambert at 17, and by 22 had formed his own company. In his performances he wore flamboyant costumes designed by the outrageous performance artiste Leigh Bowery. In 1988 Clark retired due to a serious ongoing heroin habit. The following year he fell in love with American choreographer Stephen Petronio and began to tackle his addictions and perform again.

Petula Clark
✪ b. 15 November 1932, 05.00 GMT, Epsom, Surrey, England, 51N20, 0W16.
☛ Hans-Hinrich Taeger q. Jacques de Lescaut's Encyclopedia of Birth Data, Vol. 12, no source. RR: C.

Intensely private singer, most famous for her rendition of *Downtown*, a British chart-topper. Spurred on by a dominating, controlling father, Clark was seven years old when she entered show business by entertaining British soldiers. Later she was a Rank film starlet before hitting the big time with her music. During her fame in the 60s she had great problems balancing her work and trying to raise her two small daughters, even giving up her profession for two years before the boredom sent her back to work. In 1995 she revealed that she and her husband of 34 years lived virtually separate lives, although they have remained firm friends. Perhaps her greatest romance has been with her audiences. With sales of over 70 million singles and albums, she is

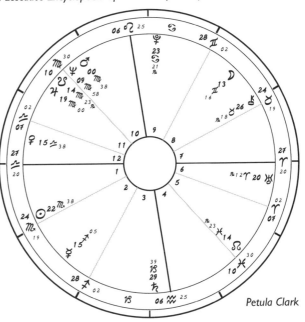

Petula Clark

one of the biggest selling British female singers ever. Clark is also adored in France. On 7 January 1996 Clark took over the role of Norma Desmond in the West End production of *Sunset Boulevard*, and in May 2002 released an album of new songs and greatest hits. Clark describes herself as a loner – remote, rootless, wary of intrusion and someone intent on keeping in control and remaining grounded. She has coped through difficulties and depression by pushing sadness out of her conscious mind and carrying on.

Q
"I'm not a monster but I'm a Scorpio, and I can get very dark. People don't expect me to get depressed. I'm supposed to be this blonde, bubbly, smiling lady. My exterior is often like that... It was just that through me [my father] was able to live out some of his fantasies. I was a nice, good little girl, smiling, trusting and at the same time very intense, and I haven't changed much... In the beginning I wanted to please my father, then it transferred into pleasing the public and pleasing [husband] Claude." (Petula Clark, *Daily Mail*, 30/12/95)

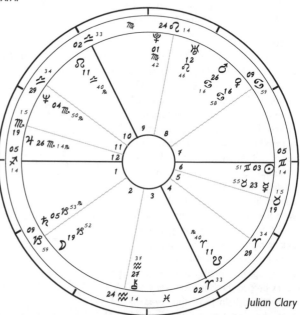

Q "Inwardly I'm driven by emotion but I'm very controlled. My father trained me to always put on a front, keep my feelings inside. He brought me up to believe that I should never cry." (Petula Clark, *Daily Mail*, 23/2/02)

Margi Clarke

Gemini Sun, Scorpio Ascendant. From her in a newspaper interview a few years ago.

Versatile actress and television presenter who gained recognition for her starring roles on TV in three series of *Making Out* and later in the films *Letter to Brezhnev* (1985) and *Blonde Fist*. With her Sun-Ascendant combination she was a natural choice to present the popular and humorous series *The Good Sex Guide*. Later Clarke made appearances in *Coronation Street* from 1997.

Julian Clary

✪ b. 25 May 1959, 21.00 GDT, Surbiton, England, 51N24, 0W18.

Sy Scholfield q. Clary personally. RR: A.

Camp stand-up comedian, compere and TV presenter, who has shocked and provoked audiences with innuendo and witty asides. Clary, the son of a traffic policeman, was very religious from an early age and went to a strict Catholic school run by Benedictine monks. He had stints as a guard on the London Underground and as a singing telegram before embarking on a career on the London comedy circuit as an in-your-face drag act (Gillian Pie-Face and later The Joan Collins Fan Club). A TV debut followed in 1988, as did his own TV series (*Sticky Moments* in 1989 and *Terry and Julian*, 1992). Clary, known for his outrageous clothes, effete and languid stance, is a master of the double entendre (Sagittarius Rising, Jupiter strong), and always

Julian Clary

delivered his bitchy barbs in a matter-of-fact manner (Moon in Capricorn). After years of being in the public spotlight, he made a sexual joke on live TV in December 1993 that involved a politician (Norman Lamont*, note their angular synastry), and many members of the Press called for his removal from TV (TR Uranus and Neptune conjunct Moon, TR Pluto conjunct Jupiter). This episode resulted in him being blacklisted for five years. He lost his partner to complications caused by AIDS in 1991. After a period of clinical depression (Sagittarius Rising) he considered taking his own life in 1993. Fanny, his beloved dog and stage companion, died in late May 1999. Clary, although often nervous on stage and forgetting his lines, appeared on stage in Jean Genet's play *Splendid's* in June 1995 and later appeared in pantomime. Clary took on the role of Leigh Bowery in the West End production of Boy George's (qv) musical *Taboo* in September 2002 and toured from March to June 2003 in his one-man show *Natural Born Mincer*. Clary presents an image to the world that is aloof, fey, self-contained, and one that does not invite physical contact or intimacy. Personally he is self-sufficient and extremely hygiene conscious. (Additional info from http://Astroqueer.tripod.com)

Q "Julian evokes strong protective feelings in those around him; he's a sensitive soul in a brutal world. But he's carved a niche for himself in the public's affection by exposing himself on his own terms." (Dermod Moore, *Bootboy*, Hot Press, 21/9/95)

---

* Norman Lamont b. 8 May 1942, 17.55 DGDT, Lerwick, Scotland, 60N09, 01W10. P. Wright q. BC. RR: AA.

John Cleese – see Monty Python
Zal Cleminson – see Nazareth

Andy Clyde
✪ b. 25 March 1892, 09.30 GMT, New Rattray, Scotland, 56N36, 03W20.
Gerard q. BC (Andrew Allan Clyde). RR: AA.
Comedian who was invited to the USA in the early 20s by James Finlayson (qv) to play a variety of
supporting comedy roles. A popular star of the early talkie era, he later became a master of the short
film at the Hollywood studio Columbia from 1934.

Joe Cocker
b. 20 May 1944, 05.00 DGDT, Sheffield, England, 53N23, 01W30.
From him to Ruth F. Nobel. RR: A.

Considered by many to be the
finest white soul vocalist in the UK,
Cocker won a recording contract
in 1964 and released his first single
that September, *I'll Cry Instead*. But
after touring he found himself
without a contract, so resumed his
job with the Gas Board. The tide
turned in 1967 and a first hit
followed in May 1968. Later that
year he hit #1 with the Beatles'
cover *With a Little Help From My
Friends* (November 1968). During
the 70s he struggled with drug
addiction and drink problems.
Cocker made a much-welcomed
return in the early 80s, and in
November 1982 topped the US
listings with the movie theme *Up
Where We Belong*. In 2004 a sober
Cocker will celebrate 40 years in
music.

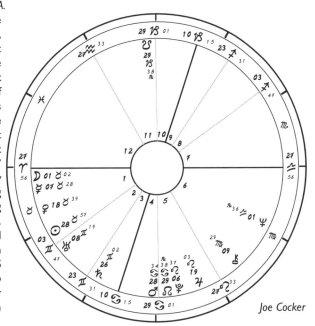
Joe Cocker

Q "In 1989 Joe sang at the inauguration of President George Bush, just one of many seals of
respectability to have laid to rest a reputation for jaw-dropping untogetherness, beverage
consumption, addictive addiction, forceful deportation and projectile vomiting second to
none in rock's checkered chronicle." (Mat Snow, Q, 05/92)

Paul Coia
b. 19 June 1955, 18.40 GDT, Glasgow, Scotland, 55N51, 04W19.
Gerard q. BC (Paul Giacomo Coia). RR: AA.
A broadcaster (at Radio Clyde, Glasgow) before he joined Channel 4 as an announcer in 1982,
colour-blind Coia moved into television with his gentle, slightly reserved (Saturn Rising) and friendly
manner as an interviewer, presenter and quiz show host. He is married to former beauty queen and
television presenter Debbie Greenwood (b. 16 September 1959, Liverpool, England). Coia devised
the daytime quiz show *The Enemy Within*.

George Cole

b. 22 April 1925, 11.00 GDT, Tooting, London, England, 51N25, 0W10.

FCC q. him. RR: A.

Actor best known as Arthur Daley, the wily used-car salesman always out for a "nice little earner" in *Minder* (107 episodes from October 1979 to February 1989, with viewing figures of up to 18 million). Cole had been a popular member of the *St. Trinians* films, in which he played Flash Harry. In September 1953 he took over the lead role in the radio comedy *A Life of Bliss* (until 3 March 1969). The show moved to television in January 1960 and his career went from strength to strength. Cole's mother abandoned him as an infant and he was later adopted. His adoptive father died when he was 15 and the youngster thereafter made having fame and a solid family his ambitions in life (Uranus on MC, the 9th/10th House emphasis,

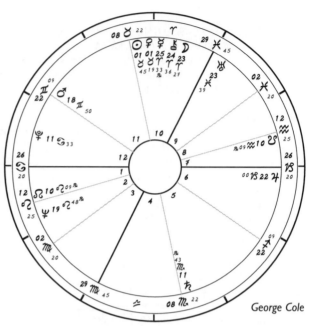

George Cole

Cancer Rising with Saturn retrograde in EQHS 4th). During 1983, as Pluto crossed the EQHS 4th cusp, he came close to giving up acting. In 1996 he starred in the seven-part drama *An Independent Man* and continues to perform on TV.

> Q "Like many good actors, he is a paradox – reclusive, yet full of joie de vivre among friends, a cautious man who owns a racehorse and loves a flutter, a devoted family man estranged for many years from his elder daughter, a performer who hates to talk about himself."
> (Andrew Duncan, *Radio Times*, 29/6/96)

Stephanie Cole

b. 5 October 1941, 12.00 Noon GDT, Solihull, England, 52N25, 01W45.

FCC q. her from her mother's memory, "twelve noon or very close to." RR: A.

A teenage Stephanie Cole knew when she was cast as a 90 year old woman (from July to September 1960, Solar Eclipse on MC and TR Neptune conjunct MC ruler Mercury) that she would never play glamorous leading ladies! After a short secretarial course to please her family, she joined the Bristol Old Vic before she turned 17 (she had auditioned in Spring 1957), winning the prestigious Sarah Siddons Award whilst studying there. Cole spent the next ten years touring the cathedral cities. At 21 she successfully traced her natural father (he had left when she was a child – Neptune natally on her MC), and 20 years later traced her half-sister. Cole married at 30 and before the birth of her daughter on 8 February 1973 had begun to battle several phobias (during her Saturn Return). After the birth she became agoraphobic but hid her illness (Mercury in 12th square Pluto). With a crisis of professional confidence, she gave up acting for nearly two years. Her mother had adopted her two cousins when Cole was 11, and during her Saturn Return (and TR Neptune conjunct Ascendant and TR Pluto over her MC), one cousin was diagnosed as schizophrenic. As with many of the difficulties in Cole's life, she has turned them into positive learning experiences and is a now a spokeswoman for mental health awareness. Cole returned to the stage in 1975 when a friend bumped into a director who was looking for her for his production (natal Uranus trine MC!). She won national fame for her remarkable performance as the austere Dr. Beatrice Mason in *Tenko* from October 1981 (after TR Saturn passed her Sun and TR Uranus was approaching her Ascendant). The show, which chronicled the suffering of expatriate British and Dutch women after the fall of Singapore in 1942, made her a household name along with Jean Anderson (qv) and Stephanie Beacham (qv). A *Talking Heads* TV monologue written by Alan Bennett, filmed in August 1988, utilised her acting gifts further. Further series (*A Bit of a Do* and five years of *Waiting For God*) made her one of the most popular performers on British television. In *Waiting for God* (28 June 1990 to 27 October 1994), she was the anarchic ex-journalist battling old age and everyone around her in a retirement home. Her performance won her the Comedy Actress of the Year at the British Comedy Awards in early December 1992 (TR Jupiter conjunct Sun). She won rave reviews onstage for *A Passionate Woman*, playing the lead role from 7 November 1994. With Mercury in Scorpio in the 12th House square Pluto, Cole moved into psycho-analysis and meditation in 1986 (TR Pluto conjunct Mercury), and her spiritual and personal development coincided with the break-up of her marriage and a growing independence (Sun in Libra, Moon in Aries). She turned to Buddhism for four years and has forged strong friendships during spiritual journeys to India (in December 1991) and the outback of Australia. Cole describes herself as a perfectionist (Virgo MC) and a hippie (Sagittarius Rising). She met up with a former colleague on 19 February 1996 and a rewarding personal relationship has since developed (Saturn retrograde on the Descendant implies a second chance at love). They married on 5 October 1998. With both a fulfilling career and a lucid spirituality (Sagittarius Rising) Stephanie Cole is following her bliss.

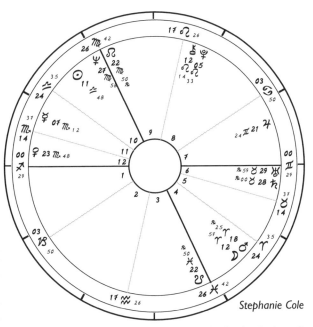

Stephanie Cole

Q "I was lucky, because I had some fire inside me that made me fight the injustices... I think if anything could drive me really mad it would be to find myself again in a place or a situation of deep injustice about which I could do nothing... I'm an optimist, a fantasist, and an idealist, which is not a frightfully realistic combination. That is to say, I'm very practical, and have my feet on the ground, except where matters of the heart are concerned. Ever since I was a child, I would weave dreams and fantasies around people... I absolutely believed, despite many contradictions to the contrary, that marriage was wonderful and that everybody always lived happily ever after." (*A Passionate Life* by Stephanie Cole, Hodder and Stoughton, 1998)

"I admire her enthusiasm and curiosity about things... [During *Tenko*] she was very funny, witty, dry; and passionate about her work. But she had a very short temper if people weren't as professional as she was. She was meticulous on detail – I remember how she relished her character's greased-back hair, yellowing teeth and sores around the nose! It didn't matter how unattractive she looked as long as it was authentic." (Veronica Roberts, c.1995)

Edwyn Collins

b. 23 August 1959, 19.20 GDT, Elsie Inglis Maternity Hospital, Edinburgh, Scotland, 55N57, 03W10. Gerard q. BC (Edwyn Stephen Collins). RR: AA.

Collins was one of the original members of the revered pop band Orange Juice, formed in the late 70s. The band had a series of minor successes and a #8 hit (released in February 1983) entitled *Rip It Up*. Collins' record company dropped him in early 1985 and his reputation as difficult and stubborn caused problems in winning a record deal as a solo performer (he was eventually re-signed in Summer 1986, as TR Saturn conjunct his MC). Success was sporadic for the next decade but his recording career was given a huge boost in Summer 1995 (TR Jupiter conjunct MC) with the worldwide hit *A Girl Like You*. He was back again on the popular music scene in early 1997 (when TR Pluto crossed his MC). In April 2002 he released *Doctor Syntax*.

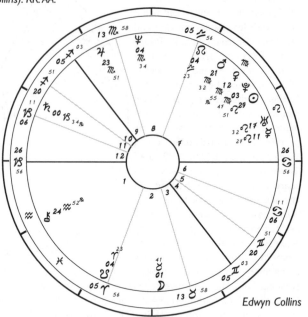

Edwyn Collins

Joan Collins

b. 23 May 1933, 07.00 GDT, Bayswater, London, England, 51N31, 0W11.

From the biography, Hollywood Sisters: Jackie & Joan Collins by Susan Crimp and Patricia Burstein (Robson Books, 1988), p. 5. Frederick Davies q. Collins for 03.00 in his book, Signs of the Stars. Her 1996 autobiography, Second Act, gives "morning." Year confirmed by FCC at Registry. Both charts are presented for the reader's discernment. RR: DD.

Glamorous, unsinkable actress whose career in bitchy melodrama is matched only by her tumultuous personal life. The daughter of a theatrical agent, Collins was RADA trained and in 1951 signed a seven year contract with Rank playing teenagers with tantrums or the leading man's bit-on-the-side before moving to Fox in the mid-50s. After a few years of forgettable roles and being replaced by Elizabeth Taylor (qv) in *Cleopatra*, she started a family and then moved into horror movies, TV commercials and glamorous guest shots on TV, such as the camp classic series *Batman*. Collins was beginning to find her niche and received a career boost when she played a super-vamp in her sister Jackie's filmed novels, *The Stud*

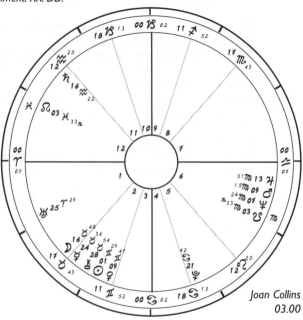

Joan Collins
03.00

(1978) and *The Bitch* (1979). (According to her birth certificate, best-selling author Jackie was born on 4 October 1937.) Collins suffered a personal setback on 2 August 1980 when her daughter was hit by a car and was in a coma for seven weeks. A survivor and hugely positive character, Collins bounced back with a role in TV's *Dynasty* (her part aired in the USA from July 1981 to May 1989) and attained fresh star status at 48, plus Golden Globe and People's Choice awards. The role easily won her the *talon* contest for the biggest bitch on American television, and she turned the series into a global phenomenon (150 million viewers in 87 countries each week). No-one could spit and roll put-downs, swear vengeance and take bites out

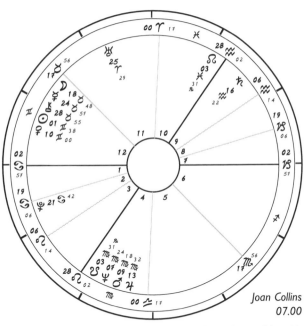

Joan Collins
07.00

of crudités with greater relish than La Collins! Her glamorous, bitchy persona (interchangeable with her TV alter-ego) was an inspiration for many older women and she remains a sex symbol for men of all ages. On 6 November 1985 (as TR Neptune crossed her 07.00 Descendant) she married Peter Holm but they separated 21 months later amid much publicity. After four marriages and four divorces (plus *Dynasty's* demise on 11 May 1989), Collins followed her sister into writing 'bonkbuster' books and won a much publicised court case against her publishers on 13 February 1996. Collins was back on centre stage with appearances in the glossy, short-lived 1997 soap *Pacific Palisades*. In 2001 she peeled off the make-up and appeared in the Badly Drawn Boy video *Spitting in the Wind*. In April 2001 she dumped her lover of 13 years for a man of 35. Collins and her new beau were married on 17 February 2002. In September 2002 she made her soap comeback in the daytime drama *Guiding Light* but Collins quit the show in December.

> Q
> "Here's a woman who already gets the joke about herself. Not only does she get it, she revels in it. Her utter narcissism feeds her perverse wit as she devours every [*Dynasty*] actor who stands in her way... Collins is a riveting self-reflection, turning *Dynasty* into *The Joan Collins Story*." (Michael McWilliams, *TV Sirens*, Perigee, 1987)
> "She's like quicksand. You can't sum her up. You never know what you're going to get with Joan." (Jackie Collins, as quoted in *A Personal Dynasty*, The Biography Channel)

Pauline Collins

b. 3 September 1940, 19.40 GDT, Exmouth, England, 50N37, 03W25.
FCC q. her letter from "mother's (excellent!) memory." RR: A.

Former English teacher who became a television favourite as the pert parlour maid Sarah in *Upstairs, Downstairs*. The late 80s brought enormous applause for this talented lady: Collins won an Olivier Award in February 1989, a Tony Award in June 1989 and a British Academy Award in March 1990 for her outstanding role in the one-woman comedy *Shirley Valentine* both on stage and screen. She had opened that show on Broadway on 16 February 1989. In October 1988 she revealed that she had given birth, in 1964, to a daughter who was adopted six weeks later, and media interest in the resulting reunion followed. Collins met her husband John Alderton (b. 27 November 1940, Gainsborough, Lincolnshire, England) on TV's *Emergency Ward 10* and they married in 1969. The couple's children are both actors.

Phil Collins – see Genesis

Ronald Colman

☞ b. 9 February 1891, 18.00 GMT, Richmond, Surrey, England, 51N28, 0W19.
From Sabian Symbols #214, no source. (Church of Light q. a speculative time of 05.45 from Miss Whitney.) (N.B. Note the L&L for Richmond.) RR: DD.

Gentlemanly and private romantic star of the silent and sound era. Following his stage debut in 1916, Colman had a hit with *Damaged Goods* (from 17 March 1917) and later moved to the USA in 1920. In 1923 he had a career turning point with the film *The White Sister*. He played swashbucklers early in his career before finding his niche as an English gentleman (Venus conjunct a possible Capricorn Ascendant), which owed more to a romantic Hollywood ideal than to his off-screen persona. In 1933 Colman successfully sued Sam Goldwyn for $2 million damages after libelous statements were issued regarding his acting and character. Colman married on 18 September 1920 (until 1935) and again on 30 September 1938. D. 19 May 1958, Santa Barbara, California.

Robbie Coltrane

✪ b. 31 March 1950, 03.00 GMT, Strathbungo, Glasgow, Scotland, 55N53, 04W16.
Gerard q. BC (Anthony Robert McMillan). RR: AA.

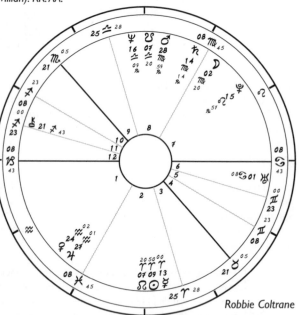

Robbie Coltrane

Actor – reputedly terse and over-sensitive – who began his career with the documentary *Young Mental Health* (Scottish Council Film of the Year Award, 1973). A stint as a nightclub entertainer and theatre work led to his comedic talents being showcased in the *Comic Strip* films (the first of these, *The Supergrass*, was released in November 1985). Coltrane later worked on *Blackadder*. His films include *Mona Lisa* (1986), *Henry V* (1989) and *GoldenEye* (released November 1995). He received recognition for his leading performance in *Tutti Frutti* (March 1987, TR Neptune over Ascendant, TR Jupiter approaching Sun) but is best known as the criminal psychologist anti-hero Fitz (note the Scorpio MC) in *Cracker* (from 27 September 1993 until 1996); the latter series earned him a Bafta award. A book on his life, *Looking For Robbie* by Neil Norman, was published in November 1999. His role as Hagrid in the *Harry Potter* films (according to her BC, author J.K. Rowling was born on 31 July 1965) and villains in two Bond films have given him a high profile with audiences worldwide. In April 2003 he was seen in *The Planman* as lawyer Jack Lennox who moonlights by planning foolproof bank raids for a local gang. On 14 April 2003 the Press reported that Coltrane's marriage was under threat (as TR Uranus approached an opposition to his Moon, ruler of the Descendant). The couple had married in December 1999.

Jason Connery

✪ b. 11 January 1963, 22.00 GMT, London, England (51N30, 0W10).
Sy Scholfield q. family records – a family tree made by his grandfather, Sir Raphael Cilento. RR: AA.

Actor, best known for his role in *Robin of Sherwood* (1984) and as son of Sean Connery (qv). His parents divorced in October 1973 and Jason recently divorced his wife, actress Mia Sara, whom he had married in 1996. Their son was born in June 1997. In February 2003, after a couple of years laying low, he began a stage tour of *The Blue Room* in the West End.

Sean Connery

b. 25 August 1930, 18.05 GDT, Royal Maternity Hospital, Edinburgh, Scotland, 55N57, 03W12.
Gerard q. BC (Thomas Connery). (N.B. No 'Sean' on BC.) RR: AA.

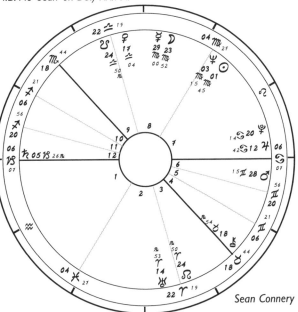

Sean Connery

Internationally esteemed actor known for his passionate beliefs, principles, sardonic wit (Saturn Rising in Capricorn), and tough guy film roles. As James Bond, Connery embodied the ultimate suave hero – dangerous and rugged both physically and sexually (brooding, potent Scorpio is on the MC). The character of James Bond was 'born' in November 1924, and the seductive, undercover spy with a license to kill is suggested by Connery's Scorpio MC. From his lonely youth, he applied strict Saturn discipline to his studies and ambitions, and began body-building at 19. He broke into acting in 1951 as a chorus boy in the London production of South Pacific, and his first starring role was in Requiem for a Heavyweight (broadcast 31 March 1957). Chosen in November 1961 (TR Uranus near Sun) to star in the first Bond film, the result, Dr. No, was filmed from 16 January 1962 and shown in late May 1963 (TR Uranus conjunct Sun). Goldfinger (September 1964), the second Bond film, began Bond-mania in 1964-5 (as TR Neptune crossed back and forth over his MC). His marriage to Diane Cilento* (from 30 November 1962) began to suffer in March 1965 and media intrusion into his private life was at its height under the same transit (in late July 1966 Connery endured a frenetic Japanese visit). Connery followed the angular Saturn and Jupiter in his chart and moved onto the (socialist) political scene in March 1967, and later developed the Scottish International Education Trust to improve the lives of Scottish people. Divorced in October 1973, he remarried in May 1975 (TR Pluto, natally in 7th, on EQHS 10th). He spent most of 1978 in litigation as TR Uranus crossed his MC and TR Saturn conjunct Sun. Although in the early 70s he said "never again" to Bond, he was persuaded to film Never Say Never Again from September 1982. Connery became a bankable film star once more with the films In the Name of the Rose (1986), The Untouchables (1987) and Indiana Jones and the Last Crusade (May 1989). Later movie successes included The Rock (June 1996), Entrapment (April 1999) and Finding Forrester. He was knighted in 2000. With Sun and Moon in Virgo, it is not surprising that he is known amongst his friends to be somewhat of a hypochondriac. With Saturn prominent he is a man who expects – and commands – respect and doesn't suffer fools. (Sean Connery by Kenneth Passingham, Book Club Associates, 1983.)

> Q "It is no belittling of Connery's talent to point out that his greatest strength on-screen is his physical authority... Connery's genius resides... in the peculiarly intense quality that he exudes even when he is standing still... He is not a man to affect an amiability that he doesn't feel, or to let his dissatisfactions go unnoticed. His brusqueness is legendary." (Zoe Heller, Vanity Fair, 6/93)

---

* Diane Cilento b. 2 April 1932, 01.30 AEST (-10), Brisbane, Australia, 27S28, 153E02. Sy Scholfield q. family records – a family tree diagram made by her father. RR: AA.

Billy Connolly

b. 24 November 1942, 04.30 GDT, Gorbals, Glasgow, Scotland, 55N51, 04W15.
Gerard q. BC (William Connolly). RR: AA.

Originally an anarchic folk singer, Connolly, known as "The Big Yin", found doors to TV fame closed because of his anti-Establishment and outrageous humour (Ascendant ruler Venus and the Sun are opposite Uranus). After his stint as a welder and later a folk singer, he won over audiences with his brand of humour. *The Great Northern Welly Boot Show* at the Edinburgh Festival in August 1972 established Connolly as an up-and-coming comic talent (TR Uranus near his Ascendant). First seen on local TV in *Dateline Scotland*, Connolly's own show first aired in 1976 along with a BBC play called *Elephant's Graveyard*. An appearance on the *Parkinson* show was his biggest break. Since then he has become one of Britain's leading

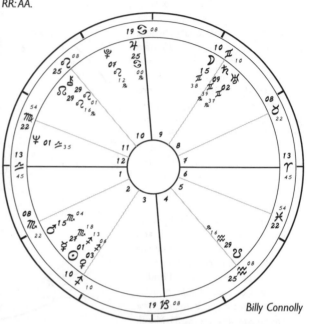

Billy Connolly

comedians (Sun in Sagittarius with ruler Jupiter on MC), offering an alternative, biting perspective on life and showing a genuine love of the ridiculous (two planets in Scorpio and the Jupiter influence is important here). He was showcased in the USA in a short-lived series and remains a cult figure there. Connolly switched pace and starred with Siobhan Redmond (qv) and Russell Hunter (qv) in a BBC drama based on the true story of Scotland's most notorious criminal in *Deacon Brodie* (aired 8 March 1997). Later he played opposite Judi Dench (b. 9 December 1934, York. FCC q. her for the date, year from Registry) in the international hit film *Mrs Brown* (released in Britain in September 1997). Connolly is married to comedian-turned-sex therapist Pamela Stephenson, who wrote an insightful book about him in 2001. In *Billy* she revealed his battle with personal demons, including drink and being molested by his father. At four Connolly's mother left home and he was sent to live with two aunts, where he endured violence and humiliation.

> Q "His technique is to make people look at all aspects of everyday life afresh, highlighting both the incongruous and the obvious in the most unexpected ways." (*Reflections on Success* by Martyn Lewis, Lennard, 1997)

Brian Connolly

✪ *b. 5 October 1945, 23.20 GDT, Govanhill, Glasgow, Scotland, 55N51, 04W14.*
Gerard q. BC. RR: AA.

Vocalist with the band Sweet. The band scored their biggest hit on 27 January 1973 with the #1 single *Blockbuster*. To the day he died, Connolly was uncertain of his family roots, and believed he was the real brother of *Taggart* actor Mark McManus (qv).

Tom Conti

b. 22 November 1941, 10.30 GDT, Paisley, Scotland, 55N51, 04W25.
Gerard q. BC (Thomas Antonio Conti). RR: AA.

Wry, velvet-voiced Italian-Scottish actor and director who learned the Scorpio art of hypnosis as a youngster. Nevertheless Conti continued without direction (Neptune elevated) until good roles in the theatre led to his 1972 breakthrough in *The Black and White Minstrels* (TR Uranus on MC) and the play *Savages*. Stardom came in 1976 (when TR Neptune crossed his Ascendant) with the TV series *Glittering Prizes* and later on stage in *Whose Life is it Anyway?* An Academy Award nomination for his portrayal of a drunken poet in *Reuben, Reuben* (1983) boosted his profile (TR Uranus on Ascendant), but a string of unsuccessful romantic farces followed. In recent years he has appeared on stage, including a lead role in *Art*. His wife, Kara Wilson (qv), is an actress.

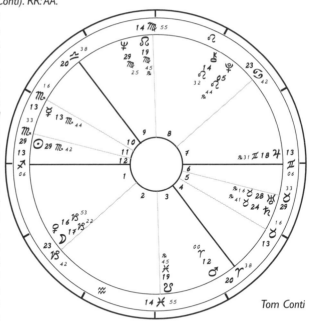

Tom Conti

Russ Conway

b. 2 September 1925, 23.30 GDT, Bristol, England, 51N27, 02W35.
From him to the Astrological Association. FCC q. BC in hand for date (Trevor Herbert Stanford). RR: A.

Conway began playing the piano in nightclubs from 1955, two years before his first chart hit. Between 1957 and 1963, he had 19 songs in the charts (including two #1s, March and June 1959). A number of difficulties befell him after his chart success. In 1963 he suffered a nervous breakdown, and a stroke in late 1965 prevented him from performing for a couple of years. In late 1971 he was close to bankruptcy and battling a problem with alcohol. In March 1995 he almost lost his thumb in an accident. Conway, who admitted to having an intense relationship with his mother, remained confused about his sexuality up to his death. On his fifteenth birthday he was sentenced to three years in Borstal for minor theft. Soonafter his

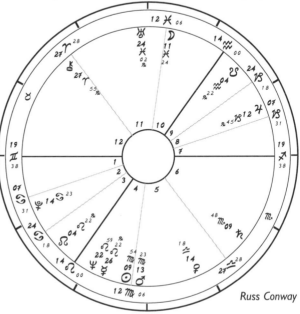

Russ Conway

mother became ill, and Conway lived with the guilt of her death for the rest of his life. He won a bout with cancer from 1989-1994, but the disease returned in 2000. He is remembered as much for his modesty and humility as for his music. D. 16 November 2000, cancer.

Peter Cook

b. 17 November 1937, 03.00 GMT, Torquay, England, 50N28, 03W30.
Data from Suzanne Michaud, original source not known. RR: C.

Acclaimed and iconic satirist, and irreverent stage, television and film actor (Moon conjunct Uranus opposite Venus in Scorpio). He was acclaimed for his comic brilliance and searing wit but was later written off as a self-destructive alcoholic and depressive recluse. Cook and Dudley Moore (qv) won a Tony Award for performances in *Beyond the Fringe* (which ran on Broadway from 27 October 1962 for almost two years). The comedy pairing was highly successful but Cook let his jealousy of Moore's Hollywood movie fame ruin their relationship (they reconciled a few years before Cook's death). Cook co-founded *Private Eye* magazine and owned a majority share. Cook later hosted the punk music show *Revolver*, but his comedy style was out of fashion in the 80s. Ben Elton (qv) helped resurrect his career and Cook made appearances in *One Foot in the Algarve* and on various TV shows. D. 9 January 1995.

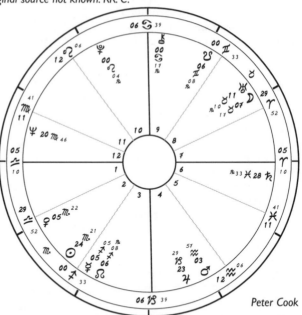

Peter Cook

> "An uncanny ability to improvise on any subject with outrageous and often tasteless absurdity. He could spin off into a world of verbal fantasy with a wit that was second to none... The intense ambition of Peter's earlier youth had dissipated... relative indolence appealed to him." (Barbara Paskin, *Dudley Moore: The Authorized Biography*, Pan, 1998)

Sue Cook

b. 30 March 1949, 16.00 GMT, Ruislip, Middlesex, England, 51N34, 0W25.
FCC q. her. RR: A.

Popular television presenter of investigative programmes such as *Nationwide* (1979-83) and *Crimewatch UK* (1984-95). Cook, who studied psychology at University, has also presented *Breakfast Time* and the annual *Children in Need* TV fundraiser. Her second husband, from 1981-7, was classical guitarist John Williams. Her personal life was in the news in April 2003 when her former best friend went public by accusing Cook of stealing her husband back in January 2002 (TR Saturn conjunct MC).

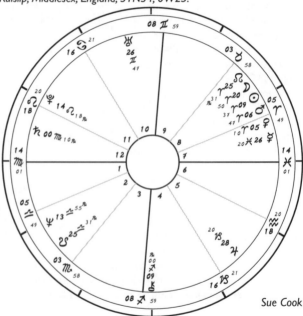

Sue Cook

Pat Coombs

✪ b. 27 August 1926, 06.30 GDT, Camberwell, England, 51N27, 0W05.
FCC q. her, from her parents. RR: A.

Highly talented and beloved comedy actress on radio, stage and television, usually cast in dithery, neurotic or spinster roles (the Virgo Sun and Ascendant influence in her horoscope!). At first Coombs was a nursery school assistant before moving into show business in the mid-50s. Comedy series included *Beggar My Neighbour* (March 1967 to March 1968) and *You're Only Young Twice* (1977-81). She was well-known for her comedy double act with Irene Handl, and for being the foil for Dick Emery (qv) and Bob Monkhouse (qv). Coombs appeared in *EastEnders* for a few years, again displaying her great talent as a character actress. After being diagnosed with osteoporosis in 1995 she campaigned to raise money for the charity. Sadly on 25 May 2002 Coombs died at Denville Hall actors' home in West London, after complications caused by emphysema.

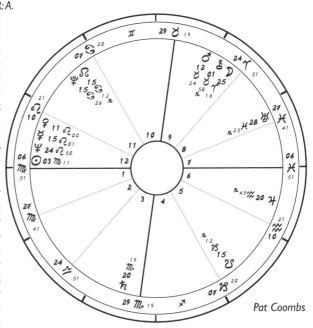

Pat Coombs

Julian Cope

✪ b. 21 October 1957, 11.30 GMT, Deri, Mid Glamorgan, Wales, 51N45, 03W22.
From him to Laura Boomer. RR: A.

After a four-year stint with The Teardrop Explodes (and a variety of chart hits), Julian Cope dissolved the band in November 1982 and embarked on a solo career in 1984. The first hit from his solo efforts was the song *World Shut Your Mouth*, a chart entry in October 1986 when re-recorded. He published a first volume of autobiography, *Head On*, in September 1991. Cope is considered a maverick because of his refusal to play the music business game (note Mars on the MC).

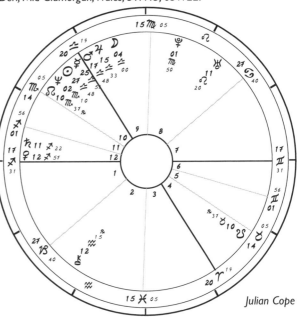

Julian Cope

Ronnie Corbett

b. 4 December 1930, 21.40 GMT, Royal Maternity Hospital, Edinburgh, Scotland, 55N57, 03W12.
Gerard q. BC (Ronald Balfour Corbett). RR: AA.

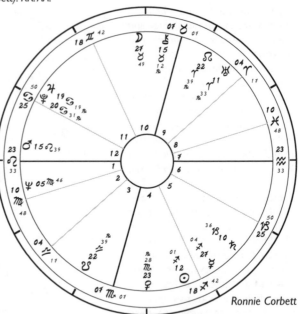

Ronnie Corbett

Spotted by David Frost (qv), diminutive and lively comedian Corbett appeared regularly on Frost's show, *The Frost Report* in 1966. Corbett had arrived in London in 1951 and began his career miscast as a children's comedian in *Crackerjack* (1955-9). In 1962 Terry Thomas picked him out to appear in the film *Operation Snatch*. In 1970 he and long-term comedy partner Ronnie Barker (qv) stole the show at the Bafta awards when a technical breakdown forced the duo to improvise for the audience. The Controller of BBC1 was in the audience and later offered them a peak-time TV slot on a Saturday night. Corbett is best known for his funny, drawn-out monologues and his enduring TV success (often in pompous roles, Leo Ascendant) with Barker in *The Two Ronnies* (1971-87). He has starred in a number of tailor-made comedy series, including *Sorry* (March 1981 to October 1988) as the hen-pecked impertinent son, *Now Look Here...* (two series from 15 November 1971 – TR Jupiter conjunct Sun – and January 1973) and its follow-up *The Prince of Denmark* (April 1974), as well as the star-making vehicle produced by Frost, *No – That's Me Over Here* (November 1967, when TR Neptune conjunct MC ruler Venus, until late 1970). Corbett was invited to appear regularly on Ben Elton's (qv) 1998 BBC TV series, which aired in late spring. Known for his mischievous sense of fun, his comedy is vaudeville jollity and cheekiness (note the strong Mars and Sagittarius). Corbett likens his temperament to that of his father's ("Jolly with a short fuse" – Mars Rising), and explains that he and Ronnie Barker had a very comfortable professional partnership and shared a strong sense of reserve (Corbett has Moon in Taurus whilst Barker has Saturn Rising). For synastry, although comedy acts tend to have alternate signs highlighted in their charts (each providing what the other lacks), note that Corbett's Sun is on Barker's Ascendant and his Mercury is conjunct Barker's Saturn. The Nodal axis is also prominent in significant alliances: Corbett's Nodal axis links up with Barker's MC-Mars-Mercury. Corbett published his autobiography, *High Hopes*, in October 2000.

Judy Cornwell

b. 22 February 1940, 15.55 GMT, London, England, 51N30, 0W10.
FCC q. her, "3.45 – 4.00 pm." RR: A.

After being cast in seductive roles, Judy Cornwell was offered a long-term Hollywood contract when she was 27. Three years later she appeared in the film *Wuthering Heights*. After years of TV and theatre work, the actress with the infectious giggle returned to a high-profile role as the slob Daisy in *Keeping Up Appearances* (with Patricia Routledge, qv), for five years from 29 October 1990. The films *Persuasion* (1995) and *The Wind in the Willows* (1996) followed.

CORONATION STREET

The Street began on 9 December 1960 at approximately 19.00, Manchester (where the series is set), and over time became a British television institution. It was one of the first series to present strong women on television (Aries MC), and has had its share of prima donnas (Leo Moon) and long-suffering matriarchs (MC ruler in Cancer). With Mars and Venus dominant, it has managed to combine high drama with gentle comedy from social interaction, usually centred around the Rovers Return pub. In early 1997 the show was criticised for lacking realism, and the producers promptly made changes to its storylines and characters. For further information see the profiles of Jean Alexander,

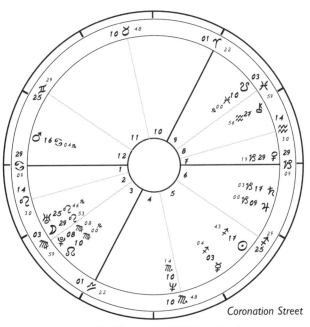

Coronation Street

Margi Clarke, Joanna Lumley, Sue Nicholls, Lynne Perrie, Pat Phoenix and William Roache.

Adrienne Corri

☻ b. 13 November 1931, 07.45 GMT, Glasgow, Scotland, 55N53, 04W15.
Gerard q. BC (Adrienne Riccoboni). RR: AA.

Corri, a redhead often cast in seductive roles, made her stage debut in 1948. She became famous in science fiction and horror films, and most notably as the rape victim in *A Clockwork Orange* (1971).

Tom Courtenay

b. 25 February 1937, 07.15 GMT, Hull, England, 53N45, 0W20.
FCC q. him. RR: A.

Shy, talented actor with a down-to-earth approach to his stardom, despite the international fame he has enjoyed since his meteoric rise in the early 60s playing non-conformist and misunderstood young men. With a Virgo Moon he is a perfectionist and voracious reader and once considered teaching. Out of RADA in 1960, he joined the Old Vic Company and made his debut in *The Seagull* at the Edinburgh Festival in August 1960 (when TR Jupiter conjunct MC). He became famous overnight in June 1961 (when TR Pluto conjunct Moon and opposed Sun) after replacing Albert Finney in *Billy Liar* on stage for nine months (he repeated the role later in the film version). By 1971, although he continued to act on stage, his

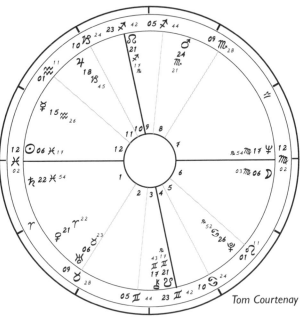

Tom Courtenay

career had stalled. Courtenay made a comeback and a Broadway debut in 1977 with *Otherwise Engaged*. In 1982 he scored a personal triumph on Broadway in *The Dresser* (TR Neptune on MC), and in early 1983 he tackled the musical *Andy Capp*. He came close to retiring in the late 80s (TR Uranus on MC) when offers dried up, and he became disenchanted with acting and uncertain of his ability – despite having been described as extraordinary by so many critics. He has revealed himself to be an uncomfortable mixture of strength and weakness (the Saturn and Pisces emphasis), the latter formed as a child under the burden of expectation from a bullying father (Saturn), who died in 1984. His mother, who battled cancer throughout Tom's childhood, longed for him to be successful, but tragically died a week before the film opening of the landmark *Loneliness of the Long Distance Runner* (US premiere, October 1962). In 1999 he appeared in *King Lear*, won a Bafta Best Actor award for his role in *A Rather English Marriage*, and starred in a film, *Whatever Happened to Harold Smith?* The following year he published *Dear Tom*, a volume of letters written to him by his mother in the late 50s. In Spring 2003 he starred in the West End in his tribute to Philip Larkin, *Pretending to Be Me*.

> Q "Where his father – although intelligent – was laconic and found it hard to give praise, his mother was lively, ebullient, emotional and expressive. Tom took after her in character... In his voice you can still hear the ambition of the gifted working-class boy, dead set on making his mark. Yet the strain of trying to fulfil his parents' dream while trying to follow his own took its toll." (Angela Lambert, *Daily Mail*, 27/3/2000)

Robin Cousins

> b. 17 August 1957, 12.15 GDT, Bristol, England, 51N27, 02W35.
> Mary Lee Lewis q. him. RR: A.

Olympic-winning ice-skater who took on the stage role made famous on film by Tim Curry (qv) in *The Rocky Horror Picture Show* from 30 May 1995.

Noel Coward

> b. 16 December 1899, 02.30 GMT, Teddington, England, 51N26, 0W20.
> From *Noel Coward and His Friends* by Cole Leslie, Graham Payn and Sheridan Morley (Weidenfeld & Nicolson, 1979), p. 10, which reproduces Coward's baby book in his mother's handwriting.
> (*Astrological Quarterly*, Winter 1938, q. his mother for "just before 4.30 am.") RR: AA.

Playwright, screenwriter, director, actor, producer, composer and novelist – the master entertainer of the British theatre. From the age of four Coward was in constant demand to sing and dance at school concerts (spurred on by a powerful bond with his dominant mother – note the Moon-Pluto conjunction). With great confidence he gave his first public performance at seven to an enraptured audience. On 13 September 1910 his mother sent him to audition for *The Goldfish*, which was to be staged by a children's theatre company. He won the part and appeared from October 1910 to rave reviews (TR Jupiter over Ascendant, TR Neptune conjunct EQHS 10th). The prodigious Coward would soon become a provocative, waspish, controversial and acclaimed

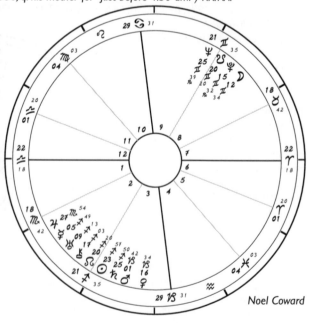

Noel Coward

performer-playwright of sophisticated comedies. Perhaps his most productive period was between 1928 and 1931 with *Bitter Sweet*, *Private Lives* and *Cavalcade*, which followed a short period during which British theatregoers had booed his plays off the stage. His extraordinary see-saw horoscope points to his creative and lasting influence on the British theatre (a prominent Pluto, conjunct Moon – the ruler of the MC – and opposite Sun and Mercury). The Moon-Uranus opposition, ruling the MC and 5th, suggests his power to ignite controversy (and accounts for his three nervous breakdowns by age 30) – add Mercury to the equation and you have an acerbic, often devastating, wit and a talent for flippant repartee. The Venus overtone as well as a Libran Ascendant suggest a reputation for being smooth, elegant, erudite and socially scandalous. Coward won a special Academy Award for *In Which We Serve* (released 23 December 1942). When he died on 26 March 1973 Coward left behind over 50 plays, 25 films, hundreds of songs, two autobiographies, a novel, several volumes of short stories and countless poems, recordings and paintings.

Q "He was a radical innovator with form, an acute observer of social patterns and a brilliant cartographer of the human heart. More than that – these are talents, his was a gift – he wrote from a private place, a granary of poisoned dreams and soured romances, that defies understanding... In his frivolity he nailed our greatest shame: that many of us are frivolous too." (Dominic Dromgoole, c.2001)

Brian Cox
b. 1 June 1946, 14.15 GDT, Maternity Hospital, Dundee, Scotland, 56N28, 02W58.
Gerard q. BC (Brian Denis Cox). RR: AA.
Actor who won great notices at the Royal Court in *Rat in the Skull* (1984). He has worked mainly in the theatre since his London debut as Orlando in *As You Like It* in 1967. He teaches drama in London and his book *From Salem to Moscow* (1990) chronicled his stint at the Moscow Art Theatre – he was the first British actor to teach there. After playing *King Lear* at the National Theatre in 1990, he swore never to return to the stage, a vow he broke in February 1997, when he returned to fringe. In April 2003 he starred in *X-Men 2*.

Andy Crane
b. 24 February 1964, 22.30 GMT, Morecambe, England, 54N04, 02W53.
FCC q. him, from his parents. RR: A.
Former radio presenter Crane moved into Phillip Schofield's (qv) chair at Children's BBC, and has since hosted TV series, including *Bad Influence!* (1992-5) and *Take Two* (1995-6).

Kenneth Cranham
b. 12 December 1944, 22.25 GDT, Maternity Hospital, Dunfermline, Scotland, 56N04, 03W28.
Gerard q. BC (Kenneth Raymond Cranham). RR: AA.
Actor often cast as rough-diamond characters. Cranham's stage debut was with Sadler's Wells Theatre in 1962. His principal appearances have included the lead in *Shine On Harvey Moon* (January 1982 to August 1985), *Oranges Are Not the Only Fruit* (1990), and *El C.I.D.* (from February 1990).

Beverley Craven
✪ *b. 28 July 1963, 15.00 IST (-5.5 = -5 hrs 30 mins), Colombo, Sri Lanka, 6N56, 79E51.*
FCC q. her, February 1997. (N.B. Her birth month has occasionally been given incorrectly as June.)
RR: A.
Craven left the Home Counties of England and moved to London at 19. Waitressing and squatting followed as she auditioned unsuccessfully for numerous bands. She waited four more years before winning a recording contract. The results of recording sessions led to the release of a landmark debut album in 1990 (her song *Promise Me* became a classic). It established her as a fine contemporary singer-songwriter of ballads, and won her the Best British Newcomer honour at the 1992 Brit Awards. A year after the birth of her daughter in March 1992, Craven embarked upon a well-received European tour. A second, less successful album followed, as did further touring, which helped her become more comfortable performing on stage.

Michael Crawford

○ b. 19 January 1942, 04.00 GDT, Salisbury, England, 51N05, 01W48.
His autobiography *Parcel Arrived Safely: Tied with String* (Century, September 1999) recounts a telegram that was sent announcing his birth. (Previously astrologer Carol Kanada had quoted him personally in March 1991 for 06.00.). RR: A.

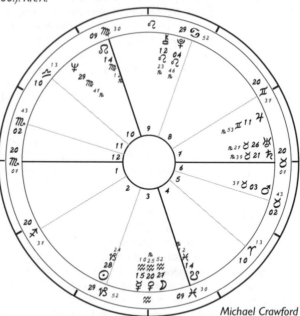

Michael Crawford

Dedicated craftsman and boyish star of stage, screen and television. Crawford is known for tackling a number of physically demanding roles (note the Scorpio Ascendant and Sun square Mars) and for his meticulous attention to detail (MC in Virgo). His father (or rather, the man he thought was his father until he discovered otherwise in his mid-teens) was killed during the Battle of Britain before Michael was born, and Michael's own unrealised ambition was to be a test pilot in the RAF. He endured some difficult times in childhood, including a violent stepfather and bullying at school from ages 9 to 10. His performance debut was in April 1965 (when TR Uranus moved over the MC and TR Neptune hit the Ascendant) and Crawford later dropped out of education at 15 to move into radio, TV and theatre full-time (making his New York debut in February 1967). In 1969 he flew to Hollywood to co-star with Barbra Streisand in *Hello, Dolly!* but his three-film contract produced little. He endured a trying period in 1971 (the year of his June stage triumph *No Sex Please – We're British*) when his marriage was beginning to break down (he left the family home in November 1972). In his determined and steady climb towards his goals, the brilliant Crawford has produced flashes of exceptional artistry in a variety of acting choices, most notably as the infantile, accident-prone (Virgo MC) poltroon Frank Spencer in *Some Mothers Do 'Ave 'Em* (from 15 February 1973, when TR Jupiter conjunct Sun, to November 1978). Although only 18 episodes were made, the show attracted between 20 and 25 million viewers and continues to be a favourite with audiences. His private life was not without difficulty and in July 1978 Crawford was given the all-clear when doctors discovered tumours in his breast tissue. In February 1983 he told a court how he had lost £250,000 in a dodgy investment earlier in the decade, his money mishandled by his personal manager. Crawford was almost declared bankrupt. Professionally Crawford walked the tightrope for five tricky years as circus performer *Barnum* (from June 1981) and on the last day of its run was offered the tormented lead in *The Phantom of the Opera*, which began in the West End on 9 October 1986 (and opened on Broadway on 26 January 1988, later winning him a Tony Award). He completed 1069 performances up to its close in Los Angeles in 1990. In August 1996 an injury he had sustained to his hip in late 1995 (TR Uranus conjunct Sun) finally put him out of his hectic £26 million Las Vegas show *EFX*, which he had started at New Year 1995. The show had made Crawford a bigger draw than any American star at Vegas, although the injury and disinterest of the money men in Vegas left him "profoundly depressed". On 10 December 1996 he had hip replacement surgery. In 1998 he released a new album and video and embarked upon a US concert tour. In October 2002 he was named the 17th Greatest Briton of all time.

Q | "A complex man who keeps his true personality carefully hidden behind guffaws and well-intentioned platitudes. He is that most unusual celebrity: genuinely pleasant and unassuming." (Andrew Duncan, *Radio Times*, 19/8/95)

> "I guess people are intrigued and want to analyse me because I won't discuss [my life]. I like to be private when I'm not on stage... I was on the verge of bankruptcy but didn't feel bitter, I was just furious I'd been so stupid and blind, and far too trusting. But it was business – something I never did, and never will, understand." (Michael Crawford, *Radio Times*, 19/8/95)
>
> "I'm not ashamed to say that I was fairly innocent as a child, but my innocence and childhood ended when I was 21 and my mother died." (Michael Crawford, *Night & Day*, 19/9/99)

Bernard Cribbins

b. 29 December 1928, 00.35 GMT, Oldham, England, 53N33, 02W07.
FCC q. him. RR: A.

Comedy actor who joined the Oldham Repertory as an assistant stage manager before touring in revues. He appeared in the hugely popular film *The Railway Children* (1970) and is fondly remembered for narrating *The Wombles*, as well as for lending his voice to many commercials and radio comedy productions. He appeared in three *Carry On* films: *Jack*, *Spying* and *Columbus*. Cribbins is a keen angler.

Quentin Crisp

✪ *b. 25 December 1908, 13.00 GMT, Carshalton, England, 51N22, 0W10.*
David Fisher q. Zerda Barlow, from Crisp by letter, "at about one in the daytime." Richard Geyman q. him for "between Noon and 1 pm." RR: A.

Witty and original eccentric-turned-writer, known for his purple hair, effeminacy and exotic dress sense (Uranus on the MC sets one apart and can provoke enormous hostility). After years of ridicule and abuse, Crisp achieved prominence after his 1968 autobiography (reprinted in 1977) was adapted for film. *The Naked Civil Servant*, starring John Hurt (qv), was shown on the 17 December 1975. (Taurus certainly outlasts their critics and objectors!) Since then he has become an outrageous British institution (Uranus on a Capricorn MC), appearing in a number of diverse roles such as Queen Elizabeth I in the film *Orlando*, and Lady Bracknell. He gave an alternative Queen's Speech on Channel Four at Christmas 1994.

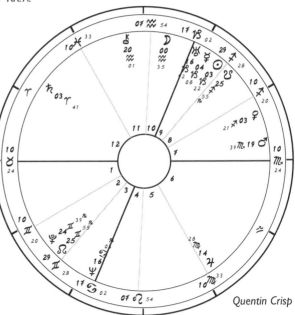

Quentin Crisp

Crisp is often celebrated for being a famous homosexual, although his major appeal lies in his articulate matter-of-fact unconventionality (a mixture of the Saturn and Uranus influence). Personally he was languid (his ambition was to be a chronic invalid), always needing to please, very traditional and concerned with money. He was plagued by guilt but played the exhibitionist and martyr to his new-found adoring public, becoming a "Stately Homo of England". He was awarded the Unique Theatrical Experience Award for *An Evening with Quentin Crisp* (1978). Crisp moved to New York City in mid-September 1981. In September 1999 he suddenly decided to undertake a punishing two-week tour of England and died on 21 November 1999 in a suburb of Manchester, on the eve of his first performance. (*The Naked Civil Servant* by Quentin Crisp, Flamingo edition, 1985.)

> Q
>
> "How Quentin Crisp became an icon is a puzzlement. A self-destructive eccentric with no self-esteem, he did survive his hard times to emerge not a hero, just a martyr. Eventually a gay Uncle Tom, who not only feels we deserve no equal rights but not even the right to exist. He's going from bad to worse to senile... [and] is one of the worst cases of siding with one's oppressors." (Allen Ginsberg, as quoted in *In or Out: Stars on Sexuality* by Boze Hadleigh, Fusion, 2001)
>
> "Someone wrote to me and said, "You're a lonely, embittered old queen who's never interested in anything that matters to anyone else." And I thought, That's true." (Quentin Crisp, as quoted in the short film *The Significant Death of Quentin Crisp*)

Annette Crosbie

b. 12 February 1934, 05.10 GMT, Gorebridge, Scotland, 55N51, 03W02.

Gerard q. BC. RR: AA.

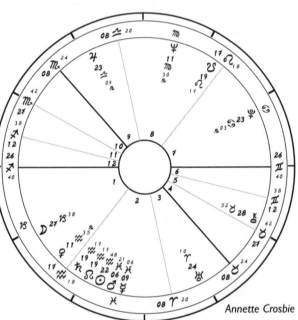

Annette Crosbie

Straight-talking, indomitable but withdrawn actress with a wide-range of credits. Crosbie won national attention as the long-suffering wife of Victor Meldrew (Richard Wilson, qv) in the high-rating comedy *One Foot in the Grave* (five series from January 1990 to December 1995). She appeared in four series of *Doctor Finlay* from September 1993 to 1996. Other television projects included *The Six Wives of Henry VIII* (January 1970, TR Pluto on EQHS 10th), and a Bafta award-winning portrayal of Queen Victoria in *Edward the Seventh* (1975). Crosbie trained at the Bristol Old Vic Theatre School. She worked with Bernard Cribbins (qv) on the radio comedy *Mind Your Own Business* in December 1987 (TR Uranus on Ascendant). In 2003 she appeared in a female *Full Monty*-inspired film, *Calendar Girls* with Julie Walters (qv). Crosbie admits to being intolerant, a trait she inherited from her undemonstrative, unfulfilled mother.

Graham Crowden

b. 30 November 1922, 00.20 GMT, Walker St., Edinburgh, Scotland, 55N57, 03W13.

Gerard q. BC (Clement Graham Crowden). RR: AA.

Television actor popular in the 60s and later in *A Very Peculiar Practice* (May 1986, when TR Saturn conjunct Sun, to April 1988). *Waiting For God* belatedly gained him millions of fans. Crowden, cast as an eccentric dreamer, joined Stephanie Cole (qv) to form a formidable geriatric duo who brought anarchy to a retirement home (five series from June 1990). In April 2003 he appeared in *The Planman* with Robbie Coltrane (qv).

Andrew Cruickshank

b. 25 December 1907, 13.40 GMT, Aberdeen, Scotland, 57N09, 02W05.

Gerard q. BC. (Andrew John Maxton Cruickshank). RR: AA.

Classical actor who gave up his ambitions of becoming a civil engineer to make his London debut in Paul Robeson's production of *Othello* (1930). He is best known for his role as the crusty Dr Angus Cameron in *Dr Finlay's Casebook* (August 1962 to January 1971). D. 29 April 1988.

Barry Cryer

b. 23 March 1935, 03.00 GMT, Leeds, England, 53N50, 01W35.
Brian Kelly q. him. RR: A.

Sketch-writer for some of the world's most renowned comedians (including George Burns and Bob Hope) and wry stand-up comic in his own right. Cryer has also written humour for *The Morecambe and Wise Show*, *The Kenny Everett Show* and *The Two Ronnies*. He is now often seen on television with adult stand-up routines on night-time TV and in game shows on daytime TV. The Aries-Scorpio overtone contributes a sharp, incisive humour, as do the prominent placements of the Moon and Mars.

Alan Cumming

b. 27 January 1965, 08.20 GMT, Aberfeldy, Perthshire, Scotland, 56N37, 03W52.
Gerard q. BC. RR: AA.

Eclectic actor known for oddball roles in *The High Life* (a comedy about two airline stewards, in which he wrote and starred) and *Circle of Friends*. His part in *Circle of Friends* brought him to the attention of Bond producers and he was cast as a computer wizard in the Bond film *GoldenEye* in November 1995, one year after a deep depression during which he had broken up with his wife. His impact in the film brought offers from America, including the Hollywood version of *Emma*. He played the Emcee in *Cabaret* on Broadway (TR Uranus over Ascendant, and later a Tony Award for his role). In April 2003 he appeared in *X-Men 2*. Cumming is scheduled to host his own talk show in America, star in a gay detective series and has written a

Alan Cumming

novel, *Tommy's Tales*. A lonely child whose parents rarely spoke during their 20-year marriage, Cumming started out working for a teen magazine interviewing pop stars such as Bucks Fizz, and later became a model for teenage photo-stories. Cumming began his acting career as part of the comedy duo Victor and Barry – the surprise hit of the Edinburgh Festival in August 1988. A stint with the RSC led to award-winning stage performances in *Accidental Death of an Anarchist* (Olivier Award) and *Hamlet*. His chart demonstrates his youthful brilliance (double Aquarian), marketability and ease in all media (Moon on MC, earth grand trine of Jupiter to Mercury/Venus to Uranus/Pluto, tying up nine houses including the EQHS 2nd, 10th, 5th and Ascendant).

> **Q**
> "For years the lonely little boy played unnoticed in the remote forests and glens of Scotland, lost in his own world of make-believe. With only his dog for company, Alan Cumming could shed the anonymous persona of a sensitive and gentle child who preferred his own company to become James Bond, all-action superhero." (Jane Preston, *Mail on Sunday*, 17/12/95)
>
> "I have no vanity playing weird, unsympathetic oddballs. To me, they're the more enjoyable parts because you can cut loose... I was called a frolicky pansexual sex symbol for the new millennium, and I'm happy to go along with that. I find labels like 'gay' and 'bisexual' too limiting, But I'm wary of discussing [my sexuality]... because I was so disappointed with the way they sensationalised what I said in a recent interview. I [called myself pansexual] because I was so fed up with being asked about my sexuality, but also because I don't think I've got anything to be ashamed of." (Alan Cumming, *You*, 13/8/2000)

JOHNNY & PHIL CUNNINGHAM

Brothers who joined 70s folk band Silly Wizard and pursued solo projects in the 80s. In 1988 Pianist Phil teamed up with Aly Bain (qv) and fiddler Johnny moved to the US and toured with Bonnie Raitt.

Johnny Cunningham

○ b. 27 August 1957, 21.44 GDT, Edinburgh, Scotland, 55N57, 03W12.
  Gerard q. BC (John James Cunningham). RR: AA.

Phil Cunningham

○ b. 27 January 1960, 06.25 GMT, Edinburgh, Scotland, 55N57, 03W12.
  Gerard q. BC (Philip Martin Cunningham). RR: AA.

Tom Cunningham – see Wet Wet Wet

Alannah Currie

b. 20 September 1957, 05.00 NZT (-12), Auckland, New Zealand, 36S52, 174E46.
Babs Kirby q. Currie's record company. RR: A.

Currie joined the Thompson Twins on percussion in August 1981 (Jupiter Return) during a promo tour, a year after she began dating lead singer Tom Bailey (b. 18 June 1957, Halifax). The band hit its stride in 1983-4 with major success in the US and UK (and a #1 album in February 1984). In 1986 she was made an Honorary Cultural Ambassador for New Zealand. After on-going personal problems had forced her out of a tour in January 1987, Currie became pregnant, giving birth in April 1988.

Finlay Currie

b. 20 January 1878, 04.00 GMT, central Edinburgh, Scotland, 55N57, 03W12.
Gerard q. BC (William Finlay Currie). RR: AA.

Currie developed a music-hall act that took advantage of his vast vocal range which extended from baritone to soprano (Pluto contacts to the Ascendant or ruler suggest a vast vocal range – Currie's Pluto opposed Scorpio Rising). 3 May 1898 saw his stage debut. He wed American performer Maude Courtney and they formed a variety act. He was a recognisable character actor on film (from 1932-65), cast in authoritative roles, including Great Expectations (1946) and Ben-Hur (1959). D. 9 May 1968.

Justin Currie – see Del Amitri

Tim Curry

b. 19 April 1946, 12.00 Noon GDT, Cheshire, England, 53N15, 02W30.
Frederick Davies q. Curry. RR: A.

An articulate and private actor, now cast in American productions as a British stereotype: malevolent, comedic and much-thwarted. The son of a naval chaplain, Curry moved with his family every 18 months (Neptune on the IC suggests, among other things, rootlessness). He later sold leather belts at a market in Notting Hill before joining a touring production of Hair. His reputation is inextricably bound with the full-on sexual image of Frank-N-Furter (Aries MC), a role he played for two years in the campy stage production The Rocky Horror Show. He also starred in the film version, which began the audience-participating cinema cult from April 1976, as TR Pluto crossed his IC. Astrologically,

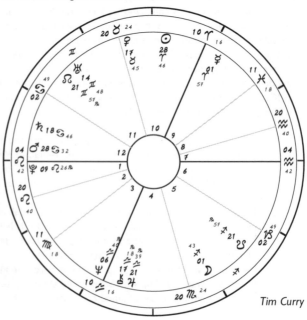

Tim Curry

cult underground shows are invariably linked to Pluto (Curry has the planet conjunct the Ascendant in his horoscope) and to Neptune, for longevity and adoration. He also starred as Mozart in the Broadway production of *Amadeus*, which opened on 17 December 1980. Later films have included *Annie* (1982), *Clue* (1985), *Stephen King's It* (1990), *The Hunt for Red October* (1990) and *Home Alone 2* (1992).

Q "When I was 12 my father died from pneumonia following two strokes. It was an extremely violent thing to happen. If you lose a parent when you are embarking on adolescence, from that moment on you know too much. A major part of your innocence is taken away. After that, my friends were always older than me." (Tim Curry, *Night & Day*, 19/5/96)

Peter Cushing
○ b. 26 May 1913, 07.00 GMT, Kenley, England, 51N19, 0W06.
◑ Jane Struthers q. his autobiography, stating he was born in Kenley, Surrey, "in time for an early breakfast." RR: C.

A refined actor and screen legend during the great age of British horror films with Christopher Lee (qv). Cushing made his stage debut in 1935 and then appeared on Broadway on 21 November 1941, two years before his West End debut on 6 August 1943. Cushing was devastated when his wife (whom he had married on 10 April 1943) died in January 1971 and contemplated suicide (in his memoirs Cushing revealed that his life had started at age 29 when they met). Cushing died from cancer in August 1994. On the eve of the 40th anniversary of his first Hammer horror film *The Curse of Frankenstein*, Cushing's long-time, trusted secretary spoke of him as a private man, riddled with insecurities and very dependent upon his wife, and later on her.

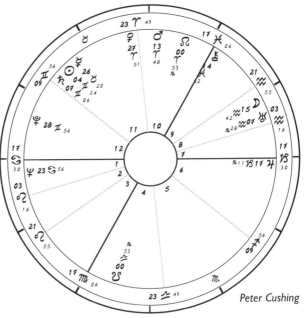

Peter Cushing

Iain Cuthbertson
b. 4 January 1930, 06.15 GMT, Glasgow, Scotland, 55N52, 04W19.
Gerard q. BC. RR: AA.
Actor-director Cuthbertson began his career in radio and moved into theatre in 1955 (*The Man Upstairs*). TV and film work include *Budgie* (1971-2) and *Gorillas in the Mist* (1989).

Ivor Cutler
○ b. 15 January 1923, 08.40 GMT, Govan, Glasgow, Scotland, 55N51, 04W19.
Gerard q. BC (Isadore Cutler). RR: AA.
Cutler, the eccentric poet, humourist and cartoonist, began recording surreal records in 1959.

Andrew Dallmeyer
b. 10 January 1945, 06.00 GDT, St. Boswells, Scotland, 55N34, 02W38.
Gerard q. BC (Andrew Victor Dallmeyer). RR: AA.
Actor and highly regarded director (Ascendant ruler Jupiter on MC). Considered a playwright without equal (Moon and Jupiter angular), two of his most popular works have been the political satire, *The Boys in the Backroom* (1982) and *A Grand Scam* (1991), the latter a parody of theatrical life.

Paul Daniels

b. 6 April 1938, 04.30 GMT, Middlesbrough, England, 54N35, 01W14.

FCC q. him, from his parents. RR: A.

Magician and television presenter. Daniels's love of magic and total engrossment in learning the art began at the age of eleven. At 22 he worked in a miming act with his brother Trevor (as Ted & Trevor Daniels) at various working men's clubs, whilst retaining his day-job as an internal auditor in local government. Daniels moved full-time into show business in 1969, the year his first marriage broke up. His television debut was on *Opportunity Knocks* and his catchphrase, "You'll like it – not a lot, but you'll like it" has been well-known since. He arrived on the TV scene at a time when magicians were stale and being phased out. Daniels managed to corner the market (success in his chart is suggested in part by MC and

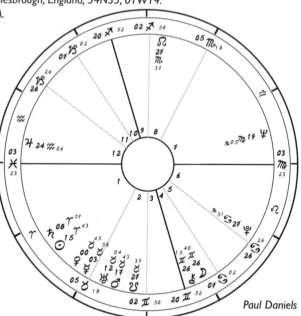

Paul Daniels

Ascendant co-ruler Jupiter Rising trine 5th House ruler Moon) and for a number of years remained the only high-profile magician on TV, fiercely guarding his territory from other acclaimed magicians. His TV series *The Paul Daniels Magic Show* began in 1979 (TR Neptune over MC) and lasted 16 years. It won a Golden Rose at the 1985 Montreux Television Festival. Although his magic feats are modest compared to his American counterparts, Daniels is a popular performer. He has also acted as quizmaster on several TV shows. The Press have made much of the difficult relationship he has with his eldest son Paul (born 9 September 1960), who served six months inside in June 1998 for running a bogus insurance firm. After a five year absence from regular TV, Daniels, who was in semi-retirement, was challenged by the BBC in July 2001 to make a name for himself in the USA as Eldani the Unusualist. On 25 March 2003 Daniels was in hospital suffering from an infection. Neptune is traditionally the planet of magic (deception/illusion as a form of entertainment), although Jupiter is more essential for public exhibition and performance (and throw in Saturn for countless hours of rehearsal). In Daniels's chart Neptune rules his Pisces Ascendant, Jupiter is rising and Saturn conjuncts Sun. Neptune should tie in with his need to be heard (3rd House) and his audience (5th House): Neptune makes a square to 5th House ruler Moon and sesquisquare to Mercury in EQHS 3rd.

> Q
>
> "Those who, through no fault of their own, have built up an irrational antipathy towards this perky little conjuror will find little evidence in his autobiography to alter their impression of a chippy, self-righteous, bullying, single-minded, mirthless and stunningly vain performer, whose undoubted skill as a magician may well be the natural result of a compulsion to control other people." (Craig Brown, *Mail on Sunday*, 18/6/2000)

Alec Dankworth

b. 14 May 1960, 22.00 GDT, London, England, 51N30, 0W10.

From his mother's autobiography, Cleo (Simon & Schuster, 1994), p. 171, "at about 10 p.m." RR: B.

A short while after completing his music course in Boston in 1978, bassist Alec Dankworth joined his father John Dankworth and mother Cleo Laine (qv) on tour in America (from 1980-3). By 1990 he had established a firm musical reputation in his own right on both sides of the Atlantic. He continues touring with his father in their Generation Band, which was formed in early 1993.

John Dankworth – see Cleo Laine

Nigel Davenport

> b. 23 May 1928, 08.00 GDT, Great Shelford, Cambridge, England, 52N09, 0E09.
> FCC q. him, January 1995, "approximately 8.00 am." RR: A.

Actor known for tough and tetchy characters on film, TV and stage (perhaps easily expressed with Moon-Pluto on his Cancer Ascendant). His film debut was in 1959. He had a continuing role in the soap *Howard's Way* in 1987 and in the series *South Riding* (1974), *Bird of Prey* (1982), and *Trainer* (1991-2).

Jim Davidson

> b. 13 December 1953, 07.30 GMT, Blackheath, England, 51N28, 0E01.
> David Fisher q. Davidson's agent. (N.B. L&L for Blackheath.) RR: A.

At first, Davidson wanted to be a hairdresser rather than the often offensive and vulgar, yet popular, comedian he became (Davidson is a double Sagittarian with Sun opposite Jupiter). He won *New Faces* on 9 March 1976 (TR Neptune conjunct Ascendant) and some 20 years later in mid-February 1997 was the Variety Club's Showbiz Personality of the Year. He took over *The Generation Game* on 21 October 1995 and hosted a snooker-based TV game show for a few years. He has married four times (from 1971) and his latest union was overshadowed by accusations of violence.

Linda Davidson

> b. 18 June 1964, 01.00 EDT (+4), Toronto, Canada, 43N39, 79W23.
> FCC q. her letter stating the birth time (01.00) is "approximate as neither of my parents can remember... (they) agreed it was the early hours of the morning." RR: C.

After a period living rough in Liverpool when she left home at 16, dancer and actress Linda Davidson moved to London to train at drama school. In February 1985 she debuted on the then-new soap *EastEnders* as illiterate punk Mary Smith, who juggled single-motherhood with stripping and prostitution, whilst walking around with a huge chip on her shoulder. The character – and Davidson – left the soap in May 1988.

Dave and Ray Davies – see The Kinks

DEACON BLUE

Singer-songwriter Ricky Ross formed the band in 1985 to perform his socialist-inspired, soul compositions. Soon after winning a recording contract, the band were joined by vocalist McIntosh and released a commercially successful album, *Raintown*, in May 1987 (500,000 copies sold, Ross's Saturn Return). Six singles were released from the album, with one Top Ten success. A second album went straight to the top of the charts in mid-April 1989 (as TR Jupiter passed Ross's EQHS 10th) and sold 900,000 units. The EP *Four Bacharach & David Songs* made #2 in the UK in September 1990. McIntosh and Ross, joint-lead vocalists in the band, were later married (professionally, her Sun conjuncts his MC, and personally, her Saturn lies on his Descendant). Ross went solo in 1994.

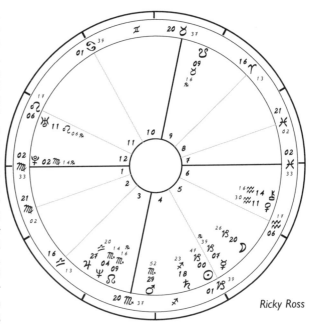

Ricky Ross

Graeme Kelling

> b. 4 April 1957, 06.05 GMT, Barshaw Hospital, Paisley, Scotland, 55N51, 04W23.
> Gerard q. BC (Graeme Hunter Kelling). RR: AA.

Lorraine McIntosh

> b. 13 May 1964, 06.03 GDT, Belvidere Hospital, Glasgow, Scotland, 55N50, 04W14.
> Gerard q. BC (Lorraine Marie McIntosh). RR: AA.

James Prime

> b. 3 November 1960, 07.30 GMT, Maternity Hospital, Kilmarnock, Scotland, 55N37, 04W29.
> Gerard q. BC (James Miller Prime). RR: AA.

Ricky Ross

> b. 22 December 1957, 21.20 GMT, Maternity Hospital, Dundee, Scotland, 56N28, 02W58.
> Gerard q. BC (Richard Alexander Ross). RR: AA.

Ewan Vernal

> b. 27 February 1964, 07.13 GMT, Balornock Road, Glasgow, Scotland, 55N53, 04W14.
> Gerard q. BC. RR: AA.

Dougie Vipond

> b. 15 October 1966, 01.40 GDT, Thornhill Hospital, Elderslie, Scotland, 55N50, 04W28.
> Gerard q. BC (Douglas Vipond). RR: AA.

Letitia Dean

> b. 14 November 1967, 08.00 GMT, Wild Hill, near Potters Bar, England, 51N44, 0W11.
> FCC q. Russell Grant's All-Star Show with Dean, and information derived from it. RR: A.

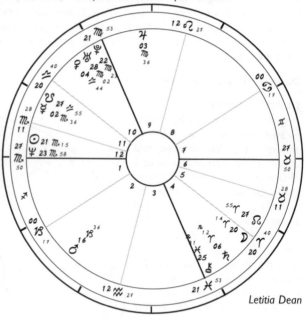

Letitia Dean

A major player in the BBC soap *EastEnders*, Letitia Dean appeared in the series from its beginning in February 1985 (when TR Saturn conjunct her Ascendant). The series made her one of the most recognisable faces on TV. In November 1986 she had a hit record from the show. After leaving *EastEnders* in June 1996 (she had made the decision to quit back in Autumn 1994) she starred in two series of *The Hello Girls*. Dean was threatened with jail and given a two and a half year driving ban after drink-driving on 12 April 1996 (note the prominent Neptune). She returned to *EastEnders* in March 2001 (TR Saturn conjunct her Descendant). Dean met her future husband in June 2001 and they were married on 30 September 2002.

Chris DeBurgh

> ☙ b. 15 October 1948, 02.20 ASD (+3), Venado Tuerto, Argentina, 33S45, 61W58.
> From the biography, *Chris DeBurgh – The Authorized Biography* by Tony Clayton-Lee (1996), p. 8, "born in the early hours." Speculative time. RR: C.

After touring in late 1973, DeBurgh signed a record contract in September 1974. Although enormous success followed in late 1975 in Brazil, and during 1979 in South America and Europe, he had to wait until his album *The Getaway* was released October 1982 before cracking the US market. In February 1985 he was brought to a wider audience in the UK, and his smash hit *The Lady in Red* topped the charts in August 1986. He has contributed his time and musical proceeds to many worthwhile causes. During early 1995, the media had a field day when his marriage almost broke up.

DEL AMITRI
Cult semi-acoustic rock band known for wry political lyrics (written by Currie). Formed in 1981, their debut album was released in 1985 but disputes with the recording label led to a forced hiatus. The band's following organised and promoted gigs until they were signed to A&M in 1987 (TR Saturn over Currie's Sun). Their first single to chart was in August 1989.

Justin Currie
> b. 11 December 1964, 04.04 GMT, Queen Mother Maternity Hospital Hospital, Glasgow, Scotland, 55N52, 04W19.
> Gerard q. BC (Justin Robert Currie). RR: AA.

Iain Harvie
> b. 19 May 1962, 12.20 GDT, Beckford Lodge, Hamilton, Scotland, 55N46, 04W03.
> Gerard q. BC (Iain Wallace Harvie). RR: AA.

Judi Dench – see Billy Connolly

Les Dennis
> b. 12 October 1953, 20.20 GMT, Liverpool, England, 53N25, 02W55.
> Marjorie Orr q. him. RR: A.

Dennis (Leslie Heseltine) won *Opportunity Knocks* before moving full-time into TV with popular comedy shows such as *Russ Abbot's Madhouse* and *Who Do You Do?*, two shows to which his comedy partner Dustin Gee (qv) also leant his talents. His double act with Gee (which included *Coronation Street's* Vera and Mavis impersonations) made them both familiar TV faces in the early 80s, and one of the most successful comedy acts in Britain. It came to an abrupt end when Gee died of a heart attack aged 43 on 3 January 1986. Dennis took over the game show *Family Fortunes* in 1987 (Gemini is prominent in the chirpy, perma-smiling world of the game show). Dennis, who has acted in various stage shows, married actress

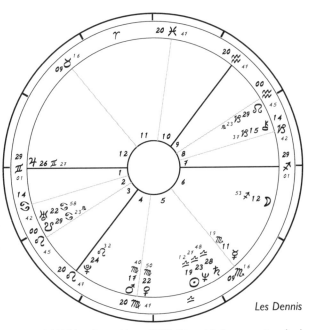

Les Dennis

Amanda Holden (b. 16 February 1971, Bishop's Waltham) on 4 June 1995 (Dennis's first marriage had ended in divorce in 1990). Dennis and Holden's marriage break-up was a tabloid sensation in early May 2000 (as TR Uranus hit his MC, TR Pluto on Moon, and TR Jupiter-Saturn square MC), when Holden was romantically linked with actor Neil Morrissey (see Elizabeth Carling). Dennis, who was appearing in the West End production of *Chicago* at the time, was embarrassed by the publicity and hurt by the affair. The relationship survived and he returned to acting in the Alan Ayckbourn play *Just Between Ourselves* in July 2002. Appearing in *Celebrity Big Brother* in late November 2002 (TR Saturn on Jupiter), the media were keen to make much of his battle with depression (Moon in Sagittarius) and his on-screen 'romance' with a fellow contestant. Dennis and Holden announced their separation on 27 December 2002.

Sandy Denny

   b. 6 January 1947, 16.00 GMT, Wimbledon, London, England, 51N25, 0W12.
   From her to Ruth Elliot. RR: A.

Acclaimed singer Denny joined Fairport Convention in July 1968, which later developed into a band blending folk with rock. She completed a couple of notable albums with the group (plus a few solo albums in the early 70s) before she left in January 1976 (as TR Neptune squared the MC). On 21 April 1978, after a fall at a friend's house, Denny suffered a cerebral haemorrhage and died.

DEPECHE MODE

•1980, May – Gahan joins the group Composition of Sound, later renamed Depeche Mode.

•1981, Apr – Their debut single is released.

•1981, Oct – First Top Ten UK hit.

•1982, Jan – Wilder joins the group (TR Neptune had just passed MC).

•1985, August – Gahan attempts suicide.

•1996, May 28 – Gahan is arrested after an apparent cocaine overdose.

•2003, June – Gahan supports Bon Jovi on tour.

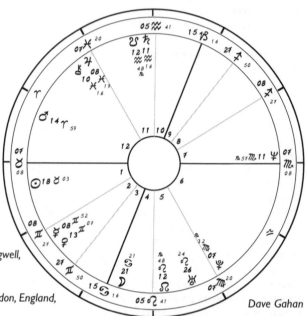

Dave Gahan

Dave Gahan

   b. 9 May 1962, 05.00 GDT, Chigwell, England, 51N38, 0E05.

Alan Wilder

   b. 1 June 1959, 02.00 GDT, London, England, 51N30, 0W10.
   Marjorie Orr q. both. RR: A.

Jimmy Deuchar

   b. 26 June 1930, 15.15 GDT, Dundee, Scotland, 56N28, 02W57.
   Gerard q. BC (James Deuchar). RR: AA.

Composer, arranger on BBC projects during the mid-60s, bandleader and leading jazz trumpeter from 1950. Deuchar was a member of the Johnny Dankworth Seven and in 1953 joined Ronnie Scott's nine-piece orchestra. From 1957-71 his reputation enabled him to travel with many big bands in Europe and the USA (3rd ruler Jupiter conjunct Sun in 9th). Throughout the 80s and early 90s he continued to write, notably for the Jack Sharpe Big Band. His last composition, *Concerto for Joe*, was released in 1995, two years after his death on 9 September 1993.

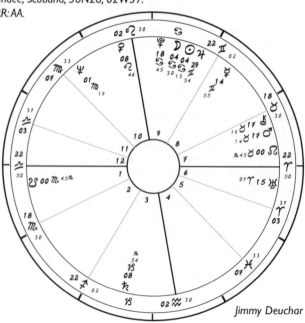

Jimmy Deuchar

Jim Diamond

b. 28 September 1951, 14.30 GDT, Maternity Hospital, Glasgow, Scotland, 55N51, 04W14.
Gerard q. BC (James Diamond). RR: AA.

Former vocalist with PhD on the top three hit *I Won't Let You Down* in May 1982 (TR Pluto near MC). Diamond went on to score a #1 hit on 1 December 1984 with *I Should Have Known Better*. Both singles were in the top 25 best sellers of their respective years. A few chart releases followed including a #5 hit, *Hi Ho Silver*, in March 1986.

Barbara Dickson

b. 27 September 1947, 23.00 GDT, Maternity Hospital, Dunfermline, Scotland, 56N04, 03W28.
Gerard q. BC (Barbara Ruth Dickson). RR: AA.

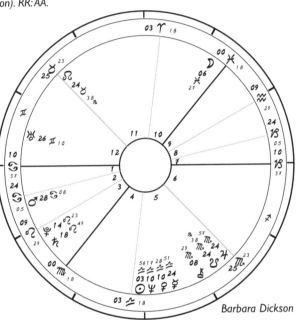

Barbara Dickson

At 21 Dickson gave up her civil service job and took off for a six week music engagement in Denmark, when TR Uranus crossed her Sun. In 1973 she got her first big break in the musical *John, Paul, George, Ringo and Bert* (TR Pluto conjunct Sun). She first hit the charts in January 1976, and *Another Suitcase, Another Hall* charted in February 1977. Originally considered a folk singer, she adopted a more eclectic repertoire and later went to #1 in February 1985 with *I Know Him So Well*. She was applauded for her continuing lead role on stage in *Blood Brothers* from January 1983 (Best Actress in a Musical from the Society of West End Theatres), as well as *The 7 Ages of Woman* and *Spend, Spend, Spend*. She moved into television acting with the gritty *Band of Gold* (1995-6) and *Taggart*. Dickson's enduring popularity (MC ruler Neptune conjunct Sun, and Moon on MC) has seen her become a regular concert performer, although she is known to be very private and shy in person (note the Cancer Ascendant and Moon in Pisces).

Joan Dickson

b. 21 December 1921, 05.30 GMT, Edinburgh, Scotland, 55N57, 03W11.
Gerard q. BC (Katherine Joan Dickson). RR: AA.

Cellist who studied in Rome and Paris and performed a debut recital in 1953 in London. A leading concert soloist, she also taught at the Royal Scottish Academy of Music (1954-81) and the Royal College of Music (1967-81).

Phil Differ

b. 6 May 1956, 04.00 GDT, Maternity Hospital, Stirling, Scotland, 56N07, 03W56.
Gerard q. BC (Philip Differ). RR: AA.

Experimental and mainstream comedian who debuted on BBC2 in January 1997 with his comedy show *Beg to Differ*. A clerical officer in accounts for six years, he quit and joined a media course at Glasgow College. He had early work with Robbie Coltrane (qv) in *A Kick Up the Eighties* and 13 years working on BBC Scotland's Comedy Unit before winning his own series.

Jonathan Dimbleby

b. 31 July 1944, 14.00 DGDT, Aylesbury, England, 51N50, 0W50.
FCC q. him. RR: A.

Renowned television journalist and presenter. Editor of his University paper, Dimbleby went to Bristol as a trainee newspaper reporter. In 1969 he followed in the footsteps of his father Richard Dimbleby (qv) by joining the BBC. In 1971 he joined Thames Television's *This Week* team (first report – 27 January 1972). He won a special award in 1973 for his outstanding contribution to factual television (for *The Unknown Famine*, broadcast 18 October 1973 during his Saturn Return). He has Saturn prominent (for professional esteem) and a stellium of MC-Sun-Pluto (highlighting the importance of his famous, distinguished father), and 3rd-9th rulers Jupiter-Mercury conjunct (for media success).

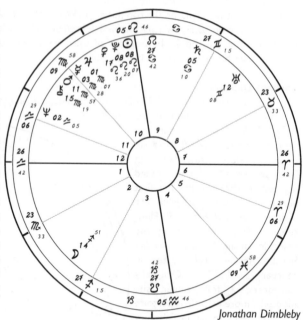

Jonathan Dimbleby

Richard Dimbleby

✪ b. 25 May 1913, 12.00 Noon GMT, Richmond-upon-Thames, London, England, 51N27, 0W20.
From the biography by his son, Jonathan Dimbleby, "midday." RR: B.

During the 50s and 60s Richard Dimbleby was the personification of British TV current affairs broadcasting (Sun-Saturn crowns the MC for respect and professional gravitas, and Moon-Uranus in Aquarius in 5th trines MC for a successful following in the new medium of TV). He joined the BBC as a radio news observer in 1936 and became their first war correspondent, bringing the reality of warfare into the homes of millions of Britons. When he moved to TV he covered important state occasions, such as the funerals of Kennedy and Churchill. In 1955 he was selected as anchor of *Panorama* (1955-63) and became a defender of public interest. Viewers trusted him to grill all politicians with equal severity and Dimbleby became a

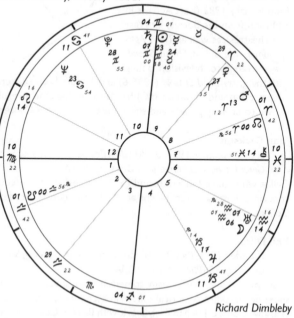

Richard Dimbleby

"bastion of fairness and perspicuity in political debate" (Sun-Saturn on the MC). He became almost synonymous with the BBC* itself (which used to be very Saturn-Capricorn!) and the synastry is

---

* BBC (corporation registration) b. 1 January 1927, 00.00 GMT, central London, 51N30, 0W06. From *The History of Broadcasting in the UK*, vol. ii by Asa Briggs (OUP, 1965), p. 3.

interesting. A standard-setter who was instrumental in developing broadcast journalism, Dimbleby was also popular with his radio shows *Twenty Questions* and *Down Your Way*. D. 22 December 1965, approximately 21.00, London, cancer.

Q "It fell to Richard Dimbleby to take the television audience by the hand and guide it gently into more tolerant, liberal ways. Intuitively sensitive to public attitudes, frequently sharing them himself, he had an acute sense of what was felt to be proper. Sharing many of the doubts and anxieties of his audience, having discarded yesterday the prejudices they held today, he was the perfect television mentor... his instinct was to inform and entertain, while gently pushing back the barriers of ignorance and intolerance... so accurately did he touch the public pulse that he soon attained the status of a televisual father of the people." (Jonathan Dimbleby, as quoted in *The Draconic Chart* by Rev. Pamela Crane, Flare 2000)

DIRE STRAITS

Mainstream blues-based band initially led by brothers David and Mark Knopfler. Allegedly the band's formation was a result of Mark Knopfler's relationship breakdown and the birth of his wife's child by another man in May 1976. Mark, a former *Yorkshire Evening Post* journalist, gathered together a band and recorded a five-song demo in July 1977 (as TR Saturn approached his Sun). He developed his own style through fusion and synthesis, often playing rockabilly and R&B music. The band were signed in October 1977, after Mark had quit his day job and taken a bus trip around America. A debut album appeared in September 1978 and hit #2 in the US album charts in April 1979 (both dates, his Saturn Return). Their recording *Sultans of*

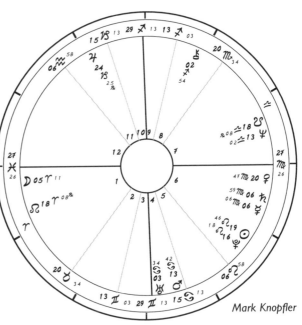

Mark Knopfler

Swing led to a 51-date sold out tour of the US. Before the major 80s success that was to come, David Knopfler left the band in July 1980 to begin a solo career. Despite his brother's departure, Mark continued recording with the band whilst writing for other artists (he wrote *Private Dancer* for Tina Turner) and pursuing solo film projects (*Local Hero*) in 1983-4 (TR Neptune over MC). The band hit the commercial stratosphere in August 1985 with the release of *Brothers in Arms*, a chart-topping album worldwide and the biggest selling CD of all time in Britain (by November 1987, over three million sales) – a product of successful global marketing. As a songwriter Mark was a late developer but by the late 80s he had the Midas touch. He became a father of twins in January 1988 (when TR Saturn and Uranus moved over the MC). Dire Straits have sold over 105 million records, including 26 million albums of *Brothers in Arms*. On 17 March 2003 Mark suffered a broken collarbone and six broken ribs when his motorcycle collided with a car.

David Knopfler
b. 27 December 1952, 22.15 GMT, Broomhill Drive, Glasgow, Scotland, 55N52, 04W20.
Gerard q. BC. RR: AA.

Mark Knopfler
b. 12 August 1949, 21.50 GDT, Great Western Road, Glasgow, Scotland, 55N53, 04W19.
Gerard q. BC (Mark Freuder Knopfler). RR: AA.

DOCTOR WHO

✪ The first episode of this unique TV phenomenon, *An Unearthly Child*, was televised on 23 November 1963, from Shepherd's Bush, London at 17.16.20 GMT (Adam Fronteras q. official BBC documentation). Note the Moon-Saturn conjunction crowning the MC in the sci-fi, futuristic and eccentric sign of Aquarius. See profiles on actors who appeared in the series: Sophie Aldred, Tom Baker, Lynda Bellingham, Liza Goddard, Bonnie Langford, Jean Marsh and Sylvester McCoy. (The show was first broadcast one day after the infamous assassination of President John F. Kennedy.)

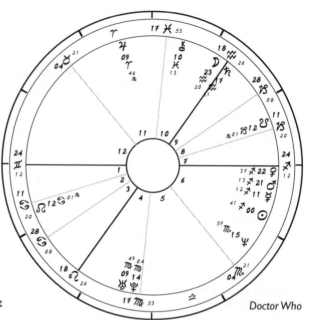

Doctor Who

Howard Donald – see Take That

James Donald

✪ b. 18 May 1917, 23.25 GDT, Aberdeen, Scotland, 57N10, 02W04.
Gerard q. BC (James Robert MacGeorge Donald). RR: AA.

Actor, best known for his cultivated but humourless, stiff-upper lip, gent roles in films (between 1942 and 1978). He appeared in *The Bridge on the River Kwai* and *The Great Escape*. D. 3 August 1993, stomach cancer.

Lonnie Donegan

b. 29 April 1931, 03.00 GDT, Glasgow, Scotland, 55N52, 04W13.
Gerard q. BC (Anthony James Donegan). RR: AA.

Donegan was the King of Skiffle in the 50s and a self-confessed "decisive, hard and total bastard." A rhythm-based singer-guitarist, he changed his name in tribute to blues performer Lonnie Johnson. He achieved 17 Top Ten hits (including three #1s) from February 1956 (TR Saturn heading towards MC) to May 1962. Saturn, conjunct a Capricorn Ascendant, overshadows Donegan's chart, character and his life history: his poverty-stricken family moved to London in 1933 and he was diagnosed with a heart problem at four, but decided at eleven to have a full, rather than long, life. His father had musical talent but was broke and gave up his dream. Donegan's career, however, always took precedence over his personal

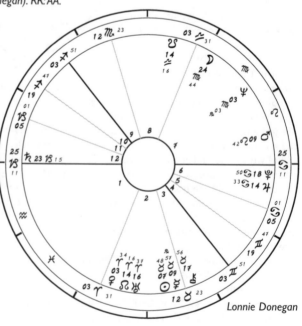

Lonnie Donegan

life and health. A tireless performer for 40 years, he travelled the cabaret circuit after suffering two heart attacks (the first in 1976), three strokes, open heart surgery (1985) and two broken marriages. He admitted music and the perfection he sought through it (Moon in Virgo) was his substitute for a stable home (Sun, Mercury and Chiron in EQHS 4th). Donegan was awarded with the Ivor Novello award, Outstanding Contribution to British Music, in May 1995 (when TR Neptune hovered over his Ascendant). A new album was released in July 1997 (TR Pluto on MC). After five heart bypasses, Donegan died on 3 November 2002.

> "Donegan's life has been characterised by passionate commitment to his work and terrible failure in his personal life. He believes that for much of his life music was a substitute for the thing he most wanted but couldn't find – a stable home." (Jane Kelly, *Daily Mail*, 10/5/96)
>
> "Since my first hit in 1956, I've lived on adrenaline. It's rotted my heart and liver. I've never lived on love or affection. I've hardly had any of that. I have to try to get that from audiences. I really didn't have a home until I was 25 and then I destroyed it." (Lonnie Donegan, *Daily Mail*, 10/5/96)

Donovan

b. 10 May 1946, 06.15 GDT, Glasgow, Scotland, 55N54, 04W18.
Gerard q. BC (Donovan Phillips Leitch). RR: AA.

Donovan Leitch was dubbed the British Bob Dylan, a title he did not welcome. Leitch, a flower-power rebel icon for the 60s, became a millionaire at 20. He was catapulted to fame after three consecutive weeks performing on *Ready, Steady, Go* in February 1965 (TR Jupiter conjunct Sun, TR Uranus conjunct Moon), and his first hit appeared one month later (TR Saturn over EQHS 10th). Seven Top Ten UK hits and four US smashes (including a chart-topper in September 1966) followed, as well as five appearances at Carnegie Hall. Donovan was returned to the pop scene by the group Happy Mondays on their tour in November 1990 (TR Pluto opposite Sun), which led to other music opportunities (TR Saturn passed over his MC in early

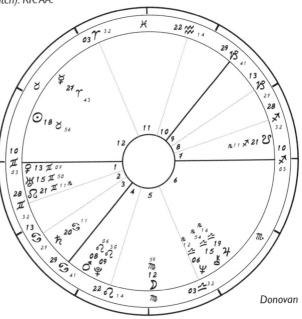

Donovan

1991). A solo UK tour followed in April 1992 and a CD box set was issued in January 1993. Donovan met former model Linda Lawrence in April 1965 and after an on-off relationship they married in October 1970, a short while after his nervous breakdown (a second collapse occurred in the early 1980s).

> "His music, with its spiritual lyrics and mystic messages, appealed to a generation of discontented youngsters looking for an alternative to the rampant materialism of the Sixties. Donovan became their voice: a beatnik rebel of his times... He will talk for hours about the significance of his contribution to the world – he has an unshakeable belief in his own self-importance." (Lester Middlehurst, *Daily Mail Weekend*, 12/10/96)

Danny Dorrian

b. 8 September 1922, 23.30 GDT, Leith, Scotland, 55N59, 03W10.
Gerard q. BC. RR: AA.

Jazz pianist (Sun opposite Uranus, Mercury conjunct Saturn) with an illustrious 50-year career. At four he was playing the harmonica and by the age of seven he had passed all the examinations set by the London School of Music. Working as an electrician to support his talent, Dorrian finally left his day job at 20 to focus on his music. In 1948 he established a quartet and formed a seven-piece band for the first Edinburgh International Festival. During the 70s and 80s he was a freelance solo piano player in many of Edinburgh's hotels and restaurants. Dorrian married in 1956. D. 5 October 1995.

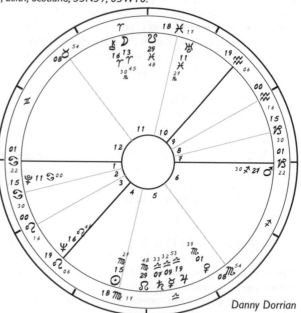

Danny Dorrian

Diana Dors

b. 23 October 1931, 07.00 GMT, Swindon, England, 51N34, 01W47.
Astrological Quarterly Review (Winter 1956) gave "around sunrise," original source not known. RR: C.

Leading lady of British films, educated at RADA and famous for her hour-glass figure. With a screen debut at 14, Dors was soon labelled England's playgirl answer to Monroe, and like her American counterpart struggled against typecasting and had difficulty winning serious acting roles. With three planets in Scorpio her private life was more scandalous than any of her roles, and Dors's infamous orgy parties in the 50s and 60s were legendary. On 24 January 1960 (TR Uranus conjunct Jupiter, TR Neptune approaching Venus) an exposé of her social exploits was published, prompting the Archbishop of Canterbury to brand her a "wayward hussy". Dors objected to the label, saying she thought she was more of a "dreary

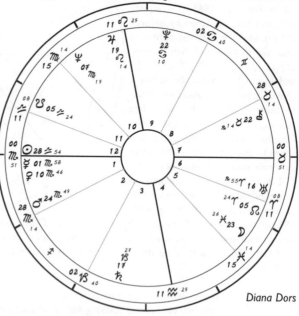

Diana Dors

tart". A TV film of her life, *Blonde Bombshell*, aired in 1999. At the time her son spoke of his mother as a shrewd, ambitious woman who controlled her life path and her money with an iron fist. D. 4 May 1984.

DOUBLE ACTS

With double-acts we can expect some basic synastry between charts to reflect their on-stage chemistry (simple connections – usually conjunctions – between Sun/Moon/Ascendant/MC). More often than not, however, there is a marked difference in horoscopes (with each partner having a set of different signs for the major chart planets and points), suggesting that one performer complements the other, the result hopefully producing a successful and humorous act. The nodal axis is often important, too. A few of the great double-acts in British comedy are featured in individual profiles elsewhere in this book: Eric Morecambe and Ernie Wise, The Two Ronnies (Barker and Corbett), Peter Cook and Dudley Moore, plus the comedy duos Les Dennis and Dustin Gee, and Little & Large.

Lesley-Anne Down

b. 17 March 1954, 16.15 GMT, Clapham, London, England, 51N27, 0W08.
Edwin Steinbrecher q. her secretary (letter in hand). RR: A.

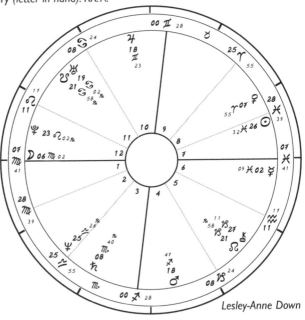
Lesley-Anne Down

From the age of 13 Down was being propositioned by men as old as 45, and by 17 was modelling nude for *Playboy*. Soon her self-confidence was being boosted by drugs. With Pisces able to swim upstream to creative success or downstream into addiction, wisely she moved into acting and broke a million hearts on TV as the flighty Georgina Worsley in *Upstairs, Downstairs*. Down settled in America in the early 80s to marry, but the union was to end in 1986 in one of Hollywood's most vicious custody battles. The case lasted two and a half years, and she was portrayed in court as promiscuous and drug-dependent. Down remarried soon after. By late 1996 she had revived her career with a hammy role in the new daytime soap, *Sunset Beach*, and was celebrating ten good years of marriage. On 11 March 1998 at 21.55 in Malibu she gave birth to a son, and was back to work on the soap four weeks later.

> Q "I was always scared. I was not a confident human being. That's why I took drugs. From the age of 12 onwards I had nothing to do with people my own age. You spend your time trying to feel as important as you think everyone else is... I wanted to be reassured. I felt like I was Sleeping Beauty, a sweet little wafty thing just waiting to be awakened by my prince." (Lesley-Anne Down, *Style*, 2/3/97)

Paul Downing

b. 14 December 1945, 15.58 GMT, Hull, England, 53N45, 0W20.
Lois Rodden q. him in 1979, from his BC (a twin born three minutes earlier lived a few days). RR: AA.
Guitarist and keyboard player from 1966 with bands in Europe and the USA. He is also a record producer.

Nick Drake

✪ b. 19 June 1948, 07.15 LT (-6.5 hrs = -6 hrs 30 mins), Rangoon, Burma, 16N47, 96E10.
John Etherington q. a letter from Drake's mother, Molly Drake. RR: A.

Hugely influential singer and songwriter. After his birth Drake and his family moved to Bombay but in 1952 the family relocated to Tanworth-in-Arden, England. Drake spent much of his youth on his own, displaying a melancholy and self-containment that would later be characteristic in his musical recordings. His album *Five Leaves Left* (1969) was considered unusually mature for a debut release and heralded a great future for the prodigy. When his second release failed commercially, a bout of severe depression followed. Nevertheless he released *Pink Moon* in 1972. In April 1972 he checked himself into a psychiatric hospital, saying he didn't understand the point of living. He felt no emotion, simply "numb –

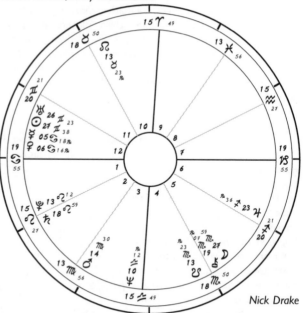

Nick Drake

dead inside." On 25 November 1974 (as TR Saturn hovered near the Ascendant) he was found dead in his bedroom. The verdict was suicide but relatives and friends felt his overdose was accidental.

Q

"His heart often carried him away. He carried other people's troubles and worries on his shoulders, and was always terribly depressed when something happened to somebody he knew... Of himself he rarely spoke." (Father Rodney Drake, as quoted on the website www.algonet.se/~iguana/DRAKE/DRAKE.html)

"Nick was very obstinate as a little boy. He knew absolutely what he wanted, always. He was much quieter than I was in many ways. I think Nick was both a loner and a leader. Whereas I would be a follower and seek friends, Nick would go off on his own and people would follow him. He'd definitely be a leader. Nick never shouted. If Nick shouted it was really bad, he was deeply upset. I think it would take a lot to make Nick angry and then when he was he wouldn't be able to get over it quickly. And I think he found it difficult in some ways to separate his aggression from his hostility." (Sister and actress Gabrielle Drake, as quoted on the above website)

Molly Duncan – see Average White Band
Andy Dunlop – see Travis

Joe Dunlop

b. 16 February 1942, 09.30 GDT, Galston, Ayrshire, Scotland, 55N36, 04W23.
Gerard q. BC (Joseph Johnston Strain Dunlop). RR: AA.

Film, Stage and TV actor with credits with the RSC and noted appearances in *Take the High Road* and four series of *Don't Wait Up* (which ran from 1983-1990). Dunlop trained at the Royal Academy of Music and Drama.

John Dunn

b. 4 March 1934, 21.50 GMT, Hillhead, Glasgow, Scotland, 55N53, 04W18.
Gerard q. BC (John Churchill Dunn). RR: AA.
Radio Disc Jockey.

EASTENDERS

Daring, controversial and aiming for social reality, the series began on 19 February 1985 at 19.00. It was created by Julia Smith and Tony Holland who had met in September 1971, and were approached to create the series in March 1983. They presented the format to TV bosses at 19.00 on 1 February 1984. One highlight in the series came in October 1985 with television's longest single scene, when viewers discovered the identity of the father of Michelle's baby. The series topped the ratings for the first time three weeks later. 1986-7 were pivotal years with viewing audiences of over 20 million (the two Christmas Day 1986 episodes enjoyed audiences of 29 and 31 million). Julia Smith, who controlled the show's direction until 1989, died on 19 June 1997 (TR Saturn conjunct the show's EQHS 8th). For further information, see the profiles of the following *EastEnders'* actors: John Altman, June Brown, Michael Cashman, Pat Coombs, Linda Davidson, Letitia Dean, Leslie Grantham, Martin Kemp, Sophie Lawrence, Sean Maguire, Barbara Windsor, Anna Wing. (*The EastEnders Programme Guide* by Josephine Munro, Virgin, 1994.)

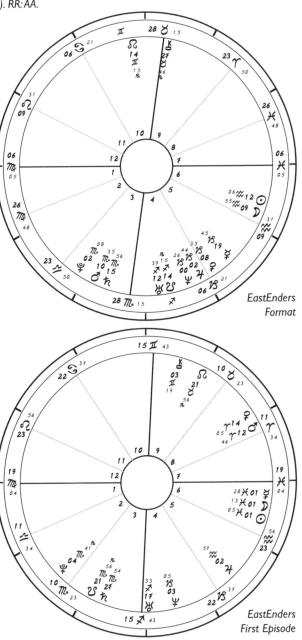

EastEnders
Format

EastEnders
First Episode

Sheena Easton

b. 27 April 1959, 15.40 GDT, Bellshill, 55N49, 04W01.
FCC q. BC in hand (Sheena Shirley Orr). RR: AA.

Plucky singer Sheena Easton was packaged for a wide, commercial audience (Sun opposite Neptune) and, with the help of a TV show documenting her bid for fame, was TV's original manufactured pop star (Venus-MC in Gemini) – polished, preened and packaged for the British public. In a profession where fame is fleeting, Easton, much to the critics' surprise, reinvented herself and refused to be categorised (although with Venus on the MC, she has had to fight to be taken seriously). With Sun opposite Neptune and a versatile Gemini MC, her varied musical interests led to a US chart feat: she is the only artist to have had Top Five hits in the US pop, adult contemporary, R&B, dance and country charts. In May 1979 she auditioned

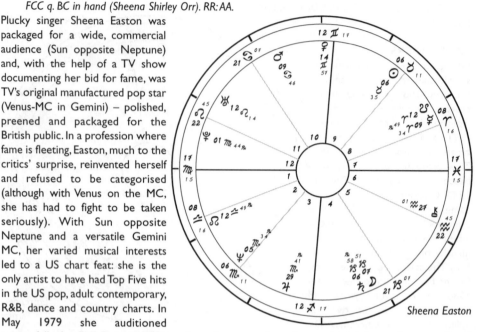

Sheena Easton

successfully for EMI Records, and graduated as a teacher of speech and drama from the Royal Scottish Academy of Music and Drama the following month. A minor chart release with EMI in April 1980 was followed on 2 July 1980 at 20.10 by a magic wand documentary, *The Big Time* presented by Esther Rantzen (qv), which chronicled her search for stardom. By September, with the release of *9 To 5* (a US chart-topper in May 1981) and the re-release of *Modern Girl*, spandex queen Easton had two simultaneous UK Top Ten hits (as TR Jupiter crossed the Ascendant). (It is interesting to note the synastry between Easton and presenter Rantzen: Rantzen's Jupiter conjuncts Easton's Sun (the starmaker), and if Rantzen's birth time is reliable, their Ascendants and Midheavens are conjunct.) Commentators noted how fearless, focused and hungry for success the young Easton was (her ambition and backbone can be attributed to a Moon-Saturn conjunction in Capricorn opposite Mars in the 10th). In 1981 her Bond theme hit the charts (propelled by a landmark appearance in the film's opening credits), and the following year she performed in the most melodramatic musical number the Academy Awards had ever seen! Nevertheless chart success continued. With Virgo Rising and MC ruler Mercury in a T-Square, she had to fight her wholesome, girl-next-door image and is known to be tough, prickly and straight-talking. Her association with Prince in 1985 and 1987 brought further hit records with a new, raunchier look (Mars in 10th) when she invited listeners inside her *Sugar Walls*. Approaching 30 Easton decided to be less reliant on chart positions and airplay, mellowed out and even considered retiring. Instead she took the decision to concentrate on theatre and live performances (Sun opposite Neptune). In October 1996 she began a scheduled ten-week stint on Broadway in the musical *Grease* (her first Broadway outing had been in March 1992 in the panned revival of *Man of La Mancha*, which had come after a trial run in Chicago in November 1991). Since her last chart success, she has married, divorced, made occasional appearances on television, and become a US citizen. Easton's success in the US and Japan has always been greater than in the UK and she survived a June 1990 homecoming concert in Glasgow, during which she was pelted with bottles from the rowdy, drunk crowd. In 1994 she adopted the first of two children. By the mid-90s she was listed as one of Britain's wealthiest women with an eight-figure fortune, and has designed a collection of dolls. Easton has married three times (at 18 for 8 months, in 1984 for 18 months and in August 1997 for 11 months). In 2000 she was performing with David Cassidy at a glitzy Las Vegas show and released her 16th album, *Fabulous*.

"If my only motivation was money I'd have given up after the first million. I have a desire to create – which curses and blesses your life. I was more of a people-pleaser when I started, but at least now I'm tougher and say no... 'Artistic temperament' is a cliche because it's true. Mostly we're attention junkies who go on stage to escape something in ourselves. I'm escaping a lot of things." (Sheena Easton, *Radio Times*, 11/11/2000)

"I have to take full responsibility – for my diabolical choices, for my inability to compromise, for my lack of maturity, for everything I brought to the table... I'm a 40-year-old woman in all other aspects of my life, but I'm 15 when it comes to being married." (Sheena Easton, *The Times Magazine*, c.2000)

Valerie Edmond
✪ *b. 12 October 1967, 11.20 GDT, Glasgow, Scotland, 55N54, 04W11.*
Gerard q. BC. RR: AA.
Tall (six foot) actress who won TV roles in *The Crow Road* (1996) and *Kavanagh QC* (1997).

Joe Egan
b. 18 October 1947, 22.45 GDT, Barshaw Hospital, Paisley, Scotland, 55N51, 04W23.
Gerard q. BC. RR: AA.
Egan formed Stealers Wheel with long-time friend Gerry Rafferty (qv) and released two albums (and a hit in May 1973) before quitting, disillusioned by management problems.

Kenneth Elliott
b. 28 November 1929, 02.00 GMT, Dundee, Scotland, 56N28, 03W00.
Gerard q. BC (Kenneth James Elliott). RR: AA.
Editor, musician and scholar. An authority on early Scottish music.

Michael Elphick
b. 19 September 1946, 11.10 GDT, Chichester, England, 50N50, 0W48.
FCC q. him. RR: A.

A popular face on TV, Elphick had a long list of comedy series to his credit, including *Auf Wiedersehen, Pet* (November 1983 – TR Saturn on Venus and Ascendant – to May 1986), *Three Up, Two Down* (April 1985 to June 1989, with Angela Thorne, qv) and *Boon* (1986-92). As a young trainee technician Elphick was encouraged by Laurence Olivier (qv) to apply to the Central School of Speech and Drama in London. After many years on stage and in small TV parts, he won the lead role in the comedy *Private Schulz* (May to June 1981). His final role was in the soap *EastEnders* in the summer of 2001. Elphick often spoke of his alcoholism (Moon square Neptune) in interviews before his death on 7 September 2002.

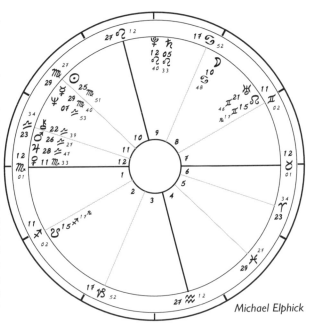

Michael Elphick

Ben Elton

b. 3 May 1959, 23.30 GDT, Catford, London, England, 51N26, 0W00.
FCC q. him. RR: A.

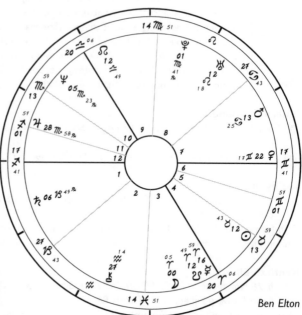

Ben Elton

Highly successful left-wing stand-up comedian (vehemently anti-Thatcher, Sun square Uranus), scriptwriter and novelist. This intelligent motormouth performer (Mercury in Aries square Mars) with a Sagittarian optimistic streak was originally influenced by P.G. Wodehouse and the glamour of Noel Coward's (qv) life (Coward's Ascendant is conjunct Elton's MC). Elton was approached by Rik Mayall (qv) in January 1981 to write *The Young Ones*, and since then he has written comedies from *Blackadder* to *The Thin Blue Line*. He married in 1994. Six of his novels have been bestsellers, and his fourth book, *Popcorn*, was published on 5 August 1996 and addressed the connection between film and violence. A stage play of the book premiered on 20 March 1997, and since then he has become equally famous for his TV scripts, novels and plays. His film, *Maybe Baby*, based on his novel *Inconceivable*, was released in June 2000 and dealt with IVF treatment, which Elton and his wife went through before their twins were born on 13 August 1999. Elton wrote the musical *The Beautiful Game* with Andrew Lloyd Webber (qv), which premiered on 26 September 2000. A tribute to the band Queen, *We Will Rock You*, opened in London on 14 May 2002. *High Society*, his latest novel, was published on 7 November 2002.

Q

"When he teamed up with the famously conservative Lloyd Webber... Elton-bashers saw it as proof that he'd sold out. They missed the point. Despite having an overdeveloped social conscience, Elton has always been an entertainer rather than a polemicist... He has a mortal fear of causing offence." (Nick Curtis, *Evening Standard*, 3/5/02)

"The angry cynic is always admired more than the enthusiast, and I'm an enthusiast. I'm not cool. I've never been cool." (Ben Elton, *Evening Standard*, 3/5/02)

"For all his triumphs, Ben Elton has an image problem which at times makes him frantic with denial and rebuttal, his good nature straining to contain what he perceives as a wild slur on his character... He is temperamentally unsuited to confrontation... too twitchy, too intense, too dark with the complexity he denies. He compensates by being sweepingly nice." (Lesley White, *The Sunday Times Magazine*, c.2000)

Keith Emerson

✪ b. 2 November 1944, 22.15 GDT, Todmorden, England, 53N43, 02W05.
Amy Rodden q. him, 1977. RR: A.

A former member of Nice, Emerson founded the supergroup Emerson, Lake and Palmer in the early 70s (first gig – 25 August 1970), and developed a reputation for fusing classical sound with rock music. Emerson is known for his wild and dramatic antics on stage (note Moon-Uranus opposite Venus in EQHS 5th).

Dick Emery

✪ b. 19 February 1915, 23.50 GMT, St. Pancras, London, England, 51N32, 0W07.
From the book Ooh You Are Awful... But I Like You: The Story of Dick Emery by Faye Hillier (Sidgwick & Jackson, 2001), which states he was born just before midnight. RR: B.

Comedy great. Emery worked with Tony Hancock (qv) on stage in 1948 before gaining a reputation for comedy on the radio show *Educating Archie*. But it was his appearances in *The Army Game* (from 27 September 1960) as camp Chubby Catchpole that made him a star (TR Uranus conjunct MC, and TR Neptune near Ascendant). *The Dick Emery Show* began on 13 July 1963 and ran for 18 years. In the feel-good sketch show he played a variety of hilariously over-the-top characters (MC ruler Sun conjunct Jupiter-Mercury) including Camp Clarence, Kitchener Lampwick and Randy Mandy (who uttered Emery's most famous line "Ooh, you are awful, but I like you"). In 1972 he was Television Entertainer of the Year. At an early age Emery

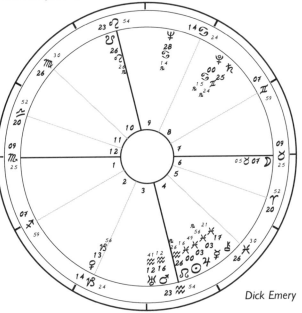

Dick Emery

joined his parents' entertainment act, which provided him with invaluable experience in variety and pantomime (Jupiter). Post-war he guested on the Goons' (qv) radio show. He was married five times. Hospitalised in December 1982, after taking pills for gout, he died on 2 January 1983.

Harry Enfield

✪ b. 30 May 1961, 00.30 GDT, Horsham, England, 51N04, 0W21.
Maggie Hyde q. his letter. RR: A.

Comic chameleon Enfield began his TV career contributing voices to the satire *Spitting Image*, and took to the stage doing stand-up in *Saturday Live* (1986) and *Friday Night Live*. In the latter he introduced the definitive 80s get-rich-quick yuppie Loadsamoney and the naive kabab house owner Stavros, both of which were immensely popular and iconic comedy characters in Britain. Enfield is also famous for his other comic creations Tim Nice-but-Dim, The Slobs and Smashy and Nicey, all from the sketch-based *Harry Enfield's Television Show* (1990). In 2000 he starred in the film *Kevin and Perry Go Large*. Note Enfield's Moon-MC square Pluto and Jupiter-Saturn conjunction on the Ascendant (suggesting his ability to reflect and influence the 80s mood with comical stereotypes).

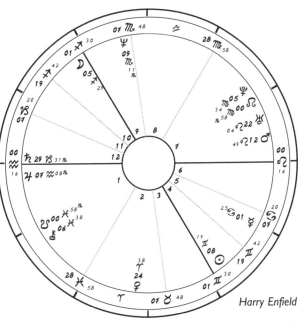

Harry Enfield

Brian Eno

> b. 15 May 1948, 03.50 GDT, Melton, England, 52N06, 01E20.
> Tony Matthews q. Eno's mother. RR: A.

In January 1971 androgynous electronics whiz Brian Eno joined Roxy Music as a technical advisor, later assuming a more substantial role in the look and direction of the group. A personality clash with Bryan Ferry (qv) led to his departure from the group on 21 June 1973 to embark on solo projects. He has become a much sought-after producer due to acclaimed work with various bands – his credits including the best-selling U2 albums *The Unforgettable Fire* (October 1984) and *The Joshua Tree* (1987).

Roger Eno

> b. 29 April 1959, 18.00 GDT, Woodbridge, Suffolk, England, 52N06, 01E19.
> Tony Matthews from Eno's mother. RR: A.

Pianist and younger brother of Brian Eno (qv).

John Entwistle – see Who

Brian Epstein

☄ b. 19 September 1934, 04.30 GDT, Liverpool, England, 53N25, 02W55.
> From *New World Astrology*, October 1967, no source (Marc Penfield speculates 19.00). RR: C.

Manager famous for his role in creating the musical phenomenon of the century, The Beatles (qv). Since his death by accidental overdose on 27 August 1967, there has been much speculation around his sexuality and excessive drug use.

David Essex

✪ b. 23 July 1947, 06.20 GDWT, West Ham, London, England, 51N31, 0E01.
> Penny Thornton, in *Romancing the Stars*, q. him. (N.B. Sy Scholfield q. his autobiography *A Charmed Life* (Orion, 2002). p. 1, for "I was born just before dawn... in West Ham." If his quote to Thornton was "dawn", the statement in his book would suggest the birth occurred 10-15 minutes earlier than 06.20. According to *The Times*, dawn was at 06.09.) RR: A.

As a child, singer-actor Essex was a virtual recluse until he won a place in his first rock band at 16 in 1963. A recording contract came his way the following year, but it took seven long years before he hit the music charts. As a stage performer, Essex became a star 'overnight' when he appeared as Jesus in the rock musical *Godspell* from 17 November 1971 (he was cast in Summer 1971 following an Eclipse on his Sun/Ascendant). Two years later he wrote the single *Rock On*, which became his first major hit. Between 1973-5 Essex was one of Britain's most popular performers, becoming the teenage heartthrob and pinup of the time and enjoying the sexual benefits his status offered him (MC in Aries). From June 1978 he moved to the West End, playing Che Guevara* in the

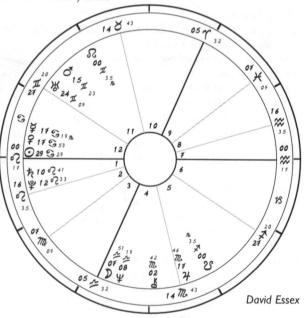

David Essex

* Che Guevara b. 14 May 1928, 03.05 AST (+4), Rosario, Argentina, 32S57, 60W40. From his mother's records (BC stated 14 June to hide her pregnancy outside marriage). RR: AA.

production of *Evita* (Guevara's Uranus-Ascendant is conjunct Essex's MC and conjunct the Moon of Antonio Banderas, who later played the role). Essex's father died in January 1994 and his mentor/manager died in June 1996 (as TR Saturn crossed his MC). On 10 December 1996 (a short while after TR Uranus crossed his Descendant) Essex divorced his wife of nearly 30 years, although they had been separated for 17 of those years. He began a 50-date tour of Britain in May 1997 and married on 4 July 1997 (TR Neptune on Descendant opposite Sun). His autobiography, *A Charmed Life*, was published on 29 August 2002.

> Q "It's imperative to me to believe that there are more adventures ahead... I like to feel there are new situations ahead, a new trip, a new job, and another woman, who knows?" (David Essex, *Daily Mail*, 17/8/02)

Don Estelle

b. 22 May 1937, 05.15 GDT, Manchester, England, 53N30, 02W15.
Rosemary Shields q. him personally. RR: A.

Lovable actor most widely known for his role in *It Ain't Half Hot Mum* from 1974-81. With Jupiter on the MC, he remains a popular star from the show's success.

Lee Latchford Evans – see Steps

Kenny Everett

b. 25 December 1944, 03.00 GDT, Crosby, England, 53N30, 03W02.
From his autobiography The Custard Stops at Hadfield (Willow Books, 1982), p. 8. RR: B.

Famous on TV from 1978, Everett was an iconoclastic, camp and outrageous performer (note the Sagittarian and Aquarian planets) known for his brilliant, outlandish creations (Sun-Mercury square Neptune), which included biker Sid Snot, Marcel Wave, and busty starlet Cupid Stunt, who crossed her legs with "an extravagant lack of discretion." Everett had a mix of zany, mischievous and dry humour (Venus in Aquarius and the strong Saturn), and he was known for single-handedly transforming the fledgling art of music radio (MC ruler Moon square Pluto). A master of bad taste, Everett had embarked upon a career in pirate radio in 1964 and had the opportunity to travel with The Beatles (qv) during their last tour in August 1966. He

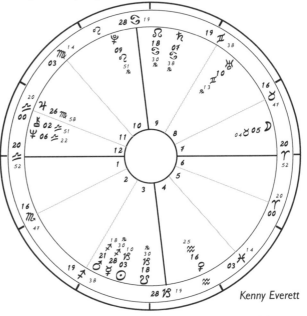

Kenny Everett

joined Radio One from 25 December 1967 but annoyed bosses by being too controversial. A tame joke told on air (on 18 July 1970, about a Cabinet Minister's wife) gave them the chance to fire him three days later (with Sun opposition Saturn he was made a target by those in authority). As a child Everett (born Maurice Cole) was cherubic and inquisitive, dismantling everything in the house. At 12 he had spent two years training for the priesthood (note the prominent Saturn). His personal life appeared to be a constant battle to reconcile his homosexuality with his religious beliefs (his Venus-Pluto opposition suggests this emotional dilemma was always at the forefront), a battle hindered by an inability to deal with emotion and make up his mind (Libra). On 14 May 1975 the newspapers reported a suicide attempt. During the Summer of 1975 he decided to come out of the closet to himself and his wife (TR Saturn crossed EQHS 10th and MC). Finally in the mid-80s he spoke openly to the Press about his sexuality. His wife Lee said, "Everyone wanted to mother him," and Kenny has been described as naive and hygiene-obsessed. He loved to escape to the quiet countryside, often giving God marks out of ten for particular nature spots. He had a long-standing love-hate friendship with Freddie Mercury (qv), formed after he gave Queen a platform by promoting their song *Bohemian Rhapsody*. Although his TV show (with voluptuous vamp Cleo Rocos* regularly by his side) attracted 15 million viewers, he quit in 1989 and admitted to always having preferred the spontaneity of radio (three planets in the 3rd House). Everett died on 4 April 1995 of an AIDS-related illness having just reconciled with the church, which allowed him to have the requiem mass he craved. Half-Greek Rocos, whose Sun-Mercury conjunction flanks Everett's MC, wrote a fond memoir of their friendship, *Bananas Forever*, and is now a TV host of travel programmes and a producer of stage shows.

> Q "One of the funniest and most inventive broadcasters that Britain has produced. Yet he was also an angst-ridden depressive who tried to take his own life. [He] was a rebel who defied the establishment... yet he was also deemed a Thatcherite... [He] was a glittering socialite... yet he suffered continual crises of confidence over his appearance, his ability and his popularity." (*In the Best Possible Taste* by David Lister, Bloomsbury, 1996)

Pat Fairley – see Marmalade

Al Fairweather
b. 12 June 1927, 11.30 GDT, Portobello, Edinburgh, Scotland, 55N57, 03W07.
Gerard q. BC (Alister Fairweather). RR: AA.
Bandleader, arranger, songwriter and jazz trumpeter. His partnership with architect-musician Sandy Brown began in 1941. From 1954 Fairweather performed with the West Indian-influenced Fairweather-Brown All-Stars for ten years. He suffered a heart attack in 1983. D. 21 June 1993.

Marianne Faithfull
☉ b. 29 December 1946, 12.30 GMT, Hampstead, London, England, 51N34, 0W11.
☙ Nick Dagan Best q. her personally for between "noon and one in the afternoon," from her mother's recollection. An inebriated Faithfull added that she was born on Boxing Day (26). Sy Scholfield q. The Times, "FAITHFULL. – On Dec. 29, 1946, to Eva, wife of R. Glynn Faithfull, 13 Gayton Crescent, N.W.3 – a daughter." (*Times*, 3 January 1947, p. 1). RR: C.

Iconic singer and captivating symbol of the swinging sixties. Ex-convent schoolgirl Faithfull is most famous for her doomed relationship with Mick Jagger (qv, Rolling Stones), as well as her battle with drugs and suicide attempts (including one on 8 July 1969). Following her discovery in June 1964, her first pop single, *As Tears Go By*, hit the Top Ten in September that year. She appeared on stage in *Three Sisters* (April 1967) and in the title role on film in *Girl on a Motorcycle*. Faithfull married artist John Dunbar on 6 May 1965 but the couple split in early 1966 when she became involved with Mick Jagger (their affair lasted almost four years). She suffered a personal loss when she miscarried Jagger's baby on 22 November 1968. She

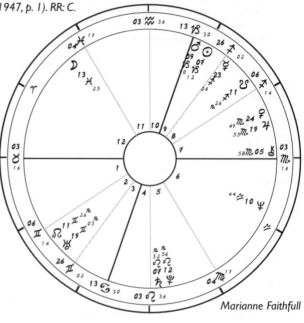

Marianne Faithfull

* Cleo Rocos b. 24 July 1962, 23.40 BZT (+3), Rio de Janeiro, Brazil, 22S54, 43W14. From her to Laura Boomer. RR: A.

reemerged in November 1975 with *Dreamin' My Dreams*. Faithfull resumed her career in May 1990 with a heralded performance at the Dominion Theatre, her first concert since 1981.

Simon Fanshawe

✪ *b. 26 December 1956, 04.45 GMT, Devizes, England, 51N22, 01W59.*
From him to Laura Boomer. Birthplace confirmed at Registry. RR: A.

A witty comedian, Fanshawe was a co-presenter (with Esther Rantzen, qv) on *That's Life* for one season, with a popular and bitchy review of the week's odd events. Since this initial stint on TV he has been a regular and excellent writer for many magazines. He has also given a great deal of time to fund-raising for various charities. Fanshawe began his career as a live stand-up comedian, becoming a regular at the Edinburgh Fringe.

Eric Faulkner – see Bay City Rollers

Craig Ferguson

✪ *b. 17 May 1962, 18.10 GDT, Balornock Road, Glasgow, Scotland, 55N53, 04W14.*
Gerard q. BC. RR: AA.

Comedian Ferguson was known for his merciless alter-ego Bing Hitler in the 80s before moving to the US in January 1995 and finding fame on *The Drew Carey Show* in 1996 and in Hollywood films (including *The Big Tease*, 1999 and *Saving Grace*, 2000, for which he wrote the screenplay and co-produced). He plays the lead in *Bob the Builder*, due for cinema release in 2004. He married in July 1998.

Steve Ferrone – see Average White Band

Bryan Ferry

b. 26 September 1945, 11.30 GDT, Washington, Tyne & Wear, England, 54N55, 01W30.
Ian Richards q. him. RR: A.

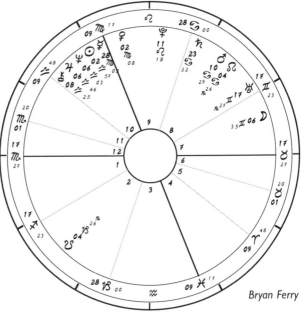

After studying Fine Art and working as a teacher (he was fired for turning some classes into music sessions), smooth crooner Bryan Ferry formed Roxy Music in November 1971 (TR Pluto approaching a conjunction to his Sun, ruler of EQHS 10th). The group began attracting attention in early 1973. Ferry later spent time developing his own solo career after the release of an album in October 1973. In December 1977 he spent three months in Montreux recording a new album, *The Bride Stripped Bare*, released in October 1978 (as TR Saturn conjunct his MC). With the prominent Jupiter and Neptune, Ferry admits to having been a "slave to drugs." He married on 26 June 1982 but the couple split in August 2002, and around this time his new album, *Frantic*, was receiving an enthusiastic response from critics. In March 2003 the couple were facing a bitter divorce battle.

Bryan Ferry

Q "I think I am often regarded as a bit aloof, rather snooty, serious and humourless." (Bryan Ferry, *Style, The Sunday Times*, 14/7/02)
"Ferry can be catty, camp, hilariously self-deprecating, shameless, vain and wickedly amusing – particularly on matters sartorial." (Simon Mills, *Style, The Sunday Times*, 14/7/02)

Fenella Fielding

b. 17 November 1927, 22.40 GMT, Euston, London, England, 51N32, 0W08.
Calculated from a birth chart in Penny Thornton's *Sons and Lovers* which had no data; the reprint, *Romancing the Stars*, p. 342, incorrectly gave 11 July 1927, 10.44 pm. Both editions, however, present a chart that corresponds with the data given above. Data from Fielding to Thornton. RR: A.

Known for her devastating wit, sexy voice and a campy vamp's persona to match, Fielding, with three planets in Scorpio, became a sensation performing as the nymphomaniac in the musical *Valmouth* (with Cleo Laine, qv) from October 1958, earning the 'sexy' tag which has kept her employed and typecast ever since. She made her mark in two *Carry On* films and her acrimonious relationship with co-star Kenneth Williams (qv) was legendary. Remarkably kept, with the same gothic hairstyle framing an unlined face, fabulous Fielding is still active in the entertainment industry and a regular contributor to *Carry On* debates and reunions.

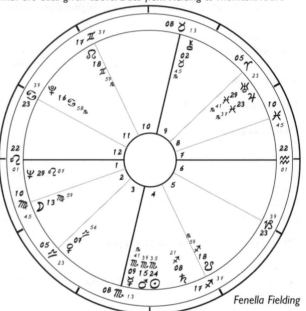

Fenella Fielding

Gracie Fields

✪ b. 9 January 1898, 01.15 GMT, Rochdale, England, 53N38, 02W09.
Astrological Quarterly (Spring 1951) q. her mother. (N.B. Sabian Symbols #337 gives 07.00; Margaret Hone used a time of 23.00.) RR: A.

In her time Gracie Fields, with Jupiter and the Moon prominent, was one of the highest paid entertainers in the world (both rulers of the audience-based EQHS 5th are conjunct in the 2nd House of money and resources). A comedienne and entertainer from the early 30s, she had begun performing at 13 in music-halls. (Note the impressive 3rd stellium in Capricorn with a Leo Moon on the MC, a sign of lasting popularity and her pushy, ambitious mother.) She became an overnight sensation on 25 February 1924 when the revue *Mr Tower of London* opened in the West End. Fields brought optimism, hope and energy to audiences during the Depression years, and her fame spread to the USA only

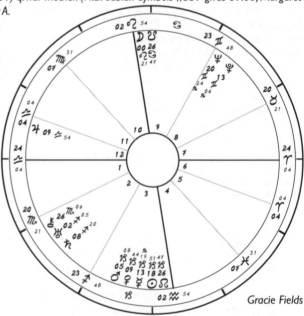

Gracie Fields

after a tailor-made role in *Holy Matrimony* in 1943. Her personal life was host to tragedy and violence: she was raped at 12, and in June 1939 she had a hysterectomy to rid cervical cancer (TR Pluto conjunct Moon). The first of three marriages took place on 21 April 1923. D. 27 September 1979.

Joseph Fiennes

✪ b. 26 May 1970, 22.30 MET, Salisbury, England, 51N05, 01W48.
FCC q. BC in hand (a twin, Joseph Alberic Twisleton-Wykeham-Fiennes). RR: AA.

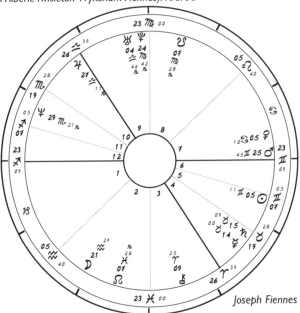

Joseph Fiennes

After a screen debut in 1996, Fiennes wooed audiences in the film *Shakespeare in Love* (released December 1998), yet Fiennes was the only major cast member to be overlooked when award nominations were announced. With Jupiter-MC and Sagittarius Rising, he was looking for more meaning and retreated from the limelight for a while, travelling to India for six months, seemingly uncomfortable with show business and celebrity. Later he returned to theatre and independent films. His film *Enemy at the Gates* was released in England on 16 March 2001 and the film *Killing Me Softly* followed. In 2003 he was on the London stage with *Love's Labours Lost*. The youngest of six children, Fiennes and his famous older brother Ralph lived an unconventional, bohemian childhood, moving 14 times in nearly as many years. Joseph left school at 16 to study art but turned to the theatre with stints at the Young Vic, Guildhall and the RSC.

Q "I wanted to be true to my word about jumping from one extreme to the other and not get caught up in the need to 'follow up'." (Joseph Fiennes, *Evening Standard*, 27/2/01)

Peter Finch

b. 28 September 1916, 14.00 GDT, South Kensington, London, England, 51N30, 0W12.
From *Peter Finch: A Biography* by Trader Faulkner (Angus & Robertson, 1979), p. 20, q. an interview with Finch's mother, "She told me Finchie made his first appearance at two in the afternoon of September 28th, 1916... South Kensington." RR: A.

Based in Australia from the age of ten, Finch became a comedian's stooge in vaudeville and starred in his first film in 1936. He also made an impact as an actor on radio (Moon and Mercury on the MC). He had had a nomadic childhood after his parents' divorce when he was two. From 1949 he returned to London as a protege of Laurence Olivier (qv) and won acclaim in the theatre almost immediately. Good film roles emerged in the mid-50s (he was later to collect four British Academy Awards). His role as the homosexual doctor in *Sunday Bloody Sunday* won much notice and an Oscar nomination. Finch also played the lead in *The Trials of Oscar Wilde** (released in the US on 27 June 1960) and their synastry is startling: Finch's Mercury-Moon-MC conjuncts Wilde's Sun in Libra, Finch's Mars is on Wilde's Mercury, his Sun hits Wilde's Venus, and his Venus is near to Wilde's Moon in Leo. Whilst promoting the film *Network* he suffered a fatal heart attack on 14 January 1977. The film, released in November 1976, won him a posthumous Academy Award on 29 March 1977. Finch married three times (on 21 April 1943, 4 July 1959 and 9 November 1973).

---

* Oscar Wilde b. 16 October 1854, 03.00 LMT (03.25 UT), Dublin, Ireland. Cyril Fagan q. Wilde's baptismal certificate. RR: AA.

James Finlayson

b. 27 August 1887, 22.50 GMT, Larbert, Scotland, 56N01, 03W50.

Gerard q. BC (James Henderson Finlayson). (N.B. Paul Wright's Scottish Birth Data collection gave 31 January 1877 in error.) RR: AA.

Finlayson was touring the US in a Scottish production when, in 1916, he decided to stay in Los Angeles and try his luck in films. His most memorable appearances were with Hal Roach from 1923 and with Laurel and Hardy from 1927. D. 9 October 1953, Los Angeles.

Linda Finnie

b. 9 May 1952, 17.45 GDT, Paisley, Scotland, 55N50, 04W24.

Gerard q. BC (Linda Agnes Finnie). RR: AA.

Mezzo-soprano concert and opera singer (Saturn strong, conjunct the Ascendant). Finnie studied at Royal Scottish Academy of Music and Drama, made her debut in 1976, and was the winner of the Kathleen Ferrier Prize in 1977. From 1979, she was a guest at Covent Garden and on European tours.

Fish

b. 25 April 1958, 17.07 GDT, Simpson Memorial Maternity Pavilion, Edinburgh, Scotland, 55N57, 03W12.

Gerard q. BC (Derek William Dick). RR: AA.

Bombastic front-man with progressive rock band Marillion from January 1981. The band won a following from continuous gigging and they hit the charts in late 1982. Fish was known for structuring a series of elaborate concept albums. Their most successful album, *Misplaced Childhood*, topped the charts in its first week of release in June 1985, the same month they hit #2 on the singles chart with *Kayleigh*. Fish, who acquired his nickname from a landlord who objected to the lengthy periods he spent in the bath, announced his intention in September 1988 (Saturn Return) to pursue a solo career. In 2000 he began an acting career.

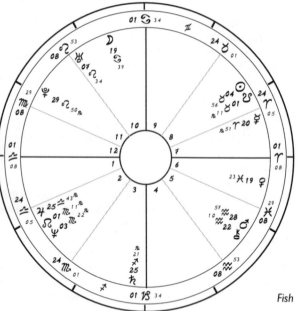

Fish

Archie Fisher

b. 23 October 1939, 05.05 GDT, Redlands Hospital, Glasgow, Scotland, 55N53, 04W17.

Gerard q. BC (Archibald MacDonald Fisher). RR: AA.

Pioneering composer, folk-singer and acoustic guitarist who released an eponymous debut album in 1956. Fisher was artistic director from 1988-1992 of the Edinburgh International Folk Festival. He formed a successful partnership with Barbara Dickson (qv) on some of her earlier recordings (his Moon falls on Dickson's MC).

Lesley Fitz-Simons

b. 23 September 1961, 07.30 GDT, Glasgow, Scotland, 55N53, 04W17.

Gerard q. BC. RR: AA.

Actress best known for her continuing role as Sheila Ramsey in *Take the High Road* from 1983.

Tom Fleming

b. 29 June 1927, 10.20 GDT, north Edinburgh, Scotland, 55N59, 03W13.
Gerard q. BC (Thomas Kelman Fleming). RR: AA.

Poet, director and actor, whose stage debut was in India during 1945. He directed and starred in plays at the Gateway Theatre in Edinburgh from 1953 until 1962, when he joined the RSC (*Cymbeline*, 1962 and *The Tempest*, 1963). Since 1952 he has worked as a commentator on radio and TV.

Derek Forbes – see Simple Minds
Dean Ford – see Marmalade

Bill Forsyth

b. 29 July 1946, 11.00 GDT, Medwyn Street, Glasgow, Scotland, 55N52, 04W20.
Gerard q. BC (William David Forsyth). RR: AA.

A filmmaker since 1963. Acclaim came from 1979 at the Edinburgh Film Festival with *That Sinking Feeling*. He also won praise for *Gregory's Girl* in 1980 and *Local Hero* in 1983.

Bruce Forsyth

✪ *b. 22 February 1928, 03.30 GMT, Edmonton, London, England, 51N37, 0W04.*
FCC q. his autobiography Bruce (2001), breech birth (same information from Peter West). RR: B.

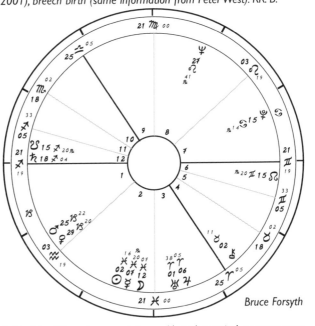

Bruce Forsyth

Forsyth is Britain's most recognisable game show host. His ability to ad-lib, cajole contestants and laugh at himself have guaranteed top ratings over five decades. He began entertaining at 14 as Boy Bruce, the Mighty Atom and joined various double acts before landing his first TV appearance in 1954. Jaunty Forsyth was asked by Lew Grade to host *Sunday Night at the London Palladium* (from 1958 to 1971, plus a short-lived revival in 2000) and introduced the first of his many catchphrases, "I'm in charge." He became an overnight sensation and an unlikely sex symbol. His celebrity was tainted by an acrimonious public dispute with his wife because of his alleged philandering. From 2 October 1971 he presented *The Generation Game* (with 26 million viewers at its peak) and married co-presenter Anthea Redfern. (After it's demise in 1977, Forsyth later returned to present the show in 1990 for five years before being replaced by Jim Davidson, qv.) In 1995 he took over at the helm of *Bruce's Price is Right*, the popular game show. When the show was scheduled out of primetime and *Play Your Cards Right* was facing the axe, Forsyth staged a press conference in October 2000 to announce his retirement. He was brought out of retirement in August 2002 by TV bosses to host a new series of *Play Your Cards Right*. Forsyth is a master of the catchphrase ("You're so much better than last week's audience" and "Nice to see you, to see you nice") – he was born with Mercury-Moon as well as Saturn Rising in Sagittarius. He also has an enviable ability to put people at ease whilst mocking them with gentle sarcasm (the Sagittarian Ascendant). He has been married three times and has six children.

Samantha Fox

○ *b. 15 April 1966, 04.30 GDT, London, England, 51N30, 0W10.*

● *FCC q. Shiloh Costa, a webmaster for a Fox site, who believes the data ("about 04.30... Mile End Hospital, London") came from a diary that was sold as fan merchandise back in the mid-80s, no source was given inside. (Helene Schnitzer q. Fox personally for 06.00, which may simply be an estimate, although TRs 'fit' extremely well using this time). Both charts are presented for the reader's discernment. RR: DD.*

Former Page Three girl and voted the Face and Body of 1983, Samantha Fox, with her cheeky smile, girlish looks and adult body, was a media sensation as a topless model from age 16 (February 1983) with an exclusive contract with *The Sun*, until she quit in June 1987 (TR Jupiter conjunct Sun). (Note Neptune trines Mercury and squares the Moon for tabloid interest and media sensation.) Fox's imposing physical assets were her two finer points: Sun conjunct Mars in Aries. From March 1986 Fox, who had ambitions to be the next Stevie Nicks (see Peter Green), had a successful singing career (30 million albums sold), and found music fame as an unlikely icon in India. A famous low-point back in the UK was presenting the embarrassing Brit Awards ceremony on 13 February 1989, in which she and Mick Fleetwood waded through a disastrous, incoherent show — she's never been able to live down the fiasco. In May 1988 the tabloids reported that she fallen out with her father, accusing him embezzling much of her fortune. She took further steps to recover then money in 1992 and won £125,000 in late July 1993. She was awarded damages in May 1995 (her Saturn Return) and her father died in September 2000 without a reconciliation. Fox became a born again Christian in the mid-90s and shocked readers in September 2001 by announcing that she was living with her female manager-lover (Venus opposes Uranus-

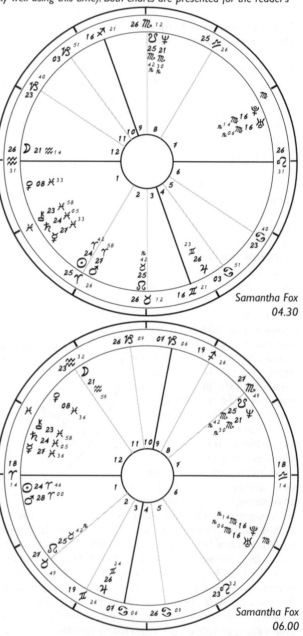

Samantha Fox
04.30

Samantha Fox
06.00

Pluto). (The Press had reported her possible lesbianism in May 1999, as TR Jupiter crossed her Sun). Fox still appears on TV, is writing her autobiography, and surprised the audience during Paris Fashion Week in October 2002 when she took to the catwalk and modelled a *Cabaret*-inspired outfit. A documentary and a presenter's job on TV followed.

Roddy Frame

b. 29 January 1964, 10.05 GMT, Maternity Hospital, Glasgow, Scotland, 55N51, 04W14.
Gerard q. BC. RR: AA.

Singer-songwriter and founder, in 1980, of pop group Aztec Camera. April and August 1981 saw the release of the band's first two singles, both of which were big on the Indie circuit. Their pop breakthrough occurred in 1983. The band was always a vehicle for Frame's songwriting talents and many members came and went until it was established in early 1986 (TR Neptune over MC) that Frame would be working without assistance (his independence is shown by Jupiter Rising in Aries and a Sun-Mars conjunction in Aquarius in 10th). His most hailed album came in May 1993 with *Dreamland*. A new recording, *Surf*, was released in August 2002.

Peter Frampton

⚙ b. 22 April 1950, 06.30 GDT, Beckenham, Kent, England, 51N24, 0W02.
The biography Peter Frampton: The Man Who Came Alive by Steve Clarke (Bunch Books Package, 1977), p. 6 gives place, time and an incorrect date of 20 April. FCC q. BC in hand for 22 April. RR: B.

Guitarist, singer and songwriter – a 70s pretty boy rock star and pinup. At 11 Frampton formed his own band, jammed with David Bowie (qv) and later played demos for Bill Wyman (qv). After the photogenic Frampton became the Face of 68 in teenage magazines, his band Humble Pie was signed to A&M records in the USA in 1969. The band achieved their breakthrough in February 1971 but Frampton had decided to leave the previous November to go solo (TR Jupiter conjunct Descendant, TR Saturn conjunct Ascendant). In Autumn 1974 he flew to the Bahamas to write songs. The pressure was mounting to produce a hit and Frampton was inspired to write *Baby I Love Your Way*. From 1975 he spent almost a year on tour and his

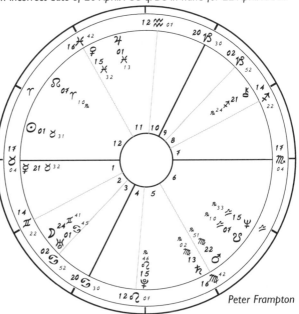

Peter Frampton

album *Frampton Comes Alive!* (topping the US charts on 10 April 1976, TR Jupiter conjunct Sun) became (and remains) the biggest-selling live pop album of all time (15 million copies sold). In January 1977 he was exhausted and had the pressure of a preordered three million units of an album he hadn't completed. When the new album was released mid-1977 the critics panned it. On 29 June 1978 he was involved in a near fatal car accident when he fell asleep at the wheel. Over the coming months (during his Saturn Return) he had time to reexamine his life direction and look into his mishandled finances. Follow-up albums and a film role in *Sgt. Pepper's Lonely Hearts Club* Band were critical and commercial disappointments, and he went broke after the 19 October 1987 Stock Market crash (as TR Uranus opposed Moon in 2nd). In April 1987 he was invited by David Bowie to tour with him as his lead guitarist. Frampton married for the third time in January 1996 and his Spring 2000 CD and DVD *Live in Detroit* (and a film role in *Almost Famous*) won critical praise. Frampton describes himself as unrealistic and a dreamer, and someone who has finally learned to put his family first and say "no".

Alasdair Fraser

⚙ b. 14 May 1955, 15.50 GDT, Alloa, Scotland, 56N08, 04W47.
Gerard q. BC (Alasdair Buchanan Fraser). RR: AA.

Musician and respected fiddle teacher. Fraser's recording career began in November 1983.

Elizabeth Fraser – see Robin Guthrie

John Fraser
> b. 18 March 1931, 01.15 GMT, Glasgow, Scotland, 55N51, 04W16.
> Paul Wright q. BC. RR: AA.

Actor of film, TV, and stage from age 16. Most of his films were made between 1953-1968.

Marjory Fraser
> b. 15 July 1857, 19.00 GMT, Garlin, Abernethy, Scotland, 56N20, 03W19.
> Gerard q. BC. RR: AA.

Folk performer who trained in Paris as a concert singer. In 1882 she studied in Gaelic music and began collecting a huge catalogue to which she added modern harmonic settings. In 1909 she published *Songs of the Hebrides*. D. 22 November 1930.

Dawn French – see Lenny Henry

David Frost
> b. 7 April 1939, 10.30 GMT, Tenterden, England, 51N05, 0E42.
> Paul Rosner q. Diahann Carroll, from Frost. RR: A.

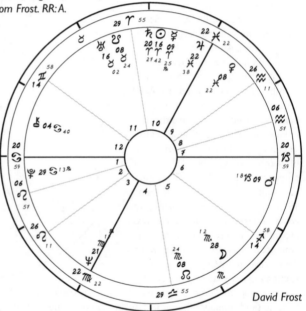

David Frost

Unflappable, urbane TV presenter and interviewer who has moved from being the voice of an emergent young generation to a recognised media institution (Sun-Saturn mocks – then joins – the establishment). He was instrumental in launching a number of comedy careers, with the results being The Goodies, Monty Python and The Two Ronnies, and created LWT (dominating the TV night lineup himself). David Frost was brought up in a supportive and Puritan atmosphere by a Methodist minister father (Jupiter-MC) and was himself a trainee evangelist preacher before moving into TV. He joined the Cambridge Footlights revue (he had entered Cambridge in October 1958) and later won national attention hosting the topical, biting satire show *That Was The Week That Was* from 24 November 1962 until 28 December 1963. Such was the show's influence, it was taken off the air in case its content affected the result of the 1964 General Election. Frost's deadpan delivery (the strong Saturn) was perfect for lampooning the establishment. He began *Frost Report* on 10 March 1966 (as TR Saturn hit the MC and Jupiter) and often indulged in 'trial by television', as it was coined. His confidence on screen was matched by his own personal integrity, an upbeat and positive philosophy and strong moral code (Jupiter-MC). In the US he moved into political interviewing as host of *The Next President?*, a syndicated series of interviews with presidential candidates which began in March 1968 (as Saturn approached his Sun). In February 1969 (during his Saturn Return, TR Saturn conjunct EQHS 10th, and TR Neptune conjunct Moon) it was announced that he would host his own chat show in the US. Fronting TV shows on both sides of the Atlantic, he was soon suffering from over-exposure (when TR Uranus opposed his Sun) and was off the air for some time. Later Frost scooped a number of prestigious and exclusive interviews, including a series with disgraced President Nixon in May 1977. He was one of the famous five when ITV launched TV-AM on 1 February 1983. In recent years he has presented a Sunday breakfast show (from 1993) and *Through the Keyhole* with the drawling Loyd Grossman (b. Massachusetts; an Evening Standard article q. him for being a "double Virgo"). Frost's media success and distinguished career is demonstrated in his

EQHS horoscope: MC/9th rulers Jupiter and Neptune are on the MC/IC axis; four planets in EQHS 9th (including 3rd ruler Mercury); Pluto Rising trine Moon in 5th, Grand Trine MC; Saturn conjunct Sun. Although free of the sort of scandal that might affect Jupiter conjunct MC in Pisces opposite Neptune, Frost's personal life has been eventful. Before his marriage he was cited as one of the world's most eligible playboys and had dated some of the world's most beautiful women, including glamorous actress Diahann Carroll (they fell in love on his show in June 1968 as TR Neptune hit his Moon). Carroll broke off their engagement but remains a close friend. Frost married in 1981 for 17 months (June 1982) and for the second time in early 1983.

> Q "Mr. Frost's technique can be deceptive. His interviewing style seems so harmless, and often it can be infuriatingly docile. His strongest talent is for being able to put someone so at ease they practically forget they're awake." (N.R. Kleinfield, *New York Times*, as quoted in *Let's Talk* by James Robert Parish, Pioneer, 1993)

Rikki Fulton
b. 15 April 1924, 12.30 GDT, Glasgow, Scotland, 55N52, 04W13.
Gerard q. BC (Robert Kerr Fulton). RR: AA.
Comedian, actor and broadcaster. Fulton did pantomime from the 50s and his stage act Francie and Josie was legendary. He was successful on TV from 1978.

Will Fyffe
b. 16 February 1885, 03.40 GMT, Dundee, Scotland, 56N28, 02W57.
Gerard q. BC (William Fyffe). (N.B. The date of birth, almost illegible on the BC, is presented incorrectly in Scottish Birth Data.) RR: AA.
Comedian, actor and singer from childhood. By 1910 he was playing Polonius in *Hamlet*. He wrote sketches for Harry Lauder (qv), but upon rejection, he performed them himself. Fyffe's London debut came in 1916. By 1921 he was top of the bill at the Palladium. Four Royal Variety Performances followed from 1922 and he made his film debut in 1930.

Peter Gabriel – see Genesis
Dave Gahan – see Depeche Mode

Charlotte Gainsbourg
b. 21 July 1971, 22.00 MET, London, England, 51N30, 0W10.
Grazia Bordoni q. Patrick Deimar, from Gainsbourg. RR: A.

Compelling actress usually in French films, and the daughter of Serge Gainsbourg and Jane Birkin (qv). The subject of press attention since her birth, Charlotte grew up to be quiet and self-protective (Venus-Moon-Sun in Cancer), and altogether more conventional than her parents (who both have dominant Sun-Uranus contacts). At age twelve she became an actress (specialising in wayward adolescents) and went on to win two Cesar awards, the French Oscar. She survived a kidnap plot at age 15. In September 1996 the film *Jane Eyre*, directed by Zeffirelli, was released in the UK, with Charlotte in the lead role.

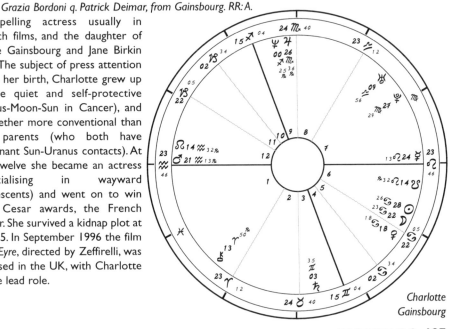

Charlotte Gainsbourg

Benny Gallagher – see Gallagher and Lyle

GALLAGHER AND LYLE

This folk-based songwriting team began their professional careers in 1964, before moving to London and becoming in-house composers at the Apple label. From April 1970 the duo enjoyed a successful partnership with McGuinness Flint, before forming their own group. During 1976 they achieved two Top Ten hits from an album *Breakaway* in April and June. They split in 1980. Lyle continued writing songs, including compositions for Tina Turner (*What's Love Got to Do With It*, a chart-topper in September 1984, and *We Don't Need Another Hero*, August 1985), and Jim Diamond (qv) in December 1984. On 26 February 1985 Lyle won a Song of the Year Grammy for Turner's 1984 #1 smash.

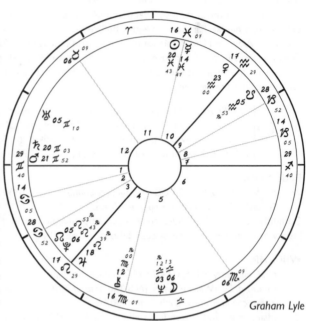

Graham Lyle

Benny Gallagher
b. 21 January 1944, 15.15 GDT, Pierhouse, Blairmore, Argyll, Scotland, 56N00, 04W53.
Gerard q. BC (Benjamin Gallagher). RR: AA.

Graham Lyle
b. 11 March 1944, 11.20 GDT, County Hospital, Bellshill, Lanarkshire, Scotland, 55N50, 04W01.
Gerard q. BC (Graham Hamilton Lyle). RR: AA.

Jim Galloway
b. 28 July 1936, 05.40 GDT, Maternity Home, Kilwinning, Scotland, 55N39, 04W42.
Gerard q. BC (James Braidie Galloway). RR: AA.
Jazz saxophonist and bandleader (Uranus in EQHS 10th square Sun, Mercury, Venus), and a regular performer at international venues. Galloway was an art teacher before concentrating on a musical career. Based in Toronto, Canada from 1964, he played at the Montreux Jazz Festival in 1976.

James Galway
✽ b. 8 December 1939, 06.00 GDT, Belfast, Ireland, 54N35, 05W55.
Lois Rodden q. Dori Sipper from Galway, who said "Scorpio Rising." Speculative. (N.B. Scorpio was rising from approximately 05.18 to 08.14.) RR: C.
Popular performer known for his mastery of the flute. During late Summer 1977 he was seriously injured in an accident. One of his most popular albums was *Sometimes When We Touch* with Cleo Laine (qv).

Graeme Garden
b. 18 February 1943, 08.50 GDT, Aberdeen, Scotland, 57N08, 02W08.
Gerard q. BC (David Graeme Garden). RR: AA.
Garden is best known for the slapstick and speeded-up action sequences in *The Goodies* with Tim Brooke-Taylor (qv). The series was highly influential, ground-breaking British comedy (Garden himself has Pluto conjunct Moon, opposite Mercury, whilst Brooke-Taylor, regardless of his birth time, has Mercury conjunct Pluto). Nine seasons of this anti-establishment television farce were broadcast between November 1970 and February 1982.

Mary Garden

b. 20 February 1874, 10.30 GMT, Charlotte St., Aberdeen, Scotland, 57N09, 02W06.

Gerard q. BC. RR: AA.

Legendary soprano (Saturn on the MC), brought to America at age six. Garden studied singing in Chicago and later in Paris. She had a sensational, life-changing start when she took over mid-performance as Charpentier's Louise on 13 April 1900. Two years later she performed at Covent Garden. In 1907 she made her debut in America. From 1910 she began a 20-year association with the Chicago Grand Opera, becoming a leading opera singer of her generation. Although a prima donna assoluta in the lyric repertoire she also excelled in coloratura roles. Garden was known to be glamorous, capricious, publicity-minded, imperious and indomitable. D. 3 January 1967, Aberdeen.

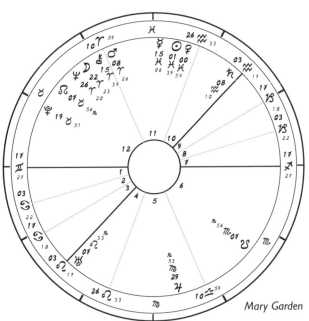

Mary Garden

Bamber Gascoigne

b. 24 January 1935, 16.30 GMT, London, England, 51N30, 0W10.

FCC q. him. RR: A.

Gascoigne is considered the doyen of quizmasters for his enduring stint on *University Challenge*, a TV quiz institution from September 1962 until it was axed on 25 August 1987 (later to be revived and fronted by Jeremy Paxman). Composed, attractive and intelligent to (at its height) almost eleven million viewers, Gascoigne was neither patronising nor offensive to the student contestants. During the 978 editions of the quiz show, he set many of the questions and fine-tuned others with Virgoan (and Mercury-Saturn) pedantry. (Aquarius Sun + Virgo Moon + Leo Ascendant = authoritative boffin!) Gascoigne is also well known as a presenter of authoritative documentaries. He was the first

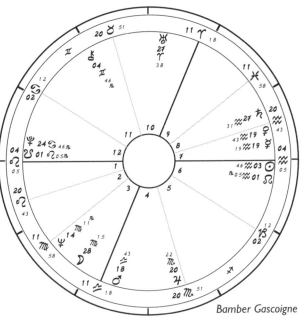

Bamber Gascoigne

presenter of the magazine show *Cinema* in 1964 and was a drama critic for *The Spectator* and *The Observer*. Born into a theatrical family, he was educated at Eton and Oxford. One of his first plays was *Share My Lettuce*, starring Kenneth Williams (qv).

Jill Gascoine

b. 11 April 1937, 19.00 GMT, London, England, 51N30, 0W10.

Marjorie Orr q. her. RR: A.

Lively actress-turned-writer, with a third book published in Spring 1997. She moved to Los Angeles in 1993 with husband Alfred Molina (b. 24 May 1953, London). They had first met eleven years earlier (Molina's Venus is conjunct Gascoine's Sun, and his Saturn-Neptune opposes it). Gascoine's acting career peaked with two detective dramas, *C.A.T.S. Eyes* (1985-7) and *The Gentle Touch* (1980-4). Both provided significant roles and began a trend for dramatic productions depicting women as efficient and intelligent professionals (MC and EQHS 10th rulers are both in Aries), rather than glamour bimbos. Alternative medicine helped Gascoine to contain cancer discovered in Summer 1996 and operated on in

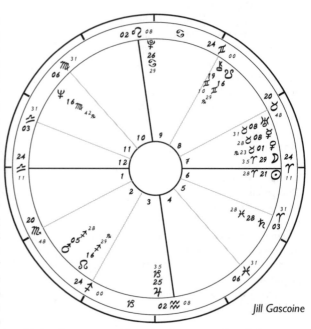

Jill Gascoine

June (TR Uranus conjunct IC), but her life has been scarred by a battle against clinical depression (Moon square Pluto on the MC, Moon-Venus-Mercury-Uranus conjunction) and has written about it in a book, *Lillian*.

> Q
>
> "She is a lively, open person with a ready smile. She is so disarmingly honest about her sensitivity and lack of self-esteem that you feel quite protective towards her. However, she has a tenseness and vulnerability that makes you tread warily." (Angela Levin, *Daily Mail*, 13/12/95)
>
> "It never occurred to me that I couldn't do anything a man could do, but I also love to care for my man... [Alfred] is the only man in my life who has supported me. I've always had to help the men in my life... I remember feeling depressed as a child, but thought I was just being moody. I always overreacted to things. When I fell in love I fell so heavily I wanted to die of misery when whoever it was left me." (Jill Gascoine, *Daily Mail*, 13/12/95)

Dick Gaughan

b. 17 May 1948, 08.45 GDT, Maternity Hospital, Glasgow, Scotland, 55N51, 04W14.

Gerard q. BC (Richard Gaughan). RR: AA.

Singer-songwriter and renowned interpreter of contemporary and traditional folk. In 1972 he released his debut album entitled *No More Forever*. He has retained a strong following on the music circuit with his blend of political and social songs, including the classic *World Turned Upside Down*.

Dustin Gee

b. 24 June 1942, 12.00 Noon DGDT, York, England, 53N58, 01W05.

David Fisher q. a letter from Gee's agent, "the time of Dustin's birth was mid-day." RR: A.

Comedian and impersonator best known for his professional partnership with Les Dennis (qv), which made them both famous on TV in the early 80s. D. 3 January 1986, heart attack.

Ron Geesin

✪ b. 17 December 1943, 06.00 GDT, Maternity Hospital, Kilwinning, Scotland, 55N39, 04W42.
Gerard q. BC (Ronald Frederick Geesin). RR: AA.

Geesin recorded a film soundtrack (*Music From The Body*) in 1970 with Roger Waters (b. 9 September 1944, Great Bookham, England).

Bob Geldof

b. 5 October 1951, 14.20 GDT, Dublin, Ireland, 53N20, 06W15.
David Fisher q. Jo Logan's letter, who obtained the data from Geldof. RR: A.

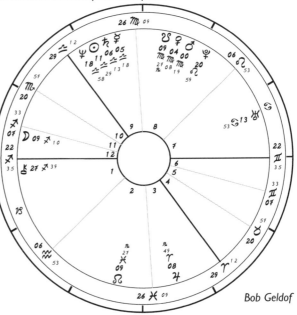

Bob Geldof

Geldof was a music journalist before forming The Boomtown Rats in mid-1975 (TR Uranus conjunct MC, TR Pluto conjunct Saturn, TR Neptune conjunct Moon). The band signed a recording contract in October 1976 (TR Pluto conjunct Sun, Solar Eclipse on MC) and a first single was released in September 1977, followed by an extensive ten-month tour. The Rats hit #1 in October 1978 and July 1979 but their popularity had waned by 1981 (TR Saturn conjunct Sun and TR Neptune conjunct Ascendant). Geldof later starred in the film *The Wall* (released in August 1982) and went solo in November 1986 (TR Uranus conjunct Ascendant). In October-November 1984 (as TR Pluto moved past his MC), he turned his attention towards raising money for famine victims in Ethiopia. Celebrity interest developed and on 25 November 1984 the song *Do They Know It's Christmas?* was recorded by 36 pop artists. It became the biggest selling single of all time in Britain (3.5 million copies, only surpassed in 1997 by Elton John's *Candle in the Wind*). Live Aid, the fund-raising concert, began at 12.01 on 13 July 1985 in Wembley, England (spokesman Geldof's Mercury lies on the concert's Ascendant). Geldof – known to be confrontational and abrasive when dealing with political matters – was a frank, articulate, if unorthodox, campaigner and someone the public trusted with their money. The fund-raising efforts, however, led to great personal debt for Geldof. He married Paula Yates (qv) on 31 August 1986 but they split in February 1995 when Yates's relationship with Michael Hutchence (qv, Australian Data) developed. Geldof was devastated by the break-up and lost his confidence. As TR Uranus squared his MC, they began an acrimonious divorce and custody battle, which was still unresolved at the time of Yates's death in September 2000 (TR Pluto near Moon). On 14 December 2000 he was awarded custody of Yates and Hutchence's daughter Tiger Lily, after a court battle with Hutchence's family. Geldof became an TV entrepreneur, owning the company behind the hit shows *Survivor* (2001) and the long-running show *The Big Breakfast* (from September 1992, as TR Jupiter conjunct EQHS 10th). In 2002 he returned to the stage, singing songs from his latest solo album *Sex, Age and Death*. Geldof's mother died of a brain haemorrhage when he was seven and he was frequently beaten by his father. Geldof is wry, anarchic and open. He has battled depression (the Sagittarian Ascendant), is known to love a good argument, and is a strict disciplinarian to his children.

Q "If he comes across as essentially lugubrious and occasionally ill-tempered, his intelligence and lust for life have never been in doubt... When he took over the afternoon stint as DJ on XFM [in 1999]... we were offered a glimpse of his personality and it was charismatic, rebarbative, foul-mouthed and charming." (Alison Roberts, *Evening Standard*, 20/9/2000)

GENESIS

• 1966, Sep – Rutherford, Gabriel and Banks record a demo with other band members.

• 1967, Dec – Having approached Jonathan King (qv) in January, the group are renamed Genesis and sign a recording contract.

• 1969, Mar – Their first album is released (650 copies are sold).

• 1969, July – The band members leave school and turn professional.

• 1970, Sep – Former child actor Collins joins as drummer.

• 1972, Oct – First chart hit.

• 1975, May – Gabriel quits and Collins takes over as drummer and lead vocalist.

• 1976, Mar – Album hits UK #3.

• 1977, Mar – Gabriel's first of four eponymous albums is released.

• 1979, Nov – Banks's solo album hits the charts.

• 1981, Feb – Collins's solo hit In The Air Tonight hits #2 on the UK charts.

• 1982, Oct 2 – Gabriel joins Genesis for a one-off reunion.

• 1983, Jan – Collins's song You Can't Hurry Love tops the UK charts. He tops the US charts in April 1984 with the movie song Against All Odds.

• 1985, Mar – Collins's album No Jacket Required tops the US charts (TR Jupiter conjunct Sun) and spawns #1 hits.

• 1985, July 13 – Collins performs on Live Aid in Wembley and Philadelphia.

• 1986, May – Gabriel's single Sledgehammer hits the UK Top Five, and his album So enters the UK chart at #1. In July the single reaches #1 in the USA.

Phil Collins

Peter Gabriel

• 1986, June – Rutherford's spin-off band, Mike & the Mechanics, has a US Top Five singles smash. Genesis' album Invisible Touch tops the charts in the UK and the title track hits US #1.

• 1988 – Collins stars as Buster Edwards, the former Great Train Robber, in the film Buster.

• 1989, Mar – Mike & the Mechanics top the US charts.

• 1994, June – Collins is on the Queen's Birthday Honours List.

• 1996, Mar 28 – Collins officially quits Genesis.

• 2000 – Collins wins a Grammy, Oscar and Golden Globe for his musical contribution to the Disney film Tarzan.

• 2002, Nov 11 – Collins releases a new album, Testify.

Tony Banks
> b. 27 March 1950, 07.30 GMT, East Hoathly, England, 50N55, 0E10.
> Marjorie Orr q. him. RR: A.

Phil Collins
> b. 30 January 1951, 00.05 GMT, Hounslow, London, England, 51N29, 0W22.
> Garry Heaton q. his record company, who obtained the data from Collins's mother (same data in biography, but birthplace given as Chiswick). RR A.

Peter Gabriel
> b. 13 February 1950, 16.30 GMT, Woking, England, 51N20, 0W34.
> From him to T.J. Andrews, a friend. RR: A.

Mike Rutherford
> b. 2 October 1950, 19.30 GDT, Guildford, England, 51N14, 0W35.
> Marjorie Orr q. him. RR: A.

Liam Genockey
✪ b. 12 August 1948, 09.00 GDT, Dublin, Ireland, 53N21, 06W18.
> Lesley Griffiths q. him personally. RR: A.
The drummer of the band Steeleye Span.

Susan George
> b. 26 July 1950, 02.00 GDT, Surbiton, London, England, 51N24, 0W18.
> Letter in hand from her husband Simon MacCorkindale to Edwin Steinbrecher (same from her to Marjorie Orr). RR: A.

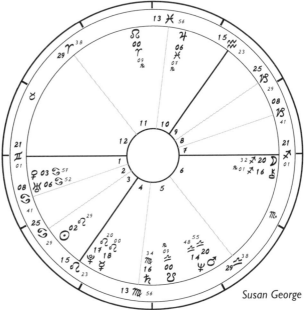

Susan George

An actress who, at the age of twelve, appeared in the West End production of *The Sound of Music* and later won a range of TV roles. She developed a sex-kitten image in productions on both sides of the Atlantic, and the media were always kept busy with her tumultuous love life (MC ruler Uranus conjunct Venus), including romances with Andy Gibb (qv) and Prince Charles, and an intense relationship with singer Jack Jones. Although she had been working since age four (as a model) and feeling responsible for everyone around her, the relationship with Jones left her fearful and dependent for a while. Since the mid-80s her husband has been actor Simon MacCorkindale (qv), and they live a rural life running a film production company together (her Sun conjuncts his Ascendant and her MC hits his Mercury).

> Q "Much of her life has been defined by [men], from her long, intense love affairs to the masculine reaction to her sex-kitten appeal. The notorious rape scene in *Straw Dogs*, the 1971 Sam Peckinpah film that pushed back the barriers of sex and violence, cast her as an archetype in the classic male fantasy of Woman As Victim." (Anne de Courcy, *Daily Mail*, 4/2/95)
>
> "I shall never forget how, when [Jack Jones and I] broke up, I became a child. Without him I felt small and totally lost. I almost didn't know how to cross the street." (Susan George, *Daily Mail*, 4/2/95)

Andy Gibb

b. 5 March 1958, 06.30 GMT, Manchester, England, 53N30, 02W15.

Tashi Grady q. his mother for Birth Record. RR: AA.

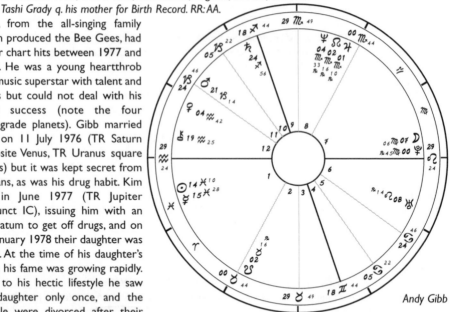

Andy Gibb

Gibb, from the all-singing family which produced the Bee Gees, had major chart hits between 1977 and 1980. He was a young heartthrob and music superstar with talent and looks but could not deal with his early success (note the four retrograde planets). Gibb married Kim on 11 July 1976 (TR Saturn opposite Venus, TR Uranus square Venus) but it was kept secret from his fans, as was his drug habit. Kim left in June 1977 (TR Jupiter conjunct IC), issuing him with an ultimatum to get off drugs, and on 25 January 1978 their daughter was born. At the time of his daughter's birth his fame was growing rapidly. Due to his hectic lifestyle he saw his daughter only once, and the couple were divorced after their child's tragic death. Gibb and the Bee Gees' releases often passed each other up and down the American charts and Andy was determined to prove that he could be famous independently from his older brothers. His first three releases topped the US charts (July 1977, March and June 1978, as TR Neptune crossed the MC) but he began running up enormous debts, particularly after the failure of his 1980 album. In February 1981 (TR Uranus conjunct EQHS 10th and TR Neptune conjunct Saturn) he met and fell in love with pneumatic actress Victoria Principal, who described him as sweet, kind and gentle. His fortunes seemed to be on the upswing with a role as host of *Solid Gold* and performing in the stage show *The Pirates of Penzance*. But his addictions caused him to be erratic and he was fired from both shows. At 24 his career seemed over and young Andy found peace and solitude by sailing and fishing. On 23 July 1982 he confessed a recent nervous breakdown and on-going battle with drugs and alcohol on *Good Morning America*, blaming it on the disintegration of his relationship with Principal (although his habit had in fact destroyed their partnership). Later in 1982 he won a Broadway role but was soon fired because of his unreliability. He took his show on the road in late 1985 (TR Uranus conjunct MC) but by January 1986 his addiction was doing irreparable damage to his heart. Gibb had heart disease, which was kept secret from friends and family, and battled low self-esteem, drink problems and drug addiction (the downside of the creative urges of Pisces, Venus square Neptune and the intensity of a Moon-Pluto conjunction). A stint at the Betty Ford Clinic and AA meetings followed in Spring 1987 (after TR Saturn crossed his MC) but on 9 September 1987 he filed for bankruptcy (TR Saturn square Sun), citing debts of over one million dollars (by contrast Gibb had earned two million dollars at the peak of his career). In late 1987 he began writing new songs with his brothers (during his Saturn Return) but the pressure from living up to the family name (Saturn conjunct MC) was too strong and Andy suffered from writer's block and depression. On 7 March he fell violently ill and died from a heart attack three days later.

Barry, Maurice and Robin Gibb – see Bee Gees

A.A. Gill

✪ b. 28 June 1954, 19.55 GDT, Edinburgh, Scotland, 55N57, 03W12.
Gerard q. BC (Adrian Anthony Gill). RR: AA.

Food critic, features and travel writer for *The Sunday Times* and *GQ* magazine. He was voted Critic of the Year by *What the Papers Say*. He has published the books *Sap Rising* and *Star Crossed*, as well as a collection of 22 travel pieces in *A.A. Gill is Away*. He is known to be a waspish and unsparing restaurant critic and a master of vitriol (note Mercury is conjunct Uranus and square Neptune for electrifying bitchiness, contrary opinions and a highly creative pen). Gill, who is married with two children, 'came out' as a gay-straight man who loves Streisand and camp classics!

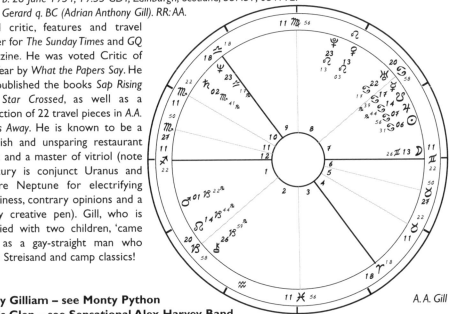

A. A. Gill

Terry Gilliam – see Monty Python
Chris Glen – see Sensational Alex Harvey Band

Iain Glen

b. 24 June 1961, 19.10 GDT, Edinburgh, Scotland, 55N57, 03W12.
Gerard q. BC (Iain Alan Sutherland Glen). RR: AA.

Actor. In 1988 the TV series *The Fear* first brought Glen to public notice. In 2000 he starred alongside Nicole Kidman on stage in *The Blue Room* and went to the Edinburgh Festival in August 2002 with *The Seagull*. The high-profile role and him stripping totally naked in the play brought film and TV offers of roles that focused on various facets of sexuality (including TV's *Glasgow Kiss* and *Anchor Me*). Glen was a winner of a Silver Bear award and Best Actor at the Berlin Film Festival for his convincing portrayal of the murderer Larry Winters* in *Silent Scream* (1990). Winters was convicted in 1964 of the murder of a barman in London. He received a life sentence and further terms whilst in prison (15 years for attempted murder, 2 years for his part in a prison riot). Winters died in 1977 of an overdose. The synastry between actor and murderer is remarkable: Glen's Descendant conjunct LW's Uranus, Glen's Mars conjunct LW's Moon, Glen's MC conjunct LW's Neptune, Glen's Jupiter conjunct LW's Mercury.

Iain Glen

* Larry Winters b. 23 January 1943, 16.30 GDT, Glasgow, Scotland, 55N52, 04W14. From BC. RR: AA.

Evelyn Glennie

b. 19 July 1965, 12.41 GDT, Aberdeen, Scotland, 57N08, 02W05.
Gerard q. BC. RR: AA.

Remarkable and bloody-minded percussionist who suffered a gradual loss of hearing from age eight and was classified profoundly deaf at twelve. Her parents taught her to be independent and not to feel handicapped by her deafness. Glennie trained at the Royal Academy of Music in 1982 (after battling prejudice to be granted an audition) and became an Honorary Doctor of Music, 1991. Her autobiography, *Good Vibrations*, was published in 1990. Many composers have written especially for her and she is considered an outstanding percussion player even by the harshest of critics. She was the first percussionist to go solo and now plays up to 40 instruments in the course of a single concert. She has performed with an eclectic number

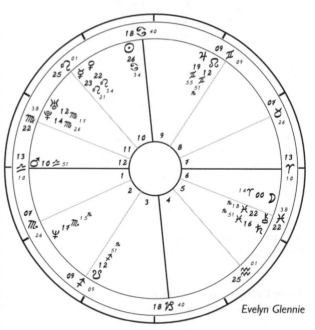

Evelyn Glennie

of people ranging from the New York Philharmonic to Bjork. Glennie played at the Rio carnival and won a Grammy at age 21. The cardinal signs in her chart (Libra Ascendant, Aries Moon and Cancer Sun on the MC) point to a sense of adventure and an indefatigable spirit, as does stubborn Mars on the Ascendant. She considers the healthy development of her marriage partnership to be one of the greatest signs of success.

> Q
>
> "I am very single-minded. I am rather stubborn... Everything I do, I do in a very focused way." (Evelyn Glennie, as quoted in *Reflections on Success* by Martyn Lewis, Lennard, 1997) "Nothing was ever given to me or my brothers for free. To this day, I work very hard for everything and expect nothing to come to me without a struggle. Working hard as a youngster has ensured that I have a very strong work ethic. I still feel guilty about taking holidays... and because I'm a bit of a workaholic anyway I can be quite a difficult person to live with... [My parents] instilled in me a great deal of confidence and never mollycoddled me, even when I started losing my hearing. It made me become very independent and responsible." (Evelyn Glennie, *Night & Day*, 9/7/2000)

Julian Glover

(Confidential data)

Character actor notable for villainous roles in films including *Indiana Jones and the Last Crusade* (Glover has strong Sagittarian leanings in his chart). From 31 October 1996 he starred alongside his son Jamie Glover in the Norwich Playhouse Theatre's production of *Hamlet*.

Liza Goddard

b. 20 January 1950, 09.00 GMT, Smethwick, England, 52N30, 01W58.
FCC q. her for time. Date and place from BC in hand (Louise Elizabeth Goddard). RR: A.

Goddard emigrated to Australia in 1965 and began acting there before her return to Britain four years later. She has appeared in *The Brothers* (1972-6), *Doctor Who* and had a popular recurring role in *Bergerac* as a diamond thief. She regularly appears on TV quiz shows and adverts. Sporadic appearances in TV dramas serve as a reminder that Goddard is not just a pretty face. She married in

1995 (after knowing her partner for 14 years) and finished an intensive course of radiotherapy to treat breast cancer in July 1997.

Jimmy Gold

    b. 21 April 1886, 04.00 GMT, Glasgow, Scotland, 55N51, 04W15.
    Gerard q. BC (James McGonigal). RR: AA.

Comedian who had a double-act with Charles Naughton (qv) from 1908. From the early 30s the duo were given star-billing. The synastry between the pair is interesting: Gold's Mercury opposes Naughton's Uranus, Gold's Sun opposes Naughton's Jupiter, Gold's Moon conjuncts Naughton's Mercury, and Gold's MC is flanked by Naughton's Sun-Venus.

THE GOONS

The Goons began in 1951 as a conventional radio show with sketches and music. But Milligan (Uranus Rising in Aquarius) was allowed to experiment with his absurd, bizarre and surreal brand of comedy, which led to The Goons being considered the finest comedy team on air and a significant influence on others in the genre.

Whilst at Eton, shy **Michael Bentine** suffered from a severe stammer until the age of 16 (Mercury in 3rd sesquisquares Saturn and Pluto suggesting his talents for communication were formed under great stress). Remaining at heart a big kid himself, he created the popular TV puppet series The Bumblies in 1954. Known as much for his frenetic monologues as his paranormal experiences and healing gifts, Bentine faced prostate cancer with a reliance on humour rather than medicine. With Scorpio Rising he dealt with the deaths of his three children with courage – his son was killed in an air crash in 1971 and his daughter died from cancer in 1983. Another child died in late February 1987. D. 26 November 1996, London, cancer.

Spike Milligan was a director and writer whose books and comedy recordings are still immensely popular. He was known to be demanding and suffered from manic depression. He was awarded a Lifetime Achievement award at the British Comedy Awards in December 1994. When he died on 27 February 2002 he left his family battling over his estate.

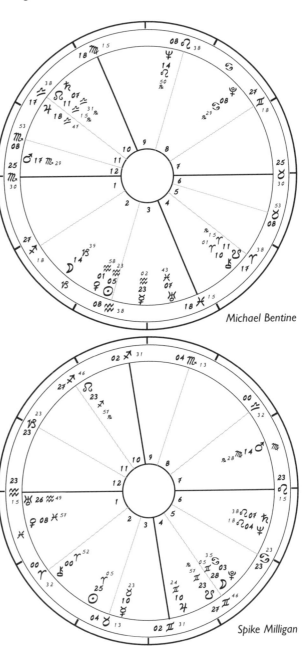

Michael Bentine

Spike Milligan

Jovial **Harry Secombe** followed his radio stint with the Goons with various variety shows, although he is now best remembered for his weekly religion-based show *Highway* (1983-93), which offered an outlet for his vocal gifts through hymns (as well as for his religious Moon in Sagittarius). He suffered a stroke in late January 1999 and died on 11 April 2001.

Peter Sellers was as neurotic as Milligan, but whereas Milligan fought depression (Moon-Pluto, Uranus Rising in Aquarius), Sellers, a chameleon on-screen, battled to establish a concrete self-image off-screen (Neptune in 12th conjunct Mercury, ruling Ascendant, square Moon). Many believed that out of character he was a hollow man, waiting for a role to bring him back to life. Sellers was both charming and volatile, the latter accompanied by a raging temper (Sun-Mars opposite Uranus, he had four wives and twice as many heart attacks). Dominated by his manipulative mother, he was known to be deeply insecure and a control freak, and continued to make contact with her through ritual and seance after her death. He sought perfection both in his personal and professional lives (note the Virgo – Sun and Ascendant – influence). Between 19 February 1964 and 18 December 1968 he was married to Swedish sex symbol and model Britt Ekland*. He was memorable impersonating a bumbling Indian in *The Millionairess* and *The Party*, and even hit #3 on the UK charts in November 1960 with his

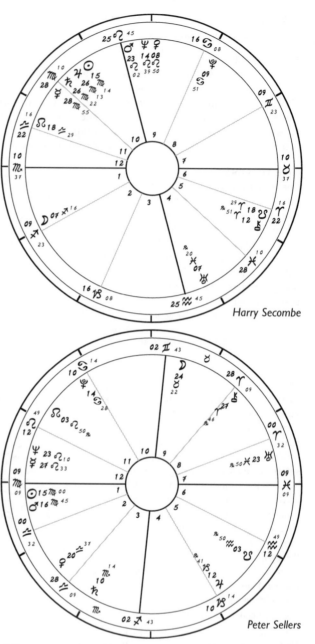

Harry Secombe

Peter Sellers

catchphrase *Goodness Gracious Me*. Sellers's later film comedies as Inspector Clouseau revolved around Virgoan humour – chaos and constant misunderstandings. Clouseau's outrageous French accent was inspired by the hairdresser of his one-time lover Princess Margaret. On 5 April 1964 he suffered a heart attack and at 04.32 the following day in Los Angeles his heart stopped beating. Later that day he had seven further heart attacks. D. 24 July 1980, London, heart attack.

> Q "If you ask me to play myself, I will not know what to do... There used to be a me behind the mask, but I had it surgically removed." (Peter Sellers, as quoted in *Radio Times*, 24/8/02)

---

* Britt Ekland b. 6 October 1942, 00.20 MET (-1), Stockholm, Sweden, 59N20, 18E03. *American Astrology* (December 1986) q. her hospital record. RR: AA.

The Pluto stamp of black humour is evident here, as is the acerbic, frank wit of Mars and its signs:
• Bentine – Pluto opposite Moon, Mars Rising in Scorpio.
• Milligan – Moon conjunct Pluto in the 5th, Sun in Aries.
• Secombe – Scorpio Rising, Mars conjunct MC.
• Sellers – Mars conjunct Sun on the Ascendant.

Michael Bentine
   b. 26 January 1922, 03.00 GMT, Watford, England, 51N40, 0W25.
   David Fisher q. his letter. RR: A.
Spike Milligan
☉   b. 16 April 1918, 03.00 IST (-5.5 = -5hrs 30 min), Ahmadnagar, India, 19N05, 74E44.
   Astrological Journal, August 1967, q. him in a Sunday newspaper article. N.B. David Fisher q. a
   biography which gives "2 am or 2.30." RR: A.
Harry Secombe
   b. 8 September 1921, 12.00 Noon GDT, Kilvey Hill, Swansea, Wales, 51N38, 03W57.
   From his autobiography, Arias and Raspberries, p. 11. RR: B.
Peter Sellers
   b. 8 September 1925, 06.00 GDT, Southsea, Portsmouth, England, 50N46, 01W05.
   Edwin Steinbrecher q. him (place confirmed by FCC at Registry). RR: A.

Hannah Gordon
   b. 9 April 1941, 00.15 GDT, Edinburgh, Scotland, 55N57, 03W13.
   Gerard q. BC (Hannah Campbell Grant Gordon). RR: AA.

Theatre, radio and TV actress. Hannah Gordon studied to be a drama teacher at the Glasgow College of Dramatic Art, then moved on to the Dundee Repertory Company and performed in 22 plays. Since her TV debut in 1965 she has often been cast in middle-class suburban roles (including *Upstairs, Downstairs*) to which she has bestowed both depth and charm. Gordon's father was absent from her life (Neptune-MC), and later thrown into an asylum because he had Parkinson's disease. By age 11 Gordon had suffered the loss of both parents (her mother had died two years earlier) and by age 14 she was forced to be self-sufficient and live on her own. In 1994 she lost her husband of 25 years – he was many

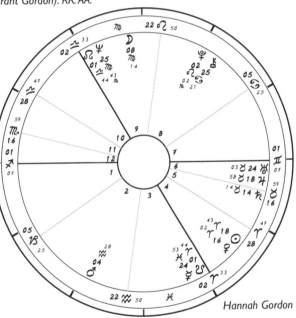

Hannah Gordon

years older and also acted as her protector. In 1998 she began presenting the series *Watercolour Challenge*, in which she toured Britain meeting amateur artists and watching them work. In March 2003 she joined the cast of *My Fair Lady* in the West End and was in love again. (N.B. Gordon was born two days after TV actress Cornelia Frances, see Australian Data.)

Q   "She's known much tragedy in her life but she has a superficial calm which I suspect comes more from an iron self-control than a fundamental tranquillity. She learned from a very early age to keep any hurt to herself." (Lynda Lee-Potter, *Daily Mail*, 12/4/03)

Harry Gordon

> b. 11 July 1893, 00.20 GMT, Aberdeen, Scotland, 57N09, 02W07.
> Gerard q. BC (Alexander Ross Gordon). RR: AA.

Comedian and pantomime performer known for his rich array of comedy creations (Jupiter conjunct Ascendant). Gordon made his stage debut in 1912 and a London debut at the Palladium in 1929. D. 21 January 1957, 16.10 GMT, Glasgow, 55N51, 04W14 (Gerard q. Death Certificate).

Dave Gorman

✪ b. 2 March 1971, 01.55 MET, Stafford, England, 52N48, 02W07.
> Kim Farnell q. him (a twin). RR: A.

British comedian who presented a humorous show on Sun Sign astrology, *Dave Gorman's Important Astrology Experiment*, from 1 September 2002. He set himself a 40-day task to follow advice from 20 popular horoscope daily columns to see if astrology could improve his health, love and wealth. The result? "I have proved astrology is the best way to run your life... We will take no responsibility, we have found a better way! We have the knowledge – astrology works!"

Alan Gorrie – see Average White Band
Luke and Matt Goss – see Bros

Eve Graham

> b. 19 April 1943, 04.50 DGDT, Damside Cottages, Auchterarder, Scotland, 56N19, 03W42.
> Gerard q. BC (Evelyn May Beatson). RR: AA.

Member of the wholesome band New Seekers, who enjoyed chart success in the US from 1970, and particularly later with *I'd Like to Teach the World to Sing*, a US million-seller and a UK chart-topper in early 1972. Their six Top Ten UK hits over three years were all massive commercial buys (as TR Neptune passed over her MC). Graham has MC ruler Jupiter in the 6th House, a key indicator of her short burst of professional success.

Stewart Granger

> b. 6 May 1913, 02.00 GMT, Old Brompton Road, London, England, 51N29, 0W11.
> From his autobiography, *Sparks Fly Upward* (Granada, 1981), p. 8, q. his mother to a psychic. RR: A.

Granger began as an extra in British films from 1933 and won his first leading screen role in 1939. He became a top box office star in Britain during the 40s. Virile and swashbuckling roles were offered by Hollywood during 1950-57 and Granger performed his own stunts. Television welcomed Granger as a leading man in the early 70s. He was born at a New Moon (Sun conjunct Moon), indicating that his life would be divided into clear-cut phases. Granger's life was indeed marked by distinct periods, both in his working life and relationships (in his chart, the Moon rules 6th, Sun rules 7th). He had three marriages, including one to Jean Simmons (qv) from December 1950 to August 1960. During the 70s he owned millions of dollars worth of real estate before the markets crashed. D. 16 August 1993, Santa Monica, California.

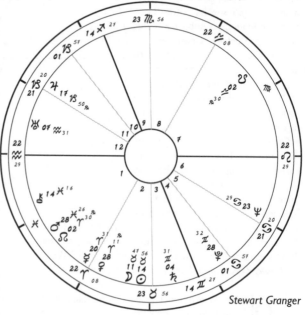

Stewart Granger

Angus Grant

b. 13 September 1931, 20.30 GDT, Edinburgh, Scotland, 55N57, 03W13.

Gerard q. BC (Angus William Grant). (N.B. The birth was registered in Fort Augustus.) RR: AA.

Fiddler at Scottish folk festivals, as well as across Europe and the USA, and a notable exponent of the West-Highland Fiddling style. An album, *Highland Fiddle*, was released in 1978.

Cary Grant

b. 18 January 1904, 01.00 GMT, Bristol, England, 51N27, 02W35.

From *Evenings with Cary Grant* by Nancy Nelson (William Morrow, 1991), p. 27, q. him "around 1:00 am on a cold January morning" (year confirmed by FCC at Registry). RR: A.

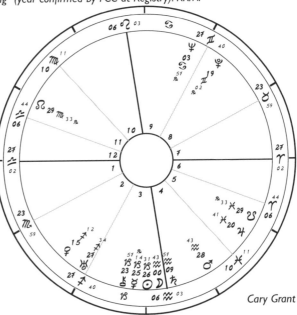

Cary Grant

Born Archibald Leach, Grant was a leading actor of the 30s, 40s and 50s with a flair for playing smooth, charming bachelors (the MC in Leo and Libra Ascendant) in dramas, thrillers, slapstick and screwball comedies (although Grant himself had a dry sense of humour). He is best remembered as Hollywood's most debonair, suave and sophisticated leading man, an image he built up from scratch. Grant had an unstable childhood (Moon and Saturn flanking the IC), during which his mother suffered a nervous breakdown. Her husband committed her to an asylum, with nine year old Archie thinking his mother had abandoned him (later when he discovered the truth, he purged his ghosts with the help of LSD drug therapy). He joined an acrobatic troupe (as a stilt-walker) on 16 March 1918 (as TR Saturn and Neptune flanked the MC), before undertaking a three-year vaudeville stint in the USA from 21 July 1920. Discovered by Arthur Hammerstein in the late 20s, he signed a five-year Hollywood contract on 7 December 1931 and changed his name. Grant married on 9 February 1934 but his wife filed for divorce in December that year (TR Uranus conjunct Descendant), citing extreme possessiveness. It was Mae West who picked him to star with her in *She Done Him Wrong* (1933, his Saturn Return) and *I'm No Angel* (1934), and these proved to be the turning points in his career. When his contract ended in 1935 (TR Pluto conjunct EQHS 10th) he had enough professional clout to refuse to be held down by one studio. Grant went freelance by choice and by 1937 (when TR Pluto had made its last pass over the EQHS 10th) he was a star. He found his niche in madcap comedy as a charming, light comedy lead (films included *Bringing Up Baby* and *The Philadelphia Story*). After TR Pluto crossed his MC in 1942 he took on more serious roles and began his 'Hitchcock phase' of suspense films (*Notorious, To Catch a Thief* and *North by Northwest*). Grant was known to suffer from depression and insecurity, as well as a strong need to be recognised and accepted. He was considered a shrewd businessman and tight with money (Sun and Mercury in Capricorn) and was always aware of his image as a star, keeping his private life beyond reach (Leo MC, Moon-Saturn on IC). He quit films after his daughter's birth on 26 February 1966 and began a lecture tour in the 1980s. In October 1984 he suffered a stroke. Years after his death it is now believed by some that he was a British spy during the Second World War. He was married five times and partners accused him of verbal cruelty, meanness and a controlling instinct. D. 29 November 1986, Davenport, Iowa, stroke. (*Cary Grant: A Class Apart* by Graham McCann, Fourth Estate, 1996.)

Russell Grant

✪ b. 5 February 1951, 21.45 GMT, Hillingdon, Middlesex, England, 51N32, 0W27.
FCC q. him, from his mother. (N.B. Grant's first astrology teacher Pamela Crane rectified this to 21.39.) RR: A.

Until he presented the Queen Mother with her horoscope at an exhibition in 1979, Grant had not found his career niche. Born at a New Moon (suggesting, along with Uranus-MC, that his life would be made up of distinct, separate phases), as an actor he was cast in more than 30 musicals and comedies before becoming Britain's first high-profile, ubiquitous and competent TV pop astrologer (his big break occurred on BBC's *Breakfast Time* in 1983). At one stage Grant had columns in 250 publications worldwide (MC ruler Moon opposite Pluto suggests the popularity and daily influence he exerted over people's lives). He has written over 100 books. Grant has recently branched out into a variety of TV shows, including travel and sport series, leaving many of his tabloid columns behind him. For a number of years he has suffered from tinnitus and Méniere's syndrome.

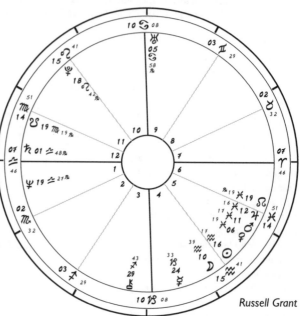

Russell Grant

Leslie Grantham

b. 30 April 1947, 04.00 DGDT, Camberwell, London, England, 51N27, 0W05.
FCC q. him, from his parents. RR: A.

At 15 Grantham became a junior research lab technician for six months, and later moved into the Army, posted to Germany. Three days after his first appearance in the soap *EastEnders*, he became the show's first actor to suffer media intrusion when his past as a convicted murderer was exposed on 22 February 1985 – he had served nearly twelve years for the murder of a German taxi driver in 1967. Later when he appeared in the murder TV show *Cluedo*, critics were quick to suggest that there'd be little suspense: the culprit every week would be Leslie Grantham, with a revolver... in the back of a cab! As 'Dirty Den' Watts in *EastEnders* Grantham was involved in some of the highest-rating and most captivating episodes, and

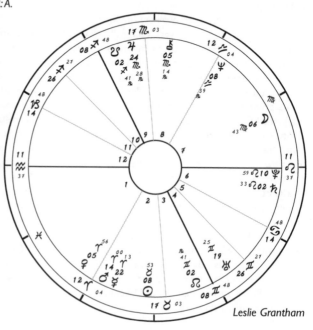

Leslie Grantham

many memorable scenes with screen-wife shrew Angie. His character was written out of the show in February 1989. Other notable appearances in series include *The Paradise Club* (1989-90) and *99-1* (1994-5), as well as being mean and moody for the game show *Fort Boyard*. In April 2003 it was announced that Grantham would return to *EastEnders* in the autumn.

Elspet Gray

b. 12 April 1929, 22.00 GMT, Inverness, Scotland, 57N29, 04W12.

Gerard q. BC (Elspet J. MacGregor Gray). RR: AA.

Seasoned actress and wife of Brian Rix (qv) from 14 August 1949. Gray has often acted alongside Rix (including the radio comedy series, *One Man's Meat*, from June 1964). She appeared in the comedy series *Solo* (from January 1981) and the first series of *Blackadder* (June-July 1983).

Muriel Gray

b. 30 August 1958, 17.50 GDT, East Kilbride, Scotland, 55N45, 04W11.

Gerard q. BC (Muriel Janet Gray). RR: AA.

Witty, acerbic and short-tempered TV presenter and outspoken journalist (with Mercury conjunct Pluto and square Mars, both rulers of the MC). Feminist Gray is a graduate of the Glasgow School of Art and a former illustrator. The latter experience and the treatment she received from work colleagues toughened up her Pisces Moon and helped her develop a combative, aggressive streak. Later Gray was a member of the rock group The Family Von Trapp. In 1982 she won an audition to present the pop series *The Tube* with Jools Holland and Paula Yates (qv). On this show she developed a reputation for aiming painfully direct comments and questions at guests (fools are rarely entertained when Capricorn rises). Later she

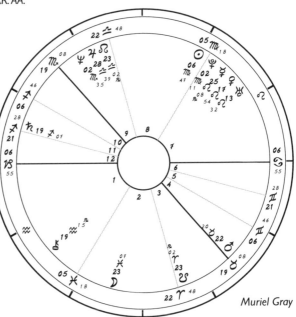

Muriel Gray

appeared in *The Media Show* and *Frocks on the Box*. Gray formed her own production company in 1989 and three years later married film director Hamish Barbour. She suffered post-natal depression after the birth of both her children. On 6 March 1997 (with TR Pluto square Sun and TR Saturn on her EQHS 4th) her two year old daughter was rushed to hospital after being found face down in a pond – the child suffered brain damage and is now severely handicapped. Gray has also written horror novels (even Stephen King is a fan) and gave birth again in January 1999.

> Q
>
> "Muriel, who seems to have chips the size of mountains on her shoulders, knows what we should all put up with, how we should behave and what we should believe in... You would be unwise to tackle her too fiercely. Muriel, with her thin face and fox-like features, looks as if she has a bite even worse than her bark." (Angela Levin, *Daily Mail*, 18/11/96)
>
> "I can't describe that first year after [my child's] accident. I spent a lot of time lying face down on the floor. Nothing can ever get as low as that again... Everyone talks about not bottling up your feelings, but I've learned that one of the most brilliant human abilities is being able to bottle things up and put them away in a box. Either crumble and be destroyed, or put them in a box." (Muriel Gray, *Daily Mail*, 15/3/99)

Larry Grayson

b. 31 August 1923, 08.30 GDT, Banbury, England, 52N04, 01W20.

From Prediction (January 1979), original source not known. RR: C.

Once a music-hall drag performer, camp Grayson won a following through one-off guest appearances on TV and later for his own series, *Shut That Door* (named after his catchphrase). His humour, often telling of his state of health, was pure Virgo hypochondria. In 1978 he joined Isla St. Clair (qv) to host *The Generation Game*, which they did until 1982. He made two cameo appearances in the much-loved and ridiculed soap *Crossroads* (1973 and 1975) and was respected and adored by colleagues. His catchphrase from his cream cake advert ("It's naughty but nice") was coined by copy-writer Salman Rushdie. D. 7 January 1995.

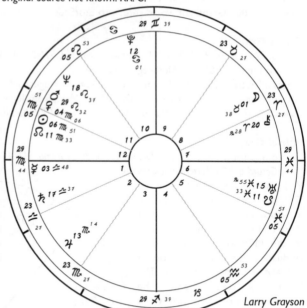

Larry Grayson

Peter Green

b. 29 October 1946, 21.59 GMT, Bethnal Green, London, England, 51N32, 0W03.

Bettina M. Lee q. him, confirmed by Green's mother. RR: A.

Green stood in for Eric Clapton (qv) in the Bluesbreakers in late 1965 and replaced him from July 1966. He was a founding member of Fleetwood Mac in July 1967. The latter band had a few hits in the late 60s before the pressures of fame proved too much for Green, who quit on 11 April 1970 (playing his last gig on 24 May). His mental decline worsened in 1973 and again in late 1976 (after TR Uranus had crossed his Ascendant ruler Sun in EQHS 4th). He was committed to a mental hospital on 26 January 1977. Green's Saturn-Pluto conjunction in the 1st (ruling EQHS 4th and 6th) squares Sun-Jupiter, suggesting he put tremendous pressure upon himself to achieve. Uranus makes a sesquisquare to Sun (Ascendant ruler) and to Jupiter (ruler of EQHS 5th) suggesting flashes of brilliance on stage but an instability in his personal life and interaction with others (Sun-Jupiter in 4th, Uranus rules 7th).

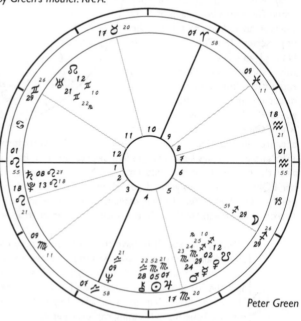

Peter Green

Other members of Fleetwood Mac (Lindsey Buckingham, Stevie Nicks and Bob Welch) are included for reference:

Fleetwood Mac's Stevie Nicks

b. 26 May 1948, 03.02 MST (+7), Phoenix, Arizona, USA, 33N27, 112W04.

Tashi Grady q. her, from BC. RR: AA.

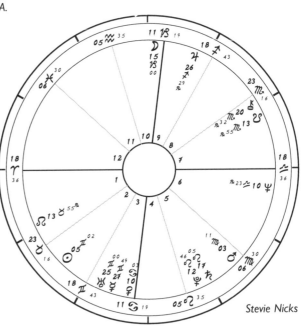

Stevie Nicks

With the departure of Bob Welch (qv), Nicks brought her vocal and songwriting skills to Fleetwood Mac in December 1974, after the commercial failure of an album with companion Lindsey Buckingham (qv). Fleetwood Mac went on to produce one of the top selling albums of all time in America, *Rumours* (#1 for 31 weeks from April 1977). In 1981 Nicks took time out from the group to record a solo album, *Bella Donna*, which became a best seller in September of that year. She married on 29 January 1983 (until April 1984, TR Jupiter conjunct MC). Nicks entered the Betty Ford Clinic in November 1986 to kick a drug habit. Fleetwood Mac reunited to record *Tango in the Night*, which was released in April 1987.

Fleetwood Mac's Bob Welch

b. 31 August 1945, 15.03 PWT (+7), Los Angeles, California, USA, 34N03, 118W15.

FCC q. BC (Robert Lawrence Welch). (N.B. 31 July 1946 is usually given as his date of birth.) RR: AA.

Welch joined Fleetwood Mac in April 1971, after a stint with the soul show-band the Seven Souls in Las Vegas. He was involved in a legal wrangle in November 1973 over the group's right to their name. Welch left Fleetwood Mac in December 1974 to form the band Paris, and he was replaced by Stevie Nicks (qv) and Lindsey Buckingham (qv). In 1977 he went solo and achieved further success, hitting the Top Ten in America at Christmas 1977 (TR Jupiter conjunct Moon). During the 80s he worked on film soundtracks.

Fleetwood Mac's Lindsey Buckingham

b. 3 October 1949, 01.53 PST (+8), Palo Alto, California, USA, 37N27, 122W09.

FCC q. BC in hand (Lindsey Adams Buckingham). RR: AA.

A chance meeting in December 1974 led to Buckingham joining Fleetwood Mac with Stevie Nicks (qv), whom he partnered both personally and professionally during the group's most successful period. His solo album hit the US Top 40 in December 1981.

Robson Green

✪ b. 18 December 1964, 22.00 GMT, Hexham, England, 54N58, 02W06.

☾ Sy Scholfield q. Green's official website, www.robsongreen.com, "born at Dilston Hospital in Hexham, Northumberland at approx. 10 pm." FCC received an email (16/5/03) confirming the data came from Green's mother. (Terry Lamb q. Green, 1999, for 02.00.) Both charts are presented for the reader's discernment. RR: DD.

Actor and singer who, with no formal training, has emerged as the preeminent small screen performer of his generation and been in some of the highest rated TV shows of the late 90s. In June 1999 he signed a golden handcuffs £1.75 million deal with ITV to star in a succession of TV dramas, many to be produced by his own company. He has also set up a youth theatre for 350 students in Newcastle. Back in 1984 Robson Golightly Green, working at a shipyard, won the starring role in a professional theatre company production. What followed, though, was a long period of unemployment. His big break came on TV in *Casualty* (1989-91), and he acted and sang in *Soldier Soldier* (1991-5) with Jerome Flynn. *Soldier Soldier* garnered 14 million viewers and there were constant requests to release songs from the show. Two singles *Unchained Melody* (May 1995) and *I Believe* (November 1995) hit the charts and sold 2.9 million records in the UK (earning Green a cool £2 million in four months). Between 1995 and 1998 he won numerous Best Actor awards. Green's success has also meant inevitable tabloid intrusion into his personal life, with numerous accounts of alleged infidelities. Following their split in July 1999 (at a time when he went into therapy), Green announced his intention to divorce his wife (they had married on 22 June 1991). He married again on 10 March 2001. Robson's parents had divorced when he was 11, and during his childhood he was a loner.

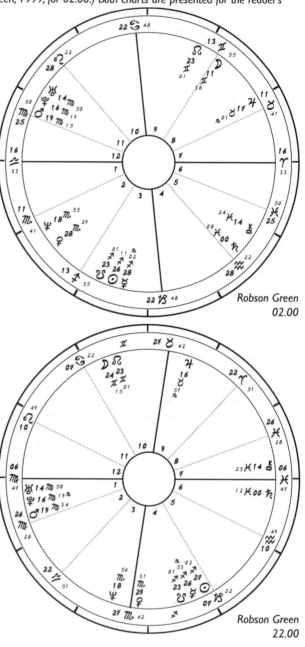

Robson Green
02.00

Robson Green
22.00

Q "Even when I was working at the shipyard, I never went out with the lads. I instinctively felt there was a certain sadness, a lack of individuality, about being part of a group." (Robson Green, *You*, 6/5/2001)

"It was never a question of loving acting. It was more a question of hating having no money." (Robson Green, *Radio Times*, 25/4/98)

Sarah Greene

⊗ b. 24 October 1957, 09.10 GMT, London, England, 51N30, 0W10.
   FCC q. her letter for all data except year. Year obtained by FCC from Registry. RR: A.

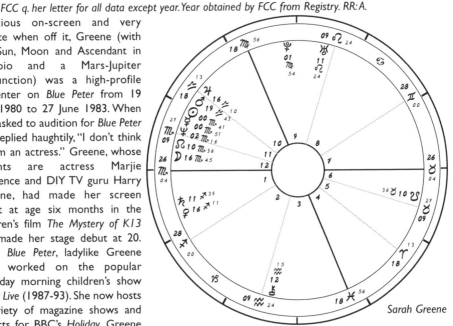

Sarah Greene

Vivacious on-screen and very private when off it, Greene (with the Sun, Moon and Ascendant in Scorpio and a Mars-Jupiter conjunction) was a high-profile presenter on *Blue Peter* from 19 May 1980 to 27 June 1983. When first asked to audition for *Blue Peter* she replied haughtily, "I don't think so. I'm an actress." Greene, whose parents are actress Marjie Lawrence and DIY TV guru Harry Greene, had made her screen debut at age six months in the children's film *The Mystery of K13* and made her stage debut at 20. After *Blue Peter*, ladylike Greene later worked on the popular Saturday morning children's show *Going Live* (1987-93). She now hosts a variety of magazine shows and reports for BBC's *Holiday*. Greene survived a horrific helicopter crash with her husband Mike Smith (whom she had met in early 1981) on 11 September 1988 (Solar Eclipse exactly on her MC).

Debbie Greenwood – see Paul Coia

Anne Gregg

   b. 11 February 1940, 08.00 GDT, Belfast, Northern Ireland, 54N35, 05W55.
   FCC q. her. RR: A.

A popular writer and TV anchorwoman for *Holiday*. When she was forced to resign after ten years on the show in 1991, the BBC received a record 1000 complaints from viewers. She was also fired from her Radio 4 show *Breakaway* (last broadcast on 4 January 1997).

Joyce Grenfell

🖤 b. 10 February 1910, 02.52 GMT, London, England, 51N30, 0W10.
   Speculative time from Charles Harvey, rest of data are from various film and comedy books. RR: C.

A journalist and radio critic with *The Observer* before she made a stage debut with her monologues on 21 April 1939. Chirpy, bright and popular, Grenfell appeared in many films, most notably those of the *St. Trinian's* series and appeared to epitomise British gentility. Grenfell married on 12 December 1929 and during 1944-5 she travelled with ENSA touring hospitals in Algeria, Malta, Italy, Iran, Egypt and India. Her witty one-woman shows were acclaimed across the world (particularly her shows in June 1954 in London and in October 1955 on Broadway) – she has a Mercury-Uranus conjunction and stellium in Aquarius. Her very last performance of songs and monologues was given on 21 June 1963 at Windsor Castle, before she retired and wrote two volumes of autobiography. In mid-1994 Maureen Lipman (qv) recreated Grenfell's funniest moments in *Re-Joyce*, another one-woman show for the stage.

Sheila Grier
> b. 11 February 1959, 23.45 GMT, Redlands Hospital, Glasgow, Scotland, 55N53, 04W17.
> Gerard q. BC (Sheila Jean Grier). RR: AA.

Soap actress best known for a two-year stint in *Brookside* (as Sandra Maghie) and *Take the High Road*.

John Grierson
> b. 26 April 1898, 07.00 GMT, Deanstown, Kilmadock, Scotland, 56N11, 04W04.
> Gerard q. BC. RR: AA.

Renowned documentary film maker and sociologist. Aware that film would shape cultural and moral attitudes, and keen to use it to educate (MC in Aquarius, strong EQHS 11th), Grierson founded the documentary film movement. In 1924 he studied the effects of media on public opinion in the US and became a specialist in the psychology of propaganda (note Neptune is conjunct a Gemini Ascendant). Grierson coined the term 'documentary' in February 1926. In 1927 he worked to establish an organisation that could make education and propaganda films. From 1930-3 his unit produced 100 documentaries. His philosophy was to "exploit the powers of natural observation, to build a picture of reality, to bring the cinema to its destiny as a social commentator, inspirator and art." D. 1972.

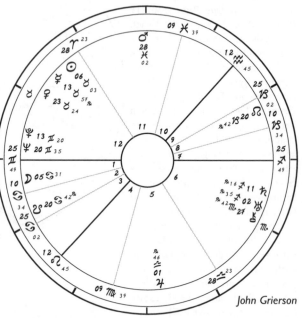

John Grierson

John Grieve
> b. 14 June 1924, 13.30 GDT, Glasgow, Scotland, 55N58, 04W17.
> Gerard q. BC (John Muirhead Grieve). RR: AA.

Acclaimed comic and dramatic actor. Grieve appeared at the Edinburgh Festival in August 1984 and August 1985.

Jimmy Grimes – see Sensational Alex Harvey Band

Clare Grogan
> b. 17 March 1962, 05.25 GMT, Merryland Street, Glasgow, Scotland, 55N51, 04W19.
> Gerard q. BC (Clare Patricia Grogan). RR: AA.

Elfin lead singer of the 80s pop band Altered Images. Grogan was cast in *Gregory's Girl* (1980) before touring with the pop group in June 1980. The band was signed in the autumn and released a pop hit in October 1981, the infectious *Happy Birthday*. By July 1983 the band's appeal had worn thin and Grogan moved into acting. Grogan, who also works as a presenter on satellite television, moved into the popular soap *EastEnders* in 1997 for a short while.

Pippa Guard
> b. 13 October 1952, 20.25 GDT, Edinburgh, Scotland, 55N57, 03W17.
> Gerard q. BC (Philippa Ann Guard). RR: AA.

An award-winning actress at RADA before she made her debut in 1978 on TV in *The Mill on the Floss*. Guard has also featured in Shakespearian productions for television.

Alec Guinness

- b. 2 April 1914, 05.45 GMT, London, England, 51N30, 0W10.
  Chryss Craswell q. Astrological Quarterly Vol. 5, #4. No source. (Astrological Quarterly, Winter 1958, gives 05.54 GMT, possibly a typo). RR: DD.

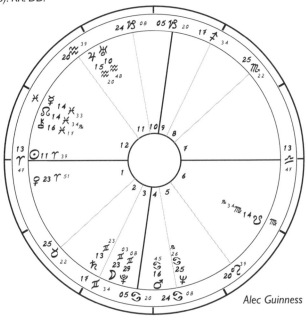
Alec Guinness

A former copywriter, Guinness first performed on the professional stage on 2 April 1934 and later gained experience from September 1936 working at the Old Vic. He made his New York stage debut in 1942 and was on screen regularly from 1946 with roles such as *Bridge on the River Kwai* (1957), *Oliver Twist* (1948), *The Ladykillers* and *Great Expectations* (1946). Guinness was known for his chameleon-like acting persona and his disguises, both of which are highlighted in the classic Ealing comedy film *Kind Hearts and Coronets* (1949). Kenneth Tynan labelled him "the man without a face." Royalties from appearances in *Star Wars* ensured his status as one of Britain's richest actors. Guinness was a shy man and a devout Catholic. D. 5 August 2000, cancer.

> Q "Almost in penance for the iconic fame such roles brought him, Guinness developed an extreme outward serenity that was like the curtain which a penitent draws after stepping into the confessional. He regarded the stage a safer place than the screen because he was more in control of what he revealed there... His talents lay in playing characters who, in Tynan's words, 'are nine-tenths concealed and whose fascination lies not in how they look, but in how their minds work.'" (Alexander Walker, *Evening Standard*, 7/8/2000)

Robin Guthrie

- b. 4 January 1962, 10.30 GMT, Royal Infirmary, Falkirk, Scotland, 56N00, 03W48.
  Gerard q. BC (Robin Andrew Guthrie). RR: AA.

Enigmatic performer with a contemporary sound. Guthrie formed The Cocteau Twins with Elizabeth Fraser (b. 29 August 1958, Grangemouth) and moved to London in search of a break in November 1981. In their early years they were one of the few bands to remain independent of large record companies, releasing through a small label, 4AD (from which they departed in March 1991, when TR Uranus conjunct Guthrie's Sun). A debut album was released in June 1982 and made #2 on the Indie chart. From April 1984 (TR Jupiter conjunct Sun), the band hit the mainstream UK charts. Fraser's voice has always been the major instrument of the band's appeal.

'H' (Ian Watkins) – see Steps

Georgina Hale

- b. 4 August 1943, 16.05 DGDT, Essex, England, 51N48, 0E40.
  Rectified by her friend, astrologer Penny Thornton in *Romancing the Stars*, "about tea-time, but before 5 pm," p. 221. RR: C.

Enigmatic stage and film actress who began her professional life as a hairdresser before successfully auditioning for RADA. By 21 she had married and divorced a fellow actor and completed training with the Royal Shakespeare Company, where she discovered stage fright that would keep her out of the theatre for the next nine years. In 1970 she was discovered by Ken Russell (qv) who cast her in

The Devils and made her a film star. As highly regarded as she is controversial within her profession (the Scorpio Ascendant), Hale won a best comedy performance for the lead role of Josie on stage in *Steaming*. In 1984 Hale entered two years of professional complications that delayed her film career.

Geri Halliwell

✪ b. 6 August 1972, 14.30 GDT, Watford, London, England, 51N40, 0W25.
Barry Street of The Astrology Shop, 78 Neal Street, London q. her personally. RR: A.

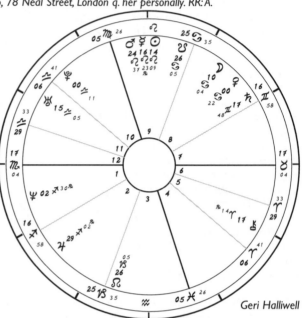

Geri Halliwell

With naked ambition and a talent for self-promotion, Halliwell was catapulted to fame as the ballsy, brassy Ginger Spice of the Spice Girls (qv) and was the driving force behind Girl Power and the group phenomenon (note the prominent Mars). Girl Power, the worldwide commercialism of the world's best-selling girl group, began in July 1996 (TR Jupiter opposite Moon) with their single *Wannabe*, which topped the charts in 21 countries. When she left the band on 28 May 1998 she embarked upon a highly publicised solo career on her own terms (note the MC ruler is retrograde giving her a second shot). In a TV documentary that followed, she revealed herself to be warm, needy and insecure (note the tight Venus-Pluto square, ruling the Ascendant-Descendant). In October 1998 she was appointed a Goodwill ambassador to the United Nations. Halliwell has also transformed herself from buxom Ginger Spice to a slimline solo artist, giving rise to speculation and fears about her lifestyle (she had an ongoing battle with bulimia: Moon square Uranus). After the relative commercial failure of *Scream if You Wanna Go Faster*, she moved into TV as a judge of the series *Pop Stars: The Rivals* in 2002 and released a second yoga fitness video and another autobiography. She is a sharp, driven businesswoman with a penchant for publicity coups (Moon in Cancer, Descendant ruler Venus square Ascendant ruler Pluto), but is also known for her eccentric habits, idiosyncrasies and battles with mental health (Moon square Uranus). Halliwell's parents split when she was nine and she battled breast cancer in her late teens.

> Q "Halliwell is an exasperating muddle of hang-ups and ego, sharp insights and dense ineptitude, but there is something about her – a warmth, a sense that her heart is fundamentally in the right place even when her judgment has deserted her – that can't help but make you wish her well." (Ginny Dougary, *The Times Magazine*, 28/9/02)

Tony Hancock

☄ b. 12 May 1924, 11.00 GDT, Birmingham, England, 52N30, 01W50.
From David Fisher, original source not known. RR: C.

Comic genius. Hancock's first success was on radio with *Hancock's Half Hour*, from 2 November 1954 (when TR Pluto moved over the Moon of the 11 am birth time) to 29 December 1959. On the show his character had a lugubrious, pompous manner – a megalomaniac with delusions of grandeur and a capacity for self-deception (suggestive of the possible Neptune Rising and the Leo Ascendant and Moon). The show moved to TV on 6 July 1956 (until 30 June 1961). Critics suggest that most of Hancock's popularity was due to the excellent writing of Ray Galton and Alan Simpson (qv), with whom Hancock broke ties in 1963. Anthony John Hancock gave his first performance at 17 in a local church hall, found an agent in 1948 and won his big break with the radio series *Educating Archie*.

Despite his popularity with audiences and critics, he had a fear of failure and an on-going battle with alcohol (note the prominent Neptune). Hancock married his first wife in September 1950 after a five-month courtship. Hancock wed again in December 1965 and admitted his alcohol problem later that month, as TR Neptune opposed Sun. His second wife, who attempted suicide five times in their marriage, was often injured by Hancock when he was drunk. In March 1968 Hancock fled to Sydney and attempted to revive his flagging career, but committed suicide on 25 June 1968. On 8 May 1999 (as TR Jupiter hit MC) a book serialisation asserted that Hancock lived his later years as a closeted bisexual.

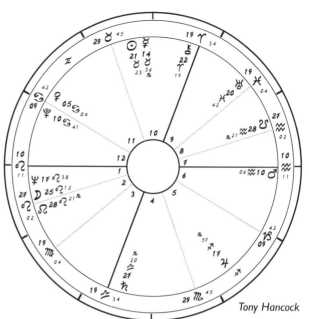

Tony Hancock

John Hannah

b. 23 April 1962, 14.30 GDT, East Kilbride, Scotland, 55N46, 04W10.
Gerard q. BC (John David Hannah). RR: AA.

Popular actor and reluctant star of television and film. Hannah had the lead role in the TV series *McCallum* and a role as the lover of Simon Callow (qv) in the blockbuster film *Four Weddings and a Funeral* (released March 1994). He then appeared in *Sliding Doors*, which led to well-received appearances in two US box office hits, *The Mummy* and *The Hurricane*. Hannah left school at 16 and went straight into a four-year apprenticeship with the Scottish Electricity Board until he had a revelation at 19 when a friend suggested he try acting. What followed was a place at the Royal Scottish Academy of Music and Drama and then eight years as a struggling actor in bit parts and repertory (later joining the National

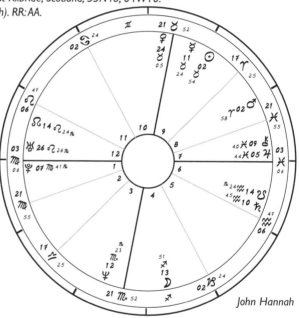

John Hannah

Theatre and the RSC). Hannah married his girlfriend of six years, Joanna Roth, in January 1996 and they appeared together in a sitcom, *See You Friday*, and in a detective drama, *Rebus*, which aired in April 2000.

Bill Hardie

b. 21 August 1916, 07.45 GDT, Aberdeen, Scotland, 57N09, 02W06.
Gerard q. BC (William James Hardie). RR: AA.

Fiddler and teacher with family fiddling roots dating back to the Eighteenth Century. He made his first BBC broadcast at 16.

Forsyth Hardy

b. 12 February 1910, 03.00 GMT, Bathgate, West Lothian, Scotland, 55N54, 03W38.
Gerard q. BC (Henry Forsyth Hardy). RR: AA.

Film and documentary maker and the first film critic of *The Scotsman* from 1932-41.

Anita Harris

b. 3 June 1942, 07.00 DGDT, Midsomer Norton, England, 51N18, 02W28.
From Roger Elliot in *TV Times*, 5 May 1973, original source not known. Place from Registry. RR: C.

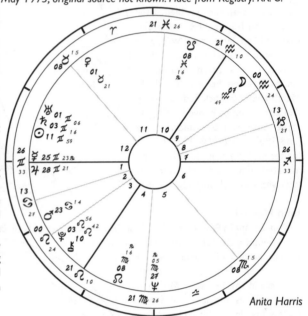
Anita Harris

Popular, ever-youthful all-round entertainer, known (from 1972) for her regular appearances in pantomime. For two years Harris trained as a dancer and was an ice-skating champion when growing up. At 16 she auditioned for a chorus line and travelled to Las Vegas with the show. Her first hit record, *Just Loving You*, made the Top Ten in the summer of 1967. In the 70s she was cast in plays and musicals, including *Cats*. In the late 70s Harris's legs were insured for £2 million. But she and her theatre director husband faced near bankruptcy in the years that followed. In December 1996 she spoke of her upset at not being able to have children (she suffered her first of three miscarriages in 1976).

Richard Harris

b. 1 October 1930, 11.20 GDT, Limerick, Ireland, 52N40, 08W38.
His astrologer Kathleen Johnson q. him (N.B. Harris gave the same data but 1932 to M. Scudieri. *National Enquirer*, March 1972, gave 1933 and 10.20, but often reports times in GMT.). RR: A.

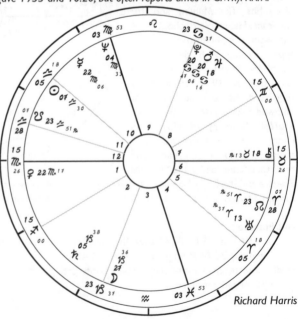
Richard Harris

Legendary actor and hell-raiser. Richard Harris was known for being reclusive off-screen and for many flashes of brilliance on screen (Sun opposite Uranus in 5th, and Neptune conjunct MC). Harris's robust, rebellious and pugnacious portrayals made him a star from 1963 with the film *This Sporting Life*. He is best remembered for *Camelot* (1967) on both stage and screen. He wrote and sang *MacArthur Park* (a hit in June 1968). With his health ravaged by drink (Neptune on MC, Scorpio Rising), Harris discovered religion in the early 80s in the Bahamas and resumed his film career in the late 80s, including a charismatic role in *Gladiator* and the lead in *To Walk with Lions*. Over the years he made sound financial investments and rejected offers to tell-all in an autobiography. Harris was diagnosed with Hodgkin's Disease in August 2002 and died two months later. His last films were the hugely successful *Harry Potter* tales.

George Harrison – see The Beatles

Rex Harrison
> b. 5 March 1908, 05.00 GMT, Huyton, England, 53N25, 02W52.
>
> Blanca Holmes, in American Astrology January 1957, q. Lili Palmer, Harrison's former wife. RR: A.

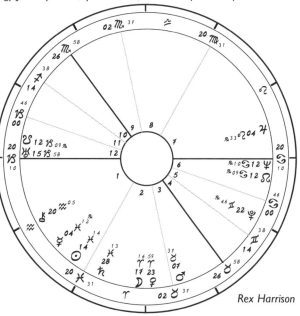

Rex Harrison

Debonair stage and screen star known for charming British gentlemen roles, polished characters without feeling and for his serious dedication to his work. He made his stage debut at 16 in September 1924 with the Liverpool Repertory Theatre and moved onto the London stage in November 1930, where he began establishing a strong reputation as an actor. He began working in film that year and went to Broadway on 2 March 1936 in *Sweet Aloes*, but the show failed and he was home by the end of the month. Harrison spent two years in photographic reconnaissance with the RAF from 1942. He began acting in Hollywood in 1945 and following actress Carole Landis's suicide on 5 July 1948, he was involved in a scandal because of his relationship with her (Descendant ruler Moon square Neptune on the Descendant). On 26 November 1970 his fourth ex-wife Rachel Roberts committed suicide (TR Uranus conjunct MC). Harrison won a second Tony in June 1957 for his stage work from 15 March 1956 in *My Fair Lady* (which he took to London in April 1958), and an Oscar for the film version in 1964. He returned to the show and his most famous role in 1981. D. 2 June 1990, New York City, pancreatic cancer.

Tony Hart
> b. 15 October 1925, 07.30 GMT, Maidstone, England, 51N17, 0E32.
>
> FCC q. him. RR: A.

Artist who presented children's art TV shows, which included *Take Hart* (with plasticine sidekick Morph) and *Hartbeat*. Dapper and friendly, Hart was also a member of the team fronting *Vision On* (1964-76). After a stint in the army, Hart began painting murals in London restaurants to earn a free meal before he persuaded a BBC producer to take him on. The result was at least one TV show each year for the next 50 years.

Alex Harvey – see Sensational Alex Harvey Band

Leslie Harvey
> b. 13 September 1945, 09.55 GDT, Glasgow, Scotland, 55N51, 04W15.
>
> Gerard q. BC (Leslie Cameron Harvey). RR: AA.

Guitarist and younger brother of Alex Harvey (qv, Sensational Alex Harvey Band). He played with Maggie Bell (qv) from 1967 and later with her in Stone the Crows. On 3 May 1972 in Swansea, Harvey died after being electrocuted on stage.

Iain Harvie – see Del Amitri

Nigel Havers

> b. 6 November 1951, 03.00 GMT, London, England, 51N30, 0W10.
> David Fisher q. a postcard from Havers's mother, Lady Carol Havers. Year confirmed by FCC. RR: A.

A former researcher for a radio show, Havers's big break came in *Don't Wait Up*, the long-running TV sitcom and the film *Chariots of Fire*. He has wowed audiences on both sides of the Atlantic with suave, aristocratic roles, especially as the smooth-talking con merchant in *The Charmer* (expressing the deadliest sides of Venus conjunct the Ascendant and a Scorpio Sun!). He has also been seen recently in the series *Dangerfield* (1998-9) and *Manchild* (from 2002). Havers's second wife was diagnosed with ovarian cancer in May 2000 and completed chemotherapy that November. (His first marriage had lasted from 1975 to January 1989.)

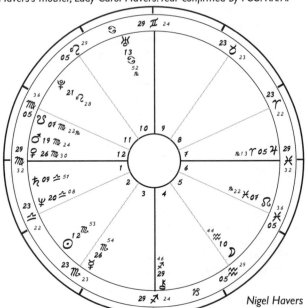

Nigel Havers

Nigel Hawthorne

> b. 5 April 1929, 07.00 GMT, Coventry, England, 52N25, 01W30.
> FCC q. him, from his parents (same from him to David Fisher). RR: A.

Distinguished actor of film and TV, known to be quiet, courteous and self-effacing. After emigrating with his family at the age of two, Hawthorne arrived back in England from South Africa in 1951 with £12 in his pocket. He was hired as stage manager in a small repertory theatre until he began winning small roles on stage. When work dried up he returned to South Africa in 1957 only to return to England again in 1963, after confidence-boosting roles on the South African stage. Hawthorne is best known for his role in the classic BBC TV comedies *Yes, Minister* and *Yes, Prime Minister* (February 1980 to January 1988, Bafta award in 1987 for the latter show). Hawthorne made his stage debut in America in 1974 and won

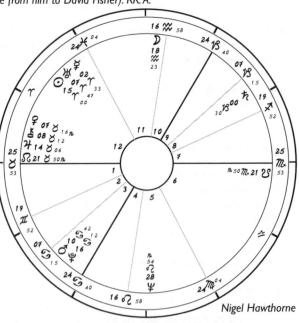

Nigel Hawthorne

a Tony Award for playing C.S. Lewis in *Shadowlands* in June 1991, but like a number of his stage roles, the part was later given to another actor to portray on film. His West End stage performance in *The Madness of King George*, however, not only earned him an Olivier Award but also the movie role, for which he was nominated for an Academy Award. Despite leading a quiet life with his male partner of

17 years, Trevor Bentham, false press reports before the Oscar ceremony in March 1995 threatened to overshadow his achievement by stating he would use a winning speech at the show to come out of the closet (TR Neptune over MC). The experience was hurtful for both men, as the media had a field day publishing homophobic and sometimes ridiculous articles. Later, caustic reviews of his *King Lear* in 1999 led to Hawthorne refusing to act on stage again. In March 2000 he was diagnosed as having blood clots on his lungs which led to doctors finding a malignant tumour in his pancreas (TR Uranus conjunct Moon). Hawthorne was operated on in June (TR Jupiter and Saturn on Ascendant). In April-May 2001, while fighting another bout of cancer, he was the subject of a poison pen campaign, apparently started by a disgruntled gardener he had once employed. After his death from cancer in December 2001, he left a book of candid memoirs, *Straight Face*, about the personal life he had fought so long and hard to keep private. The book was published on 6 June 2002. D. 26 December 2001, 09.30 GMT, near Ware, Hertfordshire, heart attack/cancer.

Q "For years I suffered from depression because I thought I was a complete failure. I could not seem to find love, in fact I found neither love nor success until I was 50. When I met my present partner it seemed as though everything fell into place. Suddenly life made more sense and when I relaxed about myself, success came." (Nigel Hawthorne, *Mail on Sunday*, 27/8/2000)

"He was one of nature's innocents, who rather liked being seen as the urbane country gent – which of course he wasn't. Jane Lapotaire [the actress] called him 'a bit of a fusspot', which he certainly was about his work. He could be difficult, and in private he could also be quite a dark person. We had a way of joking each other out of things." (Trevor Bentham, *The Times*, 25/5/02)

"He was fiercely intelligent but gifted with a painterly skill rather than intellect. Instinct governed his latter years: he could 'smell' his way into a part and give it a living, breathing reality – unchoreographed, unpredictable and always dynamic." (Trevor Bentham, *The Times*, 2/6/02)

Colin Hay

b. 29 June 1953, 10.20 GDT, Maternity Hospital, Kilwinning, Scotland, 55N39, 04W42. Gerard q. BC (Colin James Hay). RR: AA.

Lead singer of the pop band Men at Work, which was hugely successful in the early 80s. Hay emigrated with his parents to Australia at 14 and in 1979 founded the group. An initial single release topped the charts in Australia in March 1982 (Saturn Return and TR Uranus conjunct EQHS 4th), before also reaching the summit in America that October. What followed in 1983 was a chart invasion resisted only by Michael Jackson. Their album *Business as Usual* spent 15 consecutive weeks at the top of the charts (from November 1982) and another single, *Down Under*, topped the charts in Australia, the UK and US during January 1983. Two albums were certified million-sellers in the US (*Business as Usual*

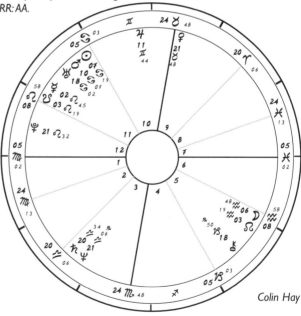

Colin Hay

sold six million). The band had lost momentum by the time a new single was released in June 1985. Hay moved onto a solo music career (a March 1987 album release failed to crack the US Top 100, TR Neptune opposite Sun) and later took up acting, appearing on Australian TV and film.

Calvin Hayes

> b. 23 November 1962, 05.00 GMT, Edgware, London, 51N37, 0W17.
>
> FCC q. Hayes's mother. RR:A.

Guitarist of Johnny Hates Jazz, a short-lived pop band that secured four UK chart placements from April 1987 to March 1988 and produced a best-selling album (#1 on 23 January 1988). In 1992 Hayes, the son of producer Mickie Most and his successful entrepreneur wife (Mars on MC), was seriously hurt in a car accident with a record company executive. Recovered, he lives with his wife and child in America, where he produces music. Hayes's famous father died on 30 May 2003.

David Hayman

> b. 9 February 1948, 21.15 GMT, Maternity Hospital, Glasgow, Scotland, 55N51, 04W14.
>
> Gerard q. BC. RR:AA.

Actor-director, Hayman was a steelworker at 16 before studying at the Royal Scottish Academy of Music and Drama. The TV film *A Sense of Freedom* (1981) brought him acclaim. He directed *Silent Scream* (1990) starring Iain Glen (qv).

Justin Hayward

> b. 14 October 1946, 08.00 GMT, Swindon, England, 51N34, 01W47.
>
> Garry Heaton q. Hayward's letter, from his mother and Birth Record. RR:AA.

Hayward joined The Moody Blues in November 1966, in the band's second musical phase, and together they released Hayward's classic *Nights in White Satin*. In 1974 the band split to pursue solo projects and Hayward formed part of the Blue Jays (from December 1974 to January 1977). The group achieved a UK hit with *Blue Guitar*. The Moody Blues reunited in June 1978 for the album *Octave*. In July 1978 Hayward had a solo Top Five single, *Forever Autumn*. The group is still touring to sell-out audiences.

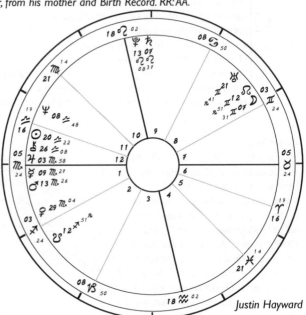

Justin Hayward

Fran Healy – see Travis

Hamish Henderson

> b. 11 November 1919, 07.00 GMT, Blairgowrie, Scotland, 56N36, 03W21.
>
> Gerard q. BC (James Scott Henderson). RR:AA.

Folk singer, poet and composer. His early poetic work in 1948 won him the Somerset Maugham Award.

Joe 'Mr Piano' Henderson

> ✪ b. 2 May 1920, 14.35 GDT, Glasgow, Scotland, 55N53, 04W15.
>
> Gerard q. BC (Joseph Turner Henderson). RR:AA.

Laid-back pianist and composer popular in the late 50s and early 60s. D. 4 May 1980.

Lenny Henry

b. 29 August 1958, 03.00 GDT, Sedgley, England, 52N33, 02W08.

FCC q. him, from his mother's memory (most sources give Dudley as the birthplace). RR: A.

Best known for both his own comic characterisations and impersonations of famous entertainers, Henry stood alone for some time as the only black comedy entertainer on television (note the pioneering Aries MC). He was discovered on *New Faces* in 1975 and on 20 October that year became the first black man to appear on *The Black and White Minstrel Show* (as TR Saturn crossed the Ascendant). In April 1981, following a stint on the children's TV show *Tiswas*, Henry was picked to co-star with Tracey Ullman (qv) in the comedy sketch show *Three of a Kind*, which aired that summer. He graduated to his own TV shows and a comedy series *Chef*, popular on both sides of the Atlantic from its first showing in January 1993, in

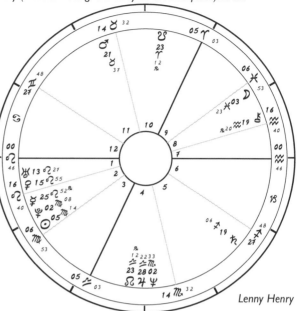

Lenny Henry

which Henry rivalled Basil Fawlty as the rudest man of comedy. Henry married comedienne Dawn French (b. 11 October 1957, Holyhead, Anglesey) on 20 October 1984, and they first adopted in March 1991. French has been credited with developing Henry's act as an alternative comedian. After travelling to the Amazon rain forests and making trips for Comic Relief in Africa, he became seriously ill with malaria in mid-February 1997. On 10 June 1999 he checked into a clinic to be treated for depression and an emotional collapse, following two weeks of allegations that he had cheated on his wife (TR Uranus opposed his Venus). Henry continues to do stand-up as well as appear in straight roles on TV. (N.B. Henry was born on the same day as singer Michael Jackson, whom he was famous for impersonating.) (*Lenny Henry* by Jonathan Margolis, Orion, 1995.)

Douglas Henshall

☉ *b. 19 November 1965, 17.35 GMT, Maternity Hospital, Johnstone, Scotland, 55N50, 04W31.*

Gerard q. BC (Douglas James Henshall). RR: AA.

Leading stage, TV, radio and film actor. Henshall starred in the drama series *Psychos*, set in a Glasgow psychiatric hospital. His films include *Orphans* (1997), *The Man With Rain in His Shoes* (1998), *Silent Cry* (2002), *It's All About Love* (2003) and *Loving You* (2003).

Eileen Herlie

b. 8 March 1918, 02.45 GMT, Clarkston, Scotland, 55N46, 04W16.

Gerard q. BC (Eileen Isobel Herlihy). RR: AA.

Stage actress who always provoked extreme reactions from critics – over the years they either loved or hated her. Herlie made her stage debut in 1938 and in 1942 toured with *Rebecca*. In November 1945 she appeared at the Lyric in *The Trojan Women* and became a star there in September 1946 when she played in *The Eagle Has Two Heads* (TR Jupiter had crossed the MC, TR Pluto opposed MC ruler Venus and Herlie was approaching her Saturn Return). Herlie made a belated Broadway debut in December 1955 in *The Matchmaker*. She also made a few impressive films, most notably *Hamlet* in 1948 and a filmed Broadway stage production of the play alongside Richard Burton (qv) in 1964. She married on 12 August 1942.

Mike Heron

◐ b. 27 December 1942, 17.30 GDT, Edinburgh, Scotland, 55N57, 03W10.

Neal Meredith q. BC. (N.B. The data given in previous editions was for another Mike Heron.) RR: AA.
Instrumentalist, singer and songwriter who founded the Incredible String Band with Robin
Williamson (qv) before the latter quit in 1974. Heron was a Scientologist from 1968 to 1983. They
played a reunion concert in 1997 and again in January 2001. Heron resurfaced with two albums,
Where the Mystics Swim (February 1996) and *Conflict of Emotion* (April 1998).

Nick Heyward

b. 20 May 1961, 08.03 GDT, Beckenham, England, 51N24, 0W02.

Marjorie Orr q. him. RR: A.
Heyward was the front man for the teen pop band Haircut 100, who scored chart hits between
October 1981 and October 1982 (including four Top Ten hits). In January 1983 he left to launch a
solo career. Between 1983 and 1988 Heyward had ten consecutive chart entries. In 2002 he
performed in an 80s revival tour with Ben Volpeliere-Pierrot (qv) and others.

Alex Hill

b. 9 August 1954, 14.35 GDT, Redlands Hospital, Glasgow, Scotland, 55N53, 04W17.

Gerard q. BC (Alexander Hunter Aga Hill). RR: AA.
Meteorologist before entering TV as a weather presenter on *Scotland Today* (1981-4). Since 1989 he
has also presented ITV and LWT weather bulletins.

Benny Hill

b. 21 January 1924, 08.15 GMT, Southampton, England, 50N55, 01W25.

Russell Grant q. him, TV Times, 4 April 1986 (year confirmed by FCC at Registry). RR: A.

With a humorously self-confessed
mental age of 17, Benny Hill became
an icon for his naughty schoolboy
sketches and mild vulgarity. He
provided titillation and sauce on TV
for 40 years (Mars and Jupiter flank
his Sagittarian MC) and was
anathema to Women's Lib. 111
episodes of his show were made
and they were eventually shown in
140 countries. A double Aquarian,
Hill possessed an inventive and
idiosyncratic streak, was a loner and
recluse who craved public
adoration and feared authority of all
kinds. (Hill also had an uneasy
relationship with his Victorian father
and a close, loving partnership with
his mother, who died in February
1976.) Work devoured him and Hill
dedicated his entire life to his
showbiz obsession, studying others

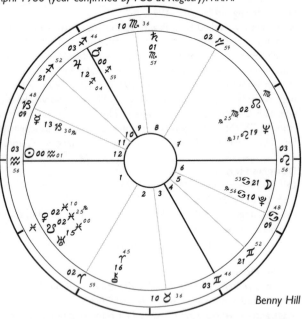

Benny Hill

and transforming it into comedy skits (Mercury-Pluto). Alfred Hawthorne Hill moved to London in
1941 with £10 and after stints as a milkman, army driver and drummer, he began performing in
theatres and clubs. He soon realised that he couldn't perform in front of a live audience (5th House
ruler Mercury in 12th opposes Pluto). He first performed on radio in September 1947. Hill started
writing scripts at 27 and soon showed a natural ability to know what TV viewers would find popular
(Aquarius, Moon in Cancer). He made his first television appearance in 1951 poking fun of others and
pushing the boundaries of censorship with his cheeky mimes. Within four years he was voted
Outstanding TV Personality and began his own Saturday night BBC series on 15 January 1955. After a
self-exile from TV to concentrate on films in 1966, he returned to star in his own TV comedy show.

He even hit #1 in Britain with *Ernie (The Fastest Milkman in the West)* in December 1971 (TR Neptune conjunct MC). Mars and Jupiter on the MC suggest very visual humour, relying on exaggeration and manic-paced farce, and Hill's comedy indeed was evocative of cheeky seaside postcards and bawdy music hall, as well as silent film comedy. His humour was universal because it was slapstick, based on sight gags, funny costumes and naughtiness. When he wasn't chasing bikini-clad Barbie dolls in speeded-up sequences (Mars), his use of word-play was brilliant (Mercury-Pluto). Finally after 30 years (natal Saturn on EQHS 10th) he became a cult favourite in USA from Autumn 1979 (EQHS 10th ruler Pluto opposes Mercury, ruling the 5th House of audience following), and where American success has eluded so many British comics, 100 of his half-hour shows were sold in February 1980 for $3.5 million. In May 1989 (as TR Saturn and Neptune hit Mercury) his association with Thames TV ended abruptly after 22 years. Hill never recovered from being dropped and took to comfort eating and staying at home watching TV. In February 1992 he was put in hospital after a series of heart attacks. Always an enigma to the Press, Hill spoke French, German and Spanish, lived a frugal life alone, hated to be imposed upon and never allowed others to get too close. D. 19 April 1992.

Q "Very few people saw the genuine Benny Hill because he had the façade that he dropped down to protect himself... He was totally self-contained; he needed nobody." (Hill's agent, gent Peter Charlesworth, as quoted in TV's *The Unforgettable Benny Hill*)
"Money didn't mean anything to Benny at all. He used to have cheques arrive through the post and he just would leave [them] lying around the flat." (Sue Upton, as quoted in TV's *The Unforgettable Benny Hill*)
"For him solitude was a genuine joy... he was an obsessive, an obsessive eccentric... a man supremely at home with himself." (Bob Monkhouse, TV's *The Unforgettable Benny Hill*)

Thora Hird

☙ *b. 28 May 1911, 17.45 GMT, Morecambe, England, 54N04, 02W53.*
Date and place from This Is Your Life. Time is speculative, from her autobiography, born in late afternoon "when church bells...ringing" (generally between 17.30 and 18.00). RR: C.

Original comedy actress much-loved nationally for her piety, as well as a career of spot-on, often heartrending, comic characterisations (Mercury-Saturn and Venus-Neptune). She won acclaim (and awards) for two of Alan Bennett's *Talking Heads, A Cream Cracker Under the Settee* shown in Spring 1988 and *Waiting for the Telegram* in 1999. In 1998 she was given a lifetime achievement award at the British Comedy Awards. For nearly two decades she presented the BBC religious show *Praise Be!* Hird died on 15 March 2003, after suffering a serious stroke on 10 March at a retirement home for actors.

Joseph Hislop

b. 5 April 1884, 20.30 GMT, Edinburgh, Scotland, 55N57, 03W11.
Gerard q. BC (Joseph Dewar Hislop). RR: AA.

Operatic tenor with strong ties to Sweden. In 1914 he made his debut at the Royal Swedish Opera as *Faust* in Gounod's opera. During 1927 and 1931 he toured South Africa and Australia. He taught from 1937-47 at the Royal Academy and the Opera School in Stockholm. D. 6 May 1977.

Alfred Hitchcock

☙ *b. 13 August 1899, 03.15 GMT, London, England, 51N30, 0W10.*
Tony Joseph q. Wangemann for time, original source not known (Marc Penfield gives 20.00 as 'personal'). Date from Hitchcock by John R. Taylor. RR: DD.

Meticulous director-storyteller of the macabre and suspenseful, and master manipulator of audiences (note the Mercury-Uranus square and the Moon-Jupiter conjunction in Scorpio, which describes the psychosexual coding embedded in his films and the voyeuristic, look-but-don't-touch atmosphere). The master of suspense was born to an intimidating, controlling mother. Personally he was known to be mischievous and obsessed with order and control. In early 1920 he began his career as a title card illustrator. Hitchcock was making films by the mid-1920s before he found his niche in thrillers. In September 1926 his third film, *The Lodger* (made in April 1926), caused a sensation. Hitchcock sailed to New York in August 1937 and was courted by studio heads. He signed with David O. Selznick in July 1938, moving to Los Angeles in Spring 1939. His battles with Selznick were titanic and

Hitchcock jumped ship, signing a contract with Warner Brothers on 3 January 1949. From 2 October 1955 his weekly anthology series *Alfred Hitchcock Presents* made him a star on TV and very wealthy. Hitchcock suffered ill health with a diseased gall bladder in early 1957, and in April 1958 his wife (since 2 December 1926) was diagnosed with cancer, later suffering a stroke. Of his 53 films his most famous include (US release dates): *The 39 Steps* (September 1936), *The Lady Vanishes* (December 1938), *Rebecca* (March 1940), *Strangers on a Train* (July 1951), *Dial M For Murder* (May 1954), *Rear Window* (August 1954), *Vertigo* (May 1958), *Psycho* (June 1960) and *The Birds* (March 1963). He was married on 2 December 1926 and his wife died in early July 1982, two years after his death. Hitchcock, the most famous director of his age, was knighted on 3 January 1980. D. 29 April 1980.

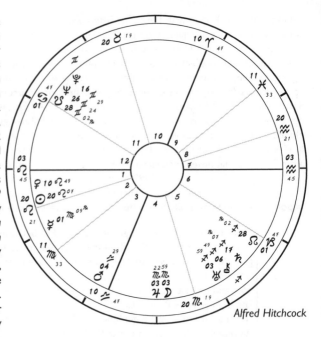

Alfred Hitchcock

Q "Hitchcock was too popular, self-publicising and successful to win the admiration of the more self-consciously intellectual critics until late in his career... Throughout his career, critics seized on elements of voyeurism, fetishism and sadism in his work... Even Hitchcock's most light-hearted films are accounts of people suffering mental torture, usually centring on the concept of guilt or loss of identity." (Christopher Tookey, *Daily Mail*, 12/8/99)

Roger Hodgson

b. 21 March 1950, 10.50 GMT, Portsmouth, England, 50N48, 01W05.
Linda Clark q. him. RR: A.

Hodgson was picked in 1969 as bass player for the newly formed Supertramp. The band's greatest success was in May 1979 when their album *Breakfast in America* topped the US charts for six weeks.

Amanda Holden – see Les Dennis

Anthony Hopkins

b. 31 December 1937, 09.15 GMT, Margam, Wales, 51N34, 03W44.
From Hopkins to his astrologer David Hayward, 1991, but Hopkins gave 10.30 to Joan Abel in 1978. (N.B. Events and synastry suggest the 09.15 time, but both charts are presented for the reader's discernment.) RR: DD.

Actor in a class of his own. Versatile, intense and neurotic, Hopkins made his film debut in *The White Bus* in 1967, seven years after first appearing on stage. Hopkins had an idyllic childhood until he went to school, where he resented authority figures. Nevertheless he was driven to be something better and, spurred on by Richard Burton (qv), wanted both fame and money. He went to RADA in 1961 and in 1965 auditioned successfully for Laurence Olivier (qv) at the National Theatre. Frightened about acting he sought comfort and courage in drink. He understudied Olivier in *The Dance of Death* and in September 1967 gave a remarkable performance when Olivier was taken ill. Olivier cast him in the leading role in his next stage production, yet Hopkins never fit in to the theatre group dynamic and turned his back on the stage to film *The Lion in Winter* in 1968. Later he returned to the stage, only to walk out of the National Theatre again and marry his wife the following day. He featured in the successful US drama series *QB VII* (1974) and in the same year made a sensational Broadway debut in *Equus* (appearing for nine months from 24 October 1974). Two years later he moved to Los Angeles and joined Alcoholics Anonymous (Moon square Neptune). Hopkins believes the rebel in him came from his agitator father. He has spoken of an underlying fury in his nature and has, over the years, wrestled with a number of personal demons. He used this all-consuming anger in his Oscar-winning portrayal in *Silence of the Lambs* (February 1991, TR Saturn conjunct Jupiter and following TR Uranus conjunct Sun). (His most famous role of Hannibal Lecter is suggestive of the possible Scorpio MC.) Winning the Oscar on 30 March 1992 was one of the finest nights of his life (eleven years to the day his father died, TR Neptune conjunct Moon). Despite (or perhaps due to) a personal crisis of confidence during 1995-6, he continued to make remarkable transformations for the screen – in *Nixon* and *Surviving Picasso*, tackling the latter with a ferocious energy. Director Oliver Stone said, "Tony can morph without the assistance of computer-generated effects," which suggests the prominent Neptune square Moon. Actress Emma Thompson remarked that he has a volcanic personality, and

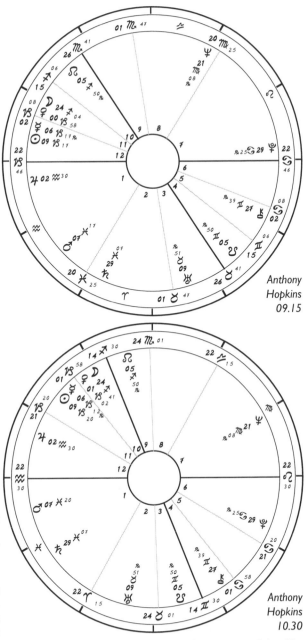

Anthony
Hopkins
09.15

Anthony
Hopkins
10.30

others have described Hopkins as unpretentious, pugnacious, restless and self-destructive. Other film roles include the repressed butler in *The Remains of the Day* and the writer C.S. Lewis in *Shadowlands*. He has made a career out of playing unfeeling characters determined to ward away intimacy and control their madness – memorable portraits of simmering, smouldering restraint (the possible Capricorn/Scorpio angles). By delving deeply into his characters' possible motivations during rehearsals, Hopkins allows room for a certain spontaneity when filming. After retiring in 1998 he returned to play *Hannibal* in May 2000, one month after he became a US citizen. He kicked a drinking habit in 1975 (Moon square Neptune) and readily admits to being more suited to his work than to fatherhood. Hopkins has a passion for music and composes. Recently he relinquished his voluntary position as honorary mayor of Pacific Palisades and devoted his time to his new relationship, and the couple tied the knot on 1 March 2003 (his second marriage had been dissolved in May 2002).

Q

"I think success has been very important to me. I wanted it to heal some inner wound of some kind. I wanted revenge; I wanted to dance on the graves of a few people who made me unhappy – and I've done it... I'm physically strong; I can be a tyrant; I'm ruthless, single-minded. I want what I want... I'm just very, very selfish. If somebody doesn't like what I am, I don't hang around trying to win anybody's approval... I'm a roamer. I think I'm a bit of a nihilist, really." (Anthony Hopkins, *Vanity Fair*, 10/96)

"He is by nature a terrifyingly angry man. I think it's to do with perfectionism in his art. He can't bear not to be on top of his game all the time. I think all Tony basically cares about is acting, and whenever he falls short he becomes incredibly angry with himself." (David Hare, *Vanity Fair*, 10/96)

"I love that bleakness [of travelling by car across America] because it is part of myself. I love the coldness of life. I love the inevitability of it all... When I went to school I discovered I was on the wrong planet because I was so academically retarded. I guess I misused my education... I was the one who didn't fit in... It's a romantic fantasy I have of the loner, the lone wolf who doesn't need any affection. That's part of my life, actually, I think I can do very well without any affection and love... I am capable of withdrawing from people and closing myself off. Maybe it's a form of martyrdom... I tend to be very unpredictable and moody... I'm Mr Friendly, Mr Nice Guy because I want to be liked, I want to be pleasant to everyone. Then somebody steps on my toes and I go off like a firecracker. So what I've learned to do recently is to say "no" to people." (Anthony Hopkins, as quoted in TV's *A Taste for Hannibal*)

Fred Housego

b. 25 October 1944, 21.15 GDT, Dundee, Scotland, 56N28, 03W00.
Gerard q. BC. RR: AA.

Taxi-driver Housego won *Mastermind* in 1980 (before the final he had collapsed with pericarditis). He became an instant celebrity and began a career in TV presenting. Housego can still be heard on LBC.

Renee Houston

b. 24 July 1902, 07.55 GMT, Johnstone, Scotland, 55N50, 04W29.
Gerard q. BC (Catherine Rita Murphy Gribbin). RR: AA.

Comedienne-actress who debuted in 1920. A London debut followed five years later and a Royal Variety Performance in 1926. Houston was a character actress who appeared in over 40 films. D. 9 February 1980.

Bruce Robert Howard

b. 2 May 1961, 04.20 GDT, Memorial Hospital, Haddington, Scotland, 55N57, 02W47.
Gerard q. BC. RR: AA.

Dr. Robert of the Blow Monkeys. Howard and his band hit the charts from 1986 (as TR Uranus reached the EQHS 10th) and in February 1987 had a Top Five chart hit. Outspoken and political, Howard released one of the first songs about AIDS (*Digging Your Scene*) and a pop record with strong anti-Thatcher leanings was banned from the BBC airwaves until after the General Election in June 1987 (TR Uranus was moving close to the MC, and Uranus is prominent at times of censorship). Howard reached the Top Ten again in early 1989.

Leslie Howard

☄ b. 3 April 1893, 10.27 GMT, London, England, 51N30, 0W10.
From Ralph Kraum in National Astrological Journal, August 1934, original source not known. RR: C.

Actor, producer and director born to Hungarian immigrants. He established a reputation in America as the perfect English gentleman on screen – charming and educated. During the 30s he co-starred with Hollywood's most glamorous leading ladies, including Vivien Leigh (qv) in *Gone With the Wind* (December 1939). In 1943 he was returning from a secret war-mission when his plane was shot down by Nazi raiders. D. 1 June 1943.

Frankie Howerd

✪ b. 6 March 1917, 15.00 GMT, York, England, 53N58, 01W05.
Penny Thornton q. Howerd, via his agent. RR: A.

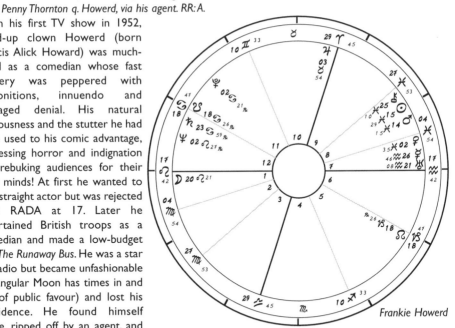

Frankie Howerd

Given his first TV show in 1952, stand-up clown Howerd (born Francis Alick Howard) was much-loved as a comedian whose fast delivery was peppered with admonitions, innuendo and outraged denial. His natural nervousness and the stutter he had were used to his comic advantage, expressing horror and indignation and rebuking audiences for their dirty minds! At first he wanted to be a straight actor but was rejected from RADA at 17. Later he entertained British troops as a comedian and made a low-budget film *The Runaway Bus*. He was a star on radio but became unfashionable (an angular Moon has times in and out of public favour) and lost his confidence. He found himself broke, ripped off by an agent, and underwent psychotherapy using LSD when his mother died. In 1962 he joined Peter Cook (qv) in his nightclub The Establishment and was reinvented as a cult comedian. This led to appearances on *That Was The Week That Was*, in which he reflected on current political events. Writer Barry Cryer (qv) said that Frankie "could reduce everything to a domestic level" (note the strong Moon). A few *Carry On* films in the late 60s brought him back to the large screen but he wasn't a team player and didn't fit in. From September 1969, with *Up Pompeii!*, he was back at the top of his profession and the first to have his own personal scriptwriter. By the late 70s he was unfashionable again until he was discovered by the student generation in the late 80s. There are classic astrological indications of comedic talent in Howerd's chart: Moon Rising opposite a strong Uranus, and Jupiter on the MC. Privately Howerd was an insatiable, indiscriminate flirt with most men he encountered, yet had a loving and enduring relationship with his manager, Dennis Heymer. His personal life was tormented by childhood abuse, depression, a battle with drink, and also blackmail threats at a time when being openly homosexual was professional suicide. Howerd had an intense bond with his mother and his father was often away from the family home. He was known to be very ambitious, moody, frightened of failure and a worrier. He loved psychoanalysing people, yet he always felt on trail, as though he had to prove himself to the public over and over again. D. 19 April 1992.

> Q
> "As a stand-up comedian, Howerd was audaciously inventive... he engaged his audience with gossipy confidences. He told stories, drawing on a repository of put-downs, catch phrases and stammered expletives that became his trademark." (Frances Hardy, *Daily Mail Weekend*, 8/6/02)
> "He would take the audience into his confidence as if everybody else were funny people." (Scriptwriter Alan Simpson, as quoted in BBC's *Reputations*, 2002)

Mick Hucknall

b. 8 June 1960, 06.30 GDT, Manchester, England, 53N30, 02W15.

Garry Heaton q. him personally, "I'm pretty sure." Place confirmed. RR: A.

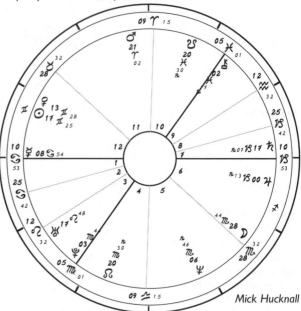

Mick Hucknall

Hucknall is the lead singer of the successful pop band Simply Red, who had their first UK hit in July 1985. Twelve months later the band scored the #2 UK smash *Holding Back the Years* (it topped the US charts later that month). In July 1989 the band secured a second US chart-topper. Hucknall and the band won greater commercial acclaim after the release of the album *Stars* in October 1991. With the band Hucknall has sold 45 million albums (Moon in EQHS 5th squares Pluto). Their latest album, *Home*, was released in March 2003. The release of *Stars* (1991) also signalled the start of a growing-up period for Hucknall, who had gained a 'wild' reputation on tour in the late 80s (the chart ruler is the Moon in Scorpio in EQHS 5th).

That reputation has stuck with him and speculation about his private life and relationships with the numerous beautiful women seen on his arm continues to this day (MC in Pisces). On 26 November 2000 he was falsely accused of rape (TR Pluto opposing Venus, TR Uranus opposing Uranus), but was cleared the next day. The police cautioned him for possessing cocaine and cannabis, found when his home was searched. Hucknall, who also has a passion for politics, grew up in Denton, Manchester and at age three his mother left home, leaving him with his father. (*Red Mick* by Mick Middles, Headline, 1993.)

> Q
>
> "The women who were around when I was growing up were never given the licence to be surrogate mothers. It meant that, right from the start, I was made to feel like an outsider, this odd kid with red hair who loved music and had no mum." (Mick Hucknall, *Daily Mail*, 4/12/2000)
>
> "I have a fear of getting involved with anybody in an intense way, a fear of getting into a deep relationship... I have a fundamental fear that someone is going to leave me again, so, in order to stop them doing that, I leave first." (Mick Hucknall, *Night & Day*, 23/2/03)
>
> "He is astonishingly candid. He used to be perceived as aggressive, arrogant, a prickly hedgehog of a man who kept people at a distance." (Rebecca Hardy, *Night & Day*, 23/2/03)

HUE AND CRY

Brothers Gregory and Patrick Kane formed Unity Express before moving on to the name Hue and Cry in 1985, with a first single release in 1986. The following year they achieved their first success. Patrick Kane, outspoken and articulate, has also worked as a TV presenter and music journalist since 1985 and is a vocal supporter of the Scottish Nationalist Party (his chart shows a dramatic political opposition of MC-Pluto-Uranus to his Mars-Mercury-Sun). He was elected the Rector of Glasgow University in 1990. When the financial partnership went into receivership in late 2001 Patrick continued writing and performing while Gregory worked as a DJ and producer.

Gregory Kane
> b. 11 September 1966, 07.55 GDT, Maternity Hospital, Glasgow, Scotland, 55N51, 04W14.
> Gerard q. BC (Gregory Philip Kane). RR: AA.

Patrick Kane
> b. 10 March 1964, 00.03 GMT, Maternity Hospital, Glasgow, Scotland, 55N51, 04W14.
> Gerard q. BC (Patrick Mark Kane). RR: AA.

Engelbert Humperdinck
> b. 2 May 1936, 23.48 IST (-5.5 = -5 hours 30 mins), Madras, India, 13N05, 80E17.
> Joan McEvers q. his fan club president, who obtained the data from Humperdinck's personal
> secretary. RR: A.

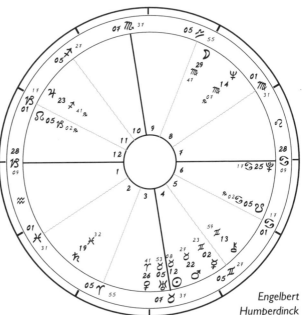

Engelbert
Humperdinck

Silk-voiced Humperdinck, the king of the romantic ballad, began his musical career as Gerry Dorsey. His first love was the saxophone and he had ambitions to be a Big Band leader. At 17, influenced by Nat King Cole, he gave up the sax and began singing at working men's clubs at weekends. After a two-year army stint he launched his fledgling career in 1956. He enjoyed moderate success until 1963, when offers dried up and he fell ill with tuberculosis. He changed name and his career was revitalised in 1966. The following year he began a run of eight Top Ten hits in Britain up to 1969, including two #1s (*Release Me* in March 1967, and *The Last Waltz* in September 1967, combined sales topping 2.5 million). He took great steps to preserve his mysterious, elusive celebrity image (note the Scorpio MC), often exiting venues via a bathroom window! Since the early 70s he has been a star attraction on the Las Vegas circuit. He has always been seen as a mellow, more 'square' alternative to former friend Tom Jones, less likely to change with the times and preferring to keep his fans happy with his classic ballads and impressive vocal range. Humperdinck has sold over 130 million albums, boasts the world's largest fan club membership (note the MC ruler Pluto conjunct the Descendant) and even more paternity suits than his rival Jones (Pluto-Descendant square Venus). Yet he has been married for 40 years to wife Patricia and they share a pad in Los Angeles, the former pink palace of the late Jayne Mansfield. Humperdinck discovered healing powers after a viral infection in 1989 (natal Neptune sesquisquare Ascendant).

Gareth Hunt – see Joanna Lumley

Russell Hunter
> b. 18 February 1925, 23.25 GMT, Glasgow, Scotland, 55N51, 04W14.
> Gerard q. BC (Adam Russell Hunter). RR: AA.

Character repertory actor, professional from 1946 after amateur dramatics with the Glasgow Unity Theatre. Hunter has staged one-man shows at the Edinburgh Festival and also starred in pantomime. He appeared in *Callan* from February 1967 to May 1972. Hunter's third wife, since 1991, is Una McLean (qv).

Noah Huntley

b. 7 September 1974, 08.42 GDT, Hammersmith, London, England, 51N30, 0W13.
FCC q. BC (a twin). RR: AA.

In early 1994 Huntley (born Noah Cornelius Marmaduke Huntley) was recruited (as part of the new generation of characters) for the soap *Emmerdale* (formerly *Emmerdale Farm*). He soon won a huge following as the rebellious son of a doctor. Huntley was raised with seven siblings in a bohemian environment after his father quit the legal profession for a relatively nomadic lifestyle. After months of travelling they settled in a commune. Huntley was brought up to be an independent child and repeated his father's move when, two years after winning the soap role (as TR Saturn hit Jupiter in EQHS 6th), he quit and found contentment by investing his time and money in a health farm. He was

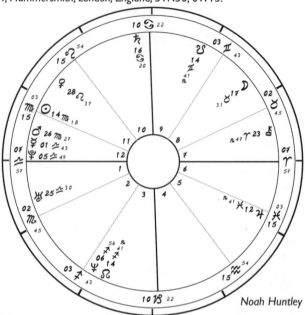

Noah Huntley

keen to avoiding typecasting by following his own Saturn-MC path. Yet Huntley returned to TV and now appears in a number of TV adverts and the football-based drama *Dream Team*.

John Hurt

b. 22 January 1940, 17.30 GMT, Shirebrook, England, 53N12, 01W13.
David Fisher q. a letter from Charlotte Pilcher of Hurt's agency. RR: A.

A charismatic and outspoken actor, John Hurt wanted to be a painter, training at Grimsby Art School and St. Martin's School of Art, before enrolling at RADA. He made stage and film debuts in 1962. He has been praised for his role in *I, Claudius* (September to December 1976) and, with Sun opposite Pluto, has also produced vivid, intense and acclaimed portrayals based on the 'unloved' and their traumatic lives: he was John Merrick in *The Elephant Man*, Quentin Crisp (qv) in *The Naked Civil Servant* (1975), and in *Champions* (1984), he played jockey Bob Champion*. (Crisp's Aquarian Moon falls on Hurt's Sun. Champion's Pluto falls on Hurt's Ascendant.) Hurt has been nominated for two Academy Awards. His recent films have

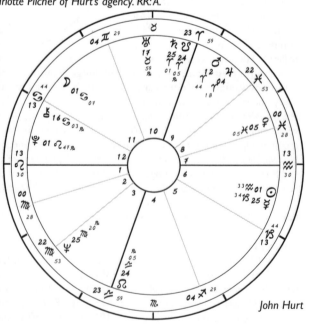

John Hurt

* Bob Champion b. 4 June 1948, 11.10 GMT, Tunbridge Wells, 51N07, 0E16. From him to Penny Thornton.
(N.B. Most sources give Manchester as Champion's birthplace.) RR: A.

included *Rob Roy* (1995) and *Captain Corelli's Mandolin* (2001). Hurt's father, who died in November 1999, was a peripatetic High Church priest and Hurt was sent away to school at age seven. He was first married at 22 (a union that lasted 18 months), then lived with a model for 15 years until her accidental death in 1983. A second marriage lasted a year and his third wife bore him a son on his 50th birthday. That marriage ended in 1994. Hurt has lived in Ireland for many years and has appeared in over 110 films, including *Alien* (released in the US on 25 May 1979).

> "I need a lot of space and will behave very well if I'm given it. The trouble is if I don't watch it, I also have a tendency when I'm in a relationship to become very dependent... I have a strong female side myself; I am quite intuitive and I like women's company and the way they think. I also have big mood swings, often related to the moon... Mine was not a touching or cuddly family... but my loneliness was also to do with being a clergyman's son. Everyone is wary of you." (John Hurt, *Daily Mail*, 15/5/95)
> "I hold back from emotional involvement in characters as I hold back in life. Acting without control is, I think, unwatchable. Art is not in any sense reality, it is a creation of reality." (John Hurt, *Evening Standard*, 12/9/02)

Chrissie Hynde – see Simple Minds
Kenny Hyslop – see Simple Minds

Armando Iannucci
✪ b. 28 November 1963, 15.00 GMT, Charing Cross, Glasgow, Scotland, 55N51, 04W17.
Gerard q. BC (Armando Giovanni Iannucci). RR: AA.
Comedy actor-writer who had his own self-titled show in 2001. Iannucci has written comedy shows with Steve Coogan for over ten years.

David Icke
b. 29 April 1952, 19.15 GDT, Bond Street Maternity Hospital, Leicester, 52N38, 01W05.
Judy Hall, in The Astrology of a Prophet?, p. 29 (Mendip Publishing, 1993), q. his mother, who is sure the birth time is "fairly accurate". RR: A.

The middle of three brothers, Icke had a huge power struggle and personality clash with his father. Icke was a keen goalkeeper before a succession of injuries in his youth (February 1968 and July 1973) and rheumatoid arthritis ended a promising football career. In late 1973 (TR Uranus on Ascendant) he began in sports broadcasting and set his goal to front *Grandstand*, which he began appearing on in late 1980 (his Saturn Return). His big break occurred in July 1982 when he commentated for the World Cup in Madrid (Solar Eclipse on 10th). When he'd fulfilled his ambition the challenge had gone so he turned his attention to environmental issues. In 1984 he joined Greenpeace (and for one year, the Liberal Party) and made a rousing closing speech at their Spring Conference on 5 April 1990 (he resigned in March 1991, TR

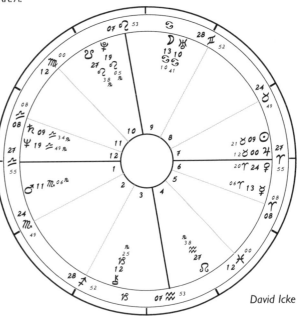

David Icke

Uranus square Mercury). A meeting with healer/medium Betty Shine in February 1990 (Solar Eclipse on IC, Lunar Eclipse conjunct Pluto) revealed a mission from Socrates and led Icke down a spiritual path to 'heal the earth' and promote awareness of ecological disaster. On 3 February 1991 (TR Jupiter on MC), Icke had a 'take-over experience'. The books he has since written offer a valuable alternative perspective on life and the cosmos (Moon conjunct Uranus in 9th, and part of a T-square), despite their author's ridicule by the more ignorant members of British TV and sensationalist Press (note the Mercury-Neptune opposition). This ridicule destroyed his fear of what others thought of him. In May 1992 the Press had a field day when a baby was born of an extra-marital affair with his spiritual partner Mari. In 1999 Icke produced his most controversial book, *The Biggest Secret*, which followed on from his assertions in *...And The Truth Shall Set You Free*.

> Q "All my life I've seen the world differently from other people... my saviour was this obsession with sport from a very early age." (David Icke, as quoted in TV's *Mystic Challenge*)

Eric Idle – see Monty Python

Gordon Inglis
> b. 13 May 1962, 22.00 GDT, Glasgow, Scotland, 55N53, 04W19.
> Gerard q. BC (Ian Gordon Inglis). RR: AA.
Chosen from 6000 applicants to present *The Disney Club*, Inglis was originally a video camera operator for BBC Scotland and a studio-audience and rock concert warm-up man.

John Inman
> b. 28 June 1935, 06.00 GDT, Preston, England, 53N46, 02W42.
> FCC q. him (David Fisher had been given 17.45 some years earlier scribbled on a letter from his
> agency. 06.00 was confirmed by Inman in February 1997 when asked about both birth times). RR: A.

Ex-window dresser Inman won cult status as the precious Mr. Humphries in the long-running BBC comedy *Are You Being Served?* Although character actor Inman had been performing since 13, it would be the mincing Humphries ("I'm free!") who would make him a star (when Saturn is angular it's hard not to be typecast or blessed/burdened with a catchphrase, and with the MC in Pisces the sexuality of Inman and his character has sparked some debate over the years, too). He was approached to play the part in December 1971 and the first series was transmitted on 21 March 1973 (the pilot had been shown the previous September), completing its 69 episodes on 1 April 1985. Preoccupied with measuring inside legs, the character was the subject

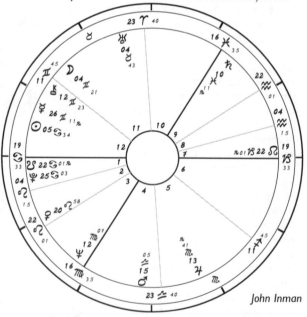

John Inman

of negative feedback from the gay community (October 1977, TR Jupiter conjunct Sun) but years later given cult status in the US almost on a par with Garland and Streisand. When the series was shown in the USA from Summer 1987 (TR Neptune opposite Sun), it became the highest rated prime-time public TV programme in many cities (and most successful British comedy ever aired). Inman, who is mobbed during his tours of the USA, won a favourite comedy character award there in 1991. Inman made two series of an Australian version and even hit the pop charts in 1975 with the theme song. 1976 marked the peak of his popularity in Britain with two top entertainment awards. Inman is a seasoned pantomime dame (especially as one of *Cinderella's* Ugly Sisters). *The Are You Being Served?* team, including Molly Sugden (b. 21 July 1922, Keighley, England) and Frank Thornton (b. 15 January 1921, London, England, FCC q. him), appeared with Inman in the comedy sequel *Grace and Favour* (January 1992-February 1993).

Jill Ireland
b. 24 April 1936, 19.00 GDT, Hounslow, England, 51N29, 0W22.
Grazia Bordoni q. INFOsophia, original source not known. RR: C.
Courageous international leading lady who trained as a dancer from 15. Her screen debut was in 1955 and TV and films followed. In 1984 Ireland lost a breast to cancer and became a spokeswoman for the American Cancer Society. Her son died of a drug overdose in 1989. She was married to David McCallum (qv) from 1957-67 and to Charles Bronson from 1968. D. 18 May 1990, Malibu, cancer.

Jeremy Irons
b. 19 September 1948, 02.00 GDT, Ventnor, England, 50N36, 01W11.
Penny Thornton, in *Romancing the Stars* (aka *Suns and Lovers*), q. him. RR: A.

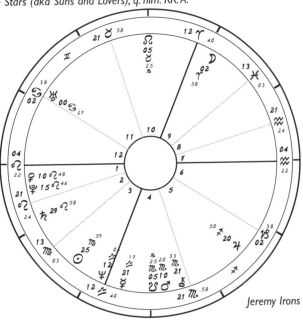

Jeremy Irons

With the Virgo-Leo combination in his chart, Jeremy Irons is the quintessential Englishman on screen. His first ambition was to become a vet but upon failing his school exams, he moved to London and into social work (both professions are associated with Virgo). Later he joined the Bristol Old Vic and although at 30 he contemplated giving up the profession, the following year he won the role of John the Baptist in the West End production of *Godspell*. Irons was also a children's presenter on *Playaway*. It was his haunting performance as the romantic lead in *Brideshead Revisited* that won him 'overnight' fame in 1981. Irons won a Tony Award in 1984 for *The Real Thing* (which opened on 5 January 1984) and an Oscar for Best Actor in *Reversal of Fortune* (released 1990). He caused controversy by appearing in the 1998 film version of *Lolita*. Now he is often seen or heard playing evil characters for big-budget American films (including *Die Hard: With a Vengeance* and *The Lion King*). In early September 1996 he was involved in two car crashes but was not seriously hurt in either.

> Q "As soon as you stop risking, something dies in your work, because you have to have the bravery to fail in order to have the possibility of succeeding... I have never been a group person... I wanted to be in a career which kept me outside the stream, so to speak. I wanted to be an observer, a watcher, someone who could pack his bags and move on without anybody noticing or minding... I think I have whittled away at my natural charm, really from very early on in my career, because I distrusted it, I disliked how it made people think of me – the lightness in it. I have a feeling that is why I have become a little bit spiky, which I never used to be. I want to get away from that 'charming Englishman' image that I once had." (Jeremy Irons, as quoted in *Reflections on Success* by Martyn Lewis, Lennard, 1997)

Jeremy Isaacs

b. 28 September 1932, 21.30 GDT, Glasgow, Scotland, 55N52, 04W18.
Gerard q. BC (Jeremiah Israel Isaacs). RR: AA.

TV presenter, producer and executive of current affairs series. Isaacs became producer of Granada TV's *What the Papers Say* in 1958. He joined BBC's *Panorama* in 1965 and was at Thames Television from 1968 to 1978. Isaacs was the first chief executive of the alternative TV station Channel 4 from 1981 to 1987. His eight-year tenure as general director of the Royal Opera House from 1988 was dogged by controversy. In recent years he has presented the TV interview show *Face to Face*.

Eddie Izzard

○ b. 7 February 1962, 19.00 (-3), Aden, Yemen, 12N45, 45E12.

From his website, www.izzard.com, which gives the date and, "Pluto was ascending at the time." If 'ascending' includes a planet in the 1st, this suggests a time between 17.30 and 20.00. RR: C.

Izzard, the irreverent, 'rambling' stand-up comedian, decided in December 1969 whilst at school to become a performer, a year after he had lost his mother to cancer. Izzard began on the London comedy circuit in 1980 launching his own club in Soho called Raging Bull. He performed at the Edinburgh Festival and in 1991 was nominated for the prestigious Perrier Award. Two years later he took his show to the West End and won the British Comedy Award for Best Stand-Up Comedian. Izzard played Lenny Bruce on stage in *Lenny* (July 1999), played in *A Day in the Death of Joe Egg* (from December 2001) and made film appearances in *The Avengers*, *Velvet Goldmine* and *Mystery Men*. His video *Dressed to Kill*, filmed in

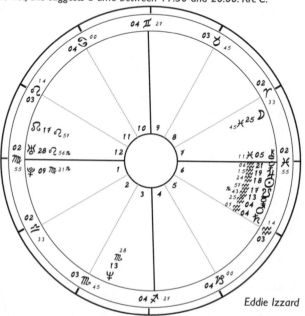

Eddie Izzard

September 1998, won two Emmys in September 2000. Izzard is also famous for being a heterosexual transvestite and jokingly calls himself a male lesbian.

Glenda Jackson

b. 9 May 1936, 08.00 GDT, Birkenhead, England, 53N24, 03W02.
Ruth Hale Oliver q. her, "about 8.00 am." RR: A.

A fascinating and significant talent, Glenda Jackson is an intense, sharp-tongued, forceful and eloquent actress-turned-politician. She is ineffably cool and known to be as wilful and catty as her toughest on-screen characters. A contrary personality with little time for charm, she almost always begins answering questions with a "no" (very Taurean!). She remains in the select band of actresses to have won two Best Actress Oscars. Jackson's Venus-Uranus conjunction in Taurus in the 11th House implies she has no qualms about nudity (indeed, she was known as the 'First Lady of the Flesh'), and with Saturn elevated squaring Ascendant-ruler Moon in the 6th, she understood from early on that everything she wanted would need to be worked hard for. Her Cancer Ascendant suggests a worrier with strong defences (the prickly, protective armour of the crab's shell) and her Taurean planets can turn the most boring of household chores into relaxing pleasures. She inherited her mother's restless spirit (Moon conjunct Jupiter in Sagittarius) and although known to be unconcerned with glamour or vacuous vanity, she has been preoccupied with her physical appearance since childhood. Despite being a bright student Jackson went off the rails at 13. Leaving school at 16 she worked at a chemist's before joining amateur dramatics, which led to her leaving home for a place at RADA in January 1955

(TR Pluto on IC). She made her stage debut at Worthing in February 1957. Moving to LAMDA Miss Jackson was invited to join the RSC, as TR Saturn approached her MC, in January 1964. Despite once being told that she would have to wait until her forties for work (her looks were not 'right' – MC in Aquarius), she became the talk of New York during Christmas 1965 touring with the play *Marat/Sade*. She married in August 1958 (TR Saturn on Moon) and divorced 17 years later (TR Uranus opposite Venus). *Women in Love* (November 1969) brought fame and her first Oscar. At Christmas 1971 a celebrated comedy performance in *The Morecambe and Wise Show* (Jupiter Return) led to more diverse acting roles, including *A*

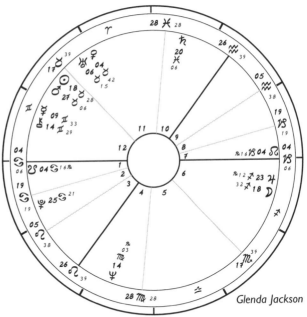

Glenda Jackson

Touch of Class (released June 1973). She gave a bravura performance as actress Patricia Neal*. Jackson's Jupiter falls on Neal's Ascendant and MC on Neal's Venus – the film focused on Neal's life following the traumatic stroke on 17 February 1965. Glenda Jackson won many awards for her starring role in the BBC's *Elizabeth R*** (February to March 1971 – again the chart of Jackson blends well with her subject's: Jupiter conjunct Jackson's Moon-Jupiter, Moon on Jackson's Uranus). An (EQHS) 11th emphasis often translates into a political calling or social sensibility and by 1983 Glenda Jackson was working with a Labour Party candidate, and in March 1990 she announced her decision to run for Parliament herself. Elected in May 1992, Jackson gave her maiden Parliamentary speech ("the most frightening experience of my life") on 11 May 1992 at 20.22 and later became Labour's transport spokesperson. When Jackson was elected to Parliament, Britain may have lost one of its finest actors but Parliament gained an articulate politician intent on working at the grass-roots level of politics. Unafraid to attack the professional stance of fellow politicians, she has made an impact in her own constituency but has not courted enough admirers to do so across a broader arena. In late March 2002 she broke her wrist and hip (TR Uranus conjunct MC).

Q

"She's direct, uncomplicated, honest, very alive. She's absolutely without machination or ulterior motives... Of all the actors I've worked with she has a capacity for work that's phenomenal. There's immense power of concentration, a great deal of attack, thrust, determination. She searches hard. It's quite ruthless." (Trevor Nunn, as quoted in *Glenda Jackson* by David Nathan, Spellmount, 1984)

"I work to live and I have a strong puritan ethic. I was taught to earn my pleasure and to earn through work. To work at my best I have to be interested, and what interests me more than anything are the difficulties the work presents." (Glenda Jackson, as quoted in *The Great Stage Stars* by Sheridan Morley, Facts on File, 1986)

"She was always sharp as razors under the cosy mateyness: articulate, opinionated and a bare-knuckle fighter with anybody who presumed to argue the toss... All her life, despite the tough 'I can cope' exterior which she presents to the world, Glenda Jackson has been a chronic worrier. She is a born pessimist." (*Glenda Jackson – A Study in Fire and Ice* by Ian Woodward, Weidenfeld and Nicolson, 1985)

* Patricia Neal b. 20 January 1926, 04.30 CST, Packard, Kentucky, USA, 36N40, 84W03. *Gauquelin Book of American Charts* q. BC (placed confirmed in autobiography). RR: AA.
** Elizabeth I b. 17 September 1533 NS (7 September OS), 15.00 LMT, Greenwich, England, 51N29, 0W00. Martin Harvey q. Latin records. RR: AA.

Gordon Jackson

b. 19 December 1923, 03.15 GMT, Glasgow, Scotland, 55N53, 04W16.

Gerard q. BC (Gordon Cameron Jackson). RR: AA.

A child star on radio before leaving school at 15 to work for Rolls Royce, Gordon Jackson went on to have a distinguished career on the stage (from 1943) and as a character actor on film and TV. In 1969 a New York debut as Horatio in *Hamlet* won him the Clarence Derwent Award. With Saturn on the Ascendant he is best remembered (and typecast) for his portrayal of the butler Hudson in *Upstairs, Downstairs* from October 1971 (his Jupiter Return) to December 1975, and won an Emmy for the role in May 1976 (TR Saturn on EQHS 10th). The character was described as "craggy, reserved, supremely dignified... [with] an unquestioned authority over the servants' hall" (Leo MC, Saturn Rising). Jackson was also very popular as the crusty Cowley of CI5 in *The Professionals* (December 1977 to February 1983) with Martin Shaw (qv). D. 14 January 1990, spinal cancer.

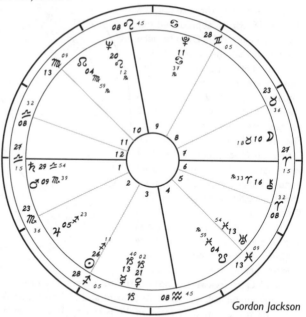

Gordon Jackson

Joe Jackson

b. 11 August 1954, 04.30 GDT, Burton-upon-Trent, England, 52N49, 01W36.

From him to Magpie Latham (he also said it could have been 08.30). RR: DD.

Jackson signed a recording deal in February 1978 and had a first single released that October. The following year he began to hit the charts. He moved to the USA in 1982 following the breakup of his marriage. His most successful album to date, *Night and Day*, was released that year, hitting the Top Five in the UK and USA. In October 1982 he had his biggest singles hit in the US, *Steppin' Out*. He changed record company in early 1991 after the failure of his 1989 album and now works as a classical composer. In 1999 he published his autobiography, *A Cure for Gravity*, and in Summer 2002 he performed a series of gigs with the original line-up of the Joe Jackson Band. In March 2003 he released a new album and toured in June.

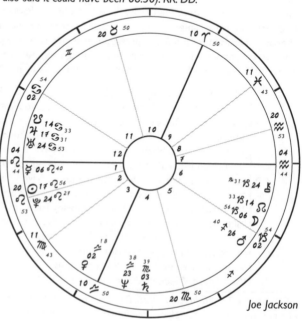

Joe Jackson

Derek Jacobi

b. 22 October 1938, 04.00 GMT, London, England, 51N30, 0W10.

Joan Abel (Mercury Hour, January 1979) q. him by letter. RR: A.

Jacobi began his career with the National Youth Theatre before his professional debut in September 1960. Laurence Olivier (qv) adopted Jacobi as his protege after spotting him on TV playing *Henry VIII* and invited him to go to Chichester for the start of an eight-year alliance with the National Theatre. Known mostly for Shakespearean roles, Jacobi also specialises in obsessive or emotionally inhibited characters (MC/Ascendant ruler Mercury in Scorpio square Pluto, Moon opposite Saturn). His title role in the TV series *I, Claudius* (September to December 1976) was a revelation and universally acclaimed (TR Uranus conjunct MC/Ascendant ruler Mercury). Whilst performing in Sydney in 1980 (as TR Saturn moved towards Mars-Ascendant), he froze

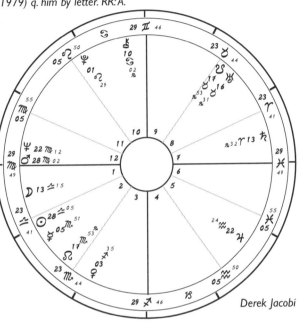

Derek Jacobi

on stage and the experience began a build-up to a nervous breakdown resulting in a two-year retirement from the theatre. His recovery took four years. Placid and non-confrontational (Libran male), he is a natural worrier off-stage (Virgo Ascendant), but a warrior on stage, passionate and intense (Mars on the Ascendant). Jacobi won a Tony Award for *Much Ado About Nothing* in June 1985.

Mick Jagger – see Rolling Stones

Sid James

b. 8 May 1913, 01.05 2E (-2), Johannesburg, South Africa, 26S15, 28E00.

FCC q. his daughter, astrologer Reina James-Reinstein. Time is speculative, from her. RR: C.

Crag-faced James entered radio and television comedy in the 50s and cornered the market in cockney barrow boys, wide-boys and con men. He scored a hit as the perfect foil for Tony Hancock (qv) in *Hancock's Half Hour* (radio: 2 November 1954 to 29 December 1959; television: 6 July 1956 to 30 June 1961). The success with television audiences led to James's own sitcom *East End – West End* (beginning 4 February 1958). Other memorable series include *Citizen James* (24 November 1960 to late 1962) and *Bless This House* (2 February 1971 to 1976). James won his greatest number of fans as the lecherous lead with the dirty chuckle in numerous *Carry On* films. He chased and loved co-star Barbara Windsor (qv). D. 26 April 1976, heart attack.

Charles Jamieson

b. 12 March 1952, 18.15 GMT, Rutherglen, Scotland, 55N50, 04W12.
Gerard q. BC (Charles Reginald Wingate Jamieson). RR: AA.

Actor, narrator and a television voice-over regular (Jamieson has a strong Mercury, ruler of the MC and Ascendant). He studied art at both the Glasgow School of Art and the Texas Christian University.

Bert Jansch

b. 3 November 1943, 14.30 GDT, Glasgow, Scotland, 55N53, 04W14.
Gerard q. BC (Herbert Jansch). RR: AA.

Seminal singer and inventive guitarist whose eponymous debut album is considered by many to be a landmark recording in British folk music. Jansch influenced a generation (Pluto square Sun/Mercury) including Jimmy Page (qv) and Donovan (qv).

Derek Jarman

b. 31 January 1942, 07.30 GDT, Northwood, Middlesex, England, 51N37, 0W25.
From his autobiography At Your Own Risk (Vintage, 1993). RR: B.

Innovative film-maker and maverick (note the strong Saturn-Uranus influence in the chart: Capricorn Rising, Sun in Aquarius, Saturn and Uranus on the IC). Jarman was known for his vivid imagery and ground-breaking depiction of homosexuality on screen (Scorpio MC, ruler Pluto conjunct Moon and opposite Sun). Jarman studied painting at the Slade School in London between 1963 and 1967, and exhibited in various galleries soon after. He moved into film in 1970 as the production designer for Ken Russell's (qv) The Devils. His first film as director was Sebastiane (1976). Jarman was diagnosed as HIV positive on 22 December 1986 and was one of the first public figures to discuss openly the disease, which he did with

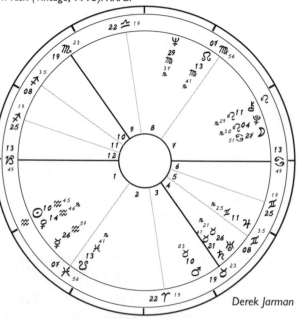

Derek Jarman

frankness and eloquence. In January 1991 (TR Neptune conjunct his Ascendant, TR Pluto conjunct MC) he criticised actor Ian McKellen (qv) for accepting a knighthood. His attack prompted a response (published on 9 January) from a number of well-known gay actors, distancing themselves from his comments. Jarman died on the eve of a House of Commons vote to lower the homosexual age of consent. His final film was Blue, a "stunning artistic interpretation of his illness." D. 20 February 1994.

> Q "Derek was handsome, funny, stimulating intellectually and irrepressibly energetic. His sexual magnetism to men and women alike was legendary... He loved to share his passionate enthusiasm about life and art and although he had a rigorous critical mind he was never malicious despite his demonic public image." (Don Boyd, The Independent, 21/2/94)

David Jason

○ b. 2 February 1940, 03.00 GMT, Finchley, London, England, 51N36, 0W10.

David Fisher q. a letter from Jason's agent. FCC q. date and place from BC. RR: A.

TV favourite with the Midas touch who has created some of the strongest characterisations in British TV sitcom and drama. Young David White always felt an outsider and lacked confidence but at 14 he won an award for best actor in a school drama contest. Nevertheless he became an electrician to support his family, but when he was made redundant at 20 he enrolled in drama school. He changed his name and his first professional break came in Noel Coward's *South Sea Bubble*. After struggling for recognition for many years, workaholic David Jason had six TV hits in a row, all of which demonstrated his immense versatility, popularity and impeccable taste in roles – *Open All Hours* (February 1976 to December 1985), *Only Fools and Horses* (from 8

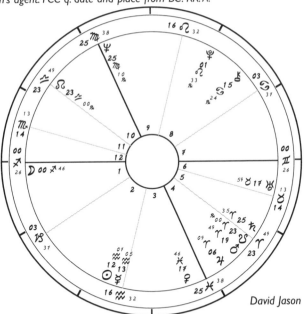

David Jason

September 1981 at 20.30 GDT to Christmas 1996), *Porterhouse Blue* (June 1987), *A Bit of A Do* (1989), *The Darling Buds of May* (April 1991 to April 1993), and *A Touch of Frost* (from 1992). With great comic timing and gentle humour (Moon conjunct his Sagittarian Ascendant) Jason is happy to play ordinary folk to whom the public can easily relate ("He's the perfect underdog, the touchstone of the national character" – Moon conjunct the Ascendant, Neptune on MC). On 8 October 1996 the National Television Awards gave Jason special recognition for lifetime achievement in television (his EQHS chart shows a strong 3rd and 5th, necessary for an audience and following). Although he is fiercely protective of his private life, he has spoken about his actress-companion Myfanwy Talog (b. 31 March 1945 – Sun in Aries, Moon in Scorpio), who died after a five-year battle on 11 March 1995 (when Jason had TR Pluto on his Ascendant). In early 2000 a TV show aired that explored his lifelong passion for deep-sea diving and was accompanied by a book. On 13 April 2003 he was honoured with a Bafta Fellowship.

> Q "Once he has taken a part on board, he builds it carefully. His characters become rounded human beings – figures we know at once from ordinary life, all, of course, quintessentially English... Jason's strength lies in his impish ordinariness, his way of being just a bit out of order." (Malcolm Bradbury, *Daily Mail*, 12/2/97)

Michael Jayston

○ b. 29 October 1935, 03.00 GMT, Nottingham, England, 52N58, 01W10.

FCC q. him, from his parents. RR: A.

Stage and screen actor. Jayston appeared in adaptations of classics (*Jane Eyre*, BBC 1980) and popular TV dramas (*Callan* in June 1970, *Tinker, Tailor, Soldier, Spy* in 1979). He has been married three times.

JESUS & MARY CHAIN

Brothers Jim and William Reid founded the controversial band in 1983 and signed a record deal in May 1984. Their debut single *Upside Down* (released in November 1984) topped the Indie charts. The brothers broke up the band in October 1999.

Jim Reid

○ b. 29 December 1961, 16.00 GMT, Glasgow, Scotland, 55N51, 04W14.

Gerard q. BC (James McLeish Reid). RR: AA.

William Reid

✪ b. 18 October 1958, 18.00 GMT, Possil Road, Glasgow, Scotland, 55N52, 04W16.
Gerard q. BC (William Adams Reid). RR: AA.

Richard Jobson

b. 6 October 1960, 18.20 GMT, Maternity Hospital, Kirkcaldy, Scotland, 56N07, 03W09.
Gerard q. BC. RR: AA.

Singer-songwriter with the Skids (1977-81), who now often appears on terrestrial and satellite television as an entertainment media presenter. Jobson is epileptic.

Elton John

b. 25 March 1947, 16.00 GDT, Pinner, England, 51N36, 0W23.
Ruth Dewey states "confirmed by him." (N.B. Other unsourced references have given 00.30 (28 Scorpio Rising) and 02.00 (15 Sagittarius Rising), which both emphasise the flamboyant, hedonistic planet Jupiter.) RR: A.

Legendary singer-songwriter and flamboyant, theatrical entertainer ("the Carmen Miranda of Pop"). Elton John was hailed as the definitive rock performer of the 70s with his unique and spectacular live shows (Leo Rising). A substantial musical talent, he was the world's biggest-selling act in the 70s (between 1972 and 1976 one in every four albums sold worldwide was by John). He is camp, dramatic and flamboyant, and sings in an unmistakable Southern drawl. A fascinating personality conflict exists within him: a driven, self-destructive, excessive and self-indulgent character is melded with an frank, self-effacing kid with self-doubt and an inferiority complex (the Moon-Pluto square, and Sun in Aries). He left school on 5 March

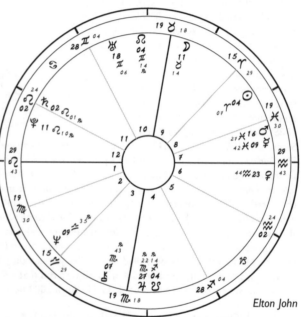

Elton John

1965 (TR Jupiter conjunct MC) to work as an office boy, formed his own group, Bluesology, and signed a recording contract in June of that year. He teamed up with Bernie Taupin in 1967 and had an initial release in March 1968. By September 1970 he was the biggest British star since The Beatles and had played his first US show. By the end of 1975 (Saturn Return) had he reached a professional high and a personal nadir (which included drugs, a suicide attempt and eating disorders). Years later he would adopt a healthier lifestyle and enjoy his passions for tennis and football (Elton was involved with Watford FC from 1973 to May 2002). Elton moved to Geffen Records, signing on 21 September 1980 and his 1983 work brought him further acclaim. He surprised fans by marrying on 14 February 1984 (a union that lasted four years) having 'come out' in 1976. In late October 1993 he met David Furnish (TR Saturn conjunct Venus, TR Pluto square Venus) and the couple have been together ever since (the only celebrity gay couple who regularly appear in newspapers, where their relationship rather than their sexuality is the issue). In March 1987 John successfully sued a tabloid over false allegations involving rent boys. He was awarded £1 million in October 1988 (TR Pluto opposite Moon). He continues to be highly driven to remain at the top and have major commercial hits (over 45 Top 20 hits in the UK alone). He scored a best-seller in January 2003 with the boy band Blue. His candid video diary entitled Tantrums and Tiaras (directed by Furnish) was broadcast in July 1996, giving viewers a glimpse into his explosive moods and to a lifestyle both lavish and mundane (Leo Rising, Moon in

Taurus on MC). The Taurean Moon (in the Virgo decan) also describes his domesticated, fastidious side and why, for him – a self-confessed anally-retentive control freak – vacuuming and tidying are therapeutic. Elton's biggest hit came with the song *Candle in the Wind*, performed at the funeral of Princess Diana. Released on 20 September 1997 it sold over 650,000 on its first day of UK release, ultimately selling 4.86 million copies in the UK and 33 million worldwide. His contributions to *The Lion King* won him a Grammy, Oscar and Golden Globe. In February 2003 *The Mail on Sunday's Rich Report* estimated his fortune at £215 million. In March 1998 (with TR Uranus, the Descendant ruler, square Moon and opposite Pluto) his relationship with manager John Reid (qv) soured after details of Elton's finances were leaked to the Press. Two months later he fired Reid and began court proceedings (claiming financial negligence) in July 1999. The case began in November 2000 (TR Saturn conjunct EQHS 10th) but Reid (and other advisors) emerged victorious in April 2001 (TR Saturn conjunct EQHS 10th, TR Uranus, ruler of the Descendant, conjunct Venus, ruler of the MC).

> Q "Despite his huge fame and wealth, he has contrived to remain – at least, to outward appearance – simple, straightforward and down to earth. Despite his displays of excess, on- and off-stage, he remains paradoxically self-effacing and shy... He is also known for hedonism, a spender and self-indulger on an epic scale... He suffers from chronic self-doubt and insecurity, periodic nervous prostration, attacks of self-destructive anger and dark fits of fathomless despair." (Philip Norman, *Elton*, Arrow, 1992)

Brian Johnson – see AC/DC

David Johnson
> b. 27 October 1942, 07.20 GDT, Edinburgh, Scotland, 55N56, 03W13.
> Gerard q. BC (David Charles Johnson). RR: AA.

Cellist and music historian educated at Cambridge. Johnson taught at Edinburgh University in 1988.

Holly Johnson
○ b. 9 February 1960, 16.30 GMT, Wavertree, Liverpool, England, 53N25, 02W55.
> Sy Scholfield q. him. (In 1997 Johnson gave FCC, "before 12 noon". In an email (1 July 2002) to FCC, Johnson stated, "after a conversation with my father I now believe "about half past four in the afternoon" to be correct.") RR: A.

Vocalist Johnson was the openly gay front man of the band Frankie Goes To Hollywood (note the Aries MC, with ruler Mars conjunct Venus, indicating he's known for his overt sexuality). The band played their first gig in August 1980. With the release of the 'sexually explicit' song *Relax* (released 31 October 1983), the band became famous overnight when the disc was banned in January 1984 (censorship is Uranian in nature, and Johnson has Uranus Rising opposite Sun). It went on to top the charts later that month selling 1.9 million copies in total. Two other #1s (with further sales of two million copies) and an enormous amount of media hype followed, but the band was dissolved in March 1987. Johnson won a lawsuit against his record company in February 1988 (TR

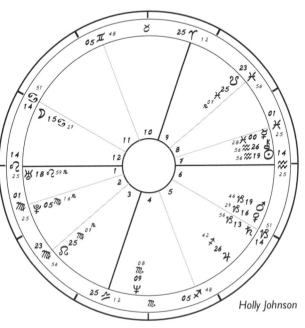

Holly Johnson

Jupiter conjunct MC), and released a solo single twelve months later. In April 1993 he revealed that in late 1991 (as TR Pluto squared Sun, and TR Neptune crossed his planets in Capricorn) he had been diagnosed as HIV positive and then a week later as having AIDS. Johnson later wrote an articulate and amusing autobiography, *A Bone in My Flute*. He now records music under his own record label Pleasuredome.

Sue Johnston

b. 7 December 1943, 07.20 GDT, Warrington, England, 53N24, 02W37.
FCC q. her from her mother's memory, who was "very sure about the time, how can anyone ever forget?" RR: A.

As the frumpy, put-upon but emotionally sturdy Sheila Grant in *Brookside* (from November 1982 to 1990), Sue Johnston proved herself an exceptional, versatile actress (Jupiter falls in a Gauquelin Plus Zone). The plot lines allowed her to run the gamut from rape victim to anguished wife-mother in times of other trauma. Johnston went through a second divorce shortly after the series began — the separation was in 1979. Since leaving *Brookside* in 1990 she has appeared in *Inspector Morse* and *Medics* (1992-5). Johnston also featured in the film *Brassed Off*, released 1 November 1996, and on 1 March 1997 she starred in an eight-part time-travelling mystery series called *Crime Traveller*. Johnston moved into comedy with

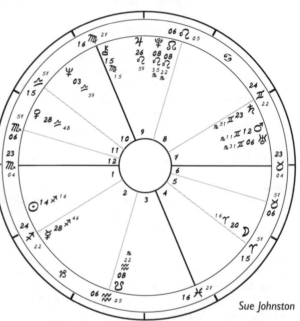

Sue Johnston

The Royle Family in 1998 and now appears as the psychological profiler Dr Grace Foley in the series *Waking the Dead* (which began as a two-part thriller on 4 September 2000). She is known to be a worrier who has a constant fear of getting into debt (MC ruler Mercury in 2nd opposes Saturn in EQHS 8th). (*Brookside*, based around a housing estate in Liverpool, began at 20.00 GMT on the first day of Channel 4's transmission, 2 November 1982. After the show's rocky start, it developed a strong, regular audience and has in recent times adopted the more sensational aspects of soap – MC in Pisces – including a religious cult, a helicopter crash and a dead body under the patio! As a defining actor in the series, it is not surprising that Johnston's chart strongly connects with the show's horoscope.)

> Q "I loved being an only child much as I love now being on my own. The pattern of my life was probably established in childhood. I'm a bit selfish about being on my own. I don't like to be too invaded with company except on my own terms... I always wanted a relationship and then when I got it fought against it. I don't want to be owned. If anyone ever gets too loving with me, I back off." (Sue Johnston, *Evening Standard*, 15/6/01)

Brian Jones – see Rolling Stones
Kenny Jones – see Who
Malcolm Jones – see Runrig
Terry Jones – see Monty Python

Tom Jones

b. 7 June 1940, 00.05 GDT, Pontypridd, Wales, 51N37, 03W22.

His parents, interviewed in Motion Picture, 1970, state "he was born just after midnight." RR: A.

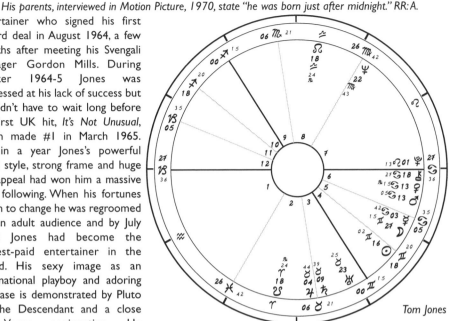

Tom Jones

Entertainer who signed his first record deal in August 1964, a few months after meeting his Svengali manager Gordon Mills. During Winter 1964-5 Jones was depressed at his lack of success but he didn't have to wait long before his first UK hit, *It's Not Unusual*, which made #1 in March 1965. Within a year Jones's powerful vocal style, strong frame and huge sex appeal had won him a massive teen following. When his fortunes began to change he was regroomed for an adult audience and by July 1970 Jones had become the highest-paid entertainer in the world. His sexy image as an international playboy and adoring fan base is demonstrated by Pluto on the Descendant and a close Mars-Venus conjunction. He relocated to California in late 1975 when the pop hits evaporated and began a 12-year reign as the king of Las Vegas. Thanks to his manager-son he reinvented himself and made successful revisits to the charts including an entry in May 1987 and a revamped version of Prince's *Kiss* in October 1988. As TR Neptune crossed his Ascendant Jones scored an international hit in Autumn 1997 with a track from the successful British film *The Full Monty*. This began a career resurgence along with an iconic status awarded by the current batch of British pop stars and a best-selling album *Reload* in September 1999 (during his Jupiter Return, and five million copies sold worldwide). In February 2003 *The Mail on Sunday's Rich Report* estimated his fortune at £180 million and on 20 February he was awarded the Outstanding Contribution to Music prize at the Brit Awards. Jones grew up a sickly boy, contracting TB as a boy and bedridden between 12 and 14. He was also dyslexic and hated school. In 1961 he joined a local band and was driving the crowds wild with his masculine sex appeal. Jones married at 16, the couple had their son in April 1957 and have stayed together ever since. Jones had a two year affair with Supreme Mary Wilson* (Wilson's Mars is on his Sun and her MC conjuncts Jones's Ascendant – her name will forever be linked romantically to his).

Junior

b. 6 June 1957, 07.30 GDT, Balham, London, England, 51N27, 0W08.

Marjorie Orr q. him. RR: A.

Grammy-winning vocalist with sporadic chart entries from his initial 1982 Top Ten hit *Mama Used To Say*. He was the first black British artist to appear on the US show *Soul Train*. He is the uncle of British comedian Richard Blackwood.

Penny Junor

✪ *b. 6 October 1949, 05.25 GDT, Leatherhead, England, 51N18, 0W20.*

From her autobiography Home Truths, about her and her father, p. 45 (Harper Collins, 2002). RR: B.

Writer and regular royal TV commentator best known for her biographies of Prince Charles and John Major. Junor has also written about Princess Diana and Margaret Thatcher.

---

* Mary Wilson b. 6 March 1944, 10.11 CWT (+5), Greenville, Mississippi, 33N25, 91W04. Lois Rodden q. her, from BC. RR: AA.

Gregory and Patrick Kane – see Hue and Cry
Graeme Kelling – see Deacon Blue

David Kelly

> b. 24 December 1923, 08.20 GMT, Kilmarnock, Scotland, 55N37, 04W30.
> Gerard q. BC (David Gray Kelly). RR: AA.

Renowned principal bass with the Royal Opera House, Covent Garden from 1954 (as TR Saturn crossed his MC). He performed some 82 performances in his second year alone. Kelly taught and inspired students at the Scottish Academy of Music and Drama with theatrical elegance and he took pride in moulding young talent (the Moon-Pluto in 7th opposite Mercury is important here, as well as the Sagittarian influence for teaching, and prominent Saturn for respect). During his professional life he gave over 700 performances in more than 50 roles. D. 24 October 1996, Troon.

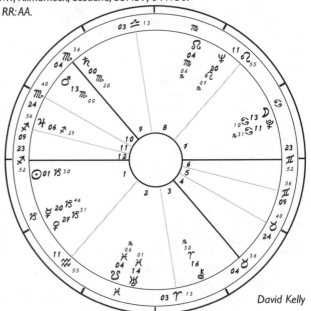

David Kelly

Lorraine Kelly

> b. 30 November 1959, 10.45 GMT, Maternity Hospital, Glasgow, Scotland, 55N51, 04W14.
> Gerard q. BC. RR: AA.

A newspaper journalist and BBC Scotland researcher (1983) before she joined *TV-am* (1984-92), Kelly is popular with viewers for her buoyant and professional manner (a Sun-Moon-Jupiter conjunction and Saturn Rising in Capricorn). Kelly impressed bosses with the speed at which she and her cameraman managed to arrive at the scene of a news story before other journalists – he was her boyfriend and always at hand! She was quietly and gradually brought to attention as the Scottish correspondent for *TV-am*, especially during 1988, a high-profile year in news. Kelly remained with breakfast television when *GMTV* took over the franchise on 1 January 1993. She has followed in a long line of upbeat female breakfast television presenters, including Anthea Turner (qv). Kelly was pleasantly surprised when many viewers thought her the sexiest woman on TV. Her daughter Rosie was born in June 1994 and Kelly presented many shows during the latter stages of her pregnancy. Sadly she suffered a miscarriage in early June 2000. Kelly has her own half-hour daily slot on morning TV and remains refreshingly down to earth and free of ego.

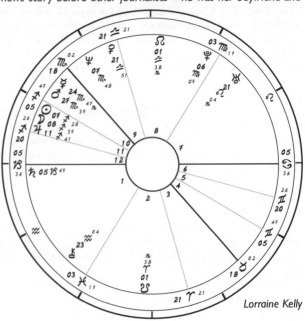

Lorraine Kelly

Matthew Kelly

b. 9 May 1950, 14.00 GDT, Urmston, Manchester, England, 53N27, 02W21.
FCC q. him (same to David Fisher). RR: A.

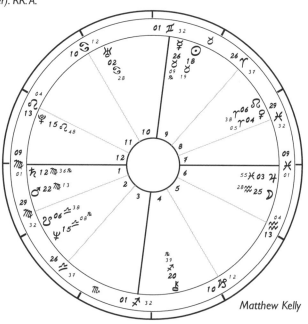

Matthew Kelly

After a teacher-training course Kelly embarked upon ten years of variety and repertory theatre with occasional stints in the West End before working on the comedy series *Holding the Fort* (shown from 5 September 1980). He was one of four presenters in the original practical joke series *Game for a Laugh* (1981-4). On 14 January 1985 the first episode of his sitcom *Relative Strangers* attracted a record-breaking Channel 4 audience of eight million. Kelly has also appeared in *You Bet!* (five series from 1991) and is the genial, lightweight host (Mercury on a Gemini MC) of *Stars in Their Eyes* (a lookalike talent competition which began in 1992). With Saturn on the Ascendant and Sun in Taurus, Kelly has distanced himself from media interest in his private life. But on 15 January 2003 (as TR Uranus passed his Moon, and following the Lunar Eclipse conjunct his Mercury) he was arrested over child-sex allegations and endured weeks of vicious gossip and innuendo. In an unprecedented move, over 40 high-profile actors signed a letter defending him. All charges were dropped on 24 February 2003.

Martin Kemp

✪ b. 10 October 1961, 07.30 GDT, Islington, London, England, 51N33, 0W06.
FCC q. him, November 2002. RR: A.

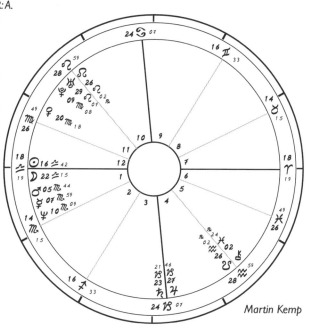

Martin Kemp

In July 1979 (as TR Pluto crossed his Sun) Kemp joined his brother Gary Kemp to form a new band, Spandau Ballet. Brought in because of his looks, he later learned to play on bass and perform with the band. Kemp, who was painfully shy as a child, wasn't preoccupied with the music, he was interested in the fame and fashion (a triple Libra!). Playing the pub circuit the band were spotted in December 1979. By March 1980 they were fast becoming the darlings of the New Romantic movement and had a growing fanbase. They signed a deal with Chrysalis Records in April with a debut hit single released in November (TR Pluto conjunct MC ruler Moon). Hits continued, including their signature tune, *True*, which topped the charts in April

1983. By this time they were rivalling Duran Duran as the top UK band and filling huge stadiums. By 1987 Spandau's hits had dried up (ten years later Gary Kemp was in court defending a fight for royalties from three other members of Spandau Ballet, a battle he won on 30 April 1999). Martin and his brother Gary moved into acting in May 1988, announcing their intention to star in the movie *The Krays*. Martin played the ruthless murderer Reg Kray*. After a number of forgettable film and TV roles, he was diagnosed with a brain tumour in February 1995 (TR Neptune conjunct IC and Saturn) and underwent four operations to save his life. Martin Kemp returned to acting in September 1998 in the TV drama *Supply and Demand* before landing the role of evil Steve Owen in *EastEnders* (the character appeared after Christmas 1998). The *EastEnders* part brought him back under the spotlight. Kemp's character made a dramatic exit from the show on 1 March 2002, with Kemp defecting to ITV and new TV roles. His autobiography *True* was published in March 2000.

Helena Kennedy
b. 12 May 1950, 05.35 GDT, Govan Road, Glasgow, Scotland, 55N52, 04W21.
Gerard q. BC (Helena Ann Kennedy). RR: AA.
Writer, broadcaster and barrister known for her erudition and powers of persuasion. Kennedy has appeared in *The Heart of the Matter* and *Blind Justice*, a TV drama loosely based on her own legal experiences. A Q.C. from 1991, her legal career has had a number of landmark cases with Kennedy having represented a member of the Guildford Four and Myra Hindley.

Ludovic Kennedy
b. 3 November 1919, 07.20 GMT, Edinburgh, Scotland, 55N57, 03W13.
Gerard q. BC (Ludovic Henry Coverley Kennedy). RR: AA.

Oxford-educated playwright and naval historian known for his campaigns against miscarriages of justice (Moon-Uranus conjunction is the handle of his chart, and Mercury, ruler of 11th, is at the first degree of Sagittarius). A librarian and later an editor for the BBC, Kennedy is also a documentary maker, author of naval books and travel anthologies, and a TV presenter. He was an ITN newscaster (1956-8) and presenter of *Panorama* (1956-8), *This Week* (1958-60) and *Did You See..?* for 8 years. He married in 1950. Kennedy contested a by-election in 1958 and the 1959 general election. He stood as an independent at the 2001 general election. His book *36 Murders and 2 Immoral Earnings* was published in June 2002.

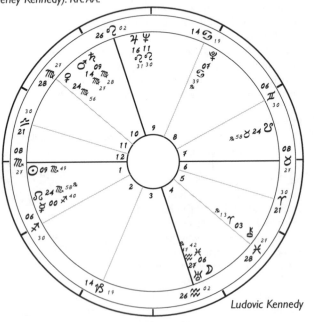

Ludovic Kennedy

Tamara B. Kennedy
b. 23 May 1962, 07.40 GDT, Edinburgh, Scotland, 55N56, 03W11.
Gerard q. BC (Tamara Brooks Kennedy). RR: AA.
Actress who attended the National Youth Theatre in London before appearing in the award-winning *Orpheus Through the Ages* (winner at the 1984 Cannes Film Festival). From 1986 she was seen in the popular soap *Take the High Road*.

Patsy Kensit – see Simple Minds

---

* Reg Kray b. 24 October 1933, 20.00 GMT, Hoxton, England, 51N32, 0E04. John E. Greig q. BC (schizophrenic brother Ron was born ten minutes later). RR: AA.

Paul Kermack

> b. 2 November 1932, 20.30 GMT, Edinburgh, Scotland, 55N57, 03W11.
> Gerard q. BC (George Stewart Auchinleck). RR: AA.

Actor from *Take the High Road* who also played John Logie Baird* on TV.

Deborah Kerr

> b. 30 September 1921, 07.40 GDT, Glasgow, Scotland, 55N53, 04W18.
> Gerard q. BC (Deborah Jane Trimmer). RR: AA.

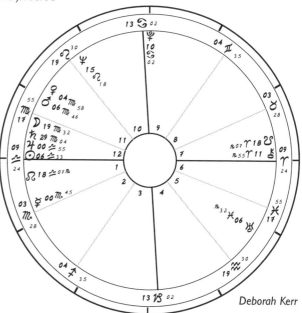

Deborah Kerr

Kerr trained as a dancer with Sadler's Wells ballet school (debut 1938 in the corps de ballet of *Prometheus*). After signing a film contract in the UK on 1 November 1939, she made her film debut in 1940 with *Contraband*, although her role was left on the cutting room floor. With the release of *Major Barbara* in August 1941, her star was on the rise. Kerr won a Hollywood contract in November 1946 (TR Neptune conjunct Ascendant) and starred with Clark Gable in *The Hucksters*, which premiered 15 July 1947 (TR Neptune conjunct Ascendant). In the star-making vehicle *From Here to Eternity* (August 1953, following TR Uranus on MC) she played an adulterous nymphomaniac. Despite this she was soon being typecast in well-bred ladylike roles in classic films. In June 1956 *The King and I* premiered, *An Affair to Remember* was released in July 1957, and *Night of the Iguana* in July 1964. A six-time Oscar nominee, Kerr retired from film in 1969 to return to the stage before a one-off film 'comeback' in 1985. She married on 28 November 1945 to 9 July 1959, marrying again on 23 July 1960 (TR Pluto conjunct Venus). She gave birth to a daughter, Melanie Jane, on 27 December 1947.

Jim Kerr – see Simple Minds

Eddie Kidd

> b. 22 June 1959, 01.15 GDT, London, England, 51N30, 0W10.
> Date and place from *The Birthday Book* by Mark James (Futura, 1988). On Russell Grant's All-Star Show, he revealed to Kidd he was born under the sign of Gemini (the Sun left Gemini at approximately 04.50 GDT that day). Speculative time. RR: C.

Popular model, playboy and dare-devil often seen on television, usually successfully claiming world records for motorcycle stunt jumps. Kidd stunt doubled for actors Harrison Ford and Pierce Brosnan. He was involved in a near-fatal accident on 11 August 1996; comatose, he had sustained head and pelvic injuries. He emerged from the coma on 26 September 1996 but occupational and speech therapy followed for years after. In August 1999, now divorced from his second wife, Kidd walked again in public at a charity event.

---

* John Logie Baird b. 13 August 1888. 08.00 GMT, Helensburgh, Scotland, 56N01, 4W44. Paul Wright q. BC. RR: AA.

Jonathan King

> b. 6 December 1944, 03.00 GDT, London, England, 51N30, 0W10.
>
> Greg Young q. King to astrologer Robert Currey live on Talk Radio in 1996. RR: A.

An unlikely pop star, King first hit the charts in 1965 with his protest song *Everyone's Gone to the Moon.* He was later a talent-spotter, award-winning producer and has released many pop singles under a number of pseudonyms (Neptune conjunct the Ascendant). King appeared regularly on TV in the 80s reporting from America in his weekly show *Entertainment USA.* He is also known as a controversial, outspoken music columnist (Sun in Sagittarius in 3rd opposite Uranus). On 23 November 2000 King was charged with child sex offences dating back 25 years. He appeared in court on 30 November 2000 amid a media circus. A year later a court heard that King took advantage of his celebrity status to 'lure' young men aged between 14

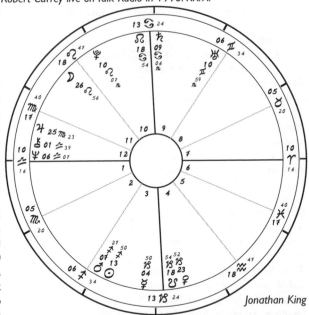

Jonathan King

and 16 into performing sex acts with him. Though only five victims were involved in his trial, police believed hundreds more suffered at his hands over many years. King was found guilty and sentenced on 21 November 2001 (note the stunning set of transits: TR Jupiter conjunct MC, TR Saturn opposite Sun, TR Pluto conjunct Sun). With natal Saturn on the MC, a defiant King, who continues to protest his innocence, is paying the piper by currently serving a seven-year stint. In February 2002 police were investigating further child sex allegations.

Ross King

> b. 21 February 1962, 06.15 GMT, Balornock Road, Glasgow, Scotland, 55N53, 04W14.
>
> Gerard q. BC (Derek Ross King). RR: AA.

Ross King is most familiar to viewers as co-presenter of the mid-day chat show *Pebble Mill* from 1991. A DJ at 15, King became Britain's youngest daytime presenter on Radio Clyde, Glasgow. He is popular and has many series (radio and TV) to his credit.

THE KINKS

• 1962, Dec – Ray Davies joins the Hamilton King/Dave Hunt Band (TR Saturn conjunct Ascendant, TR Uranus square MC). His first gig with them is in January 1963 and he continues playing with brother Dave in the Ray Davies Quartet.

• 1963, Sep – The quartet signs a management contract. Two months later Avory joins the band.

• 1963, Dec 31 – They first appear as The Kinks.

• 1964, Jan – They sign a recording contract.

• 1964, Feb 7 – Their performance on *Ready Steady Go!* attracts much attention.

• 1964, Sep – First chart-topper in the UK.

• 1964, Dec 12 – Ray Davies marries. The couple separate in June 1973 (TR Neptune on MC).

• 1965, July – They tour the USA.

• 1967, May – Ray Davies announces his departure but changes his mind three days later. It is the first of many threats to leave.

• 1970, Aug – Their song *Lola* hits #2 in the UK.

• 1971, Nov – They sign a $1 million deal for five albums.

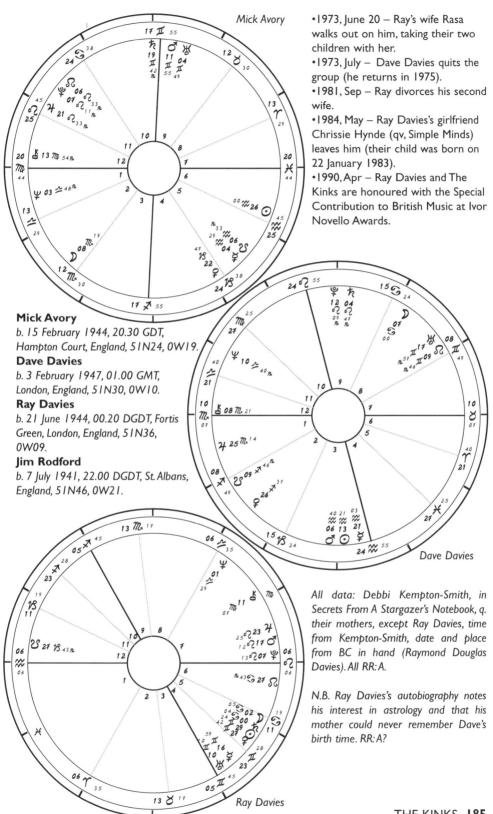

Mick Avory

- 1973, June 20 – Ray's wife Rasa walks out on him, taking their two children with her.
- 1973, July – Dave Davies quits the group (he returns in 1975).
- 1981, Sep – Ray divorces his second wife.
- 1984, May – Ray Davies's girlfriend Chrissie Hynde (qv, Simple Minds) leaves him (their child was born on 22 January 1983).
- 1990, Apr – Ray Davies and The Kinks are honoured with the Special Contribution to British Music at Ivor Novello Awards.

Mick Avory
b. 15 February 1944, 20.30 GDT, Hampton Court, England, 51N24, 0W19.
Dave Davies
b. 3 February 1947, 01.00 GMT, London, England, 51N30, 0W10.
Ray Davies
b. 21 June 1944, 00.20 DGDT, Fortis Green, London, England, 51N36, 0W09.
Jim Rodford
b. 7 July 1941, 22.00 DGDT, St. Albans, England, 51N46, 0W21.

Dave Davies

All data: Debbi Kempton-Smith, in Secrets From A Stargazer's Notebook, q. their mothers, except Ray Davies, time from Kempton-Smith, date and place from BC in hand (Raymond Douglas Davies). All RR: A.

N.B. Ray Davies's autobiography notes his interest in astrology and that his mother could never remember Dave's birth time. RR: A?

Ray Davies

THE KINKS **185**

Graham Knight – see Marmalade
David and Mark Knopfler – see Dire Straits

THE KRANKIES

Husband and wife comedy team, particularly popular in the late 70s and early 80s with their own television shows and numerous guest appearances on children's television. In their sketches pint-sized Janette Tough played 'wee Jimmy', the cheeky, excitable schoolboy. The Krankies were voted the Comedy Act of the Year, 1978.

Ian Tough
> b. 26 March 1947, 12.50 GDT, Crown Terrace, Glasgow, Scotland, 55N52, 04W19.
> Gerard q. BC. RR: AA.

Janette Tough
> b. 16 May 1947, 08.00 DGDT, Queenzieburn, Stirlingshire, Scotland, 55N59, 04W06.
> Gerard q. BC (Janet Anderson). RR: AA.

Cleo Laine

> b. 28 October 1927, 04.05 GMT, Southall, England, 51N31, 0W23.
> FCC q. her for data and "early morning." Rectified. RR: C.

Remarkable singer who joined the Johnny Dankworth Seven in April 1951 (TR Uranus on MC) and, under the guidance of future-husband Dankworth, blossomed into one of the most acclaimed interpreters of song of her era (EQHS 3rd and 5th House rulers are conjunct in 6th on the Descendant). With a vocal range encompassing throbbing contralto and the highest recorded note by a human voice, Laine achieved musical immortality in the USA after a series of stunning concerts from September 1972 (a superb live album at Carnegie Hall was recorded on 17 October 1973), and was hailed by many critics as the greatest singer in the world. Her scat singing ranks up there with the best, audiences often only

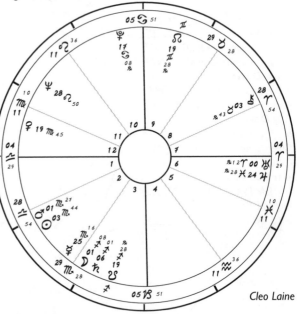

Cleo Laine

distinguishing her voice from an instrument by accepting it as the finer of the two tools. Laine moved into professional acting in March 1958 (TR Neptune conjunct Sun), the month she married John Dankworth (b. 20 September 1927, Walthamstow, Essex, England), the pioneer craftsman of British Jazz with a distinguished and inventive career spanning six decades. The 50s established Laine musically as Britain's finest female vocalist, the 60s brought constant television exposure (she was, for many years, the only black face regularly on British TV), the 70s opened with her capturing America and Australia, and the 80s saw a successful move to Broadway theatre (from December 1985). Her extensive musical repertoire (from Shakespeare to ee cummings and Spike Milligan in one album!) has often seen her excluded from lists of jazz greats because she has sung everything. Laine remains the only singer to have been nominated for classical, jazz and pop Grammys (she won in 1986 for her *Carnegie 10th Anniversary* album). From 1971 Dankworth was Laine's musical director as they triumphed on tour across the world, and with Laine's Sun-Mars conjunction in Scorpio, Dankworth is very much the equal musical partner rather than Svengali. Some of Laine's most interesting collaborations with Dankworth include *Turkish Delight, Song Without Words* and *The Compleat Works* (and Laine herself wrote the vocal accompaniment to the classic composition *Cavatina*, and the track was retitled *He Was Beautiful*). The couple bought a home in Wavendon and established a musical school there in late 1969. Both are recipients of over one hundred top accolades and Cleo was made a Dame of the British Empire in 1997. She acted in *The Last of the Blonde Bombshells*, which aired on 3 September 2000. Their joint 75th birthdays and golden jubilee in music culminated in a memorable concert at the Royal Albert Hall on 20 October 2002. (*Cleo* by Cleo Laine, Simon & Schuster, 1994.)

> Q
>
> "When I was small, I looked on Mum as a goddess. I used to watch her on stage and I would be transfixed. It was strange to have a mother who was so overpowering and I don't think it helped our early relationship... I think I was scared of Mum and probably still am, as she is such an intense person. If she's feeling unhappy, or something is bothering her, she can't cover it up... She's a bit like a cat – self-absorbed and independent." (Jacqui Dankworth, *Daily Mail*, 7/2/95)

Bonnie Langford

b. 22 July 1964, 01.15 GDT, Hampton Court, Surrey, England, 51N24, 0W19.

David Fisher q. her letter, December 1985. RR: A.

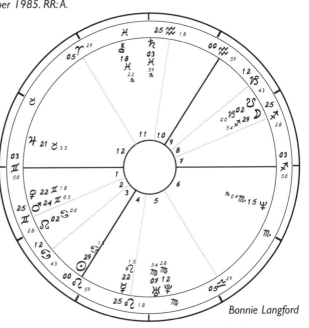

Bonnie Langford

With Jupiter prominent, Langford is a former child star who has kept a precocious, bubbly and self-assured image. At the age of 6 she won *Opportunity Knocks* with her version of *The Good Ship Lollipop*, performed with her trademark saccharine-sweet smile and red curly hair. A gifted and driven singer-dancer-actress, her performances on the West End and Broadway by 11 years of age led to the TV series *Just William* (nine episodes over two series from 6 February 1977, her Jupiter Return). She played the lisping Violet Elizabeth Bott. Roles in *Cats* at 16 and *Oklahoma* followed. Langford went off the rails at 24-5 during a tour of *42nd Street*, posing for 'raunchy' publicity shots to prove she'd come of age. She left home at 28. She first met her partner in March 1987 (the same year she starred in *Me and My Girl* on stage) and married him in September 1995. Langford spent two weeks at The Cafe Royal's Green Room singing a sophisticated set in May 1996 and appeared on stage in *Sweet Charity*. She remains a perennial pantomime performer but struggles with the public's long-standing perception of her. Langford describes herself as very homely and spends much time running her own production company and website. On 19 October 2000 at 15.20 in London she gave birth by Caesarean to her first child, a daughter named Biana.

Angela Lansbury

b. 16 October 1925, 00.45 GMT, London, England, 51N30, 0W10.

Karen Christino q. her. RR: A.

Unflappable, ageless and elegant star who moved to Hollywood during World War II and has played character parts ever since. In the 1990s she became one of television's highest earning stars. Angela Lansbury has reinvented herself over the years (maintaining a sense of mystery as well as a private life – Neptune Rising in Leo), moving gracefully through film, TV and theatre roles. Her Broadway career is unrivalled by any British performer. She has won four Tony Awards (1966, 1969, 1975, 1979) for performances in musicals (two of them were for *Sweeney Todd*, which opened on Broadway on 1 March 1979, and *Mame*, premiered 24 May 1966 and again on 24 July 1983). Other major Broadway roles include *Anyone Can Whistle* (opened 4 April 1964) and *Gypsy* (London: 29 May 1973, Broadway: 24 September 1974). At first Angela signed to MGM and won a Best Supporting Actress Oscar nomination for her debut role at 19 in *Gaslight*. But the studio didn't know what to do with her – she wasn't their idea of a glamorous leading lady so she was cast as Cockneys and then shrews. For a number of years she made villainy into an art form and her icily ambitious role in *The Manchurian Candidate* (1963) was unforgettable. Yet she moved into mundane, busybody parts and brought British ham to television (the 'let them know you're acting' school of drama) with her long-running detective series *Murder She Wrote* from 30 September 1984. The series was highly successful and on 15 May 1991 she was awarded the Lifetime Achievement award from the British Academy of Film and Television, and she received an American Golden Globe Award in 1992. She became a CBE in June 1994 and even released her own fitness video, *Positive Moves*, in 1988. Her longevity as well as her stage presence is suggested by the prominent Neptune. Lansbury's twin brothers, Bruce and Edgar Lansbury (qv), have been highly successful behind the camera. The children were taught to be independent and self-reliant from an early age and the family escaped to New York in 1940. Angela's mother, an actress who struggled to find work, died on 25 November 1975, following an Eclipse on Angela's IC and with TR Pluto conjunct IC ruler Mars. Following a difficult period in the 60s when her son battled drug addiction, Lansbury suffered a major loss when her Malibu home was destroyed by fire in September 1970 (as TR Saturn hit the EQHS 10th and TR Jupiter headed towards the IC). Lansbury underwent her second hip surgery in May 1994. She has married twice, first to the gay actor Richard Cromwell (from 27 September 1945 to 11 September 1946) and then to agent Peter Shaw (from 12 August 1949 to his death on 29 January 2003). Lansbury is a class act who has been untainted by scandal, instead using the strong Neptune to develop an enduring body of work. (*Angela Lansbury – A Life on Stage and Screen* by Rob Edelman and Audrey E. Kupferberg, Birch Lane Press, 1996.)

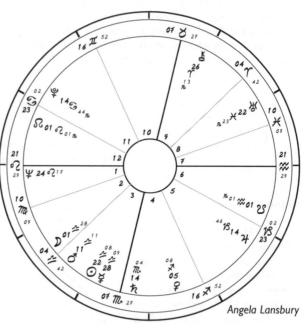

Angela Lansbury

Q "She is happy to call herself a battle-axe and beneath the gracious and very private veneer there has been heartbreak... She's like a porcelain vase with a hand grenade concealed inside it." (Andrew Duncan, *Radio Times*, 3/2/01)

> "I love owning the stage and that unbelievable feedback from an audience... It's got nothing to do with egotism. I always wanted to act, but not for recognition, nor to think I amounted to something. I did it because I adored becoming someone else, escaping my own personality... [My mother] was enormously encouraging and such a glamorous woman, totally immersed in the theatre. I think she felt a little shafted – well, jealous – by my huge success. In the end it was difficult for her to deal with because she never gave up hoping she'd get another break." (Angela Lansbury, *Radio Times*, 3/2/01)

Bruce Lansbury

b. 12 January 1930, 06.25 GMT, Paddington, London, England, 51N32, 0W12.
FCC q. BC in hand (a twin, William Bruce Magesan Lansbury). RR: AA.
Producer Lansbury joined CBS in 1959 and went on to produce *Mission Impossible* and *Murder She Wrote*.

Edgar Lansbury

b. 12 January 1930, 05.45 GMT, Paddington, London, England, 51N32, 0W12.
FCC q. BC in hand (a twin, Edgar George McIldowie Lansbury). RR: AA.
Lansbury began his career as a scenic designer and art director, working as the latter at CBS from 1955 to 1960. On Broadway he had produced *Gypsy, Waiting for Godot, The Subject Was Roses* (also for film) and the film version of *Godspell*.

Eddie Large – see Little and Large

Harry Lauder

b. 4 August 1870, 02.45 GMT, Portobello, Edinburgh, Scotland, 55N57, 03W07.
Gerard q. BC (Henry Lauder). RR: AA.
International singer and songwriter, who debuted as a comedian. He was knighted in 1919 for war entertainment services. Lauder toured America from 1907. D. 25 February 1950.

Charles Laughton

b. 1 July 1899, 06.00 GMT, Scarborough, England, 54N17, 0W24.
Church of Light q. Raphael's Almanac, 1936, original source not known (22.40 GMT has also been given). RR: DD.
Character actor Laughton was a Gold medal winner at RADA in 1927 and made his stage debut the following year. His first film came in 1929 and he won an Oscar for *The Private Life of Henry VIII* (1933). His acting peak occurred with three memorable roles in 1935. Laughton married Elsa Lanchester on 9 February 1929 but throughout his life he was tormented by his homosexuality. D. 15 December 1962.

John Laurie

b. 25 March 1897, 23.45 GMT, Maxwelltown, Scotland, 55N04, 03W37.
Gerard q. BC (John-Paton Laurie). RR: AA.
Idiosyncratic actor whose stage debut in 1921 was in J.M. Barrie's *What Every Woman Knows*. A film debut followed in 1930. Films include *The 39 Steps* (1935) and he was later popular on TV in *Dad's Army* (July 1968, when TR Uranus crossed his MC, to December 1977).

Phyllida Law

b. 6 July 1932, 16.00 GDT, Glasgow, Scotland, 55N53, 04W17.
Gerard q. BC (Phyllida Ann Law). RR: AA.
Character actress known for her portrayals of flinty, dry-witted women. In recent years she has appeared in TV's *Emma* (1996), *The Winter Guest* and *Saving Grace* (2000) on screen. Law is also the mother of Emma Thompson (see Kenneth Branagh). She was widowed in 1982.

Peter Lawford

b. 7 September 1923, 08.00 GDT, London, England, 51N30, 0W10.

Edwin Steinbrecher q. astrologer Betty Collins from Lawford, with a time from his mother. RR: A.

An actor from the age of eight, Lawford graduated to charming leads and supporting characters from 1942 through to the 50s. Perhaps his greatest role was that of playboy and jet-setter in his personal life. He moved into a TV career from the mid-50s after film offers became unsatisfactory. His connection with the Kennedys (he was married to Patricia from 24 April 1954 to 1966) is legendary, especially his infamous role in the events on the night of Monroe's death (4-5 August 1962). He became a regular on *The Doris Day Show* during 1971-2. D. 24 December 1984, Los Angeles, heart attack.

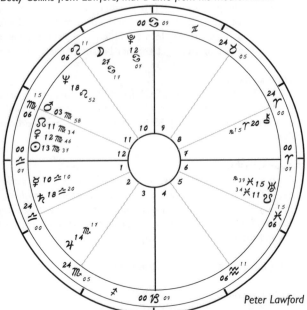

Peter Lawford

Sue Lawley

b. 14 July 1946, 18.00 GDT, Dudley, England, 52N30, 02W05.

FCC q. her. RR: A.

TV newsreader, journalist and, most recently, host of radio's *Desert Island Discs*. After a three year stint as a graduate trainee for the BBC in Plymouth, Lawley made her name in *Nationwide* during the 70s and was once described as the "mink-clad Boadicea of the Beeb." She is a forceful interviewer, although a few gaffs brought her into the news in 1996. On 1 November 1995 she joined the TV current affairs programme *Here and Now*. Her first marriage ended in divorce in 1981 after six years. She married again in December 1987. Lawley's personal relationships (alleged and otherwise) have always attracted media attention (Neptune conjunct MC in Libra) and her presenting style has been described as "matronly yet flirtatious, obsequious yet condescending." She is also known for her obsessive tidiness and passion for list-making.

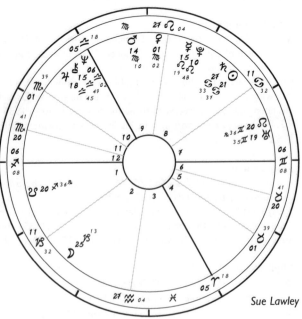

Sue Lawley

Gertrude Lawrence

b. 4 July 1898, 11.00 GMT, London, England, 51N30, 0W10.

Astro-Data II q. Old File, an anonymous file of data without sources; The Penfield Collection speculates 10.30; other sources give the year as 1900 and 1901. RR: DD.

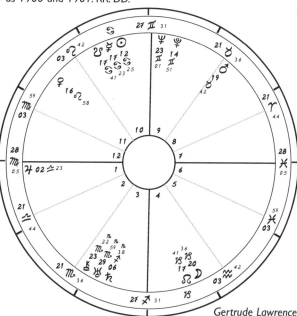

Gertrude Lawrence

Lawrence was a popular, charming actress of British films and a memorable, magnetic star of the London and Broadway stage (and for a while the First Lady of both). For her the Gershwins wrote *Oh, Kay*, childhood friend Noel Coward (qv) wrote *Private Lives* and *Tonight at 8.30*, and Rodgers and Hammerstein wrote *The King and I*. Lawrence had started out as one of 150 child choristers in *The Miracle* in 1911. Her New York debut came in 1924 in *Charlot's Revue*. She starred in *The Glass Menagerie* (1950), five years after she had published her memoirs, *A Star Danced*. In 1968 she was portrayed by Julie Andrews (qv) in *Star!*

Josie Lawrence

b. 6 June 1959, 14.00 GDT, Dudley, England, 52N30, 02W05.

FCC q. her. RR: A.

Actress and alternative comedienne who, after impressive performances at London's Comedy Store, was first brought to national attention in the improvisation TV show *Whose Line is it Anyway?* (which began in 1988). She has also appeared in the situation comedies *Outside Edge* (from March 1994 to 1996) and *Not with a Bang* (March to May 1990). Lawrence's chart has a prominent Mercury influence, aiding her improvisational skills, quick wit and versatility.

Sophie Lawrence

b. 12 June 1972, 18.27 GDT, Ilford, Essex, England, 51N33, 0E05.

From her to Laura Boomer. RR: A.

Lawrence joined the cast of *EastEnders* in 1988 but left to pursue a singing career in 1991. She reappeared in the series briefly during August 1993 and in Autumn 1997. In April 2003 Lawrence was appearing in *Boogie Nights: The 70s Musical*.

Denis Lawson

b. 27 September 1947, 11.55 GDT, Govan Road, Glasgow, Scotland, 55N52, 04W21.

Gerard q. BC (Dennis Stamper Lawson). RR: AA.

Versatile actor who trained at the Royal Scottish Academy of Music and Drama in Glasgow. He made his film debut in 1976 and appeared in the *Star Wars* trilogy. Lawson had a personal triumph on stage in *Pal Joey* (1981-2) and was cast in *Local Hero* (1983). He is the uncle of Ewan McGregor (qv).

Evelyn Laye

b. 10 July 1900, 07.30 GMT, London, England, 51N30, 0W10.

From her to Joan Revill. RR: A.

Star of the musical stage who worked continuously over many decades. Laye made her theatre debut at age 15 and first appeared on the London stage on 24 April 1916. By 1929 she was the biggest musical star in Britain. Known as Boo, her autobiography was entitled *Boo To My Friends*. D. 17 February 1996.

Christopher Lee

b. 27 May 1922, 14.45 GDT, Lower Belgrave Street, London, England, 51N30, 0W08.
His autobiography, Tall, Dark and Gruesome (W.H. Allen, 1977), pp. 9 & 12, q. his father from the attending doctor. RR: A.

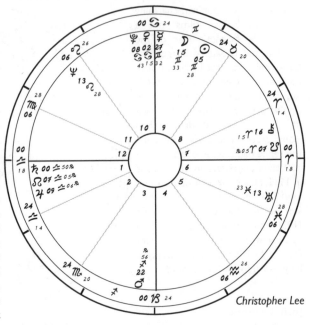

Christopher Lee

Although from a privileged background, with Saturn closely conjunct the Ascendant Lee grew up surrounded by deprivation, firstly because his parents divorced when he was 4, and later at 16 because his step-father was made bankrupt. Lee has made a name for himself in sinister roles in horror films (Saturn conjunct Ascendant, Venus conjunct Pluto on MC), with fame beginning in 1957 with The Curse of Frankenstein. He was featured in Bond's The Man with the Golden Gun in 1973. He has made over 280 pictures (of which only 20 have been terror films, but an angular Saturn typecasts easily). In 1997 he appeared in the BBC series Ivanhoe and released an album of arias sung in a few of the eight languages in which he is fluent (Lee's great ambition was to be a singer). His appearances in The Lord of the Rings and Star Wars films have introduced him to a new audience.

Q "He is a strong believer in responsibility and a proud workaholic, naively astonished that there are people "who don't want to work", who are content to sponge off the taxpayers. But there's a touch of Victor Meldrew about him when he gets on one of his rants." (Kathy Brewis, Sunday Times Magazine, 3/12/2000)

Jan Leeming

b. 5 January 1942, 20.20 GDT, Barnhurst, Kent, England, 51N27, 0E10.
Liz Medler q. her letter. RR: A.

Glamorous, perfectly coiffured BBC newsreader (the Capricorn-Leo mix!), voted newscaster of the year. On 17 February 1987 Leeming was the victim of an ammonia attack when she disturbed intruders at the BBC Television Centre. She left the BBC that year and went freelance but soon gave up her career for her fifth husband. With MC ruler Venus on the Descendant and square Saturn-Uranus in the EQHS 10th, her erratic romantic life is often in the news and Leeming has been married five times (in 1961 for seven months, 1971 for eight months, 1982 for three years, in 1988 until December 1995, and October 1997 to July 2001, as TR Neptune squared MC). She revealed the devastating breakup of her fifth marriage in late October 2001, when TR Uranus crossed her Venus-Descendant.

Vivien Leigh

○ b. 5 November 1913, 17.30 LMT (-5.53), Darjeeling, India, 27N02, 88E16.
The biography The Oliviers by Felix Barker, p. 77, states "not long after the sun had disappeared"
(sunset calculated as 17.16). RR: B.

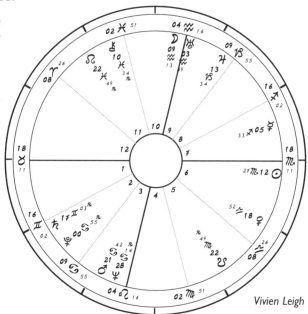

Vivien Leigh

Vivien Mary Hartley was the brilliant, erratic and beautiful star of film and theatre. She was the star of the biggest film ever made, a part she pursued with a single-mindedness and ruthlessness befitting a Scorpio and her most famous role, Scarlett O'Hara. She won the role in Gone With the Wind on 25 December 1938 (it premiered 15 December 1939 and she won the Oscar on 29 February 1940, both when TR Uranus conjunct her Ascendant). The character was wilful, self-possessed, fiery and unpredictable, with little regard for the consequences of her actions – much like Leigh herself. Her two most famous roles (in GWTW and Streetcar) were strangely prophetic, given her tumultuous private life and health.

Leigh grew up headstrong and spoilt amongst lavish surroundings in India. She arrived in England to attend a convent school and didn't see her mother for almost 2 years until her parents returned to England in 1927. She joined RADA in February 1932 but married on 20 December 1932 (until 26 August 1940) and fell pregnant, so career ambitions were put on hold for a while (TR Saturn conjunct MC). Her daughter was born on 12 October 1933. Returning to acting she made her professional stage debut on 25 February 1935 before her stunning performance in The Mask of Virtue (from 15 May 1935, as TR Jupiter conjunct her Descendant). Upon meeting Laurence Olivier (qv) at the Old Vic in June 1935, they began a scandalous affair. Leigh appeared both on stage and screen with him, although Olivier avoided sharing the screen with her once he saw how magnetic she was on celluloid. They married on 31 August 1940 (TR Pluto conjunct IC) and stayed together for 20 years (a Jupiter-Saturn cycle), but during that time the biggest celebrity couple of the day often refused to play the publicity game. In May 1945 she developed TB and spent nine months convalescing. Sexually insatiable, she deserted Olivier and fell in love with Peter Finch (qv), whom she found sensual and sexually instinctive (her Venus conjuncts his Mercury-Moon conjunction, and her Sun conjuncts his Mars in Scorpio). Leigh won a second Oscar for A Streetcar Named Desire (released 18 September 1951), but filming proved traumatic when fact and fiction became dangerously blurred. Once again Leigh struggled to hold on to reality. By completion her mental health had declined rapidly (TR Neptune conjunct Venus). After a miscarriage and difficult shoot in Ceylon in March 1953 she was carted off to an asylum. By this time she was suffering from full-blown manic depression and continued to do so until her untimely death on 7 July 1967. Leigh was known equally for her brilliant performances as for her mental instability (natal Moon conjunct MC ruler Uranus, both on the MC).

Lemmy

☉ b. 24 December 1945, 08.30 GMT, Stoke, England, 51N27, 0E37.

From him to Laura Boomer. RR: A.

Intense lead vocalist and bass player of the heavy metal band Motorhead. Lemmy (Ian Kilminster) sang with the band Hawkind from August 1971 until his dismissal in May 1975, after a brief period in a Canadian prison. He formed Motorhead in June 1975 with Phil Taylor and Eddie Clarke and they played their first gig in July. During these months TR Pluto, ruler of the MC, crossed his EQHS 10th House and TR Neptune hit Mercury. Motorhead's song *Ace of Spades* is considered one of the definitive heavy metal performances and they held a reputation as the best live band of their generation. Brian Robertson (qv) replaced Clarke in May 1982. Lemmy acted in the *Comic Strip* film *Eat the Rich*.

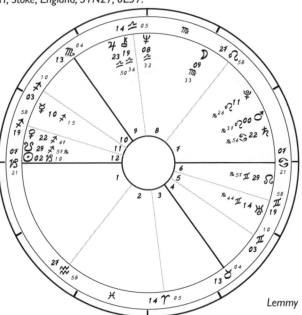

Lemmy

Angus Lennie

b. 18 April 1930, 04.10 GDT, Glasgow, Scotland, 55N52, 04W12.

Gerard q. BC (Angus Wilson Lennie). RR: AA.

Lennie began his career as a dancer before becoming a familiar face in dozens of TV shows, including comedy, children's and drama. He was a favourite as chef Shughie McFee in the soap *Crossroads*.

John Lennon – see The Beatles

Annie Lennox

☉ b. 25 December 1954, 23.10 GMT, Aberdeen, Scotland, 57N09, 02W07.

FCC q. BC in hand (Ann Lennox). (N.B. A new biography, Annie Lennox, p. 1, quotes Lennox saying that she's a Capricorn with Sagittarius Rising.) RR: AA.

A highly talented, enigmatic, volatile and private singer-songwriter. Lennox met Dave Stewart (b. 9 September 1952, Sunderland, England) in Autumn 1976, signed a record contract in June 1979 and formed The Tourists (the contract would later provoke legal conflict until 1987). Her first hit was in October 1979 (TR Saturn conjunct Ascendant). The group disbanded twelve months later (TR Jupiter over Ascendant, TR Neptune conjunct IC) and Lennox formed Eurythmics in December 1980 with ex-partner Stewart. She suffered from agoraphobia and had a nervous breakdown during late 1981 (TR Neptune conjunct 4th).

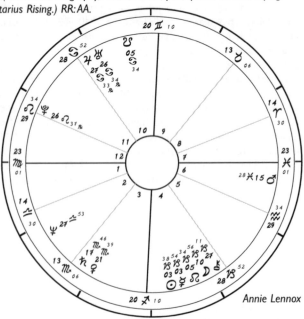

Annie Lennox

Eurythmics garnered their first chart success with the massive hit *Sweet Dreams (Are Made of This)* in March 1983 (a US #1 in September) and Lennox's (often) androgynous look (Virgo) and ballsy delivery won the band much attention. One memorable performance was at the 1984 Grammy Awards (28 February) when she appeared before a shocked audience dressed as Elvis (Lennox's Ascendant is conjunct Presley's MC). After a whirlwind romance in February 1984 (TR Jupiter conjunct Sun and Mercury), she married on 14 March. The partnership soured six months later (again TR Jupiter conjunct Sun) and the couple officially separated in February 1985 (TR Neptune conjunct Sun-Mercury). Annie suffered a personal tragedy on 4 December 1988 (TR Saturn conjunct Sun) when her baby was stillborn. After numerous pop hits she announced a two-year sabbatical in February 1990 to work for the homeless charity Shelter – Lennox has Uranus-Jupiter in EQHS 11th – and gave birth in December 1990. A year later she confirmed the professional split with Stewart (but the couple emerged with a new album and tour in October 1999). Her first two solo albums *Diva* (April 1992) and *Medusa* (March 1995) shot to the top of the UK charts. Lennox has won the Brit Award for Best Female Singer an unprecedented six times. In April 2000 her 12 year marriage broke up (TR Uranus square Venus). Annie is known to be a mixture of prickly emotional extremes (Venus conjunct Saturn in Scorpio, the stellium in Capricorn and Virgo Rising) and never felt in childhood as though she fitted in, developing a complex of superiority and inferiority.

> Q
>
> "I took a lot of risks in my personal life. I always lived in a very full way, I can't do anything half-heartedly. I'm not grey, I'm either black or white. I always ran the risk of getting badly hurt through my experiences and destroying myself... I was never one of the gang. I felt myself to be a loner." (Annie Lennox, as quoted in *Annie Lennox* by Lucy O'Brien, Sidgwick & Jackson, 1992)
>
> "She's a perfectionist (almost to the point of obsessiveness) who consequently can't stand people who are slow witted, who lack punctuality and who are untidy... Very precise and anxious to be appreciated fully, which is why – even now – she can appear cautious or restrained in interview." (*Eurythmics: Sweet Dreams* by J. Waller, Virgin Books)

Rula Lenska

b. 30 September 1947, 02.00 GDT, St. Neots, England, 52N14, 0W17.

FCC q. her, from her mother. RR: A.

Flame-haired actress. Her mother, a Polish countess, had survived a Nazi concentration camp (rescued by the Red Cross) and moved to England in exile (in Lenska's chart, both Pluto, ruler of EQHS 4th, and Saturn are conjunct the Ascendant). Lenska became a household name in Britain in the late 70s when she starred in the TV drama series *Rock Follies*. In 1980 she turned down the chance for possible stardom in America. She had a long-term turbulent and passionate relationship with Dennis Waterman from 1981. They married in 1987 but he left her in 1990 for 18 months and the marriage was on the rocks again in December 1996. They divorced in 1998, with Lenska accusing him of being cruel and selfish. Waterman fought back in October 2000 with

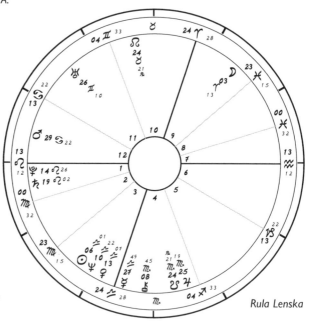

Rula Lenska

the publication of his autobiography stating Lenska could never admit being wrong nor could she ever apologise (perhaps the fixed Leo Ascendant!). In September 1996 Lenska spoke of her role in two expeditions to Nepal to halt the extinction of rare elephants. Her book, *Mammoth Hunt*, was published in September 1996. Lenska is known to get a thrill out of both emotional and physical danger (note the Aries MC and ruler Mars prominent). At 19 she was arrested and imprisoned for six months on a drug charge in Sardinia. Lenska speaks five languages fluently.

John Leslie

✪ *b. 22 February 1965, 00.30 GMT, Edinburgh, Scotland, 55N57, 03W14.*
Gerard q. BC (John Leslie Stott). RR: AA.

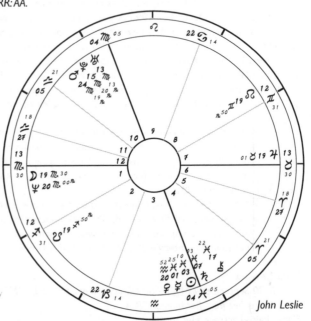

John Leslie

Leslie began his TV career on 20 April 1989, being plucked out of obscurity to present the children's show *Blue Peter* (when TR Pluto conjunct Ascendant). A popular presenter, who was dating Catherine Zeta-Jones (qv) at the time, he stayed with the programme until 20 January 1994. With natal Uranus on the MC overnight discoveries are as common as (and often followed by) sudden reversals of fortune. Leslie's career was effectively destroyed in October 2002 (TR Jupiter conjunct EQHS 10th) by leaked allegations of rape, which were kick-started by an anonymous chronicle of events in Ulrika Jonsson's autobiography (note scandalous Neptune conjuncts Moon on the Ascendant, squares Venus, T-Square Jupiter-Descendant). When a number of women came forward to make complaints of assault and a tabloid printed pictures of him allegedly snorting cocaine, TV bosses sacked him on 28 October from his well-paid presenter's job on *This Morning* (he'd been there a year). He was arrested on 5 December 2002 but in mid-May 2003 he was set to be cleared of the rape charges (TR Jupiter returning to EQHS 10th). With TR Uranus approaching Sun/IC and TR Neptune conjunct EQHS 4th, is the scandal over?

Martyn Lewis

b. 7 April 1945, 15.50 DGDT, Swansea, Wales, 51N38, 03W57.
From him to an Astrological Association member. RR: A.

Newsreader formerly with BBC Belfast (from 1967) and ITN (1970-86). From 1986 he was one of the news frontmen for the BBC until 1999, when TR Saturn crossed the MC. In September 1999 he signed a new deal on ITV.

Robert Lindsay

b. 13 December 1949, 09.30 GMT, Ilkeston, England, 52N59, 01W18.
FCC q. his letter. RR: A.

Lindsay, a leading stage and TV actor in both classical drama and comedy, won an Olivier Award and later a Tony in June 1987 (TR Neptune on Ascendant) for his performance in *Me and My Girl* (after a tour, it premiered on Broadway on 10 August 1986, and during early 1987 TR Saturn and Uranus both crossed over his Sagittarian Sun). He took over the role of Fagin in *Oliver!* at the London Palladium in November 1996 (after TR Jupiter had crossed his Ascendant), winning the Olivier Award in early 1997. As a TV comedy actor Lindsay is best known for the BBC sitcom *Citizen Smith*

(November 1977, as TR Uranus approached the MC, to July 1980). With Jupiter conjunct Venus in Aquarius and a Sagittarian Sun, Lindsay was more than capable of getting laughs in absurd situations. In December 1996 he donned a peroxide wig to play a vain businessman in *Brazen Hussies*, a character he based on a well-known media personality. Lindsay currently stars in the comedy *My Family*.

Shona Lindsay

> b. 4 December 1969, 19.51 MET, Elsie Inglis Maternity Hospital, Edinburgh, Scotland, 55N57, 03W10.
> Gerard q. BC. RR: AA.

Actress who made her professional debut at 11 in a national tour of the stage version of *Annie*. She has starred on stage in *The Phantom of the Opera* and worked on the soap *Crossroads* for two years (1986-8).

Maureen Lipman

○ b. 10 May 1946, 00.00 Midnight (of 9/10th) GDT, Hull, England, 53N45, 0W20.

● FCC q. her, but her friend, astrologer Sasha Fenton uses a 13.00 chart and 9 May (with no source) for Lipman in her book *Understanding Astrology* (the data for the various profiles were not collected by Fenton herself). RR: A?

From March 1979 (TR Saturn conjunct the 'midnight' Moon) to March 1981, Lipman appeared as a newspaper advice columnist in the star-making vehicle *Agony*, a popular TV comedy that ran for three series. The break was the result of an earlier short-lived comedy series *A Soft Touch* (from July to September 1978). From 1989 to 1992 she was very popular (and won awards) as the fussing Jewish mother Beattie in the British Telecom series of adverts. On 31 August 1995, in *Agony Again*, she returned to the role of Jane Lucas, which she had established 16 years earlier. Yet in 1996 she was left without any further TV offers, so Lipman moved to the theatre. In March 1997 she earned favourable reviews for *Maureen Lipman: Alive*

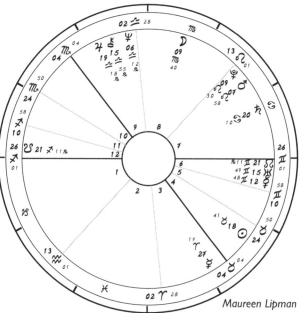

Maureen Lipman

and Kicking, which featured her consistently good anecdotes, sketches and clever songs, all delivered with impeccable timing. In early 1999 she was appearing in *Oklahoma!* to rave reviews. Lipman is known by friends and family to be chaotic, hypersensitive and employed in full-time guilt (Moon in Virgo). During 1984 she suffered a deep depression (her Moon squares an emotional see-saw of Venus conjunct Uranus). In mid-1994, whilst touring with *Re:Joyce* (a tribute to Joyce Grenfell, qv), she faced paralysis from a tumour at the top of her spine (Solar Eclipse conjunct Sun) and was quickly operated on. In May 1997 she underwent a complicated operation to remove another tumour on her spine. Lipman married writer Jack Rosenthal (b. 8 September 1931) in February 1973.

> Q "Maureen Lipman says she's anxious to please, but there's something quite formidable about her. She's witty, spiky and clever, and one doesn't want to irritate her." (Lynda Lee-Potter, *Daily Mail*, 6/2/99)

Celia Lipton
> b. 25 December 1923, 10.10 GMT, Edinburgh, Scotland, 55N57, 03W13.
>
> Gerard q. BC (Cecilia May Lipton). RR: AA.

Singer and actress who sang with her father Sidney Lipton from the age of 16. She debuted in 1939 at the London Palladium and in 1941 she went solo in variety performances. Lipton made a singing comeback in 1980.

Syd Little – see Little and Large

LITTLE AND LARGE

This comedy pair began in 1962 under their real names of McGinnis and Mead, and won *Opportunity Knocks* in 1971. In 1977 they were given their first TV series and were hugely popular in the 70s and early 80s. Syd often played the intelligent straight man to Eddie's daft loud-mouth. Little was a former painter and decorator before deciding to entertain on guitar in clubs. In January 1995 his troubled son was the victim of a heroin overdose.

Syd Little
> b. 19 December 1942, 01.30 GDT, Blackpool, England, 53N50, 03W03.
>
> FCC q. him. RR: A.

Eddie Large
> b. 25 June 1941, 01.00 DGDT, Maternity Hospital, Glasgow, Scotland, 55N51, 04W14.
>
> Gerard q. BC (Edward Hugh McGinnis). RR: AA.

Laurence Llewelyn-Bowen
> ✪ b. 11 March 1965, 23.30 GMT, London, England, 51N30, 0W10.
>
> From a chart presented to him by a guest on his show, data presumably from him. RR: A.

Flamboyant presenter of TV shows including *Changing Rooms* and *Fantasy Rooms*.

Frank Lloyd
> ✪ b. 23 September 1886, 18.00 GMT, Glasgow, Scotland, 55N50, 04W08.
>
> Gerard q. BC. RR: AA.

Emigrating to Canada in 1910 Lloyd worked steadily as an actor before eventually moving to Hollywood. After portraying villains on film he switched to film-making and directed over one hundred films, winning two Best Director Oscars for *The Divine Lady* and *Cavalcade* (1929 and 1933). He adapted literary classics including *A Tale of Two Cities* (1917), *Les Miserables* (1918) and *Oliver Twist* (1922).

Andrew Lloyd Webber
> ✪ b. 22 March 1948, 16.00 GDT, Westminster, London, 51N30, 0W09.
>
> Pamela Crane q. his mother Jean in July 1987; meeting recounted in, and the following dates are taken from, The Draconic Chart by Rev. Pamela Crane (Flare, 2000). RR: A.

The prodigious son of a director of the London College of Music and a music teacher, at the age of seven Andrew composed his first musical, *The Toy Theatre*. By age 17 he had written eight more. After winning a scholarship to Oxford to read history he dropped out a term later, intent on carving out a career in musical theatre. He began collaborating with EMI trainee Tim Rice (qv) in 1968. On 9 November 1968 a performance of *Joseph* at St. Paul's Cathedral led to him meeting managing agent David Land (TR Uranus opposite Sun). On 9 November 1970 (TR Jupiter conjunct IC, TR Saturn near MC) *Time* magazine ran an article about his work, which generated much interest in his shows and led to enormous success in the USA. *Jesus Christ, Superstar* made its debut on Broadway on 12 October 1971 (TR Pluto approaching an opposition to his Sun) and its London debut on 9 August 1972. *Evita* opened on 21 June 1978 (TR Saturn heading towards the Moon-Ascendant). *Cats*, Lloyd Webber's most famous musical, ran on the West End stage from 11 May 1981 to May 2002, four months after another hit, *Starlight Express*, closed. *The Phantom of the Opera* debuted in London on 9 October 1986 and on Broadway on 26 January 1988, with Michael Crawford (qv) taking the lead role in both productions (their synastry is extraordinary). Recent stage successes include *Bombay Dreams* and his collaboration with Ben Elton (qv), *The Beautiful Game*, which opened on 26 September 2000. Lloyd Webber is known for his work ethic and sense of humour, as well as his romantic life (MC ruler Venus on MC) and numerous public bust-ups with his performers (MC ruler squares Pluto-Saturn-Mars). His insistence on leaving the business side of his empire in the hands of advisors (11th House) has resulted in many acrimonious legal wrangles (11th ruler Mercury is weak and 8th ruler Neptune is in 2nd). He first married on 24 July 1971. His second wife, singer Sarah Brightman, auditioned for his show *Cats*, and married him two years later on 22 March 1984 (TR Saturn conjunct IC, opposite Venus). Lloyd

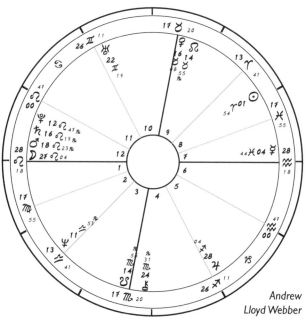

Andrew
Lloyd Webber

Webber lives in Berkshire with his third wife Madeleine. In February 2003 *The Mail on Sunday's Rich Report* estimated his fortune at £310 million.

John Locke – see Nazareth
Craig Logan – see Bros

Jimmy Logan
> b. 4 April 1928, 00.10 GMT, Glasgow, Scotland, 55N52, 04W13.
> Gerard q. BC (James Allan Short). RR: AA.

Member of The Logan Family musical group. He debuted in pantomime in 1944. After his first film in 1949, he became active in all aspects of entertainment. His credits include *Carry On Abroad* in 1972. A stage show, *Lauder*, was created by Logan in honour of his idol Sir Harry Lauder (qv). Logan's Mercury-Venus conjunction falls on Lauder's MC.

Phyllis Logan
⊗ b. 11 January 1956, 09.30 GMT, Paisley, Scotland, 55N50, 04W26.
> Gerard q. BC. RR: AA.

Actress with numerous film credits including *Secrets and Lies*.

Janice Long
> b. 5 April 1955, 08.10 GMT, Liverpool, England, 53N25, 02W55.
> From her to astrologer Laura Boomer. RR: A.

A popular Radio One disc jockey for six years, until it was announced on 14 December 1987 that she would not be returning to the radio station following her pregnancy (Lunar Eclipse on Sun). She turned to quiz shows a few years after the birth of her baby. Long, who is the sister of Keith Chegwin (qv), is married to an astrologer and from 2000 began presenting a weekday show on Radio 2.

Alan and Derek Longmuir – see Bay City Rollers
Gerard Love – see Teenage Fanclub

Lulu

b. 3 November 1948, 01.30 GMT, Lennox Castle, Scotland, 55N59, 04W14.

Gerard q. BC (Marie McLaughlin McDonald Lawrie). RR: AA.

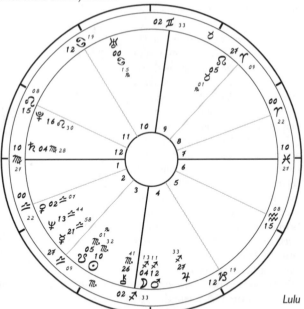

Lulu

A gutsy, diminutive 60s singer with a big voice, Lulu could belt out a song at two years old, louder and more raucous than any other child. Starmaker Mickie Most furthered her career and helped this dynamic performer become one of the UK's most recognisable singers. A 15 year old wonder, she became one of British music's stars of the decade. Lulu's hits include *Shout* (June 1964) and *To Sir With Love* (US million seller and chart-topper for five weeks in October 1967). In March 1969 she won the Eurovision Song Contest (tying with three other countries!), and was married to Maurice Gibb of the Bee Gees (qv) from 18 February 1969 for four years, and married hairdresser John Frieda in 1977 until 1995. Her career stood still in the 70s but she returned in August 1986 with a remake of *Shout*, reaching #8 in the UK. In the 90s her career was reignited with a new album (*Independence*, March 1993) and by teen sensation Take That (see Jason Orange) when she was asked to feature on their #1 smash *Relight My Fire* (October 1993). She also wrote the theme song for the biopic *What's Love Got To Do With It*, which was also the name of her 2002 autobiography, *I Don't Want to Fight*. In November 1999 an aggressive publicity campaign promoted her return to TV with a National Lottery show, but (with TR Saturn opposite her Sun) the plan backfired and the viewers vanished. In May 2002 she released a new album and her TV show, *An Audience with Lulu*, aired.

> Q "She's very girlie... and then suddenly you'll see a tough, steely side. She can switch from shoes to death in a heartbeat. Sometimes she talks in eclectic therapy speak, not in a scary way, but in a feeling-her-way, learning way, as if she really is an articulate, sharp mind... She says she was treated very much like a grown-up from the age of 10 or younger, so it didn't seem as though it would be such a terrible displacement to leave home and tour, because she had imbued in her, from a very early age, a strong work ethic." (Chrissy Iley, *Sunday Times Magazine*, c.1999)

Jamie Lumley

b. 16 October 1967, 22.15 GDT, Canterbury, England, 51N17, 01E05.

From his mother's autobiography *Stare Back and Smile*. RR: B.

Son of actress Joanna Lumley (qv). The identity of his father had been kept a closely guarded secret by his Scorpio Rising mother to prevent media intrusion. His own father blew the gaff on 17 February 1997, as Jamie approached his Saturn Return (and TR Saturn conjunct Moon).

Joanna Lumley

b. 1 May 1946, 19.30 IST (-5.5 = -5 hrs 30 mins), Srinagar, Kashmir, 34N05, 74E49.
From her to Joan Revill. Her autobiography, *Stare Back and Smile*, gives "early evening...arriving promptly...the doctor was pleased, as he was off to have dinner with my grandparents." RR: A.

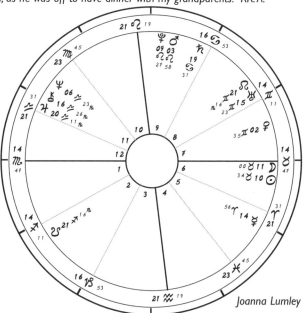

Joanna Lumley

Lumley is known to be intensely private, with a razor-sharp mind and an enviable combination of wit, style and intelligence. She is seen as an independent, glamorous woman who is self-assured, posh and dignified (Leo MC). Lumley's childhood was nomadic until she settled with an English relative on 2 June 1954 (as TR Pluto passed over her MC). Her son Jamie (qv) was born in October 1967, just after Lumley began winning parts in films (TR Jupiter over MC) following a modelling stint. In the summer of 1968 she had a small role in a Bond movie and was cast as the posh girlfriend of Ken Barlow (played by William Roache, qv) in 1973 in *Coronation Street*. On 23 May 1970 (as TR Saturn conjunct Descendant) she married writer Jeremy Lloyd but the union lasted four months and they divorced in February 1971 (TR Saturn returned to the Descendant and TR Neptune opposed Venus). In October 1986 she married conductor Stephen Barlow. She became a national sensation when she won the role of Purdey in *The New Avengers* with Patrick Macnee (qv) and Gareth Hunt (b. 7 February 1943, London) in early March 1976. The first episode was shown in late October 1976 (TR Saturn on EQHS 10th). After *The New Avengers* Lumley won another substantial role in the inventive series *Sapphire and Steel* (July 1979, when TR Jupiter conjunct her EQHS 10th, to August 1982). Her career was resurrected when she was asked to play the vulgar hedonist Patsy Stone in *Absolutely Fabulous* (beginning November 1992). Since then Lumley has happily tackled ghastly roles and parodies of Patsy. She has often used her hair as an expressive tool in her acting (from the Purdey bob to the *Ab Fab* beehive). She won two British Comedy Awards in December 1993 and a Bafta for her role in *Absolutely Fabulous*. In recent years she has revived her *Ab Fab* role and made numerous nature documentaries.

> Q | "She is most men's fantasy lover... combined with the paradoxes of the perfect pre-feminist female – clever without being intellectual, tarty with class, dizzy yet efficient, honest yet flattering, haughty yet solicitous." (Andrew Duncan, *Radio Times*, 22/1/94)

Ida Lupino
💣 b. 4 February 1918, 23.00 GMT, London, England, 51N30, 0W10.
Marc Penfield q. her personally? RR: C.
Known as a "poor man's Bette Davis," Lupino made over 60 films and was married three times. A pioneer, she was Hollywood's first woman film director. D. 3 August 1995, Burbank, California, stroke, cancer of the colon.

John Lydon – see Sid Vicious
Graham Lyle – see Gallagher and Lyle

Edith MacArthur

> b. 8 March 1926, 11.00 GMT, Ardrossan, Scotland, 55N39, 04W49.
> Gerard q. BC. RR: AA.

MacArthur began her career on stage in 1948. She won a following as Elizabeth Cunningham in *Take the High Road* from 1980. In 1987 her character was dramatically killed off in a car accident, much to the horror of the millions who had followed the series religiously.

Simon MacCorkindale

> b. 12 February 1952, 15.00 GMT, Ely, England, 52N24, 0E16.
> Letter in hand from MacCorkindale to Edwin Steinbrecher. RR: A.

Intense actor of TV and film who often works behind the camera with his second wife Susan George (qv) for their production company. As an actor his credits include *I, Claudius* (September-December 1976), *Jesus of Nazareth* (1977), *Quatermass* (October-November 1979), *Manimal* (Autumn 1983) and the glossy-turned-gory soap *Falcon Crest* from 1984 to 1986. He was back on TV in mid-2002 in the series *Casualty* and continues to produce TV with Susan George, including the series *Relic Hunter*. His first ambition was to follow in his Air Force father's footsteps. MacCorkindale was married to Fiona Fullerton from July 1976 to 1981. He married Susan George on 5 October 1984.

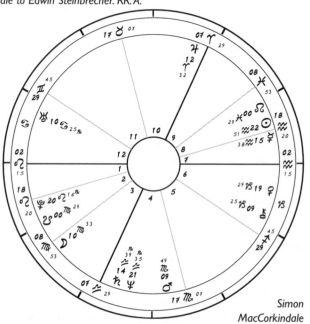

Simon MacCorkindale

Robin MacDonald

> b. 18 July 1943, 02.15 DGDT, Balvenie Place, Nairn, Scotland, 57N36, 03W52.
> Gerard q. BC (Robin Fingal MacDonald). RR: AA.

Member of Billy J. Kramer and the Dakotas, a band that had two UK #1 hits (August 1963 and March 1964).

Rory MacDonald – see Runrig

Jimmie MacGregor

> b. 10 March 1930, 15.00 GMT, Springburn, Glasgow, Scotland, 55N53, 04W14.
> Gerard q. BC (James MacGregor). RR: AA.

Folk singer and former teacher, MacGregor worked with folk-singer Robin Hall in 1937 for 21 years releasing 20 albums. As a broadcaster he has presented many radio magazine programmes.

Jillie Mack

✪ b. 25 December 1957, 03.30 GMT, Devizes, England, 51N22, 01W59.
> Lorri dePasqua q. an article in *Good Housekeeping* (October 1988), p. 60. RR: B.

Actress and dancer who married actor Tom Selleck in August 1987.

Fulton MacKay

> b. 12 August 1922, 00.55 GDT, Paisley, Scotland, 55N51, 04W25.
> Gerard q. BC (William Fulton Beith McKay, note spelling). RR: AA.

Actor who stage debuted in 1947. He is best known for his portrayal of the officious prison warden in the much-loved TV comedy *Porridge* (September 1974 to March 1977).

Billy MacKenzie

○ b. 27 March 1957, 19.20 GMT, Dundee, Scotland, 56N28, 03W01.
> Gerard q. BC (William MacArthur MacKenzie). RR: AA.

Prodigious singer with a distinctive falsetto. MacKenzie formed the band The Associates in October 1979. With five planets retrograde and after several years of chart hits and media interest, MacKenzie, unprepared for success, retreated to Dundee in Spring 1985, only emerging occasionally from his self-imposed exile to appear on other performers' records. In his chart MC ruler Moon opposes Pluto for influence and his personal withdrawal in 1985 (when TR Saturn squared this opposition). D. 22 January 1997.

Neil Mackie

> b. 11 December 1946, 07.00 GMT, Holburn, Aberdeen, Scotland, 57N08, 02W07.
> Gerard q. BC. RR: AA.

Concert tenor singer and international soloist, Mackie made his debut in 1986 at New York's Lincoln Center.

Cameron Mackintosh

○ b. 13 October 1946, 04.30 GMT, Aberdeen, Scotland, 57N09, 02W06.
> Gerard q. BC. RR: AA.

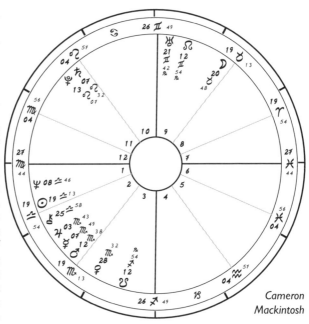

Cameron
Mackintosh

Producer and owner of seven West End theatres, Mackintosh has been responsible for many of the major productions to be staged in London over the last two decades. He is known to be intensely loyal to friends and family, independent, and personally very frugal ("I compare prices when I go shopping in the supermarket") – in spite of the £10 million-a-year salary he affords himself. The son of a Scottish timber-merchant and jazz trumpeter and a Maltese mother, Mackintosh decided at age eight to join the theatre, later training at London's famous Central School of Speech and Drama. After working as a stagehand, he began producing low budget touring shows of West End and Broadway musicals. The Lloyd Webber (qv) musicals of the early 1980s (including *Les Miserables* and *Phantom of the Opera*) turned the tide in his favour. Recent West End successes include *My Fair Lady* and he plans to introduce *Mary Poppins* to the stage. The theatre impresario now invests his vast fortune (an estimated £350 million) in property.

Roddy Macmillan

b. 27 March 1923, 16.45 GMT, Smerclate, South Uist, Scotland, 57N06, 07W23.
Gerard q. BC (Roderick Macmillan). RR: AA.

Actor from age 12 and later a playwright, Macmillan turned professional in 1946 with the Glasgow Unity Theatre. He was the TV Personality of the Year in 1972 for the TV programme *The View from Daniel Pike.*

Alan MacNaughton

b. 4 March 1920, 11.30 GMT, Bearsden, Glasgow, Scotland, 55N55, 04W20.
Gerard q. BC. RR: AA.

Comedy actor with credits including *Yanks Go Home* (from November 1976) and *Conjugal Rites* (from April 1993, when TR Saturn crossed his MC).

Patrick Macnee

b. 6 February 1922, 01.00 GMT, London, England, 51N30, 0W10.
Dana Holliday q. him personally. RR: A.

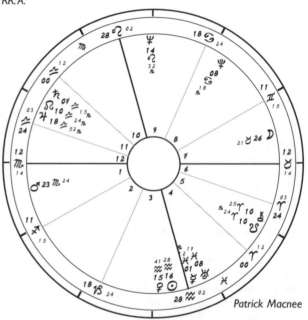

Patrick Macnee

Charming and self-effacing actor, best known for his role as the debonair, suave and classy John Steed (note the unflappable Leo MC) in *The Avengers*, a cult favourite that began on 7 June 1961. Although Macnee was with the series from the beginning, it was not until 1962, with the addition of Honor Blackman (qv), that it began attracting attention and became a TV phenomenon (TR Neptune over his Ascendant, TR Uranus on MC). Note that Blackman's Sun and Ascendant fall exactly on Macnee's MC, implying the mutual professional benefit of their TV partnership. In *The Avengers*, Macnee's capable female sidekicks also included Diana Rigg (qv) and Joanna Lumley (qv). Macnee had an unsettling childhood, brought up by his mother and her female partner before being sent off to Eton. Macnee, who suffered from tremendous guilt after leaving his first wife and young children, married for the third time in 1988. (*Blind in One Ear* by Patrick Macnee, Harrap, 1988.)

Mick MacNeil – see Simple Minds

Duncan MacRae

✪ *b. 20 August 1905, 16.00 GDT, Glasgow, Scotland, 55N53, 04W15.*
Paul Wright q. BC. RR: AA.

TV comedy actor. D. 23 March 1967.

Sean Maguire

b. 18 April 1976, 04.00 GDT, Ilford, England, 51N33, 0E05.
FCC q. him, from his parents. RR: A.

Maguire, who made his film debut with Laurence Olivier (qv) at age five, became a popular television personality after appearing in the children's drama *Grange Hill* for four years. He moved into

EastEnders for a year in 1993, before achieving further success as an actor in *Dangerfield* and pop singer (eight hit singles and four UK tours). Maguire has Moon and Neptune on a Sagittarian MC, and in 2000 (when TR Pluto crossed the MC) he moved to the US and appeared in *Prince Charming* and the sitcom *Off Centre*.

Bernard Manning

✪ b. 13 August 1930, 04.30 GDT, Manchester, England, 53N30, 02W15.
From the well-researched biography *Bernard Manning* by Jonathan Margolis (Orion, 1997). (N.B. Manning had given Marjorie Orr the time 06.00.) RR: B.

A successful exponent of the more offensive side of stand-up comedy, Manning has caused controversy with his live performances (Uranus conjunct MC) and even had his autobiography banned by major book retailers. Astrologically the Uranus-MC suggests his abusive, racist and crude comedic style, as well as the resulting censorship he faced in the politically correct 1990s ("In private, people tell the sort of jokes I do"). After first appearing on TV's *The Comedians* in 1971, and before the onset of political correctness, Manning became synonymous with racist, chauvinistic and bigoted material. Though unofficially barred from appearing on television these days, Manning is still a grand favourite with those for whom flat caps and

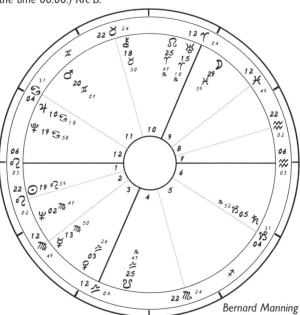

Bernard Manning

racing pigeons represent high culture. He was married for 36 years (widowed in 1986) and states that he has never had a holiday during his working life. In November 2002, at 72 with angina and diabetes, Manning appeared on the documentary series *The Entertainers*. He was also invited by Madonna to entertain at her husband's birthday party. In mid-April 2003 he played two shows in Bombay to a less than enthusiastic crowd. Manning owns a club in Manchester, which has made him a millionaire.

Shirley Manson

✪ b. 26 August 1966, 17.35 GDT, Edinburgh, Scotland, 55N57, 03W12.
Gerard q. BC (Shirley Ann Manson). RR: AA.

Charismatic Manson was recruited to sing with the US band Garbage after the members had seen her fronting the band Angel Fish. Garbage's music borrowed from punk, glam rock, techno and art rock. They topped the album charts in the UK in May 1998 and the following year were commissioned to write the theme tune to the Bond movie *The World is Not Enough*.

MARMALADE

Commercially successful band who had their first hit in the UK in May 1968 and later endured a long list of changes in their line-up. Knight joined the group, which had been formed three years earlier, in late 1964. After four years of struggling for recognition, the band hit the charts and had a #1 hit in January 1969 (and six more Top Ten hits). Fairley quit the group in November 1971. In early 1972 the band suffered a major embarrassment with a sex exposé involving their female fans. They continued into the 80s on the cabaret circuit.

Pat Fairley
   b. 14 April 1944, 20.50 DGDT, Duke Street, Glasgow, Scotland, 55N51, 04W14.
   Gerard q. BC (Patrick Fairley). RR: AA.

Dean Ford
   b. 5 September 1945, 13.00 GDT, Airdrie, Scotland, 55N52, 03W59.
   Gerard q. BC (Thomas McAleese). RR: AA.

Graham Knight
   b. 8 December 1943, 05.45 GDT, Balarnock Road, Glasgow, Scotland, 55N53, 04W14.
   Gerard q. BC (John Graham Knight). RR: AA.

Jean Marsh
   b. 1 July 1934, 12.15 GDT, Stoke Newington, England, 51N34, 0W05.
   Dana Holliday q. the date in Theater Almanac; Ruth Dewey q. the time from Marsh in an interview,
   July 1979. RR: A.

Intelligent, stylish actress and writer, who knew early on that she wanted to be involved in the arts. Marsh entered dance school at 12 and specialised in mime. Later, with her best friend Eileen Atkins, she created both *Upstairs, Downstairs* and *The House of Elliot.* Marsh had brief stints in *Doctor Who* and was a regular in the US spin-off TV series of the film *Nine to Five.* In 1996 she sold her beloved country cottage and moved to London, where she completed her first novel, *Fiennders Keepers.* Married (from 19 to 22) to actor Jon Pertwee and involved with a number of famous men, Marsh has been single since 1989.

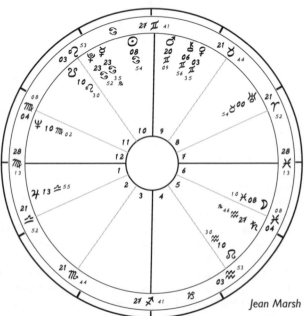

Jean Marsh

Margaret Marshall
   b. 4 January 1949, 01.35 GMT, Stirling, Scotland, 56N08, 03W55.
   Gerard q. BC (Margaret Anne Marshall). RR: AA.
Soprano with a London debut in 1975, and USA and Covent Garden debuts in 1980.

Jessica Martin
   b. 25 August 1962, 19.30 GDT, London, England, 51N30, 0W10.
   FCC q. her, from her parents. RR: A.
Within a year of leaving university Martin was starring on TV. Her credits include *Copycats,* working with Rory Bremner (qv), and showing off her natural talents for mimicry on TV (Jupiter, ruler of the MC, opposes her Sun). Influenced by Judy Garland she learned to develop her own image after years of hiding behind carefully constructed characters. At 26 she moved from impressionist to the more personally satisfying position of actress after winning the role of Sally Smith in *Me and My Girl.* A long-lasting personal relationship ended in 1993.

Forbes Masson

b. 20 March 1965, 00.40 GMT, Chalmers Hospital, Banff, Scotland, 57N40, 02W31.
Gerard q. BC (Alan Forbes Masson). RR: AA.

Popular actor featured in the slick, cult TV comedy *The High Life* and later in the soap *EastEnders*.

Donald Maxwell

b. 12 December 1948, 03.00 GMT, Perth, Scotland, 56N24, 03W27.
Gerard q. BC (Donald Maxwell MacAlpine). RR: AA.

Operatic and concert baritone with the major British opera companies. In 1991 he appeared as Falstaff in Paris and Vienna.

Rik Mayall

✪ *b. 7 March 1958, 03.30 GMT, Harlow New Town, Essex, England, 51N47, 0E08.*
FCC q. his agent, November 2002. RR: A.

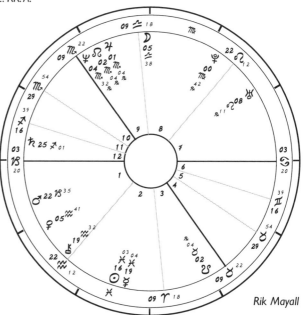

Rik Mayall

Mayall starred in the BBC sketch series *A Kick Up the Eighties* before finding national fame in the anarchic comedy *The Young Ones*, which he also co-wrote. His wild, brash and violent characters have stamped their mark on the public's consciousness. Mayall's parents were drama teachers and he made his debut at age six in a crowd scene of *The Good Woman of Setzuan*. Teaming up at college with Adrian Edmondson, Mayall formed a comedy group called Twentieth Century Coyote. Together they made their name at a club called The Comic Strip, which was also the launching ground of other 80s comedians. After *The Young Ones* (9 November 1982, following TR Jupiter conjunct MC, to June 1984, TR Saturn conjunct MC), Mayall moved into new comedy series: *Bottom* (17 September 1991 to 29 October 1992), *Filthy Rich and Catflap* (January to February 1987, TR Pluto conjunct MC) and played the ruthless and amoral Thatcherite politician (Scorpio MC) Alan B'stard in *The New Statesman* (September 1987, as TR Pluto approached the MC and TR Neptune square Moon, to 26 December 1992). He was in critical condition after a serious road accident in April 1998 (TR Jupiter conjunct Sun) but recovered fully. Mayall married in 1985 and the couple have three children. (Additional information from the website www.orangeneko.com)

> Q
>
> "I've always played thoroughly unpleasant people and I like that. It's probably something to do with expunging all the things you disapprove of about yourself. I tried to be a nice, normal bloke... but when you've got this mass of things you've suppressed in yourself – vanity, violence, selfishness, lust – you've got a garage full of high-octane emotions. When I'm in character, I get rid of all the things I disapprove of about myself." (Rik Mayall, *The West Australian*, 26/7/2000)
>
> "I'm quite a political animal, but, although I'm 30 next year, I still think of myself as a kid." (Rik Mayall, *TV Times*, 12/9/87)

Hector McAndrew

    b. 21 July 1903, 06.00 GMT, Fyvie, Aberdeenshire (between Oldmeldrum and Turriff), Scotland, 57N26, 02W23.

    Gerard q. BC. RR: AA.

Fiddler and gardener with an unconventional approach to music.

Dan McCafferty – see Nazareth

David McCallum

    b. 19 September 1933, 02.00 GDT, Hillhead, Glasgow, Scotland, 55N53, 04W18.

    Gerard q. BC (David Keith McCallum). RR: AA.

Television leading actor. The son of a concert violinist, McCallum trained at RADA (1949-51) and made his film debut in 1957. His greatest success was on TV in *The Man From U.N.C.L.E.* (1964-7), with an Emmy nomination in 1966. McCallum, who also starred in the wartime drama *Colditz*, is known to be very health conscious (Sun and Moon in Virgo in EQHS 2nd).

Eileen McCallum

    b. 2 December 1939, 04.30 GMT, Redlands Maternity Hospital, Glasgow, Scotland, 55N51, 04W14.

    Gerard q. BC (Eileen Fairweather McCallum). RR: AA.

McCallum's professional debut was at 12 in radio's *Scottish Children's Hour*. She was later the Gold Medal winner at the Scottish Academy of Music and Drama in 1959. From 1980 she played a shop owner in the long-running soap *Take the High Road*.

Brian McCardie

✪   *b. 22 January 1965, 21.38 GMT, Bellshill Maternity Hospital, Bellshill, Scotland, 55N50, 04W01.*

    Gerard q. BC (Brian James McCardie). RR: AA.

Actor with credits in *Forget About Me* and *Doctor Finlay* as well as the epic film *Rob Roy*.

Paul and Linda McCartney – see The Beatles

Ian McCaskill

    b. 28 July 1938, 22.00 GDT, Govan, Glasgow, Scotland, 55N51, 04W19.

    Gerard q. BC (John Robertson McCaskill). RR: AA.

McCaskill was a meteorologist before moving into BBC Television in 1978 to become their quaint and popular weatherman.

Sylvester McCoy

    b. 20 August 1943, 05.00 GDT, Dunoon, Scotland, 55N57, 04W56.

    Gerard q. BC (Percy James Kent-Smith). RR: AA.

An imaginative actor equally at ease with comic or dramatic roles. McCoy accepted the role as the seventh *Doctor Who* in 1986 and his three series as the character were aired from September 1987 (as TR Jupiter hovered near his Moon-MC) to December 1989. Previously he had worked in children's TV programmes. He was seen as kidnapper Michael Sams in the dramatised *The Stephanie Slater Story* (1997).

Martine McCutcheon

✪   *b. 14 May 1976, 07.40 GDT, Clapton, London, England, 51N33, 0W03.*

    From her autobiography Who Does She Think She Is? (N.B. The birth was induced.) RR: B.

Actress best-known for her role in *EastEnders*. A Cinderella rags-to-riches image (the MC is more likely to be in Pisces), McCutcheon endured a tough childhood to earn a place at stage school when she was ten. Her first attempt at fame was as part of the girl group Milan, which disbanded in April 1994 after five pop releases failed to make an impact on the charts. In January 1995 (as TR Pluto conjunct her Moon) she made her first appearance in the BBC soap *EastEnders*, which brought her into contact with over 15 million regular viewers. From the start the public warmed to the vulnerability she expressed through her character Tiffany, the sensitive martyr of Albert Square. Soon after her dramatic departure (over 22 million watched Tiffany die on 31 December 1998, the victim of a road accident) Martine released a song, *Perfect Moment*, which went to #1 in April. She leant her pleasant voice to a number of classic songs on her well-received debut album. Her much-publicised starring role on stage in *My Fair Lady* in March 2001 (MC ruler Uranus square Sun) was dogged by ill health and false rumours, yet she was determined to battle on and she picked up an Olivier Award in February 2002 for her role. The Press continue to be fascinated by her private life and professional tribulations.

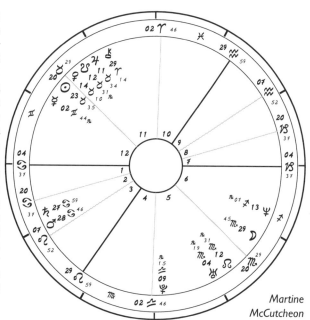

Martine
McCutcheon

Jane McDonald
✪ b. 4 April 1963, 23.30 GDT, Wakefield, England, 53N42, 01W29.
   David Fisher q. her autobiography *Follow Your Dreams* (Harper Collins, 2000), p. 10. RR: B.

McDonald was a cruise line cabaret singer when she was discovered and included in the documentary series *The Cruise*. She met her future husband in March 1996, when she was resident entertainer on board The Century. That December (TR Saturn conjunct Jupiter) she won a contract to sing on The Galaxy and luckily for her it coincided with the BBC filming of their fly-on-the-wall docusoap. When *The Cruise* aired in January and February 1998 (as TR Saturn crossed Sun) her voice and bubbly personality made her the star of the show, which was watched by an average of 12 million viewers. She married on 26 May 1998 (TR Pluto square Venus) and the BBC filmed a special episode in July featuring their wedding. Since *The Cruise* she has had a handful of successful albums, UK tours and a best-selling autobiography. She was the ideal choice to host the talent show *Star for a Night*, which began in 2000.

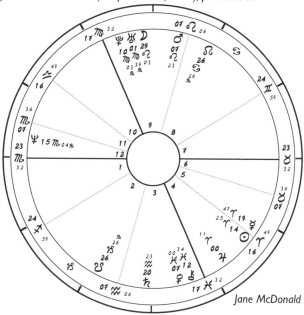

Jane McDonald

Sheena McDonald

✪ *b. 25 July 1954, 06.55 GDT, Dunfermline, Scotland, 56N04, 03W28.*
Gerard q. BC. RR: AA.

News presenter. Whilst crossing the road in Islington (51N33, 0W06) TV and radio presenter Sheena McDonald was hit by a police van answering an emergency call. The time of the accident was 00:15 on 27 February 1999 (as TR Saturn conjunct her Aries MC). The van was on the wrong side of the road and later discovered to be mechanically defective. McDonald suffered serious head injuries and was in a coma for 72 hours. In February 2002 her solicitors issued a writ against the Metropolitan Police.

Peter McDougall

b. 17 August 1947, 18.05 GDT, Greenock, Scotland, 55N58, 04W47.
Gerard q. BC. RR: AA.

Screenwriter for TV, most memorably for the award-winning *Just Another Saturday*.

Roddy McDowall

b. 17 September 1928, 21.00 GDT, London, England, 51N30, 0W10.
Paul Rosner q. him. RR: A.

Actor with a career that spanned seven decades (30s-90s) and 130 films. McDowall's ambitious 'stage' mother enrolled him as a child model at 4. By 10 he had made his film debut and moved to Hollywood two years later. In the early 40s McDowall was very popular in Hollywood films such as *Lassie Come Home* and *How Green Was My Valley*. By 18 he was more or less washed up in films so he moved to New York and acted on stage. McDowall, a Virgo with Moon in Scorpio, was often cast as critical, sniping, androgynous characters. A private collector of film memorabilia and a social historian, he was also a highly regarded stills photographer. In 1990 McDowall battled prostate

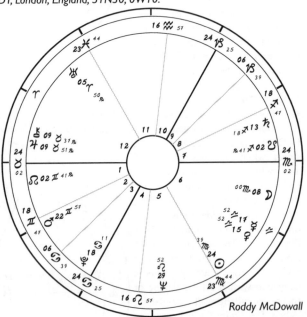

Roddy McDowall

cancer. In mid-September 1998 he was diagnosed with terminal cancer and died in October 1998. A close confidant of many film and TV stars (note the Taurus-Scorpio emphasis and Mercury square Descendant ruler Pluto), he left behind an autobiography (containing his and their secrets) to be published in 100 years. D. 3 October 1998, cancer.

Joe McFadden

✪ *b. 9 October 1975, 13.05 GDT, Glasgow, Scotland, 55N51, 04W14.*
Gerard q. BC (Joseph Martin McFadden). RR: AA.

On TV from the age of 12 (in *Taggart*), McFadden won attention in the soap *Take the High Road*. He left the series in 1997 to take up television and film offers. He joined the cast of the West End musical production of *Rent*.

Alan McGee

✪ *b. 29 September 1960, 19.40 GDT, Redlands Hospital, Glasgow, Scotland, 55N53, 04W17.*
Gerard q. BC (Alan John McGee). RR: AA.

Singer, guitarist and entrepreneur who launched the careers of Jesus & Mary Chain (qv) and Oasis.

Brian McGee – see Simple Minds
Raymond McGinley – see Teenage Fanclub

Matt McGinn
>   b. 17 January 1928, 22.30 GMT, Glasgow, Scotland, 55N51, 04W14.
>   Gerard q. BC (Matthew McGinn). RR: AA.
Singer and prolific songwriter, educated at Oxford.

Pat McGlynn – see Bay City Rollers

Ewan McGregor
✪   b. 31 March 1971, 20.10 MET, Perth, Scotland, 56N24, 03W27.
>   Gerard q. BC (Ewan Gordon McGregor). RR: AA.

Talented, intense and outspoken actor who established his reputation in the cult blockbuster film *Trainspotting* (February 1996), which made him a spokesman and posterboy for his generation (note the strong Uranus). He has since appeared in several other film successes, including *Velvet Goldmine*, based in part on the real-life icon Iggy Pop. In 1997 he guested on the television medical drama *ER* as part of his bid to break into the US market, and won a handful of Hollywood roles. It was his leading role in *Star Wars Episode One* (May 1999) that established him as an international star, yet he continues to appear in low-budget projects. Recent Hollywood films have included *Moulin Rouge*. He is also noted for appearing in uninhibited nude scenes and known for his patriotism (Cancer MC) and his unjaded, fresh approach to acting.

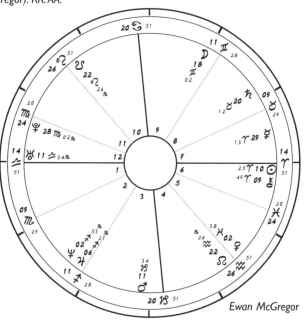

Ewan McGregor

> Q
> "As the wild-eyed junkie, McGregor gave an astonishing performance – a speed-ball of scruffy sexual charm and manic energy that managed to inject the weary concept of "the lovable rogue" with a peculiarly 90s vigour... Together with nudity, a permissive, polymorphous sort of libidinousness has been a regular characteristic of McGregor's film roles thus far. One of his interesting and peculiarly modern talents is his capacity for communicating a sexuality that is distinctively male yet devoid of machismo." (Zoe Heller, *Vanity Fair*, 12/98)
> "He is wild, uninhibited, buzzing with stories... He is very, very sexy... dizzy with his own potential, crackling with energy and enthusiasm, devoid of cynicism." (Shane Watson, *Hot Tickets*, 9/10/97)

Edward McGuire
>   b. 14 February 1948, 22.05 GMT, Lennox Castle, Scotland, 55N59, 04W14.
>   Gerard q. BC (Edward Patrick McGuire). RR: AA.
Classical instrumentalist and flautist with the Whistlebinkies folk group in 1973.

Loraine McIntosh – see Deacon Blue
Robbie McIntosh – see Average White Band
Onnie McIntyre – see Average White Band

Billy McIsaac
> b. 12 July 1949, 04.30 GDT, Victoria Cottage Hospital, Rothesay, Isle of Bute, Scotland, 55N50, 05W03.
> Gerard q. BC (William McIsaac). RR: AA.
Member of the bands Slik and Zones.

David McKail
> b. 13 March 1938, 10.00 GMT, Glasgow, Scotland, 55N52, 04W13.
> Gerard q. BC (David Frederick Mohr McKail). RR: AA.
Writer of solo plays under the pseudonym Frederic Mohr. McKail is also an actor with a number of TV credits. His film appearances include *Heavenly Pursuits* with Tom Conti (qv) and *Silent Scream*.

Kenneth McKellar
> b. 23 June 1927, 20.15 GDT, Paisley, Scotland, 55N50, 04W25.
> Gerard q. BC. RR: AA.
Composer and concert singer from age 13. Many TV appearances followed and McKellar had his own radio series, *A Song for Everyone* (1973-4). In the 90s he became a director for Radio Clyde.

Ian McKellen
⊘ b. 25 May 1939, 21.30 GDT, Burnley, England, 53N48. 02W14.
> From his website, which states "Ian Murray McKellen was born at 20.30 Greenwich Mean Time." RR: B.

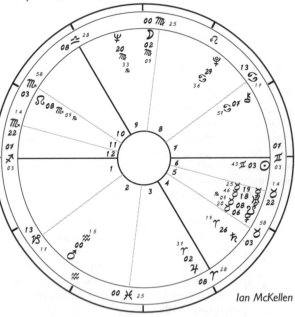

Ian McKellen

With remarkable portrayals in *Bent* (from May 1979, when TR Saturn stationed on the EQHS 10th and TR Uranus opposed Uranus-Mercury), *Amadeus* (from 17 December 1980, TR Jupiter and Saturn on MC, later winning a Tony Award) and many Shakespearean plays, McKellen has developed a reputation as the greatest theatre actor of his generation. He has also appeared in over 50 films including *And the Band Played On* (Emmy nomination), *Richard III*, *Gods and Monsters* (13 Best Actor awards) and *Lord of the Rings* (December 2001). McKellen lost his mother when he was 13 and became more shy and dependent on home life. He was bullied at school and wanted to escape into the make-believe world of acting. After Cambridge he joined the theatre in 1961 (as TR Pluto hit his EQHS 10th) and made his London debut in September 1964 and his Broadway debut in November 1967 (TR Jupiter conjunct Moon). August 1968 (TR Jupiter into the EQHS 10th) saw the beginning of a well-received tour in which he played the title roles in Shakespeare's *Richard II* and Marlowe's *Edward II*, arriving in London in September 1969 (TR Jupiter conjunct MC) and switching theatres in January 1970 (TR Uranus conjunct MC). His performances were described as having "sheer animal magnetism and interpretive intelligence," and his reputation as one of Britain's finest actors was growing, although his performance as *Hamlet* from March to July 1971 (TR Neptune opposing Sun and TR Saturn conjunct Sun) was criticised.

McKellen set up the Actors' Company in 1972 but became bored with playing small parts and joined the RSC and debuted with them as *Dr Faustus* in August 1974 (TR Neptune conjunct Ascendant). Big screen success remained elusive until he wrote the seminal screen version of *Richard III* (released April 1996), which won him an award for European Film Actor of the Year (to add to his five Olivier Awards). In 1989, one year after he publicly 'came out', McKellen became co-founder of Stonewall, a lobby group campaigning to improve the positions of gays in Britain, and two years later he was knighted.

Hugh McKenna – see Sensational Alex Harvey Band

Paul McKenna
✪ *Scorpio Sun, Scorpio Ascendant.*
From astrologer Russell Grant to McKenna on Russell Grant's All Star-Show. No other details given.
McKenna was born in Enfield (51N40, 0W05).
Britain's premier TV hypnotist. In July 1998 McKenna found himself in court defending his reputation (he was accused of turning a man who took part in his live stage performances into an "aggressive schizophrenic". McKenna was cleared on 14 August. In 2003 he was promoting self-hypnosis and positive thinking in newspapers and on *This Morning*.

Ted McKenna – see Sensational Alex Harvey Band
Leslie McKeown – see Bay City Rollers

Norman McLaren
b. 11 April 1914, 20.10 GMT, Stirling, Scotland, 56N07, 03W57.
Gerard q. BC (William Norman McLaren). RR: AA.
Pioneer documentary animator. McLaren began making amateur short films at 19. He moved to Canada and soon became the country's leading director of animated film. McLaren was known for perfecting the techniques of drawing directly on to film. He made 72 films and was the recipient of over one hundred awards, including an Academy Award for the cartoon *Neighbors* (1952). D. 26 January 1987.

Murray McLauchlan
✪ *b. 30 June 1948, 07.40 GDT, Paisley, Scotland, 55N51, 04W26.*
Gerard q. BC (Murray Edward McLauchlan). RR: AA.
Musician-composer.

Lex McLean
b. 30 April 1907, 09.30 GMT, Clydebank, Scotland, 55N54, 04W25.
Gerard q. BC (Alexander McLean Cameron). RR: AA.
Comic entertainer who elicited the public's adoration – he was Scotland's highest-paid comedian for many years.

Una McLean
b. 12 Jan 1930, 17.30 GMT, Strathaven, Scotland, 55N41, 04W04.
Gerard q. BC (Agnes Green McLean). RR: AA.
McLean, who made her professional debut in 1955, is an actress, comedian and veteran of pantomime and TV shows (including *Dreaming*, 1990). In 1991 she married Russell Hunter (qv).

Mark McManus

b. 21 February 1935, 16.20 GMT, Bellshill, Lanarkshire, Scotland, 55N49, 04W00.

Valerie Matthews q. BC via a genealogist friend. RR: AA.

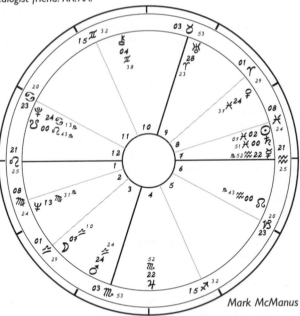

Mark McManus

McManus began his career as a boxer before emigrating to Australia. His first professional acting job was in 1964. Nine years later he won TV fame in *Sam*. He was in the crime series *The Strangers* from June 1978 to October 1982. In times of bland police series, his much-loved show *Taggart* (from 1983) offered a convincing sense of community and genuine drama; it was a cult series in France and highly popular in Britain. McManus brought a lack of pretension to the title role: he was hard-hitting, sharp and skeptical; an authority figure who was also a rebel. A heavy drinker all his life, McManus was known also for his quick wit and wicked sense of humour. He and Brian Connolly (qv, of the 70s glam pop band Sweet) were brought up by the same extended family (McManus was 13 years older). Although there remains confusion after both Connolly (qv) and McManus's deaths as to whether or not they were actually brothers, close relatives of McManus deny the direct blood link. McManus's second wife Marion died of cancer in Autumn 1993 (Solar Eclipse on 4th, TR Saturn near Descendant), seven months before his own death. D. 6 June 1994, pneumonia, alcohol abuse.

Gillian McNeill

b. 25 September 1965, 05.40 GDT, Mayfield Hospital, Dundee, Scotland, 56N28, 02W58.

Gerard q. BC (Gillian Margaret McNeill). RR: AA.

Regular cast member of the popular Scottish soap *Take the High Road* from 1987-94, in which she played Lynne McNeil.

Tommy McQuater

b. 4 September 1914, 16.30 GMT, Maybole, Ayr, Scotland, 55N21, 04W41.

Gerard q. BC (Thomas Mossie McQuater). RR: AA.

A jazz trumpeter, McQuater moved to London in the 30s to work with dance orchestras. One of Britain's most acclaimed soloists, he has worked with George Chisholm (qv).

Ian McShane

b. 29 September 1942, 03.00 GDT, Blackburn, England, 53N45, 02W29.

From him to Dana Holliday. RR: A.

A familiar TV and film actor, whose first film was *The Wild and the Willing* in 1962. McShane starred in the original 1965 production of Joe Orton's *Loot*. McShane's landmark role was that of Judas in *Jesus of Nazareth* (1977) on TV. In 1989 he appeared in the soap *Dallas* as a film director who wooed Sue Ellen away from J.R. Ewing. He was even more popular for his role as a roguish antiques dealer in *Lovejoy* (the MC ruler is Venus conjunct Neptune in the EQHS 2nd!), which spanned six series from 1986-94. In 1992 he released an album, *Both Sides Now*. In January 2001 he appeared in the film *Sexy Beast* (as TR Saturn stationed close to the EQHS 10th). A heartthrob in the 70s McShane was once as well known for his off-screen bad boy behaviour and battle with drink (MC ruler Venus conjunct Neptune) as his leading roles. In August 1980 he married for the third time and the couple have stayed together ever since.

Norris McWhirter

b. 12 August 1925, 19.40 GDT, London, England, 51N30, 0W10.
Dana Holliday q. People magazine. RR: B.

Along with twin brother Ross (born 20 minutes later), Norris McWhirter wrote *The Guinness Book of Records*. He also often appeared on the TV show *Record Breakers* with Roy Castle (qv). On 12 September 1954 the brothers were running a fact and figure agency in London (Moon in Gemini, Mercury in Virgo) when they were approached to begin the first edition of the book of records. The first copy was printed on 27 August 1955. It has been a best seller each year since (except 1957 and 1959, when it was not published). By the late 80s the yearly reference book had been translated into 35 languages and is now the world's best-selling book. Norris McWhirter was the editor for 30 consecutive years. When Ross was

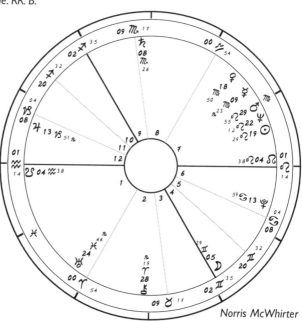

Norris McWhirter

gunned down at his front door on 27 November 1975 (for offering a reward for the capture of IRA bombers), surviving twin Norris said it felt more like an amputation than a bereavement. He continues with the controversial organisation they set up, The Freedom Association.

George Melly

b. 17 August 1926, 09.15 GDT, Liverpool, England, 53N25, 02W55.
From his mother to the Astrological Association. RR: A.

Larger-than-life and hedonistic jazz personality, vocalist, journalist and author. Melly's early career (from 1950) revolved around Mick Mulligan's band but he achieved prominence in the 60s after relaunching himself as a solo artist. From the 70s to the present his live brand of jazz and his witty repartee have made him hugely popular with audiences. In one of his autobiographies, *Rum, Bum and Concertina*, he describes his unemotional approach to life, his bisexuality and his 'open' marriage in the 60s (Venus in EQHS 11th trine 7th House Uranus on Descendant). He is now committed to a companionable old age. His first volume of autobiography, *Owning Up*, chronicles in hilarious detail his early jazz career in the 50s.

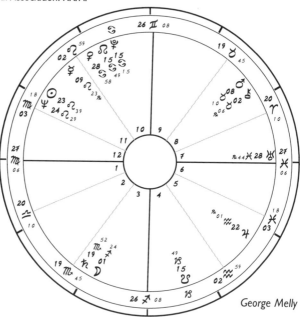

George Melly

Sheila Mercier

  b. 1 January 1919, 03.00 GMT, Hull, England, 53N45, 0W20.

    From Russell Grant's article in TV Times, 14 January 1983, original source not known. RR: C.

Mercier is best known for her role as Annie Sugden from 1972 in *Emmerdale Farm*. On 12 November 1985 the soap celebrated its 1000th episode. Both actress and character do not suffer fools gladly, but Mercier admits to being nervous and more timid than her TV alter-ego. She began acting at Randle Evans College of Drama in Stratford Upon Avon, then worked in repertory in Hull before moving to London. She appeared for 12 years with actor brother Brian Rix (qv) at the Whitehall Theatre.

Freddie Mercury

  b. 5 September 1946, 05.10 (-3), Zanzibar, Tanzania, 6S10, 39E11.

    Date and place from biographies. Birth time speculative (around 21 degrees of Fixed Signs appear to be significant). N.B. There is no longer a record of his birth held in the Zanzibar Registry. RR: C.

A singer and icon who was most vivid and alive onstage, Mercury was an outstanding contributor to British music. He joined the band Queen in 1970, with a first gig in June 1971, and they were launched to a wider audience in April 1973. 1975 was a banner year, bringing with it the masterpiece *Bohemian Rhapsody* (November 1975). Queen topped the USA charts in February 1980 and frequently hit the upper end of the British charts. After Freddie's death *A Concert for Life* (20 April 1992) celebrated his music and spirit. A statue was erected in his honour in Montreux (a haven for Mercury in later years) on 25 November 1996. D. 24 November 1991.

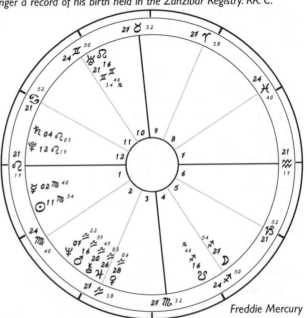

Freddie Mercury

George Michael

  b. 25 June 1963, 06.00 GDT, Finchley, London, England, 51N36, 0W10.

    Janey Stubbs q. a confidential source, verified by FCC. RR: A.

With school friend Andrew Ridgeley, George Michael formed The Executive (making their debut on 5 November 1979). They were renamed Wham when the duo signed a long-term contract on 24 March 1982 (eight months after they had left school). Their first smash hit came that October. By 1984 Wham was one of Britain's most successful pop outfits with million-selling albums and singles, including the perennial favourite *Careless Whisper* (July 1984). In April 1985 they were the first Western pop band to perform live in China. They fought a legal battle to be released from their original record contract and were successful on 22 March 1984. Michael, who had known Ridgeley since 9 September 1975, announced he was going solo in November 1985 (as TR Neptune opposed his Sun and TR Uranus squared MC). The band's farewell concert in front of 80,000 fans took place on 28 June 1986. Michael moved into a successful solo career, which has included recording a duet with Aretha Franklin in December 1986 (when TR Jupiter conjunct his MC). His rockabilly album *Faith*, released in October 1987, established him as a singer-songwriter of note and by 1988 he had conquered the US market. In September 1990 (TR Saturn conjunct Descendant), with the release of *Listen Without Prejudice*, Michael began rejecting the rock star lifestyle and grew disgruntled with his record company's management of his music. He served a writ on 21 October 1992 (TR Neptune conjunct Descendant, with TR Uranus following suit) and a court case claiming restraint of trade began on 12 October 1993 (his Saturn Return). Michael, who dared to fight the system and risk his future recording career (Chiron conjunct MC), lost the case on 21 June 1994. He was, however, bought out of his contract by Dreamworks/Virgin on 13 July 1995, and in January 1996 released a single (and in May the album *Older*) to rave reviews. His horoscope demonstrates some of the key indicators of on-going legal action where one's reputation is at stake: 7th and 8th house ruler Saturn is retrograde in the EQHS 8th, opposing Moon in a heavily tenanted EQHS 2nd house. Michael has always guarded his personal life.

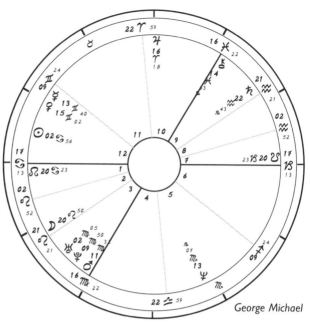

George Michael

In January 1991 (TR Pluto square Moon), when singing in Brazil, he met Anselmo Feleppa, who, as Michael's first male long-term partner, changed his life. In March 1993 (his Saturn Return) Michael was devastated when Feleppa died of a brain haemorrhage. In February 1997 his mother died of cancer. In November 1996 his first interview for six years (in which he discussed his life and sexuality – Venus/Mercury in the EQHS 11th) was ripped off by a major newspaper before publication in a charity magazine. Michael's sexuality (an open secret in music circles and the subject of much media speculation – MC in Pisces) was exposed worldwide when he was arrested for lewd conduct in a toilet in Los Angeles on 7 April 1998 at 16.48 (as TR Jupiter, known for spotlighting indiscretions, approached his MC). Michael claimed entrapment and, although fined and sentenced to 81 hours of community service, got his revenge on the LAPD with his provocative video *Outside*. In July 2002 (as TR Pluto opposed Venus) he released *Shoot the Dog*, an anti-Bush/Blair single, and in early 2003 he was vocal about his anti-war stance – both were considered 'career suicide' by journalists. With a strong Cancer influence (Sun and Ascendant in this sign), Michael has always had the ability to strike a popular chord and to be in tandem with public taste – although his image can range from sullen to smug, and taking life ever-so-seriously. The strong Cancer partly accounts for the secretive, solitary and private side to his personality (George has been described as introspective, undemonstrative, analytical, shrewd and cautious), and the Moon in Leo points to his pride, optimism, arrogance and obsession with his appearance.

Q | "I'm not an arrogant person but I have a real inner confidence... I really am an optimist... I feel a very great need to be away from George Michael most of the time." (George Michael, as quoted in *The Sunday Times Magazine*, 5/12/93)
"I created a man... who could realize my dreams, and make me a star. I called him George Michael." (George Michael, *Bare* by George Michael and Tony Parsons, Penguin, 1992)

Sarah Miles

b. 31 December 1941, 23.45 GDT, Fryerning, England, 51N41, 0E22.
Penny Thornton, in Romancing the Stars, p. 433, q. the nurse who delivered Miles for between 23.30 and midnight. RR: A.

A rebellious, sporty and dyslexic teenager, Miles sought attention whilst immersing herself in a fantasy world (Neptune conjunct Ascendant). *Term of Trial* (1963) and *The Servant* (late 1963) established her as a serious actress and movie star. She emulated that acclaim with *Ryan's Daughter* in November 1970. Neptune Rising in Virgo reflects Miles's paranormal experiences and her embroilment in an on-going scandal. On 11 February 1973 (following an Eclipse on MC ruler Mercury), her business manager was found dead in Miles's bathtub after roughing her up a few hours earlier. Speculation surrounding his death was to haunt Miles and her career, especially as she chose to remain silent about the incident for 20 years. On 20 February 1995 her

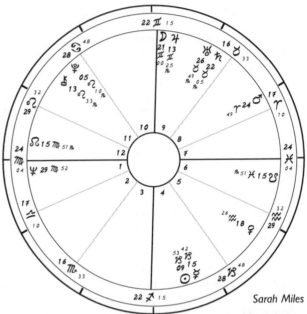

Sarah Miles

husband, playwright Robert Bolt, died marking the end of a passionate relationship spanning almost 30 years, in which they had married and separated and reconciled a number of times. Miles's liaisons with famous men have kept her in the spotlight, and some, including affairs with Laurence Olivier (qv), James Fox and Steven Spielberg, were well-kept secrets. She has related much of her extraordinary life story over three volumes of autobiography. Miles has a contradictory horoscope with a strong earth overtone (responsible and disciplined Sun-Mercury in Capricorn, methodical Virgo Rising) but also an unorthodox, free-spirited Venus in Aquarius and a flighty, curious Moon in Gemini. Despite her numerous roles and beguiling persona (Neptune Rising) she is remembered as much for her acting as for the daily routine of drinking her own urine.

Spike Milligan – see The Goons

Hayley Mills

b. 18 April 1946, 23.40 GDT, London, England, 51N30, 0W10.
From her father's autobiography, Up in the Clouds, Gentlemen Please (Weidenfeld & Nicolson, 1980) p. 197, which quotes an entry in his diary. RR: AA.

Hayley Mills first appeared on screen at 13 in *Tiger Bay* (1959). She signed a five-year Walt Disney contract and one result was *Pollyanna*, for which she won a special Oscar. Her sweet and innocent image was finally shattered when she appeared nude in *The Family Way* (1967) and dated producer-director Roy Boulting*, some 32 years her senior. Under great pressure from her fame Mills developed bulimia. She split from her partner in February 1997, despite admitting she had found spiritual and romantic contentment with this younger man. In 1998 she fell in love with actor Firdous Bamji.

---

* Roy Boulting *b. 21 December 1913, 03.30 GDT, Brookmead Bray, Maidenhead, England. FCC q. BC in hand, a twin. RR: AA.*

John Mills

☞ b. 22 February 1908, 02.35 GMT, North Elmham, Norfolk, England, 52N45, 0E56.
His autobiography, *Up in the Clouds, Gentlemen Please* (Weidenfeld & Nicolson, 1980), p. 3, states the date and place and "during the early hours". Speculative time. (N.B. Most film books incorrectly state the birthplace as being Felixstowe.) RR: C.

Mills was a leading film personality during the Second World War with many stiff upper-lip portrayals to his name. His professional debut was in the chorus of *The Five O'Clock Girl* in 1929 and films followed from 1932. He won numerous awards for the 1970 film *Ryan's Daughter* (including an Oscar and Golden Globe Award) and was knighted in 1977. In 2003, at the age of 95, he was promoting a new film, *Bright Young Things*, and celebrating 62 years of marriage.

Juliet Mills

☞ b. 21 November 1941, 23.00 GDT, Holloway Road, London, England, 51N33, 0W07.
From her father's autobiography, *Up in the Clouds, Gentlemen Please* (Weidenfeld & Nicolson, 1980), p. 174-5, which suggests the birth took place between 21.00 and 23.30. Speculative time. RR: C.

The daughter of John Mills (qv), Juliet made her screen debut at eleven weeks old. She is best known for her stage work in London and on Broadway. She won an Emmy for her performance in *QB-VII* (May 1975). She married actor Maxwell Caulfield, her third husband, in 1981.

George Mitchell

✪ b. 27 February 1917, 09.30 GMT, Carron, Scotland, 56N02, 03W47.
Gerard q. BC. RR: AA.

Lead singer of the George Mitchell Singers and creator of *The Black and White Minstrel Show* in 1958.

Ian Mitchell – see Bay City Rollers
Neil Mitchell – see Wet Wet Wet
Alfred Molina – see Jill Gascoine

Bob Monkhouse

b. 1 June 1928, 02.00 GDT, Beckenham, England, 51N24, 0W02.
David Fisher q. his letter (same in his autobiography *Crying with Laughter*, Arrow, 1994). RR: A.

Sensitive and thoughtful actor-writer-comedian. Monkhouse was ruled out of his unaffectionate mother's life when he married and chose a career in show business at 21. A beloved grandfather had died when Monkhouse was eight, leaving him with two emotionally-retarded parents. As a youngster he received tremendous advice about joke construction from Max Miller and during the Second World War, at 16, he was an able compere for the *Britain Can Take It* concert in Kent. At 18 he bluffed his way into an audition with the BBC. In Autumn 1955 Bob Monkhouse was at the forefront of the British TV phenomenon when ITV began its successful bid to rival the BBC. Monkhouse's sharp Scorpio Moon may add to his Gemini sharpness, but it also accounts for his strong

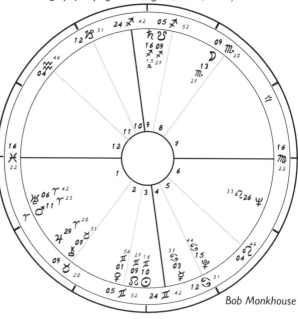

Bob Monkhouse

sex drive during a promiscuous youth. With brilliant improvisational skill (he also has a photographic memory) Monkhouse showed he was the sharpest ad-libber on TV with his 1994 BBC word-association stand-up show, which did much to rid the public's view of him as an orange-tinted smarmy quiz host (Gemini). At 65 he banished many ghosts by writing his autobiography, which told of his cold, complicated mother. In July 1995 his treasured book of comedy material went missing until November 1996, provoking many a joke from rival comedians as to the worth of its content. Monkhouse suffered a personal loss when his estranged son died of an accidental heroin overdose on 10 May 2001 (as TR Jupiter opposed TR Pluto over his EQHS 4th/10th cusps). In early 2002 he was diagnosed with advanced prostate cancer and went public in late April, following TR Saturn conjunct Sun.

Alec Monteath

b. 22 May 1941, 18.30 DGDT, Doune, Perthshire, Scotland, 56N12, 04W03.
Gerard q. BC (Alexander William Monteath). RR: AA.

Actor who played the reliable shepherd Dougal Lachlan in *Take the High Road* from 1980-91. His one-man show *Shylock Triumphant* was well-received at the annual Edinburgh Festival in August 1992 and 1993.

MONTY PYTHON

Monty Python's Flying Circus, first broadcast by the BBC on 5 October 1969 (and produced until November 1974), redefined the boundaries of TV comedy. Its often shapeless sketches combined slapstick (Jupiter) with intellectual humour, and the result was a highly visual, innovative and even anarchic television product (Uranus). The show has maintained its cult status since the 70s, spawning many spin-offs and imitations. It drew to a close after the departure of Cleese in 1973 in the penultimate series. The team made a successful transition to cinema in the 80s and each member moved on to a successful TV or film career. We can expect to see satirical and biting wit with a strong Mars and/or its signs prominent in the charts of the Python members, as well as a strong Uranus for anarchy, surreal humour and originality and Pluto for generational influence.

Outrageous satirist **Graham Chapman** (Uranus conjunct Moon), who was known (with Cleese) for sketches high in physical and verbal abuse, had written for many TV series up to his death, of spinal cancer, on 4 October 1989, in Maidstone.

John Cleese (three planets in Scorpio, Moon in Aries, Uranus opposite Mercury, Pluto square Sun) went on to write and star in the celebrated *Fawlty Towers* and has appeared in the films *A Fish Called Wanda* and *Fierce Creatures* (premiered mid-February 1997). His humour is based around farce, rudeness and chaos (Virgo Ascendant). Eric Idle noted, "John's always had that streak – half-caught by the English class system, half despising it."

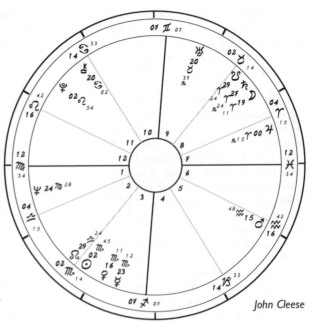

John Cleese

Rubber-faced **Terry Gilliam** (Mars and Mercury in Scorpio, Uranus opposite Sun and square Moon, Pluto square Mercury) provided surreal animation for Monty Python and later directed *Brazil* (1985), *12 Monkeys* (1995) and *Time Bandits* (1981).

Eric Idle (Sun and Mercury in Aries on the MC, Pluto on Ascendant) worked independently from the Python team, and from the late 80s appeared in Hollywood films (including *Casper*, 1995) and is set to star in Spielberg's rumoured revival of *Doctor Who*.

Terry Jones (Aries Rising, Mars square Sun, Moon and Venus, Uranus square Mercury, Pluto conjunct Moon and opposite Sun) went on to direct feature films.

Michael Palin (Uranus conjunct Moon and Mercury, Pluto conjunct Ascendant) made good use of his adventurous spirit (Jupiter prominent) by sailing into BBC documentaries such as *Around the World in 80 Days* in 1988 and *Pole to Pole* in 1992. He turned to straight acting in *GBH* with Julie Walters (qv). Palin won the Peter Sellers' Award for Best Comedy Performance in 1985. Palin survived a difficult childhood and the burden of great expectation from an unfulfilled father who abused Palin's mother.

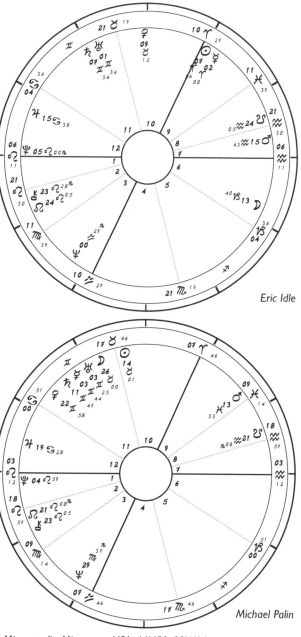

Eric Idle

Michael Palin

Graham Chapman

✪ b. 8 January 1941, 07.30 GDT,
☙ Leicester, England, 52N38, 01W05.
   Eve Jackson q. Chapman's mother over the telephone for "early morning, about breakfast." RR: C.

John Cleese

   b. 27 October 1939, 03.15 GDT, Weston-Super-Mare, England, 51N21, 02W59.
   Eve Jackson q. Cleese's mother over the telephone. RR: A.

Terry Gilliam

   b. 22 November 1940, 00.35 CST, Minneapolis, Minnesota, USA, 44N59, 93W16.
   Eve Jackson q. Gilliam's mother over the telephone. RR: A.

Eric Idle

   b. 29 March 1943, 13.20 GDT, South Shields, England, 55N00, 01W25.
   Eve Jackson q. him. RR: A.

Terry Jones

   b. 1 February 1942, 11.00 GDT, Colwyn Bay, Wales, 53N18, 03W43.
   Eve Jackson q. him. RR: A.

Michael Palin

   b. 5 May 1943, 11.45 DGDT, Sheffield, England, 53N23, 01W30.
   Eve Jackson q. him. RR: A.

Dudley Moore

> b. 19 April 1935, 18.30 GDT, Dagenham, England, 51N32, 0E10.
>
> *Tashi Grady q. him, from his father, who remembers having come home from work. RR: A.*

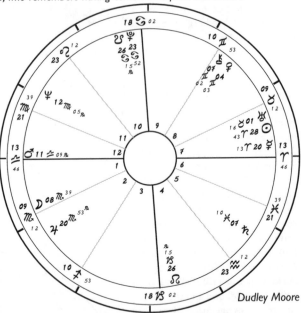

Dudley Moore

The diminutive actor-comedian-musician Dudley Moore was born with a club foot and spent most of his childhood convalescing in hospitals, feeling like an outsider and later tortured by self-doubt. His mother, described as an intense, funny woman who could "turn on you", harboured guilt about her son's disability. A classical scholar, he wrote a string quartet for his finals but his first love was always jazz. In his early twenties he found his forte with the piano, and in early 1959 was Cleo Laine's (qv) jazz pianist before moving *Beyond the Fringe* (when TR Neptune conjunct MC ruler Moon), the popular satire presented at the Edinburgh Festival in August 1960. It moved to the West End (10 May 1961) and on to Broadway in October 1962. It was Moore's partnership, until 1989, with master-improviser Peter Cook (qv) that provided him with comic longevity, although their act was said to have peaked by 1971. Both have the key astrological significators for comic talent (Uranus) and generational influence and satire (Pluto): Cook has Uranus-Moon and Moon square Pluto; Moore has Sun-Uranus, Uranus opposite Moon, and Mercury square Pluto. As a film actor Moore made two high-grossing films *Arthur* (July 1981, winning a Golden Globe Award in 1982) and *10* (filmed in November 1978, released in October 1979), the latter turning him into a sex 'thimble'. Women adored him and Moore reciprocated. His role in *Arthur* is said to have been based on Peter Cook. Moore had open-heart surgery in September 1997, three years after he began a volatile fourth marriage. He contributed to the publication of Barbara Paskin's no-holds-barred book, which examined his recent chaotic personal life, which began as TR Uranus squared his Sun in the 7th House. Paskin described him as morose, melancholic and exceptionally generous. With TR Neptune following suit in 1998, his health declined and in September 1999 he announced that he had the brain disease PSP (progressive supranuclear palsy). Moore was paid tribute by his peers and celebrity friends in April 2001, a year before he died on 27 March 2002 in Plainfield, New Jersey.

> Q
>
> "Dudley had always worn the face of a clown and, like all clowns, he wore laughter as his mantle and kept the tears inside." (Barbara Paskin, *Dudley Moore: The Authorized Biography*, Pan, 1998)
>
> "Deep down Dudley has never liked the thought of being the little man, because inside himself he's such a big chap." (Barbara Moore, as quoted in *Dudley Moore: The Authorized Biography* by Barbara Paskin, Pan, 1998)
>
> "I never agonized over music. I did with comedy; it always prompted so much soul-searching, it never came easy. I wanted to be loved and accepted by the world. I was melancholically disposed towards gaining love and friendship because I felt if I was myself, people would reject me because I was deformed." (Dudley Moore, as quoted in *The Entertainers* by Timothy White, Billboard Books, 1998)

Roger Moore

b. 14 October 1927, 00.45 GMT, London, England, 51N30, 0W10.
Edwin Steinbrecher q. Moore to Talia Shire, August 1989 (Robert Skeetz q. Mary Frances Woods, who gave 01.00, original source not known). RR: A.

Moore began his professional life as an animator before going on to work as an extra. Upon moving to America he won a contract with MGM in 1954 and starred in a number of highly successful TV series: *Ivanhoe* (1957-8), *The Alaskans* (October 1959, TR Uranus on MC, to September 1960), *Maverick* (1960-1), *The Saint* (May 1967 to September 1969) and *The Persuaders* (September 1971 to June 1972). Taking over from Sean Connery (qv), Moore was a suave, less physical James Bond in seven films of the on-going series. His first Bond film was *Live and Let Die* (June 1973, TR Uranus conjunct Sun), the last, *A View to a Kill* (May 1985). In January 1995 Moore announced the end of his marriage, which has prompted several bitter public outbursts over

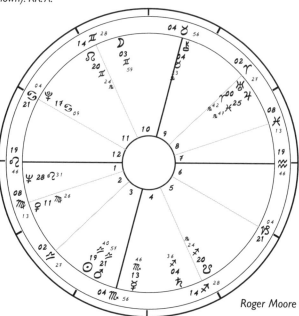

Roger Moore

the years from his wife (they were together for 38 years and married for 27). On 3 October 1999 his new partner (and, from March 2002, his fourth wife) was accidentally hit by the couple's chauffeur. After collapsing on stage in New York, Moore was fitted with a pacemaker in May 2003.

Kenneth More

b. 20 September 1914, 14.30 GMT, Gerrards Cross, England, 51N35, 0W34.
David Fisher q. him, "time is accurate." RR: A.

Popular British actor who made his stage debut in 1936. From the 50s two film comedies, *Genevieve* (1953) and *Doctor in the House* (1954, British Academy Award for Best Actor), established him as a character actor usually cast in bemused, ingenuous roles. He became the likeable gentleman of post-war British cinema and an icon of decency. Later he appeared on TV in *The Forsyte Saga* (26 episodes, shown from January to July 1967). As a young lad the death of his father and mounting family debts had put an end to his ambitions to become a civil engineer. D. 12 July 1982, Parkinson's disease.

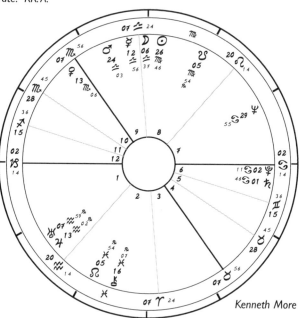

Kenneth More

Eric Morecambe

☉ b. 14 May 1926, 12.00 GDT, Morecambe, England, 54N04, 02W53.

☀ Joan Revill in Prediction, November 1975, gives 12.00 Noon, original source not known. The biography Morecambe and Wise by Graham McCann (4th Estate, 1998) p. 22, gives 12.30. RR: C/B.

Morecambe, along with Ernie Wise (qv) was one of the top attractions in British comedy from the 60s to his death in 1984. Morecambe and Wise, whose sunshine comedy bordered on pantomime, had the ability to bring out the unexpected best in their eminent guests (including Glenda Jackson, qv). Their Christmas Day show in 1977 pulled in a record 28 million viewers. There was an all-star tribute to the brilliance of Eric Morecambe on 14 May 1995. In late 2001 a show about Morecambe and Wise, The Play What I Wrote, debuted in the West End and was directed by Kenneth Branagh (qv). In October 2002 Morecambe was named the 32nd Greatest Briton of all time. Before meeting Wise he had been spurred on by an ambitious mother to perform (note the Fixed Grand Cross in angular houses) and worked as a comic through men's clubs and chapel socials. D. 28 May 1984, Gloucestershire, heart attack.

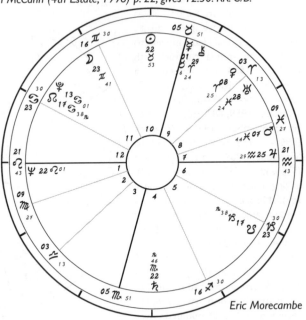

Eric Morecambe

Sarah Jane Morris

b. 21 March 1959, 15.30 GMT, Bassett, Southampton, England, 50N57, 01W24.

FCC q. her. RR: A.

Gifted and intense singer, songwriter and actress. Morris studied drama at Stratford before teaming up with a jazz pianist in 1980 to earn her Equity card. Following a brief stint with an Italian blues band later that year, she joined the world music band The Republic which, despite much hype, failed to make an impact. In 1984 Morris joined the 20-piece big band The Happy End for an association that lasted five years. In late 1985 Morris leant her husky voice to a duet with Jimmy Somerville (qv) at a fund-raiser. Their voices attracted interest from record producers and she was asked to sing on the album being recorded by Somerville's new group Communards. The group performed on the left-wing Red

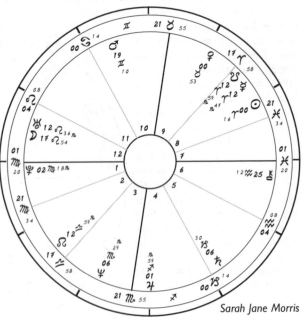

Sarah Jane Morris

Wedge tour and recorded a belting remake of *Don't Leave Me This Way*. The song hit #1 in Britain in September 1986 and became the biggest selling single of the year. On 28 October 1986 she was the subject of a mild tabloid exposé. Morris split from the group the following year and embarked upon a solo career. In 1988 she pursued acting work on stage and in the BBC drama *Thin Air* (which aired in April). After a critically-acclaimed debut album released on 3 April 1989, she began to gather a following in Europe (especially Italy, Greece and Germany, where her records hit the top of the charts). In March 1991 she wrote and performed the winning entry at the Sanremo International Song Festival. That year she also wrote and performed *I Am A Woman*, an anthem celebrating womanhood, for the TV series *The Men's Room*. Others' mismanagement of her career led to great difficulties in August 1992, although Morris released a second album, *Heaven* (which proved popular in Europe), and in mid-August, married her long-time boyfriend, David Coulter. Her third album, *Blue Valentine*, was released shortly after the birth of her son, Otis, in February 1995. A political and fast-talking performer, flame-haired Morris (with Pluto Rising and Ascendant/10th House ruler Mercury in 8th) has had to struggle for recognition in Britain, where she has sometimes been considered too controversial and outspoken. Her 20 February 1989 release of the classic *Me and Mrs Jones* was banned and she has suffered further poor press due to her unwillingness to be pigeonholed (Moon-Uranus, Pluto Rising). Morris continues to perform all over the world and her voice (a four octave seismic instrument) develops and broadens with every album she records. Morris released *Fallen Angel*, a collection of songs exploring her anger and madness (Moon-Uranus) and set up her own record label, Fallen Angel Ltd. to release her own albums, challenging her fanbase to explore new styles with her. The first result was the acclaimed *August* with Marc Ribot and in May 2003 *Love and Pain* followed.

Q "When I'm singing I get possessed by something. I'm floating above, yet still in control. Music is my expressive side. It seeps through my veins." (Sarah Jane Morris, *Diva*, March 2001)

"All the bands up until my solo career were political... Politics has always found me... but I don't think I am a very political thinker but, because there weren't many women in the music industry that were part of that kind of 80s thing, I think I've been held up to be far more important politically that I ever was. I was terrified of letting people down." (Sarah Jane Morris, as quoted in an interview with Mike Thorne on www.stereosociety.com)

Van Morrison
   b. 31 August 1945, 23.59 GMT, Belfast, Ireland, 54N35, 05W55.
   Lois Rodden q. a colleague, from Morrison (probably stated as "midnight"). RR: A.
A legendary singer-songwriter with a huge and loyal following, Morrison was originally a saxophonist with the band Monarchs from the age of 15. He began a solo career in 1967 with a US Top Ten hit that September.

Neil Morrissey – see Elizabeth Carling
Jon Moss – see Boy George

Alison Moyet

✪ b. 18 June 1961, 09.30 GDT, Billericay, England, 51N38, 0E25.
From Moyet to astrologer Fiona Graham (FCC confirmed this with Moyet's personal manager Deborah Rawlings). Previously Babs Kirby q. Moyet's record company, information from her mother (letter in hand) for 04.30, which was likely a typo or misreading of a handwritten '4' and '9'. RR: A.

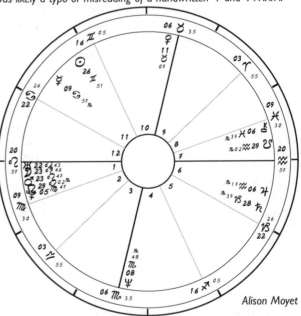

Alison Moyet

A highly regarded singer-songwriter, Moyet began with the short-lived synthesiser band Yazoo, a duo that enjoyed four major hits from May 1982 before splitting on 24 May 1983. She committed her acclaimed blues voice to a solo album, *Alf*, which topped the British charts in January 1985. She struggled against the pop star image and wanted to be taken seriously (Venus conjunct MC), embarking on a tribute to Billie Holiday in June 1985, which was not particularly well-received. Moyet admits during this time she was living a wild life and struggled with self-esteem about her weight. Two years later, after the birth of her first child and the break-up of her marriage (mid-1986, official on 19 May 1989), Moyet returned with another smash album, *Raindancing*.

After another long hiatus, during which time she suffered a lack of musical confidence, Alison Moyet returned with an album in April 1991. In June 1995 a compilation album, *Singles*, went straight to #1 in the British charts. She made a triumphant return to the spotlight in the West End with the musical *Chicago* from 13 August 2001 (to March 2002), facing head-on her agoraphobia and nervousness that had plagued her during her pop success. After the lengthy litigation that followed her 1994 album *Essex*, she delivered her album *Hometime* to Sony in November 2000 but the company rejected it two months later (TR Uranus conjunct Descendant). She persevered, knowing the project represented her musically, and the album was released to great critical acclaim on 19 August 2002 (TR Saturn conjunct Sun). (N.B. Moyet was born four days after another 80s pop star, Boy George, qv.)

> Q "I'm a bit of a chancer because I don't think I've ever really worked hard at anything in my life, which on one level is a good thing, but on another level, I wonder how much further I could have taken my skills and talents." (Alison Moyet, *Culture*, *Sunday Times*, c.2001)
> "[The album *Alf*] established me. But unfortunately in the wrong light, I think; a lot of people got the wrong impression of me. They see me as some Earth Mother, torch song singer – a would-be soul singer, which is not what I am about at all." (Alison Moyet, *Q*, 02/87)

Alex Munro

b. 6 March 1911, 03.30 GMT, Glasgow, Scotland, 55N51, 04W11.
Gerard q. BC (Alexander Nielson Horsburgh). RR: AA.
Comedian, with a debut in 1917. Munro was originally an acrobat.

Donnie Munro – see Runrig

Chic Murray

b. 6 November 1919, 13.15 GMT, Greenock, Scotland, 55N57, 04W46.
Gerard q. BC (Charles Thomas McKinnon Murray). RR: AA.
Unique comedian loved for his absurd view of the world.

Pete Murray

b. 19 September 1925, 13.30 GDT, London, England, 51N30, 0W10.

The Astrological Association q. him from his mother. RR: A.

Radio disc jockey and regular panelist on the music review show *Juke Box Jury* from 1959.

Linda Myles

b. 2 May 1947, 07.45 DGDT, Kerrlee Nursing Home, Arbroath, Scotland, 56N34, 02W35.

Gerard q. BC (Linda Robbie Myles). RR: AA.

Film and TV producer and director of the Edinburgh International Film Festival (1973-80). Co-author of the 1979 book *The Movie Brats*, she later worked for Channel 4. In 1981 Myles received a BFI Award for services to the film industry. She was Senior Vice-President of European Production for Columbia Pictures under David Puttnam (qv) before working for the BBC. In the early 90s she moved into independent film production and her credits include *The Commitments* (1991).

Mystic Meg

b. 27 July 1942, 08.45 DGDT, Accrington, England, 53N46, 02W21.

David Fisher q. her letter (copy in hand). Date and place confirmed by BC in hand. RR: A.

Mystic Meg began life as working-class Northern girl Margaret Lake and developed an interest in psychic phenomena from the age of seven. After a stint as a journalist and sub-editor of the *News of the World*, she reinvented herself as the newspaper's ethereal occult columnist in 1986. She is known to be very private and ambitious. Her close partner died around 1976.

Steve Nallon

b. 8 December 1960, 14.00 GMT, Leeds, England, 53N50, 01W35.

FCC q. him, from his aunt. RR: A.

Brilliant impersonator best known for his spot-on impersonations of Margaret Thatcher* in talent shows and later in *Spitting Image* from 26 February 1984 to February 1996 (coinciding with both Nallon's Jupiter Returns). Nallon, a Sagittarian, has Jupiter and Saturn on his MC so was able to pinpoint characteristics of this Saturnine politician and both exploit and exaggerate them (Jupiter). It is interesting to note the connections between his and Thatcher's horoscope. His MC falls on her Jupiter, facilitating the spot-on caricature which she obligingly grew into. Thatcher's departure from the political scene coincided with Nallon's TR Neptune conjunct MC. His infamous creation was as redundant as the former PM

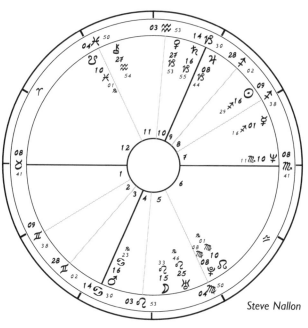

Steve Nallon

herself. *Steve Nallon's Big Odyssey*, his one-man show, debuted at the Edinburgh Festival in August 2002. (For other Thatcher impersonators see profiles on Angela Thorne and Janet Brown.)

---

* Margaret Thatcher b. 13 October 1925, 09.00 GMT, Grantham, England. Charles Harvey q. her, via her personal secretary. RR: A.

Daniela Nardini

✪   b. 26 April 1966, 12.59 GDT, Irvine, Scotland, 55N38, 04W41.
   Gerard q. BC. RR: AA.

Stage and TV actress who shot to national attention as the sardonic lawyer Anna in the BBC2 series *This Life* (1997) and won a Bafta for the role. The character was sexy, bitchy and tough (Mars on the MC) and following the series Nardini was offered similar roles.

Graham Nash

   b. 2 February 1942, 01.50 GDT, Blackpool, England, 53N50, 03W03.
   Linda Clark q. him. RR: A.

In July 1968 Nash joined music veterans Stephen Stills* and David Crosby** in a jamming session and together they decided to form a 'supergroup'. A debut album was released in June 1969. Despite numerous internal conflicts, the band would reconcile at various times.

Charles Naughton

   b. 15 December 1886, 11.30 GMT, Glasgow, Scotland, 55N51, 04W15.
   Gerard q. BC (Charles John Naughton). RR: AA.

Comedian known for his partnership with Jimmy Gold (qv) and the catchphrase "Turn it round the other way." He starred in many Royal Variety Performances from the 30s.

NAZARETH

Popular 70s band, originally formed in 1968. They had hits from 1973-9 on the UK pop charts. Cleminson, formally of the Sensational Alex Harvey Band (qv), joined the group for a short period.

Pete Agnew

   b. 14 September 1946, 17.30 GDT, Dunfermline, Scotland, 56N05, 03W28.
   Gerard q. BC (Peter Agnew). RR: AA.

Zal Cleminson

   b. 4 May 1949, 02.40 GDT, Govan Road, Glasgow, Scotland, 55N52, 04W21.
   Gerard q. BC (Alistair Cleminson). RR: AA.

John Locke

   b. 10 August 1943, 18.10 DGDT, Great Western Road, Glasgow, Scotland, 55N53, 04W19.
   Gerard q. BC. RR: AA.

Dan McCafferty

   b. 10 June 1946, 13.45 GDT, The Pleasance, Edinburgh, Scotland, 55N57, 03W10.
   Gerard q. BC (Daniel McCafferty). RR: AA.

Liam Neeson – see Natasha Richardson

Andrew Neil

   b. 21 May 1949, 09.45 GDT, Paisley, Scotland, 55N51, 04W26.
   Gerard q. BC (Andrew Fergusson Neil). RR: AA.

High profile, feisty and flamboyant former editor of *The Sunday Times*, Andrew Neil is considered to be both pugnacious and genial. Neil held the post from 1983 (after a long stint with *The Economist* from age 24) until his fall from grace in 1994 following a clash with Rupert Murdoch. When he joined he was Britain's youngest editor of a national newspaper (MC in Aries), and with no previous experience he realised that he would need to be totally ruthless, instinctive and prepared to gamble in order to survive. He also had no patience or skill for massaging bruised egos and playing the charm game. His frank and indiscreet autobiography, *Full Disclosure*, detailing his eleven years with *The Sunday Times*, was released on 25 October 1996, taking full opportunity of the chance to seek revenge in

---

* Stephen Stills b. 3 January 1945, 00.15 CWT (+5), Dallas, Texas, 32N47, 96W48. From him to Linda Clark. RR: A.
** David Crosby b. 14 August 1941, 21.02 PST (+8), Hollywood, California, 34N06, 118W20. From him to Linda Clark. Birth verified by FCC. RR: A.

print. Neil was made Executive Chairman of Sky Television in 1988, which was launched on 5 February 1989, but he left the enterprise in January 1990. That month he was awarded £1000 libel damages against *The Sunday Telegraph* – the paper had attacked his reputation when a former girlfriend (whom he had met in March 1988) turned out to be a call girl (an Aries MC suggests sexual escapades could be linked to one's reputation). Neil is also a political commentator and TV presenter and fronts BBC2's *The Daily Politics* and BBC1's *This Week*.

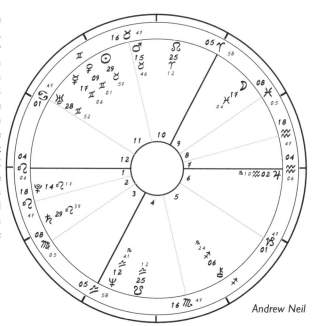

Andrew Neil

Q

"It is by opposition and confrontation that he is defined. His job is to provoke, to be out there irritating people and demanding responses." (An unnamed journalist quoted in *Reflections on Success* by Martyn Lewis, Lennard, 1997)

"I learned more than anything else – and it took me a while to do so – that the team is all important, a really strong team which is not afraid to disagree with you, full of people who want your job and one day will get it." (Andrew Neil, as quoted in *Reflections on Success* by Martyn Lewis, Lennard, 1997)

Anthony Newley

○ b. 24 September 1931, 10.00 GDT, Hackney, London, England, 51N33, 0W03.
● Marc Penfield, 'personal' (same from Lescaut). RR: C.

Versatile singer, director, lyricist and actor, Anthony George Newley was one of Britain's best known all-round entertainers. On stage and film he was often cast in comic roles and as lovable rogues. He made his stage debut in April 1946 and was the Artful Dodger in the 1948 film *Oliver Twist*. He became a pop idol in the 60s but is perhaps now best remembered for being the husband of Joan Collins (qv) from 27 May 1963 to August 1970. In November 1995 Newley appeared onstage in the title role in *Scrooge The Musical*, before opening in the West End in October 1996. He had been promised a leading part in *EastEnders* but died of cancer on 14 April 1999.

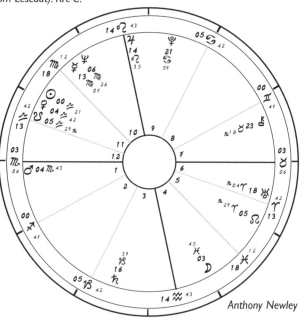

Anthony Newley

David Newton

✪ b. 2 February 1958, 14.50 GMT, Newton Mearns, Scotland, 55N46, 04W19.
Gerard q. BC (David Ritchie Newton). RR: AA.

Jazz pianist, accompanist and composer from 1978 (natal Uranus opposes Sun-Venus in Aquarius).

Olivia Newton-John

b. 26 September 1948, 06.00 GDT, Cambridge, England, 52N13, 0E08.
Debbi Kempton-Smith q. her. RR: A.

A very popular light entertainer in the 70s and early 80s. Newton-John released her first single in May 1966 and in September that year was offered to star in the pantomime *Cinderella* with Cliff Richard (qv). She declined and had to wait five years before her professional partnership with Cliff Richard finally put her in the spotlight (note their fascinating synastry). Between 1972 and 1975 she hit the US charts, had #1 records and won a Grammy for Best Country Vocal Performance, Female. Her career peak came with the lead in the film *Grease* in June 1978 (she was offered the role in May 1977). The music releases from the film (recorded mostly with John Travolta) were big sellers in 1978 across the world (their two #1s

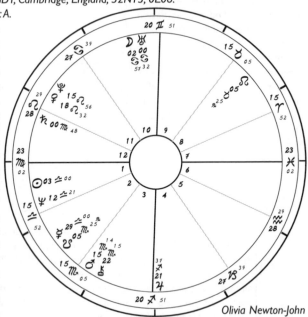

Olivia Newton-John

sold 3.5 million copies in the UK alone). From then on Newton-John's film career never matched her musical popularity, a fact underscored with the US #1 smash, *Physical* – a keep-fit anthem at the summit for ten weeks from November 1981. She also battled others' perceptions of her as sweet, prim and virginal (note she shares her Sun-Ascendant combination with Julie Andrews). In July 1992, days after losing her father from liver cancer, she learned that she too was battling cancer. She married Matt Lattanzi in 1984 but by April 1995 the couple had split and later divorced in secret.

> Q "Most of us are a certain type who don't know how to express ourselves. We try to be everything to everybody, we give, we don't take care of ourselves emotionally... I don't think I had a happy childhood. My parents' divorce [at 10] made me feel insecure. I tried to blank out what was going on, and I was always the happy child trying to keep everyone else happy." (Olivia Newton-John, *Daily Mail*, 25/1/95)

Paul Nicholas

b. 3 December 1944, 06.00 GDT, Peterborough, England, 52N35, 0W15.
Russell Grant q. him on Russell Grant's All-Star Show. RR: A.

Tough and athletic actor with a little-boy-lost image. Nicholas (born Paul Oscar Beuselinck) is best known for his comedy role as the cheeky chancer Vince in the hit TV show *Just Good Friends* (three series from September 1983) – note the MC ruler conjunct Mars in Sagittarius. Nicholas has long been a prominent figure in musical theatre and co-produced the highly successful revival of *Grease*. Nicholas quit school and went on tour with Screaming Lord Sutch and the Savages as their pianist. He married in 1965 but his career came first. When success arrived with the stage show *Hair* in September 1968 the marriage went into decline. Nicholas fell in love with performer Linzi Jennings and split from his wife in 1970. On 23 June 1972 it was announced that he would star on stage in *Jesus Christ, Superstar*. The role made him a star. In mid-1975 his new partnership began to suffer (TR Neptune conjunct Sun). In 1976 he had two Top Ten hits but in February that year he was devastated when his ex-wife (and mother of their two children) was killed in a car accident (TR Uranus near his Ascendant). The trauma brought him and his second wife back together. The couple now have two children. In 1995 he toured in the stage musical *Singin' in the Rain* and in Autumn 1999 he published his autobiography *Behind the Smile*. In February 2003 he opened in the stage production of *Fiddler on the Roof*.

Sue Nicholls

(Confidential data)

The elegant Sue Nicholls, a regular in *Coronation Street*, is fondly remembered for her previous roles in *Crossroads* (1964-8), *Rentaghost* and *The Fall and Rise of Reginald Perrin* (and the September 1996 follow-up). She won her first rave reviews in July 1964. As the scatty social-climber Audrey she made her first appearance in the soap *Coronation Street* on 14 April 1979. In February 1999 the actor who played her long-time screen husband died (as TR Saturn conjunct her Descendant). The actress, with Libra strong in her chart, is adored by fans and colleagues alike. On 6 July 1993 she married her boyfriend of ten years, actor Mark Eden (they had originally met on 31 July 1983). On 10 May 2003 (TR Jupiter near MC) she won two British Soap Awards (including Best Actress) for acting in a series of harrowing storylines in *Coronation Street*.

Derek Nimmo

♣ *b. 19 September 1933, 07.00 GDT, Liverpool, England, 53N25, 02W55.*

From BBC North's LifeLines, 24 February 1982, original source not known. RR: C.

British actor of theatre and TV known for his (Virgoan) dithery roles (especially the flustered, stammering monk in *Oh Brother!* – a celibate twit he played from 13 September 1968). Nimmo was already a familiar face from January 1967 when he starred in *All Gas and Gaiters*, another comedy at the Church's expense, and that year began on the London stage with *Charley Girl* for six years. Despite an exhausting TV and stage schedule, he found time to be a contestant on the radio show *Just a Minute* with Kenneth Williams (qv). Virgo is the true eccentric and Nimmo was very Virgoan (Sun, Moon and possibly the Ascendant placed here). He was married for 43 years. In December 1998 he suffered a fall and developed a blood clot on the brain. D. 24 February 1999.

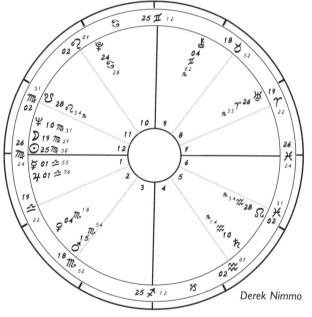

Derek Nimmo

Q "A certain special vein of British humour has died with him; gently quizzical, idiosyncratic but kindly, and utterly middle-class... His comedy was all about [the Church's] rules breaking down, and the tension and anxiety caused to young and inexperienced men, in his case clerics, as they struggled to keep the rules in the face of terrible adversity." (Jane Kelly, *Daily Mail*, 25/2/99)

Rab Noakes

b. 13 May 1947, 00.55 DGDT, Craigmount Nursing Home, St. Andrews, Scotland, 56N20, 02W48. Gerard q. BC (Robert Ogilvie Noakes). RR: AA.

Noakes was a member of the short-lived pop band Stealers Wheel with Gerry Rafferty (qv) and Joe Egan (qv).

Peter Noone

✪ b. 5 November 1947, 21.00 GMT, Manchester, England, 53N30, 02W15.
Dana Haynes q. him. RR: A.

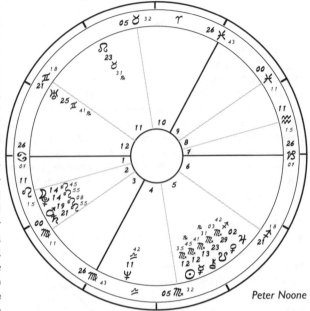

Peter Noone

A former child star who appeared in *Coronation Street*, Noone joined a Manchester beat group, The Heartbeats, in 1963. They became Herman and the Hermits and signed a record deal in August 1964. Noone was made lead singer and soon became a teen pop idol during their most successful year, 1965 (note Pluto conjunct Moon and squares Mercury for popularity and influence). The band had their first US #1 hit in May 1965 and sold 52 million records. Noone married on his twenty-first birthday. After splitting with the group he began a solo career in April 1971. In 1982 he was seen on Broadway in *The Pirates of Penzance*, which transferred to London the following year. Noone has acted in various TV shows, including *Married with Children*, *Quantum Leap* and *Laverne and Shirley*. He was the host of VH1's *My Generation* for four years.

Steve Norman

b. 25 March 1960, 15.00 GMT, London, England, 51N30, 0W10.
Marjorie Orr q. him. RR: A.

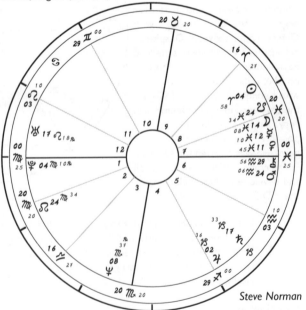

Steve Norman

Norman was with New Romantic band Spandau Ballet (see Martin Kemp, qv) from its conception in 1976. He played rhythm guitar, sax and percussion with the group. After signing a record contract in April 1980, Spandau Ballet enjoyed a number of hits over the next several years, including the UK chart-topper *True* (April 1983) and the smash *Gold* (August 1983). The band were the best of friends until Norman and two other members of the band (Tony Hadley and John Keeble) went to court in late January 1999 suing songwriter Gary Kemp for publishing royalties going back to 1988. They lost the case on 30 April 1999 and were left with a huge legal bill. In January 2003 Norman, Hadley and Keeble were now being sued by Gary and brother Martin Kemp (qv) for using the name Spandau Ballet during a recent UK tour. The case was scheduled for mid-June 2003.

Gary Numan

○ b. 8 March 1958, 22.30 GMT, Hammersmith, London, 51N30, 0W13.
From his autobiography, *Praying To The Aliens*, p. 1. RR: B.

Leather-clad eccentric synthesising superstar who hit #1 in June 1979 with *Are Friends Electric?* under the name Tubeway Army (their first hit single was released in February 1978). In September that year he had another chart-topper, *Cars*. Two of his albums entered the UK charts at #1, making him one of the biggest selling UK acts of the time. With Neptune Rising, Numan's image was always strong and often he was perceived as surly and arrogant (Leo MC). In September 1981 he attempted to fly around the world in his light aircraft and was arrested in India on suspicion of spying! The charge was later dropped and he returned in December. By 1984 the tide had turned and he was shunned by record-buyers, sneered at for his

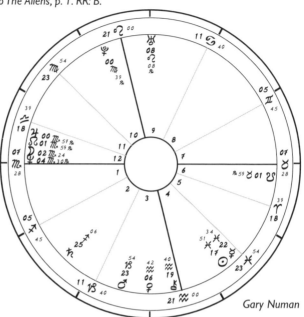

Gary Numan

avowed Thatcherism, hair transplants and boyish enthusiasm for planes and fast cars. After attracting an unusual amount of abuse (Scorpio Ascendant) he started his own label. In February 1996 his anthem *Cars* was used for a lager commercial and suddenly he was back in vogue. On 1 October 2001 he presented a show on cars for Granada *Men and Motors*.

Daniel O'Donnell

○ b. 12 December 1961, 19.30 GMT, Dungloe, Ireland, 54N57, 8W22.
Mary McFadden q. O'Donnell's mother. RR: A.

O'Donnell is the clean-cut crooner (Ireland's Ambassador of Song) with a huge fanbase of devoted (mostly middle-aged female) admirers (note the strong 5th House of following and Jupiter conjunct Descendant – ardent fans want him single, too!). He is famous for his accessibility, rapport with fans and the personal time he gives them (note the four planets in Sagittarius). His nationwide tours sell out within hours and his albums go platinum. O'Donnell joined his sister's band Margo at age 19, after dropping out of teacher training. His first major release came with *Two Sides of Daniel O'Donnell* (1985) and subsequent albums have entered the UK Country Charts at #1. In 1991 he gave a lauded concert at Carnegie Hall.

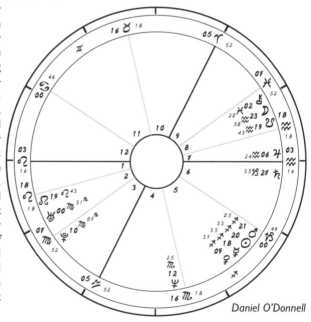

Daniel O'Donnell

Sean O'Farrell

○ b. 9 September 1966, 13.20 GDT, Dublin, Ireland, 53N20, 06W15.
Mary McFadden q. O'Farrell's mother. RR: A.

Singer.

Mike Oldfield – see Richard Branson

Laurence Olivier
b. 22 May 1907, 05.00 GMT, Dorking, England, 51N14, 0W20.
From his baby book, reproduced in his autobiography *Confessions of an Actor* (Weidenfeld & Nicolson, 1982), following p. 50. RR: AA.

Laurence Olivier

Peerless actor, producer and bold director of international film and stage productions. Olivier, considered by many to be the greatest Shakespearean interpreter of the century (MC ruler Saturn in EQHS 10th for respect and standing), was the son of an Anglican clergyman and his wife, who died when Olivier was 12. He joined the Central School in July 1924 and then the Birmingham Repertory from April 1926 but left in mid-June 1928 (TR Saturn conjunct Descendant) when only offered a small part. After a number of terrible stage roles (as TR Neptune squared Sun-Mercury) he made his Broadway debut on 11 September 1929 (TR Jupiter conjunct Ascendant). The show flopped but he was reconciled with his partner Jill Esmond, who was working in New York. In September Olivier was part of an unexpected stage success, *Coward's Private Lives*, and the show moved to Broadway in January 1931. The couple signed a Hollywood contract in Spring 1931 but made only a few films before he returned to the stage. His first major theatre success was in April 1933 in *The Rats of Norway* and in October 1933 another successful show began on Broadway (note TR Saturn on the MC). Theatre box office success in *Romeo and Juliet* followed from October 1935 and from January to November 1937 he played *Hamlet* (as TR Saturn moved into EQHS 10th and completed its return). Olivier's star was on the rise and over the next decade he became the most admired actor of his generation. He was also appearing on screen in acclaimed films from the mid-30s. He adapted the critical and commercial success *Henry V* (Spring 1946, TR Uranus conjunct Ascendant), which became the first such work of the talking era to make a large profit. In June 1947 he was knighted. In September 1948 *Hamlet* was released in the USA. In January 1950 (TR Jupiter conjunct MC) he launched Laurence Olivier Productions and in October 1963 he was the head of the National Theatre Company at its inaugural production at the Old Vic. His horoscope suggests a genuine craftsman who had unparalleled influence (Moon in Virgo square Pluto on the Ascendant) and great charisma (EQHS 10th rulers Jupiter and Neptune are conjunct opposite MC ruler Uranus in – a opposition also evident considering his history of unstable relationships). Olivier met Vivien Leigh on 17 June 1935 and married her on 31 August 1940. The union lasted until 2 December 1960. He had two other marriages, from 25 July 1930 to 29 January 1940 and from March 1961. His Uranus-Mars conjunction offers a clue to his bisexual leanings. Olivier preferred the stage to film work (note the dominant Neptune-Jupiter opposition, which suggests an ability to 'project' to a live audience). But in 1964 (as

TR Neptune moved into the EQHS 6th) he was overcome with a stage fright that lasted for five years. Oliver's advice to young thespians was, "Imitate the great actors – be a thief, be a magpie," which is descriptive of his Gemini Ascendant. D. 11 July 1989, Steyning, West Sussex, England.

Yoko Ono – see The Beatles

Jason Orange
☀ b. 10 July 1970, 07.30 MET, Manchester, England, 53N30, 02W15.
   From a TV programme on Italia Uno, original source not known. RR: C.
Dancer and one of the members of five-year pop sensation Take That, British counterparts to New Kids On The Block. Hand-picked by manager Nigel Martin-Smith, the group released their first single in July 1991 and soon acquired a teenage following not seen in Britain since The Beatles (qv). The members (Gary Barlow – 20/1/71, Frodsham, Cheshire; Robbie Williams – 13/2/74, Stoke-on-Trent; Howard Donald – 27/4/70, Droylsden, Manchester; Mark Owen – 27/1/74, Oldham; and Orange) had an unprecedented eight UK instant chart-toppers (and 14 Top 20 hits). Between June 1992 and March 1996 they sold nine million albums and ten million singles. The announcement of the departure of Robbie Williams on 17 July 1995 sounded the death knell for Take That (the band would have to wait until the autumn to hit in America), who announced their own split on 13 February 1996. Orange was the only member not to provide lead vocals for a hit song. Barlow, Williams and Owen followed solo music careers, while Orange worked as a stage (from March 1999) and TV actor.

THE OSBOURNES
✪ *The Osbournes* debuted on TV on 5 March 2002 (in New York at 22.30) and soon became a cultural phenomenon – reality TV in an unreal, celebrity setting. Mum **Sharon**, who rules the house with a rod of iron, was born on 9 October 1952. She battled colon cancer in mid-2002 and viewers were granted an insight into her predicament as she underwent chemotherapy in late July. Eccentric rocker dad of Black Sabbbath fame **Ozzy Osbourne** was born on the morning of 3 December 1948 in Birmingham, England (52N30, 01W50). His daughter, pop wannabe and professional troublemaker, **Kelly Osbourne** (b. 27 October 1984, 20.00 GDT, London, England, 51N30, 0W10) recorded a cover version of

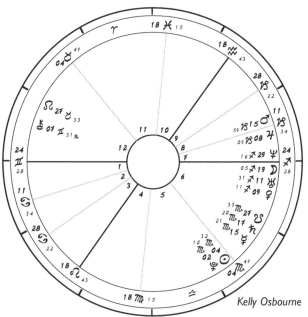

Kelly Osbourne

Madonna's *Papa Don't Preach*. The show began when TR Pluto hit Kelly's Moon, ruler of her 2nd House. Completing the dysfunctional domestic set-up is youngest member, son and part-time scout for Epic Records, **Jack Osbourne** (b. 8 November 1985, 21.20 GMT, London, England, 51N30, 0W10.) Eldest daughter **Aimee Osbourne** (b. 2 September 1983, 15.30 GDT, London, England, 51N30, 0W10) was the only member of the family who refused to take part in the reality show. All data are from the biography *Officially Osbourne* by Todd Gold (2002). RR: B.

Mark O'Toole

⊘ b. 6 January 1964, 00.20 GMT, Liverpool, England, 53N25, 02W55.
Bettina Lee q. him. (N.B. The last edition had 16 January in error.) RR: A.

Band member with Frankie Goes To Hollywood, which formed in 1980. O'Toole was with the band as they became the biggest act in the UK during 1984 with three #1s from January of that year. Acrimonious lawsuits followed in 1987 and O'Toole spent a while in America before returning to Liverpool in early 1992.

Peter O'Toole

⊘ b. 2 August 1932, 00.20 GDT, Leeds, England, 53N50, 01W35.
B. Granite q. him to actor David Mauro, given as "shortly after midnight" (Wicklow, 52N59, 06W03 and Galway, Connemara, 53N16, 09W03, have also been given as his birthplace; Terence Stamp's biography of him states that O'Toole bemoans the fact that he was not born in Ireland; FCC confirms England from a private source and the year from Birth Registry). RR: A.

A copy boy for the *Yorkshire Evening Post* at 14, O'Toole made his amateur stage debut three years later. After training at RADA he joined the Bristol Old Vic company in September 1955 and stayed until 1959, by which time his acting had garnered much notice. He was in films from 1960, graduating to major roles in 1962 with the epic *Lawrence of Arabia* being his star-making vehicle. During the 60s and 70s he was a leading box office attraction before a drinking problem (and sporadic depression) prompted a career decline. A charismatic film legend and egocentric personality, O'Toole refers to himself as having "enlightened self-interest" (Leo). In September 1980 he returned to the London stage after a 17 year absence. He moved into villainous roles in the 80s and was given an honorary Oscar on 23 March 2003 (TR Uranus conjunct EQHS 10th).

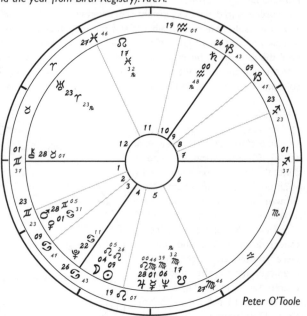

Peter O'Toole

Mark Owen – see Take That

Jimmy Page

b. 9 January 1944, 04.00 GDT, Heston, England, 51N29, 0W23.

From him to Jenni Harte (time rectified to 04.17 by an astrologer friend of Page). RR: A.

A renowned and distinctive guitarist, Page was the driving force behind Led Zeppelin, a band which enjoyed phenomenal record sales at its peak in the 70s. He is known to possess a sharp mind, icy temperament, and a desire for absolute privacy (Scorpio Ascendant). He made his debut with The Yardbirds in June 1966 and remained with the band until its split on 7 July 1968. Led Zeppelin made its live debut on 25 October 1968 and an eponymous album was released in early 1969. Page reunited with Robert Plant (qv) for the *Unledded* project and collaborated with Puff Daddy on the August 1998 hit *Come With Me*.

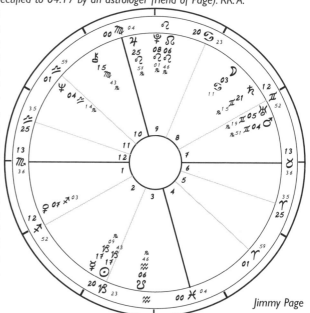

Jimmy Page

Nicola Pagett

b. 15 June 1945, 17.55 EEDT (-3), Cairo, Egypt, 30N03, 31E15.

FCC q. her, from her parents. RR: A.

Convent-educated actress with numerous roles on stage and TV. Pagett became famous overnight for her role in *Upstairs, Downstairs* and went on to appear in *A Woman of Substance* (January 1985) and *A Bit of a Do* in 1989. In 1995 (as TR Pluto crossed her Ascendant) she was in a clinic after having been arrested for an incident following a road accident. On 28 May 1996, after a stint in a psychiatric ward for three weeks in April, she revealed her private life had long been ravaged by manic depression and paranoia. One result was that Pagett had begun a obsessive letter writing campaign to an influential figure in British politics. Her husband (since 1977) wrote of her time in hospital and together they

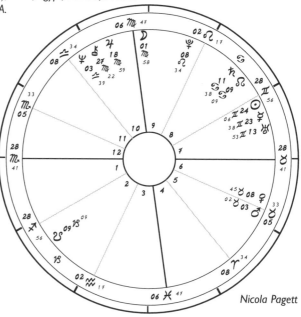

Nicola Pagett

published *Diamonds Behind My Eyes* (September 1997). With the book, the couple hoped to fight the prejudice and assumptions that accompany mental illness.

Q | "Since [12] I haven't really known what it is like to have an unmemorable, ordinary day. I would wake up either very joyful or very fearful of life." (Nicola Pagett, *Daily Mail*, 16/8/97)

Michael Palin – see Monty Python

Bill Paterson
> b. 3 June 1945, 06.00 DGDT, Glasgow, Scotland, 55N52, 04W13.
> Gerard q. BC (William Tulloch Paterson). RR: AA.

Actor of film, TV and theatre from the early 70s. Paterson trained at the Royal Scottish Academy of Music and Drama (1966-9) straight after three years as an apprentice quantity surveyor. He has had major roles in many TV productions, including *Auf Wiedersehen, Pet* (February to May 1986), *The Singing Detective* (November to December 1986) and *Licking Hitler* (1978). Films include *The Killing Fields*, *A Private Function*, *Chaplin* and *Truly Madly Deeply*.

Owen Paul
> b. 1 May 1962, 05.25 GDT, Robroyston Hospital, Glasgow, Scotland, 55N54, 04W11.
> Gerard q. BC (Owen McGee). RR: AA.

Principled and earthy brother of Simple Minds' drummer Brian McGee (qv), Owen Paul had his big break on BBC2's *The Oxford Roadshow* and signed to Epic. His first couple of releases failed but he reached #3 with his third single, the catchy pop tune *My Favourite Waste of Time* (released in May 1986). He then went on strike, refusing to play the music promotional game. A one-hit wonder, Paul lectured in Florida before returning to England with his wife and three children in 1991.

Cynthia Payne
> b. 24 December 1932, 21.00 GMT, Bognor Regis, England, 50N47, 0W41.
> FCC q. her. RR: A.

Cheeky madam turned celebrity. Payne held parties for middle-aged and wealthy men (from vicars to barristers), who bought luncheon vouchers for films, live shows, food, drink and sex. She made the headlines across the country after the police raided her establishment at 16.10 on 6 December 1978, Streatham, London (when TR Uranus moved towards her IC). She was made an example of at her court case in April 1980 and sent to prison for 18 months (from 21 April), despite the fact that so many of her clients were directly connected to the professions that condemned her. An appeal was heard on 15 May and the sentence was reduced to six months (she was released on 20 August). Payne's antics inspired two films, *Personal*

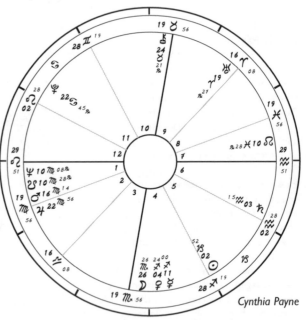

Cynthia Payne

Services starring Julie Walters (qv) and *Wish You Were Here*. The latter depicted her early years following her mother's death when Cynthia was ten years old. Her home was raided again in 1986 after an 'end of filming' party for *Personal Services*. Taken to court on ten charges of controlling prostitutes, she won a resounding victory on 11 February 1987. In 1992 she played to packed houses in a one-woman show at the Edinburgh Fringe Festival. A video documentary, *Cynthia Payne's House of Cyn*, was released in 1996. That same year she was called for jury service and was elected foreman! In July 1998 she stood for parliament in the Kensington by-election as a candidate for the Payne and Pleasure Party. The loudly assertive Payne may not have brought the Government down but she certainly raised a few carefully positioned eyebrows! She once said that she should have been given an OBE for her personal services to the country. Sun in 5th and Leo Rising suggest a marked flair for personal publicity, fanfare and showmanship, and a woman with a Capricorn Sun and Scorpio Moon aims to keep the influential happy whilst running an efficient, discreet business as the best hostess in town! Payne's MC ruler Venus in 4th is sesquisquare Uranus (ruling 7th) pointing to the fact she was known for her private situation, and the disruption (sesquisquare) of it led to celebrity. The former Madam Cyn is a regular, entertaining TV guest and a sex law campaigner.

Q "It's amazing how I've kept [public interest] going for 15 years since 1980, because I'm only re-hashing the same thing over and over again… I've got a young cult following coming up now. My agent thought it would be all over in a couple of years, but I'm still going years later. A lot of it is my own personality and being very single-minded… I'm the only one who can talk about sex in England without people getting upset… In my 30s I was doing it, in my 40s I was organising it, and in my 60s, unfortunately, I'm only going to talk about it." (Cynthia Payne, *Telegraph Magazine*, 19/1/98)
"She was jealous from the start… There's only one thing in Cynthia's life and that's sex." (Her sister Melanie, as quoted in *An English Madam* by Cynthia Payne and Paul Bailey, Fontana, 1982.)

Dougie Payne – see Travis

John Peel

b. 30 August 1939, 07.30 GDT, Heswall, Cheshire, England, 53N20, 03W06.
Garry Heaton q. him, "around breakfast time." RR: C.

Influential BBC Radio One DJ (born John Ravenscroft) who gave many new bands a start by offering them airplay. Atfer completing military service Peel headed to Texas in 1960 and soon had his own radio show. He married a 15 year old on 29 September 1965 and divorced her on 28 March 1973. On his return to Britain he became a disc jockey at the pirate station Radio London before joining Radio One at its launch on 30 September 1967. In recent years he has hosted the Saturday morning show *Home Truths* on Radio Four, where he discusses the eccentricities of family life. In March 2003 there was a bidding war to secure rights to his autobiography, which were eventually sold for a reputed £1.5 million.

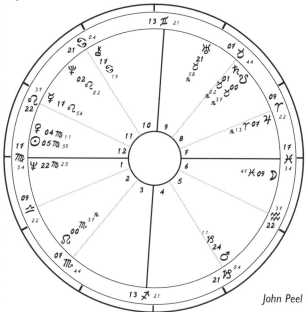

John Peel

Marti Pellow – see Wet Wet Wet

Lynne Perrie

☿ *b. 7 April 1931, 14.00 GMT, Rotherham, England, 53N26, 01W20.*
Russell Grant, in Russell Grant's All-Star Show, told her she had Leo Rising. Date and place from
Who's Who on Television. Leo was rising from approximately 11.17 to 14.10. Speculative. RR: C.

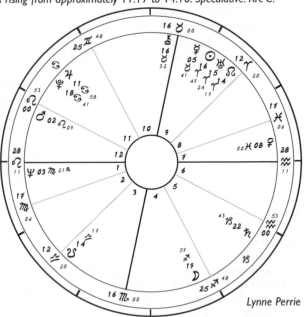

Lynne Perrie

Actress, best known for feisty roles, who played waspish 'Poison Ivy' Tilsley (later Brennan) in *Coronation Street* from 1971 to 1994. Perrie incurred the wrath of Granada bosses and was sacked, the official statement being that it was because of her decision to have lip implants without consulting the producers. Her roller-coaster life has seen great tragedy (including her son's battle with AIDS) as well as her facing up to her alcohol problem (the possible Neptune Rising) and string of adulterous love affairs. Pint-sized Perrie was once a successful cabaret singer (a Little Miss Dynamite) and has admitted to being addicted to an audience's applause, and being totally wrapped up in herself and her work. Since leaving the soap, Perrie has been fighting the enormous ghost of her character and clutching at various career opportunities, from cabaret and TV appearances (including an embarrassing spot belting out *I Will Survive* on *The Word*) to spoof exercise videos.

Q "There have been loads of times when I haven't known who I am. Am I Lynne Perrie or Ivy Tilsley? You do lose yourself... At one time I could always rely on Ivy if Lynne wasn't feeling quite right; Ivy could take over." (Lynne Perrie, as quoted in *The Ghost of Ivy Tilsley*, Channel 4 documentary, 5/10/96)

Jimmy Perry

◎ *b. 20 September 1923, 02.00 GMT, Barnes, England, 51N29, 0W15.*
Rev. Pamela Crane q. his autobiography A Stupid Boy (Century, 2002), p.9. RR: B.
Comedy scriptwriter best known for the TV series *Dad's Army*.

Patricia Phoenix

◎ *b. 26 November 1923, 08.00 GMT, Manchester, England, 53N30, 02W15.*
☿ *From Chryss Craswell, November 1978, original source not known. (N.B. Other sources state Port Humna, County Galway.) RR: C.*
Extravagant, much-loved TV star and flame-haired sex symbol of *Coronation Street* from its start in December 1960 until she left the show in January 1984. She was labelled the sexiest woman on TV by Prime Minister Jim Callaghan and became an iconic figure in Britain, the Queen of British Soap for 25 years (note Sun-Jupiter and Moon-Pluto). After her father was jailed for bigamy, Phoenix moved to London and began playing femme fatales in the theatre and wrote scripts for comedian Harry Worth. She married Tony Booth (father of British PM's wife Cherie) on her deathbed. When she died of lung cancer it caused tabloid hysteria and fans lined in the street to give her a send-off fit for royalty. D. 17 September 1986.

Jacqueline Pirie

✪ *b. 10 October 1974, 12.45 GDT, Stirling, Scotland, 56N07. 03W55.*
Gerard q. BC. RR: AA.

Actress best known for her roles in *Emmerdale* (29 December 1994, with TR Jupiter approaching Ascendant and TR Saturn conjunct Jupiter, to 24 December 1996) and *Coronation Street* (14 October 1998, TR Uranus opposite Moon and TR Pluto conjunct Ascendant, to 3 September 2001). Pirie made her debut at age eleven in the soap *Crossroads* and became a regular in the kids TV show *Palace Hill* (1988-91) before getting her major break in *Emmerdale*. She left the show after two years when she discovered she was pregnant with her daughter. She left another meal ticket when she gave up her bitchy role (note Pluto-Venus-Mars on the MC — viewers loved to hate her scheming character) on *Coronation*

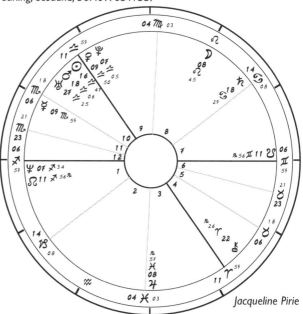

Jacqueline Pirie

Street when pregnant with her son. Pirie, who is also a talented painter, married Simon Chadwick in April 2001, and now has adopted his name for professional purposes. She has two children (April 1997 and October 2001) and the tabloids had a field day when it was discovered her first child's father was a convicted violent criminal many years her senior. Her love life has often featured in the press (Venus-Pluto on the Libran MC and Neptune Rising for tabloid fodder).

Robert Plant

b. 20 August 1948, 15.05 GDT, West Bromwich, England, 52N31, 01W56.
Ananda Bagley q. Plant's ex-girlfriend, Charlotte Martin. RR: A.

Dynamic vocalist Plant had dreamed of being a star by the age of 20 and readily accepted Jimmy Page's (qv) invitation to form Led Zeppelin in July 1968 (TR Uranus approaching MC). He married in November of that year. The number of bizarre and tragic accidents connected to Plant and the group led some to speculate that Page had made a costly pact with the devil: 5 August 1975 — Plant was involved in a car accident; 27 July 1977 — Plant's son (Karac Pendra Plant, b. 20 April 1972, Bromsgrove, England, 52N20, 02W03. FCC q. BC for date and place.) died of a virus; 25 September 1980, group member John Bonham choked to death at Page's home. The heavy metal band split in 1980. In 2001 Plant began

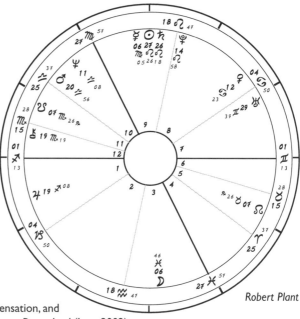

Robert Plant

touring with his new band, Strange Sensation, and released his first solo album in ten years, *Dreamland* (June 2002).

Su Pollard

b. 7 November 1949, 05.05 GMT, Nottingham, England, 52N58, 01W10.

Marjorie Orr q. her. RR: A.

As a singer on *Opportunity Knocks!* in 1974, Pollard came second to a performing dog. A zany, madcap (Ascendant ruler Venus opposite Uranus) and ubiquitous actress-singer, Pollard began with amateur theatrics at 11 and worked in public relations before a production of *The Desert Song* provided her with a big break at 24. Soon after she appeared in *Godspell*. Five years later she was a nationally recognised star as the dizzy Peggy in *Hi-De-Hi!* (January 1980, when TR Pluto crossed her Ascendant, to January 1988). The woman with 82 pairs of glasses had an unexpected pop hit in March 1986 with *Starting Together*, which went to #2 on the British charts. With Neptune Rising in Libra and Venus opposite Uranus, extrovert Pollard has had a string of difficult and ambiguous relationships.

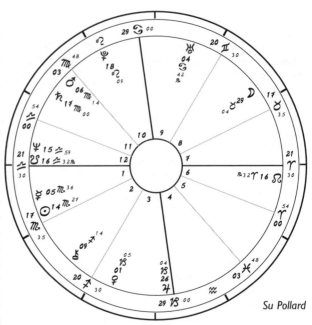

Su Pollard

Q "All the men I have loved have let me down. None of them has been able to cope with me – they always want to rein in my free spirit or take me over in some way. The truth is that none of them has really been my equal – I just fall in love and delude myself that they are. The trouble is, I get involved too quickly. I dive in, then I get half-drowned... I get taken advantage of. I don't play games, I make myself available... but in return they treat me appallingly." (Su Pollard, *Daily Mail*, 27/6/96)

Gail Porter

✪ b. 23 March 1971, 19.18 MET, Edinburgh, Scotland, 55N57, 03W12.

Gerard q. BC. RR: AA.

Pinup TV presenter who bared all for *GQ* (February 1999) and other men's magazines, becoming a teenage boy's fantasy. Porter began her career as a runner for a video production company before presenting children's TV. The shows *Fully Booked*, *Live and Kicking* and *The Movie Chart Show* followed.

John Power

✪ b. 14 September 1967, 11.15 GDT, Liverpool, 53N24, 02W59.

From *Power to astrologer D'Aste, as reported in the music magazine Melody Maker. RR: A.

Bass player for the British band La's, formed in 1986 in Liverpool. Power was replaced before the band achieved commercial success in 1990 and later joined the band Cast.

Fay Presto

✪ b. 17 May 1948, 23.50 GDT, Highgate Hill, London, 51N34, 0W09.

FCC q. her, from mother's recollection of just before midnight. RR: A.

An entertaining magician, Fay Presto (Letitia Winter) has been in the business of innovative illusions for over 20 years. She is credited for bringing much-needed glamour, humour and fun to the art of close-up magic (her Sun in the EQHS 5th of audience sesquiquadrates 3rd House ruler Neptune in the 10th). Royalty and many top celebrities are amongst her admirers and supporters, and she works tirelessly for children's charities. Other indicators of a gifted live performer include: Neptune square Venus (ruler of the EQHS 5th) on Descendant, and 3rd House co-ruler Jupiter conjunct Ascendant. Presto left school in 1963 and worked as a tailor, sales rep and then sold forklift trucks. At 32 she moved into show business and, after a sex-change operation, was the first female member of the Inner Magic Circle (ruffling the establishment's feathers along the way). A documentary, *Illusions of Grandeur*, was broadcast in 1994. She was Party Entertainer of the Year in 1998 as voted by *Tatler*. Fay, who has overcome much adversity and learned to be self-protective, says that she was brought up with unconditional love from both parents.

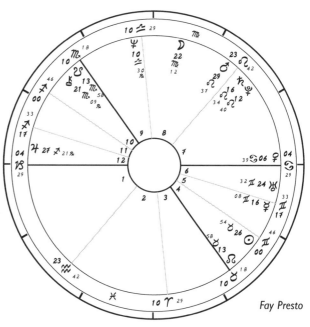

Fay Presto

Q "Believe me, I know all about reality and I won't have anything to do with it. Or as little as possible anyway! You learn to keep your lip zipped... and it explodes sooner or later. I had to completely restructure my life or die. I had been trying to live it by society's rules for too long, and it was killing me." (Fay Presto, as quoted in TV's *Illusions of Grandeur*, 1994)

Alan Price
✪ *b. 19 April 1942, 07.00 DGDT, Fairfield, County Durham, England, 54N47, 01W34.*
Nandon Bosma q. him, 1996. (N.B. L&L is for Durham, Fairfield not found.) RR: A.
Pianist with The Animals. Price formed the Alan Price Combo in 1960 to play R&B and rock 'n' roll before recruiting Eric Burdon (qv) to form The Animals.

James Prime – see Deacon Blue
Neil Primrose – see Travis

THE PROCLAIMERS
Twin acoustic performers who formed the band in 1983 and refused to compromise their strong Caledonian accents for the pop market. Their first album was released in 1986 and they made their TV debut on *The Tube* on 30 January 1987. They gained a strong following with a single release in November 1987 (*Letter from America*, produced by Gerry Rafferty, qv) and for their second album (a Top Ten album in October 1988). A tour was announced for Summer 2002.
Charles Reid
b. 5 March 1962, 20.05 GMT, Eastern General Hospital, Leith, Scotland, 55N58, 03W09).
Gerard q. BC (Charles Stobo Reid). RR: AA.
Craig Reid
b. 5 March 1962, 20.35 GMT, Eastern General Hospital, Leith, Scotland, 55N58, 03W09).
Gerard q. BC (Craig Morris Reid). RR: AA.

Jonathan Pryce

○ *b. 1 June 1947, 02.30 DGDT, Holywell, Wales, 53N17, 03W13.*
FCC q. him, February 2003. RR: A.

Acclaimed stage and film actor. Pryce won a RADA scholarship before joining the Liverpool Everyman Theatre. His role in *Comedians* was well-received in London and won him a Tony Award for his Broadway stint in 1976. In 1980 he won the prestigious SWET Best Actor Award for his performance as *Hamlet* at the Royal Court Theatre. Musicals *Miss Saigon* (Tony and Olivier Awards) and *Oliver!* (Best Actor nomination) followed, establishing Pryce as an actor of great stage presence often cast in Machiavellian roles (MC ruler Jupiter in Scorpio is elevated). In 1985 he won a Cannes Film Festival Best Actor award for his portrayal of writer Lytton Strachey in *Carrington*. Pryce has appeared in over 25 films, including *Evita* with

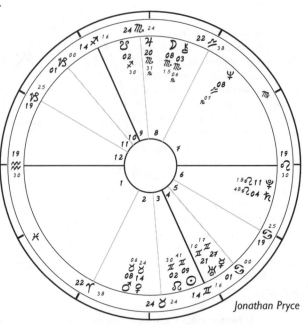

Jonathan Pryce

Madonna, in which he played Juan Peron*. The synastry between politician and actor is remarkable. Pryce's Moon conjunct's Peron's Saturn-Mercury (opposed by Pryce's Mars), and Pryce's Sun conjunct's Peron's Moon-Pluto. (Pryce's MC is conjunct Peron's Ascendant, too.)

Libby Purves

b. 2 February 1950, 09.00 GMT, London, England, 51N30, 0W10.
Marjorie Orr from her. RR: A.

A writer and TV regular. Purves is a contributor to newspapers including *The Times*.

David Puttnam

b. 25 February 1941, 13.00 GDT, London, England, 51N30, 0W10.
Bettina Lee q. him. RR: A.

British film producer (known for *Chariots of Fire* and *The Killing Fields*). Puttnam had a brief stint as chairman of Columbia Pictures from 1 September 1986 to 16 September 1987 (TR Neptune on Descendant).

Caroline Quentin

○ *b. 11 July 1960, 08.30 GDT, Reigate, England, 51N14, 0W13.*
Kim Farnell q. her on TV's The Best of British, 15/11/2000. RR: A.

Quentin's first ambition was to be a dancer and her first professional job was dancing in the chorus line of *Les Miserables*. Quentin joined the cast of *Casualty* in 1989 playing a social worker. With natal Uranus conjunct Ascendant opposite Moon in Aquarius, comedy was more her forte and she made the switch when working with playwright Arthur Smith, who wrote theatre parts for her alongside Paul Merton (to whom she was married for six years). Her first major TV comedy role came in 1992 when she appeared as a long-suffering girlfriend in the huge hit *Men Behaving Badly* opposite Martin Clunes and Neil Morrissey (see Elizabeth Carling). The series began on 18 February 1992. The 'battle of the sexes' comedy show (note Mars-MC and Moon-Descendant opposite Uranus) was a big

---

* Juan Peron b. 8 October 1895, 08.30 LT (12:46 UT), Lobos, Argentina, 35S11, 59W06. From Peron to his astrologer Boris Cristoff, 1972. RR: A.

ratings winner and lasted until 1998. Quentin has also appeared in *Jonathan Creek* (1997-2000), *Kiss Me Kate* (1998-2001), *Hot Money* (2001), *Blood Strangers* (2002) and *Blue Murder* (2003). She and Paul Merton announced their separation on 14 April 1997. Quentin remarried and gave birth to a second child, a son William, in April 2003. In the late 90s she discovered that her former agent had embezzled almost half a million pounds from her (2nd and 11th House ruler Mercury in 12th square Neptune, ruler of 8th).

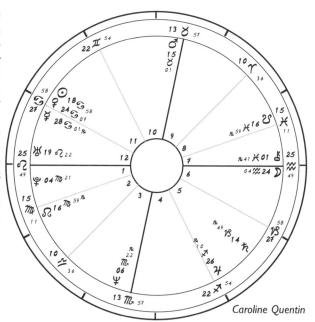

Caroline Quentin

Gerry Rafferty

b. 16 April 1947, 10.55 DGDT, Paisley, Scotland, 55N51, 04W25.
Gerard q. BC (Gerald Rafferty). RR: AA.

Songwriter and pop singer. Rafferty launched his career with Billy Connolly (qv) in the folk group The Humblebums, actively recording from 1969-70. He had a solo album in 1971 before forming Steelers Wheel with Rab Noakes (qv). The band recorded for four years and spent the next three in litigation over managerial disputes. A solo album, *City to City*, topped US charts in July 1978, breaking the Bee Gees' (qv) stranglehold with the soundtrack to *Saturday Night Fever*. The previous month (when TR Jupiter crossed the Ascendant), Rafferty's single *Baker Street* had hit #2 in the US behind a hit by Andy Gibb (qv).

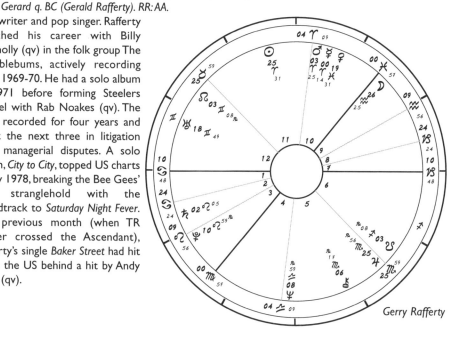

Gerry Rafferty

Charlotte Rampling

○ b. 5 February 1946, 07.45 GMT, London, England, 51N30, 0W10.
Lois Rodden q. a colleague, from Rampling. (N.B. Catherine Aubier's book Dictionaire Pratique d'Astrologie, 1986, gives 07.20, original source not known) RR: A.

Charismatic and coolly attractive actress with over 40 films to her credit, often drawn to bold and meaningful roles. Her acting career began in *The Avengers* in 1961. She is best remembered for her performance as a concentration camp survivor in *The Night Porter* (1974) with Dirk Bogarde (qv), as well as for the films *Georgy Girl* (1966), *The Damned* (1969) and *Stardust Memories* (1980). In 1996 she separated from her husband of 20 years, musician Jean-Michel Jarre. They have a son, David, who is a magician. In 2001 she was back in the limelight with the film *Signs and Wonders*. The last few years have seen her make numerous films, including *The Statement* and *Trilogy*.

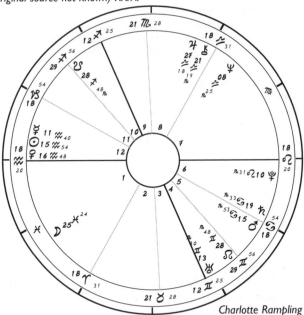

Charlotte Rampling

Esther Rantzen

✎ b. 22 June 1940, 12.00 Noon GDT, Berkhamstead, England, 51N46, 0W35.
John Naylor in Annabel, January 1975, original source not known. RR: C.

Petite television chat-show host (of *Esther*) and presenter of the consumer show *That's Life* (from 1973 to 1994, with 22 million viewers at its peak in the late 70s). Rantzen was, for a long time, a powerful woman within BBC ranks and influential with her large audience (Pluto conjunct Mercury, opposing Moon – "She taught the world how to complain to the gas board"!). Even at the age of six she was encouraged by her father to attend University, and Rantzen later read English at Somerville College, Oxford. Although her first ambition was to be a teacher, she joined the BBC as a secretary in 1963. Ending up in sound effects she resigned and reapplied as a TV researcher. TV fame with *That's Life* followed. A chronic list-maker, her diary is packed with meetings to help and organise publicity for fund-raising events, although she has admitted

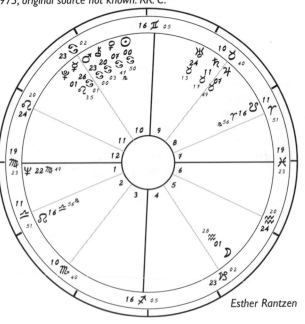

Esther Rantzen

to always putting her family first. Opinions of Rantzen range from condescending bully to caring and honest campaigner, and she was criticised for her ethics and partiality whilst holding televised debates (*The Rantzen Report*) in 1996. She made 600 episodes of her eponymous BBC2 chat show until May 2002. Labelled formidable and patronising, she did however patronise Childline, a worthwhile telephone service provided for abused children. As well as Childline (which celebrated its 15th anniversary in March 2001), Rantzen has given much time to hands-on charities (including Chronic Fatigue Syndrome – aka M.E. – which her daughter suffers from), and her television interests include shows *Drugwatch* and *Hearts of Gold* (note the strong Cancer influence and a strongly aspected Pluto). After her husband's death (TV producer and writer Desmond Wilcox died on 6 September 2000) and the publication of her autobiography (March 2001), Rantzen's stepdaughter attacked her savagely in print. Her final show for the BBC aired in May 2002 (as TR Saturn and Pluto conjunct her possible MC/IC axis).

Q "Whatever you feel about her personal style, it has been immensely successful... The fact is, it is she who, more than anyone else, forced everybody to admit that child sexual abuse is a common and serious problem... it was an incredibly important development in the history of psychology in this country. She managed to do what Freud couldn't." (Clinical psychologist Oliver James, as quoted in *Night & Day*, 8/9/96)
"The whole premise of Esther is bullying television. It's a massive and bleakly amusing irony that Esther is famous for having set up Childline, which is about bullies, while she is the biggest bully." (AA Gill, as quoted in *Night & Day*, 8/9/96)
"Esther has 'I can cope' stamped through her like Brighton rock... She's both steely and schmaltzy... She's a rare amalgam of glittering confidence and insecurity, and with Desmond she felt empowered in every way." (Lynda Lee-Potter, *Daily Mail*, 27/4/02)

Eddi Reader

b. 29 August 1959, 23.05 GDT, Glasgow, Scotland, 55N53, 04W13.
Gerard q. BC (Sadenia Reader). RR: AA.
Jazz and country-inspired Reader was a former background vocalist with the likes of Annie Lennox (qv) and Alison Moyet (qv) after moving to London in 1983. A collaboration with guitarist Mark Nevin led to the formation of Fairground Attraction, a pop band who would have their greatest success in May 1988 (Saturn Return and TR Uranus conjunct Saturn, both rulers of MC) with the #1 hit *Perfect*. Two Brit Awards – best single and album – followed in early 1989. Reader's career was put on hold during pregnancy, and when the band split, she pursued a solo singing career (Brit Award in 1995) and acting work (*Your Cheatin' Heart*, 1990).

Noel Redding

b. 25 December 1945, 06.30 GMT, Folkestone, England, 51N05, 01E11.
Time from him to Jenni Harte, without specifying am or pm (a pm time would give 5 Leo Rising). RR: DD.
Bassist, guitarist and songwriter. In September 1966, after travelling to London in the hope of auditioning for The Animals, he was recruited to perform with the Jimi Hendrix Experience. Redding died in May 2003.

Corin Redgrave

b. 16 July 1939, 08.00 GDT, London, England, 51N30, 0W10.
From his mother, Rachel Kempson's autobiography, A Family and Its Fortunes (Duckworth, 1986). RR: B.
Actor from the distinguished Redgrave acting dynasty, he stood as a candidate for the Workers' Revolutionary Party in the May 1979 General Election (Mars in Aquarius in 6th, stellium in 11th). His Ascendant is one degree away from that of his sister, actress-activist Vanessa Redgrave (qv).

Lynn Redgrave

b. 8 March 1943, 08.15 GDT, London, England, 51N30, 0W10.

Tashi Grady q. her. RR: A.

Redgrave achieved fame in *Georgy Girl* in 1966 (US release October 1966, and New York Film Critics Best Actress award). Living in the USA from 1974, she was given a brief-run series, quiz and talk shows but this intelligent actress was branded a trouble-maker and the offers became less frequent. She made an impressive Baby Jane Hudson in the 1991 remake of *Whatever Happened to Baby Jane?* with sister Vanessa Redgrave (qv). Her 1996 acclaimed one-woman Broadway show *Shakespeare For My Father* first began in Washington in 1991, with a 27-city tour two years later. She also starred in the Oscar-winning film *Shine* (released January 1996) and gave a Golden Globe award-winning performance in *Gods and Monsters.* Redgrave

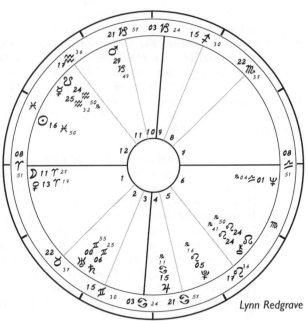

Lynn Redgrave

married her husband on 2 April 1967 but the couple split in November 1998 (TR Neptune conjunct Mars) when he revealed he had fathered a child with their son's wife. They were divorced in December 2000. In March 2003 Redgrave spoke of her successful six-month battle with breast cancer (discovered when TR Uranus hit 6th House ruler Mercury).

Vanessa Redgrave

b. 30 January 1937, 18.00 GMT, Blackheath, England, 51N28, 0E01.

From her autobiography, Vanessa Redgrave (Hutchinson, 1991), p. 1. (N.B. Correct L&L.) RR: B.

A legendary, instinctive actress, born rebel, naive idealist and political activist, Redgrave is perhaps the finest actress of her generation (part of her talent to project to an audience is shown by 5th ruler Jupiter conjunct Mercury in 5th, and Moon opposite Venus in Pisces, which gives her a "luminous transparency that makes audiences feel they can see right though a character's skin"). Despite her family's stage pedigree she was warned at drama school that she was too tall (over 5 foot 11 inches) to succeed (Uranus-MC doesn't fit the mould, so has to break it). Redgrave had a stubbornness to prove detractors wrong, which she did from July 1961 (TR Uranus conjunct Ascendant) with a

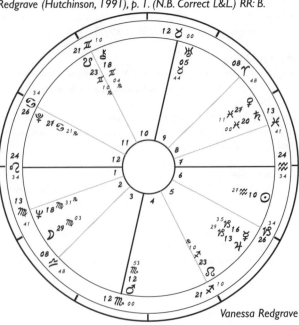

Vanessa Redgrave

sensational performance with the RSC as Rosalind in *As You Like It* at Stratford. Redgrave had made her stage debut in July 1957 (as TR Jupiter approached her Moon) and her first film came a year later. Political interests, however, would equally dominate her life. Astrologically it is hard to separate her political instincts from her acting work. With Sun in Aquarius square Uranus on the MC and T-Square Mars on the IC, she has become a high-profile figure (both revered and despised and greatly misunderstood) for her incendiary remarks against right-wing groups, even turning her acceptance speech at the Academy Awards on 29 March 1978 (when TR Saturn crossed her Ascendant) into a political statement (Uranus calls out for freedom of speech but is often blacklisted as a result). On 10 October 1974 she ran for Parliament representing the Workers Revolutionary Party. And she was back in the news in early December 2002 (TR Uranus conjunct Descendant, TR Neptune approaching Sun) when she bailed out a leading Chechen separatist. One of her most remarkable performances in recent years has been in the TV film *Second Serve* in which she portrayed Richard Raskind, the former male athlete who emerged as tennis player, coach and doctor, Renée Richards (b. 19 August 1934, "morning" from autobiography, New York City). Redgrave's Ascendant is conjunct Richards's Sun in Leo. Redgrave has also played Isadora Duncan and Mary Queen of Scots (synastry with the latter is remarkable: Redgrave's Jupiter-Mercury conjuncts Mary's MC-Mercury, and her MC-Uranus conjuncts Mary's Ascendant). The actress took *Antony and Cleopatra* to the New York stage in March 1997, after a successful run in London. She has garnered 6 Oscar nominations, 2 Cannes Film Awards, 2 Emmy wins and 12 Golden Globe nominations (she won 2). In late April 1962 (TR Saturn conjunct Sun, TR Neptune conjunct IC) she married director Tony Richardson, took time off from the stage when she fell pregnant, and the couple began their own acting dynasty. Redgrave has a son by actor Franco Nero*.

> "Redgrave's antagonistic defense of belief in her life and work directly reflects that of her foes, both political and aesthetic. Her willingness to appear ugly or naked or unappealing onscreen is a conscious political statement. She's drawn to characters who are outsiders, emotionally and socially. The more ostracized or persecuted her characters are, the freer Redgrave becomes – she seems in touch with another world." (Michael McWilliams, *TV Sirens*, Perigee, 1987)
>
> Q "There's nothing theatrical about Vanessa Redgrave – nothing pretentious or put-on. That outsize ferocity of hers isn't an act; it's the way she steers through life, devouring and confronting it, making waves, saving the world... Redgrave seems to live in a different octave from the rest of the world – higher-pitched. Life to her is more extreme, more intense, more outrageous, more dire. Everything she encounters has a rich emotional component, and yet she doesn't suffer from the nervous frailty people often have when they experience the world so keenly. She wants to feel; emotions never seem to hurt her. It's as though sorrow and anger and joy were neither positive nor negative, as though they were merely different flavors, all there for the tasting." (Stephen Schiff, *Vanity Fair*, 7/91)

Siobhan Redmond
b. 27 July 1959, 22.30 GDT, Maternity Hospital, Glasgow, Scotland, 55N51, 04W14.
Gerard q. BC. RR: AA.
Actress best known for her role in the police series *Between the Lines* (1992-4) and her work with Robbie Coltrane (qv) and Ben Elton (qv) in the comedy *Alfresco* (1987). She starred in the detective drama *Bulman* (1985-7) and won praise for her role in the comedy series *The High Life*.

Jean Redpath
b. 28 April 1937, 00.20 GDT, Royal Maternity Hospital, Edinburgh, Scotland, 55N57, 03W12.
Gerard q. BC. RR: AA.
Folk singer and academic who found success after emigrating to the USA in 1961. During the mid-70s she returned to Scotland and spends time on both sides of the Atlantic.

---

* Franco Nero b. 23 November 1941, 22.30 MEDT (-2), Lazzaro Parmense (San Lazzaro), near Parma, Italy, 44N28, 11E25. BC in hand from Grazia Bordoni (Francesco Sparanero). RR: AA.

Oliver Reed

🜨 *b. 13 February 1938, 01.00 GMT, Wimbledon, London, England, 51N25, 0W12.*
From an article by Roger Elliot in TV Times, original source not known. RR: C.

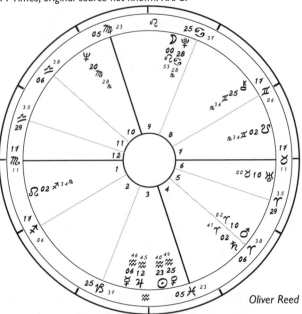

Oliver Reed

Sullen and burly actor of British films. A former boxer (who continued to exhibit macho and pugnacious behaviour on and off-screen – Mars in Aries, Scorpio Rising), Reed moved from work as an extra to a starring role in the 1961 film *The Curse of the Werewolf*. He established a strong persona on screen over the next two decades with roles in *Women in Love* (1969) and *The Devils* (1971), and was one of Britain's most recognisable actors (Moon-Pluto opposing Mercury). His hell-raising and battle with alcohol set his career back in the 80s and he often appeared the worse for drink on TV interviews, which generated much ridicule. One memorable interview under-the-influence was with Michael Aspel (qv) on 19 February 1987. By 1996 Reed – married for the second time from 7 September 1985 – was showing signs of having mellowed but his death on 2 May 1999 from a drinking binge (whilst on location in Valletta, Malta filming Gladiator) showed he was living in the fast lane to the very the end.

> Q "Oliver Reed, actor, clown and emotional prostitute – his words, not mine – was indulging in his favourite pastime... doing his damnedest to shock. It is this almost desperate, child-like urge to be the centre of attention that has landed Reed in so much trouble over the years... He has done everything possible to cultivate the image of a chauvinistic oaf and virtually nothing to dispel it." (Lester Middlehurst, *Daily Mail*, 19/6/95)

Charles and Craig Reid – see The Proclaimers
Jim and William Reid – see Jesus & Mary Chain

John Reid

b. 9 September 1949, 08.35 GDT, Barshaw Hospital, Paisley, Scotland, 55N51, 04W23.
FCC q. BC. RR: AA.

Shrewd and hard-headed entrepreneur (from age 11) who provokes extreme reactions from all quarters (Uranus conjunct MC square Moon on the Descendant). Reports of his personality range from personable to pugnacious. He worked with EMI from age 17 and the prodigious talent ran the Tamla-Motown operation in Britain from 1969. In August 1970 (TR Uranus on Ascendant) he began a friendship with Elton John (qv) and later, according to Philip Norman's biography, *Elton*, became his Svengali, manager (exclusively from March 1973) and lover (Elton's Sun falls on Reid's Descendant; Reid's MC ruler is the Moon, which is also conjunct his famous client's Sun). Reid runs his management company and had firm control over Elton's career direction until he was fired in Spring 1998 (TR Neptune opposite Mars – he lost his Aries client). It led to a court battle from November 2000, which Reid won in April 2001 (TR Pluto square Sun).

Enn Reitel

> b. 21 June 1950, 14.45 GDT, Fyfe-Jamieson Maternity Hospital, Forfar, Scotland, 56N39, 02W53.
> Gerard q. BC. RR: AA.

Actor and voice-over artist. Reitel performed in the West End in *Me and My Girl* and was also a voice impersonator on *Spitting Image* (strong Gemini influence and Jupiter opposite Moon).

Griff Rhys-Jones

> b. 16 November 1953, 15.00 GMT, Cardiff, Wales, 51N29, 03W13.
> Marjorie Orr q. him. RR: A.

A contributor to the Cambridge Footlights revues, Rhys-Jones met Mel Smith in 1979 and they were later brought together on *Not the Nine O'Clock News* (from March 1980 to March 1982). He worked with Smith in the comedy sketch series *Alas Smith and Jones* (from 1984 to 1992), in which their head-to-head sketches of idiots attempting to grasp the simplest of ideas were the most memorable. In April 2003 he appeared in the film *Puckoon*.

Tim Rice

✪ b. 10 November 1944, 17.45 GWT, Amersham, England, 51N40, 0W38.
> From his autobiography *Oh, What A Circus* (Coronet, 1999). (N.B. His father is quoted in a letter as saying he left the maternity wing at 17.00 and the birth took place "15 minutes after I had left.")
> RR: B.

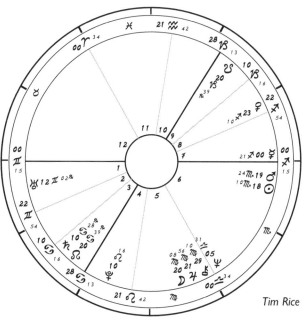

Tim Rice

Extrovert Rice (born Timothy Miles Benton Rice) has enjoyed a more varied professional life than his former collaborator, Andrew Lloyd Webber (qv). Work includes his publishing company Pavilion Books and running a local cricket team. He is also the writer of an annual guide to British hit singles and albums, and he has a massive private collection of music. Rice met Lloyd Webber at a party in 1965 and following their first collaboration, *Joseph*, were both put on a £25-a-week retainer by impresario David Land to write musicals (both Rice and Lloyd Webber have Mercury conjunct Descendant). Temperamental and artistic differences would later break up the writing pair – and their relationship remains edgy (Rice's Sun-Mars squares Webber's Saturn-Mars and opposes his MC/Venus; their Ascendants square each other). A new career in Hollywood blossomed for Rice following three music Oscars for *The Lion King* (June 1994), *Aladdin* and *Evita*. (Rice has Moon-Jupiter sextile Sun-Mars in 6th, and trine MC.) In February 2003 *The Mail on Sunday's Rich Report* estimated his fortune at £107 million.

Cliff Richard

○ *b. 14 October 1940, 21.00 IST (-5.5 = -5 hrs 30 mins), Lucknow, India, 26N51, 80E55.*

✸ *Date and place from biographies and interviews. Fowler's Compendium gave "evening." Speculative. RR: C.*

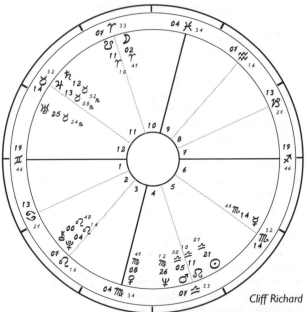

Cliff Richard

Ever-popular all-round entertainer. Particularly for the 40-80 age market nowadays, Richard's appeal lies in his clean-cut wholesome boy-next-door image (note the Virgo-Libra emphasis) rather than overt sexiness. Famously religious and celibate, both his looks and approach to life are suggestive of a real-life Peter Pan (the possible Gemini Ascendant). Yet the Cliff of the 1950s was a teenage pop sensation closely modelled on his idol Elvis Presley. He arrived in England in September 1948 and signed a record contract on 8 August 1958, with a first big hit in October of that year. He has had 14 British #1 hits and is the second most successful chart act in the UK (only Elvis has had more chart entries). Like his idol, Richard managed to combine successful music and film careers. His first films were *Serious Charge* (May 1959) and *Expresso Bongo* (December 1959). In the first two years of his career Cliff Richard had sold a staggering 5.5 million singles. On 11 January 1962 he became the first UK artist to enter the pop charts at #1 with *The Young Ones* and the film was released the same month. *Summer Holiday* followed in January 1963. Four years later (on 13 January 1967), after becoming a born again Christian, he announced his plans to retire to teach religious instruction in secondary schools. Richard postponed retirement and continues to perform to this day. After a lean commercial period in the 70s he hit the top of the charts with *We Don't Talk Anymore* (1979), *Living Doll* (1986), *Mistletoe and Wine* (December 1988) and *The Millennium Prayer* (1999). Following a national tour he performed *Heathcliff* in London from 12 February 1997. In October 2002 he was named the 56th Greatest Briton of all time and in March 2003 a musical about his life came to the West End. Although dropped from some radio playlists, Cliff is still hugely popular and Mr. Eligible to his huge female fanbase. After 45 years of fame he performs regularly and continues to be a dedicated charity worker.

Keith Richard(s) – see Rolling Stones
Claire Richards – see Steps

Ian Richardson

○ *b. 7 April 1934, 22.35 GMT, Edinburgh, Scotland, 55N57, 03W14.*

Gerard q. BC (Ian William Richardson). RR: AA.

Dazzling actor who was a Gold Medal winner in 1957 at RADA. Richardson worked at the Birmingham Rep from 1958-60 (title role in *Hamlet* in 1958) and followed this with RSC membership (he made an impact as Jean Paul Marat in the RSC's *Marat/Sade*, and repeated the role on film). Broadway appearances include *Lolita* in 1971 and *My Fair Lady* in 1976. Richardson made his TV debut in 1962 and went on to appear in several high-profile series. But it was his portrayal of the unscrupulous Machiavellian politician Francis Urquhart ("I think I'm ready for a bit of mischief now") in *House of Cards* (from November 1990) that would elicit universal praise and a Bafta Best Actor award in 1991. He also starred in the sequel, *To Play the King*. The character was a timeless political stereotype that seemed particularly appropriate in Thatcher's Britain (both actor and politician have Scorpio Rising). In fact, in an extraordinary coincidence, Thatcher ended her term of power one day after the first episode aired. Since then he has excelled when cast as merciless men who hide behind education and an air of refinement. Richardson married in 1961 and was awarded the CBE in 1989.

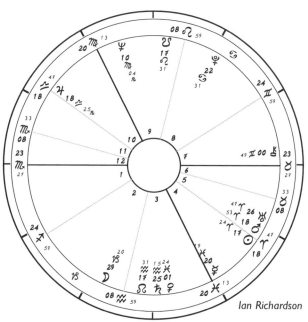

Ian Richardson

Natasha Richardson

b. 11 May 1963, 17.00 GDT, London, England, 51N30, 0W10.
From her mother's autobiography, Vanessa Redgrave (Hutchinson, 1991), p. 114. (Rachel Kempson's autobiography, A Family and Its Fortunes, notes the birth occurred early in the evening.) RR: B.

After a stint at the Leeds Playhouse, Richardson's first major roles on stage were at the London Old Vic. In 1986 she won a Most Promising Newcomer award. In 1988 Richardson won the title role in Patty Hearst, a film about the heiress who was kidnapped on 4 February 1974 by the Symbionese Liberation Army and brainwashed to carry out an armed robbery in March 1975. Patty Hearst* has Uranus on Natasha's MC, and her Sun is opposite the actress's Uranus. After appearing on Broadway in the musical Cabaret (1998), she was seen in Maid in Manhattan (2003), alongside Ralph Fiennes and Jennifer Lopez, and on stage (from 8 May) in The Lady from the Sea, a role her mother Vanessa Redgrave made famous. Richardson is married to Liam Neeson (b. 7 June 1952, Ballymena, Northern Ireland).

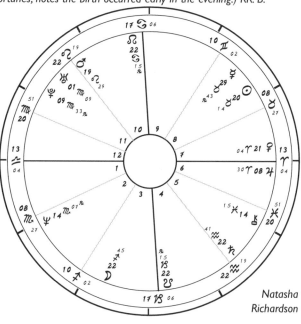

Natasha Richardson

* Patty Hearst b. 20 February 1954, 18.01 PST, San Francisco, California, 37N47, 122W25. Contemporary American Horoscopes q. BC. RR: AA.

Diana Rigg

✪ b. 20 July 1938, 04.00 GDT, Doncaster, England, 53N32, 01W07.

💣 Frederick Davies q. her for 04.00 in Signs of the Stars (FCC q. her in 1996, from her parents for 02.00). Both charts are presented for the reader's discernment. RR: DD.

Rigg travelled with her mother to India at two months old, returning at age eight. At school she developed a love of poetry and later enrolled at RADA, making her professional debut in Summer 1957. Rigg was a model until she got a job as an assistant stage manager at the Chesterfield Repertory Company. In 1959 she joined the Shakespeare Memorial Theatre Company at Stratford and made her London debut in January 1961. In April 1962 (TR Saturn conjunct the 02.00 MC) she was applauded for her role in A Midsummer Night's Dream. In May 1964 she debuted on the New York stage. On TV Rigg followed in Honor Blackman's (qv) footsteps as the female lead in The Avengers. (Whilst at the RSC she had auditioned for the series for a laugh but it was to be the turning point in her career.) She appeared from November 1965 (TR Saturn on the 04.00 MC) to late 1967. This exceptional actress's career has been in full bloom since 1992 with formidable performances on stage in Medea (1992), a West End and Broadway hit (a Tony Award in June 1994, when TR Saturn had passed over the 04.00 MC) and Mother Courage (November 1995). In October 1996 she received rave reviews for what many were calling the best part of her career, the vulgar Martha Washington in Who's Afraid of Virginia Woolf? She starred in the award-winning Mother Love (1989) on TV in October 1989, and in January 1997 returned to TV with Rebecca. Rigg's marriage ended on 14 February 1990 (TR Saturn square Moon, TR Neptune conjunct the 04.00 Descendant) when she discovered her husband was having an affair with actress Joely Richardson. Years after mourning her loss, she now lives alone in France. In a poll conducted by U.S. magazine TV Guide Rigg was voted the sexiest star in TV history ahead of George Clooney and Angie Dickinson. Rigg had her first child, a daughter, on 30 May 1977.

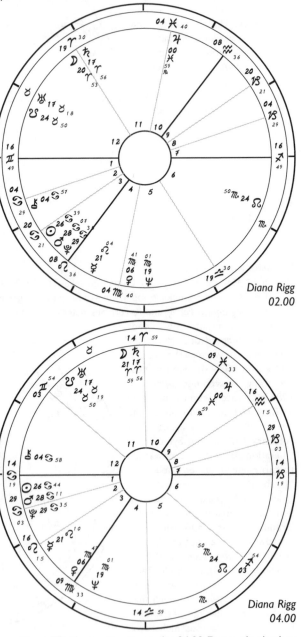

Diana Rigg
02.00

Diana Rigg
04.00

Brian Rix

b. 27 January 1924, 08.00 GMT, Cottingham, England, 53N47, 0W24.

His autobiography, *My Farce from My Elbow*, states "just in time for breakfast." RR: C.

The brother of Sheila Mercier (qv), Rix is a comedy actor known for stage farce (just like Benny Hill, qv, Brian Rix has Mars-Jupiter on a Sagittarian MC). He made his stage debut on 24 August 1942 (as TR Pluto opposed Sun) in *King Lear* and, after a four-year stint in the RAF from July 1944, made his first film in 1951. In 1948 (as TR Neptune conjunct Moon) he set up his own rep company but it failed and Rix moved on. He was seen in farces at the Whitehall Theatre, London, during the 50s and 60s and in 1976 retired after 30 years as Britain's king of farce. In 1981 he took on the full-time job of general secretary for the National Society for the Mentally Handicapped. Now Lord Rix, he married Elspet Gray (qv) on 14 August 1949.

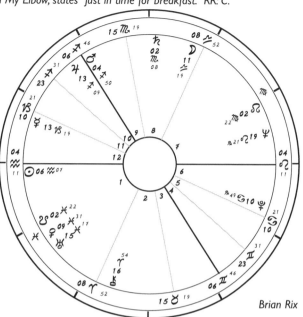

Brian Rix

Q| "He's disciplined and fanatically tidy but underneath the urbane confident charm is an emotional and driven man." (Lynda Lee-Potter, *Daily Mail*, 24/6/02)

William Roache

b. 23 April 1932, 07.30 GDT, Ilkeston, England, 52N59, 01W18.

David Fisher q. his letter (August 1980) for the data and the 25th April. His autobiography with Stan Nicholls, *Ken and Me* (Simon & Schuster, 1993), p. 2, notes the mix-up with the date of birth; his BC states 25th and is also dated the same day; Roache says he believes it to be the 23rd. RR: A?

Roache is the only member of *Coronation Street* to have remained in the series since its first episode. His character, Ken Barlow, was involved in his most dramatic storyline – a love triangle which kept the nation hooked – for the first few months of 1983 before its resolution on 23 February 1983. Roache has suffered personal tragedies during his long-haul with the soap. On 16 November 1984 (at around 23.20, Wilmslow) his 18-month old baby died (TR Uranus conjunct Descendant). A libelous tabloid article was printed in November 1990 and Roache took the transgressing paper to court (8th House ruler Saturn in EQHS 8th on MC) on 29 October 1991 (before his second Saturn Return)

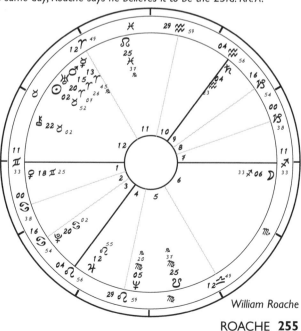

William Roache

and won. He devised a board game called *Libel* after the case but in April 1999 (TR Neptune conjunct MC, TR Pluto conjunct Descendant) he was declared bankrupt because of mounting debts from court costs (£120,000). He was in court in late June 2001 (as TR Saturn approached the Ascendant) to fight an application to pay more to clear the £600,000 debts he has since amassed.

B.A. Robertson

b. 14 June 1949, 05.40 GDT, Balarnock Road, Glasgow, Scotland, 55N53, 04W14.
Gerard q. BC. RR: AA.

Singer-songwriter Robertson is also known as a gregarious prankster (MC ruler Uranus is conjunct Venus on a Cancer Ascendant for a quirky sense of humour; the Moon also conjuncts Jupiter in Aquarius). He had three Top Ten hits between August 1979 and June 1980.

Brian Robertson

b. 12 February 1956, 21.15 GMT, Clarkston, Scotland, 55N52, 03W58.
Gerard q. BC (Brian David Robertson). RR: AA.

Guitarist with Thin Lizzy, Wild Horses, and with Motorhead from May 1982 until August 1983.

Anne Robinson

✪ *b. 26 September 1944, 23.20 GWT, Crosby, Liverpool, England, 53N30, 03W02.*
☄ *Robinson is unsure of her birth time, but in Libra fashion tried to help! She told FCC it could have been around 07.00 or just before midnight. The former time may be less reliable, as this is the time quoted for her daughter's birth in her autobiography. Place and year confirmed by FCC at Registry. RR: DD.*

In late 2001 there were reports of American viewers having recurring nightmares and requiring therapy. And the cause? The sharp rebuff, "You are the weakest link. Goodbye." Spoken by Anne Robinson, the sharp-tongued presenter of the hit quiz show, *The Weakest Link*, which first aired on US screens on 16 April 2001. Robinson, a veteran of newspaper columns, TV journalism and reporting found her niche playing the tough, acerbic dominatrix on prime time US and UK TV. Born Ann Josephine Robinson, she began as a writer in Fleet Street for the *Daily Mail* in Summer 1967 and moved the following year to *The Sunday Times* for ten years. By 1980 she was the only woman assistant editor in Fleet Street. Regular TV

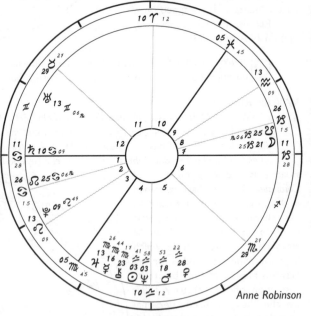

Anne Robinson

stints from 1987 (including *Points of View*) led to the high-rated live consumer programme *Watchdog* in 1993, where Robinson sharpened her tongue on callous company chiefs who were put in the hot seat. On 28 January 2000 she was presented with the concept for the TV pilot of *The Weakest Link*, which premiered in the UK in August 2000. As the leather-clad dominatrix she reinvented herself and has become a millionaire many times over, thanks to the show's success in the USA. The show is broadcast in 82 countries and some countries have employed their own red-headed Rottweiler to appal and fascinate viewers. Australia's answer is seasoned TV bitch Cornelia Frances (see Australian Data – cardinal signs obviously relish the role of the bitch, particularly when Saturn enters the fray). In Autumn 2001 Robinson released her autobiography, *Memoirs of an Unfit Mother* (Little Brown). It chronicles her life as a respected journalist, her struggle with alcoholism (Sun-Neptune) and the devastating custody battle over her daughter, which she lost on 6 April 1973 (TR Pluto conjunct Sun)

– condemned for being an ambitious working parent. A film of her life story is in production. The daughter of a self-reliant, fearless, dominating mother, in person Robinson is charming, candid and eager to please (Libra). She married on 19 January 1968 and again in March 1980 to the present day.

Tom Robinson
✪ b. 1 June 1950, 09.00 GDT, Cambridge, England, 52N13, 0E08.
Sy Scholfield q. Robinson via email, 6/6/02. (N.B. 1 July is often given in music references, but Robinson confirmed June in his email and on his official website, "A newspaper printed [my birth date] wrong once and now it's spread and seemingly impossible to stamp out.") Month confirmed by FCC at Registry. RR: A.

Robinson, a politically conscious and confrontational singer-songwriter, was a founding member of Rock Against Racism and has had an intensely controversial career. His debut album *Power in the Darkness* was released in 1978 and established him as a potent political voice. Robinson attempted suicide at 16 and spent years recovering from the breakdown until he faced his sexuality at age 23. His song *Glad to be Gay* made him one of Britain's most visible gays in the 70s (an Aries MC is often known for sexuality). Yet he stunned fans when he fell in love with a woman in 1987. He is now a respected voice on radio.

Jim Rodford – see The Kinks

Anton Rodgers
b. 10 January 1933, 16.00 GMT, Wisbech, England, 52N40, 0E10.
David Fisher q. his letter. RR: A.

A long-established actor of TV and radio. Rodgers's earliest work included a role in the BBC comedy *The Skylarks*, first broadcast in July 1958. His successful television comedy *Fresh Fields* (March 1984 to December 1986) was followed by an on-location sequel entitled *French Fields* (September 1989 to October 1991). Rodgers also starred in *May to December* (April 1989 to May 1994) and was one of the actors who played 'Number Two' in the cult 60s series *The Prisoner*. His radio work has included *Two Plus Two* with Barbara Windsor (qv) from June 1964.

ROLLING STONES
•1962, July 12 – The Rollin' Stones (with Mick Avory) make their debut at the Marquee Jazz Club.
•1962, Dec – Wyman successfully auditions for the group.
•1963, May – They sign a management contract and become The Rolling Stones.
•1963, July – First UK chart hit.
•1964, May – Their eponymous debut album hits #1 and marks the beginning of an unparalleled influence upon the music scene.
•1965, July – The single (*I Can't Get No*) *Satisfaction* hits US #1.
•1967, June 29 – Richards and Jagger are found guilty of drug offences and jailed (in July Richards's conviction is quashed and Jagger's sentence reduced).
•1969, May 28 – Jagger and Marianne Faithfull (qv) are arrested for hashish possession.
•1969, June 5 – Manager Brian Jones (b. 28 February 1942,

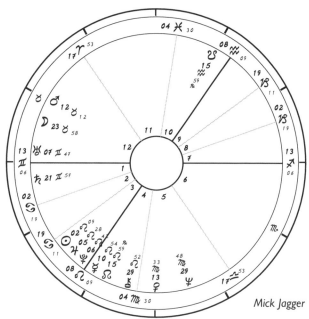

Mick Jagger

Cheltenham) is fired; Jones drowns on 2 July 1969.

•1971, May 12 – Jagger marries Bianca (they had met on 22 September 1970; and are later divorced in November 1980).

•1973, July 31 – Richards accidentally sets himself alight and his home burns down.

•1977, Feb 27 – Richards is arrested for heroin trafficking in Toronto.

•1982, Sep 2 – Richards's home is seriously damaged by fire.

•1985, Sep 7 – Jagger's duet with David Bowie (qv) hits UK #1.

•1985, Dec 12 – Ian Stewart, the 'Sixth Stone', dies of a heart attack.

•1989, June 2 – Wyman marries Mandy Smith (qv).

•1990, Nov 21 – Jagger marries Jerry Hall, although it is later revealed to be null and void. The couple have two children*.

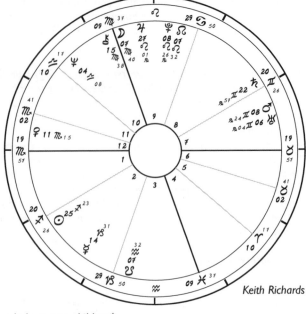

Keith Richards

•1993, Apr 21 – Wyman marries fashion designer Suzanne Accosta.

(*The Rolling Stones Chronicle* by Massimo Bonanno, Plexus, 1995.) Extra event dates from astrologer-writer Nick Dagan Best (stellardweller@hotmail.com).

Mick Jagger
🜨 b. 26 July 1943, 02.30 DGDT, Dartford, England, 51N27, 0E14.
   Ananda Bagley q. the doctor who delivered him, between "2.00 am and 3.00 am." (N.B. Although this is 'C' data, Bagley also q. two astrologers who have erected personal charts with a Gemini Ascendant for Jagger.) RR: C.

Keith Richard(s)
   b. 18 December 1943, 06.00 GDT, Dartford, England, 51N27, 0E14.
   Arthur Blackwell q. him to Ruth F. Nobel (same from other astrologers). RR: A.

Ian Stewart (the 'Sixth Stone')
   b. 18 July 1938, 01.50 GDT, Pittenweem, Fife, Scotland, 56N12, 02W44.
   Caroline Gerard q. BC (Ian Andrew Robert Stewart). RR: AA.

Bill Wyman
   b. 24 October 1936, 23.25 GMT, Lewisham, London, 51N27, 0W01.
   From his autobiography with Ray Coleman, *Bill Wyman: Stone Alone* (Penguin, 1990), q. Wyman, p. 44. RR: A.

Jack Rosenthal – see Maureen Lipman
Ricky Ross – see Deacon Blue
Johnny Rotten – see Sid Vicious

---

* Elizabeth Scarlett Jagger b. 2 March 1984, 01.37 EST (+5), New York, New York, USA, 40N43, 74W00. AFA Bulletin (v.46, no. 7) q. Los Angeles Herald Examiner, 3 March 1984. RR: A.
Leroy Augustine Jagger b. 28 August 1985, 11.30 EDT (+4), New York. David Dozier q. San Antonio Express News, 29 August 1985. RR: A.

Patricia Routledge

b. 17 February 1929, 00.30 GMT, Birkenhead, England, 53N24, 03W02.
From Old Moore's Almanac 1997, from her (verified by FCC). RR: A.

Formidable and theatrical actress with a manner that suggests fools will not be entertained (Leo MC, Scorpio Rising). Routledge began her career as an unpaid assistant stage manager at the Liverpool Playhouse in 1952. She appeared in three episodes of *Coronation Street* in 1961. She has a passionate love of language and has built up an impressive list of stage and TV credits. Routledge even won a Tony Award in June 1968 (when TR Jupiter passed over her MC) for *Darling of the Day* on the New York stage. A character actress of the highest calibre, Routledge is best as the bossy battleaxe (Leo MC) in comedies with her trademark double-takes, open-mouthed expression and animated eyebrows (the Scorpio Ascendant is easily

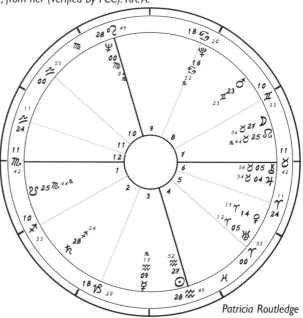

Patricia Routledge

impersonated, too). She has featured in a few of Alan Bennett's plays (including one of the *Talking Heads* monologues, *A Lady of Letters*) and was the hilarious straight-talking overnight minor-celebrity Kitty in Victoria Wood's TV show. She became a favourite for her award-winning TV run as super-snob Hyacinth Bucket (pronounced Bouquet) in *Keeping Up Appearances* from 29 October 1990 (TR Jupiter conjunct her EQHS 10th), and won the 1991 British Comedy Award for Top Comedy Actress. It ran until 1995, some time after the writers had run out of ways to explore Bucket in new comic situations (in 2003 it was being filmed in Hindi with the translated title *The Crow Who Tries to Walk like a Peacock*). The show allowed her to show off her skill at farce, physical comedy and clowning (with Jupiter angular Routledge was able to capture social pretension, which is at the heart of British comedy). Routledge successfully took to playing a local private investigator (a tough Northern Miss Marple) in *Hetty Wainthropp Investigates*. Routledge is also an accomplished and powerful singer and described her childhood as being idyllic, full of music and family sing-songs around the piano.

Q

"My ambition was to be a go-ahead headmistress by the time I was 40, with a red sports car and romances all over Europe during the holidays." (Patricia Routledge, as quoted in BBC's *Funny Women*)

"Patricia has a very strong moral streak and she has very firm views, and I think if a part doesn't conform with those she's very dubious about it." (Playwright Alan Bennett, as quoted in BBC's *Funny Women*)

"[An] ability to portray someone who seems to be a very detached and humorous observer of life, but who then reveals hidden depths either of emotion or mania." (Playwright Michael Frayn, as quoted in BBC's *Funny Women*)

"The key to understanding Patricia is her religion. Patricia's Christianity gives her this ability to know that life is both innately transient and ridiculous and deeply tragic and moving, and the secret of comedy is to be able to encompass both these things." (Director James Runcie, as quoted in BBC's *Funny Women*)

J.K. Rowling – see Robbie Coltrane

RUNRIG

Scotland's most popular rock and pop band was formed in 1973 (Munro joined the following year). With their swirling tunes Runrig have been able to win an audience outside their homeland in spite of their songs demonstrating a marked national pride and political stance. They achieved a chart hit in October 1989. Munro left the band and ran for election as a Labour candidate in May 1997 for the constituency of Ross, Skye and Inverness West. In May 1999 he stood for his home constituency of Holyrood and was narrowly beaten into second place. Wishart was a member of the band Big Country.

Iain Bayne
> b. 22 January 1960, 02.45 GMT, Craigtoun Maternity Hospital, St. Andrews, Scotland, 56N21, 02W48.
> Gerard q. BC. RR: AA.

Malcolm Jones
> b. 12 July 1959, 00.50 GDT, Raigmore Hospital, Inverness, Scotland, 57N28, 04W13.
> Gerard q. BC (Malcolm Elwyn Jones). RR: AA.

Rory MacDonald
> b. 27 July 1949, 08.35 GDT, Sutherland Road, Dornoch, Scotland, 57N53, 04W02.
> Gerard q. BC (Roderick MacDonald). RR: AA.

Donnie Munro
> b. 2 August 1953, 03.25 GDT, Portree, Isle of Skye, Scotland, 57N25, 06W12.
> Gerard q. BC (Donald Munro). RR: AA.

Peter Wishart
> b. 9 March 1962, 06.40 GMT, Maternity Hospital, Dunfermline, Scotland, 56N04, 03W28.
> Gerard q. BC. (N.B. BC stated 'pm' but was corrected to 'am' and noted on the document.) RR: AA.

Graham Russell
> b. 11 June 1950, 09.00 GDT, Arnold, England, 53N00, 01W08.
> Edwin Steinbrecher q. him from his father's memory (rectified by Steinbrecher to 09.57 GDT). RR: A.

Russell began writing poems and lyrics after his mother died when he was 10. At 13 he ran away from home when his family decided to move to Australia, and later, staying with an uncle, became the drummer for a local band. Eventually Russell also moved to Australia and performed solo before successfully auditioning for *Jesus Christ, Superstar*, where he met Russell Hitchcock (qv, Australian Data) and formed Air Supply. In 1979 they left Superstar, had a Top Five hit in Australia, and supported Rod Stewart (qv) on his Australian and American tours. Taking six months off to write songs, a rock opera and to recover from food poisoning, Russell discovered American interest in Air Supply's light, romantic songs. The duo enjoyed enormous commercial success in the early 80s.

Ken Russell
✪ b. 3 July 1927, 00.05 GDT, Southampton, England, 50N55, 01W25.
> David Fisher q. Russell's mother to the Astrological Association (Laura Boomer q. him for 00.01). RR: A.

A controversial director, Ken Russell ceaselessly dares to find new and shocking ways of portraying ideas and images on screen. He has an inspirational, rather than mechanical, approach to his writing (Pisces Ascendant). His rock opera *Tommy* debuted in London on 26 March 1975.

Mike Rutherford – see Genesis

Paul Rutherford
> b. 8 December 1959, 22.15 GMT, Liverpool, England, 53N25, 02W55.
> Bettina Lee q. him. RR: A.

Singer with the Spitfire Boys and the Opium Eaters before joining Frankie Goes To Hollywood as the leather-clad co-frontman, performing at their first gig in August 1980. From November 1983 the laddish-gay band became a sensation with their explicit hit *Relax* (banned by the BBC) being the first of three consecutive #1 hits in the UK (#1s in January, June and December 1984), two of which were double million-sellers. The band descended into lawsuits in 1987 with only Rutherford and band leader Holly Johnson (qv) escaping obscurity after quitting the band in March of that year. Rutherford signed to another label in August 1988 and had minor hits in October 1988 and September 1989.

Andrew Sachs

b. 7 April 1930, 09.00 MET, Berlin, Germany, 52N30, 13E22.
FCC q. him. RR: A.

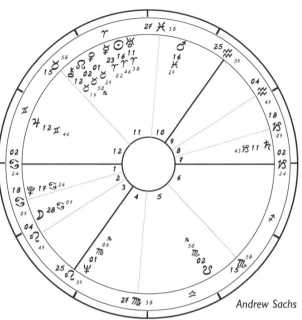

Andrew Sachs

Sachs appeared most famously as Manuel, the mad waiter from Barcelona in *Fawlty Towers* (with Prunella Scales, qv). It was a role which in times to come would unfortunately limit Sachs's career opportunities (he lost the role of Victor Meldrew to Richard Wilson (qv) in 1989). Sachs began his career as an assistant stage manager and cut his acting teeth on Brian Rix (qv) farces. He is also a writer and has created more than a dozen radio plays. When he was eight Sachs witnessed his father's arrest by an S.S. officer in a Berlin restaurant. Helped out by an influential friend and released, his father fled with the family to Britain three months later. In February 2001 Sachs presented a Radio 4 series *The Jewish Journey*, in which he took a personal look at 1,000 years of Jewish life in Britain. He has been married for 40 years.

Sandy (Alexander Cumming) from UK's Big Brother

❂ b. 12 January 1959, 01.15 GMT, Newburgh, Fife, Scotland, Scotland, 56N20, 03W15.
Gerard q. BC (Alexander Cumming). RR: AA.

Contestant in the 2002 series of Channel 4's game show *Big Brother*. Cumming, a women's personal shopper for a department store, was the second ever to walk away from the house (rather than be evicted); he escaped by climbing over the fence on day 20 (of 64) on 12 June 2002, bored with the show and his fellow contestants.

Lily Savage

(Confidential data)

Outrageous, larger-than-life performer who brazenly articulates the nation's unspeakable thoughts (both Jupiter and Uranus are prominently placed in the chart, along with an outspoken Moon sign). Savage is played by actor and comedian Paul O'Grady, who built up a strong following on the club circuit before emerging as Britain's biggest comedy draw. His alter-ego Savage – a bitchy and crude kleptomaniac ex-prostitute – was born in a pub in the Elephant and Castle during O'Grady's Saturn Return. Savage presented *The Big Breakfast* in June 1995 for 11 months, during a banner year of national recognition that saw Savage rise to the position of top comedy performer in Britain. Stage shows (*Prisoner Cell Block H – The Musical*, from October 1995), TV series, quiz shows and travel programmes followed. On 16 September 2002 O'Grady emerged from Savage's shadow and joined the cast of the West End stage show *Chitty Chitty Bang Bang*. He suffered a heart attack in April 2002, which prompted him to quit smoking and change his diet.

Prunella Scales

💣 b. 22 June 1932, 22.00 GDT, Sutton Abinger, Surrey, England, 51N12, 0W26.

FCC remembers seeing an astrological profile on Scales many years ago which mentioned a Capricorn Ascendant and Saturn in the 1st. Who's Who on Television gives the date and place. Capricorn was ascending from approximately 21.10 to 22.55. Arbitrary time. RR: C.

Making her stage debut in 1951 Scales later established herself in pleasant sitcoms such as *Marriage Lines* (1963). Substantial parts in two series of *Mapp and Lucia* (April 1985 and May 1986), *A Question of Attribution* and *After Henry* (on radio from April 1985, TV series January 1988 until August 1992) followed her *Fawlty Towers* triumph (two series from September 1975 and February 1979). She was awarded the CBE in June 1992 and continues to act on stage, film and TV.

Phillip Schofield

b. 1 April 1962, 02.00 GDT, Oldham, England, 53N33, 02W07.

FCC q. an interview with his mother, who recalled how she cried when he was born at 2 am on April Fool's Day (1st April). Same in biography. RR: A.

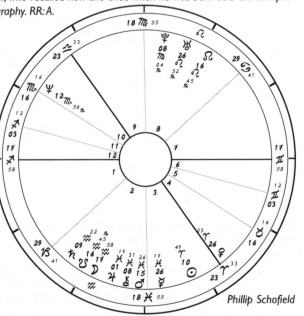

Phillip Schofield

At 17 Schofield worked as a clerk for the BBC. At 18 he emigrated to – and won his own radio and TV shows in – New Zealand (EQHS 3rd ruler Uranus in 9th opposite Moon in 3rd). Schofield returned to England at 22 and three years later was a continuity presenter for Children's BBC. He moved on to *Saturday Superstore* and *Going Live!* In 1992 Schofield took over the lead role from Jason Donovan (qv, Australian Data) in *Joseph and the Amazing Technicolour Dreamcoat*, and toured with *Doctor Doolittle* for much of the 90s. He began the entertainment show *Schofield's Quest* in 1994. In 2002 he was brought back to a larger viewing audience when he began presenting *The National Lottery: Winning Lines* and *This Morning* (TR Pluto on Ascendant, after the dismissal of John Leslie, qv, in late October).

Bon Scott – see AC/DC

Mike Scott

b. 14 December 1958, 16.45 GMT, Corstorphine, Edinburgh, Scotland, 55N57, 03W15.

Gerard q. BC (Michael Scott). RR: AA.

Vocalist and central figure of Waterboys, a band he formed in June 1981 (TR Neptune conjunct Sun). A handful of hits until the late 80s followed and Scott began making solo appearances in September 1991 (TR Uranus conjunct Descendant). In August 1993, after being unable to find new band members, Scott ended his association with the band (TR Saturn on MC).

Willie Scott

b. 7 May 1897, 12.00 Noon GMT, Canonbie, Dumfriesshire, Scotland, 55N05, 02W57.

Gerard q. BC (William James Scott). RR: AA.

Acclaimed traditional ballad singer. His only solo commercial recording was *The Shepherd's Song* (1968).

Lisa Scott-Lee – see Steps

Jenny Seagrove

b. 4 July 1958, 00.38 JT (Java Time, −7.30), Kuala Lumpur, Malaysia, 3N10, 101E42.
FCC q. an interview with her in the newspaper Evening Standard, p. 37, 18 July 1995, "I was born in hospital in Kuala Lumpur. It was exactly 38 minutes past midnight on 4 July 1958." RR: A.

Jenny Seagrove shot to fame in January 1985 with *A Woman of Substance*, a mini-series that brought Channel 4 a record-breaking audience of 14 million viewers (from 2 to 4 January). She made a sequel, *Hold The Dream*, the following year. In April 1987 (when TR Jupiter travelled over her Ascendant and she had her Saturn Return), Seagrove proved herself a real woman of substance when she left her controlling husband (natal Venus, ruler of 7th, square Pluto in 5th, and Moon opposite Uranus). She had been a virtual prisoner in the marriage and went to court for a bitterly contested divorce in July 1988, as TR Neptune, natally in 7th, conjunct her MC. On 26 May 1987 she was devastated when her new lover was killed in a car crash.

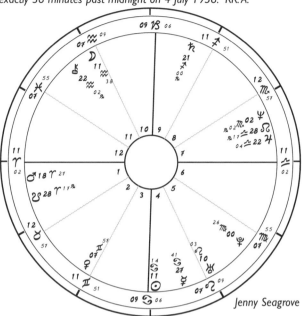

Jenny Seagrove

Seagrove had suffered with anorexia from her teenage years until her mid-20s (Uranus opposite Moon).

Harry Secombe – see The Goons

Elizabeth Sellars

b. 6 May 1921, 06.30 GDT, Hillhead, Glasgow, Scotland, 55N53, 04W18.
Gerard q. BC (Elizabeth McDonald Sellars). RR: AA.
Actress of TV and film with cinema credits from 1948-73.

Peter Sellers – see The Goons

SENSATIONAL ALEX HARVEY BAND / ALEX HARVEY SOUL BAND

Creative band known for ambitious stage shows, formed in 1972 (with Zal Cleminson of Nazareth, qv) and led by the flamboyant Harvey (Jupiter on a Sagittarian MC). They combined rock, soul and British music hall. Harvey, labelled the Tommy Steele of Scotland after a talent show win in 1956, had a recurring liver problem but rejoined the group in August 1977 after a stay in hospital. He walked out for good at the end of the year. He had a fatal heart attack on 4 February 1981.

Chris Glen

b. 6 November 1950, 08.55 GMT, Johnstone, Scotland, 55N50, 04W31.
Gerard q. BC (Christopher John Glen). RR: AA.

Jimmy Grimes

b. 26 December 1934, 19.10 GMT, Janefield Street, Glasgow, Scotland, 55N51, 04W12.
Gerard q. BC (James Grimes). RR: AA.

Alex Harvey

b. 5 February 1935, 07.15 GMT, Glasgow, Scotland, 55N52, 04W21.
Gerard q. BC (Alexander Harvey). RR: AA.

Hugh McKenna

b. 28 November 1949, 15.45 GMT, Airdrie, Scotland, 55N52, 03W59.
Gerard q. BC. RR: AA.

Ted McKenna
> b. 10 March 1950, 07.30 GMT, Lennox Castle, Scotland, 55N59, 04W14.
> Gerard q. BC (Edward McKennas). RR: AA.

John Sessions
○ b. 11 January 1953, 14.15 GMT, Bedford, England, 52N08, 0W29.
> FCC q. BC in hand (a twin). Previously Babs Kirby q. him for 14.30. RR: AA.

Popular comedian and improviser, as seen on *Whose Line is it Anyway?* and heard on *Spitting Image*. In 1994 (when TR Pluto crossed his Moon and TR Neptune conjunct his Sun) he featured in the surprise hit play *My Night with Reg*, suffered the loss of his mother, and publicly declared his homosexuality.

Jimmy Shand
○ b. 28 January 1908, 07.30 GMT, East Wemyss, Scotland, 56N09, 03W05.
> Gerard q. BC (James Shand). RR: AA.

Legendary accordion-player. Shand landed a recording deal in 1933, worked with the BBC and in 1945 formed his own band. His most successful period was 1953-65. With Moon-MC in Scorpio and Uranus Rising he was a Scottish musical institution and was also dedicated to the miners' cause (playing benefit gigs around the country during the 1984 strike). D. December 2000.

Ian Shaw
> b. 2 June 1962, 06.46 GDT, St. Asaph, Wales, 53N16, 03W26.
> FCC q. him in April 1997, time from his baby book. RR: AA.

Popular vocalist and pianist with an inventiveness and improvisational skill unequalled on the contemporary jazz scene. Shaw is also known for his hilarious sense of humour on-stage (Venus conjunct a Cancer Ascendant) and has been a tireless performer since 1984, playing in piano bars across Europe. By 1990 Shaw's reputation as a first class performer was already established and he won the Best British Jazz Singer award from *Wire* magazine. Shaw possesses a wide vocal range and an emotive voice. His third album, *The Echo of a Song*, was released in December 1996. In early 1997 Ian Shaw was being promoted in America and performing to rave reviews.

Martin Shaw
> b. 21 January 1945, 09.15 GDT, Birmingham, England, 52N30, 01W50.
> Penny Thornton q. him in Romancing the Stars, p. 480. RR: A.

Shaw began his working life in the sales office of a chemical firm before successfully auditioning for LAMDA. Shaw's acting career took off in 1969 when he landed theatre roles in Britain, received TV offers in America (*Hamlet*, 1970) and appeared in Roman Polanski's film *Macbeth* (1971). He is best known for his role as CI5 agent Ray Doyle in *The Professionals* (December 1977 to February 1983). Shaw has been married three times and was known to be a hell-raiser. In the mid-90s he contemplated retiring from acting when he studied 'polarity', based on Indian Ayurvedic medicine.

Sandie Shaw
> b. 26 February 1947, 00.00 Midnight (of 25/26th) GMT, Dagenham, England, 51N32, 0E10.
> From John Gale's interview with Shaw in The Observer, 25 February 1968. RR: A.

Shaw was discovered and signed to a management contract after an impromptu audition in April 1964 (TR Uranus opposite Sun). She hit the top of the UK charts that October (TR Neptune conjunct Ascendant), causing great interest in her style and barefooted performances. Shaw gave her first concert on 21 February 1965 (TR Saturn conjunct Sun) and spent the rest of the year trying to keep up with her manic schedule. She married fashion designer Jeff Banks on 6 March 1968, a year in which her popularity was declining rapidly. After cabaret and acting work, she signed to another record contract in June 1977 (when TR Saturn approached her EQHS 10th) but no album emerged. Since then she has made sporadic attempts to reignite her career (most notably in May 1984, September 1988, and October 1994, when TR Jupiter crossed her Ascendant and TR Saturn conjunct her Sun). She published her autobiography, *The World At My Feet*, on 9 May 1991.

Dinah Sheridan

> b. 17 September 1920, 11.00 GDT, Hampstead Garden Suburb, London, England, 51N34, 0W11.
> FCC q. her. RR: A.

Television, theatre and film actress with a career spanning seven decades from her stage debut in 1932. She has done much film work on both sides of the Atlantic, yet to British audiences this elegant actress is perhaps best known for the long-running series *Don't Wait Up* (October 1983, just before TR Saturn crossed the Ascendant, to March 1990), which also starred Nigel Havers (qv).

Jean Shrimpton

> ✪ b. 6 November 1942, 08.30 GWT, High Wycombe, England, 51N38, 0W46.
> Sally Davis q. Jean Shrimpton: An Autobiography. RR: B.

Shrimpton, known as The Shrimp, was a famous model in the 60s, often snapped by David Bailey.

Derek Shulman

> b. 11 February 1947, 03.05 GMT, Edinburgh, Scotland, 55N57, 03W12.
> Gerard q. BC (Derrick Victor Shulman). RR: AA.

With his brother Phil Shulman (qv) he formed Gentle Giant, a pop-soul band, in 1970. The group split in 1980.

Phil Shulman

> b. 27 August 1937, 05.20 GDT, Edinburgh, Scotland, 55N57, 03W12.
> Gerard q. BC (Philip Arthur Shulman). RR: AA.

Formed Gentle Giant with brother Derek Shulman (qv). His departure in the late 70s sounded the death knell for the group.

Alastair Sim

> b. 9 October 1900, 01.00 GMT, Edinburgh, Scotland, 55N57, 03W13.
> Gerard q. BC (Alastair George Bell Sim). RR: AA.

Sim was an elocution lecturer at Edinburgh University from 1925 until his stage debut on 19 May 1930. He made his film debut in 1935 and was best known for menacing and eccentric characters, including the headmistress of *St Trinian's* in a couple of films. D. 19 August 1976, cancer.

Jean Simmons

> 🐚 b. 31 January 1929, 20.00 GMT, London, England, 51N30, 0W10.
> Grazia Bordoni q. Marc Penfield, original source not known. RR: C.

Graceful film star from 14 in *Give Us the Moon* (1944) when she was picked out of a group of dance students. *Great Expectations* (1946) and *Hamlet* (1948) made her a much respected star.

SIMPLE MINDS

A leading live band (from their debut on 17 July 1978), Simple Minds did not hit the commercial big time until May 1985 with the release of *Don't You (Forget About Me)*, a chart-topper in America. The album *Once Upon a Time* debuted at #1 in UK in November 1985. McGee was replaced by Hyslop in August 1981. On 5 May 1984 Kerr married singer Chrissie Hynde*. He later married Patsy Kensit (b. 4 March 1968, London) on 3 January 1992 (TR Neptune opposite Sun, TR Jupiter on Ascendant). The band made a comeback tour in 2002, released a single, *Cry*, in March and an album in April.

Charlie Burchill

> b. 27 November 1959, 23.35 GMT, Glasgow, Scotland, 55N50, 04W14.
> Gerard q. BC (Charles Burchill). RR: AA.

Derek Forbes

> b. 22 June 1956, 15.40 GDT, Maternity Hospital, Glasgow, Scotland, 55N51, 04W14.
> Gerard q. BC. RR: AA.

---

* Chrissie Hynde b. 7 September 1951, 10.20 EDT, Akron, Ohio, 41N05, 81W31. FCC q. BC in hand (Christine Ellen Hynde). RR: AA.

Kenny Hyslop
> b. 14 February 1951, 05.15 GMT, Bholm, Helensburgh, Scotland, 56N00, 04W43.
> Gerard q. BC (Kenneth John Hyslop). RR: AA.

Jim Kerr
> b. 9 July 1959, 10.45 GDT, Glasgow, Scotland, 55N51, 04W16.
> Paul Wright q. BC. RR: AA.

Mick MacNeil
> b. 20 July 1958, 09.00 GDT, Govan, Glasgow, Scotland, 55N51, 04W17.
> Gerard q. BC (Michael Joseph MacNeil). RR: AA.

Brian McGee
> b. 8 March 1959, 15.15 GMT, Robroyston Hospital, Glasgow, Scotland, 55N54, 04W11.
> Gerard q. BC. RR: AA.

Alan Simpson
> b. 27 November 1929, 00.40 GMT, Brixton, London, England, 51N28, 0W06.
> David Fisher q. his agent, July 1986, information from Simpson. RR: A.

Premier comedy writer of such series as *Casanova* (September 1973). With Ray Galton he wrote *Citizen James* (November 1960), 102 radio editions of *Hancock's Half Hour* (November 1954 to December 1959), and TV's *Steptoe and Son* (January 1962 to December 1974).

Bill Simpson
> b. 11 September 1931, 00.08 GDT, Ayr, Scotland, 55N28, 04W37.
> Gerard q. BC (William Nicholson Simpson). RR: AA.

Newscaster before winning a role in TV's *Z Cars*. He played the lead from August 1962 (TR Uranus, MC ruler, conjunct Moon) to January 1971 in *Doctor Finlay's Casebook* for 191 episodes. After the series ended he was newsworthy for his personal life and battles with alcohol rather than for new acting roles.

Joan Sims
> ♣ b. 9 May 1930, 15.15 GDT, Laindon, England, 51N34, 0E26.
> Date and place from Who's Who in the Theatre, time calculated from Ascendant degree in a TV
> Times article by Roger Elliot. RR: C.

Actress best known for her work (and wicked laugh) in two dozen *Carry On* films, usually playing shrewish women intent on keeping their husbands away from nubile young females.

Zetta Sinclair
> b. 12 May 1920, 17.30 GDT, Buckie, Scotland, 57N41, 02W58.
> Gerard q. BC (Georzetta Sinclair). RR: AA.

Mother of Isla St. Clair (qv) and a writer, singer and poet in her own right. Born into a deeply religious family she showed early promise as a creative writer, despite battling many illnesses in childhood. The first of her three marriages lasted from 1939 to 1955. In 1961, already a keen songwriter expressing her understanding of the human condition (MC ruler Moon in Pisces conjunct Uranus), Sinclair became a founding member of a folk club in Aberdeen and introduced her daughter to folk music and performing. D. 29 December 1995, Banbury.

Valerie Singleton
> b. 9 April 1937, 23.45 GMT, Hitchin, England, 51N57, 0W17.
> FCC q. her, from her parents. RR: A.

Singleton is best known for her pioneering tenure on the children's show *Blue Peter* (once travelling on safari with Princess Anne) from 5 September 1962 to 28 September 1972. She has been awarded the OBE for broadcasting. Singleton quit Radio 4's PM programme in April 1993 and moved into TV quiz show hosting. She was once engaged to Pete Murray (qv). (*Blue Peter's* first programme aired on 16 October 1958, 17.00 GMT, London, England. Robert Nunn q. a letter from the BBC show, 19

January 1990. RR: A. Singleton's Sun is on the show's Ascendant, her Ascendant on the show's Moon, and her MC on the show's Venus – show and presenter are inextricably linked. In fact all of the *Blue Peter* presenters profiled in his book – Sarah Greene, John Leslie, Anthea Turner – have remarkable links to the show that made them famous.)

Peter Skellern
b. 14 March 1947, 23.00 GMT, Bury, Lancashire, England, 53N36, 02W17.
From his father "about 11.00 pm" (Pamela Crane rectified this to 10.45 pm). RR: A.
Entertainer known for his homely love songs and for fusing classical and popular sounds on record. In October 1972 he had his only major chart success in the UK, *You're a Lady*. He has also written for TV and in 1983 hosted a chat show.

Frank Skinner
✪ b. 28 January 1957, 17.15 GMT, West Bromwich, England, 52N31, 01W56.
From his autobiography Frank Skinner (Hodder & Stoughton, 2001), p. 10. RR: B.

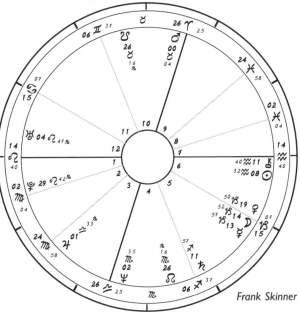

Frank Skinner

Comic Skinner (Christopher Collins), with a self-confessed chip on his shoulder, left school with ambitions to be a pop star. Instead he moved into a factory job before fighting his way out of his impoverished background (Mars-MC) and returning to education. After earning two degrees he spent three and a half years on the dole, spending much of his time drinking (Mars opposes Neptune on the IC, which squared Sun). In his best-selling autobiography he spoke of his years as an alcoholic – not as the worst time of his life, but as one of the best. He quit drinking on 24 September 1986 (two months before his Saturn Return), returned to the Roman Catholic Church, and left his long-time girlfriend. He moved into stand-up comedy, keeping it a secret from his family, and had his first gig on 9 December 1987 and first TV appearance in May 1988 (as TR Jupiter moved into the EQHS 10th). In August 1990 he supported Steve Coogan at the Edinburgh Festival and his reputation grew. Critics liked his old-fashioned, simple approach to joke telling, which proved an alternative to alternative comedy. In 1990 Skinner met comedian David Baddiel at a comedy club. Together they created *Fantasy Football League*, which led to BBC interest in their own series. They wrote the Summer 1996 football song for England. Skinner signed a deal with ITV, reputedly for £3 million a year, for his own chat show.

Carol Smillie
✪ b. 23 December 1961, 17.30 GMT, Maternity Hospital, Glagsow, Scotland, 55N51, 04W14.
Gerard q. BC (Carol Patricia Smillie). RR: AA.
TV presenter and Mensa-member who is known for her megawatt grin and chirpy disposition. Smillie beat 5000 other hopefuls to the job of co-hosting *Wheel of Fortune* in 1989. Later she hosted *Holiday Snaps* and the highly successful *Changing Rooms* (over 100 episodes) – note domestic Moon rises in its ruling sign of Cancer, giving her a girl-next-door appeal to both sexes. Smillie, who is married with three children, is attractive to men without being threatening to women. Smillie is known to be ambitious and extremely hygiene-conscious.

James Smillie

b. 28 November 1944, 21.00 GDT, Springburn, Glagsow, Scotland, 55N53, 04W14.

Gerard q. BC (James Fergus Smillie). RR: AA.

Actor of stage and TV. Smillie emigrated to Australia as a child and later worked on the Australian version of *Crackerjack*. In 1972 he returned to Britain and acted in *Z Cars* and *General Hospital* before moving back to Australia and winning a 13-week role on the cult soap *Prisoner: Cell Block H*. Since then Smillie has continued to work in both countries and starred in the lavish mini-series *Return to Eden* with Rebecca Gilling (qv, Australian Data) in September 1983 (TR Jupiter and Uranus conjunct Sun) and its sequel in February 1986 (TR Saturn conjunct Sun). Both *Edens* made him a recognisable face on TV.

Mandy Smith

b. 17 July 1970, 14.30 MET, Hackney, London, England, 51N33, 0W03.

Greg Young q. Mandy Smith to Russell Grant. RR: A.

A tabloid ran an exclusive interview on 3 August 1986 (as TR Pluto crossed her Ascendant), in which Smith revealed her two and a half year affair with Rolling Stone Bill Wyman (qv). She also battled through enormous media intrusion and speculation over her possible anorexia (Moon square Uranus). But with Scorpio Rising and a prominent Jupiter and Mars, she survived public disapproval and ridicule. Although she split with Wyman they reconciled and married on 2 June 1989. The union lasted until 24 November 1992. During their on-off relationship she wanted him tried in court for child abuse. She married again from 1993 until 1995. On 9 May 2001 she gave birth to a son. Smith had an unsettling childhood – her father abandoned her when she was three and her mother was ill through much of Mandy's early life. Smith's health has also been fragile since adolescence and she has fought depression.

David Sneddon

✪ *b. 15 September 1978, 18.46 GDT, Maternity Hospital, Paisley, Scotland, 55N51, 04W23.*

Gerard q. BC. RR: AA.

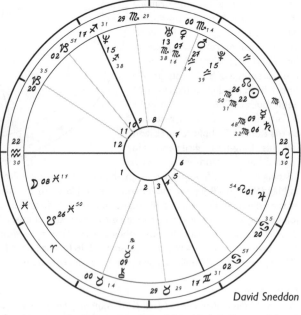

David Sneddon

After seven years of struggling for success, singer-songwriter-pianist David Sneddon became an instant star when he won BBC's TV reality show *Fame Academy*. The show began on 4 October but Sneddon lost the vote to take the final place in the house, where students were trained to sing for their supper. When a student dropped out, he joined the group on 15 October and began to make an impact. Eight weeks later, on 13 December 2002 (TR Pluto on MC), Sneddon emerged triumphant with 3.5 million votes. On 13 January his debut single *Stop Living the Lie* was released and went straight to #1. An album and follow-up were released in April 2003. With MC ruler Jupiter natally in 6th and no Pluto contacts to Moon or Mercury, Sneddon may be best remembered for this brief burst of fame.

Jimmy Somerville

b. 22 June 1961, 15.20, Possil Road, Glasgow, Scotland, 55N52, 04W16.

FCC q. BC (James William Somerville). RR: AA.

Somerville formed Bronski Beat in February 1984 and released a handful of popular hits, including a revival of *I Feel Love/Love to Love You Baby* with Marc Almond (qv). Leaving the group he formed Communards in June 1985 and that October the band released a single, *You Are My World*. They recorded a debut album later that year. A chance meeting with Sarah Jane Morris (qv) at a fund-raising event led to a musical partnership which saw a change in the band's fortunes. Morris's accompaniment on the disco standard *Don't Leave Me This Way* (her husky tones complementing his intriguing falsetto) topped the charts in September 1986 and became the best-selling single of the year. The live antics of the diminutive Somerville and statuesque Morris were a major part of the band's appeal. Communards never fully recovered from Morris's departure after an American tour in 1987, and Somerville went solo with a number of chart hits. The highest profile gay man in the UK at the time, who was once memorably

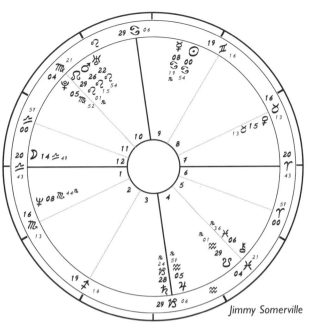

Jimmy Somerville

described as resembling an angry baked bean, Somerville was attacked and beaten up in the street on 1 January 1988. Somerville moved to San Francisco but after personal tragedies (as Uranus moved over his IC) he returned to make England his permanent base in 1996.

Sonia

b. 13 February 1971, 14.30 MET, Liverpool, 53N25, 02W55.
From her to FCC via a private source. RR: A.

Sonia first appeared in the BBC comedy *Bread* (as sex-mad Carmen) before gate-crashing Pete Waterman's live music show and demanding to be signed to his label. She won a record contract and her first hit was *You'll Never Stop Me From Loving You*, a #1 hit in July 1989 with sales of over 350,000 copies. Sonia garnered five hits from her debut album but three years later sued Peter Waterman for withheld royalties. Later she represented Britain in the 1993 Eurovision Song Contest (coming second), appeared for a year in the musical *Grease* (until April 1995) and from March 1996 toured the UK with Irene Cara and Felice Arena in the musical revue *What a Feeling!* From 8 March 2003 she began appearing in the reality TV show *Reborn in the*

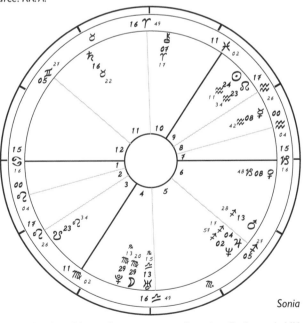

Sonia

USA, performing each week with a host of other 80s performers across America. Each week UK viewers got the chance to decide which star they'd like to send home. After a shaky start and spats with other contestants, Sonia performed well until she was sent home on 5 April. Sonia Evans is married to her tour manager.

SPICE GIRLS

The girl group phenomenon of the 90s began with an advert in The Stage on 13 May 1994. They performed a showcase for record companies on 7 December 1994. On 7 May 1995 they bolted from their creator and linked up with a record company and management agency. By July 1996 their first single, *Wannabe*, had conquered the pop charts worldwide (selling 1.27 million copies in the UK alone). Their Girl Power – with exaggerated personalities and gang-like stance – seized the headlines from Take That and Boyzone and dominated the charts for the next four years. In November 1997 they sacked their manager and began to manage their own careers. The five singers performed their last concert together in May 1998, before Geri Halliwell (qv) cut ties (Moon-Uranus) on 28 May to launch a solo career. The group survived as a quartet for two years. All members have gone on to varied solo careers and Mel C is regarded as the most successful musically, having sold three million albums and notched up a string of Top Ten hits. Her second solo album was released in March 2003. Mel B was married for 16 months to dancer Jimmy Gulzar and had a child Phoenix Chi (b. 19 February 1999, 18.42 GMT, London, 51N30, 0W10). Victoria Beckham (b. 17 April 1975 in Hertfordshire) married football pinup David Beckham and the couple have two children, Brooklyn (b. 4 March 1999, 19.48 GMT, London, England, 51N30, 0W10) and Romeo (b. 1 September 2002, 09.39 GDT, Portland Street, London, England, 51N30, 0W11). (The data of the children are from news reports.)

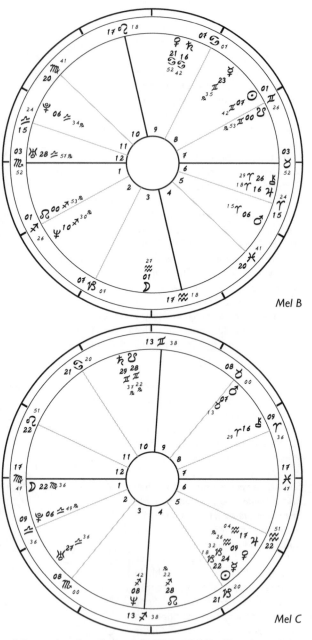

Mel B

Mel C

Mel B

○ b. 29 May 1975, 17.59 GDT, Leeds, England, 53N50, 01W35.
   FCC q. her autobiography *Catch a Fire* (Headline, 2002), p. 20. RR: B.

Mel C

○ b. 12 January 1974, 21.32 GMT, Widnes, England, 53N22, 02W44.
● From Jonathan Cainer's astrology column in *The Express*, 1 March 2000, in which he mentions meeting her. Presumably the data are from her. RR: A?

Jerry Springer

✪ b. 13 February 1944, 22.10 GWT, London, England, 51N30, 0W10.

♠ His autobiography with Laura Morton, Ringmaster (St. Martin's Press, 2000) gives "late on the evening of…" Rectified by FCC. Lois Rodden speculates 20.00. RR: C.

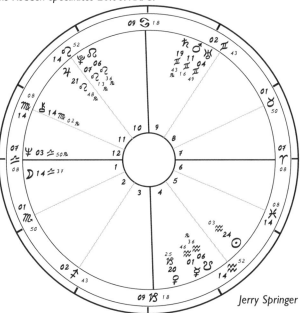

Jerry Springer

A former liberal politician, mayor and news anchor, Springer is the host/ringmaster of The Jerry Springer Show, the violent, confrontational and infamous 'talk show'. Springer was born in war-time London and some relatives were murdered in the holocaust. He and his family moved to Queens, New York in 1949 to start a new life. Springer went to law school to please his parents but politics beckoned. He idolised Democratic hopeful Robert Kennedy (Springer's Venus is on Kennedy's Venus-MC-Jupiter) and went into a deep depression when his hero was murdered on 5 June 1968. On 25 November 1969 Springer announced his candidacy for the Democratic nomination for Congress. Called up for 6 month service three days later, nevertheless he returned to win the nomination but lost the battle for Congress. In June 1970 he announced his intention to run for city council in Cincinnati and won on 1 December 1971, but almost immediately began upsetting people with his anti-war stance. Yet he was reelected two years later, becoming Cincinnati's popular public crusader and known for staging outrageous stunts to publicise his political causes. Springer's personal charm and charisma had people empathising with him, even though he always felt an outsider. In April 1974 he was about to be exposed as a client of prostitutes in Kentucky. Shattered by the revelations he resigned in late May and resumed his work as a lawyer. His indiscretion became part of local folk lore when he re-campaigned for city council in late 1975. He lost but was elected Cincinnati's youngest ever mayor in 1977. In December 1981 he resigned to run in the primary for Governor of Ohio but upon his loss moved into TV as a political news commentator, making his debut on 2 November 1982. By 1987 he was regularly voted best anchor in Cincinnati and picked up numerous Emmy Awards. In 1991 Springer, his own talk show, aired without controversy but by 1994 the show had a new angle, targeting the teenage viewers with its Friday night fraternity party stance. Soon Springer was the undisputed King of TV Sleaze. The host has become adept at justifying the show's own form of morality, although the programme has now been toned down considerably. In May 1998 a newspaper reported an alleged dalliance with a porn actress and her step-mother, casting Springer once again in the role of adulterer. Springer married on 16 June 1973 and the couple's disabled daughter was born in July 1976.

Isla St. Clair

b. 2 May 1952, 16.10 GDT, Bank Street, Grangemouth, Scotland, 56N01, 03W44.

Gerard q. BC (Isabella Margaret Dyce). RR: AA.

Making a first television appearance at 12, St. Clair was given her own radio show the following year. She was brought up with a close awareness of Scottish folk singing and was popular as a singer herself. She began a short teenage romance with fiddler Aly Bain (qv) from April 1967. From the ages of 18 to 22 she was romantically involved with singer Hamish Bayn. Isla's big TV break came in 1978 when she was chosen to co-present The Generation Game with Larry Grayson (qv), which she did until 1982. Her mother Zetta Sinclair (qv) died on 29 December 1995, and before her mother's death, Isla recorded Sinclair's work in the Radio Two series Tatties and Herrin'.

Terence Stamp

b. 22 July 1938, 12.00 Noon GDT, Stepney, London, England, 51N31, 0W02.

FCC q. him, February 1997. RR: A.

Intense, smooth actor, a star from his screen debut in 1961 as the martyr in *Billy Budd* (released in the USA in October 1962). Stamp had worked as a visualiser in an advertising agency before winning a drama scholarship. His menacing stellium in the 10th House enabled him to play a psychotic in *The Collector* in 1965 and other intense, dangerous characters. A self-confessed narcissist who considers himself "remarkably androgynous," Stamp was also dubbed the best-looking man in the world. At the height of his fame, in 1969 he disappeared to India, beginning a self-imposed five year exile (Chiron conjunct MC). In mid-1994 he starred in perhaps his finest comic role, *The Adventures of Priscilla, Queen of the Desert*. In 1993, after

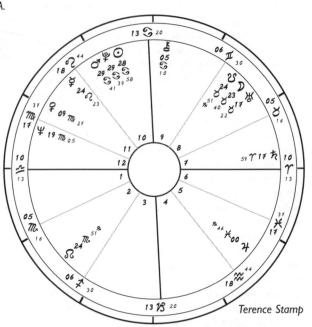

Terence Stamp

years of learning about nutrition and suffering from allergies, Stamp founded a food company, using the powerful aspects in his chart (Moon-Uranus in 8th, Sun-Pluto-Mars conjunction in 10th) to channel his energies into more spiritual pursuits than film-making. On 31 December 2002, after many publicised affairs including one with Jean Shrimpton (qv), Stamp surprised friends and colleagues by getting married to his 23 year old partner of five years.

John Stapleton

b. 24 February 1946, 23.00 GMT, Oldham, England, 53N33, 02W07.

FCC q. him, from his parents. RR: A.

Stapleton began as a journalist on the *Oldham Evening Chronicle* and joined the team of *This is Your Life* at Thames Television in 1970. He worked on *Nationwide* (1975-80), *Panorama* (1980-1) and *Watchdog* (1983-91) before winning his own TV morning talk show, *The Time The Place*, in 1993 (stellium in EQHS 5th, co-ruler of 5th is conjunct Ascendant). In 1999 he joined GMTV. He has been married to Lynn Faulds Wood (qv) since 1977 and they had a son on 15 October 1987. Wood was diagnosed with colon cancer on 22 February 1991 (TR Saturn on EQHS 4th). She was given the all-clear in Summer 1996. In the early days of their partnership Stapleton was anorexic (note the Moon in 2nd opposite Uranus).

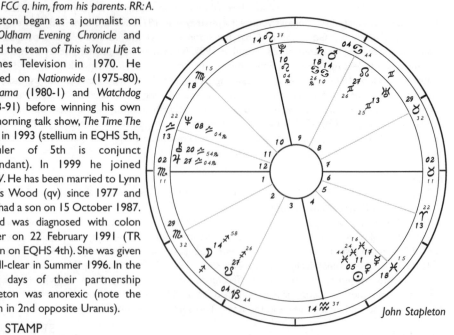

John Stapleton

Ringo Starr – see The Beatles

Alison Steadman

b. 26 August 1946, 02.30 GDT, Liverpool, England, 53N25, 02W55.
FCC q. her. RR: A.

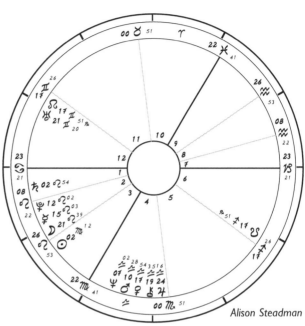

Alison Steadman

Top-notch actress who has been an audience favourite since the mid-70s, and although versatile is adept at playing women who are suburban monsters – common, loud and lewd. Steadman's talent of mastering the minutiae of mannerisms (Sun in Virgo) is legendary and has won her many top acting honours. She is a remarkable observer of people and excellent at capturing accents. The pretentious vamp Beverly in the improvisation-based play *Abigail's Party* (which opened in April 1977 and was directed by husband Mike Leigh) made her famous and won her an Evening Standard Award. A film of the play was transmitted on 1 November 1977 yet it was a repeat showing of this BBC teleplay in October 1979 (TR Jupiter conjunct Sun), during an ITV strike and watched by 16 million viewers, that finally stamped the character onto the public's consciousness with such impact that audiences still link Steadman most frequently with that role (the actress has Moon and Mercury conjunct Pluto). *Nuts in May* showed yet another side to her acting talents, as social satirist Leigh once again helped to bring her Virgo side (and his Virgo Moon) to the fore. Steadman won an Olivier Award for *The Rise and Fall of Little Voice* (1993) and acclaim for *The Singing Detective* (November to December 1986). She earned rave reviews for the play *Marvin's Room* but it closed after five weeks in October 1993. Steadman appeared on TV in *No Bananas* with Stephanie Beacham (qv) from May 1996. She was a regular member on TV's *Z Cars* in the 70s and played Mrs Bennet in the BBC's *Pride and Prejudice* (1995) as TR Saturn crossed her MC. Alternating from shy to confident (the Virgo and Leo sides), Steadman faced with dignity and honesty the storm of media intrusion into the collapse of her marriage. Her 20-year personal and professional (six projects from 1972) partnership with Mike Leigh was mutually satisfying because of their similar sense of humour and career goals, despite his infamous black moods from stress. The were married in September 1973 but broke up in April 1996 (TR Pluto square Sun), a few months after she had nursed her dying mother who was stricken with cancer (TR Saturn conjunct MC). Steadman continues to choose excellent TV roles and is often on the stage.

Tommy Steele

b. 17 December 1936, 19.30 GMT, Bermondsey, London, England, 51N30, 0W05.
Margaret Dunford q. Steele to a mutual friend, David Rees. RR: A.

Tommy Steele was discovered in July 1956, released his first hit that November and topped the charts in January 1957 with *Singing the Blues*. He was a sensation, provoking mass teen hysteria (note EQHS 5th ruler Jupiter conjunct Sun in 5th). The pop star graduated to family entertainer the following year as his record sales declined (TR Uranus on Ascendant). He married in June 1960 (engaged from June 1958) and had a final chart hit in August 1961, when TR Neptune crossed his EQHS 4th. A variety entertainer in the early 60s, Steele moved onto the stage for dramatic and musical productions (including *Half a Sixpence*, West End from 1963 for 18 months as TR Jupiter crossed his MC, and Broadway from April 1965). He had a long-running one-

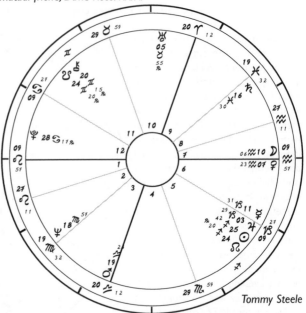

Tommy Steele

man show in the West End during 1979-80 (when TR Jupiter travelled through his 1st House) and the Variety Club named him Entertainer of the Year. He published his first novel, a thriller, in the 80s before returning in 1992 to the stage for a poorly received show, *Some Like it Hot*.

STEPS

Influenced by Abba, this pop group of singing trolley-dollies was formed after a series of auditions from Spring 1997, and later moulded by pop producer Pete Waterman. After an initial release in November 1997, Steps had 13 consecutive Top Five singles in five years, including a million-seller with *Heartbeat/Tragedy* (#1 in January 1999), and they even had their own TV show. Fans loved their easy-to-follow dance routines and sunny, cheeky personalities. An album *Steptacular* shifted two million units in the UK. The band announced their split on 26 December 2001. H (b. Ian Watkins, 8 May 1976, Llwyniphia, Wales) and Claire began a singing partnership, while Lee moved on to play in the musical *Grease* and appear in the soap *Crossroads*. Fay Tozer launched a solo career.

Lee Latchford Evans

⊘ b. 28 January 1975, 05.25 GMT, Chester, England, 53N12, 02W54.
Sy Scholfield q. data from Steps' official website. RR: B.

Claire Richards

⊘ b. 17 August 1977, 01.30 GDT, Hillingdon, Middlesex, England, 51N32, 0W27.
Sy Scholfield q. data from Steps' official website. RR: B.

Lisa Scott-Lee

⊘ b. 5 November 1975, 08.20 GMT, St. Asaph, Wales, 53N16, 03W26.
Sy Scholfield q. data from Steps' official website. RR: B.

Faye Tozer

⊘ b. 14 November 1975, 05.30 GMT, Northampton, England, 52N14, 0W54.
Sy Scholfield q. data from Steps' official website. RR: B.

Cat Stevens (Yusef Islam)

b. 21 July 1948, 12.00 Noon GDT, London, England, 51N30, 0W10.

Ruth Dewey q. Richard West, "from him." RR: A.

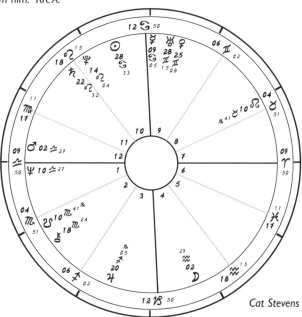

Cat Stevens

Solo singer, guitarist and eloquent songwriter of the powerfully simple song. Trained in the family restaurant business (Cancer MC), Stevens followed instead his passion for music. After an initial release in October 1966, Stevens scored his first hit in January 1967, the #2 hit *Matthew and Son*. Further hits followed that year until he was diagnosed with T.B. and depression in March 1968. One year later he had new songs, a new manager and a more positive outlook. He returned to the music charts in April 1970 and a new album, *Tea for the Tillerman*, in November 1970 (following TR Uranus on his Ascendant) established him worldwide. But by July 1973 his *Foreigner* album had alienated critics. The following year he was made a goodwill ambassador for UNICEF. His life changed in Autumn 1975 when he almost drowned in Malibu (TR Pluto conjunct Ascendant, TR Saturn conjunct Sun). He promised to repay God for saving his life. In early 1977 he travelled to Jerusalem but he was still torn between fame and faith. On 23 December 1977 he embraced Islam and changed his name. By May 1978 (his Saturn Return) the Cat Stevens era was over and he gave a final performance for charity on 22 November 1979 (TR Neptune conjunct Jupiter – suggesting the dissolution of his celebrity image). He was in the news in 1983 when he helped to create a Muslim school, but was unwittingly drawn into a controversy in February and March 1989 when Salman Rushdie was sentenced to death for writing *The Satanic Verses*. The Press turned against him, misinterpreting his views on the subject (as TR Saturn conjunct EQHS 4th, opposed Mercury and then conjunct the IC, and TR Neptune moved over the IC). Before the Gulf War in 1991 he flew to Baghdad attempting to secure the freedom of hostages by adding his voice to the call for change. On 15 November 1997 he drew world attention to the plight of the Bosnian people with his first live performance in two decades. Neptune on the Ascendant has brought some controversy yet he has been able to communicate his various forms of spirituality to a wide audience. Yusef Islam married on 7 September 1979.

Savourna Stevenson

b. 14 March 1961, 02.50 GMT, West Linton, Scotland, 55N45, 03W21.

Gerard q. BC (Ella Savourna Stevenson). RR: AA.

Versatile harpist and composer of jazz, world music and classical styles for theatre, radio and television (Uranus opposes Moon and Mercury in Aquarius).

Andy Stewart

b. 30 December 1933, 15.15 GMT, Redlands Hospital, Glagsow, Scotland, 55N53, 04W17.

Gerard q. BC (Andrew Stewart). RR: AA.

Comedian and impressionist who made his first appearance at the Edinburgh Fringe. He had his own Scottish TV series, *White Heather Club* (1960). Stewart was known for welcoming in the New Year, year after year, after year!

Belle Stewart

    b. 17 May 1906, 02.00 GMT, Dundee, Scotland, 56N28, 02W59.

    Gerard q. BC (Bella Smeaton Stewart). RR: AA.

Traditional singer who made many performances at international folk festivals. Married in 1925, she had nine children.

Dave Stewart – see Annie Lennox
Ian Stewart – see Rolling Stones

Jeff Stewart

    b. 28 October 1955, 17.00 GMT, Aberdeen, Scotland, 57N09, 02W07.

    Gerard q. BC (Jeffrey James Palmer Stewart). RR: AA.

Stewart was a bit-part player (credits include *Crossroads, Minder, Doctor Who* and *Reilly – Ace of Spies*) before winning a leading role in the TV drama *The Bill* (a series which began in October 1984) as PC Reg Hollis.

Rod Stewart

★   *b. 10 January 1945, 01.05 GDT, Highgate, London, England, 51N34, 0W09.*

●   *Dana Haynes q. Stewart for "just after the pubs closed" (apparently after 01.00). (N.B. Previously Debbi Kempton Smith q. a time of 01.17, rectified by an astrologer friend of Stewart's.) RR: C.*

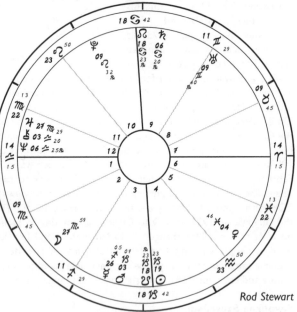

Rod Stewart

A former grave-digger at Highgate Cemetery and an apprentice at Brentford Football Club, Stewart became a leading rock star of the 70s. His voice was described as "velvet on sandpaper." In 1964, three days before his birthday, Long John Baldry heard him humming at a train station and hired him. A first single was released that September. Although he played his first major gig with his band the Soul Agents in Harrow on 19 February 1965, Stewart hit the big time six years later as a soloist after stints with the Jeff Beck Group (from March 1967) and the Faces (a first album was released in February 1970). In October 1971 his solo album *Every Picture Tells a Story* was released and the track *Maggie May* became a smash (topping the UK and US charts in November 1971). On 5 March 1975 he began an affair with actress Britt Ekland (for her data see The Goons) and relocated to America. Over the next 20 years his sexual escapades would keep tabloids busy. Later that year, in September, he scored another massive hit with *Sailing*. In 1979 *Do Ya Think I'm Sexy* hit the top of the charts but damaged his credibility. Further hits appeared in June 1983 and July 1986. He had a career resurgence with an *Unplugged* performance in 1993. Stewart was married to Alana Collins Hamilton* (ex-wife of George Hamilton) for four years from 1979. His nine-year marriage to model Rachel Hunter collapsed in January 1999. The couple have two children.

---

*Alana Stewart b. 18 May 1945, 15.15 PWT, San Diego, California, 32N43, 117W10. Lynne Palmer q. her. RR: A.

Sting

b. 2 October 1951, 01.30 GDT, Wallsend, England, 55N00, 01W31.

Arthyr Chadbourne q. him. RR: A.

Singer, songwriter and actor, former lead singer and bassist with the band Police. The band formed in January 1977 and their debut album followed in November 1978 (TR Jupiter near Ascendant, and TR Pluto conjunct IC). Between September 1979 and June 1983 Police had five British chart-toppers, the last of them, *Every Breath You Take*, being among the world's best-selling singles of 1983. The trio officially disbanded in late 1984 (and would reform in March 2003 for a one-off concert to celebrate their entry into the Rock 'n' Roll Hall of Fame). In June 1985 Sting released the solo single *If You Love Somebody Set Them Free*, together with a best-selling album. His first major acting role came in

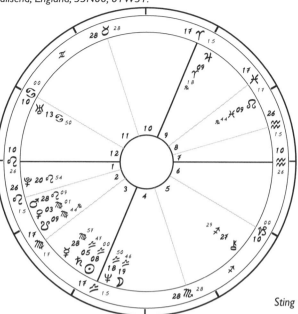

Sting

Brimstone and Treacle (a solo single from the TV film charted in September 1982) and he later appeared briefly in *Dune* (1984), but his acting has never been acclaimed. His forthright concerns for amnesty and ecological issues are well known (Uranus is the key player in a T-square, and the Moon-Neptune has been put to good use), as is his legendary Leo Rising vanity and ego (aided by a prominent Jupiter). Sting helped to raise £21 million for the rainforest. Before his music fame he was a champion athlete at school and had jobs as a filing clerk with the Inland Revenue before becoming a teacher in Autumn 1971. He married for the second time on 20 August 1992 (his first marriage had ended in September 1982) and has six children. In 1995 he was robbed of £6 million by his accountant. Besides his music and fundraising, he's remembered for boasting of his five hour tantric sex sessions! In February 2003 *The Mail on Sunday's Rich Report* estimated his fortune at £158 million.

"Did I have a happy childhood? It was stimulating... I had the streets to myself. It was a great environment for a daydreamer, which is basically what I am. And that is still the landscape of my dreams... I am from Newcastle, but not of it. You can't identify me. I belong in the world and I like that freedom. I have a very nomadic life. 'Rootless' sounds pejorative, but it's probably closer to our history." (Sting, *Radio Times*, 30/10/99)

Miriam Stoppard

b. 12 May 1937, 05.00 GDT, Newcastle-on-Tyne, England, 54N59, 01W35.

David Fisher q. her letter. RR: A.

High achiever Dr. Miriam Stoppard became a TV personality in the 70s and later hosted the medical advice show *Where There's Life* (1981-9). In late 1990 her marriage to playwright Tom Stoppard was under threat when the Press linked him to actress Felicity Kendal. The Stoppards separated in 1991. A respected medical expert, Miriam Stoppard has written a string of health books and was a columnist for the *TV Times* magazine.

Peter Stringfellow

b. 17 October 1940, 09.45 GDT, Sheffield, England, 53N23, 01W30.

Brian Kelly q. him. RR: A.

Night-club owner, ubiquitous TV guest and a cocky exhibitionist. Stringfellow has boasted of his romantic attachments with teenage girls and his voracious libido (2000 lovers and counting – if the

Libra-Scorpio combination does not move into politics or psychology, it invariably deals with sex on a regular basis!). Brought up in a supportive and loving family, he founded clubs in Sheffield, Leeds and Manchester from the age of 22, before moving to London in 1980. He was married for two years from December 1960. His second marriage (1967) lasted until 1989 and the union produced a son in January 1966. His autobiography *King of Clubs* was published in September 1996 by Little Brown.

Hamish Stuart – see Average White Band
Molly Sugden – see John Inman

Stu Sutcliffe
   b. 23 June 1940, 23.25 GDT, Simpson Memorial Maternity Pavilion, Edinburgh, Scotland, 55N57, 03W12.
   Gerard q. BC (Stuart Fergusson Victor Sutcliffe). RR: AA.
A member of The Beatles (qv), on bass from January 1960. He was ill from late 1960 and replaced in the band. D. 10 April 1962, brain haemorrhage (Mercury, ruling and placed in EQHS 6th, conjunct Pluto; Mercury-Pluto contacts are often prominent in the charts of victims of strokes/haemorrhages, either natally, by transit or direction).

Gavin Sutherland
   b. 6 October 1951, 00.20 GDT, Grange Gardens, Peterhead, Scotland, 57N30, 01W46.
   Gerard q. BC (Gavin Maurice Sutherland). RR: AA.
With his brother Iain, Gavin Sutherland was signed to a recording contract in 1972 to produce a brand of folk-based pop. The Sutherland Brothers composed Rod Stewart's (qv) massive chart hit *Sailing*. They hit the Top Five in May 1976 with *Arms of Mary*.

Kiefer Sutherland
   b. 21 December 1966, 09.00 GMT, St. Marylebone, London, England, 51N31, 0W09.
   FCC q. BC in hand (a twin, Keefer William Frederick Dempsey George Rufus Sutherland). RR: AA.

Misunderstood youths and close-to-the-edge characters are the stock in trade of actor Kiefer Sutherland, son of film star and political activist Donald Sutherland*. With a film debut in 1983, and a lead in *The Bay Boy* the following year under his belt, he moved to New York but rejected a role in a soap opera and suffered a year's unemployment. Modelling opportunities brought him back to the film arena and he quickly built an impressive volume of work, including appearances in *Stand By Me* (August 1986), *The Lost Boys* (1987) and the thriller *Flatliners* (1990). He married in September 1987 and was later engaged to temperamental and unlucky-in-love actress Julia Roberts**. Roberts shocked him when she cancelled

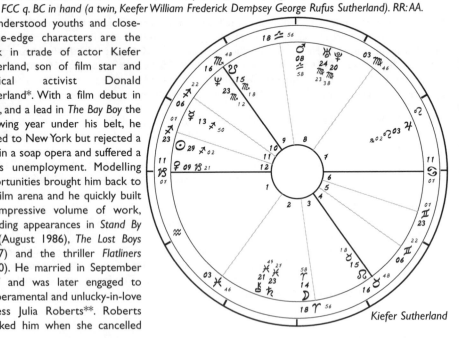

Kiefer Sutherland

* Donald Sutherland b. 17 July 1935, 11.30 ADT (+3), Saint John, New Brunswick, Canada, 45N16, 66W03. Mark Johnson q. him. RR: A.
** Julia Roberts b. 28 October 1967, 00.16 EDT (+4), Atlanta, Georgia, 33N45, 84W23. Lois Rodden q. BC. RR: AA.

the wedding on 11 June 1991 (just before TR Uranus conjunct his Ascendant). He married on 1 September 1996 but the couple split on 30 June 1999 and he filed for divorce on 20 March 2000.

Myfanwy Talog – see David Jason

Jimmy Tarbuck
◑ *b. 6 February 1940, 14.30 GMT, Liverpool, England, 53N25, 02W55.*
From Roger Elliot in TV Times, original source not known (Marjorie Orr says "early morning"). RR: DD.
A regular quizmaster on TV, Tarbuck is also a popular compere and comedian. He had overnight success from his TV debut in 1963. During the 70s he was one of the most popular faces on British television.

Chris Tarrant
b. 10 October 1946, 19.20 GMT, Reading, England, 51N28, 0W59.
Date from Who's Who on Television, time from Michael Aspel on This Is Your Life, March 1997, with Tarrant as the surprised subject. RR: A.

A former teacher, Tarrant was a presenter on the anarchic Saturday morning children's show *Tiswas*. A non-stop talker with Gemini Rising, he took over a popular slot with London's Capital Radio. He has made his fortune through TV production and voice-overs for adverts. He also presents *Tarrant on TV*, a guide to funny clips from foreign and British television a la Clive James (qv, Australian Data). His career received a huge boost when he fronted the quiz show *Who Wants to be a Millionaire?* from 1998. In late May 1999 (TR Pluto conjunct Descendant, TR Neptune conjunct MC) he was involved in the scandal surrounding the publication of pictures of him and royal bride-to-be Sophie Rhys-Jones. Tarrant was in the headlines when one contestant was convicted (in April 2003) of cheating on *Millionaire* (the infamous episode had been taped on 9 September 2001).

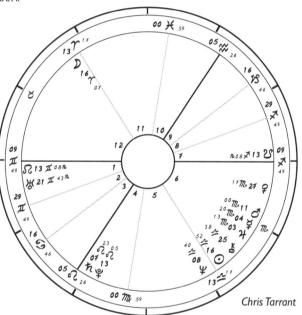

Chris Tarrant

Kathy Tayler
Aries Sun, Leo Rising. From astrologer Russell Grant to her on television. No other details available.
A sporty former presenter of breakfast show *TVam*, Tayler was a one-time athletics champion. More recently she has presented the programme *Holiday*.

Elizabeth Taylor

b. 27 February 1932, 02.00 GMT, Golders Green, England, 51N34, 0W12.

Bob Prince q. her for the time, written on a signed photo (her mother's biography, My Daughter Elizabeth, gives "around 2.00 am"; Alexander Walker's biography, The Life of Elizabeth Taylor, p. 9, gives 02.30). (N.B. The place of birth is often stated incorrectly as Hampstead.) RR: A.

A luminous star with a turbulent and glamorous life. Elizabeth Taylor, her beauty and her numerous marriages (MC in Libra, ruler Venus conjunct Uranus in EQHS 5th) have enchanted fans for six decades. Her enduring relationship with Richard Burton (qv) set the screen alight from June 1963, when they starred in *Cleopatra* (their first scene together was shot on 22 January 1962). A beautiful child with stunning violet eyes, she and her family moved to the US in April 1939. Taylor signed a movie contract with Universal (appearing in *There's One Born Every Minute*), and was then given ballet lessons and groomed for stardom. She was dropped for looking older than her years but moved to MGM where *Lassie Come Home* with Roddy

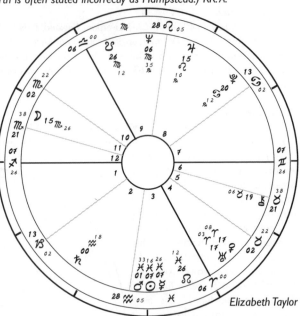

Elizabeth Taylor

McDowell (qv) brought her success. Brought up in an unreal environment and pushed by her stage mother, Taylor continued to make successful films, including *National Velvet* (which she began filming on 4 February 1944), which established her as a child star. She married Conrad Hilton on 6 May 1950, the first of her eight marriages to seven men. She reached her acting zenith when she was awarded an Oscar for *Butterfield 8* (filmed from 4 January 1960, released November 1960) and later gave a bravura performance in *Who's Afraid of Virginia Woolf?* (June 1966). She married producer Mike Todd on 2 February 1957, a decision that was to provoke profound changes in her personal life. The union was tragically cut short on 22 March 1958 when Todd was killed in a plane crash. Taylor incurred the wrath of Hollywood when she sought comfort in the arms of Eddie Fisher (who was married to her friend Debbie Reynolds) and married him in May 1959. Branded a homewrecker, nevertheless the public forgave her when she almost died shortly afterwards. She left Fisher for Richard Burton (during TR Neptune conjunct Moon), whom she married in March 1964 (TR Uranus opposite Sun-Mercury). The relationship was passionate, tempestuous and competitive. It turned toxic ("the Battling Burtons"), sunk by Taylor's battle with drink and painkillers and Burton's self-loathing negativity and addictions (their synastry reveals his Moon on her Neptune and her Moon on his Sun-Saturn). Wilful and restless in relationships (Venus-Uranus), she was known to have a strong sexual appetite (Scorpio Moon) and enjoy conflict with her partners (MC ruler Venus conjuncts Uranus in Aries). Marrying for the eighth time on 6 October 1991, she separated in September 1995 (TR Jupiter on Ascendant) and filed for divorce in February 1996. For the last 30 years her personal life has been the arena in which she has acted out some of her most dramatic storylines. Ill-health, addiction and accidents have stalked this Piscean with Sun opposite Neptune since birth, and Taylor's life reads like a jinx's diary: born with a spine defect (an operation in December 1956, TR Saturn conjunct Ascendant); May 1953 – surgery to save her sight; December 1957 – appendicitis; February 1962 – alleged overdose; December 1973 – ovarian cyst (TR Neptune over Ascendant); December 1983 and November 1988 – drug addiction; March 1994 and May 1995 – hip replacements; November 1959 (TR Pluto opposite Sun) and December 1990 – life threatening pneumonia; and February 1997 – surgery to remove a large benign brain tumour. Yet Taylor has always faced the many tragedies in her life with courage, humour, optimism and a sense of drama (Sagittarius Rising). The young Elizabeth Taylor inspired men's fantasies as a fairytale princess (the Neptune oppositions) and later helped reshape the morals of her age as an opulent star who flouted social conventions (Venus-Uranus). Joseph Mankiewicz said that for Taylor, "Living life was a kind of acting." An instinctive actress, she allowed her audience to see into her soul (the Neptune oppositions). Since her last major film in 1980 Taylor has found career avenues in promoting perfumes and, more importantly, AIDS awareness (those with Sagittarius Rising can do much to break down barriers and unite opposing factions). She is known for choosing friends who fascinate her and is still on a quest for love and adoration (Pisces). With Moon in Scorpio Taylor has always been a loyal friend and loves people she feels are misfits, and has been ready to rescue the defenceless or vulnerable. Her synastry with her famous gay friends is fascinating: James Dean (Ascendants one degree apart), Montgomery Clift (her Piscean planets on his Descendant, her Moon on his Mercury), Roddy McDowall (her Venus-Uranus opposite his Venus-Mercury) and Rock Hudson (her Ascendant on his Moon).

Q "Elizabeth is a lot shrewder than you think. I think her emotional intelligence is really high... her survival instincts are very keen." (Shirley MacLaine, as quoted in TV's *England's Other Elizabeth*)
"[She] can welcome the camera up close and can share [her] emotional intensity and passion very easily in front of the camera.. she had [it] by some kind of natural instinct." (Jeanine Basinger, as quoted in TV's *England's Other Elizabeth*)

TEENAGE FANCLUB
The band produced their first album in 1989 and the following year gave a number of drunken live rock shows. Long-supported by the music Press they have since made little impact on the charts, despite a few hopeful releases.

Norman Blake
> b. 20 October 1965, 05.52 GDT, Maternity Hospital, Bellshill, Scotland, 55N50, 04W01.
> Gerard q. BC (Norman George Blake). RR: AA.

Gerard Love
> b. 31 August 1967, 16.45 GDT, Motherwell, Scotland, 55N47, 03W59.
> Gerard q. BC. RR: AA.

Raymond McGinley
> b. 3 January 1964, 04.35 GMT, Possil Road, Glasgow, Scotland, 51N52, 04W16.
> Gerard q. BC. RR: AA.

Richard Telfer
> b. 9 January 1908, 03.50 GMT, Edinburgh, Scotland, 55N57, 03W10.
> Gerard q. BC (Richard Dodds Telfer). RR: AA.

Musician and teacher. During the 30s he was a regular performer of the Wurlitzer in many leading Edinburgh cinemas. With Alexander Gibson in 1962 he launched and had a major part in building up Scottish Opera, a professional opera company. Telfer retired from a teaching post in 1973 and moved on to lecture at the University of Edinburgh's Extra-Mural Department on opera and musical comedy. D. 22 February 1996.

Joseph Temperley
> b. 20 September 1927, 10.00 GDT, Cowdenbeath, Fife, Scotland, 56N07, 03W21.
> Gerard q. BC. RR: AA.

Versatile jazz saxophonist (Uranus opposite Sun) who moved to London in 1949.

Jake Thackray
> b. 27 February 1938, 23.30 GMT, Leeds, England, 53N50, 01W35.
> Jon Taylor q. him personally. RR: A.

A former English teacher, Thackray was a regular on the consumer show *On the Braden Beat* during the late 60s. An acquired musical taste, he was known for his satirical songs (Scorpio Rising) exploring the quirky side of life (the strong Uranian influence: Uranus on the Descendant, Moon conjunct Jupiter in Aquarius), and performed in an inimitable deadpan manner. Towards the end of his life he had marital and financial problems, eventually declaring bankruptcy. He was found dead at his home on Christmas Eve 2002.

Gerald Thomas – see Carry On Films

Dougie Thompson
> b. 24 March 1951, 06.20 GMT, Redlands Hospital, Glasgow, Scotland, 55N53, 04W17.
> Gerard q. BC (Douglas Campbell Thompson). RR: AA.

Member of rock group Supertramp from the early 70s. In May 1979 the band had a US #1 album for six weeks with *Breakfast in America*.

Emma Thompson – see Kenneth Branagh

Kennedy Thomson
> b. 4 April 1936, 14.30 GMT, Pollokshields, Glasgow, Scotland, 55N50, 04W16.
> Gerard q. BC (James Kennedy W. Thomson). RR: AA.

Continuity announcer for Grampian Television for 26 years (1970-96). He had both stage and teaching experience.

Sybil Thorndike
> b. 24 October 1882, 18.20 GMT, Gainsborough, England, 53N24, 0W46.
> Astrological Quarterly (Spring 1971) and Fowlers state "from her." RR: A.

Memorable stage actress. Thorndike had originally trained as a concert pianist but a broken wrist ended any musical ambitions. Moving into acting in 1903 she joined the Old Vic in 1914. She won acclaim as *Saint Joan* in 1924, a role especially written for her by George Bernard Shaw. Thorndike was unrivalled in her era (her EQHS chart is strongly suggestive of a 'natural' performer: Sun conjunct Mercury – rulers of 3rd and 1st – in the 5th, whilst having the 5th ruler in the 7th, and Moon in 10th, all indications of a loving and appreciative following). D. 9 June 1976.

Angela Thorne
> b. 25 January 1939, 17.20 IST (-5.5 = -5 hrs 30 mins), Karachi, India (now Pakistan), 24N52, 67E03.
> FCC q. her, from her parents. RR: A.

This refined actress is frequently cast as genteel middle-class suburbanites with a feisty streak (Saturn on an Aries MC). Starring with John Wells (qv) she had a year-long run as Margaret Thatcher (see Steve Nallon) in the stage satire *Anyone For Denis?* in 1982. (Thorne has Uranus conjunct MT's Descendant, Jupiter on MT's IC, and her IC falls on MT's Mars – her stage role focused on the PM's marriage and personal life.) Her career peak came with the highly successful series *To the Manor Born* (September 1979 to November 1981) and *Three Up, Two Down* (April 1985 to June 1989). Because her father was often away in the Indian Army (Saturn on MC), Thorne grew to be an independent

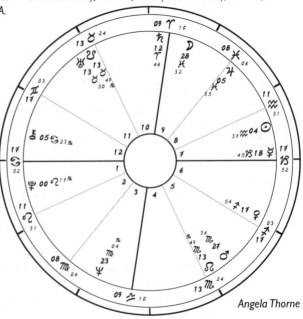

Angela Thorne

individualist (MC in Aries). From age six she was stopped from seeing her mother for eleven years after her parents' divorce (Ascendant ruler Moon in 9th opposite Neptune, ruling 9th).

Frank Thornton – see John Inman

Alan Titchmarsh
✪ b. 2 May 1949, 21.30 GDT, Ilkley, England, 53N55, 01W50.
David Fisher q. him through his assistant. (N.B. His 2002 autobiography Trowel and Error gives 21.00.) RR: A.

Friendly and accessible, Titchmarsh is famous for presenting the entertainment and interview show *Pebble Mill* from 1991 (EQHS 5th ruler Jupiter in 3rd trine MC ruler Mercury), and for his gardening expertise in magazines and on TV (*Gardeners' World* from 1996 and *Ground Force* a year later) – Scorpio Rising, Sun conjunct Venus in Taurus. In 1985 he won a Gold Medal at the Chelsea Flower Show for his country kitchen garden design. In 1998 his first novel, *Mr MacGregor* was published. Three more (plus an autobiography) followed – all were bestsellers. He has more than 30 gardening books to his credit. Two series are scheduled to air in 2003-4, one on the natural history of Britain.

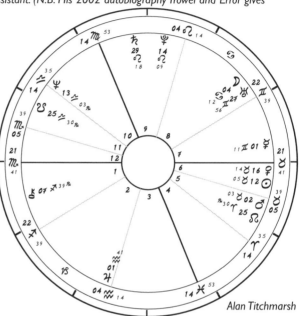

Alan Titchmarsh

TOP OF THE POPS
The dominant TV chart programme during the last 40 years has been *Top of the Pops* (first broadcast on 1 January 1964, 18.36 GMT, Manchester, England, 53N30, 02W15, from the *Daily Express*, 26 December 1988, p. 20, in the article *25 Years of Top of the Pops*). Note the Moon on the Ascendant and Jupiter conjunct the MC. The show celebrated its 2000th episode on 13 September 2002.

Ian and Janette Tough – see The Krankies
Pete Townshend – see Who
Faye Tozer – see Steps

TRAVIS
Rock quartet who first met while studying art in Glasgow. They recorded a demo for £600 and left Glasgow for London in 1996. Their debut album *Good Feeling* hit the Top Ten in 1997. Two years later *The Man Who* was released and, despite being slated by critics, topped the album charts and became the biggest selling album of 1999. A follow-up *The Invisible Band* debuted at #1 in 2001. Fran Healy was born on 23 July 1973 in Stafford (52N48, 02W07) and Andy Dunlop was born on 16 March 1972.

Dougie Payne
✪ b. 14 November 1972, 19.24 GMT, Glasgow, Scotland, 55N52, 04W08.
Gerard q. BC (Douglas William Payne). RR: AA.

Neil Primrose
✪ b. 20 February 1972, 23.10 GMT, Glasgow, Scotland, 55N53, 04W14.
Gerard q. BC (Neil Macdonald Primrose). RR: AA.

Arthur Treacher

b. 21 July 1894, 18.00 GMT, Brighton, England, 50N50, 0W08.

From Wynn's Astrology, January 1945, original source not known. RR: C.

Legally-trained Treacher became a stage actor before moving to Broadway in 1926. He was famous for playing disdainful butlers. He began a second career in 1966 offering a variety of services – from butlering to gardening – on a rental basis. D. 14 December 1975.

Anthea Turner

b. 25 May 1960, 12.30 GDT, Norton, England, 53N20, 02W40.

From Raphael's Almanac 1996 q. her agency (verified by FCC). RR: A.

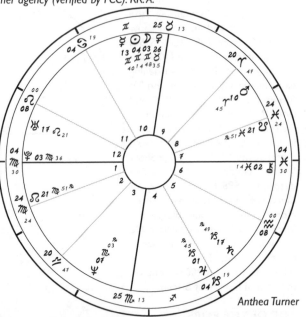

Anthea Turner

Anthea Turner became famous on TV for her light-hearted interview style, freshness and infectious, sunny nature (Gemini Sun and Moon, Venus on MC). These characteristics and her ingenue image, perfect for her stints on breakfast TV and children's programmes, hide a steely determination, ambition and an obsession with perfection (Pluto Rising in Virgo square Sun and Moon). At 18, in 1978, her sister Ruth died after a 15-year battle with spina bifida. Anthea's working life began with the AA Breakdown service before she started reading traffic news at a local radio station – being dyslexic she had to work twice as hard. Turner moved to satellite television, and later to the children's series *Up2U* and *Blue Peter* (from 14 September 1992 to 27 June 1994), where at 32 she was much older than her colleagues. As a TV presenter she struggled to be taken seriously (Venus on MC) but viewers enjoyed her effervescent girl-next-door quality. She married DJ Peter Powell on 31 January 1990 and announced the end of the partnership in early January 1998 (following a TR Pluto opposition to her Sun and Moon). Turner presented the National Lottery show from its inception whilst working each morning on *GMTV*. After two years she relinquished the morning job on 24 December 1996 and moved into various TV jobs and producing fitness videos (Virgo Rising). In 1996 she won two Personality of the Year awards. By 1995 the knives were already out with tabloids dissecting her personality and screen image. But after professional overexposure and a love triangle with new beau Grant Bovey (whom she had fallen for in September 1997, TR Pluto opposite Sun-Moon) and his wife, it was all out war. The affair became public in early 1998 and Bovey returned to his wife in April but returned to Turner in mid-December. She took a sabbatical in 1999 to start a family but failed to become pregnant after five IVF treatments. When the reunited couple married in August 2000 TV's golden girl endured 'trial by tabloid' – attacked for selling her wedding photos for £250,000 and advertising a chocolate bar. As TR Pluto opposed Mercury, work dried up and her popularity plummeted, much to the tabloids' delight.

Q | "I always wanted approval. As you grow up, for some reason you're not supposed to be like that, but the child in me will always be seeking approval, and I'm not ashamed about it... I'm a people-pleaser, which is what this business is about." (Anthea Turner, *Sunday Times Magazine*, 29/7/01)

Dorothy Tutin

b. 8 April 1930, 14.00 GMT, Paddington North, London, England, 51N32, 0W11.
Ruth Hale Oliver q. her for the time. FCC q. BC for other data. RR: A.

Actress of stage and film, known to be immensely critical of herself and protective of her privacy. As one of Britain's finest actresses she delighted audiences as Juliet, and in *Peter Pan*, *The Cherry Orchard* and various Sondheim musicals. Although she had originally left school at 15 to study music, she was pushed by her professionally unfulfilled father into acting and joined RADA. Her first stage appearance was in September 1949 and Tutin joined the Bristol Old Vic in January 1950. After leaving RADA she became a member of the Shakespeare Memorial Theatre Company (later the RSC) in April 1958 (as TR Pluto crossed her Ascendant) and went on to play most of Shakespeare's leading ladies. In April 1953 she opened in

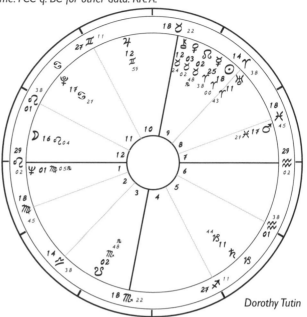

Dorothy Tutin

The Living Room, which proved to be a star-making vehicle (TR Jupiter had just crossed the MC). She married at 32 and both of her children became actors. Tutin, who was made a Dame in the 2000 New Year Honours List, died from leukaemia on 6 August 2001.

> Q
> "A negative film of darkness extends to all aspects of her life... [which] seems to come from an inner dark ogre waiting to pounce... Talking to her would have been a very daunting experience, except that her eyes – soft, sensual and very youthful – reveal quite another side. It took quite a while before she let the inner magic that she uses so skilfully on her audiences to surface." (Angela Levin, *Daily Mail*, 13/4/95)
>
> "The truth is that I hate being out of work. I'm so ashamed and bad at organising my life when I'm not working... I never wanted to act, it was just that my father wanted a daughter on the stage." (Dorothy Tutin, *Daily Mail*, 13/4/95)

Twiggy

○ *b. 19 September 1949, 01.25 GDT, Neasden, London, England, 51N33, 0W16.*
● *Rectified by Penny Thornton in Romancing the Stars, p. 264, "[She] maintains it was in the very early hours of the morning". RR: C.*

The original superwaif, 60s icon, and one of the most photographed women of all time. She was a phenomenon from Summer 1966 for three and a half years with an innocent, girl-next-door quality and effervescent personality. The media frenzy surrounding her was matched only by Beatlemania. She made an acting debut in *The Boy Friend* (filmed late 1970). Her hard-working and professional approach has enabled her to continue in various fields, including a successful stint on Broadway in *My One and Only* (from 1 May 1983). Her personal relationships have often bordered on the abusive and all-encompassing, and stories have been paraded across tabloids. Her first marriage (in June 1977) lasted a rocky six years before her husband, 18 years her senior, suffered a fatal heart attack on 30 November 1983. She remarried on 23 September 1988 and moved back to England in 1993, after a stint on an American sitcom *Princesses*. For a short while she presented *This Morning*, but viewers didn't take to her and she was sacked in October 2001.

Tracey Ullman

b. 30 December 1959, 03.15 GMT, Burnham, England, 51N33, 0W39.

Russell Grant (Stargazer, Dec. 1984/Jan. 1985) q. her (year confirmed by FCC at Registry). RR: A.

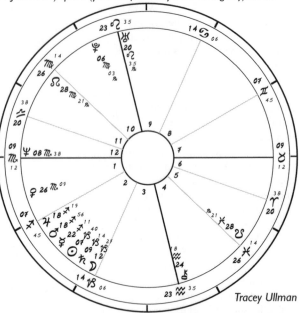

Tracey Ullman

Madcap, highly versatile performer and social satirist with a strong American following, known originally for her portrayals of inarticulate air-heads. After training at stage school from age 12 and a stint in Berlin as a dancer, Ullman was first brought to public notice in *Three of a Kind* (from Summer 1981), later starred in the hilarious *Girls on Top* (from October 1985), and performed three warbling bubble-gum Top Ten hits in Britain (two during October-November 1983, as TR Saturn crossed her Ascendant). She moved to the USA in 1984 (often Uranus-MC doesn't 'feel' at home in the country of birth). Her comedy show was conceived the following year as she prepared to make her film debut in *Plenty*. Although she refused to play the Hollywood self-promotion game, awards for her 'skitcom' *The Tracey Ullman Show* were forthcoming (an initial Emmy was won on 17 September 1989, as TR Saturn conjunct her Sun). It first aired on April 1987 (TR Pluto conjunct Ascendant, TR Neptune conjunct Sun). The show gave her a high profile until its conclusion in September 1990 (when it also won its last two Emmys). Despite her show's critical praise and Emmy Awards, Ullman has never been in the highest bracket of film deals, ratings or of media attention. Yet she remains the only British comedienne to make her mark in America. In recent years she has contributed her voice to a number of animated films, including *Happily Ever After*, and has appeared in a handful of Woody Allen films. The hugely successful cartoon *The Simpsons* was born on *The Tracey Ullman Show*, but Ullman lost a $1.3 million lawsuit in October 1992 to receive royalties from the lucrative breakaway programme and its merchandise. The edge Ullman has over her rivals is a zany unpredictability and willingness to explore new ground (Uranus conjunct MC), as well as an ability to transform herself expertly into a variety of characters (Neptune conjunct Ascendant). In early April 2003 Ullman's husband spoke of his on-going five year battle with cancer.

> Q
>
> "It is difficult to think of a time or circumstance when Ullman isn't the boss. Underneath the slightly heightened air of ordinariness that she wears like make-up, there is a skeleton of flexible steel. She may claim that she is not driven to succeed like her super-ambitious colleagues but that has not stopped her from succeeding a million times better than many of them." (Neil Norman, *Evening Standard*, 7/11/2000)

UPSTAIRS, DOWNSTAIRS

There were 68 episodes of this award-winning landmark show. *Upstairs, Downstairs*, shown between October 1971 and December 1975, was one of the few series that depicted the servant classes as more than comical characters. When it was shown in America it was a critical and ratings success, eventually notching up 16 Emmy nominations (seven wins) including four Emmys for the outstanding series of the year (1974-7) and acting wins for Jean Marsh (qv) and Gordon Jackson (qv). Other actors profiled who appeared in the series are: Pauline Collins, Lesley-Anne Down, Hannah Gordon and Nicola Pagett.

Mary Ure

> b. 18 February 1933, 08.30 GMT, Kelvinside, Glasgow, Scotland, 55N53, 04W17.
> Gerard q. BC (Mary Eileen Ure). RR: AA.

Stage actress (from 30 August 1954) who took occasional film roles. Ure was Oscar-nominated for her film role in *Sons and Lovers* (1960). She died on 3 April 1975 from an accidental mixture of alcohol and barbiturates (TR Jupiter conjunct Ascendant), a few hours after opening a new play in London. Ure was married to John Osborne.

Midge Ure

> b. 10 October 1953, 08.30 GMT, Cambuslang, Scotland, 55N59, 04W09.
> Gerard q. BC (James Ure). RR: AA.

Singer-songwriter with Ultravox from April 1979 (TR Pluto, natally at MC, conjunct MC ruler Sun). His first album with the group sold impressively from July 1980 and a #2 hit – *Vienna* – in January 1981 was the fifth best-selling single of the year. For Band Aid (Christmas 1984, TR Pluto conjunct Ascendant) he joined forces with Bob Geldof (qv), the driving force behind the venture, to release Britain's second biggest selling single of all time, *Do They Know It's Christmas?* Ure hit the top of the UK charts himself in September 1985 with *If I Was*. In May 1996 he released a Celtic-flavoured album, his first album in five years.

Robert Urquhart

> b. 16 October 1921, 04.00 GMT, Ullapool, Scotland, 57N54, 05W10.
> Gerard q. BC (Robert Alister MacLennan Urquhart). RR: AA.

Actor who starred in a three-part drama for *The Ruth Rendell Mysteries* series shown during September 1994. D. 20 March 1995.

Peter Ustinov

> b. 16 April 1921, 11.00 GDT, Swiss Cottage, London, England, 51N33, 0W10.
> From his autobiography, *Dear Me* (William Heinemann, 1977), pp. 3-4. RR: B.

Exceptional character actor, mimic and acclaimed writer of Russian and French descent. Ustinov is best remembered as the Belgian sleuth Hercule Poirot in films of Agatha Christie's novels, although he is also a playwright, designer, director, author and campaigner for UNICEF. A double-Emmy winner, off-screen he is much loved as a raconteur, master of dialects and for his witty one-man shows (Ascendant ruler Moon in Leo, conjunct MC ruler Neptune). Onstage from 17 and performing his own sketches in a 1939 revue, Ustinov made his film debut the following year. After appearing in *Spartacus* (October 1960), for which he garnered the first of two Best Supporting Actor Oscars, Ustinov produced, directed and starred in *Billy Budd* (US release October 1962). In January 1963 he was sued for walking out of *The Pink Panther* and was replaced by Peter Sellers (qv). Ustinov has married three times (1944-51, 1954-71, and from 1972). He was knighted in June 1990.

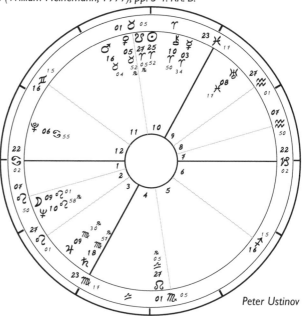

Peter Ustinov

Ewan Vernal – see Deacon Blue

Sid Vicious

✪ b. 10 May 1957, 19.09 GDT, London, England, 51N30, 0W10.

Lorraine Exley q. his mother, Anne Beverley, in person c.1980. RR:A.

Doomed youth Sid Vicious (John Simon Ritchie) was bassist for the The Sex Pistols, an anarchic, antihero punk band that defined the 70s (Vicious has Neptune Rising and attained a mythological status with his "live fast die young" creed). After building a cult following in Summer 1976, the Pistols signed a contract with EMI in October and a month later released their debut single, *Anarchy in the UK*. On 1 December 1976 the band achieved notoriety by unleashing a volley of four-letter words on tea-time TV. In March 1977 Vicious joined the band (TR Jupiter conjunct Venus, TR Uranus opposite Mercury). Dropped by EMI they moved to Virgin in May 1977 and the single *God Save the Queen* was released at the end of

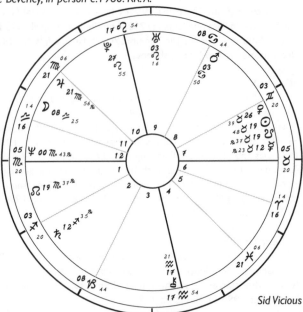

Sid Vicious

the month (TR Saturn conjunct MC followed). The single caused an uproar, as did the October release of their album *Never Mind the Bollocks*. Following their US tour the band imploded in January 1978. Vicious began dating groupie Nancy Spungen*, who introduced him to hard drugs and brought out his S&M side (Venus, ruler of the Descendant squares Pluto, and Moon squares Mars). On 12 October (TR Jupiter conjunct EQHS 10th, and following an Eclipse on his Moon) Vicious woke up to find Spungen dead in their hotel room. Out on bail accused of murder he was found dead of a heroin overdose on 2 February 1979 (TR Uranus opposite Sun). A film of their lives, *Sid and Nancy*, premiered on 20 July 1986, six weeks before his mother Anne committed suicide (TR Pluto conjunct Ascendant). Pistols' vocalist Johnny Rotten (Lydon) was born on 31 January 1956, Finsbury Park, London, 51N31, 0W05 with Mercury in Aquarius opposite Uranus, T-square Neptune.

Tim Vincent

✪ b. 4 November 1972, 22.00 GMT, Wrexham, North Wales, 53N03, 03W00.

☗ FCC q. his letter, "eve?" Speculative time. RR: C.

A part-time fitness instructor before he joined *Blue Peter* on 16 December 1993, beefcake Vincent was a welcome host of the popular children's show. He ran the New York marathon in 1995 for charity. His first role on TV had been acting in *Children's Ward*. Vincent left *Blue Peter* on 24 January 1997 and continued on TV presenting *The Clothes Show* and acting in *Dangerfield* and *Emmerdale*.

Dougie Vipond – see Deacon Blue

Ben Volpeliere-Pierrot

b. 19 May 1965, 23.25 GDT, Kensington, London, England, 51N31, 0W12.

From him to Laura Boomer on *The Astrology Show*, place and year confirmed by FCC at Registry. RR:A.

Singer and songwriter with the group Curiosity Killed the Cat, which was formed in 1983. A release in mid-1986 failed to chart but the group cracked it in December of that year, and later had a best-selling album in May 1987. He joined an 80s revival tour in 2002.

---

* Nancy Spungen b. 27 February 1958, 06.52 EST, Philadelphia, Pennsylvania, 39N57, 75W10. From her mother's biography *And I Don't Want to Live This Life*. RR: B.

Gordon Waller

> b. 4 June 1945, 07.55 DGDT, Braemar, Scotland, 57N00, 03W25.
> Gerard q. BC (Gordon Trueman Waller). RR: AA.

Supported by Paul McCartney (qv), Waller and his musical partner Peter Asher (b. 2 June 1944, London) formed Peter and Gordon and had hits on both sides of the Atlantic from April 1964 (TR Uranus on IC, and TR Saturn conjunct MC in June, coinciding with a #1 hit in America). McCartney's compositions gave the duo chart success for the next few years (he was dating Peter's sister Jane Asher, qv). Peter and Gordon split in September 1968 (TR Pluto opposite Moon). Peter Asher moved to California and became a successful producer (two Grammys by 1990), whilst Waller has pursued a solo recording career.

Julie Walters

> b. 22 February 1950, 15.00 GMT, Smethwick, Birmingham, England, 52N30, 01W58.
> David Fisher q. her letter, "according to my mother." RR: A.

One of Britain's finest actress-comediennes, blessed with the gift of mimicry, an exceptional eye for personal detail, and famous for her portrayals of flustered, blinking manic women. With three planets in Aquarius, Walters is a one-of-a-kind who gave her first performance at the Everyman Theatre in Liverpool in 1975 (after quitting nursing at 23), and has gone on to contribute some of the finest characterisations to TV. She met Victoria Wood (b. 19 May 1953, Prestwich, England) at Manchester Polytechnic in 1970 and they eventually began working on TV together ten years later. Wood and a number of top writers have queued up to utilise Walters's inimitable talents. She hides a single-mindedness (Mercury

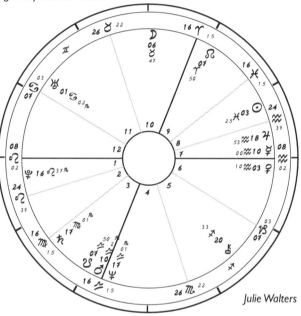

Julie Walters

opposite Pluto on the Ascendant), inherited from her unfulfilled and dominating mother, that has taken her to the top of her profession. In *Personal Services* she played a character based on Cynthia Payne (qv), whilst her hilarious antics on the soap spoof *Acorn Antiques* (from 11 January 1985) won her many admirers, proving she has the Piscean ability to fully submerge herself into characters of any age. Walters earned the lead role in *Educating Rita*, alongside Michael Caine (qv), and went on to receive Golden Globe, Variety Club and Bafta awards for her performance. She passed up the chance to appear in Hollywood films and put her ambitions on hold in 1990 when her daughter Maisie was diagnosed with leukaemia. Maisie had recovered fully by Autumn 1995. Walters has continued to make excellent dramas, such as *My Beautiful Son* (2001) and *Murder* (May 2002 – a Best Actress Bafta award on 13 April 2003), and comedies like *Dinnerladies*, and has appeared (somewhat under-used) in box office hits like *Billy Elliot* (September 2000) and *Harry Potter*. In 2003 she appeared in a female *Full Monty*-inspired film, *Calendar Girls*.

> "Her appeal is about more than a good impersonation... Walters is like a living almanac of our national idiosyncrasies... And all those tics and twitches; the unwanted information, the malapropisms and awkwardness, are so accurately and affectionately observed, she makes us feel good about ourselves." (Shane Watson, *Evening Standard*, 19/2/99)

Q

"I'm quite courageous at running away. My thirties were like most people's teens. I'd repressed everything and was a late developer. I drank – probably too much at times – and it was a way of escaping the fame and success I had from *Educating Rita*...When I was younger I felt acting defined who I was. I was driven. You can become eaten up with ambition. I felt I couldn't exist without being an actress, but I've realised that's not true... I express myself hugely through [acting], but it isn't me... There's a great relief in being someone else, but using your own feelings... Acting is my personal psychiatrist." (Julie Walters, *Radio Times*, 25/5/02)

David Ward

> *b. 3 July 1922, 06.40 GDT, Dumbarton, Scotland, 55N57, 04W34.*
> *Gerard q. BC. RR: AA.*

Operatic bass singer who studied at the Royal College of Music. His stage debut was at Sadler's Wells Opera in 1953. Ward joined the Royal Opera in Covent Garden in 1960 and was awarded the CBE in 1972.

Kirsty Wark

> *b. 3 May 1955, 16.20 GDT, Dumfries, Scotland, 55N04, 03W36.*
> *Gerard q. BC. RR: AA.*

Political television journalist who made a name for herself as a tough interrogator and serious journalist by grilling Prime Minister Thatcher in March 1990. She has gone on to present BBC's *Newsnight*. In 2000 she signed a lucrative three-year deal with the BBC. Wark began on a graduate training scheme at the BBC after completing a degree at Edinburgh University.

Roger Waters – see Ron Geesin
Ian Watkins ('H') – see Steps

Molly Weir

> *b. 17 March 1910, 08.35 GMT, Springburn, Glasgow, Scotland, 55N53, 04W15.*
> *Gerard q. BC (Mary Weir). RR: AA.*

Energetic actress and writer, and sister of Tom Weir (qv). Molly made her film debut in 1944 and created the famous radio character Tattie Mackintosh in *Itma* (1939-49). With Gemini Rising she could knock ten years off her age... and often did.

Tom Weir

> *b. 29 December 1914, 02.00 GMT, Springburn, Glasgow, Scotland, 55N53, 04W15.*
> *Gerard q. BC (Thomas Weir). RR: AA.*

Broadcaster, climber, best-selling author, wildlife observer, and brother of Molly Weir (qv). His first book was published in 1948. Weir is a staunch environmentalist.

Paul Weller

> ○ *b. 25 May 1958, 23.45 GDT, Woking, England, 51N20, 0W34.*
> *Neil Spencer q. him. RR: A.*

As leader of The Jam, Weller captured the times he lived in through his political songwriting (Scorpio MC, Moon-Pluto). His first gig was at the Woking Working Men's Club in November 1972. Weller and his band struggled to win recognition and a gig in October 1976 (after TR Pluto hit EQHS 10th) should have launched them but they received a poor review in *Melody Maker*. On 25 February 1977, following gigs at the Red Cow and Marquee, the band signed to Polydor and released a single that May, followed by a UK tour and album release in June (TR Pluto conjunct EQHS 10th). Soon The Jam were enormously successful in the UK and once had a record-breaking 13 singles simultaneously in the British charts. They were also the first act to enter the chart at #1 three times. Although in control on the business side, Weller's alcohol abuse saw him develop complicated stomach problems. On 29 October 1982 The Jam announced its split (TR Jupiter conjunct MC). Weller founded the jazz/soul band The Style Council in early 1983 and released a first album in March 1984 (TR Saturn conjunct MC). Weller joined the left-wing Red Wedge movement at its start on 21 November 1985 and the tour began on 25 January 1986. The Style Council continued until mid-1989 (TR Saturn-Neptune conjunct Ascendant). Weller officially dissolved the band in March 1990 and reemerged solo and self-financed in Autumn 1990 (TR Pluto's final cross over his MC). In February 1995 (and again in 1996) he won a Brit Award for Best Male Solo Artist. Weller suffered a personal and professional blow when in October and November 2000 he was falsely accused of having attacked and raped a woman back in 1996. The charges were dropped and Weller called for a change in the law. After two years without a record deal and band (getting his act together by playing live in small venues) Weller's latest album, *Illumination*, entered the UK charts at #1 on 22 September 2002.

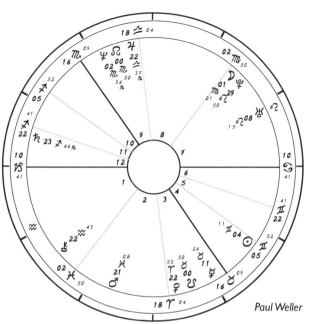

Paul Weller

Bobby Wellins

> b. 24 January 1936, 05.00 GMT, Hutchesontown, Glasgow, Scotland, 55N50, 04W14.
> Gerard q. BC (Robert Coull Wellins). RR: AA.

Jazz composer (Uranus square Sun-Moon in Aquarius) and musician of Russian and Polish roots. He was taught the alto saxophone from age 12 by his father and was a bandleader from 1976.

John Wells

> b. 17 November 1936, 08.00 GMT, Willesborough, Ashford, Kent, England, 51N08, 0E53.
> Marjorie Orr q. him. RR: A.

Wells once doubled as a teacher at Eton by day and a comedian on stage at night. A professional satirist (Scorpio emphasis, Mars on MC), Wells was associated with the magazine *Private Eye* from 1961. As TR Uranus crossed his Ascendant he wrote and starred with Angela Thorne (qv) in a hilarious play about the Thatchers, *Anyone for Denis?* (which opened on 7 May 1981, previews from 28 April), although the then-PM was unable to find humour in the farce (Wells's chart has a Moon-Jupiter conjunction in Sagittarius). He took the role of gin-happy husband Denis Thatcher. John Wells also appeared in *Kavanagh QC*. D. January 1998.

Alex Welsh

> b. 9 July 1929, 17.40 GDT, Royal Maternity Hospital, Edinburgh, Scotland, 55N57, 03W12.
> Gerard q. BC. RR: AA.

Jazz cornetist and bandleader (Uranus square Sun). Welsh moved to London in 1953 and the following year formed his own band, which remained under his leadership for 28 years.

Irvine Welsh

b. 27 September 1957, 15.20 GDT, Elsie Inglis Maternity Hospital, Edinburgh, Scotland, 55N57, 03W10.
Gerard q. BC (Irvine John Welsh). RR: AA.

Welsh wrote his decadent, seminal book *Trainspotting* in 1993, described as a "journey through the collective mental landscape of Scottish drug addicts." It was shortlisted for the Booker Prize. Welsh is known for his quirky, barbed and edgy writing as well as his black humour (note the MC, Venus and Moon are in Scorpio, and Moon squares Pluto). Great reviews and controversy surrounded the film of the book, released in February 1996. The film's star, Robert Carlyle (qv) was born with Neptune exactly on Welsh's MC. His novel *Marabou Stork Nightmares* was an exploration of a soccer hooligan's mind as he lies comatose in hospital. His works *Ecstasy*, *Filth* and *Glue* followed.

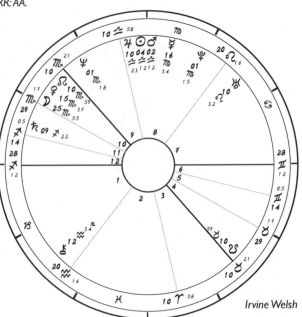

Irvine Welsh

Timothy West

b. 20 October 1934, 18.00 GMT, Bradford, England, 53N48, 01W45.
FCC q. him. RR: A.

Sincere actor with a pugnacious jaw, known for his masterful renditions of difficult biographical roles (Edward VII and playing Churchill a few times, sharing fascinating synastry with both). Brought up in a busy, impatient atmosphere, West was nevertheless a slow developer. After a stint as an office furniture salesman, he became an assistant stage manager at Wimbledon Theatre in 1956 before embarking on rep. He married Prunella Scales (qv) in October 1963.

Karen Westwood

b. 26 November 1964, 04.27 GMT, Cresswell Maternity Hospital, Dumfries, Scotland, 55N04, 03W36.
Gerard q. BC (Karen Smith). RR: AA.

Actress who appeared in two series of the Anglo-Australian soap *Families*.

Vivienne Westwood

b. 8 April 1941, 01.00 GDT, Glossop, England, 53N27, 01W57.
From her to Babs Kirby. RR: A.

Off-the-wall fashion designer, 'Queen of Outrage', eccentric icon and intellectual. Westwood, born Vivienne Swire, is in constant flux through reinventing herself. A biography released in late 1995 claimed she was a manipulative mother and partner, a charge she strenuously denied. Westwood, the high priestess of punk fashion, is famous for her see-through dresses and for her relationships (Libra MC).

WET WET WET

Signed to a recording contract in 1985, Wet Wet Wet (formed in 1982) began charting hits in April 1987 and soon became pinup idols. With the photogenic Pellow fronting the band, their debut album topped the charts in January 1988 and a charity record gave them a #1 hit that May. Amongst their hits are *Goodnight Girl* (#1, January 1992) and the movie theme song *Love is All Around* from *Four Weddings and a*

Funeral (#1 for 15 weeks from 4 June 1994, shifting 1.78 million units until their manager insisted the song be deleted). In March 1997 the band announced dates of their first tour for six years. Pellow, who surprised friends when he announced he would marry, left the group and signed a solo deal with manager John Reid (qv) in May 1999. The move occurred after stints in rehab over Summer 1998 and Spring 1999, when TR Pluto crossed his Moon (Pellow had been battling alcoholism and heroin addiction for years – Neptune Rising). In mid-2001 he released a new single and album, Smile. On 10 June 2002 Pellow joined the cast of the West End's hit musical Chicago. The show coincided with a solo album and in June 2003 Pellow was scheduled to appear on Broadway with the musical.

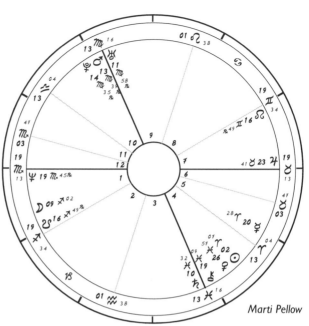

Marti Pellow

Graeme Clark
b. 15 April 1965, 00.00 Midnight (N.B. 15/16th) GDT, Possil Road, Glasgow, Scotland, 55N52, 04W16.
Gerard q. BC. RR: AA.

Tom Cunningham
b. 22 June 1964, 16.15 GDT, Kinclaven Avenue, Glasgow, Scotland, 55N54, 04W22.
Gerard q. BC (Thomas Cunningham). RR: AA.

Neil Mitchell
b. 8 June 1965, 02.00 GDT, Braeholm, Helensburgh, Scotland, 56N00, 04W43.
Gerard q. BC. RR: AA.

Marti Pellow
b. 23 March 1965, 00.15 GDT, Clydebank, Scotland, 55N54, 04W24.
Gerard q. BC (Mark McLachlan). Same data from Pellow to Laura Boomer on The Astrology Show. RR: AA.

Caron Wheeler
b. 19 January 1963, 13.00 GMT, Acton, London, England, 51N30, 0W16.
From her to Laura Boomer. RR: A.
Vocalist who featured prominently in the distinctive rap and R&B band Soul II Soul for the smash hits Keep on Movin' (March 1989) and Back to Life, the latter a UK #1 hit for four weeks in June 1989 (as TR Jupiter passed her Ascendant). Wheeler departed from the group in late 1989 to concentrate on a solo career. The first result was the UK Top 20 album UK Blak in 1990.

Alan Whicker
b. 2 August 1925, 05.30 EET (-2), Cairo, Egypt, 30N03, 31E15.
David Fisher q. his letter, September 1984. RR: A.
Whicker is best known for Yorkshire's Whicker's World (from 1958), a globe-trotting documentary series often featuring interviews with the famous and watched by over ten million viewers (Moon in EQHS 5th conjunct 5th ruler Jupiter, both opposite Pluto). Whicker was with the BBC from February 1957-68 before beginning the award-winning association with Yorkshire Television. Constantly travelling the world, it was calculated in the early 80s that on average he clocked up 100,000 miles each year. His autobiography, Within Whicker's World, was published in March 1982.

Jon Whiteley

☉ b. 19 February 1945, 18.10 GDT, Monymusk, Scotland, 57N14, 02W31.
Gerard q. BC (Jon James Lamont Whiteley). RR: AA.

Child actor who appeared in *The Kidnappers* (1953) and won a special Oscar for his performance.

WHO

•1959 – Daltrey, the bolshie leader of the group, Entwistle and the combative Townshend form the Confederates.

•1964, Apr – The manic drummer Keith Moon (b. 23 August 1946, Wembley, England. Date from BC reproduced in *Dear Boy* by Tony Fletcher) joins the group.

•1964, July – The group's first single, *I'm The Face*, is released. They are marketed as the principal mod band.

•1964, Nov – Their name is changed to the Who and they begin at the Marquee Club, becoming infamous for smashing equipment.

•1965, Apr – Who have their first radio performance and first hit in UK with *I Can't Explain*.

•1965, Nov – *My Generation*, a seminal recording, hits #2 in the UK. The band are involved in internal power struggles.

•1968, July – Townshend's life is changed by the teachings of Indian spiritualist Meher Baba. From then on his songwriting focuses on the concept of identity and God.

•1969, May – *Tommy* is launched (the concept was developed by Townshend on 15 August 1968, and the film version begins shooting in April 1974 and is released on 26 March 1975).

•1970, Jan – Moon accidentally runs down and kills his chauffeur.

•1973 – Early in the year Daltrey releases his first solo album.

•1973, Oct – *Quadrophenia* is released.

•1974, Apr 14 – Townshend's first solo gig.

•1975, Aug – The film *Lisztomania*, starring Daltrey, is released.

•1978, Sep 8 – Moon dies of an overdose.

•1979, Jan – Kenny Jones takes over Moon's role.

•1983, Feb – Townshend is honoured at the Brit Awards with a Lifetime Achievement Award.

•1983, Dec 16 – Last gig of US 'farewell' tour.

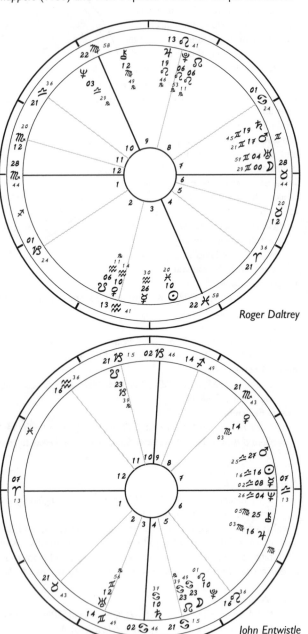

Roger Daltrey

John Entwistle

- 1989, June – Entwistle, Daltrey and Townshend embark on a new tour (until September).
- 1992 – During summer the stage version of Tommy premieres (and on Broadway from April 1993).
- 2002, June 27 – Entwistle dies in Las Vegas after a cocaine binge.
- 2003, Jan – Townshend is named in a worldwide investigation into child pornography (he denies being a paedophile, claiming he was abused as a child and is researching the subject for his autobiography).

Pete Townshend

Roger Daltrey
> b. 1 March 1944, 02.00 GDT, London, England, 51N30, 0W10.

John Entwistle
> b. 9 October 1944, 18.00 GDT, London, England, 51N30, 0W10.

Kenny Jones
> b. 16 September 1948, 20.55 GDT, London, England, 51N30, 0W10.

Pete Townshend
> b. 19 May 1945, 15.00 DGDT, London, England, 51N30, 0W10.

All data: Debbi Kempton-Smith in *Secrets From A Stargazer's Notebook*, q. their mothers. RR: A.

Extra event dates from astrologer-writer Nick Dagan Best (stellardweller@hotmail.com).

Kim Wilde
> b. 18 November 1960, 20.00 GMT, Chiswick, London, England, 51N29, 0W16.
> From her to Ananda Bagley over the telephone. RR: A.

Attractive singer, songwriter and actress – the (cover) girl-next-door with the perfect pop pout. With the backing of her father, pop idol Marty Wilde (b. 15 April 1936, London) and starmaker Mickie Most, she released her first single in February 1981, which went on to hit #2 on the pop charts the following month (it also cracked the US Top 30 in August 1982). Switching to a more overtly sexy image Wilde scored her biggest hit *You Keep Me Hangin' On* in December 1986 (#2 in Britain and later topping the US chart in June 1987). Despite further success, by 1990 she was suffering a lack of confidence. Her personal life and career were given a boost when she made a stage musical debut in the London revival of *Tommy* in March 1996 when TR Saturn hit her MC (rehearsals began in January) and married her co-star on 31 August 1996. She continued with the sell-out show until February 1997. Wilde reinvented herself, became a landscape gardener and began presenting a gardening show, *Better Gardens* (1999-2000). She also had a slot on the daytime show *This Morning* in 2001. In November 2001 she began a UK tour to coincide with the release of her greatest hits album. In May 2003 Wilde appeared on the TV show *Celebrity Detox Camp*.

Marty Wilde – see Kim Wilde
Alan Wilder – see Depeche Mode

Toyah Willcox

b. 18 May 1958, 11.57 GDT, Birmingham, England, 52N30, 01W50.
From her to Liz Medler. RR: A.

Ex-punk and flamboyant rock star with a cultivated tough image. Toyah was an out-of-control teenager downing a bottle of spirits a day by age 14. She had three Top Ten hits in Britain in 1981 (when TR Uranus opposed her Sun). She moved into films, including *Quadrophenia*, *The Tempest* and *Jubilee*, directed by Derek Jarman (qv). During 1986 she made personal and professional changes in her life (including a marriage to rock musician Robert Fripp on 16 May), and by early 1987 was playing Sally Bowles in *Cabaret* in the West End (TR Pluto conjunct IC). She has also hosted TV shows, including *The Good Sex Guide Late* and *Songs of Praise*. A believer in alternative therapies, Willcox no longer smokes and rarely drinks. She is her

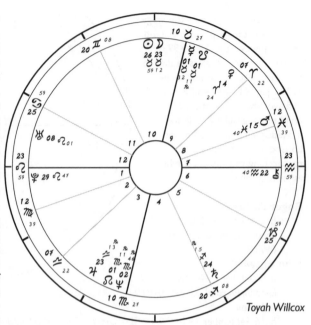

Toyah Willcox

own manager, with a production company to further her many ambitions. The rebel is still there but now she has a cause. In late April 2003 Willcox quit a stage show to join the cast of *I'm a Celebrity – Get Me Out of Here!*, with the hope that it would revamp her career.

Kenneth Williams

b. 22 February 1926, 14.30 GMT, off Caledonian Road, Islington, London, England, 51N32, 0W07.
From his autobiography, Just Williams, p. 8, from his mother's recollection ("At about 2.30...it was early closing day and Charlie (KW's father) had the afternoon off"). RR: A.

The most prolific (and most highly paid) *Carry On* star excelled on radio and stage before, during and after his stint with the Rogers-Thomas comedy film classics. A natural performer, Williams was best known on screen for his nostril-flaring, often-outraged characters, as well as his naughty innuendo and mischief (Aries MC). His humour captured the spectrum of the English class system (Aries MC, and ruler Mars in Capricorn) – Williams's voice could journey from his extravagant vowels and upper class posh tones to a guttural, snide Cockney vulgarity in a single sentence. Along with Larry Grayson (qv) and later John Inman, he was the acceptable languid face of camp. He began entertaining in World War II, acted in rep from 1948 and

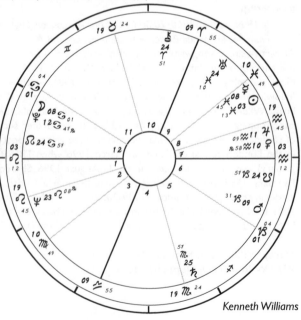

Kenneth Williams

had a breakthrough role in *St Joan* from 29 September 1954 before joining Tony Hancock (qv) on radio in *Hancock's Half Hour* in November 1954. His comic timing, phrasing and vocal characterisations made him a star, particularly when he joined the show on TV in March-April 1957 (TR Uranus conjunct Ascendant). Hancock, apparently jealous of his rival's success, removed him from the line-up and Williams recorded his last show on 7 June 1959 (TR Jupiter conjunct Saturn – a reliable indicator of career change). In April 1958 he filmed his first *Carry On* – the series of films that were to bring him fame. Early the following year his father's business was floundering, which led to Williams senior's health decline and early death on 15 October 1962 (which was rumoured, like Williams's own death, to be a suicide). (Transits at this time are revealing: Jupiter conjunct Sun, Saturn conjunct Descendant, Uranus opposite Sun.) Later he worked as the camp Sandy on the radio show *Round the Horne* (which began in March 1965) and was instrumental in making the radio show *Just a Minute* so popular. Despite his own popularity he nevertheless lived what he considered to be an unfulfilled life, continually moaning, hypersensitive at best and feeling bitter – he was torn between being a serious intellectual and an outrageously vulgar comedian. He kept a set of infamously personal and bitchy diaries (Moon-Pluto in the 12th), which were published posthumously in 1993. They revealed a lonely figure unwilling to form intimate relationships, usually preferring masturbation (his snobbery and reluctance to be physically intimate can be seen, in part, by the Venus-Jupiter conjunction in the detached air sign Aquarius in 7th). Williams, with Leo Rising, harboured a contempt for many people, loved put-downs (see his book *Acid Drops*) and hated over-familiarity – he gave his best to his audience at the expense of personal ties (the EQHS 3rd and 5th House rulers are conjunct in the 7th). Erudite and a captivating interviewee and raconteur, Williams appears to be Mercury incarnate, yet it is the Moon-Pluto conjunction (powerfully placed, having just risen) that is the key to his emotive energy, love of language and his enormous public appeal as an entertainer (as well as his instinctive sense of his audience and comic timing). This conjunction plus MC ruler Mars in the 6th suggests his comedic fascination with bodily functions and his hypochondria (tight-arsed mania almost out of control!). He maintained a love-hate relationship with his mother (Moon conjunct Pluto in 12th, ruling 12th and EQHS 4th), whom he lived with in bickering domesticity until his death on 15 April 1988 (as TR Neptune hit Mars in 6th and TR Pluto squared Jupiter-Venus). His tormented life and comedic genius were paid great tribute by actor-impersonator David Benson (qv) on stage from August 1996 (TR Jupiter on MC ruler Mars) and in a national tour January 1997 (as TR Saturn approached Williams's MC).

> Q "I settled for the books, the gramophone and an awful lot of talking to myself. My exhibitionism concealed a sense of inadequacy. The real self was a vulnerable, quivering thing which I did not want to reveal; showing-off, affectation and play-acting I used like a hedgehog uses his spines. The facade was not to be penetrated." (Kenneth Williams, *Just Williams*, Harper Collins, 1993)
> "He felt he didn't belong [with his family]. He felt a bit like a changeling, a little prince of higher birth accidentally dropped to this low-life family." (Russell Davies, as quoted in *Kenneth Williams* on TV's The Biography Channel)

Nicol Williamson

✪ *b. 14 September 1936, 04.45 GDT, Beckford Lodge Nursing Home, Hamilton, Scotland, 55N47, 04W02. Gerard q. BC (Thomas Nicol Williamson). RR: AA.*
Wilful stage actor known for being a difficult perfectionist (Mars, Uranus and Virgo strong). He made his London debut in November 1961 (TR Uranus on Ascendant) and joined the RSC in April 1962.

Robin Williamson

b. 24 November 1943, 14.50 GDT, Edinburgh, Scotland, 55N57, 03W13. Gerard q. BC (Robin Duncan Harry Williamson). RR: AA.
Composer, poet, singer and songwriter. In early 1966 he founded the distinctive The Incredible String Band with Mike Heron (qv), until he quit following their March 1974 album *Hard Rope and Silken Twine*. In 1975 he settled in Los Angeles with his wife. Williamson went solo in the early 80s. He returned to the UK and remarried in August 1989. He was impressively prolific during the mid-late 90s, the highlight of which was a reunion concert with Heron in 1997. On 26 January 2001 they stopped the show at a Celtic Connections concert in Glasgow.

Dave Willis

    b. 6 September 1894, 16.00 GMT, Glasgow, Scotland, 55N52, 04W17.

    Gerard q. BC (David Williams). RR: AA.

Comedian with film experience who debuted in 1920. His London debut was at The Pavilion in 1932.

Francis Wilson

    b. 27 February 1949, 16.30 GMT, Ayr Hospital, Irvine, Ayrshire, Scotland, 55N38, 04W40.

    Gerard q. BC (Francis Alfred Wilson). RR: AA.

Trained at RAF Farnborough with the Met Research Flight for three years, Wilson became television's favourite weatherman after joining BBC *Breakfast Time* in 1983. He now works for *Sky News*.

Kara Wilson

    b. 18 June 1944, 16.30 DGDT, Glasgow, Scotland, 55N53, 04W19.

    Gerard q. BC (Katherine Drummond Wilson). RR: AA.

Highly regarded actress and artist, whose private life is off-limits. A psychologist before moving into acting, Wilson's produced her most acclaimed television work in *MacKenzie*. She has also appeared in *Grange Hill* and several projects with her husband, actor Tom Conti (qv). Their daughter, Nina (b. late 1973), followed in both parents' footsteps by studying art and beginning an acting career in Spring 1996, before becoming an award-winning ventriloquist (BBC New Comedy Award 2002).

Richard Wilson

    b. 9 July 1936, 23.58 GDT, Greenock, Scotland, 55N56, 04W47.

    Gerard q. BC (Iain Carmichael Wilson). RR: AA.

A former research scientist (Saturn Rising), Wilson, a director and superb character actor, featured in the comedy *Only When I Laugh* (1979-83) before gaining wide acclaim as the cantankerous, disbelieving geriatric Victor Meldrew in *One Foot in the Grave*. Crabby Meldrew, an ex-security guard on the scrapheap, and self-appointed champion of the people, was first introduced to TV audiences on 4 January 1990. The final episode aired on 20 November 2000. Meldrew's personality is the epitome of Saturn-Capricorn and, indeed, Wilson has Moon-Saturn Rising to reflect the irascible character's domestic setup and misanthropic views. Wilson, who trained at RADA from age 27, adores the adulation his role has brought him.

Richard Wilson

> Q | "His highly developed work ethic and his seriousness are inherited from his father, a timekeeper at the Greenock shipyard... As a "shy, gawky, skinny" young man, he relied on alcohol to disinhibit him." (Andrew Billen, *Evening Standard*, 11/10/2000)

Barbara Windsor

    b. 6 August 1937, 19.35 GDT, Shoreditch, London, England, 51N32, 0W05.

    FCC q. her for "sometime in the evening." Rectified (birth registered in Stepney). RR: C.

Four feet ten, with a bubbling personality, infectious giggle and more front than Brighton, busty Windsor has always stood out in a crowd. A woman who has lived an adventurous life, Windsor is known for her affairs, choice of men (most famously, criminal Ronnie Knight) and being able to resurrect her career each decade (MC ruler Pluto in 7th trine MC). Sent away from her family during the war, she was abused by a foster family. At 13 she was trained for the stage when a talent scout offered her a part in a pantomime. The first taste of the limelight for this Sun-Moon Leo lady was in the Autumn of 1952 with a long-running stage show. Her career took off during Summer 1955 and she became a sensation when the stage show *Fings Ain't Wot They Used T'Be* moved to the West End on 20 March 1960. She met Ronnie Knight in the late 50s and married him on 3 March 1964, whilst she was filming her first of nine *Carry On* films. Before

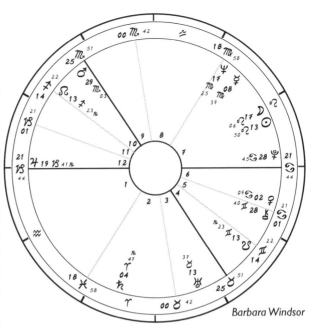

Barbara Windsor

they were separated, Knight was charged with armed robbery and arrested in January 1980, turning their lives upside down. The following ten months were a living hell until Knight was cleared on 10 November 1980. Windsor suffered a nervous breakdown in early April 1981. She ended the partnership that December and divorced in January 1985. She married again (April 1986 until 1994). Her reputation as an aging sex symbol and hammy actor was demolished when she took a role in *EastEnders* and made her first appearance on 7 November 1994. Her residence in Albert Square (*EastEnders*) has proved very popular with viewers and established Windsor as a strong acting talent, although in late 2002 she announced that she would take a rest from the soap. She left the show in April 2003 for a year. Ex-husband Ronnie Knight* fled to Spain as 'Britain's Most Wanted Man' with his third wife, but returned to face the music in the 1994, pleading guilty to handling stolen money. He served seven years for handling the proceeds of the 1983 Security Express robbery. Although he has been tried by the Press, he remains well-liked in England as a lovable rascal (Sagittarius Rising, Jupiter conjunct MC). He was wanted for robberies committed on Easter Monday 1983 and 26 November 1983 at 06.40 GMT (the £25 million Brinks-Mat gold bullion haul at Heathrow Airport – source: Daily Telegraph, 28 November 1983, p. 1). He married Sue Haylock (b. 26 November 1953) on 4 June 1987, a month before Windsor reopened old wounds by selling her story to a tabloid.

Anna Wing

b. 30 October 1914, 07.30 GMT, London, England, 51N30, 0W10.
FCC q. her. RR: A.

For three years in TV's *EastEnders* (from February 1985) Anna Wing played the tough, dominating matriarch Lou Beale, who ruled the roost with an iron hand (note Wing's Leo MC). The soap made her a household name and brought her more fame than she had enjoyed during her previous 50 years as an actress. Voicing concerns about the increasingly belligerent content and loss of East End humour, she left the series through her character's death on 21 July 1988.

Vincent Winter

b. 29 December 1947, 22.30 GMT, Aberdeen, Scotland, 57N10, 02W04.
Gerard q. BC (Vincent Frederick Winter). RR: AA.

Child actor who appeared in *The Kidnappers* (1953) and won a special Oscar for his performance.

---

* Ronnie Knight b. 20 January 1934, 06.00 GMT, Hackney, England 51N33, 0W03. From his latest autobiography. (N.B. His first autobiography Black Knight (Century, 1990), p. 10-11, states "early one bright and crisp morning on the 20th of January 1934," which was rectified by FCC to 05.50.) RR: B.

Steve Winwood

> b. 12 May 1948, 05.00 GDT, Birmingham, England, 52N30, 01W50.
> Time from him to Jenni Harte; date and place from biography *Keep on Running* by Winwood and Chris Welch (Omnibus Press, 1989), p. 29. RR: A.

A singer, composer and producer with an impressive history of work projects with the greats. Winwood was a prodigy at 15 (from August 1963) with the Spencer Davis Group. He left the group and formed Traffic in April 1967 and later Blind Faith with Eric Clapton (qv) in 1969. He released a compilation of his group work in June 1971. A serious illness in 1972 delayed new projects, as TR Neptune opposed Mercury and TR Pluto squared Moon. And Winwood took a sabbatical in December 1974 to work on music compositions. His first solo album was released in July 1977 to good reviews (during Saturn Return). A tour in July 1983 (his first since 1974) saw Winwood at his healthiest and most creative for ten years. After a string of successful albums and singles (including *Arc of a Diver*, January 1981) on both sides of the Atlantic, he moved to New York in February 1986. He divorced his wife later that year. In August 1986 he hit #1 in America with *Higher Love*, a double Grammy winner in February 1987. In August 1987 he had his second #1 in the USA, *Roll With It*.

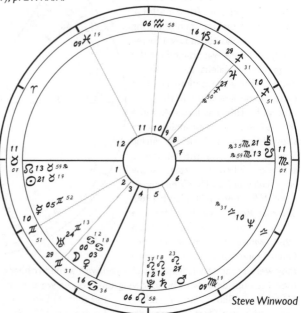

Steve Winwood

Ernie Wise

> b. 27 November 1925, 03.00 GMT, Leeds, England, 53N50, 01W35.
> Data from an article by Joan Revill in *Prediction*, November 1975, original source not known. RR: C.

Popular entertainer (born Ernest Wiseman) with comedy partner Eric Morecambe (qv). When they met, Ernie was the star – a child prodigy from 6, a gifted comic and dancer who had appeared in the West End when he was only 13. The pair were given a TV show, *Running Wild*, in 1954 but it was panned. *The Morecambe and Wise Show* began in 1961 and is considered by many to be the flagship series in the Golden Age of British Comedy. Wise was the straight man, often the butt of harmless insults on stage from Morecambe. The duo were also instrumental in establishing new performing avenues for many entertainers (including Glenda Jackson, qv) and were voted the funniest British comedians of all time in a recent BBC poll. Wise yearned to conquer Hollywood but Morecambe wasn't interested. Instead Wise contented himself with a lavish Hollywood lifestyle in England. After Morecambe's death in May 1984, Wise, always driven by money, worked in stage plays and one-man shows. He underwent a heart bypass in January 1999 following two heart attacks in December 1998 and a stroke in 1996. D. 21 March 1999, 07.00, near Slough.

Peter Wishart – see Runrig

Donald Wolfit

> b. 20 April 1902, 06.00 GMT, Balderton, England, 53N03, 0W47.
> From the biography *Sir Donald Wolfit* (1971), p. 7. RR: B.

An actor of considerable presence from his debut in 1920. Although he dedicated most of his professional life to the theatre and to Shakespeare, Wolfit appeared in 20 films. He was knighted in 1957.

Lynn Faulds Wood

b. 25 March 1948, 18.10 GDT, Redlands Hospital, Glasgow, Scotland, 55N53 04W17.
Gerard q. BC. RR: AA.

In 1991 Wood left her eight-year, high-profile post as a presenter with the consumer programme *Watchdog* when she was diagnosed with cancer of the colon (on 22 February 1991, TR Uranus – ruler of 6th – square Moon; she had an operation five days later). Despite the emotional upheaval, both she and her husband confronted the disease with courage and unity. In Summer 1996 she was given the all-clear. She is married to broadcaster (and former *Watchdog* co-presenter) John Stapleton (qv). They met on 15 December 1970, married in 1977 and Lynn gave birth on 15 October 1987. Wood avoids the invitations and trappings that the life of a public figure can bring.

Stuart Wood – see Bay City Rollers
Victoria Wood – see Julie Walters
Bill Wyman – see Rolling Stones

Paula Yates

✪ *b. 24 April 1959, 12.10 GDT, Colwyn Bay, Wales, 53N18, 03W43.*
From her baby book, excerpt published in The Sunday Times Magazine (2/11/2000). (N.B. Her mother gave a time of 12.25, as quoted in Daily Mail (24/1/98), p.42. RR: AA.

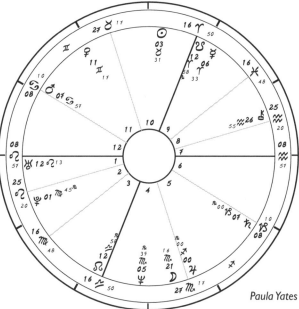

Paula Yates

Uninhibited and childlike TV presenter, Yates had a rootless childhood, never seeing much of either parent in her formative years (her 1995 autobiography claimed she was anorexic at 8 and had dabbled with heroin at 12). Always rebellious she posed for *Playboy* in 1979 and then, while a rock groupie, met musician Bob Geldof (who has been described as a dominating bully) at a party. She used her relationship with Geldof (qv) to acquire a column in a pop magazine. As a haughty, naughty pop tart Yates hosted the youth show *The Tube* in 1982 and seduced interviewees on *The Big Breakfast* (from September 1992, as TR Pluto conjunct Moon, until June 1995), using her flirtatiousness, cleavage and Aries MC to good effect. Yates was described as "the vixen and the Earth mother" (Moon in Scorpio, Sun in Taurus). She eventually married Geldof in August 1986 and they had three children together. When the man she believed to be her father died in April 1993, her outlook changed – she was not only outrageous and shocking but also worried about her age and looks. In May 1997 (when TR Saturn hit her MC and TR Uranus hit her Descendant) she discovered that in fact TV presenter Hughie Green, who had just died, was her true father. The shock sent her into a deep depression. By then Paula's romantic life was in tatters. Yates met singer Michael Hutchence (qv, Australian Data) in the 80s while presenting *The Tube*, and they rekindled their association on 31 October 1994 (on the interviewing bed of her show *The Big Breakfast*, TR Jupiter conjunct Moon in Scorpio) and began an affair soon after. She split with 'Saint Bob' in February 1995 (TR Pluto, ruler of EQHS 4th conjunct Jupiter, ruler of EQHS 5th) and tabloids made her into a national figure of hate. Although now living the life of a rock chick, Yates continued to be an earthy, ordinary mother to their daughter Tiger Lily (b. 22 July 1996). When Hutchence was found hanged on 22 November 1997 (TR Saturn conjunct South Node, near MC), Yates blamed his 'suicide' on Bob Geldof for not allowing the couple access to their children. She slipped into a deep depression, began using drugs again and, tragically, was found dead by her daughter on 17 September 2000. In November a coroner's report stated she had died of an accidental heroin overdose.

> Q "[When younger] she was also famous for her highly potent, almost camp seductiveness... she emitted a lusty, giddy vitality which many men found captivating, and which would eventually serve her well on television... [She] was herself the product of another time, a time when celebrity was little more than a hobby for a feckless peroxide blonde of semi-bohemian provenance... Yates was an English eccentric in the classic sense." (Steven Daly, Vanity Fair, 2/01)

David Yip
> b. 4 June 1951, 18.30 GDT, Liverpool, England, 53N25, 02W55.
> FCC q. him. RR: A.

With *The Chinese Detective* (1981-2) Yip broke down the barriers to become the first ethnic lead in a major television series. Whilst subsequently filming four documentaries about the Chinese community, he became more aware of the Eastern roots he had neglected as a Liverpudlian child. Yip has appeared in the Spielberg films *Empire of the Sun* (1987) and *Indiana Jones and the Temple of Doom* (1984), as well as the Bond movie *A View To a Kill* (1985).

Michael York
> b. 27 March 1942, 05.05 GDT, Fulmer, Buckinghamshire, England, 51N33, 0W34.
> From his autobiography, *Travelling Player: An Autobiography* (Headline, 1991), p. 5. RR: B.

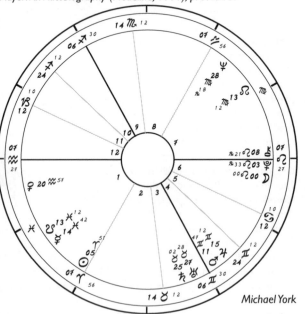

Michael York

Film and television actor usually cast in strong, leading roles. York gained experience with the National Youth Theatre and at Oxford University's Dramatic Society (he graduated in 1964). He made his film debut in 1967 (the year TR Saturn crossed his Sun) and went on to star in international films, including *Romeo and Juliet* and the highly successful cult flick *Cabaret* (released on 13 February 1972, as TR Neptune approached MC). In the last few years he has made dozens of film appearances, including the *Austin Powers* trilogy (1997, 1999 and 2002), and has leant his voice to a number of animated films. On television he appeared in *The Forsyte Saga* (January to July 1967). York married Patricia McCallum on his birthday in 1968.

Susannah York
> b. 9 January 1939, 10.00 GMT, London, England, 51N30, 0W10.
> From Suzanne Michaud, original source not known. York told astrologer Nicholas Campion that she had no idea of her birth time. Sy Scholfield reports that a Times birth announcement on 11 January 1939, p. 1 states a Miss Fletcher was born on 9 January 1939 in London: FLETCHER. – On Jan. 9, 1939, at 18, Walpole Street, S.W.3, to Joan, wife of Peel Fletcher – a daughter. RR: C.

Actress with credits ranging from international films (*Tom Jones*, 1963) to experimental fringe theatre. In January 1996 York was directed by her son in *Look Back in Anger* at Oxford. In November 1996 she joined the RSC in Stratford for her first Shakespearean role on the British stage. Although she has made numerous plays and films, she is remembered for her lesbian scene in *The Killing of Sister George*. York is also the author of books for children.

> Q "People do say I am very energetic, alive, speedy and restless, and I recognise those traits. But there is another side to me which is at odds with that. It is a pedantic side... I am incredibly slow. I don't have a natural facility for the techniques of life in any way. I think I am a fairly basic and earthy character." (Susannah York, *Daily Mail*, 16/3/96)

Angus and Malcolm Young – see AC/DC

George Young
b. 6 November 1946, 08.30 GMT, Bernard Street, Glasgow, Scotland, 55N51, 04W14.
Gerard q. BC (George Redburn Young). RR: AA.
Brother of Angus and Malcolm Young of AC/DC (qv), George Young was a member of the successful Australian group Easybeats (which had five Australian #1 hits from June 1965 to December 1966). After they split in 1969, Young worked with his brothers to develop AC/DC in 1973.

Kirsty Young
✪ b. 23 November 1968, 20.50 MET, East Kilbride, Scotland, 55N45, 04W13.
Gerard q. BC. RR: AA.

Kirsty Young, glamorous, bright and professional, is the highly respected TV news journalist who has given gravitas to mainstream news. She began making her name on Channel 5 from 1996 before being poached by ITV in 1999 (she began reading the news there on 10 January 2000). Young, however, returned to Channel 5, and has even performed as Peggy Lee on a celebrity edition of the TV talent contest *Stars in Their Eyes* (she won). Young's father deserted the family home when she was two months old but she acquired an unshakeable optimism from her mother and learned tact and kindness from her stepfather, who joined the family when she was three. She left school to become an au pair in Switzerland before working in radio and TV in Scotland and has admitted to battling bulimia for a short while.

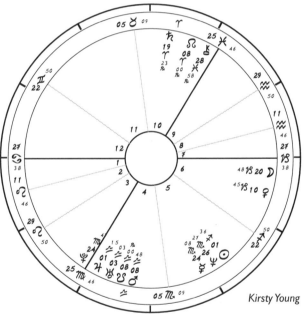

Kirsty Young

Paul Young
b. 3 July 1944, 22.25 DGDT, Elsie Inglis Maternity Hospital, Edinburgh, Scotland, 55N57, 03W10.
Gerard q. BC. RR: AA.
Actor with many television and film credits, including the soap *Take the High Road* (from 1987-90) and two series of *The Tales of Para Handy* (1994-5).

Will Young

✪ b. 20 January 1979, 21.55 GMT, Reading, England, 51N28, 0W59.
FCC q. BC in hand (a twin, William Robert Young). RR: AA.

Along with some 10,000 other pop wannabes, Will Young applied to TV's *Pop Idol* – the new 'reality' talent show – and was granted an audition on 7 August 2001. The audition took place on 5 September and when the show started soon after (as TR Pluto conjunct Venus) millions of viewers followed Young's efforts as he progressed all the way to the final. On 9 February 2002 he won a staggering 4.6 million votes to win the show and become Britain's first *Pop Idol*. His double-sided first single, *Anything is Possible/Evergreen*, debuted in the charts at #1 on 9 March 2002 and sold almost 1.78 million copies. It became the biggest selling debut single in Britain and the 12th biggest selling single in the UK of all time. Young's

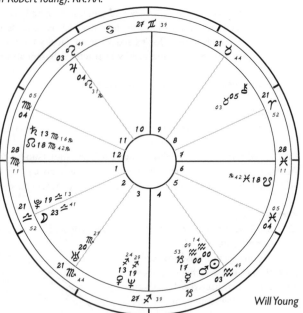

Will Young

homosexuality was made public on 10 March 2002 but the revelation had little effect on his record sales or popularity with his audience. Critics suggest that Young has the vocal talent and approach to have career longevity in pop music. Young has both key astrological signs of prominence: Moon-Pluto (conjunction) and Mercury-Pluto (square). Before his fame he worked as a personal assistant at Sony Music and had been in a TV boy band for *GMTV*, but with little success.

Lena Zavaroni

b. 4 November 1963, 00.45 GMT, Greenock, Scotland, 55N56, 04W48.
Gerard q. BC (Lena Hilda Zavaroni). RR: AA.

A talented child star who won *Opportunity Knocks* five times in a row from 6 January 1974 and had a Top Ten hit in March 1974 at the age of ten. The girl with a remarkable and powerful voice beyond her years was given her own show, toured the world and earned £300,000 a year. In Japan her song *Ma He's Making Eyes at Me* hit #1 and Lena toured Japan, sang to President Ford at the White House and met Frank Sinatra and Lucille Ball. A natural performer, Lena was nevertheless shy and worked hard at being perfect and pleasing others (Uranus). She lived away from her family, staying with her agent from age ten in London, totally focused and driven to succeed. Yet even as early as May

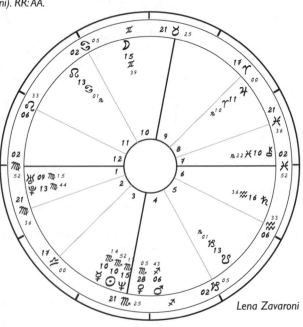

Lena Zavaroni

1974 the newspapers expressed concern at her losing considerable weight. Later she attended the Italia Conti stage school and made friends with fellow student Bonnie Langford (qv). At 13 (when TR Uranus crossed her Sun, and TR Neptune opposed her Moon), Zavaroni fell victim to anorexia nervosa (6th rulers Saturn in 6th and Uranus prominent – on Ascendant, square Moon). Her weight fell to four stone (56 pounds) and later (in Summer 1979) spent months in hospital. Between 1982 and 1984 she had little work but went public about her illness. In Summer 1985 she staged a comeback but a year later the illness stopped her working again. Sadly, although she sought treatment sporadically over the years, the illness took over her life. Eventually it destroyed her career and 18 month marriage, which ended around the time her mother committed suicide. In 1995 she went to a clinic in Canada to build her self-esteem but she was unable to cope with an empty feeling she called 'static'. At four and a half stone, depressed, broke and desperate to be well enough to make a comeback, Zavaroni underwent a brain operation (leuchotomy) to cure her anorexia on 7 September 1999, but after developing a blood infection the sweet little girl with the big voice died at 18.30 on 1 October 1999 in Cardiff, Wales. A documentary *The Real Lena Zavaroni* aired on 23 February 2000.

Catherine Zeta-Jones

b. 25 September 1969, 14.40 MET, Swansea, Wales, 51N38, 03W57.
FCC q. her. RR: A.

Statuesque, stunning and highly driven, Jones had already appeared in *Annie* in the West End by age eleven. She went in search of an Equity card at 15 with ambitions to be a showgirl. By 16 she had performed on stage in *Bugsy Malone* and *The Pajama Game* before landing the role as second understudy in *42nd Street*. In classic star-is-born fashion she went on stage the night David Merrick, the producer, was in the audience and within two weeks he had agreed to let her star in the show. Later Jones appeared in two films in Paris before securing a substantial TV role in *The Darling Buds of May* (from 7 April 1991 until 5 April 1993, with 23 million viewers at its peak). Her career has been marked by lucky breaks (Ascendant ruler

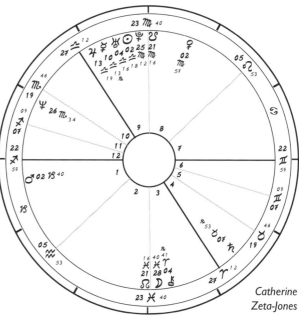

Catherine
Zeta-Jones

Jupiter is strong), although at times media interest in her love life has threatened to overshadow her professional life (MC in Libra). Her debut single was released in 1995. Her relationship with actor Michael Douglas* and commercially successful film roles (*The Mask of Zorro* – her big US break in July 1998, when TR Jupiter conjunct Moon, and *Entrapment* – April 1999) have kept her firmly in the spotlight and raised her to a A-list Hollywood celebrity (MC in Libra and Moon opposite Pluto). Michael Douglas began dating Jones in June 1998, divorced his wife of 22 years in October 1999, and married Jones in November 2000. The couple have two children**. A role in *Traffic* (January 2001)

---

* Michael Douglas b. 25 September 1944, 10.30 EWT (+4), New Brunswick, New Jersey, 40N29, 74W27. From BC in hand, from Lois Rodden. RR: AA.
** Dylan Michael Douglas b. 8 August 2000, 17.52 PDT (+7), Los Angeles, California, 34N03, 118W15. From news reports. RR: A.
Carys Douglas b. 20 April 2003, 04.50 EDT (+4), Ridgewood, New Jersey, 40N59, 74W07. From their official website and news reports. RR: A.

with Douglas earned her a Golden Globe nomination and proved she was more than Douglas's wife. In February 2003 she testified in an invasion of privacy suit brought against *Hello!* magazine, and won a Bafta and Oscar (March 2003) for her role in the musical film *Chicago*. In February 2003 *The Mail on Sunday's Rich Report* estimated the couple's fortune at £175 million.

> Q "After [*Darling Buds*] every person I had a cup of tea with was [according to the Press] the new love of my life, and all of that became much more important than me as a person or the work I did... It was like I was a pretty face and a big bust and nothing else. I never wanted to be that." (Catherine Zeta-Jones, *The Times Magazine*, 16/12/2000)

The Australian Data Section

The following section includes more than 30 profiles of successful Australian entertainers who have made an impact in Britain.

To acquire further Australian data, see:

http://Astroqueer.tripod.com
Simon-Astley Scholfield's excellent website with numerous profiles of entertainers and other public figures. Sy Scholfield has a reputation as a top rate data collector and can be contacted via his website or at syscholfield@hotmail.com

50 Australian Charts
Dennis Sutton's book of horoscopes and profiles of public figures is available from
21C Astrologer, 14 Lasburn Crescent, Carlingford, NSW 2118, Australia
The cost is $30 Australian (including postage); interntaional money orders only
email: lasburns@optusnet.com.au

The Australian Data Collection
Stephanie Johnson's ever-expanding compilation of the data collected by various astrologers is included with every copy of Solar Fire astrology software. For more details see: www.esotech.com.au

Jimmy Barnes
✪ b. 28 April 1956, 16.30 GDT, Glasgow, Scotland, 55N51, 04W14.
   Gerard q. BC (James Dixon Swan). RR: AA.
Australian rock singer. Barnes's family moved to Australia when he was 15, and after playing in a school band he replaced Bon Scott (qv) as lead vocalist in the band Fraternity. In early 1973 he joined Cold Chisel and the band won a record contract in 1976. The band became one of Australia's highest profile music acts (charting from 1978). They split in 1983 and Barnes went solo (having hits from late 1984 through 1995). Although promoted in the US in 1987, Barnes didn't make an impact there. By then he had left his wild days behind, married and toured with his family. Considered an Australian folk hero, Barnes is one of Australia's beloved 'working class men'.

Bryan Brown
   b. 23 June 1947, 08.45 AEST (-10), Sydney, Australia, 33S52, 151E13.
   Lois Rodden q. Nancy Ewart, who obtained the data "directly from him", 08.30 to 09.00. RR: A.
Brown moved to London and joined the National Theatre in 1974, before embarking on a film career back home in Australia (most notably, *Breaker Morant*, 1979). He has maintained successful careers in both Australia and America (*F/X*, *Gorillas in the Mist*, *Cocktail*) and appeared in a well-received British mini-series.

Jono Coleman

✪ b. 29 February 1956, 11.30 GMT, London, England, 51N30, 0W10.
Sy Scholfield q. him to Jane Bennett and Craig McIntosh, as presented in their book A Handbook of
Astrology for Australia and New Zealand (1986, p. 205). RR: A.

Jonathan Coleman is a larger-than-life radio personality and funnyman known in Australia and the UK.
After working in advertising and playing keyboards with various bands, Coleman moved into radio,
TV and film in the late 80s. He returned to Britain in 1990 and worked on *Power Station* on satellite
TV, Radio 4 and GLR. (Mercury is helpful for radio talk but the Moon is the key player for success in
this medium – Coleman has Ascendant ruler Moon conjunct Neptune and square MC ruler Uranus.
His Mercury is unaspected.) In April 1993 (as TR Saturn conjunct his MC) Richard Branson (qv)
chose him to present a show for his new radio station. Coleman fronted the *Russ 'n' Jono's Breakfast
Experience*, which won him a Sony Gold in 1996 for Best Breakfast Show. In February 1997 he joined
Heart 106.2 (as TR Saturn crossed his EQHS 10th)

Jason Donovan

b. 1 June 1968, 18.00 AEST (-10), Melbourne, Australia, 37S49, 144E58.
From the biography, The Jason Donovan Factfile, "exactly..." RR: B.

Son of seasoned actor Terence
Donovan and TV hostess Sue
McIntosh, who were involved in a
bitter divorce when Jason was five.
Donovan was well-known in
Australia from the age of 11 when
he won a continuing role in *Skyways*
(October 1979, TR Jupiter conjunct
MC). He was asked to join the soap
Neighbours in early 1986 and his
arrival coincided with the producer
bringing in co-star Kylie Minogue
(qv, Australian Data). Their sexual
chemistry was later to be marketed
worldwide. By 1987, as TR Uranus
crossed his Ascendant, the show
had become a phenomenon in
Australia and in England, and both
Donovan and Minogue began
releasing commercially successful
records. Donovan had his first
chart entry in September 1988 and

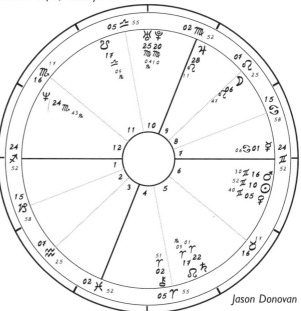

Jason Donovan

filmed his last *Neighbours* scene in April 1989. He made his UK stage debut with *Joseph and the
Amazing Technicolour Dreamcoat* on 12 June 1991. He sued a magazine in August 1991 (winning on 3
April 1992) over gay rumours and his career never fully recovered from the backlash. His teenage
audience had grown up and the gay audience were angered by the libel case and his reaction to the
gay 'slur'. Within months he'd lost his hair, youthful looks, fan base and record deal! He also lost
Minogue, his girlfriend of four years, to his musical hero Michael Hutchence (qv, Australian Data).
After amassing 17 hits (including four UK #1s) he sunk to a personal nadir in March 1995 (as TR
Saturn crossed his IC) and collapsed on numerous occasions after drug binges. He later admitted
that his four-year stint with cocaine cost him £250,000. He returned to the stage in September 1996
for the play *Night Must Fall*, but it was axed after one month, although his tour with *The Rocky Horror
Show* was well-received. The British Press had a field day with his 'fall from grace' when he began a
16-date pub tour performing his 90s hits in March 2001. In April 2002 there was talk of him returning
to TV in a new Australian medical series called *MDA*.

Bob Downe

✪ b. 4 February 1959, 11.00 AEST (-10), Melbourne, Australia, 37S49, 144E58.

   Sy Scholfield q. his email, and confirms the date and place from Melbourne's Age newspaper. RR: A.
Rubber-faced comedian and singer. Downe (Mark Trevorrow), the cabaret performer known as the
Prince of Polyester, began his career as a daily Pop columnist before leaving in 1980 to take his group
Gloria and the Go Go's (later The Globos) on tour. The group disbanded in 1984 and in January 1987
he went solo as a cabaret comedian in Sydney. After an August 1988 performance at the Edinburgh
Festival as Bob Downe, he became famous with British viewers when seen with Lily Savage (qv) on
various variety shows from 1994. Now a cult figure, he debuted his show in New York to great
acclaim in Spring 2001.

Dan Falzon

   b. 24 November 1974, 20.45 AEDT (-11), Melbourne, Australia, 37S49, 144E58.

   From his autobiography, My Diary: Intimate Secrets of Neighbour Dan Falzon (Boxtree, 1995), p. 16-
   7. Date confirmed from other sources, including birth announcement found by Sy Scholfield. RR: B.
Young actor and pop performer who appeared in Neighbours in 1992, filming the first episode on 29
April whilst still at school. His interest in acting had been aroused in school plays during the mid-80s.
He got himself a manager in April 1994 and left Neighbours in December. Falzon embarked on a UK
promotional tour in May 1995 and proved immensely popular (TR Saturn over the MC). Since then
film projects and music gigs with his band have taken his time. Falzon is known to have a hugely
positive approach to his work and life (the Sagittarian/Gemini influence). In an attempt to promote
the sponsor-a-child charity World Vision, he was mauled by a lion in April 1996.

Cornelia Frances

   b. 7 April 1941, 07.07 GDT, Liverpool, England, 53N25, 02W55.

   FCC q. her, from her mother's memory (the hospital registered her birth as 07.15). Data confirmed
   in her March 2003 autobiography And What Have You Done Lately (Pan Macmillan). RR: A.

Frances first won national fame in
Australia for her portrayal of icy
Sister Scott in the soap The Young
Doctors (from November 1976).
She was convent-educated from
the age of 4 to 16 and later trained
at drama school. She has spoken
publicly of her strict and
tumultuous childhood (Saturn
Rising and Pluto opposite Mars on
4/10th cusps) as well as her early
rebellious attitude. In 1960 Frances
won her first professional film part
when TR Saturn crossed her MC.
She moved to Australia with her
partner in 1965. In August of that
year she worked as a model and
later, in June 1966, won a job as a
TV presenter. Returning to England
Frances married in 1969 before
emigrating to Australia the
following year. She took the

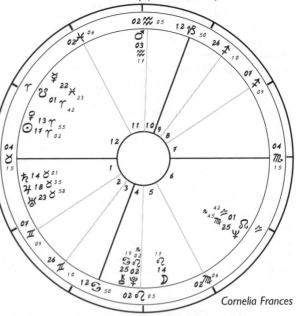

Cornelia Frances

opportunity to act and by 1976 had appeared in some 26 roles on Australian TV. Offered a part in
The Young Doctors in September 1976, she would leave the show in November 1978 when her
husband changed job (TR Pluto opposite Sun). Roles in Sons and Daughters (from November 1981 to
November 1985) and Home and Away followed. She was sacked from the latter series in June 1989
(as TR Saturn crossed her MC) when the producers decided to focus chiefly on the younger
characters (although in 2003 she was asked to return). Late 1990-1 was a year of opportunity in

Britain to act and appear in pantomime, as well as one of personal pain and adjustment (both TR Neptune and Uranus crossed her MC). Frances has a strong sense of drama and is known by friends to be something of an earth mother and traditionalist (Moon in Leo, Taurus Rising). It is also rare for her not to talk about money and her financial position in interviews. After years of non-acting jobs, her career was resurrected in December 2000 (Neptune conjunct EQHS 10th) when she was asked to take on the role of stern quizmaster in Australia's version of *The Weakest Link* – the show began on 5 February 2001 and ran for two years. Frances was made to look a carbon copy of series originator Anne Robinson (qv) and her cutting remarks and acerbic dismissals saw ratings hit the roof. After years of bitchy acting roles (Aries, Saturn prominent), TV bosses hired her because she has, "a command, a look, an attitude," and Cornelia Frances relished every moment of it.

Colin Friels
✪ b. 25 September 1952, 15.00 GDT, Kilwinning, Ayrshire, Scotland, 55N39, 04W42.
  Gerard q. BC (Colin Smith Friels). RR: AA.
Friels trained at Australia's National Institute of Dramatic Arts with fellow students Mel Gibson (qv, Australian Data) and Judy Davis, whom he later married. His films include *Monkey Grip* (1981), *High Tide* (1987) and *Class Action* (1991). In 1997 Friels battled pancreatic cancer, which almost cost him his life. His personal life was back in the news on 30 October 2002 when an Australian court ordered him not to "assault, harass, or otherwise threaten" his wife, following a domestic disturbance.

Belinda Giblin
  b. 2 March 1950, 08.30 AEST (-10), Tamworth, New South Wales, Australia, 31S05, 150E55.
  FCC q. her from her father's memory, March 1994 (Date confirmed by Sy Scholfield from The
  Sydney Morning Herald, 11/3/50). RR: A.

Cool blonde with large pale blue-eyes and cheekbones that could cut ice, Belinda Giblin captured a million hearts when she first appeared in the sexy Australian soap *The Box* (in October 1973). With Neptune-Mars on the Descendant she became one of the nation's major sex symbols but quit the show in November 1974, after the media attention left her without a private life. She was typecast in two sexy roles (*End Play*, 1975 and *Petersen*, 1976) before moving into gentle drama with *The Sullivans* in early 1977. In June 1978 the TV film *Say You Want Me* aired and she won a Sammy Award for Best Actress of the Year. In mid 1981 her daughter was born and Giblin spent two full years

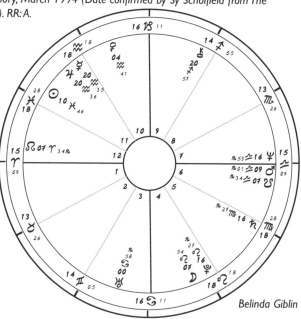

Belinda Giblin

looking after her, accepting roles only if the shoot could accommodate them both. She appeared in *The Empty Beach* (with Bryan Brown, qv, Australian Data) in November 1984, a year after she married long-time beau, stage designer Axel Bartz. With Venus in 10th, Giblin made efforts to move away from sexy roles and secured credibility as a major home-grown acting talent. Giblin has five retrograde planets and after a few years away from high-profile roles, she returned to greater and more solid success. In early April 1985 she accepted a leading role in *Sons and Daughters* and her arrival as the biggest bitch on screen became the TV sensation of the year, boosted the show's ratings, and shook up the storylines. In the role of Alison Carr (formerly Patricia Palmer), she tackled the character with a sledgehammer impact and stamped her place in Australian TV history (Giblin has Moon conjunct Pluto in EQHS 5th opposite Mercury, ruler of 3rd, for audience influence). Giblin had taken over from

Rowena Wallace (qv, Australian Data) but Giblin's Rat was sharper and bitchier (Aries Rising) than her predecessor's intense, emotional basketcase (Wallace has Virgo Rising, Moon in Scorpio). The show stopped production in April 1987 and Belinda gave birth in September of that year. She made a successful transition to theatre in October 1988 with *Move Over Mrs Markham* and carved a niche as one of Australia's most respected stage and TV actresses (often appearing in Alan Ayckbourn* farces). She is known to be direct, self-determining (Aries Rising) as well as slightly aloof (three planets in Aquarius). Her mother was an actress (Belinda has Moon-Pluto in Leo) who resembled Bette Davis. In March 1994 she began a nationwide tour of Australia in the nude play *Steaming*, proving she could still turn heads with both her acting and looks. In 1997 she appeared in the drama series *Good Guys, Bad Guys* before embarking on various stage tours and teaching. Her daughter Romy Bartz is now establishing herself as an actress.

Mel Gibson

✪ b. 3 January 1956, 16.45 EST (+5), Peekskill, NY, 41N17, 73W55.
From a news clipping announcing his birth. RR: A.

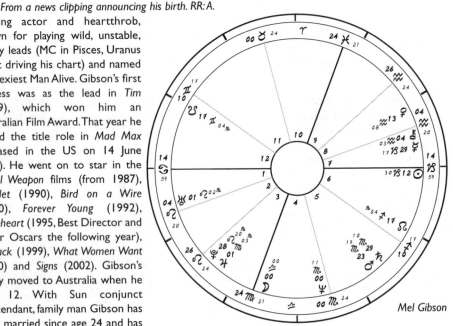

Leading actor and heartthrob, known for playing wild, unstable, wacky leads (MC in Pisces, Uranus in 1st driving his chart) and named the Sexiest Man Alive. Gibson's first success was as the lead in *Tim* (1979), which won him an Australian Film Award. That year he played the title role in *Mad Max* (released in the US on 14 June 1980). He went on to star in the *Lethal Weapon* films (from 1987), *Hamlet* (1990), *Bird on a Wire* (1990), *Forever Young* (1992), *Braveheart* (1995, Best Director and Actor Oscars the following year), *Payback* (1999), *What Women Want* (2000) and *Signs* (2002). Gibson's family moved to Australia when he was 12. With Sun conjunct Descendant, family man Gibson has been married since age 24 and has seven children.

Mel Gibson

Rebecca Gilling

b. 3 November 1953, 07.30 AEST (-10), Sydney, Australia, 33S52, 151E13.
FCC q. her, from her parents (same date and place from Sy Scholfield q. birth announcement). RR: A.
Gilling began her career as a model before moving into television on the sexy soap *Number 96*. She is best known for her starring role in the melodrama *Return to Eden* (two series from September 1983 and February 1986), as a woman who returns with a new face to wreak revenge on her adulterous husband, who had pushed her into crocodile infested waters. The soap owed more to its glossy American counterparts than to antipodean shows. Gilling's son was born in 1987. She has also made notable appearances in *Glenview High* (from September 1977), *A Dangerous Life* (November 1988) with Gary Busey, and *The Paper Man* (September 1990).

---

* Alan Ayckbourn b. 12 April 1939, 22.00 GMT, London, England, 51N30, 0W10. Laura Boomer q. him to a fellow astrologer. RR: A.

Anne Haddy

b. 5 October 1930, 17.00 ACST (-9.5 = -9hrs 30 mins), Quorn, Australia, 32S21, 138E03.

FCC q. her, September 1992 (same date and place from Sy Scholfield q. birth announcement). RR: A. An only child, Haddy was obsessed with acting from an early age but was dissuaded by her parents. She grew up inventing characters, dressing up and performing with neighbourhood kids. After leaving school she worked in radio plays and had two children from a marriage that lasted until 1968. Upon moving to Sydney in 1960 Haddy's growing reputation as an actress brought her a steady flow of parts. She appeared in the successful Australian show *Dynasty* from October 1970. Her career has seen many set-backs due to severe illness. She suffered a massive heart attack on 20 March 1979 and within six months had open heart surgery. Then routine tests revealed she had stomach cancer. She returned to work in early 1981 on *Punishment*. Early 1982 brought her the first dose of fame in the continuing saga *Sons and Daughters*, before more heart surgery forced her retirement from the series in early 1983. It wasn't until 18 March 1985 (after twenty five years in television) that she became an 'overnight success' in *Neighbours* as the elegant Helen Daniels (she won the Penguin Award for her performance in 1987). The show was originally cancelled after 171 episodes but revived by another network and went on to major success. *Neighbours'* popularity in England (where it was first shown on 27 October 1986) resulted in international recognition for this versatile actress. Plagued for years by serious illness, when diagnosed with kidney disease following a hip operation, Haddy asked the producers to kill off her character. The character's on-screen death in 1997 was one of the show's most watched episodes in the UK. Haddy died in Melbourne on 6 June 1999, survived by her husband, actor James Condon, and six children.

David Helfgott

b. 19 May 1947, 08.24 AEST (-10), Melbourne, Australia, 37S49, 144E58.

Speculative time from his astrologer wife, Gillian Helfgott, in the FAA Journal, December 1996. RR: C. Child prodigy whose love of the piano was both spurred on and crushed by a dominating father, resulting in Helfgott's nervous breakdown. In May 1986 "the mad pianist" was approached to make his life story and the film, *Shine*, premiered in January 1996. It went on to achieve international success and reignited Helfgott's career. He was a surprise performer at the Academy Awards in March 1997. He met astrologer Gillian Murray at 13.15 on 30 November 1983 in Perth. They were married on 26 August 1984. Murray was born on 10 December 1931 at 05.04 AEST (-10) in Melbourne, Australia, 37S49, 144E58 (Data from her mother, given in *FAA Journal*, December 1996. RR: A.) In the film Gillian was portrayed by Lynn Redgrave (qv). Redgrave's Mercury sits on her IC and her Sun conjuncts Gillian's EQHS 4th cusp. Redgrave's Moon-Venus falls on her Uranus, and MC on Mars-Mercury.

Russell Hitchcock

b. 15 June 1949, 07.00 AEST (-10), Melbourne, Australia, 37S49, 144E58.

Edwin Steinbrecher q. him from his father's memory. RR: A.

With musical partner Graham Russell (qv), Hitchcock formed the band Air Supply in 1976. He had met Russell during the run of *Jesus Christ, Superstar* and their first single was released in Australia in November 1976. Their major success, however, was to take place in America. From May 1980 to September 1983 they had eight Top Five singles (seven consecutive) in America and three million-sellers.

Paul Hogan

b. 8 October 1939, 09.30 AEST (-10), Lightning Ridge, New South Wales, Australia, 29S25, 147E59).

Victoria Shaw q. Hogan's mother for between "6.30 to 10.30 am." Shaw used Granville as the birthplace and rectified to 09.03 and 20 Sagittarius Asc. With the correct birthplace, rectified Ascendant degree calculates to 09.30. (N.B. Hogan later grew up, rather than was born in Granville.) RR: C.

Leather-faced Australian hero who amplified his national success with the worldwide box-office hit *Crocodile Dundee* (Moon conjunct Pluto, Pluto square MC ruler Mercury). Nonchalant, easily bored and highly intelligent, he dropped out of school at 15 and earned a modest living as a boxer, union organiser and bridge rigger. Hogan married at 19. For a dare he appeared on Australia's *New Faces* talent show in 1971 and became a sensation. His TV series *The Paul Hogan Show* ran for nine years and was syndicated in 30 countries. Hogan became spokesman for the Australian tourist industry. Whilst filming *Crocodile Dundee* in June 1986 (TR Uranus conjunct Ascendant) he suffered a cerebral haemorrhage. The film was released on 26 September 1986 and had grossed (US) \$117 million by the end of the year. He is one tall poppy no Australian has wanted to chop down.

Barry Humphries

✪   b. 17 February 1934, 06.30 AEST (-10), Camberwell, Australia, 37S50, 145E04.
    Dennis Sutton, in 50 Australian Charts, states "from him." Sy Scholfield q. his baby book for the date and place. (Previously, Suzanne Michaud gave 06.00, Melbourne, original source not known.) RR: A.

Reclusive Humphries is best known as the housewife megastar Dame Edna Everage ('born' in May 1955) and the revolting drunk Sir Les Patterson — both humorous creations are highly popular around the world. Humphries, who had a love-hate relationship with his mother (who put order and good behaviour above all else), was a precocious child who entertained the family from 18 months old. Shattered that he was unable to always please his parents (Aquarius) he rebelled in adolescence and was soon determined to be a provocative, shocking artist as he studied at University. In 1955 he joined a theatre company and soon became notorious for his racist, vitriolic characters (including Sandy Stone) — his revenge on the

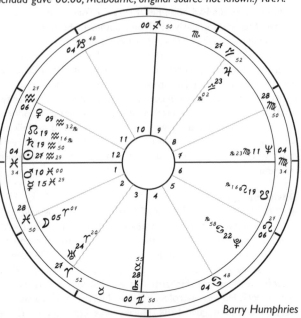

Barry Humphries

narrow-minded, suburban middle class of Australia. In doing so he broke new ground and 'created' a new Australian humour. In June 1959 he went to conquer the London stage and won a role in the musical *Oliver!* in 1960. Two years on and he was back in Australia with a one-man show of his characters, *A Nice Night's Entertainment*. The show opened in London in Spring 1963 but bombed (during his Saturn Return). Success in England began in 1964 when he was asked to write a comic strip for *Private Eye*, the satirical magazine. The result was the cult figure Barry McKenzie, which was later made into a film. Humphries raged an on-going war with the bottle and was hospitalised in 1968, the year his marriage collapsed. This led to a period of anguish, isolation and further illness. In 1976 he was back in the UK as Dame Edna Everage, a role that was to make him a household name. Success in the US eluded him until his October 1999 Broadway debut (a 2000 Tony Award winner) and appearance in *Ally McBeal* (2001-2). His personal life has often been chaotic. In October 1955 (TR Jupiter and Pluto opposite Sun) he announced he was to marry but the union went sour a year later. Humphries married in Spring 1959 (for nine years, with a daughter Tessa, born 14 May 1963) and again in June 1979. In June 1990 he married his fourth wife. Humphries sought his mother's approval right up until her death in 1984. In November 2002 he published a memoir, *My Life as Me*.

Michael Hutchence

✪   b. 22 January 1960, 05.00 AEST (-10), Sydney, Australia, 33S52, 151E13.
    Scott Whitters q. an article, A Life Lived INXS by Toby Cresswell, featured in Juice Magazine. RR: B.

A charismatic rock icon with a hypnotic stage presence, Hutchence (with Moon-Neptune in Scorpio in 10th) was the wild, flamboyant singer of INXS (note the band's name can be read in MC ruler Venus conjunct hedonistic Jupiter in Sagittarius). He had a nomadic childhood moving to Hong Kong at 5, to Los Angeles with his mother at 15 and then returning to Sydney the following year. In August 1977 Hutchence joined the band the Farris Brothers before they became INXS in September 1979

(TR Pluto conjunct MC). The band began to hit the charts in October 1980 and a year later signed to RCA Records (TR Jupiter conjunct MC). In April 1982 Hutchence travelled to the US and UK to negotiate the next stage in the group's career (TR Saturn conjunct MC) and the band began to chart in the all-important US market in March 1983 (TR Pluto conjunct EQHS 10th). By 1985 they were making their impact worldwide and an appearance at Live Aid on 13 July helped further their fame. In 1986 Hutchence made his screen debut in *Dogs in Space* and would later play Percy Shelley in *Frankenstein Unbound* (released in the US in May 1990, Hutchence's Moon is on Shelley's Descendant plus other interesting synastry). They reached

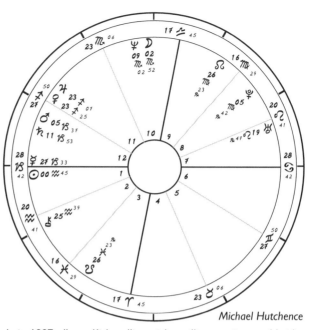

Michael Hutchence

the commercial stratosphere with their 1987 album *Kick*, selling eight million copies worldwide. Hutchence took a sabbatical from late 1988 to November 1989 (during his Saturn Return and TR Neptune conjunct Saturn). Despite the band's success the press were always more interested in his excesses and sexual escapades (MC in Libra, MC and 5th House ruler Venus conjunct Jupiter in Sagittarius), and Hutchence fought to escape from his fame through drink and drugs (Moon-Neptune in Scorpio in 10th). By 1995 he was fighting the press for the first time in his career as his affairs with Kylie Minogue (qv), Helena Christensen and Paula Yates (qv) began to overshadow his musical accomplishments. His affair with Paula Yates (wife of Bob Geldof, qv) turned the media against him and much was made of the love triangle (from February 1995, as TR Uranus crossed Mercury-Ascendant). Their daughter was born on 22 July 1996 but after erotic Polaroids were found of the couple in September (TR Uranus conjunct Sun), Yates lost custody of her three other children to father Geldof. By 1997 INXS were in decline but as they were about to embark on a new tour, Hutchence was found hanged on 22 November 1997. There is still some speculation as to whether the death was an act of accidental strangulation via auto-eroticism or suicide by hanging. (Mysterious deaths, or when the cause is in dispute, are accompanied by Neptune transits, and Hutchence had TR Neptune conjunct Mercury-Ascendant.)

Clive James
b. 7 October 1939, 21.00 AEST (-10), Sydney, Australia, 33S52, 151E13.
Taurus Ascendant with Uranus Rising as stated by an astrologer on James's television show, who was given the complete data by James himself. Date and place from Who's Who on Television. (N.B. Uranus was on a Taurean Ascendant from approx. 20.15 to 21.40.) RR: C.
Presenter and writer who casts a sharp, critical eye over other shows on television. He was the influential TV critic (Moon conjunct Pluto in 3rd) of *The Observer* (1972-82) before moving to wry, witty television commentary as well as documentary.

Maggie Kirkpatrick
b. 29 January 1941, 07.20 AEST (-10), Albury, Australia, 36S05, 146E55.
FCC q. her. RR: A.
In *Prisoner: Cell Block H* Kirkpatrick starred as the sadistic lesbian prison guard, Joan Ferguson ('The Freak') – note the Scorpio MC – the woman viewers loved to hate for nearly 500 episodes. She entered full-time acting at 19 (after winning the City of Sydney Shakespearean Championship at 16) but it wasn't until her Saturn Return that her career finally began to take off. Now a renowned theatre

and musical actress, Kirkpatrick broke many television moulds during her tenure in *Prisoner* (she began filming the show in February 1982, and her part aired from June 1982 until the final day of shooting on 29 August 1986). Kirkpatrick has a monumental presence on screen and in *Prisoner* the Freak's reign of terror and corrupt ways brought her fans from around the world (including Sammy Davis Jr., who wanted to appear in the show alongside her). So strong was her impact that finding substantial follow-up roles for Kirkpatrick proved difficult. Nevertheless the actress entered the soap fray once more with *Richmond Hill* as pretentious Ivy Hackett. What followed *Richmond Hill* were seven disappointing years without

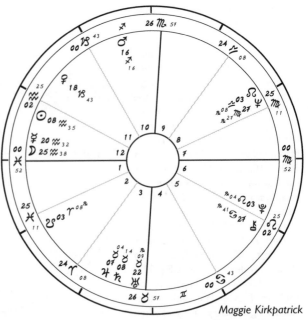

Maggie Kirkpatrick

substantial roles because she had spoken out against TV producers once too often, criticising them for the lack of opportunities for older actresses. Her chart shows many 'tough' aspects and a strong Saturn implying late success. In 1995 (as TR Pluto crossed the MC and into the EQHS 10th), Kirkpatrick's international career was resurrected by comedy queen Lily Savage (qv), who invited her to co-star in the British stage hit *Prisoner Cell Block H: The Musical* (from October 1995).

Val Lehman

✪ b. 15 March 1943, 05.00 (-9), Cottesloe, Perth, Australia, 31S59, 115E45.

🌑 FCC q. Lehman's mother, Kathleen Malta, for "In those days delivering mothers were administered 'Twilight Sleep' which effectively knocked them out for the moment of birth. However, I believe it was sometime between 4am and 6am on that morning, probably towards the latter. The place was Devonleigh Hospital, Cottesloe, Western Australia." (Same date from Sy Scholfield q. birth announcement, Valerie Kathleen Willis). RR: C.

Formidable, straight-talking actress, best-known for her continuing role in the Australian drama series *Prisoner: Cell Block H*. Lehman played double murderess Bea Smith, the prison's Top Dog, feared and loved in equal measure (note the Scorpio MC). The character bucked the system but was motherly to many of her fellow inmates (Lehman herself has Aquarius Rising and Moon in Cancer). Up until winning the role in May 1978 (the show debuted in February 1979) she had only played in minor roles and worked as an extra. At 19 Val Lehman began a 10-year stint as an army wife, but the couple split (during her Saturn Return) when she took up acting. Lehman was

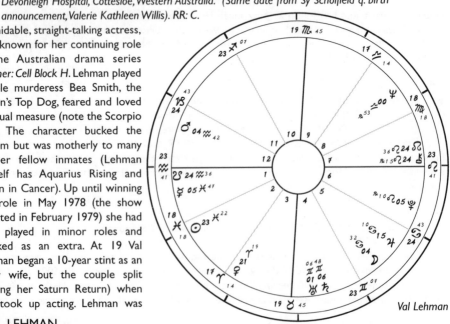

Val Lehman

immensely popular in the rebellious role, particularly when her character went up against bent warden Joan Ferguson (played by Maggie Kirkpatrick, qv, Australian Data). Off-camera she was the team leader and Equity Rep for the show's group of actresses. For the role Lehman won two Logie Awards, Australia's top TV acting prize, in March 1982 and a further Logie in 1983. In April 1983 she announced she was quitting the show (she taped the final episode on 13 May 1983, and completed work at 21.30!), and moved into theatre roles (including *Trafford Tanzi* and *Steaming*) but TV work since has been sporadic as TV bosses believed she was too identified with her *Prisoner* role. In March 1986 she starred in the big budget mini-series *A Fortunate Life*. Her stage work even took her to England in February 1996 (TR Saturn conjunct Sun) with the lead role in *Misery* and for various promotional tours with the UK's *Prisoner* fanclub (including a tour in September 1990). Lehman married playwright Charles Collins in 1989.

Julian McMahon

✪   b. 27 July 1968, 10.20 AEST (-10), Sydney, Australia, 33S52, 151E13.
     Sy Scholfield q. the Sun Herald (Sydney, 28/7/68), p. 5. RR: B.
Model (from 1987) who began acting in TV's *Home and Away* before moving to the US to star in the psychological series *Profiler*. He is the son of former Australian Prime Minister William McMahon.

Kylie Minogue

   b. 28 May 1968, 11.00 AEST (-10), Melbourne, Australia, 37S49, 144E58.
   Prue Hollinshead q. an article by Val Hopgood in Australian Women's Weekly Magazine, 5/1997. RR: B.

Petite actress and singer with a talent for reinvention. Minogue first found fame in the soap *Neighbours* (from early 1986). Some years before she had made appearances in *The Sullivans* and *Skyways*. In October 1987 she was approached by record producers Stock, Aitken and Waterman who were aware of her popularity and marketability. The first result of their collaboration was the UK release *I Should Be So Lucky*, a chart-topper for five weeks from February 1988 (TR Jupiter on EQHS 10th). Minogue became the most successful artist in the British charts during 1988-9. Her over-exposure during this time caused Minogue's career to suffer, despite her ever-changing image and the on-going media interest in all aspects of her

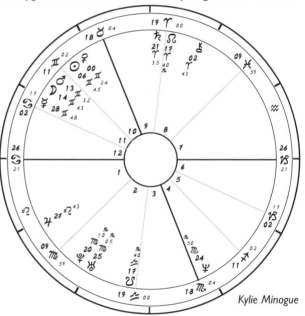

Kylie Minogue

life. She was pop's virgin until she met Michael Hutchence (qv) and soon developed a sexy, tarty image. She changed gear in 1994 with a trendier image then went Indie with Nick Cave. She resuscitated her career by signing a new deal in June 1999 (a full Jupiter cycle after her first #1) and worked on a new sexy image (famously wearing gold hot pants in her video for *Spinning Around*, which hit #1 in July 2000, TR Jupiter on Venus). Kylie also caused a sensation with her performance closing the Sydney Olympic Games. Her longevity has surprised critics and Minogue has been unafraid to take professional gambles with her music and image. Her love life has always attracted much speculation (MC ruler Venus opposite Neptune, which also suggests her ever-changing feminine image, from hot pants to pop tart). 2001 saw her biggest year to date internationally with the song *Can't Get You Out of My Head* (one million sales in the UK alone, topping the charts in late September, as TR Saturn conjunct Moon). In May 2002 Minogue split with her partner of two years (TR Pluto opposite Moon). In a VH1 poll in September 2002 she was voted the second greatest female performer of all time, behind Madonna.

Guy Pearce

b. 5 October 1967, 16.15 GDT, Ely, Cambridgeshire, England, 52N24, 0E16.
FCC q. him. RR: A.

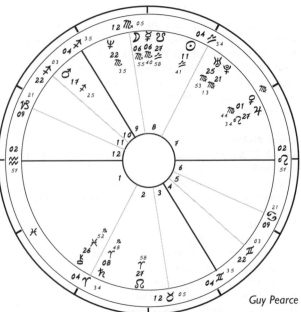

Guy Pearce

Actor and songwriter. Pearce moved to Australia at three and a half. At eight his father was killed in a plane crash (6 August 1976, TR Uranus conjunct EQHS 10th, TR Pluto approaching Sun). By the age of twelve, acting, dancing and writing were his passions. In 1984 Pearce won the UBBA Victorian Body Building Contest. In late 1985, as *Neighbours* swapped networks, Pearce was brought in for his first professional acting job with Jason Donovan and Kylie Minogue (both qv, Australian Data). His first day on the set was 3 December 1985 (TR Saturn approaching MC, TR Uranus on EQHS 10th ruler Mars, TR Pluto conjunct Mercury-Moon). It was a major turning point in his life and introduced him to a worldwide audience. The show's stars worked tirelessly from June 1986 promoting the show until ratings picked up considerably. Pearce, Donovan and Minogue stayed during the most commercially successful period of *Neighbours* (1986-9). An appearance in the film *Heaven Tonight* with Rebecca Gilling (qv, Australian Data) and six weeks in *Home and Away* followed. Many household names have given up roles in soap and met with obscurity, but Pearce's gamble paid off with an acclaimed starring role in the hilarious film *The Adventures of Priscilla, Queen of the Desert*, alongside Terence Stamp (qv). The film's release provided new career opportunities for him and coincided with the painful breakup of a long-term relationship. *Priscilla* brought offers from Hollywood and (following TR Uranus on Ascendant and TR Pluto on MC) he starred in *L.A. Confidential* (Autumn 1997), a critical and commercial success. Since his move to the US, Pearce has become a box-office star with roles such as *Rules of Engagement* (2000), *Memento* (2000), *The Count of Monte Cristo* (2002) and the #1 box-office hit *The Time Machine* (2002). His latest, *Two Brothers*, is due for a 2004 release. Pearce married in March 1997.

Tom Richards

b. 22 March 1948, 19.30 AEST (-10), Brisbane, Australia, 27S28, 153E02.
FCC q. him. RR: A.

Actor, journalist and cartoonist who trained in the theatre before becoming a familiar face on Australian television from the late 70s. Richards made appearances in the film *Dawn* (1976) and the series *Matlock Police* (shown from February 1971). In *Sons and Daughters* (appearing in over 500 episodes from November 1981 until mid-1986), his sizzling on-off again television relationship with Rowena Wallace and later Belinda Giblin (both profiles are presented in the Australian Data section) sent the ratings soaring. He returned to the show for its final episode, filmed in April 1987. Richards was so popular in Belgium in the role that he even scored a hit record, *Now I Know*. Richards spent his pre-acting days as a top swimmer, footballer and artist (he's well-known in Australia for his cartoons under the name Tomas). Richards has a heavily tenanted EQHS 10th House with Moon, Mars, Saturn and Pluto placed there, suggesting a variety of career pursuits.

Rick Springfield

✪ b. 23 August 1949, 19.00 AEST (-10), Guildford, Sydney, Australia, 33S51, 150E59.
Zein Stein q. an interview with him in 16 Magazine. (Same date and place from Sy Scholfield q. birth
announcement.) RR: A.

Springfield was a singer and American teen idol (his first track peaked in the US charts in October 1972) before becoming a TV star. After his music success evaporated he began winning guest roles in TV shows, including *Wonder Woman* and *The Incredible Hulk*. He played the highly popular role of Dr. Noah Drake on the top-ranked US daytime soap *General Hospital* for two years from 1981. Suddenly he was a star again and Springfield combined his acting success with a recording career. In August 1981 he scored his biggest pop hit with the US #1 *Jessie's Girl* (the song won him a Grammy) and four albums went platinum (note Moon-Pluto in Leo in 5th trine MC for popularity and influence). From the mid-80s Springfield's reversal of fortune

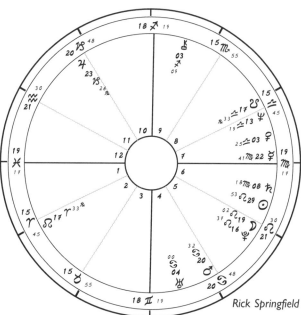

Rick Springfield

began a downwards spiral into clinical depression. Ten years later he won a guest role in the TV comedy *Suddenly Susan*. In 2000 he was arrested on charges of spousal abuse, which were later dropped.

Robert Stigwood – see Bee Gees

Gary Sweet

b. 22 May 1957, 05.57 AEST (-10), Melbourne, Australia, 37S49, 144E58.
FCC q. him from BC. RR: AA.

Actor and beefy sex symbol who first won the public's attention playing Don Bradman in the ten-part series *Bodyline*, which aired in Australia from July 1984. Other television projects include *Come in Spinner* (March 1990) and *Children of the Dragon* (May 1992) and a lead role in the highly successful *Police Rescue* series (aired in Australia from 3 September 1992, when TR Saturn moved to the EQHS 10th, and over the MC in 1993, when he won an international following) and its spin-off film released in Australia in early Spring 1994. He was back on television in 1997 with two action series *Cody* and *Big Sky*.

Nick Tate

b. 18 June 1942, 04.00 AEST (-10), Sydney, Australia, 33S52, 151E13.
FCC q. his letter (same date and place from Sy Scholfield q. birth announcement). RR: A.

A rugged actor who often appears as a maverick (Aquarian MC), Nick Tate has had major film and TV roles in Australia, the USA and Britain. He spent six years in Australian TV production and trained to become a director. At 22 he decided he belonged in front of the camera and won his first acting work the following year. One of his most high-profile roles came with *Space 1999* (from September 1976). The series, with a notable cult following, has kept him in demand (Tate has Moon conjunct Pluto in 3rd) ever since. He returned to Australia in 1981 and soon broke into films and TV series. In September 1983 he had a critically acclaimed part in the three episode mini-series *Scales of Justice*. By 1989 a trip to America for work persuaded him to change environment once again. Since then he has had numerous roles in TV series, films and voice-over film ads (note the lucrative 2nd house placements of Mercury and Sun-Jupiter). With all his planets below the horizon, Tate has kept his family life away from the public glare.

Eric Thomson

○   b. 27 April 1967, 14.00 GDT, Inverness, Scotland, 57N28, 04W12.
    Gerard q. BC (Erik Alexander Thomson). RR: AA.

An Australian actor who was raised in New Zealand, best known for his roles in *Pacific Drive* (1995), *Water Rats*, *Young Hercules*, *Xena*, *Hercules the Legendary Journeys*, and *All Saints* (from 1999). Thomson married on 7 August 1999.

Rowena Wallace

○   b. 23 August 1947, 08.10 GDT, Coventry, England, 52N25, 01W30.
    Phillip Lindsay q. her personally. RR: A.

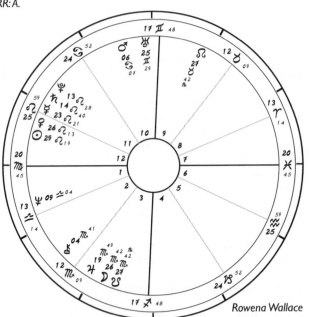

Rowena Wallace

Wallace is one of Australia's best-loved actresses and best-remembered for her neurotic, bitchy role as Patricia ('Pat the Rat') Hamilton in the soap *Sons and Daughters*, for which she won five Logie Awards. The part was a seminal role in Aussie TV history. Wallace, a shy child pushed by her ambitious mother, began her versatile career by joining the Twelfth Night Theatre in Brisbane. From 17 she worked as a voice-over announcer, children's host and weather girl before moving into TV roles in the 60s. Her TV stint in *You Can't See 'Round Corners* brought her to national attention in Australia from July 1967 (TR Uranus-Pluto conjunct Ascendant). Yet it was her role as the mercurial woman viewers loved to hate in *Sons and Daughters* that brought her international fame. During the series Wallace used her celebrity to promote World Vision and made a documentary called *Children on the Edge of Survival*. The soap role (from November 1981, and airing from 18 January 1982) was so stressful (the character survived numerous nervous breakdowns and murder attempts!) that Wallace quit the show suffering from exhaustion after three years and over 390 episode appearances. She taped her last episode on 26 September 1984 but the character survived and was later played by Belinda Giblin (qv, Australian Data). In a bid to boost ratings in its final year, Wallace returned to the show as her long-lost twin (for 10 weeks from March 1987). Since then the press have alleged that Wallace has been unable to capitalise on her high-profile soap role, struggling with financial problems, depression, painful back surgery (in January 1987) and a nervous breakdown. After promoting psychic telephone lines, Wallace moved back to TV with a role in *Home and Away* in 2002.

Jacki Weaver

○   b. 25 May 1947, 20.05 AEST (-10), Sydney, Australia, 33S52, 151E13.
    Stephanie Johnson q. Weaver by letter, quoting her parents. RR: A.

Actress whose film credits include *Alvin Purple* (1973), *Petersen* (1974), *Picnic at Hanging Rock* (1975) and *Cosi* (1996) with Greta Scacchi.

Bibliography

Blythe, Daniel, *The Encyclopaedia of Classic 80s Pop* (Allison & Busby, 2002)

Brooks, Tim and Earle Marsh, *The Complete Directory to Prime Time Network TV Shows* (Ballantine, 1999)

Brown, Gene, *Movie Time* (Macmillan, 1995)

Buckley, Jonathan and Mark Ellingham (Ed.), *Rock: The Rough Guide* (Rough Guides, 1996)

Carr, Ian, Digby Fairweather and Brian Priestley, *Jazz: The Rough Guide* (Rough Guides, 1995)

Conrad, Peter, *Feasting with Panthers or, The Importance of Being Famous* (Thames and Hudson, 1994)

Cornell, Paul, Martin Day and Keith Topping, *The Guiness Book of Classic British TV* (Guinness, 1996)

Davis, Sharon, *'80s Chart Toppers* (Mainstream Publishing, 1999)

Dempster, Nigel, *Nigel Dempster's Address Book* (Pan, 1992)

Donnelley, Paul, *Fade to Black: A Book of Movie Obituaries* (Omnibus Press, 2000)

Evans, Jeff, *The Guinness Television Encyclopedia* (Guinness, 1995)

Farkas, Anna (Ed.), *The Oxford Dictionary of Catchphrases* (Oxford University Press, 2002)

Gambaccini, Paul, Tim Rice and Jonathan Rice, *The Guinness Book of Number One Hits* (Guinness, 1994)

Genower, Peter (Ed.), *Who's Who on Television* (Boxtree, 2000)

Goring, Rosemary, *Scottish Biographical Dictionary* (Chambers, 1992)

Harris, Bob, *Bob Harris' Rock Dates* (Virgin, 1992)

Haun, Harry, *The Cinematic Century* (Applause Books, 2000)

Housham, David and John Frank-Keyes, *Funny Business* (Boxtree, 1992)

Katz, Ephraim, *The Macmillan International Film Encyclopedia* (Macmillan, 1994)

Kingsley, Hilary, *Soap Box* (Papermac, 1988)

Larkin, Colin (Ed.), *The Guinness Encyclopedia of Popular Music* (Guinness, 1993)

Lewis, Jon E. and Penny Stempel, *Cult TV* (Pavilion, 1993)

Lewis, Martin, *Reflections on Success* (Lennard, 1997)

Massingberd, Hugh (Ed.), *Third Book of Obituaries: Entertainers* (Macmillan, 1997)

McFall, Sally, Mark Bennett and Bruno MacDonald, *Guinness Rockopedia* (Guinness, 1998)

McWilliams, Michael, *TV Sirens* (Perigee Books, 1987)

Moran, Albert, *Moran's Guide to Australian TV Series* (Allen & Unwin, 1993)

Morley, Sheridan, *The Great Stage Stars* (Facts on File, 1986)

O'Neil, Thomas, *The Emmys* (Perigee, 1998)

O'Neil, Thomas, *The Grammys: For the Record* (Penguin, 1993)

Parish, James Robert, *Let's Talk* (Pioneer Books, 1993)

Rees, Dafydd and Luke Crampton, *Q Encyclopedia of Rock Stars* (Dorling Kindersley, 1996)

Roach, Martin, *Top 100 Singles* (Chrysalis, 2002)

Sackett, Susan, *Prime Time Hits* (Billboard Books, 1993)

Sheward, David, *It's a Hit* (Back Stage Books, 1994)

Simpson, Paul (Ed.), *The Rough Guide to Cult TV* (Rough Guides, 2002)

Smith, Joe, *Off the Record* (Warner Books, 1988)

Stambler, Irwin, *The Encyclopedia of Pop, Rock & Soul* (Macmillan, 1989)

Taylor, Rod, *The Guinness Book of Sitcoms* (Guinness, 1994)

Tibballs, Geoff, *First Jobs of the Famous* (Sphere Books, 1991)

Tracy, Sheila, *Who's Who in Popular Music* (World's Work, 1994)

Veitch, Margot, *Australia's Entertainers* (Child & Associates, 1990)

White, Timothy, *The Entertainers* (Billboard Books, 1998)

Wright, Steve, *Just Keep Talking* (Simon & Schuster, 1997)

Updates to this Edition

To receive a yearly update of amendments to this edition please send a SAE to Flare Publications, c/o P.O. Box 10126, London NW3 7WD. For an update by email please write to info@flareuk.com The author is grateful for any amendments and updates to the bios and data. To exchange data or copies of celebrity birth records and data notes please contact Frank Clifford at the above address.

Flare Books

✪ For books, discounted titles as well as consultations, events and giveaways, check out our website at **www.flareuk.com**

✪ Books can also be bought online at various sites including www.flareuk.com, www.amazon.com, www.amazon.co.uk and www.midheavenbooks.com

✪ If you wish to keep informed of our special offers and new books as they become available, please write to us at Flare Publications, P.O. Box 10126, London NW3 7WD or **info@flareuk.com**

Books by Frank Clifford available from Flare Publications

📖 *British Entertainers: the Astrological Profiles*   £12.99
     1-903353-01-7, 320pp, paperback, June 2003

📖 *Palmistry 4 Today: the fast and accurate way to understand yourself*
     and the people around you   £8.99
     0-7126-1584-9, 224pp, paperback, Rider, June 2002

📖 *Venus: Your Key to Love*   (see below)
     0-9530261-5-9, 36pp, paperback, November 2000

📖 *Mars: Your Burning Desires*   £3.50 *total for both*
     0-9530261-6-7, 32pp, paperback, November 2000

📖 *The Essentials of Hand Analysis*   £1.99
     0-9530261-7-5, 16pp, February 1999

Other books published by Flare

📖 *Astrology in the Year Zero* by Garry Phillipson   £15.99
     0-9530261-9-1, 272pp, paperback, November 2000

📖 *The Draconic Chart* by Rev. Pamela Crane   £16.99
     0-9530261-4-0, 278pp, comb-bound, January 2000

📖 *The Sun Sign Reader* by Joan Revill   £9.99*
     0-9530261-3-2, 224pp. paperback, January 2000

📖 *Shorthand of the Soul: the Quotable Horoscope* by David Hayward   £12.99*
     0-9530261-2-4, 256pp, paperback, November 1999

* Check www.flareuk.com for special discounts on these titles.

Please add 15% for p&p (20% outside the UK). Sterling cheques, money orders or postal orders only please.

INTRODUCING... a landmark companion volume to *British Entertainers: the astrological profiles*

Birth Charts: Horoscopes of the Famous
by Frank C. Clifford (Flare, 2004)
The ultimate astrological reference book! A brand-new volume of birth charts, data and biographies of one thousand public figures: politicians, entrepreneurs, activists, astrologers, religious leaders, criminals and victims, writers, explorers, sportspeople, artists and designers, entertainers of film, stage, tv, record and comedy. Many data are from the author's private collection and have never before been published.

www.flareuk.com
P.O.Box 10126, London NW3 7WD, England